Praise for *The Wolf of Wall Street*:

'Reads like a cross between Tom Wolfe's *Bonfire of the Vanities* and Scorsese's *Goodfellas* . . . Laugh-out-loud funny' – *Sunday Times*

'A cocky bad boy of finance recalls . . . [his] career as a master of his own universe . . . A hell of a read.' – *Kirkus*

'This book reads like The Financial World presented by Ozzy Osbourne . . . One reads a book like this for tales of excess, and Belfort certainly delivers, to the point where you long for a night in with Dad's Army and something eggy on a plate.' – *Mail on Sunday*

'A memoir that reads like fiction . . . [about a] vast amount of sex, drugs and risky physical behavior Belfort managed to survive.'
– *Publishers Weekly*

'A tour of the sort of underbelly of the financial market scene, the dark side of which, in some form, is always out there . . . plain and simple, a fun read.' – *TheStreet.com*

'Belfort's narrative is at once gleefully crass and terribly sad. By the time he gets arrested by FBI agents en route to buy his daughter a *Rugrats* video, you actually feel for the guy.' – *Rolling Stone*

About the Author

Jordan Belfort was born in Queens, New York, the son of accountants (his mother wanted him to be a doctor). He hustled ices to put himself through college, showing early entrepreneurial flair. His first business sent him bankrupt at twenty-four so he went down to Wall Street with $100 in his pocket and through a series of wild coincidences and leaps of logic ended up building one of the largest brokerages in America – the now infamous Stratton Oakmont. Ultimately indicted by the federal government, Belfort served twenty-two months in prison, spent one month in rehab, and is currently living in Los Angeles, California.

JORDAN BELFORT

The Wolf of Wall Street

First published in Great Britain in 2008 by Hodder & Stoughton
An Hachette Livre UK company

Published by arrangement with The Bantam Dell Publishing Group, a division of Random House, Inc.

First published in paperback in 2008

11

A CIP catalogue record for this title is available from the British Library

ISBN 978 0 340 95375 4

Typeset in Garamond by Hewer Text UK Ltd, Edinburgh

Printed and bound in the UK by CPI Mackays, Chatham ME5 8TD

Hodder & Stoughton policy is to use papers that are natural, renewable and recyclable products and made from wood grown in sustainable forests. The logging and manufacturing processes are expected to conform to the environmental regulations of the country of origin.

Hodder & Stoughton Ltd
338 Euston Road
London NW1 3BH

www.hodder.co.uk

To my two wonderful children, Chandler and Carter Belfort

AUTHOR'S NOTE

This book is a work of memoir; it is a true story based on my best recollections of various events in my life. Where indicated, the names and identifying characteristics of certain people mentioned in the book have been changed in order to protect their privacy. In some instances, I rearranged and/or compressed events and time periods in service of the narrative, and I recreated dialogue to match my best recollection of those exchanges.

PROLOGUE

A BABE IN THE WOODS

May 1, 1987

"You're lower than pond scum," said my new boss, leading me through the boardroom of LF Rothschild for the first time. "You got a problem with that, Jordan?"

"No," I replied, "no problem."

"Good," snapped my boss, and he kept right on walking.

We were walking through a maze of brown mahogany desks and black telephone wire on the twenty-third floor of a glass-and-aluminum tower that rose up forty-one stories above Manhattan's fabled Fifth Avenue. The boardroom was a vast space, perhaps fifty by seventy feet. It was an oppressive space, loaded with desks, telephones, computer monitors, and some very obnoxious yuppies, seventy of them in all. They had their suit jackets off, and at this hour of morning–9:20 a.m.–they were leaning back in their seats, reading their *Wall Street Journals*, and congratulating themselves on being young Masters of the Universe.

Being a Master of the Universe; it seemed like a noble pursuit, and as I walked past the Masters, in my cheap blue suit and clodhopper shoes, I found myself wishing I were one of them. But my new boss was quick to remind me that I wasn't. "Your *job*"–he looked at the plastic nametag on my cheap blue lapel–"Jordan Belfort, is a *connector*, which means you'll be dialing the phone five hundred times a day, trying to get past secretaries. You're not trying to sell anything or recommend anything or create anything. You're just trying to get business owners on the phone." He paused for a brief instant, then spewed out more venom. "And when you *do* get one on the phone, all you'll say is: 'Hello, Mr. So and So, I have Scott holding for you,' and then you pass the phone to me and start dialing again. Think you can handle that, or is that too complicated for you?"

"No, I can handle it," I said confidently, as a wave of panic overtook me like a killer tsunami. The LF Rothschild training program was six months long. They would be tough months, *grueling* months, during which I would be at the very mercy of assholes like Scott, the yuppie scumbag who seemed to have bubbled up from the fiery depths of yuppie hell.

Sneaking peeks at him out of the corner of my eye, I came to the quick conclusion that Scott looked like a goldfish. He was bald and pale, and what little hair he did have left was a muddy orange. He was in his early thirties, on the tall side, and he had a narrow skull and pink, puffy lips. He wore a bow tie, which made him look ridiculous. Over his bulging brown eyeballs he wore a pair of wire-rimmed spectacles, which made him look fishy–in the goldfish sense of the word.

"Good," said the scumbag goldfish. "Now, here are the ground rules: There are no breaks, no personal calls, no sick days, no coming in late, and no loafing off. You get thirty minutes for lunch"–he paused for effect–"and you better be back on time, because there are fifty people waiting to take your desk if you fuck up."

He kept walking and talking as I followed one step behind, mesmerized by the thousands of orange diode stock quotes that came skidding across gray-colored computer monitors. At the front of the room, a wall of plate glass looked out over midtown Manhattan. Up ahead I could see the Empire State Building. It towered above everything, seeming to rise up to the heavens and scrape the sky. It was a sight to behold, a sight worthy of a young Master of the Universe. And, right now, that goal seemed further and further away.

"To tell you the truth," sputtered Scott, "I don't think you're cut out for this job. You look like a kid, and Wall Street's no place for kids. It's a place for killers. A place for mercenaries. So in *that* sense you're lucky I'm not the one who does the hiring around here." He let out a few ironic chuckles.

I bit my lip and said nothing. The year was 1987, and yuppie assholes like Scott seemed to rule the world. Wall Street was in the midst of a raging bull market, and freshly minted millionaires were being spit out a dime a dozen. Money was cheap, and a guy named Michael Milken had invented something called "junk bonds," which had changed the way corporate America went about its business. It was a time of unbridled greed, a time of wanton excess. It was the era of the yuppie.

As we neared his desk, my yuppie nemesis turned to me and said, "I'll say it again, Jordan: You're the lowest of the low. You're not even a cold caller yet; you're a *connector*." Disdain dripped off the very word. "And 'til you pass your Series Seven, connecting will be your entire universe. And *that* is why you are lower than pond scum. You got a problem with that?"

"Absolutely not," I replied. "It's the perfect job for me, because I *am* lower than pond scum." I shrugged innocently.

Unlike Scott, I don't look like a goldfish, which made me feel proud as he stared at me, searching my face for irony. I'm on the short side, though, and at the age of twenty-four I still had the soft boyish features of an adolescent. It was the sort of face that made it difficult for me to get into a bar without getting proofed. I had a full head of light brown hair, smooth olive skin, and a pair of big blue eyes. Not altogether bad-looking.

But, alas, I hadn't been lying to Scott when I'd told him that I felt lower than pond scum. In point of fact, I did. The problem was that I had just run my first business venture into the ground, and my self-esteem had been run into the ground with it. It had been an ill-conceived venture into the meat and seafood industry, and by the time it was over I had found myself on the ass end of twenty-six truck leases–all of which I'd personally guaranteed, and all of which were now in default. So the banks were after me, as was some belligerent woman from American Express–a bearded, three-hundred-pounder by the sound of her–who was threatening to personally kick my ass if I didn't pay up. I had considered changing my phone number, but I was so far behind on my phone bill that NYNEX was after me too.

We reached Scott's desk and he offered me the seat next to his, along with some kind words of encouragement. "Look at the bright side," he quipped. "If by some miracle you don't get fired for laziness, stupidness, insolence, or tardiness, then you might actually become a stockbroker one day." He smirked at his own humor. "And just so you know, last year I made over three hundred thousand dollars, and the other guy you'll be working for made over a million."

Over a million? I could only imagine what an asshole the *other* guy was. With a sinking heart, I asked, "Who's the other guy?"

"Why?" asked my yuppie tormentor. "What's it to you?"

Sweet Jesus! I thought. Only speak when spoken to, you nincompoop! It was like being in the Marines. In fact, I was getting the distinct impression that this bastard's favorite movie was *An Officer and a Gentleman,* and he was playing out a Lou Gossett fantasy on me–pretending he was a drill sergeant in charge of a substandard Marine. But I kept that thought to myself, and all I said was, "Uh, nothing, I was just, uh, curious."

"His name is Mark Hanna, and you'll meet him soon enough." With that, he handed me a stack of three-by-five index cards, each of them having the name and phone number of a wealthy business owner on it. "Smile and dial," he instructed, "and don't pick up your fucking head 'til twelve." Then he sat down at his own desk, picked up a copy of *The Wall Street Journal,* and put his black crocodile dress shoes on the desktop and started reading.

I was about to pick up the phone when I felt a beefy hand on my shoulder. I looked up, and with a single glance I knew it was Mark Hanna. He reeked of success, like a true Master of the Universe. He was a big guy–about six-one, two-twenty, and most of it muscle. He had jet-black hair, dark intense eyes, thick fleshy features, and a fair smattering of acne scars. He was handsome, in a downtown sort of way, giving off the hip whiff of Greenwich Village. I felt the charisma oozing off him.

"Jordan?" he said, in a remarkably soothing tone.

"Yeah, that's me," I replied, in the tone of the doomed. "Pond scum first-class, at your service!"

He laughed warmly, and the shoulder pads of his $2,000 gray pin-striped suit rose and fell with each chuckle. Then, in a voice louder than necessary, he said, "Yeah, well, I see you got your first dose of the village asshole!" He motioned his head toward Scott.

I nodded imperceptibly. He winked back. "No worry: I'm the senior broker here; he's just a worthless piker. So disregard everything he said and anything he might ever say in the future."

Try as I might, I couldn't help but glance over at Scott, who was now muttering the words: "Fuck you, Hanna!"

Mark didn't take offense, though. He simply shrugged and stepped around my desk, putting his great bulk between Scott and me, and he said, "Don't let him bother you. I hear you're a first-class salesman. In a year from now that moron will be kissing your ass."

I smiled, feeling a mixture of pride and embarrassment. "Who told you I was a great salesman?"

"Steven Schwartz, the guy who hired you. He said you pitched him stock right in the job interview." Mark chuckled at that. "He was impressed; he told me to watch out for you."

"Yeah, I was nervous he wasn't gonna hire me. There were twenty people lined up for interviews, so I figured I better do something drastic–you know, make an impression." I shrugged my shoulders. "He told me I'd need to tone it down a bit, though."

Mark smirked. "Yeah, well don't tone it down *too* much. High pressure's a must in this business. People don't buy stock; it gets sold to them. Don't ever forget that." He paused, letting his words sink in. "Anyway, Sir Scumbag over there was right about one thing: Connecting does suck. I did it for seven months, and I wanted to kill myself every day. So I'll let you in on a little secret"–and he lowered his voice conspiratorially–"You only *pretend* to connect. You loaf off at every opportunity." He smiled and winked, then raised his voice back to normal. "Don't get me wrong; I want you to pass me as many connects as possible, because I make money off them. But I don't want you to slit your wrists over it, 'cause I hate the sight of blood." He winked again. "So take lots of breaks. Go to the bathroom and jerk off if you have to. That's what I did, and it worked like a charm for me. You like jerking off, I assume, right?"

I was a bit taken aback by the question, but as I would later learn, a Wall Street boardroom was no place for symbolic pleasantries. Words like *shit* and *fuck* and *bastard* and *prick* were as common as *yes* and *no* and *maybe* and *please.* I said, "Yeah, I, uh, love jerking off. I mean, what guy doesn't, right?"

He nodded, almost relieved. "Good, that's real good. Jerking off is key. And I also strongly recommend the use of drugs, especially cocaine, because that'll make you dial faster, which is good for me." He paused, as if searching for more words of wisdom, but apparently came up short. "Well, that's about it," he said. "That's all the knowledge I can impart to you now. You'll do fine, rookie. One day you'll even look back at this and laugh; that much I can promise you." He smiled once more and then took a seat before his own phone.

A moment later a buzzer sounded, announcing that the market had just opened. I looked at my Timex watch, purchased at JCPenney for fourteen bucks last week. It was nine-thirty on the nose. It was May 4, 1987, my first day on Wall Street.

Just then, over the loudspeaker, came the voice of LF Rothschild's sales manager, Steven Schwartz. "Okay, gentlemen. The futures look strong this morning, and serious buying is coming in from Tokyo." Steven was only thirty-eight years old, but he'd made over $2 million last year. (Another Master of the Universe.) "We're looking at a ten-point pop at the open," he added, "so let's hit the phones and rock and roll!"

And just like that the room broke out into pandemonium. Feet came flying off desktops; *Wall Street Journal*s were filed away in garbage cans; shirtsleeves were rolled up to the elbows; and one by one brokers picked up their phones and started dialing. I picked up my own phone and started dialing too.

Within minutes, everyone was pacing about furiously and gesticulating wildly and shouting into their black telephones, which created a mighty roar. It was the first time I'd heard the roar of a Wall Street boardroom, which sounded like the roar of a mob. It was a sound I'd never forget, a sound that would change my life forever. It was the sound of young men engulfed by greed and ambition, pitching their hearts and souls out to wealthy business owners across America.

"Miniscribe's a fucking steal down here," screamed a chubby-faced yuppie into his telephone. He was twenty-eight, and he had a raging coke habit and a gross income of $600,000. "Your broker in West Virginia? Christ! He might be good at picking coal-mining stocks, but it's the eighties now. The name of the game is high-tech!"

"I got fifty thousand July Fifties!" screamed a broker, two desks over.

"They're out of the money!" yelled another.

"I'm not getting rich on one trade," swore a broker to his client.

"Are you kidding?" snapped Scott into his headset. "After I split my commission with the firm and the government I can't put Puppy Chow in my dog's bowl!"

Every so often a broker would slam his phone down in victory and then fill out a buy ticket and walk over to a pneumatic tubing system that had been affixed to a support column. He would stick the ticket in a glass cylinder and watch it get sucked up into the ceiling. From there, the ticket made its way to the trading desk on the other side of the building, where it would be rerouted to the floor of the New York Stock Exchange for execution. So the ceiling had been lowered to make room for the tubing, and it seemed to bear down on my head.

By ten o'clock, Mark Hanna had made three trips to the support column, and he was about to make another. He was so smooth on the phone that it literally boggled my mind. It was as if he were apologizing to his clients as he ripped their eyeballs out. "Sir, let me say this," Mark was saying to the chairman of a Fortune 500 company. "I pride myself on finding the bottom of these issues. And my goal is not only to guide you into these situations but to guide you out as well." His tone was so soft and mellow that it was almost hypnotic. "I'd like to be an asset to you for the long term; to be an asset to your business–and to your family."

Two minutes later Mark was at the tubing system with a quarter-million-dollar buy order for a stock called Microsoft. I'd never heard of Microsoft before, but it sounded like a pretty decent company. Anyway, Mark's commission on the trade was $3,000. I had seven dollars in my pocket.

By twelve o'clock I was dizzy, and I was starving. In fact, I was dizzy and starving and sweating profusely. But, most of all, I was hooked. The mighty roar was surging through my very innards and resonating with every fiber of my being. I *knew* I could do this job. I knew I could do it *just* like Mark Hanna did it, probably even better. I knew I could be smooth as silk.

To my surprise, rather than taking the building's elevator down to the lobby and spending half my net worth on two frankfurters and a Coke, I now found myself ascending to the penthouse with Mark Hanna standing beside me. Our destination was a five-star restaurant called Top of the Sixes, which was on the forty-first floor of the office building. It was where the elite met to eat, a place where Masters of the Universe could get blitzed on martinis and exchange war stories.

The moment we stepped into the restaurant, Luis, the maître d', bum-rushed Mark, shaking his hand violently and telling him how wonderful it was to see him on such a glorious Monday afternoon. Mark slipped him a fifty, which caused me to nearly swallow my own tongue, and Luis ushered us to a corner table with a fabulous view of Manhattan's Upper West Side and the George Washington Bridge.

Mark smiled at Luis and said, "Give us two Absolut martinis, Luis, straight up. And then bring us two more in"–he looked at his thick gold Rolex watch–"exactly seven and a half minutes, and then keep bringing them every five minutes until one of us passes out."

Luis nodded. "Of course, Mr. Hanna. That's an excellent strategy."

I smiled at Mark, and said, in a very apologetic tone, "I'm sorry, but I, uh, don't drink." Then I turned to Luis. "You could just bring me a Coke. That'll be fine."

Luis and Mark exchanged a look, as if I'd just committed a crime. But all Mark said was, "It's his first day on Wall Street; give him time."

Luis looked at me, compressed his lips, and nodded gravely. "That's perfectly understandable. Have no fear; soon enough you'll be an alcoholic."

Mark nodded in agreement. "Well said, Luis, but bring him a martini anyway, just in case he changes his mind. Worse comes to worst, I'll drink it myself."

"Excellent, Mr. Hanna. Will you and your friend be eating today or just imbibing?"

What the fuck was Luis talking about? I wondered. It was a rather ridiculous question, considering it was lunchtime! But to my surprise, Mark told Luis that he would not be eating today, that only I would, at which point Luis handed me a menu and went to fetch our drinks. A moment later I found out exactly why Mark wouldn't be eating, when he reached into his suit-jacket pocket, pulled out a coke vial, unscrewed the top, and dipped in a tiny spoon. He scooped out a sparkling pile of nature's most powerful appetite suppressant–namely, cocaine–and he took a giant snort up his right nostril. Then he repeated the process and Hoovered one up his left.

I was astonished. Couldn't believe it! Right here in the restaurant! Among the Masters of the Universe! Out of the corner of my eye I glanced around the restaurant to see if anyone had noticed. Apparently no one had, and, in retrospect, I'm sure that they wouldn't have given a shit anyway. After all, they were too busy getting whacked on vodka and scotch and gin and bourbon and whatever dangerous pharmaceuticals they had procured with their wildly inflated paychecks.

"Here you go," said Mark, passing me the coke vial. "The true ticket on Wall Street; this and hookers."

Hookers? That struck me as odd. I mean, I'd never even been to one! Besides, I was in love with a girl I was about to make my wife. Her name was Denise, and she was gorgeous–as beautiful on the inside as she was on the outside. The chances of me cheating on her were less than zero. And as far as the coke was concerned, well, I'd done my share of partying in college, but it had been a few years since I'd touched anything other than pot. "No thanks," I said, feeling slightly embarrassed. "The stuff doesn't really agree with me. It makes me . . . uh . . . nuts. Like I can't sleep or eat, and I . . . uh . . . well, I start worrying about everything. It's really bad for me. Really evil."

"No problem," he said, taking another blast from the vial. "But I promise you that cocaine can definitely help you get through the day around here!" He shook his head and shrugged. "It's a fucked-up racket, being a stockbroker. I mean, don't get me wrong: The money's great and everything, but you're not creating anything, you're not *building* anything. So after a while it gets kinda monotonous." He paused, as if searching for the right words. "The truth is we're nothing more than sleazoid salesmen. None of us has any idea what stocks are going up! We're all just throwing darts at a board and, you know, churning and burning. Anyway, you'll figure all this out soon enough."

We spent the next few minutes sharing our backgrounds. Mark had grown up in Brooklyn, in the town of Bay Ridge, which was a pretty tough neighborhood from what I knew of it. "Whatever you do," he quipped, "don't go out with a girl from Bay Ridge. They're all fucking crazy!" Then he took another blast from his coke vial and added, "The last one I went out with stabbed me with a fucking pencil while I was sleeping! Can you imagine?"

Just then a tuxedoed waiter came over and placed our drinks on the table. Mark lifted his twenty-dollar martini and I lifted my eight-dollar Coke. Mark said, "Here's to the Dow Jones going straight to five thousand!" We clinked glasses. "And here's to your career on Wall Street!" he added. "May you make a bloody fortune in this racket and maintain just a small portion of your soul in the process!" We both smiled and then clinked glasses again.

In that very instant if someone told me that in just a few short years I would end up owning the very restaurant I was now sitting in and that Mark Hanna, along with half the other brokers at LF Rothschild would end up working for me, I would have said they were crazy. And if someone told me that I would be snorting lines of cocaine off the bar in this very restaurant, while a dozen high-class hookers looked on in admiration, I would say that they had lost their fucking mind.

But that would be only the beginning. You see, at that very moment there were things happening away from me–things that had nothing to do with me–starting with a little something called *portfolio insurance,* which was a computer-driven stock-hedging strategy that would ultimately put an end to this raging bull market and send the Dow Jones crashing down 508 points in a single day. And, from there, the chain of events that would ensue would be almost unimaginable. Wall Street would close down business for a time, and the investment-banking firm of LF Rothschild would be forced to shut its doors. And then the insanity would take hold.

What I offer you now is a reconstruction of that insanity–a satirical reconstruction–of what would turn out to be one of the wildest rides in Wall Street history. And I offer it to you in a voice that was playing inside my head at that very time. It's an ironic voice, a glib voice, a self-serving voice, and, at many times, a despicable voice. It's a voice that allowed me to rationalize anything that stood in my way of living a life of unbridled hedonism. It's a voice that helped me corrupt other people–and manipulate them–and bring chaos and insanity to an entire generation of young Americans.

I grew up in a middle-class family in Bayside, Queens, where words like *nigger* and *spick* and *wop* and *chink* were considered the dirtiest of words–words that were never to be uttered under any circumstances. In my parents' household, prejudices of any sort were heavily discouraged; they were considered the mental processes of inferior beings, of unenlightened beings. I have always felt this way: as a child, as an adolescent, and even at the height of thc insanity. Yet dirty words like that would come to slip off my tongue with remarkable ease, especially as the insanity took hold. Of course, I would rationalize that out too–telling myself that this was Wall Street and, on Wall Street, there's no time for symbolic pleasantries or societal niceties.

Why do I say these things to you? I say them because I want you to know who I really am and, more importantly, who I'm not. And I say these things because I have two children of my own, and I have a lot to explain to them one day. I'll have to explain how their lovable dad, the very dad who now drives them to soccer games and shows up at their parent–teacher conferences and stays home on Friday nights and makes them Caesar salad from scratch, could have been such a despicable person once.

But what I sincerely hope is that my life serves as a cautionary tale to the rich and poor alike; to anyone who's living with a spoon up their nose and a bunch of pills dissolving in their stomach sac; or to any person who's considering taking a God-given gift and misusing it; to anyone who decides to go to the dark side of the force and live a life of unbridled hedonism. And to anyone who thinks there's anything glamorous about being known as a Wolf of Wall Street.

BOOK I

CHAPTER I

A WOLF IN SHEEP'S CLOTHING

Six Years Later

The insanity had quickly taken hold, and by the winter of '93 I had this eerie feeling that I'd landed the starring role in one of those reality TV shows, before they came into vogue. The name of my show was *Lifestyles of the Rich and Dysfunctional,* and each day seemed to be growing more dysfunctional than the last.

I had started a brokerage firm named Stratton Oakmont, which was now one of the largest and by far the wildest brokerage firm in Wall Street history. The word on Wall Street was that I had an unadulterated death wish and that I was certain to put myself in the grave before I turned thirty. But that was nonsense, I knew, because I had just turned thirty-one and was still alive and kicking.

At this particular moment, a Wednesday morning in mid-December, I was sitting behind the controls of my twin-engine Bell Jet helicopter on my way from the 30th Street Heliport in midtown Manhattan to my estate in Old Brookville, Long Island, with enough drugs running through my circulatory system to sedate Guatemala.

It was a little after three a.m., and we were cruising along at a hundred twenty knots somewhere over the western edge of Long Island's Little Neck Bay. I remember thinking how remarkable it was that I could fly a straight line while seeing two of everything, when suddenly I began to feel woozy. Then all at once the helicopter was in the midst of a steep dive and I could see the black waters of the bay rushing toward me. There was this terrible vibration coming from the helicopter's main rotor, and I could hear the panic-stricken voice of my copilot coming through my headset, screaming frantically, "Jesus Christ, boss! Pull up! Pull up! We're gonna crash! Holy shit!"

Then we were level again.

My loyal and trusted copilot, Captain Marc Elliot, was dressed in white and sitting before his own set of controls. But he'd been under strict orders not to touch them unless I either passed out cold or was in imminent danger of smashing into the earth. Now he was flying, which was probably best.

Captain Marc was one of those square-jawed captain-types, the sort who instills confidence in you at the mere sight of him. And it wasn't only his jaw that was square; it was his entire body, which seemed to be comprised of squarish parts, unit-welded together, one atop the other. Even his black mustache was a perfect rectangle, and it sat on his stiff upper lip like an industrial-grade broom.

We'd taken off from Manhattan about ten minutes ago, after a long Tuesday evening that had spiraled way out of control. The night had started out innocently, though–at a trendy Park Avenue restaurant named Canastel's, where I'd had dinner with some of my young stockbrokers. Somehow, though, we'd ended up in the Presidential Suite at the Helmsley Palace, where some very expensive hooker named Venice, with bee-stung lips and loamy loins, had tried using a candle to help me achieve an erection, which turned out to be a lost cause. And that was why I was running late now (about five and a half hours, to be exact), which is to say I was in deep shit, once again, with my loyal and loving second wife, Nadine, the righteously aspiring husband-beater.

You may have seen Nadine on TV; she was that sexy blond who tried to sell you Miller Lite beer during *Monday Night Football,* the one walking through the park with the Frisbee and the dog. She didn't say much in the commercial, but no one seemed to care. It was her legs that got her the job; that and her ass, which was rounder than a Puerto Rican's and firm enough to bounce a quarter on. Whatever the case, I would be feeling her righteous wrath soon enough.

I took a deep breath and tried to right myself. I was feeling pretty good now, so I grabbed hold of the stick, sending a signal to

Captain SpongeBob SquarePants that I was ready to fly again. He looked a bit nervous, so I flashed him a warm, comrade in arms sort of smile and offered him a few kind words of encouragement through my voice-activated microphone. "Ooo gone get hazdiz duzy pay fuh dis, buzzy," said I, who was trying to say, "You're going to get hazardous duty pay for this, buddy."

"Yeah, that's *great,*" replied Captain Marc, releasing the controls to me. "Remind me to collect, if we should happen to make it home alive." He shook his square head in resignation and amazement, then added, "And don't forget to close your left eye before you start your descent. It'll help with the double vision."

Very shrewd and professional, this square captain of mine was; in fact, he happened to be quite the party animal himself. And not only was he the only licensed pilot in the cockpit, but he also happened to be the captain of my 167-foot motor yacht, the *Nadine,* named after my aforementioned wife.

I gave my captain a hearty thumbs-up sign. Then I stared out the cockpit window and tried to get my bearings. Up ahead I could see the red-and-white-striped smokestacks that rose up from out of the wealthy Jewish suburb of Roslyn. The smokestacks served as a visual cue that I was about to enter the heart of Long Island's Gold Coast, which is where Old Brookville is located. The Gold Coast is a terrific place to live, especially if you like blue-blooded WASPs and overpriced horses. Personally, I despise both, but somehow I ended up owning a bunch of overpriced horses and socializing with a bunch of blue-blooded WASPs, the latter of whom, I figured, viewed me as a young Jewish circus attraction.

I looked at the altimeter. It was at three hundred feet and spiraling downward. I rolled my neck like a prizefighter stepping into the ring, beginning my descent at a thirty-degree angle, passing over the rolling fairways of the Brookville Country Club and then easing the stick right and cruising over the lush treetops on either side of Hegemans Lane, where I started my final descent onto the driving range at the rear of the property.

Working the foot pedals, I brought the helicopter into a stationary hover about twenty feet above the ground and then attempted to land. A little adjustment with the left foot, a little adjustment with the right foot, a little less power to the collective, a tiny bit of back pressure to the stick, and then all at once the helicopter slammed into the ground and started rising again.

"Oh, zit!" I muttered, on the way up. Out of panic, I slammed down the collective and the helicopter began sinking like a stone. And then all at once–*SLAM!*–we landed with a giant thud.

I shook my head in amazement. *What an incredible rush that was!* It wasn't a perfect landing, but who cared? I turned to my beloved captain, and with great pride I slurred, "Am I goodz, buzzy, or am I goodz!"

Captain Marc cocked his square head to the side and raised his rectangular eyebrows high on his square forehead, as if to say, "Are you out of your fucking mind?" But then he began nodding slowly, his face breaking out into a wry smile. "You're good, buddy. I have to admit it. Did you keep your left eye shut?"

I nodded my head. "It zwork like charm," I mumbled. "You za best!"

"Good. I'm glad you think that." He let out a tiny chuckle. "Anyway, I gotta bolt out of here before we get ourselves in trouble. Want me to call the guardhouse to come get you?"

"No, I fine, buzzy. I fine." With that, I undid my safety restraints, gave Captain Marc a mock salute, and opened the cockpit door and climbed out. Then I wheeled about and closed the cockpit door and banged two times on the window, to let him know that I'd been responsible enough to close the door, which gave me a feeling of great satisfaction, insofar as a man in my condition could be sober enough to do that. Then I wheeled about once more and headed for the main house, straight into the eye of Hurricane Nadine.

It was gorgeous outside. The sky was filled with countless stars, twinkling brilliantly. The temperature was unseasonably warm for December. There wasn't a stitch of wind, which gave the air that earthy, woodsy smell that reminds you of your childhood. I thought of summer nights at sleepaway camp. I thought of my older brother, Robert, whom I'd recently lost touch with after his wife threatened to sue one of my companies for sexual harassment, at which point I took him out for dinner, got too stoned, and then called his wife an asshole. But, still, they were good memories, memories from a much simpler time.

It was about two hundred yards to the main house. I took a deep breath and relished the scent of my property. *What a fine smell it had!* All the Bermuda grass! The pungent smell of pine! And so many soothing sounds! The ceaseless croaking of the crickets! The mystical hooting of the owls! The rushing water from that ridiculous pond and waterfall system up ahead!

I had purchased the estate from the Chairman of the New York Stock Exchange, Dick Grasso, who bore an odd resemblance to Frank Perdue, the chicken salesman. Then I dumped a few million into various improvements–most of it sucked into that ridiculous pond and waterfall system and the remainder sucked into a state-of-the-art guardhouse and security system. The guardhouse was manned twenty-four hours a day by two armed bodyguards, both of whom were named Rocco. Inside the guardhouse were banks of TV monitors that received images from twenty-two security cameras positioned throughout the estate. Each camera was tied to a motion sensor and floodlight, creating an impenetrable ring of security.

Just then I felt a tremendous gust of air, so I craned up my neck to watch the helicopter ascend into the darkness. I found myself taking small steps backward, and then the small steps became bigger steps, and then . . . *Oh, shit! I was in trouble! I was about to hit the dirt!* I wheeled about and took two giant steps forward, extending my arms out like wings. Like an out-of-control ice skater I stumbled this way and that, trying to find my center of gravity. And then, all at once . . . a blinding light!

"What the fuck!" I put my hands to my eyes, shielding myself from the searing pain of the floodlights. I had tripped one of the motion sensors and was now a victim of my own security system. The pain was excruciating. My eyes were dilated from all the drugs, my pupils as big as saucers.

Then, the final insult: I tripped in my spiffy crocodile dress shoes and went flying backward and landed flat on my back. After a few seconds the floodlight went off, and I slowly lowered my arm to the side. I pressed my palms against the soft grass. *What a wonderful spot I picked to fall on!* And I was an expert at falling, knowing exactly how to do it without hurting myself. The secret was to just go with it, like a Hollywood stuntman did. Better still, my drug of choice–namely, Quaaludes–had the wonderful effect of turning my body into rubber, which further protected me from harm.

I resisted the thought that it was the Quaaludes that had made me fall in the first place. After all, there were so many advantages to using them that I considered myself lucky to be addicted to them. I mean, how many drugs made you feel as wonderful as they did, yet didn't leave you with a hangover the next day? And a man in my position–a man burdened with so many grave responsibilities–couldn't afford to be hungover, now could he!

And my wife . . . well, I guess she'd earned her scene with me, but still; did she really have that much reason to be angry? I mean, when she married me she knew what she was getting into, didn't she? She had been my mistress, for Chrissake! That spoke volumes, didn't it? And what had I really done tonight? Nothing so terrible, or at least nothing that she could prove!

And around and around that twisted mind of mine went–rationalizing, justifying, then denying, and then rationalizing some more, until I was able to build up a healthy head of righteous resentment. Yes, I thought, there were certain things that went on between rich men and their wives that dated all the way back to the caveman days, or at least back to the Vanderbilts and Astors. There were liberties, so to speak, certain liberties that men of power were entitled to, that men of power had earned! Of course this wasn't the sort of thing I could just come out and say to Nadine. She was prone to physical violence and she was bigger than me, or at least the same size, which was just one more reason to resent her.

Just then I heard the electric whir of the golf cart. That would be Rocco Night, or perhaps Rocco Day, depending on when their shifts changed. Either way, some Rocco was coming out to fetch me. It was amazing how everything always seemed to work out. When I fell down, there was always someone to pick me up; when I got caught driving under the influence, there was always some crooked judge or corrupt police officer to make an accommodation; and when I passed out at the dinner table and found myself drowning in the soup du jour, there was always my wife, or, if not her, then some benevolent hooker, who would come to my aid with mouth-to-mouth resuscitation.

It was as if I was *bulletproof* or something. How many times had I cheated death? It was impossible to say. But did I really want to die? Was my guilt and remorse eating at me that voraciously–so much, in fact, that I was trying to take my own life? I mean, it was mind-boggling, now that I thought about it! I had risked my life a thousand times yet hadn't gotten so much as a scratch. I had driven drunk, flown stoned, walked off the edge of a building, scuba dived during a blackout, gambled away millions of dollars at casinos all over the world, and I still didn't look a day over twenty-one.

I had lots of nicknames: Gordon Gekko, Don Corleone, Kaiser Soze; they even called me the King. But my favorite was the Wolf of Wall Street, because that was me to a T. I was the ultimate wolf in sheep's clothing: I looked like a kid and acted like a kid, but I was no kid. I was thirty-one going on sixty, living dog years–aging seven years for every year. But I was rich and powerful and had a gorgeous wife and a four-month-old baby daughter who was living, breathing perfection.

Like they say, it was all good, and it all seemed to work. Somehow, and I wasn't sure how, I would end up beneath a $12,000 silk comforter, sleeping inside a royal bedchamber draped with enough white Chinese silk to make silk parachutes for an entire squadron of paratroopers. And my wife . . . well, she would forgive me. After all, she always had.

And with that thought, I passed out.

CHAPTER 2

THE DUCHESS OF BAY RIDGE

December 13, 1993

The next morning–or, if you want to get technical about it, a few hours later–I was having an awesome dream. It was the sort of dream that every young man hopes and prays for, so I decided to go with it. I'm alone in bed, when Venice the Hooker comes to me. She kneels down at the edge of my sumptuous king-size bed, hovering just out of reach, a perfect little vision. I can see her clearly now . . . that lusty mane of chestnut brown hair . . . the fine features of her face . . . those juicy young jugs . . . those incredibly loamy loins, glistening with greed and desire.

"Venice," I say. "Come to me, Venice. Come to me, Venice!"

Venice moves toward me, walking on her knees. Her skin is fair and white and shimmers amid the silk . . . the silk . . . there's silk everywhere. An enormous canopy of white Chinese silk is suspended from above. Billows of white Chinese silk hang down at all four corners of the bed. So much white Chinese silk . . . I'm drowning in white fucking silk. In this very instant the ludicrous figures come popping into my mind: the silk cost $250 a yard, and there have to be two hundred yards of it. That's $50,000 of white Chinese silk. So much white fucking silk.

But that's my wife's doing, my dear aspiring decorator–or, wait, that was last month's aspiration, wasn't it? Isn't she an aspiring chef now? Or is she an aspiring landscape architect? Or is it a wine connoisseur? Or a clothing designer? Who could keep track of all her fucking aspirations? So tiring it is . . . so tiring to be married to Martha Stewart in embryo.

Just then I feel a drop of water. I look up. What the hell? Storm clouds? How can there be storm clouds inside the royal bed-chamber? Where's my wife? *Holy shit! My wife! My wife! Hurricane Nadine!*

SPLASH!

I woke up to the angry yet gorgeous face of my second wife, Nadine. In her right hand was an empty twelve-ounce water glass; in her left hand was her own balled-up fist, punctuated by a seven-carat, yellow canary diamond in a platinum setting. She was less than five feet away, rocking back and forth on the balls of her feet, like a prizefighter. I made a quick mental note to watch out for the ring.

"Why the fuck did you do that?" I yelled halfheartedly. I wiped my eyes with the back of my hand and took a moment to study Wife Number Two. *God, she was a real piece of ass, my wife!* I couldn't begrudge her that even now. She was wearing a tiny pink chemise that was so short and low cut that it made her look more naked than if she were wearing nothing at all. And those legs of hers! Christ, they looked scrumptious. But, still, that was beside the point. I needed to get tough with her and show her who was boss. Through clenched teeth, I said, "I swear to God, Nadine, I'm going to fucking kill–"

"Oh, I'm really fucking scared," interrupted the blond firecracker. She shook her head in disgust, and her little pink nipples popped out of her next-to-nothing outfit. I tried not to stare, but it was difficult. "Maybe I should go run and hide," she quipped. "Or maybe I'll just stay here and *kick your fucking ass*!" The last few words she screamed.

Well, maybe *she* was boss. Either way, she had definitely earned her scene with me; there was no denying that. And the Duchess of Bay Ridge had a vicious temper. Yes, she was a duchess, all right–a Brit by birth, who still carried a British passport. It was a wonderful fact she never failed to remind me of. Yet, it was all very ironic, since she had never actually lived in Britain. In fact, she had moved to Bay Ridge, Brooklyn, when she was still a baby, and it was there, in the land of dropped consonants and tortured vowels, where she was raised. Bay Ridge; it's that tiny corner of the earth where words like *fuck* and *shit* and *bastard* and *prick* roll off the tongues of young natives with the poetic panache of T. S. Eliot and Walt Whitman. And it was there that Nadine Caridi–my lovable English, Irish, Scottish, German, Norwegian, and Italian mutt-of-a-duchess–learned to tie her curses together, as she was learning to tie the laces on her roller skates.

It was sort of a grim joke, I thought, considering that Mark Hanna had warned me about going out with a girl from Bay Ridge all those years ago. His girlfriend, as I recalled, had stabbed him with a pencil while he was sleeping; the Duchess preferred throwing water. So, in a way, I was ahead of the game.

Anyway, when the Duchess got angry it was as if her words were bubbling up from out of the rancid gullet of the Brooklyn sewer system. And no one could make her angrier than me, her loyal and trustworthy husband, the Wolf of Wall Street, who less than five hours ago was in the Presidential Suite of the Helmsley Palace with a candle in his ass.

"So tell me, you little shit," snapped the Duchess, "who the fuck is Venice, huh?" She paused and took an aggressive step forward, and all at once she struck a pose, with her hips cocked in a display of insolence, one long, bare leg slewed out to the side, and her arms folded beneath her breasts, pushing her nipples out into plain view. She said, "She's probably some little hooker, I bet." She narrowed her big blue eyes accusingly. "You don't think I know what you're up to? Why, I oughta smash your fucking face in, you . . . you little . . . *ugghhhhh!*" It was an angry groan, and the moment she'd finished groaning she gave up her pose and began marching across the bedroom–marching on the custom-made beige and taupe $120,000 Edward Fields carpet. And she marched fast as lightning, all the way to the master bathroom, which was a good thirty feet away, where she turned on the faucet, refilled the water glass, turned off the faucet, and came marching back, looking twice as angry. Her teeth were clenched in unadulterated rage, making her square model-girl jaw really stand out. She looked like the Duchess from Hell.

Meanwhile, I was trying to gather my thoughts, but she was moving too fast. I had no time to think. It had to be those fucking Quaaludes! They had made me talk in my sleep again. *Oh, shit!* What had I said? I ran the possibilities through my mind: the limousine . . . the hotel . . . the drugs . . . Venice the Hooker . . .

Venice with the candle–*Oh, God, the fucking candle!* I pushed the thought out of my mind.

I looked over at the digital clock on the night table: It was 7:16. Jesus! What time had I gotten home? I shook my head, trying to get out the cobwebs. I ran my fingers through my hair–Christ, I was soaked! She must have dumped the water right over my head. My own wife! And then she called me little–a little shit! Why had she called me that? I wasn't that little, was I? She could be very cruel, the Duchess.

She was back now, less than five feet away, holding the water glass out in front of her, with her elbow cocked out to the side: her throwing position! And that look on her face: *pure poison.* Yet, still . . . such undeniable beauty! Not only her great mane of golden blond hair but those blazing blue eyes, those glorious cheekbones, her tiny nose, that perfectly smooth jawline, her chin with its tiny cleft, those creamy young breasts–a bit worse for the wear after breast-feeding Chandler, but nothing that couldn't be fixed with $10,000 and a sharp scalpel. And those legs . . . God almighty, those long bare legs of hers were off the charts! So perfect they were, the way they tapered so nicely at the ankle yet stayed so luscious above the knee. They were definitely her best asset, along with her ass.

It was only three years ago, in fact, when I had first laid eyes on the Duchess. It was a sight I found so alluring that I ended up leaving my kind first wife, Denise–paying her millions up front in one lump sum plus fifty thousand a month in non-tax-deductible maintenance, so she would walk away quietly without demanding a full-blown audit of my affairs.

And look how fast things had deteriorated! And what had I really done? Say a few words in my sleep? What was the crime in that? The Duchess was definitely overreacting here. In fact, at this point, I had every reason to be mad at her too. Perhaps I could maneuver this whole thing into a quick round of make-up sex, which was the best sex of all. I took a deep breath and said with complete and utter innocence, "Why are you so mad at me? I mean, you . . . you kinda got me confused here."

The Duchess responded by cocking her blond head to the side, the way a person does after they've just heard something that completely defies logic. "You're confused?" she snapped. "You're fucking confused? Why . . . you . . . little . . . bastard!" *Little, again! Unbelievable!* "Where do you want me to start? How about you flying in here on your stupid helicopter at three in the morning, without so much as a fucking phone call to say you'd be late. Is that normal behavior for a married man?"

"But, I–"

"And a father, no less! You're a father now! Yet you still act like a fucking infant! And does it even matter to you that I just had that ridiculous driving range sodded with Bermuda grass? You probably fucking ruined it!" She shook her head in disgust, then she plowed on: "But why should you give a shit? You're not the one who spent your time researching the whole thing and dealing with the landscapers and the golf-course people. Do you know how much time I spent on that stupid fucking project of yours? Do you, you inconsiderate bastard?"

Ahhh, so she's an aspiring landscape architect this month! But such a sexy architect! There had to be some way to turn this all around. Some magic words. "Honey, please, I'm–"

A warning through clenched teeth: "Don't–you–honey–me! You don't ever get to call me honey ever again!"

"But, honey–"

SPLASH!

That time I saw it coming, and I was able to pull the $12,000 silk comforter over my head–deflecting most of her righteous wrath. In fact, hardly a drop of water even touched me. But, alas, my victory was short-lived, and by the time I pulled down the comforter she was already marching back to the bathroom for a refill.

Now she was on her way back. The water glass was filled to the rim; her blue eyes were like death rays; her model-girl jaw looked a mile wide; and her legs . . . Christ! I couldn't keep my eyes off them. Still, there was no time for that now. It was time for the Wolf to get tough. It was time for the Wolf to bare his fangs.

I removed my arms from beneath the white silk comforter, careful not to get them tangled in the thousands of tiny pearls that had been hand-crocheted onto the fabric. Then I cocked my elbows, like chicken wings, giving the irate Duchess a bird's-eye view of my mighty biceps. I said, in a loud, forthright voice, "Don't you dare throw that water at me, Nadine. I'm serious! I'll give you the first two glasses out of anger, but to keep doing it again and again . . .

well, it's like stabbing a dead body when it's lying on the floor in a pool of blood! It's fucking sick!"

That seemed to slow her down—but only for a second. She said, in a mocking tone, "Will you stop flexing your arms, please? You look like a fucking imbecile!"

"I wasn't flexing my arms," I said, unflexing my arms. "You're just lucky to have a husband who's in such great shape. Right, sweetie?" I smiled my warmest smile at her. "Now get over here right this second and give me a kiss!" Even as the words escaped my lips I knew I'd made a mistake.

"Give you a kiss?" sputtered the Duchess. "What are you, fucking kidding me?" Disgust dripped off her very words. "I was an inch away from cutting your balls off and sticking them in one of my shoe boxes. Then you'd never find them!"

Jesus Christ, she was right about that! Her shoe closet was the size of Delaware, and my balls would be lost forever. With the utmost humility, I said, "Please give me a chance to explain, hon—I mean sweetie. Please, I'm begging you!"

All at once her face began to soften. "I can't believe you!" she said, through tiny snuffles. "What did I do to deserve this? I'm a good wife. A beautiful wife. Yet I have a husband who comes home at all hours of the night and talks about another girl in his sleep!" She started moaning with contempt: "Uhhhhh . . . Venice . . . Come to me, Venice."

Jesus Christ! Those Quaaludes could be a real killer sometimes. And now she was crying. It was a complete disaster. After all, what chance did I have of getting her back into bed while she was crying? I needed to switch gears here, to come up with a new strategy. In a tone of voice normally reserved for someone who's standing on the edge of a cliff and threatening to jump, I said, "Put down the glass of water, sweetie, and stop crying. Please. I can explain everything, really!"

Slowly, reluctantly, she lowered the glass of water to waist level. "Go ahead," she said in a tone ripe with disbelief. "Let me hear another lie from the man who lies for a living."

That was true. The Wolf *did* lie for a living, although such was the nature of Wall Street, if you wanted to be a true power broker. Everyone knew that, especially the Duchess, so she really had no right to be angry about that either. Nonetheless, I took her sarcasm in stride, paused for a brief moment to give myself extra time to coagulate my bullshit story, and I said, "First of all, you have the whole thing backward. The only reason I didn't call you last night was because I didn't realize I'd be getting home so late until it was almost eleven. I know how much you like your beauty sleep, and I figured you'd be sleeping anyway, so what was the point of calling?"

The Duchess's poisonous response: "Oh, you're so fucking considerate. Let me go thank my lucky stars for having such a considerate husband." Sarcasm oozed off her words like pus.

I ignored the sarcasm and decided to go for broke. "Anyway, you took this whole Venice business completely out of context. I was talking to Marc Packer last night about opening a Canastel's in Venice, Calif–"

SPLASH!

"You're a fucking liar!" she screamed, grabbing a matching silk bathrobe off the back of some obscenely expensive white fabric chair. "A total fucking liar!"

I let out an obvious sigh. "Okay, Nadine, you've had your fun for the morning. Now come back into bed and give me a kiss. I still love you, even though you soaked me."

That look she gave me! "You want to fuck me now?"

I raised my eyebrows high on my forehead and nodded eagerly. It was the look a seven-year-old boy gives his mother in response to the question: "Would you like an ice-cream cone?"

"Fine," screamed the Duchess. "Go fuck yourself!"

With that, the luscious Duchess of Bay Ridge opened the door–the seven-hundred-pound, twelve-foot-high, solid mahogany door, sturdy enough to withstand a twelve-kiloton nuclear explosion–and walked out of the room, closing the door gently behind her. After all, a slammed door would send the wrong signal to our bizarre menagerie of domestic help.

Our bizarre menagerie: There were five pleasantly plump, Spanish-speaking maids, two of which were husband-and-wife teams; a jabbering Jamaican baby nurse, who was running up a thousand-dollar-a-month phone bill, calling her family in Jamaica; an Israeli electrician, who followed the Duchess around like a love-sick puppy dog; a white-trash handyman, who had all the motivation of a heroin-addicted sea slug; my personal maid, Gwynne, who anticipated my every need no matter how bizarre it might be;

Rocco and Rocco, the two armed bodyguards, who kept out the thieving multitudes, despite the fact that the last crime in Old Brookville occurred in 1643, when white settlers stole land from the Mattinecock Indians; five full-time landscapers, three of which had recently been bitten by my chocolate-brown Labrador retriever, Sally, who bit anyone who dared go within a hundred feet of Chandler's crib, especially if their skin was darker than a brown paper bag; and the most recent addition to the menagerie–two full-time marine biologists, also a husband-and-wife team, who, for $90,000 a year, kept that nightmare-of-a-pond ecologically balanced. And then, of course, there was George Campbell, my charcoal-black limo driver, who hated me.

Yet, with all these people working at Chez Belfort, it didn't change the fact that, right now, I was all alone, soaking wet, and horny as hell, at the hands of my blond second wife, the aspiring everything. I looked around for something to dry myself off with. I grabbed one of the cascading billows of white Chinese silk and tried to wipe myself. Christ! It didn't help a bit. Apparently the silk had been treated with some sort of water repellent, and all it did was push the water from here to there. I looked behind me–a pillowcase! It was made of Egyptian cotton; probably a three-million thread count. Must've cost a fortune–*of my money!* I removed the pillowcase from the overstuffed goose-down pillow inside it and started wiping myself. Ahhh, the Egyptian cotton was nice and soft. And such terrific absorption! My spirits lifted.

I scooted over to my wife's side of the bed to get out of the wet spot. I would pull the covers over my head and return to the warm bosom of my dream. I would return to Venice. I took a deep breath . . . *Oh, shit! The Duchess's scent was everywhere!* All at once I felt the blood rushing to my loins. Christ–she was a frisky little animal, the Duchess, with a frisky little scent! No choice now but to jerk off. It was all for the best, anyway. After all, the Duchess's power over me began and ended below my waist.

I was about to do a little self-soothing when I heard a knock at the door. "Who is it?" I asked, in a voice loud enough to get through the bomb-shelter door.

"Iz Gwaayne," answered Gwynne.

Ahhh, Gwynne–with her wonderful Southern drawl! So soothing it was. In fact, everything about Gwynne was soothing. The way she anticipated my every need, the way she doted on me like the child she never had. "Come in," I replied warmly.

The bomb-shelter door swung open with a tiny creak. *"Guh mawnin, guh mawnin!"* said Gwynne. She was carrying a sterling-silver tray. There was a tall glass of light iced coffee and a bottle of Bayer aspirin resting on it. Tucked beneath her left arm was a white bath towel.

"Good morning, Gwynne. How are you this fine morning?" I asked with mock formality.

"Oh, I'm fine . . . I'm fine!" *Ahhhm fahyn . . . Ahhhm fahyn!* "Well, I see you're over on your wife's side of the bed, so I'll just walk right on over there and bring you your iced coffee. I also brought a nice soft towel for you to wipe yourself with. Mrs. Belfort told me you spilled some water on yourself."

Un-fucking-believable! Martha Stewart strikes again! All at once I realized that my erection had given the white silk comforter the appearance of a circus tent–*shit!* I elevated my knees with the speed of a jackrabbit.

Gwynne walked over and placed the tray on the antique night table on the Duchess's side of the bed. "Here, let me dry you off!" said Gwynne, and she leaned over and began dabbing the white towel on my forehead, as if I were an infant.

Holy Christ! What a fucking circus this house was! I mean, here I was, lying flat on my back, with a raging hard-on, while my fifty-five-year-old plumpish black maid, who was an anachronism from a bygone era, leaned over with her drooping jugs three inches from my face and wiped me with a five-hundred-dollar monogrammed Pratesi bath towel. Of course, Gwynne didn't look even the slightest bit black. Ohhh, no! That would be way too normal for *this* household. Gwynne, in fact, was even lighter than me. The way I had it figured, somewhere in her family tree, perhaps a hundred fifty years ago, when Dixie was still Dixie, her great-great-great-great-grandmother had been the secret love slave of some wealthy plantation owner in south Georgia.

Whatever the case, at least this extreme close-up of Gwynne's drooping jugs was sending the blood rushing out of my loins and back to where it belonged, namely, my liver and lymph channels, where it could be detoxified. Still, the mere sight of her hovering over me like this was more than I could bear, so I kindly explained to her that I was capable of wiping my own forehead.

She seemed a bit sadder for that fact, but all she said was, "Okay," which came out as, *Ohhhhkaii.* "Do you need some aspirin?" *Daya need sum airrrsprin?*

I shook my head. "No, I'm fine, Gwynne. Thanks anyway, though."

"*Ohhhhkaii,* well how 'bout some of them little white pills *fer yer* back?" she asked innocently. "Would you like me to get you some of those?"

Christ! My own maid was offering to fetch me Quaaludes at seven-thirty in the morning! How was I supposed to stay sober? Wherever I was, there were drugs close behind, chasing after me, calling my name. And nowhere was it worse than at my brokerage firm, where virtually every drug imaginable lined the pockets of my young stockbrokers.

Yet my back *did* actually hurt me. I was in constant chronic pain from a freak injury that occurred right after I'd first met the Duchess. It was her dog that did me in–that little white bastard of a Maltese, Rocky, who barked incessantly and served no useful purpose other than to annoy every human being he came into contact with. I had been trying to get the little prick to come in from the beach at the end of a summer Hamptons day, but the little bastard refused to obey me. When I tried to catch him he ran circles around me, forcing me to lunge over to try to grab him. It was reminiscent of the way Rocky Balboa had chased around that greasy chicken in *Rocky II* before his rematch with Apollo Creed. But unlike Rocky Balboa, who became fast-as-lightning and ultimately won his rematch, I ended up rupturing a disk and being bedridden for two weeks. Since then I'd had two back surgeries, both of which had made the pain worse.

So the Quaaludes helped with the pain–sort of. And even if they didn't, it still served as an excellent excuse to keep taking them.

And I wasn't the only one who hated that little shit of a dog. Everyone did, with the exception of the Duchess, who was his sole protector and who still let the mutt sleep at the foot of the bed and chew on her panties, which for some inexplicable reason made me jealous. Still, Rocky would be sticking around for the foreseeable future–until I could figure out a way to eliminate him that the Duchess wouldn't pin on me.

Anyway, I told Gwynne thanks but no thanks for the Quaaludes, and, once more, she seemed a bit sadder for the fact. After all, she had failed to anticipate my every need. But all she said was, "*Ohhhhkaii,* well, I already set the timer on your sauna so it's ready for you right now"–*raghite nahow*–"and I laid out your clothes for you late last night. Is your gray pinstripe suit and that blue tie with the little fishees on it *ohhhhkaii*?"

Christ, talk about service! Why couldn't the Duchess be more like that? True, I was paying Gwynne $70,000 a year, which was more than double the going rate, but, still . . . Look what I got in return: service with a smile! Yet my wife was spending $70,000 a month–on the low side! In fact, with all those fucking aspirations of hers, she was probably spending double that. And that was fine with me, but there had to be a certain trade-off here. I mean, if I needed to go out once in a while and swing the schlong here or dang the gong there, then she oughta cut me just a little bit of slack, shouldn't she? Yes, certainly so–in fact, so much so that I started nodding my head in agreement with my own thoughts.

Apparently, Gwynne took my nodding as an affirmative answer to her question, and she said, "*Ohhhhkaii,* well, I'll just go on out and get Chandler ready so she's nice and clean for you. Have a nice shower!" Cheery, cheery, cheery!

With that, Gwynne left the room. Well, I thought, at least she killed my hard-on, so I was better off for the encounter. As far as the Duchess was concerned, I'd worry about her later. She was a mutt, after all, and mutts were well-known for their forgiving nature.

Having worked things out in my mind, I downed my iced coffee, took six aspirin, swung my feet off the bed, and headed for the sauna. There I would sweat out the five Quaaludes, two grams of coke, and three milligrams of Xanax that I had consumed the night before–a relatively modest amount of drugs, considering what I was truly capable of.

Unlike the master bedroom, which was a testament to white Chinese silk, the master bathroom was a testament to gray Italian marble. It was laid out in an exquisite parquetlike pattern, the way only those Italian bastards know how to do it. And they sure as hell hadn't been scared to bill me! Nonetheless, I paid the thieving Italians in stride. After all, it was the nature of twentieth-century capitalism that everyone should scam everyone, and he who scammed the most ultimately won the game. On that basis, I was the undefeated world champ.

I looked in the mirror and took a moment to regard myself. Christ, what a skinny little bastard I was! I was very muscular, but, still . . . I had to run around in the shower to get wet! Was it the drugs? I wondered. Well, perhaps; but it was a good look for me, anyway. I was only five-seven, and a very smart person had once said you could never be too rich or too thin. I opened the medicine cabinet and took out a bottle of extra-strength Visine. I craned back my neck and put six drops in each eye, triple the recommended dose.

In that very instant, an odd thought came bubbling up into my brain, namely: What kind of man abuses Visine? And, for that matter, why had I taken six Bayer aspirin? It made no sense. After all, unlike Ludes, coke, and Xanax, where the benefits of increasing the dose are plain as day, there was absolutely no valid reason to exceed the recommended doses of Visine and aspirin.

Yet, ironically, that was exactly what my very life had come to represent. It was all about excess: about crossing over forbidden lines, about doing things you thought you'd never do and associating with people who were even wilder than yourself, so you'd feel that much more normal about your own life.

All at once I found myself becoming depressed. What was I going to do about my wife? *Christ–had I really done it this time?* She seemed pretty angry this morning! What was she doing right now? I wondered. If I had to guess, she was probably yapping on the phone to one of her friends or disciples or whatever the fuck they were. She was somewhere downstairs, spewing out perfect pearls of wisdom to her less-than-perfect friends, in the genuine hope that with a little bit of coaching she could make them as perfect as she was. Ahhh, that was my wife, all right–the Duchess of Bay fucking Ridge! The Duchess and all her loyal subjects, those young Stratton wives, who sucked up to her as if she were Queen Elizabeth or something. It was totally fucking nauseating.

Yet, in her defense, the Duchess had a role to play and she played it well. She understood the twisted sense of loyalty that everyone involved with Stratton Oakmont felt for it, and she had forged ties with the wives of key employees, which had made things that much more solid. Yes, the Duchess was a sharp cookie.

Usually she would come into the bathroom in the morning while I was getting ready for work. She was a good conversationalist, when she wasn't busy telling me to go fuck myself. But usually I had brought that on myself, so I really couldn't blame her for it. Actually, I really couldn't blame her for anything, could I? She happened to be a damn good wife, in spite of all that Martha Stewart crap. She must've said "I love you" a hundred times a day. And as the day progressed she would add on these wonderful little intensifiers: *I love you desperately! I love you unconditionally!* . . . and, of course, my favorite: *I love you to the point of madness!* . . . which I considered the most appropriate of all.

Yet, in spite of all her kind words, I still wasn't sure I could trust her. She was my second wife, after all, and words are cheap. Would she really be there with me for better or worse? Outwardly, she gave every indication that she genuinely loved me–constantly showering me with kisses–and whenever we were out in public, she held my hand or put her arm around me or ran her fingers through my hair.

It was all very confusing. When I was married to Denise I never worried about these things. She had married me when I had nothing, so her loyalty was unquestioned. But after I made my first million dollars, she must have had a dark premonition, and she asked me why I couldn't get a normal job making a million dollars a year? It seemed like a ridiculous question at the time, but back then, on that particular day, neither of us knew that in less than a year I'd be making a million dollars a week. And neither of us knew that in less than two years, Nadine Caridi, the Miller Lite girl, would pull up to my Westhampton beach house on July Fourth weekend and step out of that banana-yellow Ferrari wearing a ridiculously short skirt and a pair of white go-to-hell pumps.

I had never meant to hurt Denise. In fact, it was the furthest thing from my mind. But Nadine swept me off my feet, and I swept her off hers. You don't choose who you fall in love with, do you? And once you do fall in love–that obsessive sort of love, that all-consuming love, where two people can't stand to be apart from each other for even a moment–how are you supposed to let a love like that pass you by?

I took a deep breath and slowly exhaled, trying to push all this Denise business back down below the surface. After all, guilt and remorse were worthless emotions, weren't they? Well, I knew they weren't, but I had no time for them. Forward motion; that was the key. Run as fast as you can and don't look back. And as far as my wife went–well, I would right things with her too.

Having worked things out in my mind for the second time in less than five minutes, I forced myself to smile at my own reflection and then headed for the sauna. Once there, I would sweat out the evil spirits and start my day anew.

CHAPTER 3

CANDID CAMERA

Thirty minutes after beginning my morning detox, I emerged from the master bedroom feeling rejuvenated. I was wearing the very gray pinstripe suit that Gwynne had laid out for me. On my left wrist I wore an $18,000 gold Bulgari watch that was thin and understated. In the olden days, before the Duchess came to town, I had worn a solid gold Rolex that was thick and chunky. But the Duchess, being the self-proclaimed arbiter of taste, grace, and gentility, had immediately discarded it, explaining to me that it was gauche. Just how she would know such a thing I still couldn't figure out, given the fact that the nicest watch she'd seen growing up in Brooklyn probably had a Disney character on it. Nevertheless, she seemed to have a knack for these things, so I usually listened to her.

No matter, though. I still maintained my masculine pride with one holdout: a terrific pair of handmade black crocodile cowboy boots. Each boot had been cut from a single crocodile skin, making them absolutely seamless. They had cost me $2,400, and I absolutely loved them. The Duchess, of course, despised them. Today I wore them with great pride, hoping to send a clear signal to my wife that I couldn't be pushed around, in spite of the fact that she had just pushed me around.

I was on my way to Chandler's bedroom for my morning nip of

fatherhood, which was my favorite part of the day. Chandler was the only thing in my life that was completely pure. Each time I carried her in my arms it was as if all the chaos and insanity was held in harness.

As I made my way toward her room, I felt my spirits lifting. She was almost five months old and she was absolutely perfect. But when I opened Channy's door–*what a tremendous shock!* It wasn't just Channy, it was Mommy too! She'd been hiding in Channy's room all along, waiting for me to come in!

There they were, sitting in the very middle of the room on the softest, most glorious pink carpet imaginable. It was another outlandishly expensive touch from Mommy, the formerly aspiring decorator–*who was looking mighty fine, for Chrissake!* Chandler was sitting between her mother's slightly parted legs–*slightly parted legs!*–with her delicate little back resting against Mommy's firm tummy and Mommy's hands clasped around her belly for added support. The two of them looked gorgeous. Channy was a carbon copy of her mother, having inherited those vivid blue eyes and glorious cheekbones.

I took a deep breath to fully relish the scent of my daughter's room. Ahhhh, the smell of baby powder, baby shampoo, baby wipes! And then another deep breath to relish the smell of Mommy. Ahhhh, her four-hundred-dollar-a-bottle shampoo and conditioner from God only knew where! Her hypoallergenic, custom-formulated Kiehl's skin conditioner; that tiny hint of Coco perfume she wore oh so insouciantly! I felt a pleasant tingling sensation shoot through my entire central nervous system and into my loins.

The room itself was absolutely perfect, a little pink wonderland. Countless stuffed animals were scattered about, all arranged just so. To the right was a white crib and bassinet, custom-made by Bellini of Madison Avenue, for the bargain price of $60,000. (Mommy strikes again!) Above it hung a pink and white mobile that played twelve Disney songs, while strikingly realistic Disney characters went round and round at a merry clip. It was another custom-made touch of my dear aspiring decorator, this one only $9,000 (for a mobile?). But who cared? This was Chandler's room, the most favored room in the house.

I took a moment to regard my wife and daughter. All at once

the word *breathtaking* popped into my mind. Chandler was naked as a blue jay. Her olive skin looked buttery smooth and utterly flawless.

And then there was Mommy, who was dressed to kill or, in my case, to tease. Mommy wore a salmon-pink sleeveless minidress with a plunging neckline. Her cleavage was extraordinary! Her terrific mane of golden blond hair shimmered in the morning sunlight. The dress was hiked up above her hips, and I could see all the way up to the top of her waist. There was something missing from this picture . . . but what was it? I couldn't seem to place it, so I dismissed the thought and kept right on staring. Her knees were slightly bent, and I let my eyes run down the full length of her legs. Her shoes matched her dress perfectly, to the very shade and hue. They were Manolo Blahnik, probably cost a thousand bucks, but worth every penny, if you want to know what I was thinking at that particular moment.

So many thoughts were roaring through my head I couldn't keep track of them. I wanted my wife more than ever . . . yet my daughter was there too . . . but she was so little that it didn't really matter! And what about the Duchess? Had she already forgiven me? I wanted to say something, but I couldn't find the words. I loved my wife . . . I loved my life . . . I loved my daughter. I didn't want to lose them. So I made the decision right there, in that very instant: I was done. Yes! No more hookers! No more midnight helicopter rides! No more drugs–or at least not as much of them.

I was about to speak, to throw myself on the mercy of the court, but I never got the chance. Chandler spoke first. *My daughter, the baby genius!* She smiled from ear to ear and in a little tiny voice she said, "Da-da-da-da-da-da-da . . . Da-da-da-da-da-da-da-da."

"Good morning, Daddy!" said Mommy, in a little baby's voice. So sweet! So incredibly sexy! "Aren't you going to give me a good-morning kiss, Daddy? I really, really want one!"

Whuhh? Could it really be this easy? I crossed my fingers and went for broke. "Do I get to kiss both of you, Mommy *and* Daughter?" I pursed my lips and gave Mommy my best puppy-dog face. Then I said a prayer to the Almighty.

"Ohhh, no!" said Mommy, bursting Daddy's bubble. "Daddy doesn't get to kiss Mommy for a very, very long time. But his daughter's dying for a kiss. Isn't that right, Channy?"

Good Lord–she doesn't fight fair, my wife!

Mommy soldiered on in her baby's voice: "Here, Channy, now go crawl over to your daddy right now. Now, Daddy, you bend down so Channy can crawl right into your arms. Okay, Daddy?"

I took a step forward–

"That's far enough," warned Mommy, raising her right hand in the air. "Now bend down just like Mommy said."

I did as I was told. After all, who was I to argue with the luscious Duchess?

Mommy put Chandler down on all fours, ever so gently, and gave her a loving shove forward. Chandler started crawling toward me at a snail's pace, repeating: "Dadadadadadada . . . Dadadadadadada."

Ahhhh, such happiness! Such *joie de vivre*! Was I the luckiest man alive or what? "Come here," I said to Chandler. "Come to Daddy, sweetie." I looked up at Mommy, slowly lowering my gaze . . . and . . . "Holy shit! Nadine, what the . . . what the hell is wrong with you! Are you out of–"

"What's wrong, Dada? I hope you don't see anything you want, because you can't have it anymore," said Mommy, the aspiring cock-teaser, with her glorious legs spread wide open and her skirt hiked up above her hips and her panties nowhere in sight. Her pretty pink vulva was staring me right in the eye and was glistening with desire. All Mommy had was a tiny patch of soft blond peach fuzz, just above her mons pubis, and that was it.

I did the only thing any rational husband could do: I groveled like the dog that I was. "Please, honey, you know how sorry I am about last night. I swear to God I'll never–"

"Oh, save it until next year," said Mommy, with a flap of the back of her hand in the air. "Mommy knows how much you like to swear to God about this and that and everything else when you're about to burst. But don't waste your time, Daddy, because Mommy's only getting started with you. From now on it's going to be nothing but short, short skirts around the house! That's right, Dada! Nothing but short, short skirts, no underwear, and this . . ." said the luscious Mommy with great pride, as she put her palms down behind her and locked out her elbows and leaned all the way back. Then, using the very tips of her Manolo Blahnik high heels in a way the shoe designers had never imagined, she turned them into erotic pivots and let those luscious legs of hers swing open and closed and open and closed until on the third pivot she let them fall so wide open that her knees almost hit the glorious pink carpet. She said, "What's wrong, Dada? You don't look so well."

Well, it wasn't like I hadn't seen it before. In fact this wasn't the first time Mommy had pulled a fast one on me. There were elevators, tennis courts, public parking lots, even the White House. There was no venue completely safe from Mommy. It was just the fucking shock of it all! I felt like a boxer who never saw the punch coming and ended up getting knocked out cold–permanently!

Making matters worse, Chandler had stalled in mid-crawl and decided to take some time to inspect the glorious pink carpet. She was pulling on the fibers as if she'd discovered something truly wonderful, completely oblivious to what was transpiring around her.

I tried to apologize once more, but Mommy's response to that was to stick her right index finger inside her mouth and start to suck. It was then that I lost the power of speech. She seemed to know she'd just delivered the knockout punch, so she slowly pulled her finger out of her mouth and then poured on the baby voice even more: "Ohhh, poor, poor Dada. He loves to say how wrong he is when he's ready to come in his own pants, isn't that right, Dada?"

I stared in disbelief and wondered if any other married couples did things like this.

"Well, Daddy, it's too late for apologies now." She pursed her luscious lips and nodded slowly, the way a person does when they feel like they've just let you in on some great truth. "And it's such a *shame* that Daddy likes to fly around town in his helicopter at all hours of the night after doing God only knows what, because Mommy loves Daddy so, so much and there's nothing she wants to do more right now than to make love to Daddy all day long! And what Mommy's really in the mood for is for Daddy to kiss her in his favorite spot, right where he's looking right now."

Now Mommy pursed her lips again and pretended to pout. "But, ohhh . . . poor, poor Daddy! There's no chance of that happening now, even if Daddy was the very last man on planet Earth. In fact, Mommy has decided to be like the United Nations and institute one of her famous sex embargoes. Daddy doesn't get to make love to Mommy until New Year's Eve"–Whuh? Why, the impudence of it!–"and that's only if he's a very good boy between now and then. If Daddy makes even one mistake it's going to be Groundhog's Day!" What the fuck? Mommy's lost it!

I was just about to sink to unprecedented levels of groveling when all at once something hit me. *Oh, Christ!* Should I tell her? Fuck it, the show's too good!

Mommy in baby voice: "And now that I think of it, Daddy, I think it's time for Mommy to break out her silk thigh-highs and start wearing them around the house, and we all know how much Daddy loves Mommy's silk thigh-highs, don't we, Daddy!"

I nodded eagerly.

Mommy plowed on: "Oh, yes, we do! And Mommy's so sick and tired of wearing underwear . . . *uhhh!* In fact, she's decided to throw them all away! So take a good look, Dada"–time to stop her? Uhhhn, not yet!–"because you're going to be seeing an awful lot of it around the house for a while! But, of course, under the rules of the embargo, touching will be strictly prohibited. And there'll be no jerking off either, Daddy. Until Mommy gives her permission it will be hands at your sides. Is that understood, Daddy?"

With renewed confidence: "But what about you, Mommy? What are you going to do?"

"Oh, Mommy knows how to please herself just fine. Uhhhn . . . uhhhn . . . uhhhn," groaned the fashion model. "In fact, just the thought of it is getting Mommy all excited! Don't you just hate helicopters, Daddy?"

I went for the jugular: "I don't know, Mommy, I think you're all talk and no action. Please yourself? I don't believe you."

Mommy compressed those luscious lips of hers and slowly shook her head, then she said, "Well, I guess it's time for Daddy to be taught his first lesson"–ahhh, this was getting good! And Chandler, still inspecting the carpet, no comprehension–"so Mommy wants Daddy to keep his eye on Mommy's hand and watch very closely or else Groundhog's Day will become Easter Sunday faster than Daddy can say 'blue balls!' Do you understand who's in charge here, Daddy?"

I played along, getting ready to drop the bomb. "Yes, Mommy, but what are you going to do with your hand?"

"Shhh!" said Mommy, and just like that she stuck her finger in her mouth and sucked and sucked until it glistened with saliva in the morning sunlight, and then, slowly, gracefully, lubriciously headed south . . . down her plunging neckline . . . past her cleavage . . . past her belly button . . . and all the way down to her–

"Stop right there!" I said, holding up my right hand. "I wouldn't do it if I were you!"

This shocked Mommy. And infuriated her too! Apparently she had been looking forward to this magic moment as much as I had. But it had gone far enough. It was time to drop the bomb on her. But before I had the chance, Mommy began scolding me: "That's it! Now you've done it! There'll be no kissing or lovemaking until July Fourth!"

"But, Mommy, what about Rocco and Rocco?"

Mommy froze in horror. "Huh?"

I leaned over and picked Chandler up off the glorious pink carpet, held her close to my chest, and gave her a big kiss on the cheek. Then, with her safely out of harm's way, I said, "Daddy wants to tell Mommy a story, and if after he's done Mommy is glad Daddy stopped her before she did what she was about to do, then she has to forgive him for everything he's done, okay?"

No reaction. "Okay," I said, "this is the story about a little pink bedroom in Old Brookville, Long Island. Does Mommy want to hear about it?"

Mommy nodded, a look of complete confusion on her perfect little model face.

"Does Mommy promise to keep her legs spread wide, wide open while Daddy tells the story?"

She nodded slowly, dreamily.

"Good, because it's Daddy's favorite view in the whole world, and it inspires him to tell the story *just* right! Okay–now, there was a little pink bedroom on the second floor of a great stone mansion on a perfect piece of property in the very best part of Long Island, and the people who lived there had lots and lots of money. But–and this is very important to the story, Mommy–of all the possessions they had, and of everything they owned, there was one thing that was much more valuable than all the rest combined, and that was their little baby daughter.

"Now, the daddy in the story had lots and lots of people working for him, and most of them were very, very young and barely housebroken, so Mommy and Daddy decided to put up big iron gates around the entire property so all these young people wouldn't be able to stop by uninvited anymore. But, believe it or not,

Mommy, they still tried stopping by!" I paused and studied Mommy's face, which was slowly losing its color. Then I said, "Anyway, after a while, Mommy and Daddy got so sick and tired of being bothered that they went out and hired two full-time bodyguards. Now, as funny as it may seem, Mommy, they both happened to be named Rocco!" I paused again and studied Mommy's pretty face. Now she was as pale as a ghost.

I continued: "Anyway, Rocco and Rocco spent their time in a wonderful little guardhouse that was in that very backyard in the story. And since the mommy in the story always liked to do things just right, she went out and researched the very best in surveillance equipment, and she ended up buying the latest and greatest TV cameras that give the clearest and brightest and most detailed picture that money can buy. And the best part, Mommy, is that it's all in living color! Yeah!"

Mommy's legs were still spread wide open, in all their glory, when I said, "Anyway, about two months ago Mommy and Daddy were lying in bed on a rainy Sunday morning when she told him about an article she'd read about how some baby nurses and housekeepers mistreated the babies they looked after. This shocked Daddy terribly, so he suggested to Mommy that they have two hidden cameras and a voice-activated microphone installed in that very pink bedroom that I mentioned in the beginning of the story!

"And one of those hidden cameras is right over Daddy's shoulder"–I pointed to a tiny pinhole high up on the wall–"and as luck would have it, Mommy, it happens to be focused right on the very best part of your glorious anatomy"–and there go the legs, snapped shut, like a bank vault–"and since we love Channy so, so much, this is the room that they monitor on the big thirty-two-inch TV screen in the center of the guardhouse!

"So smile, Mommy! You're on *Candid Camera*!"

Mommy didn't move–for about an eighth of a second. Then, as if someone had just shot ten thousand volts of electricity through the glorious pink carpet, Mommy jumped up and screamed: "Holy shit! Holy fucking shit! Oh, my God! I can't fucking believe it! Oh-my-fuc-king-God!" She ran to the window and looked out at the guardhouse . . . then she spun around and ran back, and . . . *BOOM!* . . . down went Mommy, as one of the erotic pivots on her go-to-hell pumps collapsed.

But Mommy was only down for a second. She quickly rolled

onto all fours with the speed and dexterity of a world-class wrestler and then popped right back up. To my complete and utter shock, she opened the door, ran out, and slammed it behind her as she left, entirely unconcerned with what the bizarre menagerie of help might think of all the ruckus. And then she was gone.

"Well," I said to Channy, "the real Martha Stewart would definitely not have approved of a slammed door, now, would she, sweetie!" Then I said a silent prayer to the Almighty, asking him–no begging him, in fact–to never allow Channy to marry a guy like me, much less date one. I wasn't exactly Husband of the Year material, after all. Then I carried her downstairs and handed her to Marcie, the jabbering Jamaican baby nurse, and made a quick beeline for the guardhouse, not wanting the videotape of Mommy to end up in Hollywood as a pilot for *Lifestyles of the Rich and Dysfunctional.*

CHAPTER 4

WASP HEAVEN

Like a dog in heat, I searched all twenty-four rooms of the mansion for Mommy. In fact, I searched every nook and cranny of all six acres of the estate until, finally, reluctantly, and with great sadness, I called off my search. It was almost nine o'clock, and I had to get to work. Just where my dear aspiring cock-teaser was hiding, I couldn't figure out. So I gave up trying to get laid.

We pulled away from my Old Brookville estate just after nine a.m. I was sitting in the backseat of my midnight-blue Lincoln limousine, with my chauffeur, George Campbell, behind the wheel. In the four years George had worked for me, he'd said only a dozen words. On some mornings I found his self-imposed vow of silence rather annoying, but at this particular moment it was just fine. In fact, after my recent run-in with the luscious Duchess, a little bit of peace and quiet would be sublime.

Still, as part of my morning ritual I would always greet George in overly warm tones and try to get some sort of response out of him. Anything. So I figured I'd take another crack at it, just for shits and giggles.

I said, "Hey, Georgie! How ya doing today?"

George turned his head approximately four and a half degrees to the right, so I could barely see the whites of his blazing white eyeballs, and then he nodded, just once.

Never fails, God damn it! The guy's a fucking mute!

Actually, that wasn't true: About six months earlier George had asked me if I could loan him (which, of course, meant give him) $5,000 to get himself a new set of choppers (as he referred to them). This I gladly did, but not until I tortured him for a good fifteen minutes, making him tell me everything–how white they'd be, how many there'd be, how long they'd last, and what was wrong with his teeth right now. By the time George was done, there were beads of sweat running down his charcoal-black forehead, and I was sorry I'd ever asked him in the first place.

Today, as on every day, George wore a navy-blue suit and grim expression, the grimmest expression his inflated $60,000-a-year salary could reasonably allow for. I had no doubt that George hated me or at least resented me. The only exception to that was my wife, the aspiring people-pleaser, whom George adored.

The limo was one of those superstretch jobs, with a fully stocked bar, a TV and VHS, a fridge, a terrific sound system, and a rear seat that turned into a queen-size bed with the flip of a switch. The bed was an added touch, to ease my back pain, but it had the unintended effect of turning my limousine into a $96,000 brothel on wheels. Go figure. My destination this morning was none other than Lake Success, Long Island, the once quiet middle-class hamlet where Stratton Oakmont was located.

Nowadays, the town was like Tombstone, Arizona–*before* the Earps came to town. All these quaint little cottage industries had sprung up to service the needs, wants, and desires of the twisted young stockbrokers in my employ. There were brothels, illegal gambling parlors, after-hours clubs, and all that sort of fun stuff. There was even a little prostitution ring turning tricks in the lower level of the parking garage, at two hundred dollars a pop.

In the early years, the local merchants were up in arms over the apparent gracelessness of my merry band of stockbrokers, many of whom seemed to have been raised in the wild. But it wasn't long before these same merchants realized that the Stratton brokers didn't check price tags on anything. So the merchants jacked up their prices, and everyone lived in peace, just like in the Wild West.

Now the limo was heading west, down Chicken Valley Road, one of the finest roads in the Gold Coast. I cracked my window to let in a little fresh air. I stared out at the lush fairways of the Brookville Country Club, where I'd made my drug-assisted approach earlier this morning. The country club was remarkably close to my estate–so near, in fact, that I could hit a golf ball from my front lawn to the middle of the seventh fairway with a well-struck seven iron. But, of course, I never bothered applying for membership, what with my status as a lowly Jew, who had the utter gall to invade WASP heaven.

And it wasn't just the Brookville Country Club where I felt out of place as a Jew. No, no, no! All the surrounding clubs restricted Jews or, for that matter, anyone who wasn't a blue-blooded WASP bastard. (In fact, Brookville Country Club admitted Catholics and wasn't nearly as bad as some of the others.) When the Duchess and I first moved here from Manhattan, the whole WASP thing bothered me. It was like some secret club or society, but then I came to realize that the WASPs were yesterday's news, a seriously endangered species no different than the dodo bird or spotted owl. And while it was true that they still had their little golf clubs and hunting lodges as last bastions against the invading *shtetl* hordes, they were nothing more than twentieth-century Little Big Horns on the verge of being overrun by savage Jews like myself, who'd made fortunes on Wall Street and were willing to spend whatever it took to live where Gatsby lived.

The limo made a gentle left turn and now we were on Hegemans Lane. Up ahead on the left was the Gold Coast Stables, or, as the owners liked to refer to it, "The Gold Coast Equestrian Center," which sounded infinitely WASPier.

As we passed by, I could see the green-and-white-striped stables, where the Duchess kept her horses. From top to bottom the whole equestrian thing had turned into a giant fucking nightmare that continually sucked in money. The horses cost a fortune to buy. And if that weren't painful enough, as soon as we bought the horses, they would become afflicted with bizarre ailments. Between the vet bills, the food bills, and the cost of paying stable hands to ride the horses so they would stay in shape, it had turned into an enormous black hole.

Nevertheless, my luscious Duchess, the aspiring hunter-jumper expert, went there every day–to feed her horses sugar cubes and carrots and to take riding lessons–in spite of the fact that she suffered from intractable horse allergies and would come home sneezing and wheezing and itching and coughing. But, hey, when you live in the middle of WASP heaven you do as the WASPs do, and you pretend to like horses.

As the limo crossed over Northern Boulevard, I felt my lower-back pain breaking through the surface. It was about that time when most of last night's recreational drug medley had worked its way out of my central nervous system and into my liver and lymph channels, where it belonged. But it also meant that the pain would now be returning. It felt as if an angry, feral, fire-breathing dragon was slowly awakening. The pain started in the small of my back, on the left side, and went shooting down the back of my left leg. It was as if someone were twisting a red-hot branding iron into the back of my thigh. It was excruciating. If I tried rubbing the pain out it would shift to a different spot.

I took a deep breath and resisted the urge to grab three Quaaludes and swallow them dry. That would be completely unacceptable behavior, after all. I was heading for work, and in spite of being the boss, I couldn't just stumble in like a drooling idiot. That was only acceptable at nighttime. Instead, I said a quick prayer that a bolt of lightning would come down from out of the clear blue sky and electrocute my wife's dog.

On this side of Northern Boulevard, things were decidedly low rent, which is to say the average home went for a little over a million-two. It was rather ironic how a kid from a poor family could become desensitized to the extravagances of wealth to the point that million-dollar homes now seemed like shacks. But that wasn't a bad thing, was it? Well, who knew anymore.

Just then I saw the green and white sign that hung over the entrance ramp to the Long Island Expressway. Soon enough I'd be walking into the very offices of Stratton Oakmont–my home away from home–where the mighty roar of America's wildest boardroom would make the insanity seem perfectly okay.

CHAPTER 5

THE MOST POWERFUL DRUG

The investment-banking firm of Stratton Oakmont occupied the first floor of a sprawling black-glass office building that rose up four stories from out of the muddy marrow of an old Long Island swamp pit. In truth, it wasn't as bad as it sounded. Most of the old pit had been reclaimed back in the early 1980s, and it now sported a first-class office complex with an enormous parking lot and a three-level underground parking garage, where Stratton brokers would take mid-afternoon coffee breaks and get laid by a happy hit squad of prostitutes.

Today, as on every day, as we pulled up to the office building I found myself welling up with pride. The mirrored black glass gleamed brilliantly in the morning sunshine, reminding me of just how far I'd come in the last five years. It was hard to imagine that I'd actually started Stratton from out of the electrical closet of a used-car dealership. And now . . . *this!*

On the west side of the building there was a grand entranceway meant to dazzle all those who walked through it. But not a soul from Stratton ever did. It was too far out of the way, and time, after all, was money. Instead, everyone, including me, used a concrete ramp on the south side of the building, which led directly to the boardroom.

I climbed out of the back of the limousine, said my parting farewells to George (who nodded without speaking), and then made my way up that very concrete ramp. As I passed through the steel doors, I could already make out the faint echoes of the mighty roar, which sounded like the roar of a mob. It was music to my ears. I headed right for it, with a vengeance.

After a dozen steps, I turned the corner and there it was: the boardroom of Stratton Oakmont. It was a massive space, more than a football field long and nearly half as wide. It was an open space, with no partitions and a very low ceiling. Tightly packed rows of maple-colored desks were arranged classroom style, and an endless sea of crisp white dress shirts moved about furiously. The brokers had their suit jackets off, and they were shouting into black telephones, which created the roar. It was the sound of polite young men using logic and reason to convince business owners across America to invest their savings with Stratton Oakmont:

"Jesus Christ, Bill! Pick up your skirt, grab your balls, and make a goddamn decision!" screamed Bobby Koch, a chubby, twenty-two-year-old Irishman with a high-school diploma, a raging coke habit, and an adjusted gross income of $1.2 million. He was berating some wealthy business owner named Bill who lived somewhere in America's heartland. Each desk had a gray-colored computer on it, and green-diode numbers and letters came flashing across, bringing real-time stock quotes to the Strattonites. But hardly a soul ever glanced at them. They were too busy sweating profusely and screaming into black telephones, which looked like giant eggplants growing out of their ears.

"I need a decision–*Bill!*–I need a decision right now!" snapped Bobby. "Steve Madden is the hottest new issue on Wall Street, and there's nothing to think about! By this afternoon it'll be a fucking dinosaur!" Bobby was two weeks out of the Hazelden Clinic and had already begun to relapse. His eyes seemed to be popping right out of his beefy Irish skull. You could literally feel the cocaine crystals oozing from his sweat glands. It was 9:30 a.m.

A young Strattonite with slicked-back hair, a square jaw, and a neck the size of Rhode Island was in a crouch position, trying to explain to a client the pros and cons of including his wife in the decision-making process. "Tawk to ya wife? Waddaya, crazy a sumthin'?" He was only vaguely aware that his New York accent was so thick it sounded like sludge. "I mean, ya think your wife *tawkstaya* when she goes out and buys a new pair of shoes?"

Three rows back, a young Strattonite with curly brown hair and an active case of teenage acne was standing stiff as a ramrod with his black telephone wedged between his cheek and collarbone. His arms were extended like airplane wings, and he had giant sweat stains under his armpits. As he shouted into his telephone, Anthony Gilberto, the firm's custom tailor, fit him for a custom-made suit. All day long Gilberto would go from desk to desk taking measurements of young Strattonites and make suits for them at $2,000 a pop. Just then the young Strattonite tilted his head all the way back and stretched his arms out as wide as they could possibly go, as if he were about to do a swan dive off a ten-meter board. Then he said, in a tone you use when you're at your wits' end: "Jesus, will you do yourself a favor, Mr. Kilgore, and pick up ten thousand shares? Please, you're *killing* me here . . . you're killing me. I mean, do I have to fly down to Texas to twist your arm, because if I have to I will!"

Such dedication! I thought. The pimply-faced kid was pitching stock even while he was clothes shopping! My office was on the other side of the boardroom, and as I made my way through the writhing sea of humanity I felt like Moses in cowboy boots. Brokers parted this way and that as they cleared a path for me. Each broker I passed offered me a wink or a smile as a way of showing their appreciation for this little slice of heaven on earth I'd created. Yes, these were my people. They came to me for hope, love, advice, and direction, and I was ten times crazier than all of them. Yet one thing we all shared equally was an undying love for the mighty roar. In fact, we couldn't get enough of it:

"Pick up the fucking phone, please!" screamed a little blond sales assistant.

"You pick up the fucking phone! It's your fucking job."

"I'm only asking for one shot!"

"–twenty thousand at eight and a half–"

"–pick up a hundred thousand shares–"

"The stock's going through the roof!"

"For Chrissake, Steve Madden's the hottest deal on Wall Street!"

"Fuck Merrill Lynch! We eat those cockroaches for breakfast."

"Your local broker? Fuck your local broker! He's busy reading yesterday's *Wall Street Journal*!"

"–I got twenty thousand B warrants at four–"

"Fuck that, they're a piece of shit!"

"Yeah, well, fuck you too, and the piece-a-shit Volkswagen you drove here!"

Fuck this and fuck that! Shit here and shit there! It was the language of Wall Street. It was the essence of the mighty roar, and it cut through everything. It intoxicated you. It seduced you! It fucking liberated you! It helped you achieve goals you never dreamed yourself capable of! And it swept everyone away, especially me.

Out of the thousand souls in the boardroom there was scarcely a warm body over thirty; most were in their early twenties. It was a handsome crowd, exploding with vanity, and the sexual tension was so thick you could literally smell it. The dress code for men–*boys!*–was a custom-made suit, white dress shirt, silk necktie, and solid gold wristwatch. For the women, who were outnumbered ten to one, it was go-to-hell skirts, plunging necklines, push-up bras, and spike heels, the higher the better. It was the very sort of attire strictly forbidden in Stratton's human-resources manual yet heavily encouraged by management (yours truly).

Things had gotten so out of hand that young Strattonites were rutting away under desks, in bathroom stalls, in coat closets, in the underground parking garage, and, of course, the building's glass elevator. Eventually, to maintain some semblance of order, we passed out a memorandum declaring the building a Fuck Free Zone between the hours of eight a.m. and seven p.m. On the top of the memo were those very words, *Fuck Free Zone,* and beneath them were two anatomically correct stick figures, doing it doggy-style. Surrounding the stick figures was a thick red circle with a diagonal line running through its center: a *Ghostbusters* sign. (Certainly a Wall Street first.) But, alas, no one took it seriously.

It was all good, though, and it all made perfect sense. Everyone was young and beautiful, and they were seizing the moment. Seize the moment–it was this very corporate mantra that burned like fire in the heart and soul of every young Strattonite and vibrated in the overactive pleasure centers of all thousand of their barely postadolescent brains.

And who could argue with such success? The amount of money being made was staggering. A rookie stockbroker was expected to make $250,000 his first year. Anything less and he was suspect. By year two you were making $500,000 or you were considered weak and worthless. And by year three you'd better be making a million or more or you were a complete fucking laughingstock. And those were only the minimums; big producers made triple that.

And from there the wealth trickled down. Sales assistants, who were really glorified secretaries, were making over $100,000 a year. Even the girl at the front switchboard made $80,000 a year, just for answering the phones. It was nothing short of a good old-fashioned gold rush, and Lake Success had become a boomtown. Young Strattonites, the children that they were, began calling the place Broker Disneyland, and each one of them knew that if they were ever thrown out of the amusement park they would never make this much money again. And such was the great fear that lived at the base of the skull of every young Strattonite–that one day you would lose your job. Then what would they do? After all, when you were a Strattonite you were expected to live the Life–driving the fanciest car, eating at the hottest restaurants, giving the biggest tips, wearing the finest clothes, and residing in a mansion in Long Island's fabulous Gold Coast. And even if you were just getting started and you didn't have a dime to your name, then you would borrow money from any bank insane enough to lend it to you–regardless of the interest rate–and start living the Life, whether you were ready for it or not.

It was so out of control that kids still sporting teenage acne and only recently acquainted with a razor blade were going out and buying mansions. Some of them were so young they never even moved in; they still felt more comfortable sleeping at home, with their parents. In the summers they rented lavish homes in the Hamptons, with heated swimming pools and spectacular views of the Atlantic Ocean. On weekends they threw wild parties that were so decadent they were invariably broken up by the police. Live bands played; DJs spun records; young Stratton girls danced topless; strippers and hookers were considered honored guests; and, inevitably, at some point along the way, young Strattonites would get naked and start rutting away right under the clear blue sky, like barnyard animals, happy to put on a show for an ever-expanding live audience.

But what was wrong with that? They were drunk on youth, fueled by greed, and higher than kites. And day by day the gravy train grew longer, as more and more people made fortunes providing the crucial elements young Strattonites needed to live the Life. There were the real estate brokers who sold them the mansions;

the mortgage brokers who secured the financing; the interior decorators who stuffed the mansions with overpriced furniture; the landscapers who tended to the grounds (any Strattonite caught mowing his own lawn would be stoned to death); the exotic car dealers who sold the Porsches and Mercedes and Ferraris and Lamborghinis (if you drove anything less you were considered a total fucking embarrassment); there were the maître d's who reserved tables at the hottest restaurants; there were the ticket scalpers who got front-row seats to sold-out sporting events and rock concerts and Broadway shows; and there were the jewelers and watchmakers and clothiers and shoemakers and florists and caterers and haircutters and pet groomers and masseuses and chiropractors and car detailers and all the other niche-service providers (especially the hookers and the drug dealers) who showed up at the boardroom and delivered their services right to the feet of young Strattonites so they wouldn't have to take even one second out of their busy day or, for that matter, engage in any extracurricular activity that didn't directly enhance their ability to commit one single act: dial the telephone. That was it. You smiled and dialed from the second you came in to the office until the second you left. And if you weren't motivated enough to do it or you couldn't take the constant rejection of secretaries from all fifty states slamming the phone down in your ear three hundred times a day, then there were ten people right behind you who were more than willing to do the job. And then you were out–permanently.

And what secret formula had Stratton discovered that allowed all these obscenely young kids to make such obscene amounts of money? For the most part, it was based on two simple truths: first, that a majority of the richest one percent of Americans are closet degenerate gamblers, who can't withstand the temptation to keep rolling the dice again and again, even if they know the dice are loaded against them; and, second, that contrary to previous assumptions, young men and women who possess the collective social graces of a herd of sex-crazed water buffalo and have an intelligence quotient in the range of Forrest Gump on three hits of acid, *can* be taught to sound like Wall Street wizards, as long as you write every last word down for them and then keep drilling it into their heads again and again–every day, twice a day–for a year straight.

And as word of this little secret began to spread throughout

Long Island–that there was this wild office, in Lake Success, where all you had to do was show up, follow orders, swear your undying loyalty to the owner, and he would make you rich–young kids started showing up at the boardroom unannounced. At first they trickled in; then they poured in. It started with kids from the middle-class suburbs of Queens and Long Island and then quickly spread to all five boroughs of New York City. Before I knew it they were coming from all across America, begging me for jobs. Mere *kids* would travel halfway across the country to the boardroom of Stratton Oakmont and swear their undying loyalty to the Wolf of Wall Street. And the rest, as they say, is Wall Street history.

As always, my ultraloyal personal assistant, Janet,* was sitting before her own desk, anxiously awaiting my arrival. At this particular moment she was tapping her right index finger on her desktop and shaking her head in a way that said, "Why the fuck does my whole day revolve around when my crazy boss decides to show up for work?" Or perhaps that was just my imagination and she was simply bored. Either way, Janet's desk was positioned just in front of my door, as if she were an offensive lineman protecting a quarterback. That was no accident. Among her many functions, Janet was my gatekeeper. If you wanted to see me or even speak to me, you first had to get through Janet. That was no simple task. She protected me the way a lioness protects her cubs, having no problem unleashing her sometimes righteous wrath on any living soul who tried breaching the gauntlet.

As soon as Janet saw me she flashed a warm smile, and I took a moment to regard her. She was in her late twenties but looked a few years older. She had a thick mane of dark brown hair, fair white skin, and a tight little body. She had beautiful blue eyes, but there was a certain sadness to them, as if they'd seen too much heartache for someone so young. Perhaps that was why Janet showed up for work each day dressed like Death. Yes, from head to toe, she always wore black, and today was no exception.

"Good morning," said Janet, with a bright smile and slight hint of annoyance in her tone. "Why are you so late?"

I smiled warmly at my ultraloyal assistant. In fact, in spite of Janet's funeral ensemble and her undying urge to know every last ounce of my personal gossip, I found the sight of her immensely

*Name has been changed.

pleasing. She was Gwynne's counterpart in the office. Whether it was paying my bills, managing my brokerage accounts, keeping my schedule, arranging my travel, paying my hookers, running interference with my drug dealers, or lying to whichever wife I was currently married to, there was no task either too great or too small that Janet wouldn't gladly jump through a hoop to accomplish. She was incredibly competent and never made a mistake.

Janet had also grown up in Bayside, but her parents had both died when she was young. Her mother had been a good lady, but her father had mistreated her, a total scumbag. I did my best to make her feel loved, to feel wanted. And I protected her in the same way she protected me.

When Janet got married last month, I threw her a glorious wedding and walked her down the aisle with great pride. On that day she wore a snow-white Vera Wang wedding dress–paid for by me and picked out by the Duchess, who also spent two hours doing Janet's makeup. (Yes, the Duchess was also an aspiring makeover artist.) And Janet looked absolutely gorgeous.

"Good morning," I replied with a warm smile. "The room sounds good today, right?"

Tonelessly: "It always sounds good, but you didn't answer me. Why are you so late?"

A pushy little broad, she was, and damn nosy too. I let out a deep sigh and said, "Did Nadine call, by any chance?"

"No. Why? What happened?" They were rapid-fire questions. Apparently she sensed a juicy piece of gossip.

"Nothing happened, Janet. I got home late, and Nadine got pissed and threw a glass of water at me. That's it; although, actually, it was three glasses, but who's counting? Anyway, the rest of it is too bizarre for words, but I need to send her flowers right now or else I might be hunting for wife number three before the day is out."

"How much should I send?" she asked, picking up a spiral pad and Montblanc pen.

"I don't know . . . three or four thousand worth. Just tell them to send the whole fucking truck. And make sure they send lots of lilies. She likes lilies."

Janet narrowed her eyes and pursed her lips, as if to say, "You're breaching our silent understanding that as part of my compensation package it's my right to know all the gory details, no matter how gory they might be!" But being a professional, driven by her sense of duty, all she said was, "Fine, you'll tell me the story later."

I nodded unconvincingly. "Maybe, Janet, we'll see. So tell me what's going on."

"Well–Steve Madden's floating around here somewhere, and he seems kind of nervous. I don't think he's gonna do such a good job today."

An immediate surge of adrenaline. *Steve Madden!* How ironic it was that with all the chaos and insanity this morning it had actually slipped my mind that Steve Madden Shoes was going public today. In fact, before the day was out I'd be ringing the register to the tune of twenty million bucks. Not too shabby! And Steve had to stand up in front of the boardroom and give a little speech, a so-called dog-and-pony show. Now, that would be interesting! I wasn't sure if Steve was the sort who could look into the wild eyes of all those crazy young Strattonites and not completely choke.

Still, dog-and-pony shows were a Wall Street tradition: Just before a new issue came to market, the CEO would stand before a friendly crowd of stockbrokers and give a canned speech, focusing on how glorious his company's future was. It was a friendly sort of encounter with a lot of mutual back-scratching and phony palm-pressing.

And then there was Stratton, where things got pretty ugly sometimes. The problem was that the Strattonites weren't the least bit interested; they just wanted to sell the stock and make money. So if the guest speaker didn't captivate them from the moment he began speaking, the Strattonites would quickly grow bored. Then they would start booing and catcalling–and then spewing out profanities. Eventually, they would throw things at the speaker, starting with balled-up paper and then quickly moving to food products like rotten tomatoes, half-eaten chicken legs, and half-consumed apples.

I couldn't let such a terrible fate befall Steve Madden. First and foremost, he was a childhood friend of Danny Porush, my second-in-command. And, second, I personally owned more than half of Steve's company, so I was basically taking my own deal public. I had given Steve $500,000 in start-up capital about sixteen months ago, which made me the company's single largest shareholder, with an eighty-five percent stake. A few months later I sold off thirty-five percent of my stock for a little over $500,000, recouping my original investment. Now I owned fifty percent for free! Talk about your good deals!

In point of fact, it was this very process of buying stakes in private companies and then reselling a portion of my original investment (and recouping my money) that had turned Stratton into even more of a printing press than it already was. And, as I used the power of the boardroom to take my own companies public, my net worth soared and soared. On Wall Street this process was called "merchant banking," but to me it was like hitting the lotto every four weeks.

I said to Janet, "He should do fine, but if he doesn't, I'll go up there and bail him out. Anyway, what else is going on?"

With a shrug: "Your father's looking for you, and he seems pissed."

"Eh, shit!" I muttered. My father, Max, was Stratton's de facto Chief Financial Officer and also the self-appointed Chief of the Gestapo. He was so tightly wound that at nine a.m. he was walking around the boardroom with a Styrofoam cup filled with Stolichnaya vodka, smoking his twentieth cigarette. In the trunk of his car he kept a forty-two-ounce Louisville Slugger, autographed by Mickey Mantle, so he could smash the "fucking windows" of any stockbroker who was insane enough to park in his glorious parking spot. "Did he say what he wanted?"

"Nope!" said my loyal assistant. "I asked him, and he growled at me, like a dog. He's definitely pissed about *something,* and if I had to take a guess, I'd say it's the November American Express bill."

I grimaced. "You think?" All at once the number *half a million* came bubbling up, uninvited, into my own brain.

Janet nodded her head. "He was holding the bill in his hand and it was about yea thick." The gap between her thumb and forefinger was a good three inches.

"Hmmmmm . . ." I took a moment to ponder the American Express bill, but something caught my eye from way out in the distance. It was floating . . . floating . . . what in the hell was it? I squinted. Jesus Christ–someone had brought a red, white, and blue plastic beach ball into the office! It was as if the corporate headquarters of Stratton Oakmont were a stadium, the floor of the boardroom was the orchestra section, and the Rolling Stones were about to give a concert.

". . . of all this he's cleaning his fucking fishbowl!" said Janet. "It's hard to believe!"

I'd only caught the tail end of what Janet was saying, so I mumbled, "Yeah, well, I know whatya mean–"

"You didn't hear a word I said," she muttered, "so don't pretend you did."

Jesus! Who else besides my father would speak to me that way! Well, maybe my wife, but in her case I usually deserved it. Still, I loved Janet, in spite of her poisonous tongue. "Very funny. Now tell me what you said."

"What I said is that I can't believe that kid over there"–she pointed to a desk about twenty yards away–"what's his name, Robert something or other, is cleaning his fishbowl in the middle of all this. I mean, it's new-issue day! Don't you think that's kinda weird?"

I looked in the direction of the alleged perpetrator: a young Strattonite–no, definitely not a Strattonite–a young misfit, with a ferocious mop of curly brown hair and a bow tie. The mere fact that he had a fishbowl on his desk wasn't all that surprising. Strattonites were allowed to have pets in the office. There were iguanas, ferrets, gerbils, parakeets, turtles, tarantulas, snakes, mongooses, and whatever else these young maniacs could procure with their inflated paychecks. In fact, there was even a macaw with a vocabulary of over fifty English words, who would tell you to go fuck yourself when he wasn't busy mimicking the young Strattonites pitching stock. The only time I'd put my foot down with the whole pet thing was when a young Strattonite had brought in a chimpanzee wearing roller skates and a diaper.

"Go get Danny," I snapped. "I want him to get a load of this fucking kid."

Janet nodded and went to fetch Danny, while I stood there in utter shock. How could this bow-tied dweeb commit an act so . . . fucking heinous? An act that went against the grain of everything the boardroom of Stratton Oakmont stood for! It was sacrilege! Not against God, of course, but against the Life! It was a breach of the Stratton code of ethics of the most egregious sort. And the punishment was . . . what was the punishment? Well, I would leave that up to Danny Porush, my junior partner, who had a terrific knack for disciplining wayward Strattonites. In fact, he relished it.

Just then I saw Danny walking toward me, with Janet trailing two steps behind. Danny looked pissed, which is to say the bow-tied broker was in deep shit. As he drew nearer, I took a moment to regard him, and I couldn't help but snicker at how normal he actually looked. It was really quite ironic. In fact, dressed the way he was, in a gray pin-striped suit, crisp white dress shirt, and red silk necktie, you would have never guessed that he was closing in on his publicly stated goal of banging every last sales assistant in the boardroom.

Danny Porush was a Jew of the ultrasavage variety. He was of average height and weight, about five-nine, one-seventy, and he had absolutely no defining features that would peg him out to be a member of the Tribe. Even those steel-blue eyes of his, which generated about as much warmth as an iceberg, hadn't the slightest bit of Yid in them.

And that was appropriate, at least from Danny's perspective. After all, like many a Jew before him, Danny burned with the secret desire to be mistaken for a WASP and did everything possible to cloak himself in complete and utter WASPiness–starting with those incredibly boiling teeth of his, which had been bleached and bonded until they were so big and white they looked almost radioactive, to those brown tortoiseshell glasses with their clear lenses (Danny had twenty-twenty vision), and all the way down to those black leather shoes with their custom-fitted insteps and fancy toe caps, the latter of which had been polished into mirrors.

And what a grim joke that was–considering by the ripe age of thirty-four, Danny had given new meaning to the term *abnormal psychology*. Perhaps I should have suspected as much six years ago, when I'd first met him. It was before I'd started Stratton, and Danny was working for me as a stockbroker trainee. It was sometime in the spring, and I had asked him to take a quick ride with me into Manhattan, to see my accountant. Once there, he convinced me to make a quick stop at a Harlem crack den, where he told me his life's story–explaining how his last two businesses, a messenger service and an ambulette service, had been sucked up his nose. He further explained how he'd married his own first cousin, Nancy, because she was a real piece of ass. When I asked him if he was concerned about inbreeding, he casually replied that if they had a child who ended up being a *retard* he would simply leave *it* on the institution steps, and that would be that.

Perhaps I should have run the other way right then and there, realizing that a guy like this might bring out the worst in me. Instead, I made Danny a personal loan to help him get back on his feet, and then I trained him to become a stockbroker. A year later I started Stratton and let Danny slowly buy in and become a partner. Over the last five years Danny had proven himself to be a mighty warrior–squeezing out anyone in his way and securing his position as Stratton's number two. And in spite of it all, in spite of his very insanity, there was no denying that he was smart as a whip, cunning as a fox, ruthless as a Hun, and, above all else, loyal as a dog. Nowadays, in fact, I counted on him to do almost all my dirty work, a job he relished more than you can imagine.

Danny greeted me Mafia style, with a warm hug and a kiss on either cheek. It was a sign of loyalty and respect, and in the boardroom of Stratton Oakmont it was a greatly appreciated gesture. Out of the corner of my eye, though, I saw Janet, the cynic, rolling her eyes in the oh-brother mode, as if to mock Danny's display of loyalty and affection.

Danny released me from his Mafia embrace and muttered, "I'm gonna kill that fucking kid. I swear to God!"

"It's a bad showing, Danny, especially today." I shrugged. "I think you should tell him that if his fishbowl ain't out of here by the end of the day, then the fishbowl is staying and he's leaving. But it's your call; do what you want."

Janet the instigator: "Oh, my God! He's wearing a bow tie! Can you imagine?"

"That rat fucking bastard!" said Danny, in a tone used to describe someone who'd just raped a nun and left her for dead. "I'm gonna take care of this kid once and for all, in my own way!" With a huff and a puff, Danny marched over to the broker's desk and began exchanging words with him.

After a few seconds the broker started shaking his head no. Then more words were exchanged, and the broker began shaking his head no again. Now Danny began shaking his own head, the way a person does when they're running out of patience.

Janet, with a pearl of wisdom: "I wonder what they're saying? I wish I had bionic ears like the Six Million Dollar Woman. You know what I mean?"

I shook my head in disgust. "I won't even dignify that with a response, Janet. But just for your information, there was no Six Million Dollar Woman. It was the Bionic Woman."

Just then, Danny extended his palm toward the broker's left hand, which held a fishnet, and began waving his fingers inward, as if to say, "Hand over the fucking net!" The broker responded by dropping his arm to the side–keeping the net out of Danny's reach.

"What do you think he's gonna do with the net?" asked the aspiring Bionic Woman.

I ran the possibilities through my mind. "I'm not really sure– Oh, shit, I know exactly what . . ."

All at once, faster than would seem possible, Danny ripped off his suit jacket, threw it on the floor, unbuttoned his shirtsleeve, pushed it up past his elbow, and plunged his hand into the fishbowl. His entire forearm was submerged. Then he began thrashing his arm in all directions, trying to catch an unsuspecting orange goldfish in the palm of his hand. His face was set in stone, with the look of a man possessed by pure evil.

A dozen young sales assistants seated close to the action jumped out of their seats and recoiled in horror at the very sight of Danny trying to capture the innocent goldfish.

"Oh . . . my . . . God," said Janet. "He's gonna kill it."

Just then Danny's eyes popped wide open and his jaw dropped down a good three inches. It was a face that so much as said, "Gotcha!" A split second later he yanked his arm out of the fishbowl, with the orange goldfish firmly in his grasp.

"He's got it!" cried Janet, putting her fist to her mouth.

"Yeah, but the million-dollar question is, what's he gonna do with it?" I paused for just an instant, then added, "But I'm willing to bet you a hundred to one on a thousand bucks that he eats it. Are we on?"

An instant reply: "A hundred to one? You're on! He won't do it! It's too gross. I mean–"

Janet was cut off as Danny climbed on top of a desk and extended his arms out, as if he were Jesus Christ on the cross. He screamed, "This is what happens when you fuck with your pets on new-issue day!" As an afterthought, he added, "And no fucking bow ties in the boardroom! It's fucking . . . ridiculous!"

Janet the welcher: "I want to cancel my bet right now!"

"Sorry, too late!"

"Come on! It's not fair!"

"Neither is life, Janet." I shrugged innocently. "You should know that." And just like that, Danny opened up his mouth and dropped the orange goldfish down his gullet.

A hundred sales assistants let out a collective gasp, while ten times as many brokers began cheering in admiration–paying homage to Danny Porush, executioner of innocent marine life. Never one to miss an opportunity to ham it up, Danny responded with a formal bow, as if he were on a Broadway stage. Then he jumped off the desk into the arms of his admirers.

I started snickering at Janet. "Well, don't worry about paying me. I'll just take it out of your paycheck."

"Don't you fucking dare!" she hissed.

"Fine, you can owe me, then!" I smiled and winked. "Now go order the flowers and bring me some coffee. I gotta start this fucking day already." With a bounce in my step and a smile on my face, I walked into my office and closed the door–ready to take on anything the world could toss at me.

CHAPTER 6

FREEZING REGULATORS

It was less than five minutes later, and I was sitting in my office, behind a desk fit for a dictator, in a chair as big as a throne. I cocked my head to the side and said to the room's two other occupants, "Now let me get this straight: You guys want to bring a midget in here and toss his little ass around the boardroom?"

In unison, they nodded.

Sitting across from me, in an overstuffed oxblood leather club chair, was none other than Danny Porush. At this particular moment he seemed to be suffering no ill effects from his latest fishcapade and was now trying to sell me on his latest brainstorm, which was: to pay a midget five grand to come into the boardroom and be tossed around by brokers, in what would certainly be the first Midget Tossing Competition in Long Island history. And as odd as the whole thing sounded, I couldn't help but be somewhat intrigued.

Danny shrugged his shoulders. "It's not as crazy as it sounds. I mean, it's not like we're gonna toss the little bastard in any odd direction. The way I see it, we'd line up wrestling mats at the front of the boardroom and give the top-five brokers on the Madden deal two tosses each. We'd paint a bull's-eye at one end of the mat and then put down some Velcro so the little bastard sticks. Then we pick a few of the hot sales assistants to hold up signs–like they're judges at a diving competition. They can score based on throwing style, distance, degree of difficulty, all that sort of shit."

I shook my head in disbelief. "Where are you gonna find a midget on such short notice?" I looked over at Andy Greene, the room's third occupant. "What's your opinion on this matter? You're the firm's lawyer; you must have *something* to say . . . no?"

Andy nodded sagely, as if he were measuring the appropriate legal response. He was an old and trusted friend, who'd recently been promoted to head of Stratton's Corporate Finance Department. It was Andy's job to sift through the dozens of business plans Stratton received each day and decide which, if any, were worth passing along to me. In essence, the Corporate Finance Department served as a manufacturing plant–providing finished goods in the form of shares and warrants in initial public offerings, or new issues, as the phrase went on Wall Street.

Andy was wearing the typical Stratton uniform–consisting of an immaculate Gilberto suit, white shirt, silk necktie, and, in his case, the worst toupee this side of the Iron Curtain. At this particular moment, it looked like someone had taken a withered donkey's tail and slapped it onto his egg-shaped Jewish skull, poured shellac over it, stuck a cereal bowl over the shellac, and then placed a twenty-pound plate of depleted uranium over the cereal bowl and let it sit for a while. It was for this very reason that Andy's official Stratton nickname was Wigwam.

"Well," said Wigwam, "in terms of the insurance issues here, if we get a signed waiver from the midget, along with some sort of hold-harmless agreement, then I don't think we have any liability if the midget were to break his neck. But we would need to take every precaution that a reasonable man would take, which is clearly the legal requirement in a situation like . . ."

Jesus! I wasn't looking for a fucking legal analysis of this whole midget-tossing business–I just wanted to know if Wigwam thought it was good for broker morale! So I tuned out, keeping one eye on the green-diode numbers and letters that were skidding across the computer monitors on either side of my desk and the other eye on the floor-to-ceiling plate-glass window that looked out into the boardroom.

Wigwam and I went all the way back to grade school. Back then he had this terrific head of the finest blond hair you've ever seen, as fine as corn silk, in fact. But, alas, by his seventeenth birthday his wonderful head of hair was a distant memory, barely thick enough for the dreaded male comb-over.

Faced with the impending doom of being bald as an eagle while still in high school, Andy decided to lock himself in his basement, smoke five thousand joints of cheap Mexican reefer, play video games, eat frozen Ellio's pizza for breakfast, lunch, and dinner, and wait for Mother Nature, the bitch that she was, to play out her cruel joke on him.

He emerged from his basement three years later, a fifty-year-old ornery Jew with a few strands of hair, a prodigious potbelly, and a newfound personality that was a cross between the humdrum Eeyore, from Winnie the Pooh, and Henny Penny, who thought the sky was falling. Along the way, Andy managed to get caught cheating on his SATs, which forced him into exile to the little town of Fredonia in upstate New York, where students freeze to death in summer, at the local educational institution, Fredonia State University. But he did manage to negotiate his way through the rigorous academic demands of that fine institution and graduate five and a half years later–not one ounce smarter, yet a good deal frumpier. From there he finagled his way into some Mickey Mouse law school in Southern California–earning a diploma that held about as much legal weight as one you'd receive from a Cracker Jack box.

But, of course, at the investment-banking firm of Stratton Oakmont, mere trivialities such as these didn't mean a lot. It was all about personal relationships; that and loyalty. So when Andrew Todd Greene, alias Wigwam, caught wind of the dramatic success that had rained down on his childhood friend, he followed in the footsteps of the rest of my childhood friends and sought me out, swore undying loyalty to me, and hopped on the gravy train. That was a little over a year ago. Since then, in typical Stratton fashion, he'd undermined and backstabbed and manipulated and cajoled and squeezed out anyone who stood in his way, until he Peter-Principled himself all the way to the very top of the Stratton food chain.

Having had no experience in the subtle art of Stratton-style corporate finance–identifying fledgling growth companies so desperate for money that they were willing to sell a significant chunk of their inside ownership to me before I financed them–I was still in the process of training him. And given the fact that Wigwam possessed a legal diploma that he'd gained from an obscure school in Southern California that I'd never heard of, I started him off with a base salary of $500,000.

". . . so does that make sense to you?" asked Wigwam.

Suddenly I realized he was asking me a question, but other than it having something to do with tossing the midget, I hadn't the slightest idea what the fuck he was talking about. So I ignored him and turned to Danny and asked, "Where are you gonna find a midget?"

He shrugged. "I'm not really sure, but if you give me the green light my first call is gonna be to Ringling Bros. Circus."

"Or maybe to the World Wrestling Federation," added my trusted attorney.

Jesus H. Christ! I thought. I was up to my ears in more nuts than a fruitcake! I took a deep breath and said, "Listen, guys, fucking around with midgets ain't no joke. Pound for pound they're stronger than grizzly bears, and, if you want to know the truth, they happen to scare the living shit out of me. So before I approve this midget-tossing business, you need to find me a game warden who can rein in the little critter if he should go off the deep end. Then we're gonna need some tranq darts, a pair a handcuffs, a can of Mace–"

Wigwam chimed in: "A straitjacket–"

Danny added: "An electric cattle prod–"

"Exactly," I said, with a chuckle. "And let's get a couple of vials of saltpeter, just on general principles. After all, the bastard might pop a hard-on and go after some of the sales assistants. They're horny, the wee folk, and they can fuck like jackrabbits."

We all broke up over that. I said, "In all seriousness, though, if this gets out to the press there's gonna be hell to pay."

Danny shrugged. "I don't know, I think we can put a positive spin on the whole thing. I mean, think about it for a second: How many job opportunities are there for midgets? It'll be like we're giving back to the less fortunate." He shrugged again. "Either way, no one'll give a shit."

Well, he was right about that. The truth was that no one could care less about the articles anymore. Every one of them always had the same negative slant–that the Strattonites were wild renegades, headed by me, a precocious young banker, who'd created my own self-contained universe out on Long Island, where normal behavior no longer applied. In the eyes of the press, Stratton and I had become inexorably linked, like Siamese twins. Even when I'd donated money to a foundation for abused children, they managed to find something wrong with it–writing a single paragraph about my generosity and three or four pages about everything else.

The press onslaught had started in 1991, when an insolent reporter from *Forbes* magazine, Roula Khalaf, coined me as *a twisted version of Robin Hood, who robs from the rich and gives to himself and his merry band of brokers.* She deserved an A for cleverness, of course. And, of course, I was a bit taken aback by it, at least at first, until I came to the conclusion that the article was actually a compliment. After all, how many twenty-eight-year-olds got their own personal exposé in *Forbes* magazine? And there was no denying that all this Robin Hood business emphasized my generous nature! After the article hit, I had a fresh wave of recruits lining up at my door.

Yes, it was truly ironic that despite working for a guy who'd been accused of everything but the Lindbergh kidnapping, the Strattonites couldn't have been prouder. They were running around the boardroom chanting, "We're your merry band! We're your merry band!" Some of them came into the office dressed in tights; others wore fancy berets at jaunty angles. Someone came up with the inspired notion of deflowering a virgin–for the simple *medievalness* of it–but after a painstaking search one couldn't be found, at least not in the boardroom.

So, yes, Danny was right. No one cared about the articles. But midget-tossing? I had no time for it right now. I still had serious issues to resolve with the Steve Madden underwriting, and I still had to contend with my father, who was lurking close–holding a half-million-dollar Am Ex bill in one hand and a cup of chilled Stoli, no doubt, in the other.

I said to Wigwam, "Why don't you go track down Madden, maybe offer him a few words of encouragement or something. Tell him to keep it short and sweet and not to go off on any tangents about how much he adores women's shoes. They might lynch him over that."

"Consider it done," said Wigwam, rising from his chair. "No shoe talk from the Cobbler."

Before he was even out the door, Danny was trashing his toupee. "What's with that cheap fucking rug of his?" Danny muttered. "It looks like a dead fucking squirrel."

I shrugged. "I think it's a Hair Club for Men special. He's had the thing forever. Maybe it just needs to be dry-cleaned. Anyway, let's get serious for a second: We still have the same issue with the Madden deal, and we're out of time."

"I thought NASDAQ said they'd list it?" asked Danny.

I shook my head. "They will, but they'll only let us keep five percent of our stock; that's it. The rest we have to divest to Steve before it starts trading. That means we have to sign the papers now, this morning! And it also means we have to trust Steve to do the right thing after the company goes public." I compressed my lips and started shaking my head slowly. "I don't know, Dan–I get this feeling he's playing his own game of chess with us. I'm not sure if he'll do the right thing if push comes to shove."

"You can trust him, JB. He's a hundred percent loyal. I know the guy forever, and believe me–he knows the code of omerta as good as anyone." Danny put his thumb and forefinger to his mouth and twisted it, as if to say, "He'll keep his mouth shut nice and tight!" which is exactly what the Mafioso word *omerta* meant: silence. Then he said, "Anyway, after everything you've done for him, he's not gonna screw you. He's no fool, Steve, and he's making so much money as my rathole that he won't risk losing that."

Rathole was a Stratton code word for a nominee, a person who owned shares of stock on paper but was nothing more than a front man. There was nothing inherently illegal about being a nominee, as long as the appropriate taxes were being paid and the nominee arrangement didn't violate any securities laws. In fact, the use of nominees was prevalent on Wall Street, with big players using them to build stock positions in a company without alerting other investors. And as long as you didn't acquire more than five percent of any one company–at which point you'd be required to file a 13D disclosing your ownership and intentions–it was all perfectly legal.

But the way we were using nominees–to secretly buy large blocks of Stratton new issues–violated so many securities laws that the SEC was trying to invent new ones to stop us. The problem was that the laws currently on the books had more holes than

Swiss cheese. Of course, we weren't the only ones on Wall Street taking advantage of this; in fact, everyone was. It was just that we were doing it with a bit more panache–and brazenness.

I said to Danny, "I understand he's your rathole, but controlling people with money isn't as easy as it seems. Trust me on that. I've been doing it longer than you. It's more about managing your rathole's future expectations and less about what you've made him in the past. Yesterday's profits are yesterday's news, and, if anything, they work against you. People don't like feeling indebted to someone, especially a close friend. So after a while your ratholes start resenting you. I've already lost a few friends that way. You will too; just give it some time. Anyway, the point I'm trying to make is that friendships bought with money don't last very long, and the same goes with loyalty. That's why old friends like Wigwam are priceless around here. You can't buy loyalty like that; you know what I'm saying?"

Danny nodded. "Yeah, and that's what I have with Steve."

I nodded sadly. "Don't get me wrong, I'm not trying to belittle your relationship with Steve. But we're talking about eight million bucks here, on the low side. Depending on what happens with the company, it could be ten times that." I shrugged. "Who really knows what's gonna happen? I don't have a crystal ball in my pocket–although I do have six Ludes there, and I'll gladly split them with you after the market closes!" I raised my eyebrows three times in rapid succession.

Danny smiled and gave me the thumbs-up sign. "I'm in like Flynn!"

I nodded. "Anyway–in all seriousness–I *will* tell you that I got a really good feeling about this one. I think this company's got a shot of hitting it out of the park. And if it does, we have two million shares. So do the math, pal: At a hundred bucks a share that's two hundred million bucks. And that kind of money makes people do strange things. Not just Steve Madden."

Danny nodded and said, "I understand what you're saying, and there's no doubt that you're the master at this stuff. But I'm telling you, Steve is loyal. The only problem is how to get that kind of money from him. He's a slow payer as it is."

It was a valid point. One of the problems with ratholes was figuring out how to generate cash without raising any red flags. It was easier said than done, especially when the numbers went into the millions. "There are ways," I said confidently. "We could work some of it out with some sort of consulting contract, but if the numbers go into the tens of millions we'll have to consider doing something with our Swiss accounts, although I'd like to keep that under wraps as much as possible. Anyway, the way things are going we have bigger issues than just Steve Madden Shoes–like the fifteen other companies in the pipeline just like Madden. And if I'm having trouble trusting Steve, well, most of the people I hardly even know."

Danny said, "Just tell me what you want me to do with Steve and I'll get it done. But I'm still telling you that you don't need to worry about him. He sings your praises more than anyone."

I was well aware of how Steve sang my praises, perhaps too aware. The simple fact was that I had made an investment in his company and taken eighty-five percent in return, so what did he really owe me? In fact, unless he was the reincarnation of Mahatma Gandhi, he had to resent me–at least somewhat–for grabbing such a large percentage of his namesake.

And there were other things about Steve that bothered me, things that I couldn't share with Danny–namely, that Steve had made subtle intimations to me that he would prefer to deal directly with me than through Danny. And while I had no doubt that Steve was simply trying to earn brownie points with me, his strategy couldn't have been more off the mark. What it suggested to me was that Steve was cunning and manipulative–and, most importantly, in search of the Bigger Better Deal. If somewhere down the line he found a Bigger Better Deal than me, all bets would be off.

Right now Steve needed me. But it had little to do with Stratton raising him $7 million and even less to do with the approximately $3 million Danny had made him as his rathole. That was yesterday's news. Going forward, my hold on Steve was based on my ability to control the price of his stock after it went public. As Steve Madden's dominant market maker, virtually all the buying and selling would occur within the four walls of Stratton's boardroom–which would afford me the opportunity to move the stock up and down as I saw fit. So if Steve didn't play ball, I could literally crush the price of his stock until it was trading in pennies.

It was this very ax, in fact, that hung over the heads of all Stratton Oakmont's investment-banking clients. And I used it to ensure that they stayed loyal to the Stratton cause, which was: to issue me new shares, below the prevailing market price, which I could then sell at an enormous profit, using the power of the boardroom.

Of course, I wasn't the one who'd thought up this clever game of financial extortion. In fact, this very process was occurring at some of the US's most prestigious firms–none of whom had the slightest compunction about beating a billion-dollar company over the head if they chose not to play ball with them.

It was ironic, I thought, how America's finest and supposedly most legitimate financial institutions had rigged the treasury market (Salomon Brothers); bankrupted Orange County, California (Merrill Lynch); and ripped off grandmas and grandpas to the tune of $300 million (Prudential-Bache). Yet they were all still in business–still thriving, in fact, under the protection of a WASPy umbrella.

But at Stratton Oakmont, where our business was microcap investment banking–or, as the press liked to refer to it, penny stocks–we had no such protection. In reality, though, all the new issues were priced between four and ten dollars and weren't actually penny stocks. It was a distinction that was entirely lost on the regulators, much to their own chagrin. It was for this reason that the bozos at the SEC–especially the two who were now camped out in my conference room–were unable to make heads or tails out of a $22 million lawsuit they'd filed against me. In essence, the SEC had engineered their lawsuit as if Stratton were a penny-stock firm, but the simple fact was that Stratton Oakmont bore no resemblance to such.

Penny-stock firms were notoriously decentralized, having dozens of small offices spread throughout the country. Yet, Stratton had only one office, which made it easier to control the negativity that would spread throughout a sales force after the SEC filed a lawsuit. Usually that alone was enough to force a penny-stock firm out of business. And penny-stock firms would target unsophisticated investors, who had little or no net worth, and convince them to speculate with a couple of thousand dollars, at most. Stratton, on the other hand, targeted the wealthiest investors in America, convincing them to speculate with millions. In consequence, the SEC couldn't make their usual claim that Stratton's clients weren't suitable to risk their money in speculative stocks.

But none of this had occurred to the SEC before they filed their lawsuit. Instead, they mistakenly assumed that the bad press would be enough to drive Stratton out of business. But with only one office to manage, it had been easy to keep the troops motivated, and not a soul left. And it was only after the SEC had already filed their lawsuit that they finally got around to reviewing Stratton's new-account forms and it dawned on them that all Stratton's clients were millionaires.

What I had done was uncover a murky middle ground–namely, the organized selling of five-dollar stocks to the wealthiest one percent of Americans, as opposed to selling penny stocks (priced under a dollar) to the other ninety-nine percent, who had little or no net worth. There was a firm on Wall Street, DH Blair, that had danced around the idea for more than twenty years but had never actually hit the nail on the head. In spite of that, the firm's owner, J. Morton Davis, a savage Jew, had still made a bloody fortune in the process and was a Wall Street legend.

But I *had* hit the nail on the head, and by sheer luck I'd hit it at exactly the right moment. The stock market was just beginning to recover from the Great October Crash, and chaos capitalism still reigned supreme. The NASDAQ was coming of age and was no longer considered the redheaded stepchild of the New York Stock Exchange. Lightning-fast computers were appearing on every desk–sending ones and zeroes whizzing from coast to coast–eliminating the need to be physically located on Wall Street. It was a time of change, a time of upheaval. And as volume on the NASDAQ soared, I, coincidentally, was embarking on an intensive three-hour-a-day training program with my young Strattonites. From out of the smoldering ashes of the Great Crash, the investment-banking firm of Stratton Oakmont was born. And before any regulator knew what hit, it had ripped through America with the force of an atomic bomb.

Just then an interesting thought occurred to me, and I said to Danny, "What are those two idiots from the SEC saying today?"

"Nothing really," he replied. "They've been pretty quiet, talking mostly about the cars in the parking lot, the usual shit." He shrugged. "I'll tell you, these guys are totally fucking clueless! It's like they don't even know we're doing a deal today. They're still looking at trading records from 1991."

"Hmmm," I said, rubbing my chin thoughtfully. I wasn't all that surprised at Danny's response. After all, I'd been bugging the conference room for over a month now and was gathering counter-intelligence against the SEC on a daily basis. And one of the first things I'd learned about securities regulators (besides them being completely devoid of personality) was that one hand had no idea what the other hand was doing. While the SEC bozos in Washington, D.C., were signing off on the Steve Madden IPO, the SEC bozos in New York were sitting in my conference room, entirely unaware of what was about to transpire.

"What's the temperature in there?" I asked with great interest.

Danny shrugged. "High fifties, I think. They've got their coats on."

"For Chrissake, Danny! Why is it so fucking warm in there? I told you–I want to freeze those bastards right back to Manhattan! What do I have to do, call a fucking refrigeration guy in here to get the job done? I mean, really, Danny, I want icicles coming out of their fucking noses! What about this don't you understand?"

Danny smiled. "Listen, JB: We can freeze 'em out or we can burn 'em out. I can probably get one of those little kerosene heaters installed right in the ceiling, and we can make the room so hot they'll need salt pills to stay alive. But if we make the place too uncomfortable, they might leave, and then we won't be able to listen to them anymore."

I took a deep breath and let it out slow. Danny was right, I thought. I smiled and said, "All right, fuck it! We'll let the bastards die of old age. But here's what I want to do with Madden: I want him to sign a paper saying that the stock is still ours, regardless of how high the price goes and regardless what it says in the prospectus. Also, I want Steve to put the stock certificate in escrow, so we have control over it. We'll let Wigwam be the escrow agent. And no one has to know about this. It'll all be among friends; omerta, buddy. So unless Steve tries to screw us, it's all good."

Danny nodded. "I'll take care of it, but I don't see how it's gonna help us. If we ever try to break the agreement we'll be in as much trouble as him. I mean, there's like seventeen thousand different"–in spite of the office just being swept for bugs, Danny mouthed the words *laws we're breaking*–"if Steve ratholes that much stock."

I held up my hand and smiled warmly. "Whoa–whoa–whoa! Settle down! First of all, I had the office swept for bugs thirty minutes ago, so if it's already bugged again they deserve to catch us. And it's not seventeen thousand laws we're breaking; it's maybe three or four, or five, tops. But either way, no one ever has to know." I shrugged and then changed my tone to one of shock. "Anyway, I'm surprised at you, Dan! Having a signed agreement helps us a lot–even if we can't actually use it. It's a powerful deterrent to stop him from trying to fuck us over."

Just then Janet's voice came over the intercom: "Your father's heading this way."

A snap response: "Tell him I'm in a meeting, God damn it!"

Janet snapping right back: "Fuck you! *You* tell him! I'm not telling him!"

Why, the insolence! The sheer audacity! A few seconds of silence passed. Then I whined, "Oh, come on, Janet! Can't you just tell him I'm in an important meeting or on a conference call or something, *please*?"

"No and no," she replied tonelessly.

"Thanks, you're a real gem of an assistant, let me fucking tell you! Remind me of this day two weeks from now, when it's time for your Christmas bonus, okay?"

I paused and waited for Janet's response. Nothing. Dead fucking silence. *Unbelievable!* I soldiered on. "How far away is he?"

"About fifty yards, and closing awfully fast. I can see the veins popping out of his head from here, and he's smoking at least one . . . or maybe two cigarettes at the same time. He looks like a fire-breathing dragon, I swear to God."

"Thanks for the encouragement, Janet. Can't you at least create some sort of diversion? Maybe pull a fire alarm or something? I–" Just then Danny began rising out of his chair, as if he was attempting to leave my office. I held up my hand and said in a loud, forthright voice, "Where the fuck do you think you're going, pal, huh?" I started jabbing my index finger in the direction of his club chair. "Now, sit the fuck back down and relax for a while." I turned my head in the direction of the black speakerphone. "One second, Janet, don't go anywhere." Then I turned back to Danny. "Let me tell you something, buddy: At least fifty or sixty thousand of that Am Ex bill is yours, so you gotta put up with the abuse too.

Besides, there's strength in numbers." I turned my head back in the direction of the speakerphone. "Janet, tell Kenny to get his ass in my office right this second. He's gotta deal with this shit too. And come open my door. I need some noise in here."

Kenny Greene, my other partner, was a breed apart from Danny. In fact, no two people could be more different. Danny was the smarter of the two, and, as improbable as it might seem, he was definitely the more refined. But Kenny was more driven, blessed with an insatiable appetite for knowledge and wisdom–two attributes he lacked entirely. Yes, Kenny was a *dimwit.* It was sad but true. And he had an incredible talent for saying the most asinine things during business meetings, especially key ones, which I no longer allowed him to attend. It was a fact that Danny relished beyond belief, and seldom did he pass up an opportunity to remind me of Kenny's many shortfalls. So I had Kenny Greene and Andy Greene, no relation–I seemed to be surrounded by Greenes.

Just then the door swung open and the mighty roar came pouring in. It was a fucking greed storm out there, and I loved every last ounce of it. The mighty roar–yes, it was the most powerful drug of all. It was stronger than the wrath of my wife; it was stronger than my back pain; and it was stronger than those bozo regulators shivering in my conference room.

And it was even stronger than the insanity of my own father, who at this particular moment was getting ready to release a mighty roar of his own.

CHAPTER 7

SWEATING THE SMALL STUFF

In ominous tones, and with his brilliant blue eyes bulging so far out of his head that he looked like a cartoon character about to pop, Mad Max said, "If you three bastards don't wipe those smug fucking looks off your faces, I swear to fucking God I'm gonna wipe them off for you!"

With that, he started pacing . . . slowly, deliberately . . . with his face contorted into a mask of unadulterated fury. In his right hand was a lit cigarette, probably his twentieth of the day; in his left hand was a white Styrofoam cup filled with Stolichnaya vodka, hopefully his first of the day but probably his second.

All at once he stopped pacing, and he turned on his heel like a prosecuting attorney and looked at Danny. "So what do *you* have to say for yourself, Porush? You know, you're even more of a fucking retard than I thought you were–eating a goldfish in the middle of the boardroom! What the fuck is wrong with you?"

Danny stood up and smiled, and said, "Come on, Max! It wasn't as bad as it seems. The kid deserved–"

"Sit down and shut up, Porush! You're a fucking disgrace, not just to yourself but to your whole fucking family, may God save them!" Mad Max paused for a brief instant, then added, "And stop smiling, God damn it! Those boiling teeth of yours are hurting my eyes! I need a pair of sunglasses to shield myself, for Chrissake!"

Danny sat down and closed his mouth nice and tight. We exchanged glances, and I found myself fighting a morbid urge to smile. But I resisted it–knowing it would only make matters worse. I glanced over at Kenny. He was sitting across from me, in the same chair Wigwam had sat in, but I failed to make eye contact with him. He was too busy staring at his own shoes, which, as usual, were in desperate need of a shine. In typical Wall Street fashion, he had his shirtsleeves rolled up, exposing a thick gold Rolex. It was the Presidential model–my old watch, in fact, the one the Duchess had made me discard because of its gaucheness. Nevertheless, Kenny didn't look gauche or, for that matter, sharp. And that new military-style haircut of his made his blockhead look that much blockier. My junior partner, I thought: the Blockhead.

Meanwhile, a poisonous silence now filled the room, which meant it was time for me to put an end to this very madness, once and for all. So I leaned forward in my chair and dug deep into my fabulous vocabulary–extracting the sort of words I knew my father would respect most–and I said in a commanding voice, "All right, Dad, enough of this shit! Why don't you calm the fuck down for a second! This is my fucking company, and if I have legitimate fucking business expenses, then I'm–"

But Mad Max cut me off before I could make my point. "You want me to calm down while you three retards act like kids in a candy store? You don't think there's any end in sight, do you? It's all one giant fucking party to you three schmendricks; no rainy days on the horizon, right? Well, I'll fucking tell you something–all this cock-and-bull horseshit of yours, the way you charge your personal expenses to this fucking company–I'm sick and tired of it!"

Then he paused and stared the three of us down–starting with me, his own son. At this particular moment he had to be wondering whether or not I was actually delivered by a stork. As he turned away from me I happened to catch a terrific look at him from just the right angle, and I found myself marveling at how dapper he looked today! Oh, yes, in spite of it all, Mad Max was very snazzy–favoring navy-blue blazers, spread British collars, solid navy neckties, and tan gabardine trousers, all custom-made and all starched and pressed to near perfection by the same Chinese laundry service he'd used for the last thirty years. He was a creature of habit, my father.

So there we sat, like good little schoolchildren, waiting patiently for his next verbal assault, which I knew wouldn't come until he did one thing first: smoked. Finally, after a good ten seconds, he took an enormous pull from his Merit Ultra low-tar cigarette and expanded his mighty chest to twice its normal size, like a puffer fish trying to ward off a predator. Then he slowly exhaled and deflated himself back to normal size. His shoulders were still enormous, though, and his forward-leaning posture and thin layer of salt-and-pepper hair gave him the appearance of a five-foot-six-inch raging bull.

Then he tilted his head back and took an enormous pull from his Styrofoam cup and downed its fiery contents, as if it were no stronger than chilled Evian. He started shaking his head. "All this money being made and you three imbeciles blowing it like there's no tomorrow. It's a fucking travesty to watch. What do you three think, that I'm some sort of yes-man who's just gonna roll over and play dead while you guys destroy this fucking company? Do you three have any idea of how many people count on this place for their fucking livelihood? Do you have any idea of the risk and exposure that . . ."

Mad Max went on and on in typical Mad Max fashion, but I tuned out. In fact, I found myself mesmerized by this wonderful ability he had to tie so many curses together with such little forethought and still make each sentence sound so very fucking poetic. It was truly beautiful the way he cursed–like Shakespeare with an attitude! And at Stratton Oakmont, where cursing was considered a high art form, to say that someone knew how to tie their curses together was a compliment of the highest order. But Mad Max took things to an entirely different level, and when he really got himself on a roll, like now, it gave his verbal tirades an almost pleasant ring to the ear.

Now Mad Max was shaking his head in disgust–or was it incredulity? Well, it was probably a bit of both. Whatever it was, he was shaking his head and explaining to us three retarded schmendricks that November's American Express bill was $470,000, and only $20,000 of it, by his calculations, were legitimate business expenses; the rest were of a personal nature, or personal bullshit, as he put it. Then, in a most ominous tone, he said, "Let me tell you something right now–you three maniacs are gonna get your tits caught right in a wringer! You mark my fucking words–sooner or later those bastards from the IRS are gonna come marching down here and do a complete fucking audit, and you three retards are gonna be in deep shit unless someone puts a stop to all this madness. That's why I'm hitting each of you personally for this bill." He nodded in agreement with his own statement. "I'm not running it through the business–not one fucking penny of it–and that's fucking final! I'm taking four hundred fifty thousand right out of your inflated fucking paychecks, and don't even try to stop me!"

Why–the fucking nerve! I had to say something to him in his own language. "Hold your fucking horses right there, Dad! That's a complete load of crap, what you're saying! A lot of that shit is legitimate business expenses, whether you believe it or not. If you just stop fucking screaming for a second I'll tell you what's what and–"

But again he cut me right off, now turning his attack directly toward me: "And you, the so-called Wolf of Wall Street–the demented young Wolf. My own son! From my very fucking loins! How could it be? You're the worst of the lot! Why the hell would you go out and buy two of the same fur coat, for eighty thousand dollars apiece? That's right–I called that place, Allessandro's House of Fucking Furs, because I thought it must be some sort of a mistake! But, no–you know what that Greek bastard down there told me?"

I humored him with a response: "No, Dad, what did he fucking tell you?"

"He told me you bought two of the same mink coat–the same color and style and everything!" With that, Mad Max cocked his head to one side and tucked his chin between his collarbones. He looked up at me with those bulging blue eyes of his, and he said, "What, one coat's not enough for your wife? Or wait–let me guess–you bought the second mink for a prostitute, right?" He paused and took another deep pull from his cigarette. "I've had it up to here with all this cockamamie bullshit. You don't think I know what EJ Entertainment is?" He narrowed his eyes accusingly. "You three maniacs are charging hookers to the corporate credit card! What kind of hookers take credit cards, anyway?"

The three of us exchanged glances but said nothing. After all, what was there to say? The truth was that hookers *did* take credit cards–or at least ours did! In fact, hookers were so much a part of the Stratton subculture that we classified them like publicly traded stocks: Blue Chips were considered the top-of-the-line hooker, *zee* crème de la crème. They were usually struggling young models or exceptionally beautiful college girls in desperate need of tuition or designer clothing, and for a few thousand dollars they would do almost anything imaginable, either to you or to each other. Next came the NASDAQs, who were one step down from the Blue Chips. They were priced between three and five hundred dollars and made you wear a condom unless you gave them a hefty tip, which I always did. Then came the Pink Sheet hookers, who were the lowest form of all, usually a streetwalker or the sort of low-class hooker who showed up in response to a desperate late-night phone call to a number in *Screw* magazine or the yellow pages. They usually cost a hundred dollars or less, and if you didn't wear a condom, you'd get a penicillin shot the next day and then pray that your dick didn't fall off.

Anyway, the Blue Chips took credit cards, so what was wrong with writing them off on your taxes? After all, the IRS knew about this sort of stuff, didn't they? In fact, back in the good old days, when getting blasted over lunch was considered normal corporate behavior, the IRS referred to these types of expenses as three-martini lunches! They even had an accounting term for it: It was called *T and E,* which stood for Travel and Entertainment. All I'd done was taken the small liberty of moving things to their logical conclusion, changing *T and E* to *T and A:* Tits and Ass!

That aside, the problems with my father ran much deeper than a few questionable charges on the corporate credit card. The simple fact was that he was the tightest man to ever walk the face of the planet. And I–well, let's just say that I had a fundamental disagreement with him on the management of money, insofar as I thought nothing of losing half a million dollars at the craps table and then throwing a $5,000 gray poker chip at a luscious Blue Chip.

Anyway, the long and short of it was that at Stratton Oakmont, Mad Max was like a fish out of water–or more like a fish on Pluto. He was sixty-five years old, which made him a good forty years older than the average Strattonite; he was a highly educated man, a CPA, who had an IQ somewhere in the stratosphere, while the average Strattonite had no education whatsoever and was about as smart as a box of rocks. He had grown up in a different time and place, in the old Jewish Bronx, amid the smoldering economic ashes of the Great Depression, not knowing if there would be food on the dinner table. And like millions of others who had grown up in the thirties, he still suffered from a Depression-era mentality–making him risk-averse, resistant to change in any shape or form, and riddled with financial doubt. And here he was, trying to manage the finances of a company whose sole business was based on moment-to-moment change and whose majority owner, who happened to be his own son, was a born risk-taker.

I took a deep breath, rose from my chair, and walked around the front of my desk and sat on the edge. Then I crossed my arms beneath my chest in a gesture of frustration, and I said, "Listen, Dad–there are certain things that go on here that I don't expect you to understand. But the simple fact is that it's my fucking money to do whatever the fuck I want with. In fact, unless you can make a case that my spending is impinging on cash flow, then I would just suggest you bite your fucking tongue and pay the bill.

"Now, you know I love you, and it hurts me to see you get so upset over a stupid credit-card bill. But that's all it is, Dad: a bill! And you know you're gonna end up paying it anyway. So what's the point of getting all upset over it? Before the day is over we're gonna make twenty million bucks, so who gives a shit about half a million?"

At this point the Blockhead chimed in. "Max, my portion of the bill is hardly anything. So I'm on the same page as you."

I smiled inwardly, knowing the Blockhead had just made a colossal blunder. There were two rules of thumb when dealing with Mad Max: First, never try passing the buck–ever! Second, never point the finger, subtly or otherwise, at his beloved son, who only he had the right to berate. He turned to Kenny and said, "In my mind, Greene, every dollar you spend above zero is one too many dollars, you fucking twerp! At least my son is the one who makes all the money around here! What the fuck do you do, besides getting us tangled up in a sexual-harassment lawsuit with that big-titted sales assistant–whatever the fuck her name was." He shook his head in disgust. "So why don't you just shut the fuck up and count your lucky stars that my son was kind enough to make a twerp like you a partner in this place."

I smiled at my father and said jokingly, "Dad–Dad–Dad! Now, calm down before you give yourself a fucking heart attack. I know what you're thinking, but Kenny wasn't trying to insinuate anything. You know all of us love you and respect you and rely on you to be the voice of reason around here. So let's all just take a step back . . ."

For as long as I could remember, my father had been fighting a one-sided ground war against himself–consisting of daily battles against unseen enemies and inanimate objects. I first noticed it when I was five, with his car, which he seemed to think was alive. It was a 1963 green Dodge Dart, and he referred to it as *she*. The problem was that *she* had a terrible rattle coming from beneath her dashboard. It was an elusive son of a bitch, this rattle, which he was certain those bastards from the Dodge factory had purposely placed in *her,* as a means of personally fucking him over. It was a rattle that no one else could hear, except my mother–who only pretended to hear it, to keep my father from blowing an emotional gasket.

But that was only the start of it. Even a simple trip to the refrigerator could bc a diccy affair, what with his habit of drinking milk directly from the container. The problem there was if even one drop of milk dripped down his chin, he would go absolutely ballistic–slamming down the milk container and muttering, "That goddamn piece-a-shit motherfucking milk container! Can't those stupid bastards who design milk containers come up with one that doesn't make the fucking milk drip down your godforsaken chin?"

Of course. It was the milk container's fault! So Mad Max shrouded himself in a series of bizarre routines and steadfast rituals as protection against a cruel, unpredictable world filled with rattling dashboards and imperfect milk containers. He'd wake up each morning to three Kent cigarettes, a thirty-minute shower, and then an inordinately long shave with a straightedge razor, while one cigarette burned in his mouth and another burned over the sink. Next he would get dressed, first putting on a pair of white boxer shorts, then a pair of black knee-high socks, then a pair of black patent-leather shoes–but not his pants. Then he would walk around the apartment like that. He would eat breakfast, smoke a few more cigarettes, and excuse himself to take a world-class dump. After that he would coif his hair to near-perfection, put on a dress shirt, button it slowly, turn up his collar, wriggle on his tie, knot it, turn down his collar, and put on his suit jacket. Finally, just before he left the house, he'd put his pants on. Just why he saved this step for the end I could never figure out, but seeing it all those years must've scarred me in some undetermined way.

Odder still, though, was Mad Max's complete and utter aversion to the unexpected ringing of the telephone. Oh, yes, Mad Max hated the sound of a ringing phone, which seemed unusually cruel–considering he worked in an office that had one thousand tightly packed telephones, give or take a few. And they rang incessantly, from the moment Mad Max entered the office at precisely nine a.m. (he was never late, of course) to the moment he left, which was whenever the fuck he damn well pleased.

Not surprisingly, growing up in that tiny two-bedroom apartment in Queens got pretty wild sometimes, especially when the phone started ringing, and especially when it was for him. Yet he never actually answered the phone himself, even if he so desired, because my mother, Saint Leah, would morph into a world-class track star the moment it started ringing–making a mad dash for it, knowing that each ring she stymied would make it that much easier to calm him down after the fact.

And on those sad occasions when my mother was forced to utter those terrible words, "Max, it's for you," my father would slowly rise out of his living-room chair, wearing a pair of white boxer shorts and nothing else, and stomp his way to the kitchen, muttering, "That motherfucking cocksucking piece-of-fucking-shit phone! Who-the-fucking-hell-has-the-goddamn-fucking-nerve-to-call-the-motherfucking-house-on-a-piece-of-shit-fucking-Sunday-after-fucking-noon . . ."

But when he finally reached the telephone, the most bizarre thing would happen: He would magically transform himself into his alter ego, Sir Max, who was a refined gentleman with impeccable manners and an accent reeking of British aristocracy. It was rather odd, I'd thought, considering my father was born and raised on the grimy streets of the South Bronx and had never been to England.

Nevertheless, Sir Max would say into the telephone, "Hello? How may I help you?" And he would keep his lips puckered and his cheeks slightly compressed, which really brought out that aristocratic accent of his. "Oh, okay, then; that will be quite fine! Righty-o, then!" With that, Sir Max would hang up the phone and revert back to Mad Max. "That-motherfucking-cocksucking-piece-of-fucking-shit-friend-of-fucking-mine-who-has-the-motherfucking-goddamn-gall-to-call-this-motherfucking-house . . ."

Yet with all the insanity, it was Mad Max who was the smiling coach of all my Little League teams, and it was Mad Max who was the first father to wake up on Sunday mornings and go downstairs and throw a ball around with his kids. He was the one who held the back of my bicycle seat and pushed me down the cement walk in front of our apartment building and then ran behind me, and he was the one who came into my bedroom at night and lay with me–running his fingers through my hair as I suffered with night terrors. He was the one who never missed a school play or a parent–teacher conference or music recital or anything else, for that matter, where he could relish his children and show us that we were loved.

He was a complicated man, my father; a man of great mental capacity who was driven to succeed yet humbled into mediocrity by his own emotional limitations. After all, how could a man like this function in the corporate world? Would such behavior be tolerated? How many jobs had he lost because of it? How many promotions had passed him by? And how many windows of opportunity had been slammed shut as a result of the Mad Max persona?

But all that changed with Stratton Oakmont, a place where Mad Max could unleash his fiery wrath with complete impunity. In fact, what better way for a Strattonite to prove his loyalty than to get berated by Mad Max and suck it up for the greater good, meaning: to live the Life. So a baseball bat to your car window or a public tongue-lashing was considered a rite of passage for a young Strattonite, to be worn like a badge of honor.

So there was Mad Max and Sir Max, and the idea was to figure out a way to bring out Sir Max. My first trial balloon was the one-on-one approach. I looked at Kenny and Danny and said, "Why don't you guys give me a few minutes to talk to my father alone, okay?"

No arguments there! The two of them left with such alacrity that my father and I had barely made it to the couch, only ten feet away, when the door slammed shut behind them. My father sat down and lit up another cigarette and took one of his enormous pulls. I plopped myself down to his right, leaned back, and put my feet up on a glass coffee table in front of us.

I smiled sadly and said, "I swear to God, Dad, my back is fucking killing me. You have no idea. The pain's going right down the back of my left leg. It's enough to drive a person insane."

My father's face immediately softened. Apparently, trial balloon number one was off to a flying start. "Well, what do the doctors say?"

Hmmmmm . . . I hadn't detected any hint of a British accent in those last few words; nonetheless, my back really was killing me and I was definitely making progress with him. "Doctors? What the fuck do they know? The last surgery made it even worse. And all they do is give me pills that upset my stomach and don't do shit for the pain." I shook my head some more. "Whatever, Dad. I don't wanna worry you. I'm just venting." I took my feet off the coffee table, leaned back, and spread my arms out on either side of the couch. "Listen," I said softly, "I know it's hard for you to make sense of all this craziness around here, but trust me, there's a method to my madness, especially when it comes to the spending. It's important to keep these guys chasing the dream. And it's even more important to keep them broke." I gestured over to the plate glass. "Look at them; as much money as they make, every last one of them is broke! They spend every dime they have, trying to keep up with my lifestyle. But they can't, because they don't make enough. So they end up living paycheck to paycheck on a million bucks a year. It's hard to imagine, considering how you grew up, but, nevertheless, it is what it is.

"Anyway, keeping them broke makes them easier to control. Think about it: Virtually every last one of them is leveraged to the hilt, with cars and homes and boats and all the rest of that crap, and if they miss even one paycheck they're up shit's creek. It's like having golden handcuffs on them. I mean, the truth is I could afford to pay them more than I do. But then they wouldn't need me as much. But if I paid them too little, then they would hate me. So I pay them just enough so they love me but still need me. And as long as they need me they'll always fear me."

My father was staring at me intently, hanging on every word. "One day"–I gestured with my chin toward the plate glass–"all that will be gone, and so will all that so-called loyalty. And when that day comes, I don't want you to have any knowledge of some of the things that went on here. That's why I'm evasive with you sometimes. It's not that I don't trust you or that I don't respect you–or that I don't value your opinion. It's the opposite, Dad. I keep things from you because I love you, and because I admire you, and because I want to protect you from the fallout when all this starts to unwind."

Sir Max, in a concerned tone: "Why are you talking like this? Why does all this have to unwind? The companies you're taking public are all legitimate, aren't they?"

"Yes. It has nothing to do with the companies. And the truth is, we're not doing anything different than anybody else out there. We're just doing it bigger and better, which makes us a target. Anyway, don't worry about it. I'm just having a morbid moment. Everything will work out fine, Dad."

Just then Janet's voice came through the intercom: "I'm sorry for interrupting, but you have a conference call with Ike Sorkin and the rest of the lawyers. They're on the line right now and they have their billing clocks ticking. Do you want them to hold or should I reschedule it?"

Conference call? I didn't have any conference call! And then it hit me: Janet was bailing me out! I looked at my father and shrugged, as if to say, "What can I do? I gotta take this call."

We quickly exchanged hugs and apologies, and then I made a pledge to try to spend less in the future, which both of us knew was complete bullshit. Nevertheless, my father had come in like a lion and gone out like a lamb. And just as the door closed behind him, I made a mental note to give Janet a little something extra for Christmas, in spite of all the crap she'd given me this morning. She was a good egg–a damn good egg.

CHAPTER 8

THE COBBLER

About an hour later, Steve Madden was making his way to the front of the boardroom with a confident gait. It was the sort of gait, I thought, of a man in complete control, a man who had every intention of giving a first-class dog-and-pony show. But when he reached the front of the boardroom—that look on his face! Sheer terror!

And the way he was dressed! It was ridiculous. He looked like a broken-down driving-range pro who'd traded in his golf clubs for two pints of malt liquor and a one-way ticket to Skid Row. It was ironic that Steve's business was fashion, considering he was one of the least fashionable dressers on the planet. He was the wacky-designer type, an over-the-top artsy-fartsy guy, who walked around town holding a horrendous-looking platform shoe in his hand as he offered unsolicited explanations as to why this shoe would be what every teenage girl would be dying to wear next season.

At this particular moment he was wearing a wrinkled navy blazer, which hung on his thin frame like a piece of cheap boat canvas. The rest of his ensemble was no better. He wore a ripped gray T-shirt and white peg-legged Levi's jeans, both of which had stains on them.

But it was his shoes that were the greatest insult. After all, one would think that anyone who was trying to pass himself off as a legitimate shoe designer would have the common decency to get a fucking shine the day he was going public. But, no, not Steve Madden; he had on a pair of cheap brown leather penny loafers that hadn't seen a high-shine rag since the day the calf was slaughtered. And, of course, his trademark royal-blue baseball cap covered his few remaining strands of wispy strawberry-blond hair, which, in typical downtown fashion, had been pulled back into a ponytail and tied with a rubber band.

Steve reluctantly grabbed the microphone off a maple-colored lectern and said a couple of quick *uhh-humms* and *uhh-hoos,* sending a clear signal that he was ready to start the show. Slowly–very slowly, in fact–the Strattonites hung up their phones and leaned back in their chairs.

All at once I felt some terrific vibrations coming from my left–almost a mini-earthquake. I turned to see . . . *Christ, it was fat Howie Gelfand!* Four hundred pounds if he was an ounce!

"Hey, JB," said fat Howie. "I need you to do me real solid and flip me an extra ten thousand units of Madden. Could you do that for your uncle Howie?" He smiled from ear to ear, and then cocked his head to the side and put his arm around my shoulder, as if to say, "Come on, we're buddies, right?"

Well, I kind of liked fat Howie despite the fact that he was a fat bastard. But that aside, his request for additional units was par for the course. After all, a unit of a Stratton new issue was more valuable than gold. All you had to do was some simple math: A unit consisted of one share of common stock and two warrants, an A and a B, each of which gave you the right to buy one additional share of stock at a price slightly above the initial offering price. In this particular instance, the initial offering price was four dollars a share; the A warrant was exercisable at four-fifty and the B warrant at five dollars. And as the price of the stock rose, the value of the warrants rose right along with it. So the leverage was staggering.

A typical Stratton new issue consisted of two million units offered at four dollars per, which by itself wasn't all that spectacular. But with a football field full of young Strattonites–smiling and dialing and ripping people's eyeballs out–demand dramatically outstripped supply. In consequence, the price of the units would soar to twenty dollars or more the moment they started trading. So, to give a client a block of 10,000 units was like giving him a six-figure gift. There was no difference, which was why the client was expected to play ball–meaning: For every unit he was given at the initial-public-offering price, he was expected to purchase *ten times as many* after the deal began trading publicly (in the aftermarket).

"All right," I muttered. "You can have your extra ten thousand units because I love you and I know you're loyal. Now go lose some weight before you have a heart attack."

With a great smile and a hearty tone: "I hail you, JB. I hail you!" He did his best to take a bow. "You are the King . . . the Wolf . . . you're everything! Your wish is my–"

I cut him off. "Get the fuck out of here, Gelfand. And make sure none of the kids in your section start booing Madden or throwing shit at him. I'm serious, okay?"

Howie began taking small steps backward and bowing toward me with his arms extended in front of him, the way a person does when they're leaving a royal chamber after an audience with a king.

What a fat fucking bastard, I thought. But such a wonderful salesman! Smooth as silk he was. Howie had been one of my first employees–only nineteen when he came to work for me. His first year in the business he'd made $250,000. This year he was on pace to make $1.5 million. Nevertheless, he still lived at home with his parents.

Just then came more rumblings from the microphone: "Uh . . . excuse me, everyone. For those of you who don't know me, my name is Steve Madden. I'm the president–"

Before he could even finish his first thought, the Strattonites were on him:

"We all know who you are!"

"Nice fucking baseball cap!"

"Time is money! Get to the fucking point!"

Then came some boos and hisses and whistles and catcalls and a couple a *hoo*-yaaas. Then the room began to quiet down again.

Steve glanced over at me. His mouth was slightly parted and his brown eyes were as wide as saucers. I extended my arms, palms toward him, and moved them up and down a few times, as if to say, "Calm down and take it easy!"

Steve nodded and took a deep breath. "I'd like to start by telling you a little bit about myself and my background in the shoe industry. And then, after that, I'd like to discuss the bright plans I have for my company's future. I first started working in a shoe store when I was sixteen years old, sweeping the stockroom floor. And while all my other friends were out running around town chasing girls, I was learning about women's shoes. I was like Al Bundy, with a shoehorn sticking out my back–"

Another interruption: "The microphone's too far from your mouth. We can't hear a fucking word you're saying! Move the mike closer."

Steve moved the microphone. "Well, sorry about that. Uh–like I was saying, I've been in the shoe industry for as far back as I can remember. My first job was at a little shoe store in Cedarhurst called Jildor Shoes, where I worked in the stockroom. Then I became a salesman. And it was . . . uh . . . then . . . back when I was still a kid . . . that I first fell in love with women's shoes. You know, I can honestly say . . ."

And just like that he began giving a remarkably detailed explanation of how he'd been a true lover of women's shoes since he was in his early teens, and how somewhere along the way–he wasn't sure where–he had become fascinated with the endless design possibilities for women's shoes, insofar as the different types of heels and straps and flaps and buckles, and all the different sorts of fabrics he could work with, and all the decorative ornaments he could stick on them. Then he began explaining how he liked to caress the shoes and run his fingers along the insteps.

At this point I snuck a glance into the heart of the boardroom. What I saw were some very puzzled looks on the faces of the Strattonites. Even the sales assistants, who could usually be counted on to maintain some sense of decorum, were cocking their heads in disbelief. Some of them were rolling their eyes.

Then, all at once, they attacked: "What a fucking homo!"

"That's some sick shit, man!"

"You queer! Get a fucking life!"

Then came more boos and hisses and whistles and catcalls, and now some foot-stomping–a clear sign they were entering phase two of the torture treatment.

Danny walked over, shaking his head. "I'm fucking embarrassed," he muttered.

I nodded. "Well, at least he agreed to put our stock in escrow. It's a shame we couldn't get the papers drawn up today, but it ain't a perfect world. Anyway, he's gotta stop with this shit or they're gonna eat him up alive." I shook my head. "I don't know, though . . . I just went over this shit with him a few minutes ago and he seemed okay. He's actually got a good company. He needs to just tell the story. I mean, he's your friend and everything, but he's a fucking crackpot!"

Danny, tonelessly: "Always has been, even in public school."

I shrugged. "Whatever. I'll give it another minute or so and then I'll go up there."

Just then Steve looked over at us, and the sweat was *pouring* off him. He had a dark circle on his chest the size of a sweet potato. I waved my hand in small circles, as if to say, "Speed it up!" Then I mouthed the words: "Talk about your plans for the company!"

He nodded. "Okay–I'd like to tell everybody about how Steve Madden Shoes got started and then talk about our bright future!"

The last two words resulted in some eye-rolling and a little bit of head-shaking, but, thankfully, the boardroom remained quiet.

Steve lumbered on: "I started my company with one thousand dollars and a single shoe. It was called the Marilyn"–*Christ almighty!*–"which was sort of like a Western clog. It was a great shoe–not my best shoe, but still a great shoe. Anyway, I was able to get five hundred pairs made on credit, and I started going around and selling them out of the trunk of my car to any store that would buy them. How could I describe this shoe to you? Let me see . . . it had a chunky bottom and an open toe, but the top of it was . . . well, I guess it doesn't really matter. The point I was trying to make was that it was a really funky shoe, which is the trademark of Steve Madden Shoes: We're funky.

"Anyway, the shoe that really launched the company was called the Mary Lou, and this shoe . . . well, *this* was no ordinary shoe!" *Oh, Jesus! What a fucking fruitcake!* "It was way ahead of its time–way ahead!" Steve waved his hand in the air, as if to say, "Forget about it!" And he kept right on going. "Anyway, let me describe it to you, because this is important. Now, it was a black patent-leather variation of the traditional Mary Jane, with a relatively thin ankle strap. But the key was that it had a bump toe. Some of you girls here must know exactly what I'm talking about, right? I mean–it was really a hot shoe!" He paused, obviously hoping for some positive feedback from the sales assistants, but none came–only more head-shaking. Then there was an eerie, poisonous silence, the sort of silence you find in a small town in the middle of Kansas the moment before a tornado hits.

Out of the corner of my eye I saw a paper airplane sail across the boardroom in no particular direction. At least they weren't throwing things directly at him! That would come next. I said to Danny, "The natives are getting restless. Should I go up there?"

"If you don't, I will. This is fucking nauseating!"

"All right, I'm going." I made a beeline for Steve.

He was still talking about the Mary fucking Lou when I reached him. Just before I grabbed the microphone he was talking about how *she* was the perfect prom shoe, priced reasonably and built to last.

I grabbed the mike out of his hand before he knew what hit him, and it was then that I realized he'd gotten so absorbed in the glory of his own shoe designs that he had actually stopped sweating. In fact, he seemed completely at ease now and was entirely unaware that he was about to get lynched.

He whispered to me, "What are you doing? They love me! You can go back now. I got it covered!"

I narrowed my eyes. "Get the fuck out of here, Steve! They're about to start throwing tomatoes at you. Are you that blind? I mean, they don't give a shit about the Mary fucking Lou! They just want to sell your stock and make money. Now, go over to Danny and relax for a while, before they come up here and rip off your baseball cap and scalp the last seven hairs off your head!"

Finally, Steve capitulated, and he walked off center stage. I raised my right hand, asking for quiet, and the room fell silent. With the microphone just beneath my lips, I said in a mocking tone, "All right, everyone, let's give a big round of applause to Steve Madden and his very special shoe. After all, just hearing about little Mary has inspired me to pick up the phone and start calling all my clients. So I want every last one of you–sales assistants included–to put your hands together for Steve Madden and his sexy little shoe: the Mary Lou!" I wedged the microphone under my arm and started clapping.

And just like that–thunderous applause! Every last Strattonite was clapping and stomping and hooting and howling and cheering uncontrollably. I raised the microphone in the air again–asking for quiet–but this time they didn't listen. They were too busy seizing the moment.

Finally, the room quieted down. "All right," I said, "now that that's out of your system, I want you to know that there's a reason why Steve is so completely off the wall. In other words, there's a method to his madness. See, the simple fact is that the guy's a creative genius, and by definition Steve has to be somewhat insane. It's necessary for his image."

I nodded my head with conviction, wondering if what I'd just said made even the slightest bit of sense. "But listen to me, everyone, and listen good. This ability Steve has–this gift of his–goes far beyond being able to spot a couple of hot shoe trends. Steve's real power–what separates him from every other shoe designer in America–is that he actually *creates* trends.

"Do you know how rare that is? To find someone who can actually set a fashion trend and enforce it? People like Steve come along once every decade! And when they do, they become household names, like a Coco Chanel or an Yves St. Laurent, or a Versace, or Armani, or Donna Karan . . . or a short list of others."

I took a few steps into the boardroom and lowered my voice like a preacher driving home a point. "And having someone like Steve at the helm is exactly what it takes to launch a company like this into the stratosphere. And you can mark my words on it! This is the company we've all been waiting for since the beginning. It's the one that'll put Stratton on a whole new plateau. It's the one that we've been . . ."

I was on a roll now, and as I continued speaking, my mind started to double track. I began totaling up the profits I was about to make. The awesome number *$20 million* came bubbling up into my brain. It was a good estimate, I figured, and the calculations were pretty simple. Of the two million units being offered, one million of them were going into the accounts of my ratholes. I would buy those units back from my ratholes at five or six dollars per and then hold them in the firm's proprietary trading account. Then I would use the power of the boardroom, the massive buying this very meeting would create, to drive the units up to twenty dollars, which would lock in a paper profit of $14 or $15 million. Although, actually, I wouldn't even have to drive the units up to twenty dollars myself; the rest of Wall Street would do the dirty work for me. As long as the other brokerage firms and trading firms knew I was willing to buy the units back at the top of the market, they would drive the price up as high as I wanted! I just had to leak the word out to a few key players and the rest would be history. (And this I'd already done.) The word on the street was that Stratton was a buyer up to twenty dollars a unit, so the wheels were already set in motion! *Unbelievable!* To make all that money and not commit a crime! Well, the ratholes weren't exactly on the up-and-up, but still, it was impossible to prove. Ahhhh, talk about your unbridled capitalism!

". . . like a rocket ship and keep on going. Who knows how high this stock could go? The twenties? The thirties? I mean, if I'm even half right, those numbers are ridiculously low! They're nothing compared to what this company is capable of. In the blink of an eye the stock could be in the fifties or even the sixties! And I'm not talking about some far-off time in the future. I'm talking about right now, as we speak.

"Listen to me, everyone. Steve Madden Shoes is the hottest company in the entire women's shoe industry. Orders are going through the roof right now! Every department store in America–chains like Macy's and Bloomingdale's, Nordstrom and Dillard's–they can't keep our shoes in stock. The shoes are so hot they're literally flying off the shelves!

"You know, I hope you're all aware that as stockbrokers you have an obligation to your clients, a *fiduciary responsibility* so to speak, to get on the phone with them the second I'm finished and do whatever it takes–even if it means ripping their fucking eyeballs out–to get them to buy as much stock in Steve Madden Shoes as they can possibly afford. I sincerely hope you're aware of this, because if you're not, then you and I are going to have some serious issues together after all this is said and done.

"You have an obligation here! An obligation to your clients! An obligation to this firm! And an obligation to yourself, God damn it! You better ram this stock right down your clients' throats and make them choke on it until they say, 'Buy me twenty thousand shares,' because every dollar your clients invest is gonna come back to them in spades.

"I mean, I could go on and on about the bright future of Steve Madden Shoes. I could talk about all the fundamentals–about all the new store openings and how we manufacture our shoes in a more cost-effective way than the competition, about how our shoes are so hot that we don't even have to advertise and how the mass merchants are willing to pay us royalties to have access to our designs–but at the end of the day none of it matters. The bottom line is that all your clients wanna know is that the stock's going up; that's it."

I slowed my pace a bit and said, "Listen, guys, as much as I'd like to, I can't get on the phone and sell the stock to your clients. Only *you* can pick up the phone and take action. And at the end of the day, that's what it's all about: taking action. Without action, the best intentions in the world are nothing more than that: intentions."

I took a deep breath and plowed on. "Now, I want everybody to look down." I extended my arm and gestured to a desk just in front of me. "Look down at that little black box right in front of you. You see it? It's a wonderful little invention called the telephone. Here, I'll spell it for you: T-E-L-E-P-H-O-N-E. Now, guess what, everybody? This telephone won't dial itself! Yeah, that's right. Until you take some fucking action, it's nothing more than a worthless hunk of plastic. It's like a loaded M16 without a trained Marine to pull the trigger. See, it's the action of a highly trained Marine–a trained killer–that turns an M16 into a deadly weapon. And in the case of the telephone it's the action of you–a highly trained Strattonite, a highly trained killer who won't take no for an answer, who won't hang up the phone until his client either buys or dies, someone who's fully aware that there's a sale being made on every single phone call and that it's only a question of who's selling who. Were you the one who did the selling? Were you proficient enough and motivated enough and gutsy enough to take control of the conversation and close the sale? Or was it your client who did the selling–explaining how he couldn't make the investment right now because the timing was wrong or he needed to talk it over with his wife or his business partner or Santa Claus or the fucking tooth fairy."

I rolled my eyes and shook my head in disgust. "So don't you ever fucking forget that that phone sitting on your desk is a deadly weapon. And in the hands of a motivated Strattonite it's a license to print money. And it's the *great equalizer*!" I paused, letting those last two words reverberate around the boardroom, and then I kept right on going. "All you gotta do is pick up the phone and say the words I've taught you, and it can make you as powerful as the most powerful CEO in the country. And I don't care whether you graduated from Harvard or you grew up on the mean streets of Hell's Kitchen: With that little black phone you can achieve anything.

"That phone equals money. And I don't care how many problems you have right now, because every single one of them can be helped with money. Yeah, that's right; money is the greatest single problem-solver known to man, and anyone who tries to tell you different is completely full of shit. In fact, I'm willing to bet that anyone who says that never had a dime to their fucking name!" I held my hand up in the scout's honor mode, and said with piss and vinegar, "It's always those same people who are the first to spew out their worthless advice–it's always the paupers, who sling around that ridiculous line of bullshit about how money is the root of all evil and about how money corrupts. Well–I–mean–*really!* What a bunch of happy horseshit that is! Having money is wonderful! And having money is a must!

"Listen to me, everyone: There's no nobility in poverty. I've been rich and I've been poor, and I choose rich every time. At least as a rich man, when I have to face my problems, I can show up in the back of a stretch limousine, wearing a two-thousand-dollar suit and a twenty-thousand-dollar gold watch! And, believe me, arriving in style makes your problems a helluva lot easier to deal with."

I shrugged my shoulders for effect. "Anyway, if anyone here thinks I'm crazy or you don't feel exactly like I do, *then get the fuck out of this room right now!* That's right–get the fuck out of my boardroom and go get a job at McDonald's flipping burgers, because that's where you belong! And if McDonald's isn't hiring, there's always Burger King!

"But before you actually depart this room full of winners, I want you to take a good look at the person sitting next to you, because one day in the not-so-distant future, you'll be sitting at a red light in your beat-up old Pinto, and the person sitting next to you is gonna pull up in his brand-new Porsche, with his gorgeous young wife sitting next to him. And who'll be sitting next to you? Some ugly beast, no doubt, with three days of razor stubble–wearing a sleeveless muumuu or a housedress–and you'll probably be on your way home from the Price Club with a hatchback full of discount groceries!"

Just then I locked eyes with a young Strattonite who looked literally panic-stricken. Hammering my point home, I said, "What? You think I'm lying to you? Well, guess what? It only gets worse. See, if you want to grow old with dignity–if you want to grow old and maintain your self-respect–then you better get rich now. The days of working for a large Fortune Five Hundred company and retiring with a pension are ancient fucking history! And if you think Social Security is gonna be your safety net, then think again. At the current rate of inflation it'll be just enough to pay for your diapers after they stick you in some rancid nursing home, where a three-hundred-pound Jamaican woman with a beard and mustache will feed you soup through a straw and then bitch-slap you when she's in a bad mood.

"So listen to me, and listen good: Is your current problem that you're behind on your credit-card bills? Good–then pick up the fucking phone and start dialing.

"Or is your landlord threatening to dispossess you? Is that what your problem is? Good–then pick up the fucking phone and start dialing.

"Or is it your girlfriend? Does she want to leave you because she thinks you're a loser? Good–then pick up the fucking phone and start dialing!

"I want you to deal with all your problems by becoming rich! I want you to attack your problems head-on! I want you to go out and start spending money right now. I want you to leverage yourself. I want you to back yourself into a corner. Give yourself no choice but to succeed. Let the consequences of failure become so dire and so unthinkable that you'll have no choice but to do whatever it takes to succeed.

"And that's why I say: Act as if! Act as if you're a wealthy man, rich already, and then you'll surely become rich. Act as if you have unmatched confidence and then people will surely have confidence in you. Act as if you have unmatched experience and then people will follow your advice. And act as if you are already a tremendous success, and as sure as I stand here today–you *will* become successful!

"Now, this deal opens in less than an hour. So get on the fucking phone right this second and go A to Z through those client books and take no prisoners. Be ferocious! Be pit bulls! Be telephone terrorists! You do exactly as I say and, believe me, you'll be thanking me a thousand times over a few hours from now, when every one of your clients is making money."

With that, I walked off center stage to the sound of a thousand cheering Strattonites, who were already in the process of picking up their phones and following my very advice: ripping their clients' eyeballs out.

CHAPTER 9

PLAUSIBLE DENIABILITY

At one p.m., the geniuses down at the National Association of Securities Dealers, the NASD, released Steve Madden Shoes for trading on the NASDAQ stock exchange–the stock exchange that the Association then owned–under the four-letter trading symbol SHOO: pronounced *shoe. How cute and appropriate that was!*

And as part of their long-standing practice of having their heads up their asses, they reserved the distinguished honor of setting the price for the opening tick for me, the Wolf of Wall Street. It was just another in a long line of ill-conceived trading policies that were so absurd that in those days they all but assured that every new issue coming out on the NASDAQ would be manipulated in one way or another, regardless of whether or not Stratton Oakmont was involved in it.

Just why the NASD had created a playing field that so clearly fucked over the customer was something I'd thought about often, and I'd come to the conclusion that it was because the NASD was a self-regulatory agency, "owned" by the very brokerage firms themselves. (In fact, Stratton Oakmont was a member too.)

In essence, the NASD's true goal was to only appear to be on the side of the customer and to not actually be on the side of the customer. And, in truth, they didn't even try too hard to do that. The effort was strictly cosmetic, just enough to avoid raising the ire of the SEC, who they were compelled to answer to.

So instead of allowing the natural balance between buyers and sellers to dictate where a stock should open, they reserved that incredibly valuable right for the lead underwriter, which in this particular case was me. I could choose whatever price I deemed appropriate, as arbitrary and capricious as it might be. In consequence, I decided to be very arbitrary and even more capricious, and I opened the units at $5.50 per, which afforded me the glorious opportunity of repurchasing my one million rathole units just there. And while I won't deny that my ratholes would have liked to hold on to the units for a *weeeee* bit longer, they had no choice in the matter. After all, the buyback had been prearranged (a definite regulatory no-no), and they had just made a profit of $1.50 per unit for doing nothing and risking nothing–having bought and sold the units without even paying for the trade. And if they wanted to be included in the next deal, they had better follow the expected protocol, which was to shut the fuck up and say, "Thank you, Jordan!" and then lie through their teeth if they were ever questioned by a federal or state securities regulator as to why they sold their units so cheaply.

Either way, you really couldn't question my logic in the matter. By 1:03 p.m.–just three minutes after I'd bought back my rathole units at $5.50 per–the rest of Wall Street had already driven the units up to $18. That meant I had locked in a profit of $12.5 million–*$12.5 million! In three minutes!* I'd made another million or so in investment-banking fees and stood to make another three or four million a few days from now–when I bought back the bridge-loan units, which were also in the hands of my ratholes. Ahhhh–ratholes! What a concept! And Steve himself was my biggest rathole of all. He was holding 1.2 million shares for me, the very shares NASDAQ had forced me to divest. At the current unit price of $18 (each unit consisting of one share of common stock and two warrants), the actual share price was $8. That meant that the shares Steve was holding for me were now worth just under $10 million! *The Wolf strikes again!*

It was now up to my loyal Strattonites to sell all this inflated stock to their clients. All this inflated stock–not just the one million units they had given to their own clients as part of the initial public offering but also my one million rathole units that were now being held in the firm's trading account, along with 300,000 bridge-loan units I would be buying back in a few days . . . and then some additional stock I had to buy back from all the brokerage firms that had pushed the units up to $18 (doing the dirty work for me). They would be slowly selling their units back to Stratton Oakmont and locking in their own profit. All told, by the end of the day, I would need my Strattonites to raise approximately $30 million. That would more than cover everything, as well as give the firm's trading account a nice little cushion against any pain-in-the-ass short-sellers, who might try to sell stock they didn't even own (with the hopes of driving the price down so they could buy it back cheaper in the future). Thirty million was no problem for my merry band of brokers, especially after this morning's meeting, which had them pitching their hearts and souls out like never before.

At this particular moment I was standing inside the firm's trading room–looking over the shoulder of my head trader, Steve Sanders. I had one eye on a bank of computer monitors directly in front of Steve, while my other eye looked out a plate-glass window that faced the boardroom. The pace was absolutely frenetic. Brokers were screaming into their telephones like wild banshees. Every few seconds a young sales assistant with a lot of blond hair and a plunging neckline would come running up to the plate-glass window, press her breasts against it, and slip a stack of buy tickets through a narrow slot at the bottom. Then one of four order clerks would grab the tickets and input them into the computer network–causing them to pop up on the proprietary trading terminal in front of Steve, at which point he would execute them in accordance with the current market.

As I watched the orange-diode numbers flash across Steve's terminal, I felt a twisted sense of pride over how those two morons from the SEC had been sitting in my conference room, searching the historical record for some sort of smoking gun, while I fired off a live bazooka under their noses. But I guess they'd been too busy freezing to death, as we listened to every word they said.

By now, more than fifty different brokerage firms were participating in the buying frenzy. What they all had in common, though, was that each one fully intended on selling every last share back to Stratton Oakmont at the end of the day, at the very top of the market. And with other brokerage firms doing the buying, it would now be impossible for the SEC to make the case that I had been the one who'd manipulated the units to $18. It was elegantly simple. How could I be at fault if I hadn't been the one who'd driven the price of the stock up? In fact, I had actually been a seller the whole way. And I had sold the other brokerage firms just enough to wet their beaks, so they would continue to manipulate my new issues in the future–but not too much that it would become a major burden to me when I had to buy the stock back at the end of the trading day. It was a careful balance to strike, but the simple fact was that having other brokerage firms bidding up the price of Steve Madden Shoes created plausible deniability with the SEC. And, in a month from now, when they were subpoenaing my trading records, trying to reconstruct what had happened in those first few moments of trading, all they would see was that brokerage firms across America had bid up the price of Steve Madden Shoes, and that would be that.

Before I left the trading room, my final instructions to Steve were that under no circumstances was he to let the stock drop below $18. After all, I wasn't about to shaft the rest of Wall Street after they'd been kind enough to manipulate my stock for me.

CHAPTER 10

THE DEPRAVED CHINAMAN

By four p.m. it was one for the record books.

The trading day was over, and the news that Steve Madden Shoes had been the most actively traded stock in America and, for that matter, the world had come skidding across the Dow Jones wire service for one and all to see. *The world! Such audacity! Such sheer audacity!*

Oh, yes, Stratton Oakmont had the power, all right. In fact, Stratton Oakmont *was* the power, and I, as Stratton's leader, was wired into that very power and sat atop its pinnacle. I felt it surge through my very innards and resonate with my heart and soul and liver and loins. With more than eight million shares changing hands, the units had closed just below $19, up five hundred percent on the day, making it the largest percentage gainer on the NASDAQ, the NYSE, the AMEX, as well as any other stock exchange in the world. Yes, the world–from the OBX exchange way up north in the frozen wasteland of Oslo, Norway, all the way down south to the ASX exchange in the kangaroo paradise of Sydney, Australia.

Right now I was standing in the boardroom, casually leaning against my office's plate-glass window, with my arms folded beneath my chest. It was the pose of the mighty warrior after the fray. The mighty roar of the boardroom was still going strong, but the tone was different now. It was less urgent, more subdued.

It was almost celebration time. I stuck my right hand in my pants pocket and did a quick check to make sure my six Ludes hadn't fallen out or simply vanished into thin air. Quaaludes had a way of vanishing sometimes, although it usually had more to do with your "friends" snatching them from you–or you getting so stoned that you took them yourself and simply didn't remember. That was the fourth phase of a Quaalude high and, perhaps, the most dangerous: the amnesia phase. The first phase was the tingle phase, next came the slur phase, then the drool phase, and then, of course, the amnesia phase.

Anyway, the drug-god had been kind to me, and the Quaaludes hadn't vanished. I took a moment to roll them around in my fingertips, which gave me an irrational sense of joy. Then I began the process of calculating the appropriate time to take them, which was somewhere around 4:30 p.m., I figured, twenty-five minutes from now. That would give me fifteen minutes to hold the afternoon meeting, as well as enough time to supervise this afternoon's act of depravity, which was a female head-shaving.

One of the young sales assistants, who was strapped for cash, had agreed to put on a Brazilian bikini and sit down on a wooden stool at the front of the boardroom and let us shave her head down to the skull. She had a great mane of shimmering blond hair and a wonderful set of breasts, which had recently been augmented to a D cup. Her reward would be $10,000 in cash, which she would use to pay for her breast job, which she'd just financed at twelve percent. So it was a win-win situation for everyone: In six months she'd have her hair back, and she'd own her D cups debt free.

I couldn't help but wonder if I should've allowed Danny to bring a midget into the office. After all, what was so wrong with it? It sounded a bit off at first, but now that I'd had a little time to digest it, it didn't seem so bad.

In essence, what it really boiled down to was that the right to pick up a midget and toss him around was just another currency due any mighty warrior, a spoil of war, so to speak. How else was a man to measure his success if not by playing out every one of his adolescent fantasies, regardless of how bizarre it might be? There was definitely something to be said for that. If precocious success brought about questionable forms of behavior, then the prudent young man should enter each unseemly act into the debit column on his own moral balance sheet and then offset it at some future point with an act of kindness or generosity (a moral credit, so to speak), when he became older and wiser and more sedate.

Yet, on the other hand, we might just be depraved maniacs—a self-contained society that had spiraled completely out of control. We Strattonites thrived on acts of depravity. We counted on them, in fact; I mean, we needed them to survive!

It was for this very reason that, after becoming completely desensitized to basic acts of depravity, the powers that be (namely, me) felt compelled to form an unofficial team of Strattonites—with Danny Porush as its proud leader—to fill the void. The team acted like a twisted version of the Knights Templar—whose never-ending quest to find the Holy Grail was the stuff of legend. But unlike the Knights Templar, the Stratton knights spent their time scouring the four corners of the earth for increasingly depraved acts, so the rest of the Strattonites could continue to get off. It wasn't like we were heroin junkies or anything as tawdry as that; we were unadulterated adrenaline junkies, who needed higher and higher cliffs to dive off and shallower and shallower pools to land in.

The process had officially gotten under way in October 1989, when twenty-one-year-old Peter Galletta, one of the initial eight Strattonites, christened the building's glass elevator with a quick blow job and an even quicker rear entry into the luscious loins of a seventeen-year-old sales assistant. She was one of Stratton's first sales assistants, and, for better or worse, she was blond, beautiful, and wildly promiscuous.

At first I was shocked and had even considered firing Peter, for dipping his pen into the company inkwell. But within a week the young girl had proven to be a real team player—blowing all eight Strattonites, most of them in the glass elevator, and me under my desk. And she had a strange way of doing it, which became legendary among Strattonites. We called it the twist and jerk—where she'd use both hands at once, while she transformed her tongue into a whirling dervish. Anyway, about a month later, after a tiny bit of urging, Danny convinced me that it would be good if we both did her at the same time, which we did, on a Saturday afternoon while our wives were out shopping for Christmas dresses. Ironically, three years later, after bedding God only knew how many Strattonites, she finally married one. He was one of the original eight Strattonites and had seen her ply her trade countless times. But he didn't care. Perhaps it was the twist and jerk that had got him! Whatever the case, he'd been only sixteen when he first came to work for me. He dropped out of high school to become a Strattonite–to live the Life.

That aside, within the four walls of the boardroom, behavior of the normal sort was considered to be in bad taste, as if you were some sort of killjoy or something, looking to spoil the fun for everyone else. In a way, though, wasn't the concept of depravity relative? The Romans hadn't considered themselves to be depraved maniacs, had they? In fact, I'd be willing to bet that it all seemed normal to them as they watched their less-favored slaves being fed to the lions and their more-favored slaves fed them grapes.

Just then I saw the Blockhead walking toward me with his mouth open, his eyebrows high on his forehead, and his chin tilted slightly up. It was the eager expression of a man who'd been waiting half his life to ask a single question. Given the fact that it was the Blockhead, I had no doubt the question was either grossly stupid or grossly worthless. Whichever it was, I acknowledged him with a tilt of my own chin, and then I took a moment to regard him. In spite of having the squarest head on Long Island, he was actually good-looking. He had the soft round features of a little boy and was blessed with a reasonably good physique. He was of medium height and medium weight, which was surprising, considering from whose loins he'd emerged.

The Blockhead's mother, Gladys Greene, was a big woman.

Everywhere.

Starting from the very top of her crown, where a beehive of pineapple blond hair rose up a good six inches above her broad Jewish skull, and all the way down to the thick callused balls of her size-twelve feet, Gladys Greene was big.

The last time a person really got under Gladys's skin was while she was going through the checkout line at Grand Union. One of those typical Long Island Jewish women, with a big nose and the nasty habit of sticking it where it didn't belong, made the sorry mistake of informing Gladys that she had exceeded the maximum number of items to pass through the express lane and still maintain the moral high ground. Gladys's response was to turn on the woman and hit her full on with a right cross. With the woman still unconscious, Gladys calmly paid for her groceries and made a swift exit, her pulse never exceeding seventy-two.

So there was no leap of logic required to figure out why the Blockhead was only a smidgen saner than Danny. Yet, in the Blockhead's defense, he had had a lot on his plate growing up. His father, who died of cancer when Kenny was only twelve years old, had owned a cigarette distributorship, and, unbeknownst to Gladys, it had been grossly mismanaged–owing hundreds of thousands in back taxes. And just like that, Gladys found herself in a desperate situation: a single mother on the brink of financial ruin.

What was Gladys to do? Fold up her tent? Apply for welfare, perhaps? Oh, no, not a chance! Using her strong maternal instincts, she managed to keep the family afloat.

But that was only the beginning. When Kenny turned fifteen, he and his friends had started smoking a different type of cigarette, namely, joints, and the budding Blockhead set up as a pot dealer.

But things were only getting warmed up. After all, you could love pot or hate pot, but you had to respect it as the most reliable gateway drug in the marketplace, especially when it came to teenagers. In light of that, it wasn't long before Kenny realized there were other economic voids to be filled in Long Island's teenage drug market. Oh, yes, that Bolivian marching powder, cocaine, offered too high a profit margin for an ardent capitalist like Blockhead to resist. This time, though, he brought in a partner, his childhood friend Victor Wang.

Victor was an interesting sort, insofar as him being the biggest Chinaman to ever walk the planet. He had a head the size of a giant panda's, slits for eyes, and a chest as broad as the Great Wall itself. In fact, the guy was a dead ringer for Oddjob, the hitman from the James Bond movie *Goldfinger,* who could knock your block off with a steel-rimmed bowler cap at two hundred paces.

Victor was Chinese by birth and Jewish by injection, having been raised amid the most savage young Jews anywhere on Long Island: the towns of Jericho and Syosset. It was from out of the very marrow of these two upper-middle-class Jewish ghettos that the bulk of my first hundred Strattonites had come, most of them former drug clients of Kenny's and Victor's.

And like the rest of Long Island's educationally challenged dream-seekers, Victor had also fallen into my employ, albeit not at Stratton Oakmont. Instead, he was the CEO of the public company Judicate, which was one of my satellite ventures. Judicate's offices were downstairs on the basement level, a mere stone's throw away from the happy hit squad of NASDAQ hookers. Its business was Alternative Dispute Resolution, or ADR, which was a fancy phrase for using retired judges to arbitrate civil disputes between insurance companies and plaintiffs' attorneys.

The company was barely breaking even now–proving to be yet another classic example of a business looking terrific on paper but not translating into the real world. Wall Street was chock-full of these kinds of concept companies. Sadly enough, a man in my line of work–namely, small-cap venture capital–seemed to be finding all of them.

Nevertheless, Judicate's slow demise had become a real sore point with Victor, despite the fact that it wasn't really his fault. The business was fundamentally flawed and no one could've made a success of it, or at least not much of one. But Victor was a Chinaman, and like most of his brethren, if he had a choice between losing face or cutting off his own balls and eating them, he would gladly take out a scissor and start snipping at his scrotal sac. But that wasn't an option here. Victor had, indeed, lost face, and he was a problem that needed to be dealt with. And with the Blockhead constantly pleading Victor's case, it had become a perpetual thorn in my side.

It was for this very reason that I wasn't the least bit surprised when the first words out of the Blockhead's mouth were, "Can we sit down with Victor later today and try to work things out?"

Feigning ignorance, I replied, "Work *what* out, Kenny?"

"Come on," he urged. "We need to talk with Victor about opening up his own firm. He wants your blessing and he's driving me crazy about it!"

"He wants my blessing or my money? Which one?"

"He wants both," said the Blockhead. As an afterthought, he added, "He *needs* both."

"Uh-huh," I replied, in the tone of the unimpressed. "And if I don't give it to him?"

The Blockhead let out a great blockheaded sigh. "What do you have against Victor? He's already pledged his loyalty to you a thousand times over. And he'll do it again–right now–in front of all three of us. I'm telling you–next to you, Victor's the sharpest guy I know. We'll make a fortune off him. I swear! He's already found a broker dealer he could buy for next to nothing. It's called Duke Securities. I think you should give him the money. All he needs is half a million–that's it."

I shook my head in disgust. "Save your pleas for when you really need them, Kenny. Anyway, now is not the time to be discussing the future of Duke Securities. I think this is slightly more important, don't you?" I motioned to the front of the boardroom, where a bunch of sales assistants were setting up a mock barbershop.

Kenny cocked his head to the side and looked over at the barbershop with a confused look on his face, but he said nothing.

I took a deep breath and let it out slowly. "Listen, there are things about Victor that trouble me. And that shouldn't be news to you–unless, of course, you've had your head up your ass for the last five years!" I started chuckling. "You don't seem to get it, Kenny, you really don't. You don't see that with all Victor's plotting and planning he's gonna Sun Tzu himself to death. And all his face-saving bullshit–I haven't got the time or inclination to deal with it. I swear to fucking God!

"Anyway, get this through your head: Victor–will–never–be–loyal. *Ever!* Not to you, not to me, and not to himself. He'll cut off his own Chinese nose to spite his own Chinese face in the name of winning some imaginary war he's fighting against no one but himself. You got it?" I smiled cynically.

I paused and softened my tone. "Anyway, listen for a second: You know how much I love you, Kenny. And you also know how much I respect you." I fought the urge to chuckle with those last few words. "And because of those two things, I will sit down with Victor and try to placate him. But I'm not doing it because of Victor fucking Wang, who I detest. I'm doing it because of Kenny Greene, who I love. On a separate note, he can't just walk away from Judicate. Not yet, at least. I'm counting on you to make sure he stays until I do what I need to do."

The Blockhead nodded. "No problem," he said happily. "Victor listens to me. I mean, if you only knew how . . ."

The Blockhead started spewing out blockheaded nonsense, but I immediately tuned out. In fact, by the look in his eyes, I knew he hadn't grasped my meaning at all. In point of fact–it was I, not Victor, who had the most to lose if Judicate went belly up. I was the largest shareholder, owning a bit more than three million shares, while Victor held only stock options, which were worthless at the current stock price of two dollars. Still, as an owner of *stock*, my stake was worth $6 million–although the two-dollar share price was misleading. After all the company was performing so poorly that you couldn't actually sell the stock without driving the price down into the pennies.

Unless, of course, you had an army of Strattonites.

Yet there was one hitch to this exit strategy–namely, that my stock wasn't eligible for sale yet. I had bought my shares directly from Judicate under SEC Rule 144, which meant there was a two-year holding period before I could legally resell it. I was only one month shy of the two-year mark, so all I needed was Victor to keep things afloat a tiny bit longer. But this seemingly simple task was proving to be far more difficult than I'd anticipated. The company was bleeding cash like a hemophiliac in a rosebush.

In fact, now that Victor's options were worthless, his sole compensation was a salary of $100,000 a year, which was a paltry sum compared to what his peers were making upstairs. And unlike the Blockhead, Victor was no fool; he was keenly aware that I would use the power of the boardroom to sell my shares as soon as they became eligible, and he was also aware that he could get left behind after they were sold–reduced to nothing more than the chairman of a worthless public company.

He had intimated this concern to me via the Blockhead, who he'd been using as a puppet since junior high school. And I had explained to Victor, more than once, that I had no intention of leaving him behind, that I would make him whole no matter what–even if it meant making him money as my rathole.

But the Depraved Chinaman couldn't be convinced of that, not for more than a few hours at a time. It was as if my words went in one ear and out the other. The simple fact was that he was a paranoid son of a bitch. He had grown up an oversize Chinaman amid a ferocious tribe of savage Jews. In consequence, he must have felt like an outsider and he now resented me, the most savage Jew of all. To date, I had outsmarted him, outwitted him, and outmaneuvered him.

It was out of his very ego, in fact, that Victor hadn't become a Strattonite in the early days. So he went to Judicate instead. It was his way of breaking into the inner circle, a way to save face for not making the right decision back in 1988, when the rest of his friends had sworn loyalty to me and had become the first Strattonites. In Victor's mind, or so it seemed to me, Judicate was merely a way station to insinuate himself back into the queue, so that one day I would tap him on the shoulder and say, "Vic, I want you to open up your own brokerage firm, and here's the money and expertise to do it."

It was what every Strattonite dreamed of and something I touched upon in all my meetings–that if you continued to work hard and stay loyal, one day I'd tap you on the shoulder and set you up in business.

And then you would get truly rich.

I had done this twice so far: once with Alan Lipsky, my oldest and most trusted friend, who now owned Monroe Parker Securities; and a second time, with Elliot Loewenstern, another long-time friend, who now owned Biltmore Securities. Elliot had been my partner back in my ice-hustling days. During the summer, the two of us would go down to the local beach and hustle Italian ices blanket-to-blanket, and make a fortune. We would scream out our sales pitch as we carried around forty-pound Styrofoam coolers, running from the cops when they chased after us. And while our friends were either goofing off or working menial jobs for $3.50 an hour, we were earning $400 a day. Each summer we would each save twenty thousand dollars and use it during the winter months to pay our way through college.

In any event, both firms–Biltmore and Monroe Parker–were doing phenomenally well, earning tens of millions a year, and they were each paying me a hidden royalty of $5 million a year just for setting them up.

It was a hefty sum, $5 million, and in truth it had little to do with setting them up. In point of fact, they paid me out of loyalty, and out of respect. And at the very crux of it, what held it all together was the fact that they still considered themselves Strattonites. And I considered them such too.

So there it was. As the Blockhead stood in front of me, still rambling on about how loyal the Chinaman would be, I knew otherwise. How could someone who harbored a deep-seated resentment toward my firm's success ever stay loyal to the Wolf of Wall Street? He was a man of grudges, Victor, a man who held every last Strattonite in contempt.

It was clear: There was no logical reason to back the Depraved Chinaman, which led to another problem–namely, that there was no way to stop him. All I could do was delay him. And if I delayed too long, I ran the risk of him doing it without me–without my blessing, so to speak, which would set a dangerous precedent to the rest of the Strattonites, especially if he succeeded.

It was sad and ironic, I thought, how my power was nothing more than an illusion, how it would vanish quickly if I didn't think ten steps ahead. I had no choice but to torture myself over every decision, to read infinite detail into everyone's motives. I felt like a twisted game theorist, who spent the better part of his day lost in thought–considering all the moves and countermoves and outcomes thereof. It was emotionally taxing, my life, and after five long years it seemed to be getting the best of me. In fact, the only time my mind was quiet now was when I was either high as a kite or inside the luscious loins of the luscious Duchess.

Nevertheless, the Depraved Chinaman couldn't be ignored. To start a brokerage firm required a minuscule amount of capital, perhaps half a million at most, which was peanuts compared to what he'd make in the first few months alone. The Blockhead himself could finance the Chinaman, if he so desired, although that would be an overt act of war–if I could ever prove it, which would be difficult.

In reality, the only thing holding Victor back was his lack of confidence–or his simple unwillingness to put his enormous Chinese ego and his tiny Chinese balls on the line. He wanted assurances, the Chinaman; he wanted direction, and emotional support, and protection against short-sellers–and, most importantly, he wanted large blocks of Stratton new issues, which were Wall Street's hottest.

He would want all these things until he could figure them out on his own.

Then he would want no more.

That would take six months, I figured, at which point he would turn on me. He would sell back all the stock I'd given him, which would put unnecessary pressure on the Strattonites, who would be forced to buy it. Ultimately, his selling would drive the stocks down, which would lead to customer complaints and, most importantly, a boardroom full of unhappy Strattonites. He would then prey upon that unhappiness–using it to try to steal my

Strattonites. He would accompany it with a promise of a better life at Duke Securities. Yes, I thought, there was something to be said for being small and nimble, as he would be. It would be difficult to defend against such an attack. I was the lumbering giant, vulnerable at the periphery.

So the answer was to deal with the Chinaman from a position of strength. I was big, all right, and despite being vulnerable at the periphery I was tough as nails at the center. So it would be from the very center that I'd strike. I would agree to back Victor, and I would lull him into a false sense of security, then, when he least expected it, I would unleash a first strike against him of such ferocity that it would leave him destitute.

First thing first: I would ask the Chinaman to wait three months to give me enough time to unload my Judicate shares. The Chinaman would understand that and suspect nothing. Meanwhile, I would approach the Blockhead and squeeze some concessions out of him. After all, as a twenty percent partner of Stratton, he stood in the way of other Strattonites who wanted a piece of the pie.

And once I put Victor into business, I would bring him to the point where he was making decent money but not too much money. I would then advise him to trade in such a manner that would leave him subtly exposed. And there were ways to do that that only the most sophisticated traders would pick up on, ways that Victor certainly would not. I would play right into that giant Chinese ego of his–advising him to maintain large positions in his proprietary trading account. And when he least expected it, when he was at his most vulnerable point, I would turn on him with all my power and attack. I would drive the Depraved Chinaman right the fuck out of business. I would sell stock through names and places that Victor never heard of, names that could never be traced back to me, names that would leave him scratching his panda-size head. I would unleash a barrage of selling that was so fast and so furious that, before he knew what even hit him, he would be out of business–and out of my hair forever.

Of course, the Blockhead would lose some money in the process, but at the end of the day he would still be a wealthy man. I would chalk that one up to collateral damage.

I smiled at the Blockhead. "Like I said, I'll meet with Victor out of respect to you. But I can't do it until next week. So let's do it in

Atlantic City, when we settle up with our ratholes. I assume Victor's going, right?"

The Blockhead nodded. "He'll be anywhere you want him to be."

I nodded. "Between now and then you better straighten the Chinaman's head out. I'm not gonna be pressured into doing this before I'm good and ready. And that won't be until after I've blown out of Judicate. You got it?"

He nodded proudly. "As long as he knows you'll back him, he'll wait as long as you want."

As long as? What a fool the Blockhead was! Was it just my imagination or had he proved yet again how clueless he was? By uttering those very words, he confirmed what I'd already known–that the Depraved Chinaman's allegiance was *subject to.*

Yes, today the Blockhead was loyal; he was still Stratton through and through. But no man can serve two masters for long, and certainly not forever. And that was what the Depraved Chinaman was: another Master. He was waiting in the wings, manipulating the Blockhead's feeble mind as he sowed seeds of dissension within my very ranks, starting with my own junior partner.

There was a war brewing here. It was looming just over the horizon–heading for my doorstep in the not-too-distant future. And it was a war I would win.

BOOK II

CHAPTER II

THE LAND OF RATHOLES

August 1993
(Four Months Earlier)

Where the fuck am I, for Chrissake?

Such was the first question that popped into my mind as I woke up to the unmistakable screech of landing gear being lowered from out of the enormous belly of a jumbo jetliner. Slowly regaining consciousness, I looked at the red and blue emblem on the seat back in front of me and tried to make sense of it all.

Apparently, the jumbo jetliner was a Boeing 747; my seat number was 2A, a window seat in first class, and at this particular moment, although my eyes were open, my chin was still tucked between my collarbones in sleep mode, and my head felt like it had been smacked by a pharmaceutical nightstick.

A hangover? I thought. From Quaaludes? That made no sense!

Still confused, I craned my neck and looked out the small oval window on my left and tried to get my bearings. The sun was just over the horizon—*morning!* An important clue! My spirits lifted. I panned my head and took in the view: rolling green mountains, a small gleaming city, a huge turquoise lake in the shape of a crescent, an enormous jet of water shooting up hundreds of feet in the air—*breathtaking!*

Wait a minute. What the fuck was I doing on a commercial plane? So tawdry it was! Where was my Gulfstream? How long had I been asleep? And how many Quaaludes–*Oh, Christ! The Restorils!*

A cloud of despair began rising up my brain stem. I had disregarded my doctor's warning and mixed Restorils with Quaaludes, both of which were sleeping pills but from two competing classes. Taken separately, the results were predictable–six to eight hours of deep sleep. Taken together, the results were–what were the results?

I took a deep breath and fought down the negativity. Then it hit me–my plane was landing in Switzerland. Everything would end up fine! It was friendly territory! Neutral territory! Swiss territory! Full of things Swiss–velvety milk chocolate, deposed dictators, fine watches, hidden Nazi gold, numbered bank accounts, laundered money, bank secrecy laws, Swiss francs, Swiss Quaaludes! What a fabulous little country this was! And gorgeous from the air! Not a skyscraper in sight and thousands of tiny homes dotting the countryside in storybook fashion. And that geyser–unbelievable! Switzerland! They even had their own brand of Quaaludes, for Chrissake! Methasedils they were called, if memory served me correctly. I made a quick mental note to speak to the concierge about that.

Anyway, you had to love the Swiss–despite the fact that half the country was full of Frogs and the other half was full of Krauts. It was the end result of centuries of warfare and political backstabbing; the country had literally been divided in two, with the city of Geneva being Frog Central, where they spoke French, and the city of Zurich being Kraut Central, where they spoke German.

Insofar as my own humble Jewish opinion went, the Geneva-based Frogs were the ones to do business with–as opposed to the Zurich-based Krauts, who passed their time speaking disgusting glottal German while binge-drinking piss-warm beer and eating Wiener schnitzel until their stomachs bulged out like female kangaroos after a birthing cycle. And, besides, it didn't take any great leap of logic to realize that there had to be a few Nazi bastards still hiding out among the populace, living off the gold fillings they'd forcibly extracted from my ancestors before they gassed them to death!

Anyway, there was an added benefit to doing business in French-speaking Geneva–namely, the women. Oh, yes! Unlike your average Zurich-based German woman, who was broad-shouldered and barrel-chested enough to play for the NFL, the average French woman–who roamed the streets of Geneva with shopping bags and poodles–was slender and gorgeous, in spite of her hairy armpits. With that thought, my smile broke through the surface; after all, my destination was none other than Geneva.

I turned from the window and looked to my right, and there was Danny Porush–sleeping. He had his mouth open, in fly-catching mode, while those enormous white teeth of his blazed away in the morning sunlight. On his left wrist he wore a thick gold Rolex watch with enough diamonds on the face to power an industrial laser. The gold gleamed and the diamonds twinkled, but neither was a match for his teeth, which were brighter than a supernova. He had on his ridiculous horn-rimmed glasses, the ones with the clear lenses in them. Unbelievable! Still a Jewish WASP–even on an international flight.

Seated just to his right was the trip's organizer, self-proclaimed Swiss-banking expert Gary Kaminsky, who also happened to be the (slippery) Chief Financial Officer of Dollar Time Group, a publicly traded company of which I was the largest shareholder. Like Danny, Gary Kaminsky was sleeping. He wore a ridiculous salt-and-pepper toupee that was an entirely different color than his sideburns, which were ink black–apparently dyed that way by a colorist with a good sense of humor. Out of morbid curiosity (and habit), I took a moment to study his awful toupee. Probably a Sy Sperling special, if I had to take a guess; the good-old Hair Club for Men!

Just then, the stewardess walked by–ah, Franca! *What a hot little Swiss number! So perky!* She was gorgeous, especially the way her blond hair fell on that creamy white blouse with its high-necked collar. Such repressed sexuality! And that sexy pair of gold pilot's wings she had pinned on her left jug–a *stewardess!* What a terrific breed of woman! Especially this one, with her tight red skirt and those silky black panty hose, such a wonderful swooshing sound they made as she passed by! Cut right through the landing gear and everything!

In fact, last I could recall I was striking up quite a rap with Franca, while we were still on the ground at Kennedy Airport in New York. She liked me. Perhaps there was still a chance. Tonight! Switzerland! Franca and me! How could I ever get caught in a country where mum's the word? With a great smile and in a tone loud enough to cut through the mighty roar of the jet's Pratt & Whitney engines, I said, "Franca, my love! Come here. Could I talk to you for a second?"

Franca turned on her heel and struck a pose, with her arms folded beneath her breasts, her shoulders thrown back, her back slightly arched, and her hips cocked in a display of contempt. That look she gave me! Those narrowed eyes . . . that clenched jaw . . . that scrunched-up nose . . . absolutely poisonous!

Well, that was a bit uncalled for. Why, the–

Before I could even finish my thought, the lovely Franca spun on her heel and walked away.

What happened to Swiss hospitality, for Chrissake? I had been told that all Swiss women were sluts. Or were those Swedish women? *Hmmm* . . . yes, on second thought it was Swedish women who were the sluts. Still–that didn't give Franca the right to ignore me! I was a paying customer of Swissair, for crying out loud, and my ticket cost . . . well, it must've cost a fortune. And what had I gotten in return? A wider seat and a better meal? I had slept through the fucking meal!

All at once I felt the uncontrollable urge to urinate. I looked up at the seat-belt sign. *Shit!* It was already illuminated, but I couldn't hold it in. I had a notoriously small bladder (drove the Duchess crazy), and I must've been asleep for a good seven hours. Oh, fuck it! What could they do to me if I got up? Arrest me for going to take a piss? I tried getting up–but I couldn't.

I looked down. There wasn't one but–Christ almighty!–there were four seat belts on me. I had been tied down! Ah . . . a practical joke! I turned my head to the right. "Porush," I snapped loudly, "wake up and untie me, you asshole!"

No response. He just sat there with his head back and his mouth open, a gob of drool glistening in the morning sunlight.

Again, but louder this time: "Danny! Wake up, God damn it! *Pooorussshhhhh!* Wake up, you piece o' shit, and untie me!"

Still nothing. I took a deep breath and slowly tilted my head back, then with a mighty thrust forward I head-butted him in the shoulder.

A second later Danny's eyes popped open and his mouth snapped shut. He shook his head and looked at me through those ridiculous clear lenses. "What–what's wrong? Whaddidya do now?"

"Whaddaya mean, whaddid I do now? Untie me–you piece o' shit–before I rip those stupid glasses off your fucking head!"

With half a smile: "I can't, or else they're gonna Taser you!"

"What?" I said, confused. "What are you talking about? Who's gonna Taser me?"

Danny took a deep breath and said in hushed tones, "Listen to me: We got some problems here. You went after Franca"–he motioned his chin in the direction of the shimmering blond stewardess–"somewhere over the Atlantic Ocean. They almost turned the plane around, but I convinced them to tie you up instead and I promised that I'd keep you in your seat. But the Swiss police might be waiting at Customs. I think they plan on arresting you."

I took a moment to search my short-term memory. I had none. With a sinking heart, I said, "I haven't the slightest idea what you're talking about, Danny. I don't remember anything. What did I do?"

Danny shrugged. "You were grabbing her tits and trying to stick your tongue down her throat. Nothing so terrible if we were in a different situation, but up here in the air . . . well, there's different rules than back at the office. What really sucks, though, is that I think she actually liked you!" He shook his head and compressed his lips, as if to say, "You let a fine piece of pussy get away, Jordan!" Then he said, "But then you tried to lift up her little red skirt and she got offended."

I shook my head in disbelief. "Why didn't you stop me?"

"I tried, but you started going wild on me. What did you take?"

"Uhhhhh . . . I don't know for sure," I muttered. "I think maybe . . . uh, maybe three or four Ludes . . . and then . . . three of those little blue Restorils . . . and, uh . . . ummm–I don't know–maybe a Xanax or two . . . and, maybe some morphine for my back. But the morphine and the Restoril were prescribed by a doctor, so it's really not my fault." I held on to that comforting thought as long as I could. But slowly the reality was sinking in. I leaned back in my comfortable first-class seat and tried to draw some power from it. Then all at once, panic: "Oh, shit–the Duchess! What if the Duchess finds out about this? I'm really screwed, Danny! What am I gonna say to her? If this hits the papers–oh, God, she'll crucify me! All the apologies in the world won't–" I couldn't bear to finish the thought. I paused for a brief second, until a second wave of panic overtook me. "Oh, Jesus–the government! The whole reason for flying commercial was to be incognito! And now . . . an arrest in a foreign country! Oh, Christ! I'm gonna kill my doctor for giving me those pills! He knows I take Ludes"–desperately I looked for a doorstep to lay the blame at–"yet he still prescribed me sleeping pills! Christ, he'd prescribe me heroin for a fucking splinter if I fucking asked him to! What a fucking nightmare, Danny! What could be worse? An arrest in Switzerland–the money-laundering capital of the world! And we haven't even laundered any money yet, and we're already in trouble!" I started shaking my head gravely. "It's a bad omen, Danny.

"Untie me," I said. "I won't get up." All at once, a flash of inspiration: "Maybe I should go apologize to Franca, smooth things out with her? How much cash you have on you?"

Danny began untying me. "I have twenty grand, but I don't think you should try talking to her. It'll only make things worse. I'm pretty sure you got your hand in her underwear. Here, let me smell your fingers!"

"Shut up, Porush! Stop fucking around and keep untying me."

Danny smiled. "Anyway, give me the rest of your Ludes to hold on to. Let me take them through Customs for you."

I nodded and said a silent prayer that the Swiss government wouldn't want any bad publicity to tarnish their reputation for discretion. Like a dog with a bone I held on to that thought for dear life, as we slowly made our descent into Geneva.

With my hat in my hand and my butt in a steel-gray chair, I said to the three Customs officials seated across from me, "I'm telling you, I don't remember anything. I get very bad anxiety when I fly, and that's why I took all those pills." I pointed to the two vials resting on the gray metal desk between us. Thankfully, both vials contained my name on the label; under my present circumstances, this seemed to be the most important thing. As far as my Quaaludes were concerned, at this particular moment they were safely tucked away up Danny's descending colon, which, I assumed, had passed safely through Customs by now.

The three Swiss Customs officials started jabbering away in some off-the-wall French dialect. They sounded like their mouths were full of rotten Swiss cheese. It was amazing–even as they spoke at near light speed, they somehow managed to keep their lips tight as snare drums and their jaws locked firmly into place.

I began scoping out the room. *Was I in jail?* There was no way to tell with the Swiss. Their faces were expressionless, as if they were mindless automatons going about their lives with the mundane precision of a Swiss clock, and all the while the room screamed out, "You have now entered the fucking Twilight Zone!" There were no windows . . . no pictures . . . no clocks . . . no telephones . . . no pencils . . . no pens . . . no paper . . . no lamps . . . no computers. There was nothing but four steel-gray chairs, a matching steel-gray desk, and a wilted fucking geranium, dying a slow death.

Christ! Should I demand to speak to the U.S. embassy? *No–you fool!* I was probably on some sort of watch list. I had to stay incognito. That was the goal–incognito.

I looked at the three officials. They were still jabbering away in French. One was holding the bottle of Restorils, another was holding my passport, and the third was scratching his weak Swiss chin, as if he were deciding my fate–or did he just have an itch?

Finally, the chin-scratching Swissman spoke: "You would please repeat your story to us again."

You *would*? What was all this *would* bullshit? Why did these stupid Frogs insist on speaking in some bizarre form of the subjunctive? Everything was based on wishes, and everything was phrased in *woulds* and *shoulds* and *coulds* and *mights* and *maybes.* Why couldn't they just demand that I repeat my story? But nooo! They only *wished* I would repeat my story! I took a deep breath–but before I began speaking, the door opened and a fourth Customs official entered the room. This Frog, I noticed, had captain's bars on his shoulders.

In less than a minute the first three officials left the room, wearing the same blank expressions they had come in with. Now I was alone with the captain. He smiled a thin Frog smile at me, then took out a pack of Swiss cigarettes. He lit one up and started calmly blowing smoke rings. Then he did some sort of amazing trick with the smoke–letting a dense cloud of it escape his mouth and then sucking it up right through his own nose in two thick columns. Wow! Even in my current position I found it impressive. I mean, I had never even seen my father do that, and he wrote the book on smoking tricks! I would have to ask him about that if I ever made it out of this room alive.

Finally, after a few more smoke rings and a bit more nasal inhaling, the captain said, "Well, Mr. Belfort, I apologize for any inconvenience you would have suffered from this unfortunate misunderstanding. The stewardess has agreed not to press charges. So you are free to go. Your friends would be waiting for you outside, if you wish to follow me."

Huh? Could it be that simple? Had the Swiss bankers bailed me out already? Just to speculate! The Wolf of Wall Street–bulletproof, once more!

My mind was relaxed now, free from panic, and it went roaring right back to Franca. I smiled innocently at my new Swiss friend and said, "Since you keep talking about wishes and such, what I would really wish is if somehow you could put me in touch with that stewardess from the plane." I paused and offered him my Wolf in Sheep's Clothing smile.

The captain's face began to harden.

Oh, shit! I lifted my hands, palms facing him, and said, "Of course, only for the purposes of making a formal apology to the young blonde–I mean, the young lady–and perhaps to make some sort of financial restitution, if you know what I mean." I fought the urge to wink.

The Frog cocked his head to one side and fixed me with a look that so much as said, "You are one demented bastard!" But all he said was, "We would wish you not to contact the stewardess while you are in Switzerland. Apparently she is . . . how would you say it in English . . . she is . . ."

"Traumatized?" I offered.

"Ah, yes–traumatized. This is the word we would use. We would wish that you please do not contact her under any circumstances. I have not the slightest doubt that you will find many desirable women in Switzerland if that is your goal. Apparently you have friends in the right places." And with that, the Captain of Wishes personally escorted me through Customs, without so much as stamping my passport.

Unlike my plane flight, my limousine ride was quiet and uneventful. That was appropriate. After all, a bit of peace was a welcome respite from this morning's chaos. My destination was the famed Hotel Le

Richemond, purportedly one of the finest hotels in all of Switzerland. In fact, according to my Swiss-banking friends, Le Richemond was a most elegant establishment, a most refined establishment.

But upon my arrival I realized that *refined* and *elegant* were Swiss code words for depressing and dumpy. As I entered the lobby I noticed that the place was packed with antique Frog furniture, Louis the XIV, the doorman proudly informed me, from the mid 1700s. But to my discerning eyes, King Louis should have guillotined his interior decorator. There was a floral print on the worn carpeting, a sort of swirling pattern that a blind monkey might paint, if he became inspired to do so. The color scheme was unfamiliar to me too–a combination of dog-piss yellow and regurgitation pink. I was certain that the Frog in charge had spent a fortune on this crap, which, to a nouveau riche Jew like me, was exactly what it was: crap! I wanted new, and bright, and cheery!

Anyway, I took it in stride. I was indebted to my Swiss bankers, after all, so I figured the least I could do was pretend to appreciate their choice of accommodations. And at 16,000 francs per night, or $4,000 U.S., how bad could it be?

The hotel manager, a tall willowy Frog, checked me in and proudly gave me the lowdown of the hotel's celebrity guest roster, which included none other than Michael Jackson. Fabulous! I thought. Now I hated the place for sure.

A few minutes later I found myself in the Presidential Suite–getting the grand tour from the manager. He was an affable-enough fellow, especially after I gave him his first dose of the Wolf of Wall Street, in the form of a 2,000-franc tip, as thanks for checking me in without alerting Interpol. As he left, he assured me that the finest Swiss prostitutes were merely a phone call away.

I walked over to the terrace and opened a pair of French doors that looked out over Lake Geneva. I watched the geyser in silent awe. It must've shot up three . . . four . . . no, five hundred feet in the air, at least! What had motivated them to build such a thing? I mean, it was beautiful, but why would they have the world's tallest geyser in Switzerland?

Just then the phone rang. It was an odd ring: three short bursts, then absolute silence, three short bursts, then absolute silence. *Fucking Frogs!* Even their phones were annoying! God, how I missed America! Cheeseburgers with ketchup! Frosted Flakes! Barbecued chicken! I was scared to look at the room-service menu. Why was the rest of the world so backward, compared to America? And why did they call us Ugly Americans?

By now I had reached the phone–*Jesus!* What a sad piece of equipment. Must be an original prototype of some sort. It was off-white and looked like it belonged in the home of Fred and Wilma Flintstone!

I reached over and grabbed the ancient phone. "What's going on, Dan?"

"Dan?" snapped the accusing Duchess.

"Oh, Nae! Hi, sweetie! How ya doing, love-bug? I thought it was Danny."

"No, it's your *other* wife. How was your flight?"

Oh, Jesus! Did she already know? She couldn't! Or could she? The Duchess had a sixth sense for these sorts of things. But this was too quick, even for her! Or had there been an article? No–not enough time had lapsed between my groping episode and the next edition of the *New York Post.* Such a relief–but only for a thousandth of a second! Then, a terrible dark thought: Cable News Network! CNN! I had seen this sort of thing happen during the Gulf War. That bastard Ted Turner had some sort of crazy system worked out where he could report the news as it was actually happening, in real time! Maybe the stewardess had gone public!

"Hello!" sputtered the blond prosecutor. "Aren't you gonna answer me?"

"Oh–it was uneventful. Just the way it should be. Know what I mean?"

A long pause.

Jesus! The Duchess was testing me, waiting for me to crack under the weight of her silence! She was devious, my wife! Maybe I should start laying the blame on Danny, in anticipation.

But then she said, "Oh, that's good, sweetie. How was the service in first class? You meet any cute stewardesses on the plane? Come on, you can tell me! I won't get jealous." She giggled.

Unbelievable! Had I married the Amazing Kreskin? "No, no," I replied, "they were nothing special. Germans, I think. One of them was big enough to kick my ass. Anyway, I slept most of the way. I even missed the meal."

That seemed to sadden the Duchess. "Ohhhhh, that's too bad,

baby. You must be starving! How was it going through Customs–any problems?"

Jesus! I had to end this phone call *instantly!* "Pretty smooth, for the most part. A few questions–just typical stuff. Anyway, they didn't even stamp my passport." Then, a strategic subject change: "But more importantly, how's little Channy doing?"

"Oh, she's fine. But the baby nurse is driving me crazy! She never gets off the stupid phone. I think she might be calling Jamaica. Anyway, I found two marine biologists who'll come to work for us full-time. They said they can get the algae out of the pond by lining the bottom with some type of bacteria. Whaddaya think?"

"How much?" I asked, not anxious to hear the response.

"Ninety thousand a year–for both of them. They're a husband-and-wife team. They seem nice."

"Okay, that sounds pretty reasonable. Where did you find–" Just then, a knock at the door. "Hold on a second, sweetie. It must be room service. I'll be right back." I put the phone down on the bed and walked over to the door and opened it–*what the hell!* I looked up . . . and up . . . and *wow!* A six-foot-tall black-skinned woman, at my own door! An Ethiopian, by the looks of her. My mind started racing. Such smooth young skin she had! Such a warm, lubricious smile! And what a set of legs! They were a mile long! Was I really that short? Well–whatever. She was gorgeous. And she also happened to be wearing a black minidress the size of a loincloth. "Can I help you?" I asked quizzically.

"Hello" was all she said.

My suspicions were confirmed. It was a black hooker straight from Ethiopia, who could only say hello and good-bye! *My favorite!* I motioned her into the room and led her over to the bed. She sat down. I sat down next to her. I slowly leaned back and put my right elbow on the bed and leaned my cheek on the palm of my hand–*OH, FUCK! MY WIFE! THE DUCHESS! SHIT!* I quickly put a forefinger to my lips and prayed that this woman understood the international sign language known to all hookers, which in this particular instance translated into: "Shut the fuck up, you whore! My wife's on the phone, and if she hears a female voice in the room, I'm in deep shit and you're not getting a tip!"

Thankfully, she nodded.

With that, I picked up the phone and explained to the Duchess that there was nothing worse in the world than cold eggs Benedict. She was sympathetic and told me that she loved me *unconditionally.* I hung on this word for all it was worth. Then I told her that I loved her too, and that I missed her and that I couldn't live without her, all of which was true.

And just like that, a terrible wave of sadness came over me. How could I feel those things for my wife and still do the things I did? What was wrong with me? This wasn't normal behavior for any man. Even for a man of power–no, especially for a man of power! It was one thing to have an occasional marital indiscretion; that was to be expected. But there had to be some line, and I . . . well, I chose not to finish the thought.

I took a deep breath and tried to drive the negativity out of my head, but it was difficult. I loved my wife. She was a good girl, despite breaking up my first marriage. But I was just as much to blame for that.

I felt like I was being driven to do things, not because I really wanted to do them but because they were expected of me. It was as if my life was a stage, and the Wolf of Wall Street was performing for the benefit of some imaginary audience, who judged my every move and hung on my every word.

It was a cruel insight into the very dysfunction of my own personality. I mean, had I really given a shit about Franca? She couldn't hold a candle to my wife. And that French accent of hers–I'd take my wife's Brooklyn accent any day! Yet even after I had come out of my blackout, I still asked the Customs officer for her phone number. Why? Because I thought it was something that the Wolf of Wall Street would be expected to do. How bizarre that was. And how sad too.

I looked over at the woman sitting next to me. Did she have any diseases? I wondered. No, she looked pretty healthy. Too healthy to be carrying the AIDS virus, right? Then again, she was from Africa . . . No, no way! AIDS was an old-fashioned disease: You had to earn it by sticking your dick in a hole it didn't belong in. Besides, I never seemed to catch anything, so why should this time be any different?

She smiled at me, so I smiled back. She was sitting on the edge of the bed, thighs akimbo. So immodest! So incredibly sexy! That loincloth of hers was almost above her hips. This would be my last time, then! To pass up this chocolate-brown towering inferno would be a travesty of justice–nothing less!

With that thought, I pushed all the negative garbage out of my mind and decided right there, on the spot, that just as soon as I shot the back of her head off, I would flush the rest of my Quaaludes down the toilet and start my life anew.

And that was exactly what I did, in exactly that order.

CHAPTER 12

DARK PREMONITIONS

A few hours later, at 12:30 p.m., Swiss Frog time, Danny was sitting across from me in the back of a blue Rolls-Royce limousine that was wider than a commercial fishing trawler and longer than a hearse, which gave me this eerie feeling that I was heading to my own funeral. That was the day's first dark premonition.

We were on our way to Union Bancaire Privée for the first meeting with our prospective Swiss bankers. I was staring out the rear window–looking up at the towering geyser, still in awe of it–when Danny said with great sadness, "I still don't see why I had to flush my own Ludes down the toilet. I mean, really, JB! I'd just shoved them up my asshole a couple of hours ago! That's pretty raw, don't you think?"

I looked at Danny and smiled. He had a valid point. In the past, I had stuck drugs up my ass too–going through this country or that–and it wasn't a barrel of laughs. I had once heard that it was easier if you sealed the drugs in a vial and then coated the vial with a hefty amount of Vaseline. But the mere thought of putting that much planning into drug smuggling had precluded me from giving the Vaseline strategy a whirl. Only a true drug addict, after all, would ever consider such an undertaking.

Anyway, I also respected Danny for looking out for me, for always being there to protect the golden goose. The real question, though, was how long would he continue to protect the goose if he ever stopped laying golden eggs? It was a good question, but not one worth dwelling on. I was on a big-time roll now, and the money was pouring in faster than ever. I said, "Yeah, it's pretty raw; I won't deny that. But don't think I don't appreciate the gesture–especially you ramming them up there without any K-Y jelly or anything–but the time for getting Luded out is over. I need you to be on top of your game now, for the next couple of days, at least, and I need to be on top of my game too. Okay?"

Danny leaned back in his seat and crossed his legs insouciantly and said, "Yeah, I'm fine with that. I could use a little break myself. I just don't like things being stuck up my ass."

"We need to slow down with the hookers too, Dan. It's getting pretty disgusting already." I started shaking my head to drive my point home. "I mean, this last girl was pretty hot. You shoulda seen her. I think she was six-one, or maybe even taller! I felt like a newborn baby sucking on his mother's tit–which was kind of a turn-on, actually." I shifted in my seat uncomfortably, taking the pressure off my left leg. "Black girls taste a little different than white girls, don't you think? Especially their pussies, which taste like . . . uhhhhmm . . . Jamaican sugar cane! Yeah, it's very sweet, a black girl's pussy! It's like . . . well, it doesn't really matter. Listen, Dan–I can't tell you where to stick your dick, that's your own affair, but I, myself, am done with hookers for a while. Seriously."

Danny shrugged. "If my wife looked like yours, maybe I'd slow down too. You know what I'm saying?"

I smiled sympathetically. "Maybe the two of you should get a divorce. Everyone else seems to be doing it, so it won't be a big deal." I shrugged my shoulders. "Anyway, I don't mean to dismiss the importance of your personal problems with your wife, but we need to talk business now. We're gonna be at the bank in a couple of minutes, and there's a couple things I want to go over with you before we get there. First, you know to let me do the talking, right?"

He nodded. "What do you think, I'm the fucking Blockhead?"

I smiled. "No, your head's not square enough, and, besides, it has a brain in it. But, listen–in all seriousness–it's important that you sit back and observe. Try to figure out what these Frogs are thinking. I can't pick up anything from their body language. I'm starting to think they don't have any. Anyway, however it goes this morning, no matter how perfect the whole thing turns out to be, we're gonna leave this meeting saying we're not interested. That's a must, Danny. We say that it doesn't fit with what we're doing back in the States and we've decided it's not for us. I'll come up with some logical reason after they tell me a little bit more about the legal issues, okay?"

"No problem," he replied, "but why?"

"Because of Kaminsky," I said. "He's gonna be there at the first meeting, and I trust that toupeed bastard about as far as I can throw him. I'll tell you–I'm really negative about this whole Swiss thing as it is. I've got bad vibes for some reason. But if we *do* decide to do this, there's no way Kaminsky can ever know. That would defeat the whole purpose. Maybe we'll use a different bank if we decide to go forward, or maybe we can still use this one. I'm sure they have no loyalty to Kaminsky.

"Anyway, the most important thing is that no one in the States knows about this. I don't care how stoned you are, Danny, or how many Ludes you've taken or how much coke you've snorted. This one never slips out. Not to Madden, not to your father, and especially not to your wife–okay?"

Danny nodded. "Omerta, buddy. To the very end."

I smiled and nodded and then looked out the window without saying a word. It was a signal to Danny that I was no longer in the mood for conversation, and Danny, being Danny, picked up on it immediately. I spent the remainder of the limousine ride gazing out the window at the immaculate streets of Geneva–marveling at how there wasn't so much as a speck of garbage on a sidewalk or a brushstroke of graffiti on a wall. Pretty soon my mind began to wander, and I started wondering why on earth I was doing this. It seemed wrong, it seemed risky, and it seemed reckless. One of my first mentors, Al Abrams, had warned me to steer clear of overseas banking. He said it was a prescription for trouble, that it raised too many red flags. He said that you could never trust the Swiss–that they would sell you down the river if the U.S. government ever put any real pressure on them. He explained that all Swiss banks had branches in the U.S., which made them vulnerable to governmental pressure. All of Al's points were valid. And Al was the most careful man I had ever met.

In the early days, back when I was getting started, Al and I would meet for breakfast at the Seville Diner, a mile or so down the road from Stratton's then-headquarters at 2001 Marcus Avenue, just a stone's throw away from its current location. He would offer me a cup of coffee and a Linzer torte, along with a historical analysis on the evolution of the federal securities laws. He would explain why things were the way they were; what mistakes people had made in the past; and how most of the current securities laws were written in consequence of past criminal acts. I soaked it all up. I took no notes. After all, writing things down was forbidden. Business with Al was done strictly on a handshake. His word was his bond. And he never broke it.

Al had taught me many things, the most important of which was that every transaction–every securities trade and every wire transfer, whether from a bank or brokerage firm–left a paper trail. And unless that paper trail exonerated you from guilt–or, if not that, supported some alternative explanation that granted you plausible deniability–then sooner or later you'd find yourself on the ass end of a federal indictment.

And so it was that I'd been careful. From the earliest days of Stratton Oakmont, every trade I had consummated, and every wire transfer Janet had made on my behalf, and every questionable corporate finance deal I had participated in, had been dressed up–or padded, as the term went on Wall Street–with various documents and time stamps, even certified letters, which together yielded an alternative explanation that alleviated me of criminal liability. There would be no head shots at the Wolf of Wall Street; I would not get caught between their crosshairs. Al Abrams had taught me well.

But now Al was in jail or awaiting sentencing for, of all things, money laundering. He'd been caught withdrawing cash from a bank account in increments slightly less than $10,000, as a means of avoiding filing a form with the IRS. It was a law designed to foil drug dealers and Mafioso types, but it still applied to all U.S. citizens. Another thing Al had taught me was that if I ever received a phone call from a business associate–current or former–and they tried getting me to discuss past dealings, there was a ninety percent chance they were cooperating. And that included him. So when I received a call from Al, and that strange squeaking voice of his uttered those fateful words, "Remember the time, . . ." I knew he was in trouble. Shortly thereafter I received a phone call from one of Al's attorneys, who informed me that Al had been indicted and that it would be much appreciated if I bought him out of all the private investments we held together. His assets had been frozen and he was running short of cash. Without hesitation I bought him out of everything, at five times the current market value, funneling millions to him in cash. And then I prayed. I prayed that Al wouldn't give me up. I prayed that Al would stand up to questioning. I prayed that in spite of the fact that he was cooperating, he would give up everyone but me. But when I checked with one of New York's top criminal lawyers, I was told there was no such thing as partial cooperation; either you cooperated against everyone or you didn't cooperate at all. My heart dropped to my stomach.

Never once had I considered that he was taking money out of the bank to avoid filing an IRS form. He was too smart for that, wasn't he? He was the most careful man on the planet. One mistake–that was all it took.

Would I share the same fate? Was Switzerland going to be my one act of stupidity? For five years I had been incredibly careful–never giving the FBI a single head shot. I never talked about the past; my home and office were constantly swept for bugs; I papered every transaction I'd ever made, creating plausible deniability; and I never took small amounts of money out of the bank. In fact, I had withdrawn over $10 million in cash from various bank accounts, in increments of a quarter million or more, for the sole reason of having plausible deniability if I was ever caught with a large amount of cash. In fact, if the FBI ever questioned me I could simply say, "Go check with my bank and you'll see that all my cash is legit."

So, yes–I had been careful. But it seemed the odds were stacked against me.

And that would be my second dark premonition of the day. But at this particular moment I had no way of knowing that it wouldn't be my last.

CHAPTER 13

MONEY LAUNDERING 101

The private banking firm of Union Bancaire Privée occupied a gleaming black-glass office building that rose up ten stories from the Frog-infested marrow of Geneva. It was located on rue du Rhône, which, I assumed, translated into Rhone Street. It was in the very heart of Geneva's overpriced shopping district, merely a stone's throw away from my favorite geyser.

Unlike a U.S. bank, where you walk through the entryway and find smiling tellers hiding behind bulletproof glass, inside this particular lobby there was only a single young lady surrounded by about forty tons of gray Italian marble. She sat behind a solid mahogany desk that was large enough to land my helicopter on. She wore a light-gray pantsuit, a high-necked white blouse, and a blank expression. Her hair was blond and had been pulled back into a tight bun. Her skin was flawless, not a wrinkle or a blemish on it. Another Swiss robot, I thought.

As Danny and I walked to the desk, she eyed us suspiciously. *She knew, didn't she!* Of course she did. It was written all over our faces. Young American criminals looking to launder their ill-gotten gains! Drug dealers who made their money selling to schoolchildren!

I took a deep breath and resisted the urge to explain to her that we were just plain old stock swindlers, who were only addicted to drugs. We didn't actually sell them, for Chrissake!

But thankfully she chose to keep her opinion to herself and not address the exact nature of our crime. All she said was, "Might I help you?"

Might? Jesus H. Christ! More wishes! "Yes, I'm here for a meeting with Jean Jacques Saurel?* My name is Jordan Belfort?" Why the fuck was I phrasing everything as a question? These Swiss bastards were rubbing off on me.

I waited for the female android to answer me, but she didn't. She just kept staring at me . . . and then at Danny . . . eyeing the two of us up and down. Then, as if to reinforce how poorly I'd pronounced Mr. Saurel's name, she replied, "Ah–you mean *Monsieur Jean Jacques Saurel!*" How beautiful she made his name sound! "Yes, Mr. Belfort, they would all be waiting for you on the fifth floor." She motioned to the elevator.

Danny and I ascended in a mahogany-paneled elevator that was operated by a young man dressed like a nineteenth-century Swiss army marshal. I said to Danny in hushed tones, "Remember what I told you. No matter how this goes down, we leave the table saying we're not interested. Okay?"

Danny nodded.

We exited the elevator and walked down a long mahogany-paneled hallway that reeked of wealth. It was so quiet I felt like I was inside a casket, but I fought the urge to draw any conclusions about that particular thought. Instead, I took a deep breath and kept heading toward the tall, slender figure at the end of the hallway.

"Ahhh, Mr. Belfort! Mr. Porush! Good morning to both of you!" said Jean Jacques Saurel in warm tones. We exchanged handshakes. Then he fixed me with a wry smile and added, "I trust that your stay has improved since that nasty business at the airport. You must tell me over coffee about your adventure with the stewardess!"

He winked at me.

What a guy! I thought. He wasn't your typical Swiss Frog, that was for sure. He was definitely a piece of Eurotrash, but, still, he was so . . . *suave* that there was no way he could be Swiss. He had olive skin and dark brown hair, which he wore slicked back tight, like a true Wall Streeter. His face was long and thin, as were his features, but everything fit together nicely. He wore an immaculate navy worsted suit with chalk-gray pinstripes, a white dress shirt

*Name has been changed.

with French cuffs, and a blue silk necktie that looked expensive. His clothes hung on his frame oh so sweetly, in a way that only those European bastards could pull off.

We had a brief conversation in the hallway, during which I found out that Jean Jacques wasn't actually Swiss but French, on loan from the bank's Paris branch. That made sense. Then he impressed the hell out of me by stating that he was uncomfortable having Gary Kaminsky attend this meeting but since it was he, Gary, who had made the introduction, it was unavoidable. He suggested that we take things only so far and then meet personally either later today or tomorrow. I told him that I was already planning to end the meeting on a negative note for that very same reason. He pursed his lips and nodded approvingly, as if to say, "Not bad!" I didn't even bother looking at Danny. I knew he was impressed.

Jean Jacques escorted us into a conference room that looked more like a men's smoking club than anything else. There were six Swiss Frogs sitting around a long glass conference table, each dressed in traditional business attire. Each of them was holding a lit cigarette or had one burning in an ashtray in front of them. From top to bottom the room was filled with a giant cloud of smoke.

And then there was Kaminsky. He was sitting amid the Frogs with that awful toupee lying on his skull like a dead animal. On his fat round face was a shit-eating grin that made me want to smack him. For a brief instant I considered asking him to leave the room, but I decided against it. Better he should witness the meeting and hear with his own ears that I had decided against doing business in Switzerland.

After a few minutes of small talk, I said, "I'm curious about your bank secrecy laws. I've heard many conflicting things from attorneys back in the United States. Under what circumstances would you cooperate with the U.S. government?"

Kaminsky replied, "That's the best part of doing business in–"

I cut him off. "Gary, if I was interested in your opinion on this matter I would've fuckin–" I stopped myself, realizing that these Swiss robots probably wouldn't appreciate my usual fuck-speak. Then I humbly said, "Excuse me, everyone–I would've asked you for it when we were back in New York, Gary."

The Frogs smiled and nodded their heads. The unspoken

message was: "Yes, this Kaminsky is as great a fool as he looks." But now my mind was racing ahead. Obviously, Kaminsky was going to get some sort of finder's fee if I decided to do business with the bank. Why else would he be so anxious to mollify my concerns? Originally I had thought that Kaminsky was just another schnook who liked to show how much he knew about an obscure topic. Wall Street was full of those sorts of people. Dilettantes, they were called. But now I was convinced that Kaminsky's motivation was financial. If I were to actually open an account at the bank, he would be alerted through the receipt of his finder's fee. That was a problem.

As if he were reading my mind, Jean Jacques said, "Mr. Kaminsky has always been quick to offer his opinion on matters such as these. I find that rather odd, considering he has nothing to gain or lose on your decision. He has already been paid a small finder's fee just for bringing you here. Whether or not you choose to do business with Union Banc does not bear on Mr. Kaminsky's pocketbook one way or the other."

I nodded in understanding. I found it interesting that Saurel didn't speak in wishes. He had a complete command of the English language, idioms and all.

Saurel plowed on: "But to answer your question, the only way the Swiss government would cooperate with the U.S. government would be if the alleged crime was also a crime in Switzerland. For example, in Switzerland, there is no law regarding tax evasion. So if we were to receive a request from the United States government regarding such a matter, we would not cooperate with them."

"Mr. Saurel is entirely correct," said the bank's vice president, a thin little Frog with spectacles, who went by the name of Pierre something or other. "We have no great affection for your government. You would please not take offense at this. But the fact remains that we would cooperate only if the alleged crime is a penal offense, or, as you would say it, a felony."

Then a second Pierre chimed in, although this one was younger and was bald as a cue ball. He said, "You would find that the Swiss penal code is far more liberal than that of your own country. Many of your felonies are not considered felonies in Switzerland."

Christ almighty! The word *felony* was enough to send a shiver down my spine. In fact, it was already obvious that there were huge problems with my preconceived notion of using Switzerland as a rathole . . . unless, of course . . . well . . . could ratholes be legal in Switzerland? I ran the possibility through my mind. No, I strongly doubted it, but I would have to inquire about it when I met with Saurel in private. I smiled and said, "Well, I'm really not concerned about that sort of thing, because I have absolutely no intention of breaking any U.S. laws." That was a bold-faced lie. But I loved the way it sounded. Who cared that it was a boatload of crap? For some inexplicable reason it still made me feel more at ease about being in Switzerland. I soldiered on: "And when I say that, I speak for Danny as well. You see, our sole reason for wanting to have money in Switzerland is for asset protection. My primary concern is that in my line of work there exists a great likelihood of getting sued–wrongfully, I might add. But either way what I'd like to know–or, to put it more bluntly, what's most important to me–is that under no circumstances will you turn any of my money over to a U.S. citizen or, for that matter, any person on the planet who happens to get a civil judgment against me."

Saurel smiled. "Not only would we never do that," he mused, "but we don't even recognize anything that is–as you say–civil. Even if we were to get a subpoena from your Securities and Exchange Commission–which is a civil regulatory body–we would not cooperate with them under any circumstances." Then, as an afterthought, he added, "And that would be even if the alleged offense is a felony under Swiss law." He nodded to drive his point home. "Even then we would still not cooperate!" He smiled a conspirator's smile.

I nodded approvingly and then looked around the room. Everyone seemed to be pleased with the way things were going, everyone except me. I couldn't have been more turned off. Saurel's last comment had struck a nerve with me, sending my brain into overdrive. The simple fact was that if the Swiss government refused to cooperate with an SEC investigation, then the SEC would have no choice but to refer their request over to the U.S. Attorney's office for a criminal investigation. Talk about being the agent of your own demise!

I began playing out possible scenarios in my mind. Ninety percent of all SEC cases were settled at the civil level. It was only when the SEC felt something overly egregious was going on that they referred the case to the FBI for criminal investigation. But if the SEC couldn't run their investigation–if they were stonewalled by the Swiss–how could they decide what was egregious and what was not? In truth, much of what I was doing wasn't all that terrible, was it?

I took a deep breath and said, "Well, it all sounds reasonable to me, but I wonder how the U.S. government would even know where to look–meaning how would they know which Swiss bank to send a subpoena to? None of the accounts have names; they're just numbered. So unless someone tipped them off"–I resisted the urge to look at Kaminsky–"as to where you were keeping your money, or unless you were careless enough to leave a paper trail of some sort, then how would they even know where to start? Do they have to guess your account number? There must be a thousand banks in Switzerland, and each one of them probably has a hundred thousand accounts. That's millions of accounts, all with different account numbers. It would be like finding a needle in a haystack. It would be impossible." I looked directly into Saurel's dark eyes.

After a few moments of silence, Saurel replied, "That is another excellent question. But to answer, I would ask you to oblige me the opportunity to give you a small lesson in Swiss banking history."

This was getting good. The importance of understanding the implications of the past was exactly what Al Abrams had drilled into my head during all those early-morning breakfast meetings. I nodded and said, "Please do. I'm actually fascinated with history, especially when it pertains to a situation like this, where I'm contemplating doing business in unfamiliar territory."

Saurel smiled and said, "The whole notion of numbered accounts is somewhat misleading. While it's true that all Swiss banks offer our clients this option–as a means of maintaining their privacy–each account is tied to a name, which is kept on record at the bank."

With that statement my heart sank. Saurel continued, "Many years ago, before World War Two, that was not the case. You see, back then it was standard practice among Swiss bankers to open an account without a name being attached to it. Everything was based on personal relationships and a handshake. Many of these accounts were held in the names of corporations. But unlike corporations in the United States, these were bearer corporations, which, again, had no name attached to them. In other words, whoever was the actual bearer of the corporation's physical stock certificates would be deemed the rightful owner.

"But then came Adolf Hitler and the despicable Nazis. This is a very sad chapter in our history and one that we are not particularly proud of. We did our best to help as many of our Jewish clients as we possibly could, but in the end I would say that we did not help enough. As you know, Mr. Belfort, I am French, but I think I speak for every man in this room when I say that we wish we had done more." With that, he paused and nodded his head solemnly.

Every man in the room, including the court jester himself, Kaminsky, a Jew in his own right, nodded in sympathy. I assumed that everyone knew that Danny and I were both Jewish, and I couldn't help but wonder if Saurel had said these things for our benefit. Or had he really meant what he'd said? Either way, before he began speaking I had already gone ten steps ahead and knew exactly where he was going next. The simple fact was that before Hitler was able to sweep through Europe and round up six million Jews and exterminate them in the gas chambers, many were able to move their money into Switzerland. They had seen the handwriting on the wall back in the early thirties, when the Nazis were first coming to power. But smuggling out their money had proved to be much easier than smuggling out themselves. Virtually every country in Europe, with the exception of Denmark, denied millions of desperate Jews safe haven within their borders. Most of these countries had cut secret deals with Hitler, agreeing to turn over their Jewish populations if Hitler agreed not to attack. These were agreements that Hitler quickly reneged on, once he had all the Jews safely tucked away in concentration camps. And as country after country fell to the Nazis, the Jews ran out of places to hide. How very ironic it was that Switzerland had been so quick to accept Jewish money yet so reluctant to accept Jewish souls.

After the Nazis were finally defeated, many of the surviving children had come to Switzerland in search of their family's secret bank accounts. But they had no way to prove that they had any rights to them. After all, there were no names tied to the accounts, only numbers. Unless the surviving children knew exactly in which bank their parents had kept their money and precisely which banker they had been doing business with, there was no possible way for them to lay claim to the money. To this very day, billions upon billions of dollars were still unaccounted for.

And then my mind wandered to a darker side. How many of these Swiss bastards had known exactly who the surviving children were but chose not to seek them out? Even worse–how many Jewish children whose entire families had been wiped out had shown up at the correct Swiss bank, and had spoken to the correct Swiss banker, only to be lied to? *God!* What a fucking tragedy! Only the most noble of the Swiss bankers would have had the integrity to make sure that the rightful heirs received what had been left for them. And in Zurich–which was full of fucking Krauts–you would be hard-pressed to find many Jew-lovers. Perhaps in French Geneva things had been a bit better, but only a bit. Human nature was human nature. And all that Jewish money had been lost forever, absorbed into the very Swiss banking system itself, enriching this tiny country beyond imagination, which probably accounted for the lack of beggars on the streets.

". . . and so you see why," said Saurel, "it is now required that every account opened in Switzerland has a beneficial owner attached to it. There is no exception."

I looked over at Danny. He nodded imperceptibly. But the unspoken message was: "This is a fucking nightmare."

On the ride back to the hotel, Danny and I hardly exchanged a word. I stared out the window and saw nothing but the ghosts of a few million dead Jews, still searching for their money. By now the back of my leg was literally on fire. Christ! If only I wasn't in such terrible chronic pain I could probably beat my drug habit. I was feeling sharp as a tack. It had been more than twenty-four hours since I'd taken any pill, and my mind was so acute I felt like I could work through any problem, no matter how insurmountable it might seem. But how could I work around Swiss banking laws? The law was the law, and having watched Al Abrams go down had only served to reinforce that age-old cliché of how ignorance of the law is no excuse for breaking it. The simple fact was that if I were to open an account with Union Bancaire, I would have to give them a copy of my passport, which would then be kept on file at the bank. And if the U.S. Department of Justice issued a criminal subpoena related to stock fraud–which, of course, was also a crime in Switzerland–then my goose would be cooked. Even if the feds didn't know which account was mine or, for that matter, which bank I was doing business with, it still wouldn't slow them down. Their subpoena would go directly to the Swiss Department of Justice, which would then send out a blanket request to every Swiss bank in the country, demanding that they turn over all records for any accounts belonging to the individual referenced in the subpoena.

And that would be that.

Christ–I would be better off sticking with my own ratholes in the United States. At least if they were ever subpoenaed they could simply lie under oath! It wasn't a pleasant thought, but at least there was no paper trail.

Wait a second! Who said that I had to give the bank *my* passport? What was to stop me from having one of my ratholes come to Switzerland and open an account with their passport? What were the chances that the FBI would hit upon the name of my U.S. rathole within my Swiss rathole? It was a rathole within a rathole! A double layer of protection! If the United States issued a subpoena for records relating to Jordan Belfort, the Swiss Department of Justice would send out their request and come up with nothing!

And now that I thought about it, why would I even want to use one of my current ratholes? In the past I had chosen my ratholes based not only on their trustworthiness but also on their ability to generate large amounts of cash in ways that wouldn't alert the IRS. That was a difficult combination to find. My primary rathole was Elliot Lavigne–who was rapidly turning into a nightmare on Elm Street. Not only was he my primary rathole but he was also the man responsible for introducing me to Quaaludes. He was the President of Perry Ellis, one of America's largest clothing manufacturers. But this exalted position of his was slightly misleading. In point of fact, he was ten times crazier than Danny. Yes, as impossible as it might seem, next to him, Danny was a choirboy.

Besides being a compulsive gambler and a drug addict of the highest order, Elliot was also a sex fiend and a compulsive marital cheat. But Elliot was starting to go bad on me. His gambling and drug habits were getting the best of him. He was falling behind on his payments–as of now he owed me almost $2 million in back profits from having ratholed new issues for me. But if I were to cut him off completely, I would lose that money for sure. So I was in the process of slowly phasing him out, continuing to make him money in new issues while he paid down his debt.

In spite of that, Elliot had served his purpose well. He had kicked me back more than $5 million in cash, which was now safely tucked away in safe-deposit boxes in the United States. Just how I was going to get all that money over to Switzerland, I still wasn't so sure–although I had some ideas. I would discuss that matter with Saurel when we met in a few hours. Anyway, I had always assumed that replacing Elliot with another rathole who could generate that much cash without leaving a paper trail was going to be a problem. But now, having Switzerland as my primary rathole layer, the issue of generating "clean" cash would no longer be a concern. I would simply keep the money in my Swiss account and let it collect interest. The only issue I hadn't been able to address at today's meeting was how I was supposed to go about using all the money I would be keeping in my Swiss account. How was I supposed to spend any of it? How would I be able to funnel the post-laundered money back into the United States to make investments? There were still many questions to be answered.

But the most important thing was that by using Switzerland, I could now choose my ratholes based solely on trustworthiness. This opened up a much larger universe of prospective ratholes, and my mind quickly turned to my wife's family. None of them were U.S. citizens; they all lived in Great Britain–outside the prying eyes of the FBI. In fact, there was a little-known exemption in the federal securities laws that allowed non-U.S. citizens to invest in public companies under much more favorable terms than U.S. citizens. It was called Regulation S, and it allowed foreigners to buy private stock in public companies, while avoiding the two-year holding period required under Rule 144. Instead, under Regulation S, a foreigner had to hold their stock for only forty days. It was a ridiculous law, giving foreigners an incredible advantage over U.S. investors. In consequence–like most regulatory brain farts–it had resulted in a massive wave of abuse, as savvy U.S. investors struck up under-the-table deals with foreigners and illegally used Regulation S to make private investments in public companies, without having to wait two full years to sell their stock (under Rule 144). I had been approached numerous times by foreigners who, for a modest fee, had offered to act as my nominee–allowing me to use their non-U.S. citizenship to do Regulation S business. But I had always declined. Al Abrams's warning was in the back of my mind, always. And, besides, how on earth was I supposed to trust some foreigner with something so inherently illegal? After all, using a foreign nominee to do a Regulation S stock purchase was a serious criminal offense, one that was sure to tweak the interest of the FBI. So I had always shied away from it.

But now, with a double-layered rathole . . . with my wife's relatives as the secondary layer of protection . . . well, all of a sudden it didn't seem all that risky!

And then my mind zeroed in on my wife's aunt Patricia–no, *my* aunt Patricia. Yes, she had become my aunt too! The first time Aunt Patricia and I met, we both knew we were kindred spirits. How ironic that was–considering what she had seen the first time she laid eyes on me. It was two years ago, in the Dorchester Hotel in London, and she had walked in on me right in the middle of a Quaalude overdose. In fact, I was in the middle of drowning in a toilet bowl when she entered the hotel room. But rather than judging me, she talked me through it and stayed up with me all night, holding my head over that very toilet as my body spewed out the poison I'd put into it. Then she ran her fingers through my hair, like my mother did when I was a child, as wave after wave of anxiety hit me from all the coke I had snorted. I had been unable to keep down any Xanax to offset the anxiety from the coke. In consequence, I was crawling out of my own skin. The next day we had lunch together, and, without making me feel the least bit guilty over what she had seen, she somehow convinced me to stop using drugs. I had actually stayed sober for two straight weeks. I was vacationing in England with Nadine, and the two of us had never gotten along better. I was so happy that I had even thought of moving to England, to make Aunt Patricia a part of my life. But deep down I knew it was just a fantasy. My life was in the United States; Stratton was in the United States; my power was in the United States; which meant I had to be in the Unites States. And when I finally arrived back in the United States, under the kind influence of Danny Porush and Elliot Lavigne and the rest of my merry band of brokers, my drug habit came roaring back. And with my back pain fueling the fire, it roared back stronger than ever.

Aunt Patricia was sixty-five, divorced, a retired schoolteacher, and a closet anarchist. She would be perfect. She had contempt for all things governmental and could be trusted without question. If I asked her to do this for me, she would smile her warmest smile and be on a plane the next day. Besides, Aunt Patricia had no money. Each time I saw her I would offer her more than she could possibly spend in a year. And each time she refused. She was too proud. But now I could explain to her that since she was doing a service for me, she had more than earned her keep. I would let her spend whatever she wanted. In point of fact, I would transform her life from rags to riches. What a wonderful thought that was! And, besides, she would hardly spend anything! She was a woman who had grown up amid the rubble of World War II and was currently living on a tiny pension from her schoolteaching days. She wouldn't know *how* to burn through any serious cash–even if she wanted to! Most of what she would spend would be used to spoil her two grandchildren. And that was just fine! In fact, the mere thought of it warmed my heart.

If the U.S. government ever came knocking on Patricia's door, she would tell them to stick it up their Yankee asses! With that thought I started laughing out loud.

"What are you so happy about?" muttered Danny. "That whole meeting was a waste of time! And I don't even have any Quaaludes to drown my sorrow in. So, tell me, what's on that twisted mind of yours?"

I smiled. "I'm meeting with Saurel in a few hours. I have a few more questions for him, but I'm pretty sure I already know the answers. Anyway, what I want you to do is call Janet as soon as we get back to the hotel and tell her to have a Learjet waiting for us at the airport first thing in the morning. And tell her to book the Presidential Suite at the Dorchester. We're going to London, buddy. We're going to London."

CHAPTER 14

INTERNATIONAL OBSESSIONS

Three hours later I was sitting across from Jean Jacques Saurel in Le Jardin restaurant, in the lobby of Hotel Le Richemond. The table had some of the finest place settings I'd ever seen. A wonderful array of hand-polished sterling silver and an immaculate collection of bone-white china rested upon a heavily starched snow-white tablecloth. Really fancy stuff it was; must've cost a fortune! I thought. But, like the rest of this antique hotel, the restaurant's decor was not to my taste. It was decidedly art deco, circa 1930, which was the last time, I assumed, the restaurant had been renovated.

Still, in spite of the less-than-stellar decor–and the fact that I was jet-lagged to the point of near exhaustion–the company happened to be excellent. Saurel had turned out to be quite a whoremaster himself, and at this particular moment he was in the middle of explaining to me the fine art of bedding Swiss Frog women, who he said were hornier than jackrabbits. In fact, they were so easy to coax into bed, he claimed, that each day he would stare out his office window and watch them walk along rue du Rhône–with their short skirts and tiny dogs–while he painted imaginary bull's-eyes on their backs.

I found that to be a clever observation and was saddened by the fact that Danny hadn't been present to hear it. But the topics Saurel and I were planning to discuss this evening were so horrendously illegal that you simply couldn't have this sort of conversation in the presence of a third party–even if the third party happened to be involved in the crime. It was a patent impossibility. It was one more lesson taught to me by Al Abrams, who'd said, "Two people make a crime; three make a conspiracy."

So here I was, alone with Saurel, but my mind was drifting back to Danny and more specifically what on earth he was doing right now. He wasn't the sort of guy you just let out of your sight in a foreign country. Left to his own devices, it was almost certain that something *bad* would happen. The only saving grace was that in this particular country, there wasn't much Danny could do, short of rape or murder, that the man seated across from me couldn't fix with one phone call to the proper authority.

". . . so most of the time," proclaimed Saurel, "I take them to the Métropole Hotel, just across from the bank, and I fuck them there. By the way, Jordan, I must say that I find this English word of yours, *fuck,* to be quite satisfying. There is really no French word that gets the point across quite as well. But not to digress–the point I was trying to make is that I have made it my second profession, behind banking, of course, to bed as many Swiss women as possible." He shrugged a gigolo's shrug and smiled a warm Eurotrash smile. Then he took another deep pull from his cigarette.

"According to Kaminsky," he said through exhaled smoke, "you share my love of beautiful women, yes?"

I smiled and nodded.

"Ahhh . . . that is very fine," continued the Whoremaster, "very fine! But I was also told that your wife is very beautiful. How odd that is, wouldn't you say? To have such a beautiful wife yet to still have a wandering eye? But I can relate to that, my friend. You see, my wife is also quite beautiful, yet I feel compelled to pleasure myself with any young woman who might care to have me, as long as she is up to my standards of excellence. And in this country there is no shortage of these sorts of women." He shrugged. "But I guess this is the way of the world, the way things are supposed to be for men like us, wouldn't you say?"

Jesus! That sounded horrific! Yet I had said those same words to myself many times–trying to rationalize my own behavior. But to be on the receiving end of it made me realize how truly ridiculous it was. "Well, Jean, there comes a time when a man has to say to himself that he's proved his point. And that's the point I'm at now. I love my wife and I'm done screwing around."

Saurel narrowed his eyes sagely and nodded. "I have been to that point many times myself. And it is a fine feeling when you arrive there, is it not? It serves to remind us of what is truly important in life. After all, without a family to come home to, it would be an empty life, indeed. That is why I relish the time I spend with my family oh so much. And then, after a few days of it, I realize that I might very well slit my wrists if I were to stay around any longer.

"Don't misunderstand me, Jordan. It is not that I don't love my wife and child. Indeed I do. It is simply that I am French, and as a French man there is only so much of this wife-and-child business that I can reasonably be expected to swallow before I begin to resent them greatly. The point I make is that my time away from home makes me a much better husband to my wife and a much better father to my child." Saurel picked up his cigarette from the glass ashtray and took a tremendous pull.

And I waited . . . and waited . . . but he never exhaled. Wow, that was interesting! I had never seen my father do that one either! Saurel seemed to internalize the smoke–absorbing it into his very core. All at once it occurred to me that Swiss men seemed to smoke for different reasons than American men did. It was as if in Switzerland it was all about being entitled to partake in a simple manly pleasure, while in the United States it had more to do with having the right to kill yourself with a terrible vice, in spite of all the warnings.

It was time to get down to business. "Jean," I said warmly, "to answer your first question–on how much money I'm interested in moving to Switzerland. I think it would make sense if I started small, perhaps with five million dollars or so. Then, if things work out, I would consider bringing over a significantly larger amount–perhaps another twenty million over the next twelve months. As far as using the bank's couriers, I appreciate the gesture, but I would just as soon use my own. I have a few friends in the United States who owe me some favors, and I'm sure that they would agree to do this for me.

"But I still have many concerns, the first of which is Kaminsky. It's impossible for me to go forward if he has any knowledge of my relationship with your bank. In fact, if he even suspected I had one penny at your bank, it would be a complete deal breaker. I would close all my accounts and move my money elsewhere."

Saurel seemed entirely unfazed. "You need never raise this issue again," he said icily. "Not only will Kaminsky never know of this, but if he chooses to make any inquiries in this matter, his passport will be put on a watch list and he will be arrested by Interpol at their earliest convenience. We Swiss take our secrecy laws more seriously than you can possibly imagine. You see, Kaminsky was once an employee of our bank, so he is held to a much higher standard. I do not kid you when I say that he will wind up in jail if he discloses matters such as these–or, for that matter, sticks his nose in areas that he would be better off steering clear of. He will be locked up in a room and we will throw away the room. So let us put Kaminsky aside, once and for all. If you choose to keep him in your employ, that is your own decision. But be wary of him, because he is a babbling buffoon."

I nodded and smiled. "I have my reasons for keeping Kaminsky where he is right now. Dollar Time is losing serious amounts of money, and if I hire a new CFO he might start to dig. So, for now, it's better to let sleeping dogs lie. Anyway, we have more important issues to discuss than Dollar Time. If you give me your word that Kaminsky will never know about my account, then I will take you at it. I'll never bring it up again."

Saurel nodded. "I like the way you conduct business, Jordan. Perhaps you were European in a former life, eh?" He gave me his broadest smile yet.

"Thanks," I said with a touch of irony. "I take that as a great compliment, Jean. But I still have some important questions to ask you, mainly in reference to that crap you guys handed me this morning about giving you my passport to open up an account. I mean–come on, Jean–that's a bit much, don't you think?"

Saurel lit up another cigarette and took a deep drag. Through exhaled smoke, he flashed me his conspirator's smile, and said, "Well, my friend, knowing you now for who you are, I assume you have already figured out a way around this impediment, yes?"

I nodded but said nothing.

After a few seconds of silence, Saurel realized that I was expecting him to come clean with me. "Very well, then," he said, shrugging his shoulders. "Most of what was said in the bank was complete horseshit, as you Americans say. It was said for the benefit of Kaminsky and, of course, for the benefit of one another. After all, we must appear to abide by the law. The simple fact is that it would be suicide for you to have your name behind a numbered Swiss account. I would never advise you to do such a thing. However, I think it *would* be prudent for you to open an account with our bank–one that proudly bears your name for one and all to see. This way, if the U.S. government ever subpoenaed your phone records, you would have a plausible explanation for calling our bank. As you know, there is no law against having a Swiss account. All you would have to do is send us a small sum of money, perhaps two hundred fifty thousand dollars, which we would then invest for you in various European stocks–only the best companies, of course–and that would give you reason enough to have contact with our bank on a continuous basis."

Not bad! I thought. Plausible deniability was obviously an international obsession among white-collar criminals. I shifted uncomfortably in my seat, trying to take the pressure off my left leg, which was slowly catching fire, and I casually said, "I see your point, and I might very well do that. But just so you know what kind of man you're dealing with, the chances of me calling your bank from my own home are *less* than zero. I would sooner drive myself down to a pay phone in Brazil–with a couple of thousand cruzeiros in my pocket–before I allowed your number to appear on my phone bill.

"But to answer your question, I'm planning to use a family member with a different last name than mine. She's from my wife's side, and she's not even a U.S. citizen; she's British. I'm flying to London tomorrow morning, and I can have her back here the day after tomorrow–passport in hand–ready to open an account at your bank."

Saurel nodded once and said, "I assume you trust this woman implicitly, because if you don't, we can provide you with people who will use their own passports. These people are entirely unsophisticated–mostly farmers and shepherds from the Isle of Man or other tax-free havens such as that–and they are one hundred percent trustworthy. Furthermore, they will not be allowed access to your account. But I'm sure that you have already taken this woman's trustworthiness into consideration. However, I would still suggest that you meet with a man named Randall Franks.* He is a professional with matters such as these, especially in the creation of documents. He can create bills of sale, financial letters, purchase orders, brokerage confirmations, and almost anything else within reason. He is what we call a trustee. He will help you form bearer corporations, which will further insulate you from the prying eyes of your government and allow you to break up your ownership of public companies into smaller increments, to avoid filing any of the requisite forms for over five percent stock ownership. He would be invaluable to a man like you–in all aspects of your business–both foreign and domestic."

Interesting. They had their own vertically integrated rathole service. You had to love the Swiss. Randall Franks would act as a forger–generating documents that would support a notion of plausible deniability. "I would very much like to meet this man," I replied. "Perhaps you can arrange something for the day after tomorrow."

Saurel nodded and said, "I will see to it. Mr. Franks will also be helpful in developing strategies, which will pave the way for you to reinvest or, for that matter, to spend as much of your overseas money as you so desire, in ways that will not be, as you say, red-flagged by your regulatory agencies."

"For instance?" I asked open-endedly.

"Well, there are many ways–the most common of which is to issue you a Visa card or an American Express card, which will be tied directly to one of your accounts at the bank. When you make a purchase, the money will be automatically deducted from your account." Then he smiled and said, "And from what Kaminsky tells me, you spend quite a bit of money on your credit cards. So this will be a valuable tool for you."

"Will the card be in my name or in the name of the woman I plan on bringing to the bank?"

"It will be in your name. But I would recommend that you allow us to issue one to her as well. It would be wise to let her spend a token sum each month, if you follow my line of thinking."

I nodded in understanding. It was plainly obvious that having Patricia spend money each month would further support the notion

*Name has been changed.

that the account was actually hers. But I saw a different problem–namely, that if the card was in my name, all the FBI would have to do was follow me around while I went shopping and then walk into a store after I'd made a purchase and demand to see the credit-card imprint. Then my goose would be cooked. I found it odd that Saurel would recommend a strategy that I'd shot a broad hole through so quickly. But I chose to keep that thought to myself. Instead, I said, "In spite of my lavish spending habits, I still see that as a way to spend only a modest sum. After all, Jean, the transactions we're contemplating are in the millions. I don't think a debit card–as we call it in the U.S.–will make much of a dent in that. Are there other ways where larger amounts can be repatriated?"

"Yes, of course. Another common strategy is to put a mortgage on your home–using your own money. In other words, you would have Mr. Franks form a bearer corporation and then move money from one of your Swiss accounts into the corporate account. Then Mr. Franks would draw up official mortgage documents, which you would sign as the mortgagee and receive the money like that. This strategy has two benefits. First, you will be charging yourself interest, which will be earned in whatever country you choose to form your overseas corporation. Nowadays, Mr. Franks prefers to use the British Virgin Islands, which tend to be very lax with their paperwork requirements. And, of course, they have no income taxes. The second benefit is in the form of a domestic tax deduction in the United States. After all, in your country, mortgage interest is tax deductible."

I ran that one through my mind and had to admit it was clever. But this strategy seemed even riskier than the debit card. If I were to put a mortgage on my home, it would be recorded by the Town of Old Brookville, which meant all the FBI would have to do is go down to the town and request a copy of my deed–at which point they would see that an overseas company had funded the mortgage. Talk about your red flags! Apparently, this was the more difficult part of the game. Getting money into a Swiss bank account was easy, and shielding yourself from an investigation was easy too. But repatriating the money without leaving a paper trail would prove to be difficult.

"By the way," Jean asked, "what is the name of the woman you will be bringing to the bank?"

"Her name is Patricia; Patricia Mellor."

Saurel smiled his conspirator's smile once more, and he said, "That is a fine name, my friend. How could a woman with such a name ever break the law, eh?"

CHAPTER 15

THE CONFESSOR

Heathrow Airport! London! It was one of my favorite cities in the world, save the weather, the food, and the service–the former of which was the worst in Europe, the middle of which was the worst in Europe, and the latter of which was the worst in Europe too. Nevertheless, you still had to love the Brits, or, if not that, at least respect them. After all, it's not every day that a country the size of Ohio, with a natural-resource base of a few billion pounds of dirty coal, can dominate an entire planet for more than two centuries.

And if that wasn't enough, then you had to be awed by the uncanny ability of a few select Brits to perpetuate the longest-running con game in the history of all mankind, namely–royalty! It was the most fabulous scam ever, and the British royals had done it just right. It was utterly mind-boggling how thirty million working-class people could come to worship a handful of incredibly average people and follow their every move with awe and wonder. Even more mind-boggling–the thirty million were actually silly enough to run around the world calling themselves "loyal subjects" and bragging about how they couldn't imagine that Queen Elizabeth actually wiped her own ass after taking a dump!

But in reality none of this mattered. The simple fact was that Aunt Patricia had been spawned from the very marrow of the glorious British Isles. And, to me, she was Great Britain's most valuable natural resource.

I would be seeing her soon, right after I cleared British Customs.

As the wheels of the six-seat Lear 55 touched down at Heathrow, I said to Danny, in a voice loud enough to cut through the two Pratt & Whitney jet engines, "I'm a superstitious man, Danny, so I'm gonna end this flight with the same words I started it with: You're a real demented fuck!"

Danny shrugged and said, "From you, I'll take that as a compliment. You're not still mad at me for keeping a few Ludes off to the side, are you?"

I shook my head no. "I expect that sort of shit from you. Besides, you have this wonderful effect of reminding me how truly normal I am. I can't thank you enough for that."

Danny smiled and turned his palms up. "Heyyyy–what are friends for?"

I smiled a dead smile back at him. "That aside, I'm assuming you don't have any more drugs on you, right? I'd like to pass through Customs uneventfully this time."

"No, I'm clean–you flushed everything down the toilet." He lifted his right hand up in the scout's honor mode. Then he added, "I just hope you know what you're doing with all this Nancy Reagan crap."

"I do," I replied confidently, but deep down I wasn't so sure. I had to admit that I was slightly disappointed that Danny hadn't squirreled away a few more Ludes. My left leg was still killing me, and while my mind was dead set on staying sober, the mere thought of being able to numb out the pain with even one Quaalude–*just one!*–was a fabulous prospect. It had been more than two days since my last Quaalude, and I could only imagine how high I'd get.

I took a deep breath and pushed the thought of Quaaludes back down below the surface. "Just remember your promise," I snapped. "No hookers while we're in England. You gotta be on your best behavior in front of my wife's aunt. She's a sharp lady and she'll see right through your bullshit."

"Why do I even have to meet her? I trust you to look out for me. Just tell her that if something should happen to you–God forbid–she should take instructions from me. Besides, I wouldn't mind roaming the streets of London a bit. Maybe I'll go down to Savile Row, get a few new custom-made suits or something. Or maybe I'll even go down to King's Cross and check out some of the sights there!" He winked at me.

King's Cross was London's infamous red-light district, where for twenty British pounds you could get a blow job from a toothless hooker with one foot in the grave and a raging case of herpes. "Funny, Danny, very funny. Just remember that you don't have Saurel here to bail you out. Why don't you let me hire you a bodyguard to take you around?" It was a phenomenal idea, and I was dead serious about it.

But Danny waved me off as if I had a screw loose or something. "Stop with the overprotective crap," he exclaimed. "I'll be *juuuust* fine. Don't you worry about your friend Danny! He's like a cat—with nine lives!"

I shook my head and rolled my eyes. But what could I do? He was a grown man, wasn't he? Well, yes and no. But that was besides the point. I needed to be thinking about Aunt Patricia right now. In a couple of hours I would be seeing her. She always had a calming influence over me. And a little bit of calming would go a long way.

"So, love," said Aunt Patricia, strolling arm in arm with me along a narrow tree-lined path in London's Hyde Park, "when shall we get started on this wonderful adventure of ours?"

I smiled warmly at Patricia, then took a deep breath and relished the cool British air, which at this particular moment was thicker than a bowl of split-pea soup. To my eyes, Hyde Park was very much like New York City's Central Park, insofar as it being a tiny slice of heaven encircled by a burgeoning metropolis. I felt right at home here. Even with the fog, by ten a.m. the sun was high enough in the sky to bring the entire landscape into high relief—turning five hundred acres of lush fields and towering trees and well-trimmed bushes and immaculately groomed horse trails into a vision so picturesque it was worthy of a postcard. The park was favored with just the appropriate number of sinuous concrete walking paths, which were all freshly paved and hadn't a speck of litter on them. Patricia and I were walking on one of them at this very moment.

For her part, Patricia looked beautiful. But it wasn't the sort of beauty you see in a sixty-five-year-old woman in *Town & Country* magazine, the supposed barometer of what it means to age gracefully. Patricia was infinitely more beautiful than that. What she had was an inner beauty, a certain heavenly warmth that radiated from every pore of her body and resonated with every word that escaped her lips. It was the beauty of perfectly still water, the beauty of cool mountain air, and the beauty of a forgiving heart. Physically, though, she was entirely average. She was a bit shorter than I and on the slender side. She had shoulder-length reddish-brown hair, light blue eyes, and fair white cheeks, which bore the expected wrinkles of a woman who'd spent the greater part of her adolescence hiding in a bomb shelter beneath her tiny flat, to avoid the Nazi Blitz. She had a tiny gap between her two front teeth that revealed itself whenever she smiled, which was often–especially when the two of us were together. This morning she wore a long plaid skirt, a cream-colored blouse with gold-colored buttons running down the front, and a plaid jacket that matched her skirt perfectly. Nothing looked expensive, but it all looked dignified.

I said to Patricia, "If possible, I'd like to go to Switzerland tomorrow. But if that's not good for you, I'll wait in London as long as you like. I have some business here, anyway. I have a jet waiting at Heathrow that can have us in Switzerland in under an hour. If you want, we can spend the day together there and do some sight-seeing or some shopping.

"But, again, Patricia"–I paused and looked her dead in the eye–"I want you to promise me you're going to spend at least ten thousand pounds per month out of the account, okay?"

Patricia stopped in mid-stride, unhooked her arm from mine, and placed her right hand over her heart. "My child, I wouldn't even know where to begin to spend that much money! I have everything I need. I really do, love."

I took her hand in mine and began walking again. "Perhaps you have everything you need, Patricia, but I'm willing to bet you don't have everything you want. Why don't you start by buying yourself a car and stop taking those double-decker buses everywhere? And after you get a car, you can move to a bigger apartment that's got enough room for Collum and Anushka to sleep over. Just think how nice it would be to have extra bedrooms for your two grandkids!"

I paused for a brief moment, then added, "And within the next few weeks I'll have the Swiss bank issue you an American Express card. You can use it to pay all your expenses. And you can use it as often as you like and spend as much as you like, and you'll never get a bill."

"But who will pay the bloody bill?" she asked, with confusion.

"The bank will. And–like I said–the card will have no limit. Every pound you charge will bring a smile to my face."

Patricia smiled, and we walked in silence for a while. But it wasn't a poisonous silence. It was the sort of silence shared by two people who're comfortable enough not to force a conversation ahead of its logical progression. I found this woman's company to be incredibly soothing.

My left leg was feeling somewhat better now, but that had little to do with Patricia. Activity of any sort seemed to diminish the pain–whether it was walking, playing tennis, lifting weights, or even swinging a golf club, the latter of which seemed rather odd to me, considering the obvious stress it placed on my spine. Yet the moment I stopped, the burning would start. And once my leg caught fire, there was no way to extinguish it.

Just then Patricia said, "Come sit down with me, love," and she led me toward a small wooden bench, just off the walking path. When we reached the bench we unhooked arms and Patricia sat down beside me. "I love you like a son, Jordan, and I am only doing this because it helps you–not because of the money. One thing you'll find as you grow older is that, sometimes, money can be more trouble than it's worth." She shrugged. "Don't get me wrong, love, I'm not some silly old fool who's lost her marbles and lives in a dream world where money doesn't matter. I'm well aware that money matters. I grew up digging myself out of the rubble of World War Two, and I know what it's like to wonder where your next meal is coming from. Back in those days we weren't sure of anything. Half of London had been blown to smithereens by the Nazis, and our future was uncertain. But we had hope, and a sense of commitment to rebuilding our country. That was when I met Teddy. He was in the Royal Air Force then, a test pilot, actually. He was really quite dashing. He was one of the first people to fly the Harrier jet. Its nickname was the Flying Bedstead." She smiled sadly.

I reached my arm around the back of the bench and gently placed my hand on her shoulder.

In a more upbeat tone, Patricia said, "Anyway, the point I was trying to make, love, is that Teddy was a man who was driven by a sense of duty, perhaps too driven. In the end, he let it get the best of him. The higher he climbed, the more uneasy he became about his station in life. Do you see what I'm saying, love?"

I nodded slowly. It wasn't a perfect analogy, but I assumed her point had something to do with the perils of chasing a preconceived notion of what it meant to be successful. She and Teddy were now divorced.

Patricia soldiered on: "Sometimes I wonder if you let money get the best of you, love. I know you use money to control people, and there's nothing wrong with that. That's the way of the world, and it doesn't make you a bad soul to try to work things in your favor. But I'm concerned that you allow money to control *you*–which is not all right. Money is the tool, my child, not the mason; it can help you make acquaintances but not true friends; and it might buy you a life of leisure but not a life of peace. Of course, you know I'm not judging you. That's the last thing I'd do. None of us is perfect, and each of us is driven by our own demons. God knows I have my share.

"Anyway, getting back to this whole caper you've cooked up–I want you to know that I'm all for it! I find the whole thing rather exciting, in fact. I feel like a character in an Ian Fleming novel. It's really quite racy, this whole overseas-banking business. And when you get to my age, a little bit of raciness is what keeps you young, isn't it?"

I smiled and let out a gentle laugh. "I guess, Patricia. But as far as the raciness goes, I'll say it again: There's always a slight chance that some trouble might arise, at which point the raciness might get a bit racier than old Ian Fleming might've liked. And this won't be in a novel. This'll be Scotland Yard knocking at your door with a search warrant."

I looked her directly in the eye, and I said in a tone implying the utmost seriousness, "But if it ever comes to that, Patricia–and I swear this to you–I'll come forward in two seconds flat and say that you had no idea what was going on with any of this. I'll say that I told you to go to the bank and give them your passport and that I promised you there was nothing wrong with it." As I said those words I was certain they were true. After all, there was no way that any regulator on the planet would believe this innocent old lady would take part in an international money-laundering scheme. It was inconceivable.

Patricia smiled and replied, "I know that, love. Besides, it would be nice to spoil my grandchildren a bit. Perhaps they would even feel indebted enough to come visit me while I'm doing time in prison–after the bobbies have carted me away for international bank fraud, right, love?" With that, Patricia leaned forward and started laughing raucously.

I laughed right along with her, but inside I was dying. There were certain things that you just didn't joke about; it was simply bad luck. It was like pissing in the fate god's eye. If you did it long enough, he was certain to piss right back at you. And his urine stream was like a fucking fire hose.

But how would Aunt Patricia know that? She had never broken the law in her entire life until she met the Wolf of Wall Street! Was I really so awful a person that I was willing to corrupt a sixty-five-year-old grandma in the name of plausible deniability?

Well, there were two sides to that coin. On one side was the obvious criminality of the whole thing–corrupting a grandma; exposing her to a lifestyle she'd never needed or wanted; placing her liberty at risk; placing her reputation at risk; perhaps even causing her a stroke or some other stress-related disorder if things ever went awry.

But on the flip side–just because she'd never needed or wanted a life of wealth and extravagance didn't mean it wasn't better for her! It *was* better for her, for Chrissake! With the extra money, she'd be able to spend the twilight of her life in the lap of luxury. And (God forbid) if she ever got sick, she would have access to the finest medical care money could buy. I had no doubt that all that British nonsense about their egalitarian utopia of socialized medicine was nothing more than a bunch of happy horseshit. There had to be special medical treatment for those with a few million extra British pounds. That would be only fair, wouldn't it? Besides, while the Brits might not be as greedy as the Americans, they weren't fucking commies. And socialized medicine–*real* socialized medicine–was nothing short of a commie plot!

There were other benefits too, which, when taken together, all tipped the scale heavily in favor of recruiting the lovely Aunt

Patricia into the illicit lion's den of international bank fraud. Patricia herself had said that the sheer excitement of being part of a sophisticated money-laundering ring would keep her young, perhaps for years to come! *What a pleasant thought that was!* And, in truth, what were the chances of her really getting in trouble? Almost zero, I thought. Probably less than that.

Just then Patricia said, "You have this wonderful gift, love, to be engaged in two separate conversations at once. There's one conversation that you're having with the outside world–which, in this case, is your beloved aunt Patricia–and then there's another conversation that you're having with yourself, which you alone can hear."

I let out a gentle laugh. I leaned back and spread my arms on either side of the top wooden slat, as if I were trying to let the bench absorb some of my worries. "You see a lot, Patricia. Since the day we met, when I almost drowned in a toilet bowl, I've always felt that you understood me better than most. Perhaps you even understand me better than I understand myself, although probably not.

"Anyway, I've been lost inside my own head for as long as I can remember–from the time I was a kid, maybe even as far back as nursery school.

"I remember sitting in my classroom and looking around at all the other kids and wondering why they just didn't get it. The teacher would ask a question and I already knew the answer before she was done asking it." I paused and looked Patricia square in the eye and said, "Please don't take that as being cocky, Patricia. I don't wanna come off that way. I'm just trying to be honest with you so you can *really* understand me. But since I was small, I was always far ahead–intellectually, I mean–of all the other kids my age. The older I got, the further ahead I became.

"And from the time I was a kid, I've had this bizarre internal monologue roaring through my head, which doesn't stop–unless I'm asleep. I'm sure every person has this; it's just that my monologue is particularly loud. And particularly troublesome. I'm constantly asking myself questions. And the problem with that is that your brain is like a computer: If you ask it a question, it's programmed to respond, whether there's an answer or not. I'm constantly weighing everything in my mind and trying to predict how my actions will influence events. Or maybe *manipulate events* are the more appropriate words. It's like playing a game of chess with your own life. And I hate fucking chess!"

I studied Patricia's face for some sort of response, but all I saw was a warm smile. I kept waiting for her to respond, but she didn't. Yet by her very silence her message was crystal clear: *Keep talking!*

"Anyway, when I was about seven or eight I started getting terrible panic attacks. I still get them today, although now I take Xanax to quell them. But even thinking about a panic attack is enough to give me one. It's a terrible thing to suffer from, Patricia. They're absolutely debilitating. It's like your heart's coming out of your chest; like every moment of your life is its own eternity; the literal polar opposite of being comfortable in your own skin. I think the first time we met I was actually in the middle of one–although that particular one was induced by a couple a grams of coke, so it doesn't really count. Remember?"

Patricia nodded and smiled warmly. Her expression bore not an ounce of judgment.

I plowed on: "Well, that aside, I was never able to stop my mind from racing, even when I was small. I had terrible insomnia when I was young–and I still have it today. But it's even worse now. I used to stay up all night long and listen to my brother's breathing, watching him sleep like a baby. I grew up in a tiny apartment, and we shared a room. I loved him more than you can possibly imagine. I have a lot of good memories about that. And now we don't even talk anymore. Another victim of my so-called success. But that's another story.

"Anyway, I used to dread the nighttime . . . or actually fear the nighttime, because I knew I wouldn't be able to fall asleep. I used to stay up all night long and stare at a digital alarm clock that was next to my bed and multiply the minutes times the hours, mostly out of boredom but also because my mind seemed to force me into repetitive tasks. By the time I was six years old, I could do four-digit multiplication in my head faster than you could do it on a calculator. No kidding, Patricia. I can still do it today. But back then my friends hadn't even learned to read yet! That wasn't much conciliation, though. I used to cry like a baby when it was time to go to bed. That's how scared I was of my panic attacks. My father would come into my room and lie down with me and try to calm me down. My mother too. But both of them worked and couldn't stay up with me all night. So eventually I was left alone with my own thoughts. Over the years, most of the bedtime panic went away. But it never really left me. It still haunts me every time my head hits the pillow in the form of intractable insomnia–terrible, terrible insomnia.

"I've spent my entire life trying to fill a hole that I can't seem to fill, Patricia. And the harder I try, the bigger it seems to get. I've spent more time than . . ."

And the words started rolling off my tongue, as I began the process of spewing out the venom that had been ripping apart my innards for as long as I could remember. Perhaps I was fighting to save my life that day or, if not that, then certainly my sanity. In retrospect, it was as good a place as any for a man to bare his soul, especially a man like me. After all, on the tiny isle of Great Britain, there was no Wolf of Wall Street and no Stratton Oakmont, both of which were an ocean away. There was just Jordan Belfort–a scared young kid–who'd gotten himself in way over his head and whose very success was fast becoming the instrument of his own destruction. The only question I had was, would I get to kill myself first–on my own terms–or would the government get me before I had the chance?

Once Patricia got me started, I couldn't seem to stop. Every human being, after all, is possessed with the undeniable urge to confess his sins. Religions were built on such things. And kingdoms were conquered with the promise that all sins would be forgiven afterward.

So for two straight hours I confessed. I desperately tried to rid myself of the bitter bile that was wreaking havoc on my body and spirit and driving me to do things that I knew were wrong and to commit acts that I knew would ultimately lead to my own destruction.

I told her the story of my life–starting with the frustration I'd felt growing up poor. I told her of the insanity of my father and how I resented my mother for failing to protect me from his vicious temper. I told her how I knew my mother had done her best, but, somehow, I was still viewing those memories through the eyes of a child, so I couldn't seem to completely forgive her. I told her about Sir Max and how he was always there for me when it mattered most and how, once again, it made me resent my mother for not being there like he was at those crucial moments.

And I told her how much I still loved my mother despite that and how much I respected her too, even though she'd drilled into my head that becoming a doctor was the only honorable way to make a lot of money. I explained how I rebelled against that by starting to smoke pot in sixth grade.

I told her how I overslept for my medical boards because I had done too many drugs the night before and how as a result of that I ended up in dental school instead of medical school. I told her the story of my first day of dental school, when the dean got up before the incoming class and explained how the Golden Age of Dentistry was over and if you were becoming a dentist to make a lot of money, then you should quit now and save yourself the time and aggravation . . . and how I got up right then and there and never went back.

And from there I explained how that led me into the meat-and-seafood business and ultimately to Denise. It was at this point when my eyes began to well up with tears. With great sadness, I said, ". . . and we would get down on our hands and knees and roll up change to pay for shampoo. That's how poor we were. When I lost all my money, I thought Denise would leave me. She was young and beautiful, and I was a failure. I was never all that confident with women, Patricia, in spite of what you or anyone else might think. When I first started making money in the meat business, I assumed it would somehow make up for that. And then when I met Denise, well, I was convinced that she loved me for my car. I had this little red Porsche back then, which was a pretty big deal for a kid in his early twenties, especially a kid from a poor family.

"I tell you the truth–when I first laid eyes on Denise I was absolutely blown away. She was like a vision. Absolutely gorgeous! My heart literally skipped a beat, Patricia. I was driving my truck that day and was trying to sell meat to the owner of the haircutting shop Denise worked at. Anyway, I chased her around the hair salon and asked her for her phone number a hundred times, but she wouldn't give it to me. So I raced home, picked up my Porsche, and drove back and waited outside her shop to make sure she saw it when she came out!" At this point I flashed Patricia an embarrassed smile. "Can you imagine? What kind of man with any self-confidence does that? What a fucking embarrassment I was! Anyway, what's really ironic is that since I started Stratton, every kid in America thinks it's their fucking birthright to own a Ferrari by the age of twenty-one." I shook my head and rolled my eyes.

Patricia smiled and said, "I suspect, love, that you're not the first man to see a pretty girl and run home to get his fancy car. And I also suspect that you won't be the last. In fact, not far from here there's a section of the park called Rotten Row, where young men used to parade their horses around in front of the young ladies in the hopes of getting inside their bloomers one day." Patricia chuckled at her own statement, then added, "You didn't invent that game, love."

I smiled graciously. "Well, I'll give you that, but I still feel like a bit of a fool, anyway. As far as the rest of the story goes . . . you already know it. But the worst part is that when I left Denise for Nadine, it was all over the newspapers. What a fucking nightmare that must've been for Denise! I mean, she was a twenty-five-year-old girl who was dumped for some young hot model. And the newspapers painted her to be some old socialite who'd lost her sex appeal–like she was being traded in for a girl who still had some life left in her! That kinda stuff happens all the time on Wall Street, Patricia.

"My point is that Denise was young and beautiful too! Don't you see the irony in that? Most rich men wait to trade in their first wives. I know you're a smart lady, so you know exactly what I'm talking about. That's the way of things on Wall Street, and, as you say, I didn't invent that game. But everything in my life became accelerated. I missed my twenties and thirties and went straight to my forties. There are things that happen during those years that build a man's character. Certain struggles, Patricia, that every man needs to go through to find out what it means to really be a man. I never went through that. I'm an adolescent inside a man's body. I was born with certain gifts–from God–but I didn't have the emotional maturity to use them in the right way. I was an accident waiting to happen.

"God gave me half the equation–the ability to lead people and to figure things out in ways that most people can't. Yet He didn't bless me with the restraint and patience to do the right thing with it.

"Anyway, everywhere Denise went, people would point at her and say, 'Oh, that's the one that Jordan Belfort dumped for the Miller Lite girl.' I tell you the truth, Patricia, I should've been horsewhipped for what I did to Denise. I don't care if it's Wall Street or Main Street. What I did was in-fucking-excusable. I left a kind, beautiful girl, who'd stuck with me through thick and thin, who bet her future on me. And when her winning ticket finally came in–I canceled it on her. I'm gonna burn in hell for that one, Patricia. And I deserve to."

I took a deep breath. "You can't imagine how hard I tried to justify what I did, to place some blame on Denise. But I never could. Some things are just inherently wrong, and you can look at them from a thousand different angles but, at the end of the day, you always come to the same conclusion, which–in my case–is that I'm a dirty rotten scoundrel, who left his loyal first wife for a longer set of legs and a slightly prettier face.

"Listen, Patricia–I know it might be hard for you to be impartial in this matter, but I suspect that a woman of your character can look at things the way they oughta be looked at. The simple fact is that I'll never be able to trust Nadine the way I trusted Denise. And no one will ever be able to convince me otherwise. Perhaps forty years from now, when we're old and gray, well, then maybe I'll consider trusting her. But that's still a long shot."

Patricia said, "I couldn't agree with you more, love. Trusting any woman you met under those circumstances would require quite a leap of faith. But there's no use torturing yourself over it. You can spend your whole life looking at Nadine through narrowed eyes and wondering 'what if?' In the end you might turn the whole thing into a self-fulfilling prophecy. When it's all said and done, it's the energy we send out into the universe that often comes back to us. That's a universal law, love.

"But on a separate note, you know what they say about trust: In order to trust someone, you need to trust yourself. Are you trustworthy, love?"

Oh, boy! That was quite a question! I ran it through the mental computer and didn't like the answer the computer spit back at me. I rose from the bench and said, "I have to stand, Patricia. My left leg is killing me from sitting so long. Why don't we walk for a while? Let's head toward the hotel. I want to see Speaker's Corner. Maybe someone will be standing on a soapbox bashing John Major. He's your prime minister, right?"

"Yes, love," replied Patricia. She rose from the bench and hooked her arm in mine. We walked along the path, heading toward the hotel. Matter-of-factly, she said, "And then after we hear what the speaker has to say you can answer my last question, okay, love?"

This woman was too much! But I had to love her! My confessor! "All right, Patricia, all right! The answer to your question is: no! I'm a fucking liar and a cheater and I sleep with prostitutes the way most people put on socks–especially when I'm fucked up on drugs, which is about half the time. But even when I'm not high on drugs, I'm still a cheat. So there! Now you know. Are you happy?"

Patricia laughed at my little outburst, then shocked the hell out of me by saying, "Oh, love, everyone knows about the prostitutes–even your mother-in-law, my sister. It's somewhat of a legend. I think in Nadine's case, she's decided to take the good with the bad. But what I was really asking was if you ever had an affair with another woman, a woman you had feelings for."

"No, of course not!" I shot back with great confidence. And then, with less confidence, I took a moment to search my memory to see if I was telling the truth. I had never really cheated on Nadine, had I? . . . No, I really hadn't. Not in the traditional sense of the word. What a happy thought Patricia had placed in my head! What a wonderful lady she was!

Still, this subject was something I would just as soon avoid, so I began talking about my back . . . and how the chronic pain was driving me insane. . . . I told her about the surgeries, which had only made it worse . . . and I explained how I'd tried taking narcotics–everything from Vicodin to morphine–and how they made me nauseous and depressed . . . so I took antinausea drugs and Prozac to offset the nausea and depression . . . but the nausea drugs gave me a headache, so I took Advil, which upset my stomach, so I took Zantac, to combat my stomachache, which raised my liver enzymes. Then I told her how the Prozac affected my sex drive and made my mouth dry . . . so I took Salagen to stimulate my salivary glands and yohimbe bark for the impotence . . . but in the end I stopped taking those too. Ultimately, I explained, I had always come back to Quaaludes, which seemed to be the only drug that truly killed the pain.

We were just approaching Speaker's Corner when I said sadly, "I fear that I'm completely addicted to drugs now, Patricia, and that even if my back didn't hurt I still wouldn't be able to stop taking them. I'm starting to have blackouts now, where I do things that I can't remember. It's pretty scary stuff, Patricia. It's like part of your life has just evaporated–*poof!*–gone forever. But my point is that I flushed all my Quaaludes down the toilet and now I'm dying for one. I've actually been thinking about having my assistant send my driver over here on the Concorde, just so I can have some Ludes. That'll cost me about twenty thousand dollars, for twenty Ludes. Twenty thousand dollars! But I'm still thinking about doing it.

"What can I say, Patricia? I'm a drug addict. I've never admitted that to anyone before, but I know it's true. And everyone around me, including my own wife, is scared to confront me about it. In one way or another they all rely on me for their living, so they enable me. And cajole me.

"Anyway, that's my story. It's not a pretty picture. I live the most dysfunctional life on the planet. I'm a successful failure. I'm thirty-one going on sixty. Just how much longer I'll make it on this earth, only God knows. But I do love my wife. And I have feelings for my baby girl that I never thought I was capable of. In a way, she's what keeps me going. Chandler. She's everything to me. I swore I would stop doing drugs after she was born, but who was I kidding? I'm incapable of stopping, at least for very long.

"I wonder what Chandler'll think when she finds out that her daddy is a drug addict? I wonder what she'll think when her daddy winds up in jail? I wonder what she'll think when she's old enough to read all the articles and finds out about her daddy's exploits with hookers? I dread that day, Patricia, I sincerely do. And I have no doubt that day will come. It's all very sad, Patricia. Very, very sad . . ."

And, with that, I was done. I had spilled my guts like never before. Did I feel any better for it? Alas, not really. I still felt exactly the same. And my left leg was still killing me, in spite of the walking.

I waited for some sort of sage response from Patricia, a response which never came. I guess that's not what confessors are all about. All Patricia did was hold my arm tighter, perhaps pull me a little closer to her, to let me know that–in spite of it all–she still loved me and that she always would.

There was no one speaking at Speaker's Corner. Most of the action, Patricia told me, occurred on the weekends. But that was appropriate. On this particular Wednesday, enough words were spoken in Hyde Park to fill a lifetime. And for a brief instant, the Wolf of Wall Street became Jordan Belfort again.

But it was short-lived. Up ahead in the distance, I could see the Dorchester Hotel rising up nine stories above the bustling streets of London.

And the one thought that occupied my mind was what time the Concorde would be leaving the United States–and how long it would take to arrive in Britain.

CHAPTER 16

RELAPSE BEHAVIOR

If I earn a million dollars a week and the average American earns a thousand dollars a week, then when I spend twenty thousand dollars on something it's the equivalent of the average American spending twenty dollars on something, right?

It was an hour later, and I was sitting in the Presidential Suite in the Dorchester Hotel when that fabulous rationalization came bubbling up into my brain. In fact, the whole thing made so much sense that I picked up the phone, dialed Janet, woke her up out of a dead sleep, and calmly said, "I want you to send George over to Alan Chemical-tob's house and have him pick up twenty Ludes for me, then have him fly them over on the next Concorde, okay?" Only as an afterthought did it occur to me that Bayside was five hours behind London, which meant it was four a.m., Janet time.

But my twinge of guilt was short-lived; after all, it wasn't the first time I'd done something like this to her, and I had a sneaky suspicion it wouldn't be the last. Anyway, I was paying her five times the going rate for personal assistants, so in essence hadn't I purchased the right to wake her up? Or, if not that, hadn't I earned the right to wake her up through the love and kindness I'd extended toward her, like the father she never had? (Another wonderful rationalization!)

Obviously so–because, without missing a beat, Janet was now wide awake and eager to please. She cheerfully responded, "No problem; I'm pretty sure the next Concorde leaves early tomorrow morning. I'll make sure George is on it. But I don't have to send him to Alan's house. I have an emergency stash for you right here in my apartment." She paused for a brief instant, then added, "Where are you calling me from, the hotel room?"

Before I answered yes, I found myself wondering what sort of conclusions could be drawn about a man who could call his assistant and ask her to use supersonic transport to satiate his raging drug habit and his obvious desire to self-destruct and not even get a raised eyebrow in return. It was a troubling thought, so I chose not to dwell on it very long. I said to Janet, "Yeah, I'm in the room. Where else would I be calling you from, numnuts, one of those red phone booths in Piccadilly Circus?"

"Fuck you!" she shot back. "I was just wondering." Then she changed her tone to one of great hope and asked, "Do you like the room better than the one in Switzerland?"

"Yeah–it's much nicer, sweetie. It's not exactly my taste, but everything is new and beautiful. You did good."

I paused and waited for a response, but none came. *Christ!* She wanted a full-blown description of the room–her vicarious thrill of the day. What a pain in the ass she was! I smiled into the phone and said, "Anyway, like I was saying, the room is really nice. According to the hotel manager it's decorated in the British traditional fashion–whatever the fuck that means! But the bedroom's really nice, especially the bed. It's got a huge canopy with lots of blue fabric everywhere. The Brits must like blue, I guess. And they also must like pillows, because the room has about a thousand of them.

"Anyway, the rest of the place is stuffed with all sorts of British crap. There's a huge dining-room table with one of those sterling-silver candelabras on it. It reminds me of Liberace. Danny's room is on the opposite side of the suite from mine, but he's gallivanting around the streets of London right now–like that song 'Werewolves of London.'

"And that's it. No other info to relay, other than my precise location, which I'm sure you'd like to know too. So I'll tell you before you ask: I'm standing on the room's balcony, and I'm looking at Hyde Park and talking to you. I can't really see that much, though. It's too foggy. Are you happy now?"

"Uh-huh," was all she said.

"How much is the room? I didn't look when I checked in."

"Nine thousand pounds per night, which is about thirteen thousand dollars. It sounds like it's worth it, though, right?"

I took a moment to consider her question. It was a mystery to me why I felt compelled to always book the Presidential Suite, no matter how ludicrous the price. I was certain that it had something to do with watching Richard Gere do it in the movie *Pretty Woman,* which was one of my all-time favorites. But it was deeper than that. There was this feeling I got whenever I walked up to the check-in counter of a fancy hotel and uttered those magic words: "My name is Jordan Belfort, and I'm here to check into the Presidential Suite." Well–I knew it was because I was an insecure little bastard, but what the hell!

With sarcasm, I said, "Thanks for reminding me of the exchange rate, Ms. World Banker. I'd almost forgotten. Anyway, the room's definitely a fucking bargain at thirteen Gs a night. Although I really think it should come with a slave for that price, don't you?"

"I'll try to find you one," said Janet. "But either way I got you a late checkout for tomorrow, so we only have to pay for one night. See how I'm always watching your money? By the way, how's Nadine's aunt?"

Instantly I plunged into paranoia mode–calculating the possibility of our phone conversation being bugged. Would the FBI have the audacity to tap Janet's phone? No, it was *inconceivable!* There was a heavy cost to tapping someone's phone and nothing meaningful was ever discussed on this line, unless of course the feds were intent on busting me for being a sexual deviant or a rip-roaring drug addict. But what about the British? Was there a possibility that MI6 was trailing me for a crime I hadn't even committed yet? No, *also inconceivable!* They had their hands full with the IRA, didn't they? Why would they give a shit about the Wolf of Wall Street and his devilish plans to corrupt a retired schoolteacher? They would not. Satisfied our conversation was secure, I replied, "She's doing great. I just dropped her off at her flat. That's what they call apartments here, Janet."

"No shit, Sherlock," said the obnoxious one.

"Oh, excuse me. I was unaware that you were such a world-fucking-traveler. Anyway, I need to stay in London an extra day. I have some business here. So book the hotel for an extra night and make sure the plane is waiting for me at Heathrow on Friday morning. And tell the pilot it's gonna be a same-day turnaround. Patricia's going back that afternoon, okay?"

With typical Janet sarcasm: "I'll do whatever you say, *boss*"–why always such contempt with this word, *boss*?–"but I don't see why you feel the need to bullshit me about why you're staying in London an extra day."

How had she known? Was it really that obvious I wanted to get Luded out in privacy–outside the prying eyes of the Swiss bankers? No, it was just that Janet knew me so well. She was sort of like the Duchess in that respect. But since I didn't lie to Janet as much as to my wife, she was that much better at anticipating when I was up to no good.

Still, I felt compelled to lie. "I'm not even gonna dignify that with a response. But as long as you brought up the subject, I might as well put you to good use. It just so happens that there's this really hot nightclub in London called Annabelle's. It's supposed to be impossible to get into. Get me the best table in the house for tomorrow night, and tell them I want three bottles of Cristal waiting for me on ice. If you have any problems–"

"Please don't insult me," interrupted Janet. "Your table will be waiting for you, Sir Belfort. Just don't forget that I know where you come from, and Bayside isn't exactly famous for its royalty. Do you need me to find you anything else or are you all set for tomorrow evening?"

"*Ooooh*, you're such a little devil, Janet! You know, I was really trying to turn over a new leaf in the female department, but since *you* put the idea in my head–why don't you order two Blue Chips, one for me and one for Danny. Or, now that I think about it, you better make that three–just in case one's a bust! You never know what's gonna walk through the door in these foreign countries.

"Anyway, I'm off! I'm going downstairs to catch a quick workout, and then I'm heading over to Bond Street to do some shopping. That should make my father happy when he gets the bill next month! Now, quick–before I hang up–remind me of what a great boss I am and tell me how much you love me and miss me!"

Tonelessly: "You're the greatest boss in the whole wide world and I love you and miss you and can't live without you."

"Well, that's what I thought," I replied knowingly. Then I hung up the phone in her ear without saying good-bye.

CHAPTER 17

THE MASTER FORGER

Precisely thirty-six hours later, our chartered Learjet screamed and roared like a military fighter as it took off out of Heathrow and made its way into the Friday morning sky. Aunt Patricia was sitting to my left–a look of sheer terror frozen on her face. She was gripping the armrests so tightly her knuckles had turned white. I looked at her for thirty seconds, and she blinked only once. I felt a twinge of guilt over her obvious discomfort, but what could I do? The simple fact was that climbing inside a fifteen-foot-long, hollowed-out bullet and being shot through the air at five hundred miles per hour wasn't most people's idea of fun.

Danny was facing me, with his back to the cockpit. He would be making the trip to Switzerland flying backward, which was something I'd always found disconcerting. But, like most things in life, it didn't seem to bother Danny one iota. In fact, despite the noise and vibrations, he had already fallen asleep and was in his customary position, with his mouth wide open and his head tilted back and his enormous teeth blazing away.

I won't deny that this incredible ability he had–to be able to fall asleep at the drop of a dime–drove me absolutely bonkers. How could you just stop your thoughts from roaring through your head? It seemed illogical! Well–whatever. It was his gift and my curse.

With frustration in my heart, I leaned my head toward the tiny oval window and banged my head against it with a gentle thud. Then I pressed my nose against the window and watched the city of London grow smaller and smaller beneath me. At this time of morning–seven a.m.–a dense layer of soupy fog still sat upon the city like a wet blanket, and all I could see was the shaft of Big Ben, rising up from the fog like an enormous erection in desperate need of a morning romp. After the last thirty-six hours, the mere thought of an erection and a romp was enough to send my frazzled nerves into a complete tailspin.

All at once I found myself missing my wife. *Nadine! The lovely Duchess! Where was she right now, when I needed her most?* How wonderful it would be to lay my head upon her warm, soft bosom and draw some power from it! But, no, I could not. At this particular moment she was an ocean away–probably having dark premonitions over my recent sins and plotting her revenge.

I kept staring out the window, trying to make heads or tails of the events of the last thirty-six hours. I genuinely loved my wife. So why on earth had I done all those terrible things? Was it the drugs that made me do them? Or was it the very acts themselves that made me do the drugs so I would feel less guilt about them? It was the eternal question, one of those chicken-and-the-egg things–enough to drive a man crazy.

Just then the pilot executed a sharp left turn and brilliant rays of morning sunlight came exploding off the right wingtip, streaming into the cabin, nearly knocking me out of my seat. I turned away from the blazing light and looked at Aunt Patricia. Ahhh, poor Patricia! She was still frozen like a statue, still gripping the armrests, and still in a state of Lear-induced catatonia. I felt I owed her a few words of comfort, so in a voice loud enough to cut through the screaming engines, I yelled, "What do you think, Aunt Patricia? It's a little different than flying commercial. You can really feel the turns, right?"

I turned to Danny and took a moment to regard him–still sleeping, he was! Unbelievable! *That rat bastard!*

I considered today's schedule and what goals I needed to accomplish. Insofar as Patricia was concerned, that would be easy. It was just a matter of getting her in and out of the bank as quickly as possible. She would smile at the closed-circuit cameras, sign a few papers, give them a copy of her passport, and that would be that. I would have her back in London by four o'clock this afternoon. In a week she would get her credit card and start reaping the benefits of being my nominee. *Good for her!*

Once Patricia was taken care of, I would have a quick meeting with Saurel, tie up a few loose ends, and work out a rough timetable for smuggling over the cash. I would start with five million, or maybe a million more, and then work my way up from there. I had a few people back in the States who'd do the actual smuggling, but I would focus on that when I got back home.

With a little bit of luck, I could get all my business done today and catch an early flight out of Switzerland first thing tomorrow morning. What a happy thought! I loved my wife! And then I would get to see Chandler and hold her in my arms. Well, what was there to say to that? Chandler was perfect! In spite of the fact that all she did was sleep and poop and drink lukewarm baby formula, I could tell that she was going to be a genius one day! And she was absolutely gorgeous! She was looking more and more like Nadine every day. That was perfect, just what I'd hoped for.

Still, I needed to keep my thoughts on today, especially my meeting with Randall Franks. I'd given a lot of thought to what Saurel had said, and I had no doubt that a man like Randall Franks could be a windfall. It was hard to imagine what I could accomplish if I had someone in my corner who was an expert at generating documents that supported a notion of plausible deniability. The most obvious benefit would be using my overseas accounts to do Regulation S business–allowing me to circumvent the two-year holding period of Rule 144. If Randall could create shell companies that gave off the sanctified odor of legitimate foreign entities, it would allow me to use Regulation S to fund some of my own companies, the most important of which was Dollar Time. It needed a cash infusion of $2 million, and if Randall had the ability to generate the necessary documents, then I could use my own smuggled money to fund Dollar Time. That would be one of the main topics of discussion.

How odd it was: As much as I despised Kaminsky, it was he who'd actually led me to Jean Jacques Saurel. It was a classic example of duds leading to studs.

With that thought, I shut my eyes and pretended to sleep. Soon enough, I'd be back in Switzerland.

The offices of Randall Franks occupied the first floor of a narrow red-brick building that rose up three stories above a quiet cobblestone street. On either side of the street an assortment of mom-and-pop shops were open for business, although despite it being mid-afternoon, they didn't seem to be doing much of it.

I had decided to meet with Randall Franks alone, which seemed like the prudent thing to do–considering the topics to be discussed could land me in jail for a couple of thousand years.

But I refused to let such a morbid consideration cast a shadow over my get-together with my prospective Master Forger. Yes–Master Forger. For some inexplicable reason I couldn't seem to get those two words out my head. *Master Forger! Master Forger!* The possibilities were . . . endless! So many devilish strategies to employ! So many laws to be circumvented under the impenetrable veil of plausible deniability!

And things with Aunt Patricia had gone off without a hitch. That was a good omen. In fact, at this very moment she was on her way back to London, hopefully feeling more comfortable on the Learjet–after consuming five shots of Irish whiskey over lunch. And Danny . . . well, he was another story. The last I'd seen of him he was in Saurel's office, listening to a discourse on the frisky nature of the female Swiss animal.

In any event, the hallway leading to my Master Forger's office was dim and musty, and I couldn't help but feel slightly saddened over the austere surroundings. Of course, Randall's official title wasn't Master Forger or anything like that. In fact, I would venture to guess that I was the first human being to ever put those two words together to characterize a Swiss trustee.

On its own, the title trustee was completely innocuous and had no negative connotations whatsoever. From a legal perspective, a trustee was nothing more than a fancy title for any individual who was legally obligated to look out for another person's affairs–to be trusted, so to speak. In the United States, it was the stuff of wealthy WASPs, who used trustees to watch over the inheritances, or trust funds, that they had set up for their idiot sons and daughters. Most trustees operated under strict guidelines that had been set for them by the parent WASPs on how much money could be dispersed and when. If all went according to plan, the idiots wouldn't get their hands on the bulk of their inheritances until they were old enough to accept the fact that they were truly idiots. Then they would still have enough money left over to live out the rest of their WASP lives in typical WASP fashion.

But Randall Franks was not that sort of trustee. His guidelines would be set by me, to benefit me. He would be responsible for handling all my paperwork and for filing any official forms that needed to be filed with various foreign governments. He would create official-looking documents that would justify the movement of money as well as equity investments in entities in which I maintained secret control. He would then disperse money, per my instructions, in any country I chose.

I opened the door to Randall's office and there he was: my wonderful Master Forger. There was no reception area, just a large, well-appointed office with mahogany-covered walls and a lush maroon carpet. He was leaning against the edge of a large oak desk that was covered with countless papers . . . and he was a real Swiss tub o' lard! He was about my height, but he had a tremendous gut and a mischievous smile on his face that so much as said, "I spend the greater part of my day figuring out ways to cheat various world governments."

Just behind him, a large walnut bookcase rose up from the floor and touched the ceiling; it was a good twelve feet high. The bookcase was filled with hundreds of leather-bound books, all the same size, all the same thickness, and all the same dark-brown color. But each book had a different name on it, which was inscribed in gold-colored letters that ran down the side of the book, along its binding. I had seen books like this in the United States. They were official corporate books, the ones you received each time you formed a new corporation. Each one contained a corporate charter, blank stock certificates, a corporate seal, and so forth. Leaning against the bookcase was an old-fashioned library ladder with wheels at the bottom.

Randall Franks walked up to me and grabbed my hand before I even had a chance to lift it. He started shaking it vigorously. With a great smile he said, "Ahhh, Jordan, Jordan–you and I must become fast friends! I have heard so much about you from Jean Jacques. He tells me of your wonderful past adventures and of your future plans. There is so much to discuss and so little time, eh?"

I nodded eagerly, a bit overwhelmed by his warmth and girth, but I instantly liked him. There was something very honest about him, very forthright. He was a man who could be trusted.

Randall led me over to a black leather couch and gestured for me to take a seat, then he sat down on a matching black leather club chair. He removed an unfiltered cigarette from a sterling-silver case and tapped it on its end, to pack in the tobacco. From inside his pants pocket he pulled a matching sterling-silver lighter, ignited it, and tilted his head to the side to avoid being singed by the nine-inch butane flame. Then he took a deep pull from the cigarette.

I watched in silence. Finally, after a good ten seconds, he exhaled, but only a drop of smoke came out. *Incredible!* Where had it gone?

I was about to ask him when he said, "You must tell me about your flight over from the United States. It is the stuff of legend, as you would say." He winked at me. Then he turned his palms up and shrugged, and said, "But me–*ehhh*–I am but a simple man, and there is only one woman in the world for me: my lovely wife!" He rolled his eyes. "Anyway, I have heard much about your brokerage firm and all the companies you own. So much for a man as young as you! I would say you are still very much a boy and yet . . ."

The Master Forger kept going on and on, talking about how young and wonderful I was, but I found it hard to follow him. I was too busy trying to follow his enormous jowls, which seemed to be swaying back and forth like a sailboat on a rough ocean. Randall had intelligent brown eyes, a low forehead, and a fat nose. His skin was very white, and his head seemed to sit directly upon his chest without the benefit of a neck. His hair was dark brown, almost black, and he wore it combed straight back over his round skull. And my first impression had been right: There was a certain inner warmth that this man exuded, a *joie de vivre* of someone completely comfortable in his own skin, despite the fact that there was enough of it to carpet Switzerland.

". . . and so, my friend, that is the long and short of it. After all, appearances are what make the difference in things. Or as you would say, it is about the dotting of the *i*'s and the crossing of the *t*'s, no?" asked the Master Forger with a smile.

In spite of catching only the tail end of what he'd said, the gist of it was clear: The paper trail was everything. Speaking more woodenly than usual, I replied, "I couldn't agree with you more, Randall. I have always prided myself on being a careful man, a man who is realistic about the world in which he operates. After all, men such as ourselves can't afford to be careless. That is a luxury of women and children." My tone dripped with sagacity, but deep down I was hoping he had never seen *The Godfather*. I felt a bit guilty over stealing some of Don Corleone's thunder, but I couldn't seem to stop myself. The movie was packed with such terrific dialogue that plagiarizing it only seemed natural. In a way, I lived my life very much like Don Corleone–didn't I? I never talked on the phone; I kept my circle of confidants to a handful of old and trusted friends; I paid off politicians and police officers; I had Biltmore and Monroe Parker paying me monthly tributes . . . and countless other things too. But, unlike me, Don Corleone didn't have a rip-roaring drug habit, nor could he be so easily manipulated by a gorgeous blonde. Well, those were my Achilles' heels, and no man could be perfect.

Apparently not picking up on my plagiarism, he replied, "That is a most wonderful insight for a man your age. And I couldn't agree with you more. Carelessness is a luxury no serious man can afford. And today that shall be something we pay great attention to. As you will see, my friend, I can serve many functions for you and wear many hats. Of course, my more mundane functions–such as keeping track of paperwork and filling out corporate forms–I trust you are already familiar with. So we will move past those. The question is: Where shall we start? What is on your mind, my young friend? Please tell me, and I will help you."

I smiled and said, "I was told by Jean Jacques that you are a man who can be trusted completely, that you are the best at what you do. So rather than beat around the bush, I will operate under the assumption that you and I will be doing business together for many years to come."

I paused for a brief moment, waiting for Randall's obligatory nod and smile in response to my patronizing statement. And while I was never a great advocate of patronizing statements . . . since this was the first time I'd ever been face-to-face with a true Master Forger . . . well, it just seemed like the appropriate thing to do.

As expected, Randall turned up the corners of his mouth and nodded deferentially. Then he took another enormous pull from his cigarette and started blowing perfectly round smoke rings. *How beautiful!* I thought. They were flawless circles of light-gray smoke, about two inches in diameter, and they seemed to float effortlessly through the air.

I smiled and said, "Those are very fine smoke rings, Randall. Maybe you can shed some light on why Swiss people love smoking so much. I mean–don't get me wrong–I'm all for smoking if that's what turns you on. In fact, my father is one of the all-time great smokers, so I respect it. But the Swiss seem to take it to a different level. Why is that?"

Randall shrugged and said, "Thirty years ago it was the same in America. But your government feels compelled to stick its nose in places where it does not belong–even into the right of an individual to partake in a simple manly pleasure. They have instituted a propaganda war against smoking, which, thankfully, has not spread to this side of the Atlantic. How bizarre it is for a government to decide what and what not a man might put into his own body. What will be next, I wonder, food?" He smiled broadly and laughed, then patted his fat stomach with great relish. "If that day comes, my friend, I will surely put a pistol in my mouth and pull the trigger!"

I let out a gentle laugh and shook my head and waved my hand in the air, as if to say, "Oh, come on! You're not really that fat!" Then I said, "Well, you've answered my question, and what you say makes a lot of sense. The United States government is overly intrusive in all aspects of life, which is the exact reason I'm sitting here today. But I still have many concerns about doing business in Switzerland, most of them stemming from my lack of knowledge about your world–meaning overseas banking–and that makes me extremely nervous. I'm a firm believer, Randall, that knowledge is power and that in a situation like this, where the stakes are so incredibly high, a lack of knowledge is a recipe for disaster.

"So I must become more knowledgeable. Everyone, at some point, needs a mentor, and I look to you for just that. I have no idea how I'm supposed to operate within your jurisdiction. For example, what things are considered taboo? Where is the line of good judgment? What is considered recklessness and what is considered prudence? These are things that are very important for me to know, Randall, things I must know if I'm to steer clear of trouble. I need to understand all your banking laws down to the very letter. If possible, I would like to look at past indictments, to see what other people have gotten in trouble for and what mistakes they've made, and then to make sure I don't repeat them. I'm a student of history, Randall, and I'm a firm believer that he who doesn't study the mistakes of the past is doomed to repeat them." This was something I had done–looking through old indictments–when I started Stratton, and it had been invaluable.

Randall said, "That is another wonderful insight, my young friend, and I will be more than happy to gather some information for you. But perhaps I can shed some light on things for you right now. You see, virtually all problems Americans run into with Swiss banking have little to do with what happens on this side of the Atlantic. Once your money is safely here, I will disappear it into a dozen different corporations without raising any red flags, outside the prying eyes of your government. I understand from Jean Jacques that Mrs. Mellor was at the bank this morning, yes?"

I nodded. "Yes, and she's already on her way back to England. But I have a copy of her passport if you need it." I tapped my hand over my left suit-jacket pocket, to let him know it was on my person.

"That is excellent," said Randall, "quite excellent. If you would be kind enough to provide me with it, I will keep it on file with each corporation we form. On a separate note, please understand that Jean Jacques shares information with me only under the authorization you granted him. Otherwise, he would have never mentioned a word about Mrs. Mellor presenting herself at the bank. And I would like to add that my relationship with Jean Jacques is one-way. I will tell him nothing of our business unless you instruct me to.

"You see, I would strongly recommend that you do not put all your eggs in one basket. Do not misunderstand me, though: Union Bancaire is a fine institution, and I recommend that you keep the bulk of your money there. But there are banks in other countries as well–Luxembourg and Liechtenstein, just to name two–that will serve a useful purpose to us. Layering your transactions in many different countries will create a web so tangled it would be nearly impossible for any single government to untangle it.

"Each country has its own set of laws. So what might be penal in Switzerland might very well be legal in Liechtenstein. Depending on what sort of transaction you are contemplating, we would form separate corporate entities for each part of the transaction, doing only what is legal in each particular country. But I am painting broad strokes here. The possibilities are much greater than that."

Incredible! I thought. A true Master Forger! After a few moments of silence I said, "Perhaps you can give me a brief education on the ins and outs of things. I can't begin to tell you how much more comfortable that would make me. I mean, there are obvious benefits to doing business in a corporate name–whether it be in the United States or Switzerland–but what I'm interested in are the less obvious benefits." I smiled and leaned back deeper in my seat and crossed my legs. It was the sort of posture that so much as said, "Take your time in telling me; I'm in no rush."

"Of course, my friend; now we are getting to the heart of matters. Each of those corporations is a bearer corporation, meaning that there is no actual paperwork stating who the owner is. In theory, whoever possesses the actual stock certificates–the so-called bearer–is deemed the rightful owner. There are two ways to secure your ownership in a corporation such as this. The first is take personal possession of the stock certificates–to be the physical bearer of them. In that case, it would be *your* responsibility to find a safe place to keep them, perhaps in a safe-deposit box in the United States or something like that. The second way would be to open a numbered safe-deposit box in Switzerland and keep the certificates there. You alone would have access to this box. And unlike a Swiss bank account, a safe-deposit box is truly numbered; there will be no name attached to it.

"If you choose that route, then I would suggest that you lease a box for a term of fifty years and pay the entire fee up front. Under those circumstances there would be no way for any government to gain access to that box. Only you–and perhaps your wife, if you so desire–would be aware of its existence. And if I could offer you a piece of advice, I would recommend that you do not inform your wife. Instead, provide me with instructions on how to contact her–heaven forbid anything should ever happen to you. You have my express word that she will be notified immediately.

"But, please, my friend, do not take my statement as any indication that I question your wife's trustworthiness. I'm sure she is a fine young lady, and from what I hear, very beautiful as well. It's just that it would not be the first time a disgruntled wife led an eager IRS agent to a place he were better not led."

I took a moment to consider his statement, and it sounded awfully reminiscent of the ghosts of six million slaughtered Jews roaming the streets of Zurich and Geneva, trying to find their Swiss bankers. Although, I had to admit, Randall seemed to be the sort who would stand up and do the right thing. But how could I be sure of that? As the ultimate Wolf in Sheep's Clothing, who should know better than me that appearances could be deceiving? Perhaps I would tell my father or, better still, hand him a sealed envelope with the explicit instructions that it should be opened only in case of my untimely demise–which, given my penchant for flying stoned and scuba diving during blackouts, seemed like a distinct possibility.

I chose to keep all those stray thoughts to myself. "I prefer the second option–for many different reasons. And in spite of the fact that I've never received a subpoena from the Justice Department, it still makes sense to keep all my documents outside their jurisdiction. As you're probably aware, all my legal problems are civil in nature, not criminal, which is exactly the way it should be. I'm a legitimate businessman, Randall. I want you to know that. First and foremost, I always try to do things right. But hard as I try, the simple fact is that many of the U.S. securities laws are entirely ambiguous, with no absolute right or absolute wrong. I tell you the truth, Randall: In many cases–most cases, actually–what violates the law is more a matter of opinion than anything else." *What a crock of shit!* But it sounded awfully good. "So, occasionally, something that I thought was perfectly legal ended up biting me in the butt. It's kind of unfair, but that's the way it is. Anyway, I would say that most of my problems are directly related to poorly written securities laws, laws that are designed for selective enforcement against individuals the government feels like persecuting."

Randall laughed raucously. "Oh, my friend, you are too much! What a wonderful way to look at things. I don't think I have ever heard someone state their outlook in such a compelling manner. Most excellent that was–most excellent!"

I chuckled and said, "Well, from a man like you I take that as a great compliment. I won't deny that from time to time, like any businessman, I step over the line and take a risk or two. But they're always calculated risks–heavily calculated, I might add. And every risk I take is always supported by an airtight paper trail, which supports a notion of plausible deniability. You're familiar with the term, I assume?"

Randall nodded his head slowly, obviously enthralled with my ability to rationalize the breaking of every securities law ever invented. What he wasn't aware of was that the SEC was in the process of inventing new ones to try to stop me.

I soldiered on: "I figured you'd be. Anyway, when I opened up my brokerage firm five years ago, a very smart man gave me some very smart advice. He said, 'If you want to survive in this crazy business of ours, then you have to operate under the assumption that every one of your transactions will eventually be scrutinized by a three-lettered government agency. And when that day comes, you'd better be damn sure that you have an explanation as to why the transaction doesn't violate any securities laws or, for that matter, any laws.'

"Now, that being said, Randall, I'll tell you that ninety-nine percent of what I do is on the up and up. The only problem is that the other one percent kills you every time. Perhaps it would be wise to put as much distance between myself and that one percent as humanly possible. I assume you'd be the trustee of each of these corporations, correct?"

"Yes, my friend. Pursuant to Swiss law, I will be empowered to sign documents on the corporation's behalf and to enter into any contracts that I believe are in the best interest of the corporation or its beneficiaries. Of course, the only transactions that I will deem appropriate will be the ones you recommend. For example, if you were to tell me that you thought I should invest my money in a certain new issue or in a parcel of real estate–or anything, for that matter–then I would be obliged to follow your advice.

"And this is where my services will become most valuable to you. You see, with each investment we make, I will put together a file filled with research documents and correspondence–coming from various securities analysts or real estate experts or whoever else need be–so I have an independent basis for making my investment. Sometimes I might retain the services of an outside auditor, whose job it would be to furnish me with a report stating that the investment is a sound one. Of course, this auditor will always come to the appropriate conclusion, but not until he has issued a fancy report with bar charts and colored graphs. In the end, it is these things that truly support a notion of plausible deniability. If someone should ever raise a question as to why I made a particular investment, I would simply point to a two-inch-thick file and shrug my shoulders.

"Again, my friend, we are only scratching the surface here. There are many strategies I will share with you that will allow you to go about your business behind a cloak of invisibility. In addition, if there should ever come a time when you wish to repatriate any of this money–to bring it back into the United States, without so much as a trace–this is another area where I can be most helpful."

Interesting, I thought. This was what I was having the most trouble getting my arms around. I moved forward to the edge of the couch, closing the distance between us to less than three feet. Then I lowered my voice and said, "That's something I'm very much interested in, Randall. I tell you the truth–I was less than impressed with the scenarios Jean Jacques laid out for me; he outlined two different options, and, to my way of thinking, they were amateurish at best and suicidal at worst."

"Well," replied Randall, with a shrug of his shoulders, "that doesn't really surprise me. Jean Jacques is a banker; his expertise lies in the marshaling of assets, not in the juggling of them. He is an excellent banker, I might add, and he will manage your account well, with the utmost discretion. But he is not well versed in the creation of documents that allow money to flow back and forth between countries without raising eyebrows. That is the function of a trustee"–a Master Forger!–"such as myself. In fact, you will find that Union Bancaire will heavily discourage the movement of money out of the account. Of course, you will always be able to do with your money as you please; they will not actually try to stop you. But do not be surprised if Jean Jacques tries to dissuade you from moving money out of the account, perhaps using the excuse that moving money raises red flags. But this is not something to be held against Jean Jacques. All Swiss bankers operate in that fashion, and it is a self-serving one, I might add. The simple fact, my friend, is that with three trillion dollars a day flowing in and out of the Swiss banking system, there is no amount of activity in your account that could possibly raise a red flag. As smart a man as you can easily see the bank's motivation for wanting to keep their account balances as elevated as possible.

"Out of curiosity, though, what ways did Jean Jacques suggest to you? I am interested to hear the bank's latest rhetoric in this area." With that, Randall leaned back and interlaced his fingers over his belly.

Mirroring his body language, I slid back from the edge of the couch and said, "Well, the first way he recommended was through a debit card. That seemed fucking outlandish to me, if you'll pardon my fucking French. I mean, running around town with a debit card tied to a foreign account leaves a paper trail a mile wide!" I shook my head and rolled my eyes, to drive my point home.

"And his second recommendation was equally ridiculous: I would use my overseas money to take out a mortgage on my own home, in the United States. Anyway, I trust that none of this will be repeated to Saurel, but I have to admit I was extremely disappointed with this part of his presentation. So tell me, Randall–what am I missing here?"

Randall smiled confidently. "There are many ways to do this, all of which leave no paper trail whatsoever. Or, to be more accurate, they leave a very wide paper trail, but it's just the sort of trail you would like to see, the sort that supports a position of complete innocence and will stand up to the most intense scrutiny, on both sides of the Atlantic. Are you familiar with the practice of transfer pricing?"

Transfer pricing? Yes, I knew what it was, but how would–all at once a thousand nefarious strategies went flashing through my brain. The possibilities were . . . limitless! I smiled broadly at my Master Forger and said, "Actually, I do, Master For–I mean, Randall, and it's a brilliant idea."

He seemed shocked that I knew about the little-known art of transfer pricing, which was a financial shell game where you would engage a transaction, either underpaying or overpaying for a particular product, depending on which way you wanted your money to flow. The rub lied in the fact that you were actually on both sides of the transaction: You were both the buyer and the seller. Transfer pricing was used mostly as a tax dodge, a strategy employed by billion-dollar multinational corporations–whereby they would alter their internal pricing strategies when selling from one wholly owned subsidiary to another–which resulted in the *transfer* of profits from countries with heavy corporate income-tax burdens to countries with none. I had read something about it in an obscure economics magazine–an article about Honda Motors, which was overcharging its U.S. factories for automotive parts, thereby minimizing its U.S. profits. For obvious reasons, the IRS was in an uproar.

Randall said, "I am surprised you know about transfer pricing. It is not a widely known practice, especially in the United States."

I shrugged. "I can see a thousand ways to use it, to move money back and forth without raising any eyebrows. All we have to do is form a bearer corporation and interposition it in some sort of transaction with one of my U.S. companies. Right off the top of my head I'm thinking about a company called Dollar Time. They're sitting on a couple of million dollars of worthless clothing inventory that I couldn't sell even for one dollar, just like the name says.

"But what we *could* do is form a bearer corporation and give it a name that sounds clothing-related, like Wholesale Clothing Inc. or something along those lines. Then I can have Dollar Time enter into a transaction with my overseas company, which would buy the worthless inventory, moving my money from Switzerland back into the United States. And the only paper trail would be a purchase order and an invoice."

Randall nodded and said, "Yes, my friend. And I have the ability to print up all sorts of invoices and bills of sale and anything else that might be needed. I can even print brokerage confirmations and date them back as of a year ago. In other words, we can go back to last year's newspaper and pick a stock that has gone up tremendously, then create records that indicate a certain trade was made. But I am getting ahead of myself here. It would take me many months to teach you everything.

"On a separate note, I can also make arrangements to have large amounts of cash available to you in many foreign countries, simply by forming bearer corporations and then creating documentation for purchases and sales for nonexistent commodities. At the end of the day, the profit will end up in the country of your choosing, where you may retrieve the cash. And all that will be left is an airtight paper trail that points to the legitimacy of the transaction. In fact, I have already formed two companies on your behalf. Come, my boy, and I will show you." With that, my Master Forger raised his enormous bulk from his black leather club chair, led me to the wall of corporate books, and removed two of them. "Here," he said. "They are both chartered in the British Virgin Islands, where there will be no taxes to pay and no regulation to speak of. All I need is a copy of Patricia's passport and then I will handle the rest."

"No problem," I said, smiling, and I reached into my inside suit-jacket pocket and handed the copy of Patricia's passport to my wonderful Master Forger. I would learn everything I could from this man. I would learn all the ins and outs of the Swiss banking world. I would learn how to hide all my transactions within an impenetrable web of foreign bearer corporations. And if the going ever got rough, the very paper trail I would create would be my salvation.

Yes–it all made sense now. As different as Jean Jacques Saurel and Randall Franks were, they were both men of power, and they were both men who could be trusted. And this was the land of Switzerland, the glorious land of secrets, where neither of them would have any reason to betray me.

Alas, I would be wrong about one of them.

CHAPTER 18

FU MANCHU AND THE MULE

It was a gorgeous Saturday afternoon in Westhampton Beach, on Labor Day weekend, and we were lying in bed, making love, just like any other husband and wife–sort of. The Duchess was lying flat on her back with her arms extended over her head and her head resting upon a white silk pillow, the perfect curve of her face framed by her luxurious mane of golden blond hair. She looked like an angel sent down from heaven just for me. I was lying on top of her with my arms extended like hers, and I was holding down her hands with my hands, our fingers interlaced. A thin film of perspiration was all that separated us.

I was trying to use the full weight of my skinny body to keep her from moving. We were pretty much the same size, so we fit together like bookends. As I breathed in her glorious scent, I could feel her nipples pushing against mine, and I could feel the warmth of her luscious thighs against my thighs, and I could feel the silky smoothness of her ankles rubbing against mine.

But in spite of being soft and slender, and ten degrees hotter than a raging campfire, she was stronger than an ox! Hard as I tried, I couldn't seem to keep her in one spot. "Stop moving!" I sputtered, with a mixture of passion and anger. "I'm almost done, Nae! Just keep your legs together!"

Now the Duchess's voice took on the tone of a child about to throw a temper tantrum: "I'm–not–comfortable! Now–let–me–up!"

I tried kissing her on the lips, but she turned her head to the side and all I caught was a high cheekbone. I craned my head and tried catching her from a side angle, but she quickly turned her head to the other side. Now I had the other cheekbone. It was so chiseled I almost cut my lower lip.

I knew I should release her–that would be the right thing to do–but I wasn't up for a location change right now, especially when I was so close to the Promised Land. So I tried changing tactics. In the tone of the beggar, I said, "Come on, Nae! Please don't do this to me!" I offered her a pout. "I've been a perfect husband for two weeks now, so stop complaining and let me kiss you!"

As the words escaped my lips, I took great pride in the fact that they were actually true. I had been a near-perfect husband since the day I'd arrived home from Switzerland. I hadn't slept with one prostitute–not even one!–not to mention the fact that I hadn't even been staying out late. My drug intake was down–way down!–cut by more than half, and I'd even skipped a few days. In fact, I couldn't recall the last time I'd entered the drool phase.

I was in the middle of one of those brief interludes where my outrageous drug addiction seemed somewhat under control. I'd had these periods before, where my uncontrollable urge to fly higher than the Concorde was greatly diminished. And during these periods even my back pain seemed less severe, and I would sleep better. But, alas, it was always temporary. Something or someone would set me off on a rampage–and then it would be worse than before.

With a bit of anger slipping out, I said, "Come on, God damn it! Hold your head still! I'm almost ready to come, and I want to kiss you while I'm coming!"

Apparently the Duchess didn't appreciate my selfish attitude. Before I realized what was happening, she had placed her hands on my shoulders and with one swift movement of her slender arms she thrust upward–and my penis quickly disinserted itself and I was flying off the bed, heading for the bleached-wood floor.

On my way down, I caught a pleasant glimpse of the dark blue Atlantic Ocean, which I could see through a solid wall of plate glass that ran the entire length of the back of the house. The ocean was about a hundred yards away, but it looked much closer. Just before I hit the dirt I heard the Duchess say, "Oh, honey! Watch out! I didn't mean–"

BOOM!

I took a deep breath and blinked, praying for no broken bones. "Ughhhhhhhhhhh . . . why'd you do that?" I groaned. I was now lying flat on my back, stark naked, with my erect penis glistening in the early-afternoon sunlight. I tilted my head up and took a moment to regard my erection. . . . It was still intact. That lifted my spirits a bit. Had I thrown my back out? . . . No, I was pretty sure I hadn't. But I was too dazed to move a muscle.

The Duchess poked her blond head over the side of the bed and stared at me quizzically. Then she pursed those luscious lips of hers, and in a tone that a mother would normally use on a child who'd just taken an unexpected tumble in the playground, she said, "Oh, my poor little baby! Come back into bed with me, and I'll make you feel all better!"

Never one to look a gift horse in the mouth, I ignored her use of the word little and rolled over onto all fours and stood up. I was about to climb back on top of her when I found myself mesmerized by the incredible sight before me: not just the luscious Duchess but also the $3 million in cash she was lying upon.

Yes–it was $3 million on the nose. The big three-O!

We had just finished counting it. It was wrapped in stacks of $10,000, and each stack was about an inch thick. There were three hundred stacks, and they were spread out over the entire length of the king-size mattress–one atop the other, a foot and a half in the air. At each corner of the bed, an enormous elephant tusk rose up three feet, setting the motif for the room, which was an African safari come to Long Island!

Just then Nadine scooted over to the side of the bed, sending $70 or $80,000 onto the floor. It joined another quarter million or so that had gone flying off the bed along with me. Still, it didn't make a dent in the picture. There was so much green on the bed it looked like the floor of the Amazon rain forest after a monsoon.

The Duchess fixed me with a warm smile. "I'm sorry, sweetie! I didn't mean to throw you off the bed . . . I swear!" She shrugged innocently. "I just had this terrible cramp in my shoulder, and I guess you don't weigh that much. Let's go into the closet and make love there. Okay, love-bug?" She flashed me another lubricious smile, and with one athletic move she popped her naked body right out of bed and stood beside me. Then she crooked her mouth to the side and started chewing on the inside of her own cheek. It was something she did whenever she was having trouble making sense of something.

After a few seconds, she stopped chewing and said, "Are you sure this is legal, 'cause I don't know. There's something about it that seems . . . wrong."

At this particular moment I had little desire to lie to my wife about my money-laundering activities. In fact, my only current desire was to bend her over the side of the bed and fuck her brains out! But she was my wife, which meant she had earned the right to be lied to. With the utmost conviction, I said, "I told you, Nae–I took all the cash out of the bank. You've seen me do it. Now, I'm not denying that Elliot hasn't given me a few dollars here and there"–a few dollars? Try $5 million!–"but that has nothing to do with this money. All this money is strictly legit, and if the government were to come charging in here right now, I would simply show them my withdrawal slips, and that would be that." I put my arms around her waist and pressed my body against hers and kissed her.

She giggled and pulled away. "I know you took the cash out of the bank, but it just seems illegal. I don't know . . . having this much cash . . . well, I don't know. It just seems weird." She started chewing on the inside of her mouth again. "Are you sure you know what you're doing?"

I was slowly losing my erection, which deeply saddened me. It was time for a location change. "Just trust me, sweetie. I got it under control. Let's go in the closet and make love. Todd and Carolyn are gonna be here in less than an hour, and I wanna make love without rushing. Please?"

She narrowed her eyes at me, then all at once she took off into a run and said over her shoulder, "I'll race you to the closet!"

And off we went–without so much as a care in the world.

There was no denying that some very wacky Jews had fled from Lefrak City in the early 1970s.

But none of them was wackier than Todd Garret.

Todd was three years older than me, and I can still remember the first time I laid eyes on him. I had just turned ten years old, and Todd was standing in the one-car garage of the garden apartment he had moved into with his two wacky parents, Lester and Thelma. His older brother, Freddy, had recently died of a heroin overdose, the rusty needle still in his arm when they'd found him sitting on the toilet bowl, two days postmortem.

So, relatively speaking, Todd was the normal one.

Anyway, he was kicking and punching a white canvas heavy bag–wearing black kung fu pants and black kung fu slippers. Back then, in the early seventies, there weren't karate centers in every local shopping center, so Todd Garret quickly developed a reputation as being somewhat of an oddity. But at least he was consistent: You could find him in his tiny garage, twelve hours a day, seven days a week–kicking and punching and kneeing the bag.

No one took Todd seriously until he turned seventeen. It was then that Todd found himself standing in the wrong bar somewhere in Jackson Heights, Queens. Jackson Heights was only a few miles away from Bayside, but it might just as well have been on another planet. The official language was broken English; the most common profession was unemployment; and even the grandmas carried switchblades. Anyway, inside the bar, words were exchanged between Todd and four Colombian drug dealers–at which point they attacked him. When it was all over, two of them had broken bones, all four had broken faces, and one had been stabbed with his own knife, which Todd had taken from him. After that, everyone took Todd seriously.

From there, Todd made the logical leap into big-time drug dealing, where through a combination of fear and intimidation, along with a healthy dose of street smarts, he quickly rose to the top. He was in his early twenties–making hundreds of thousands of dollars a year. He spent his summers in the south of France and the Italian Riviera–and his winters on the glorious beaches of Rio de Janeiro.

All was going well for Todd until one day five years ago. He was lying on Ipanema Beach and got bitten by an unidentified tropical insect–and just like that, four months later, he found himself on the waiting list for a heart transplant. In less than a year he was down to ninety-five pounds, and his five-foot ten-inch frame looked like a skeleton's.

After Todd spent two long years on the waiting list, a six-foot six-inch lumberjack, who apparently had two left feet and an unusually short lifeline, fell from a California redwood tree and plunged to his death. And, as they say, one man's curse was another man's blessing: His tissue type was a perfect match for Todd.

Three months after his heart transplant Todd was back in the gym; three months after that he was back at full strength; three months after that, Todd became the biggest Quaalude dealer in America; and three months after that, he found out that I, Jordan Belfort, the owner of the fabled investment-banking firm of Stratton Oakmont, was addicted to Quaaludes, so he reached out to me.

That was more than two years ago, and since then Todd had sold me five thousand Quaaludes and given me five thousand more–free–in exchange for all the money I was making him in Stratton new issues. But as the profits on the new issues soared into the millions, he quickly realized that he couldn't possibly reciprocate with Quaaludes. So he began asking me if there was anything he could do for me, anything at all.

I had resisted the impulse to have him beat up every kid who had looked at me wrong since the second grade, but after the three thousandth time of him saying, "If there's anything I could ever do for you, even if it means killing someone, you just let me know," I finally decided to take him up on the offer. And the fact that his new wife, Carolyn, happened to be a Swiss citizen made things seem that much more natural.

At this particular moment Todd and Carolyn were standing in my master bedroom doing what they always did: arguing! At my urging, the Duchess had gone into town to do some shopping. After all, I didn't want her to see the very insanity that was now transpiring before me.

The very insanity: Carolyn Garret was wearing nothing but white silk panties and white Tretorn tennis sneakers. She was standing less than five feet from me, with her hands clasped behind her head and her elbows cocked out to the side, as if a policeman had just screamed, "Put your hands behind your head and freeze, or I'll shoot!" She had a set of terrific blue eyes, a broad forehead, and a face that was pretty enough. She was a bombshell, all right–a Swiss bombshell.

"Tahad, you are zdupid fool!" said the Swiss Bombshell, whose thick accent dripped with Swiss cheese. "You are hutting me weeth zees tape, you ahhs-zole!" *Hurting me with this tape, you asshole.*

"Shut up, you French wench," replied her loving husband, "and stay fucking still, before I slap you!" Todd was circling his wife, holding a roll of masking tape in his hand. With each complete revolution, the $300,000 of cash already taped to her stomach and thighs grew that much tighter.

"Who do you call wench, you imbecile! I have the right to smash you one for making such a comment at me. Right, Jordan?"

I nodded. "Definitely, Carolyn–you go right ahead and smash his face in. The problem is, your husband's such a sick bastard that he'll probably enjoy it! If you really want to piss him off, why don't you go around town telling everyone how kind and nice he is, and how he likes to lie in bed with you on Sunday mornings and read the *Times*?"

Todd flashed me an evil smile, and I couldn't help but wonder how a Jew from Lefrak could end up looking so much like Fu Manchu. The simple fact was that his eyes had become slightly slanted and his skin had turned slightly yellow and he had a beard and mustache that made him a dead ringer for Fu Manchu. Todd always wore black, and today was no exception. He had on a black Versace T-shirt, with an enormous black leather V on the front, and black Lycra bicycle shorts. Both the shirt and the shorts hugged his heavily muscled body like a second skin. I could see the outline of a gun, a .38 snub-nose that he always carried, bulging out from beneath his bicycle shorts over the small of his back. On his forearms was a thick coating of coarse black hair that looked like it belonged on a werewolf.

"I don't know why you encourage her," muttered Todd. "Just ignore her. It's much easier."

The Bombshell gritted her white teeth. "Oh, go ignore yourself, you douche-a-bag-a!"

"It's douche bag," snapped Todd, "not *douche-a-bag-a,* you Swiss nitwit! Now shut the fuck up and don't move. I'm almost done."

Todd reached over to the bed and picked up a handheld metal detector–the kind used when you pass through airport security. He began sweeping it up and down the full length of the Bombshell's body. When he reached her enormous breasts, he paused . . . and both of us took a moment to regard them. Well, I was never really much of a breast man, but she did happen to have an unusually fine pair of jugs.

"You see, I tell you," said the Bombshell. "It make no sound! This is paper money, not silver. Why you think metal detector make difference, huh? You just feel like wasting money buying zdupid device, after I tell you no, dog-man!"

Todd shook his head in disgust. "The next dog-man is your last dog-man, and if you think I'm kidding then just go ahead and say it. But to answer your question, every hundred-dollar bill has a thin strip of metal in it, so I just wanted to make sure that when they were all wrapped together it wouldn't set off the detector. Here, look." He slid a single hundred-dollar bill from one of the stacks and held it up to the light. Sure enough, there it was: a thin metal strip, perhaps a millimeter wide, that ran from the top of the bill to the bottom.

Pleased with himself, Todd said, "Okay, genius? Don't ever doubt me again."

"Okay, I give you this one, Tahad, but nothing more. I will tell you that you need to treat me better, because I am nice girl and I could find other man. You big show-off in front of your friend, but me wear the pants in this family and that . . ."

And the Swiss Bombshell went on and on about how *Tahad* mistreated her, but I stopped listening. It was becoming painfully obvious that she alone couldn't smuggle nearly enough cash to make a real dent in things. Unless she was willing to stick the cash in her luggage, which I considered too risky, it would take her ten round-trips to get the full $3 million there. That would mean clearing Customs twenty times, ten on each side of the Atlantic. The fact that she was a Swiss citizen all but assured she would slip into Switzerland without incident, and the chances of her being stopped on the way out of the United States were virtually nil. In fact, unless someone had tipped off U.S. Customs, there was no chance whatsoever.

Still, to keep sticking your hand in the cookie jar over and over again seemed reckless–almost bad karma. Eventually something had to go wrong. And $3 million was just what I was starting with; if all went well, I was planning to smuggle five times that.

I said to *Tahad* and the Swiss Bombshell, "I hate to interrupt you guys from killing each other, but, if you'll excuse me, Carolyn, I need to take a walk on the beach with your husband. I don't think you can bring enough cash there alone, so we need to rethink things, and I'd prefer not to talk in the house." I reached over to the bed, picked up a pair of sewing scissors, and handed them to Todd. "Here–why don't you cut her loose and then we'll go down to the beach."

"Fuck her!" he said, handing his wife the scissors. "Let her uncut herself. It'll give her something to do besides complain. That's all she ever does, anyway–shop and complain, and maybe spread her legs once in a while."

"Oh, you funny man, Tahad. Like you such great lover! Hah! That is big joke. Go, Jordan–you take big shot to beach so I have moment of peace. I unwrap myself."

With skepticism, I said, "Are you sure, Carolyn?"

Todd said, "Yeah, she's sure." Then he looked Carolyn right in the eye and said, "When we bring this money back to the city, I'm gonna recount every dollar of it, and if there's so much as one bill missing, I'll slit your throat and watch you bleed to death!"

The Swiss Bombshell started screaming: "Ohhh, this is last time you make threat at me! I will flush all your medicine and replace with poison . . . you . . . you *fuck*! I will smash . . ." and she kept cursing at Todd in a combination of English and French, and perhaps a little bit of German, although it was hard to tell.

Todd and I exited the master bedroom through a sliding glass door that looked out over the Atlantic. In spite of the door being thick enough to withstand a Category 5 hurricane, I could still hear Carolyn screaming when we reached the back deck.

At the far end of the deck, a long wooden walkway jutted out over the dunes and led down to the sand. As we made our way over to the edge of the water I felt calm, almost serene–despite the voice inside my head that screamed, "You're in the midst of making one of the gravest errors of your young life!" But I ignored the voice and instead focused on the warmth of the sun.

We were heading west with the dark blue Atlantic Ocean off to our left. There was a commercial fishing trawler about two hundred yards offshore, and I could see white seagulls dive-bombing in the trawler's wake, trying to steal scraps from the day's catch. In spite of the obvious benign nature of the vessel, it still occurred to me that there might be a government agent hiding atop the flybridge–pointing a parabolic mike at us, trying to listen to our conversation.

I took a deep breath, fought down the paranoia, and said, "It's not gonna work with just Carolyn. It'll take too many trips, and if she keeps going back and forth Customs will eventually flag her passport. And I can't afford to spread the trips out over the next six months either. I have other business in the States that's contingent on me getting the funds overseas."

Todd nodded but said nothing. He had enough street smarts not to ask what sort of business I had or why it was so pressing. But the fact remained that I had to get my money overseas as quickly as possible. As I'd suspected, Dollar Time was in much worse shape than Kaminsky had let on; it needed an immediate cash infusion of $3 million.

If I tried to raise money through a public offering, it would take at least three months and I would be forced to do an interim audit of the company's books. Now *that* would be a nasty picture! Christ! At the rate the company was burning cash, I was certain that the auditor would issue a going-concern opinion–meaning, they would add a footnote to the company's financials stating that there were serious doubts the company could stay in business for another year. If that happened, NASDAQ would delist the company, which would be the kiss of death. Once off NASDAQ, Dollar Time would become a true penny stock, and all would be lost.

So my only option was to raise money through a private offering. But that was easier said than done. As formidable as Stratton was at raising money for public offerings, it was weak at raising money for private offerings. (It was an entirely different business, and Stratton wasn't geared up for it.) In addition, I was always working on ten or fifteen deals at the same time, and each of them required some amount of private money. So I was already spread thin. To sink $3 million into Dollar Time would put a serious damper on my other investment-banking deals.

But there *was* an answer: Regulation S. Through the legal exemption of Regulation S I could use my "Patricia Mellor accounts" to buy private stock in Dollar Time, then forty days later turn around and sell it back into the United States at a huge profit. It was a far cry from having to buy stock privately–in the United States–and then wait two full years to sell it under Rule 144.

I had already run the Regulation S scenario by Randall Franks, and he assured me that he could create all the necessary paperwork to make the transaction bulletproof. All I had to do was get my money to Switzerland, and then everything would take care of itself.

I said to Todd, "Maybe I should fly it over in the Gulfstream. Last time I went through Swiss Customs they didn't even stamp my passport. I don't see why this time would be any different."

Todd shook his head. "No way, I won't let you put yourself at risk. You've been too good to me and my family. What I'll do is have my mother and father carry money over too. They're both in their early seventies, so there's no way Customs will suspect them. They'll slip right through on both sides without a problem. I'll also get Rich* and Dina* to do it. That'll be five people, three hundred thousand each. In two trips it'll be done. Then we'll wait a few weeks and do it again." He paused for a few seconds, then added, "You know, I would do it myself but I think I'm on a watch list from all the drug stuff. But I know my parents are totally clean, and so are Rich and Dina."

We walked in silence while I thought things through. In truth, Todd's parents were perfect mules; as old as they were, they would never get stopped. But Rich and Dina were a different story. They both looked like hippies, especially Rich, who had hair down to his ass and the strung-out look of a heroin junkie. Dina also had a junkie's look, but, being a woman, perhaps Customs would mistake her for a washed-out hag in desperate need of a makeover. "Okay," I said confidently. "There's no doubt your parents are a safe bet, and probably Dina as well. But Rich looks too much like a drug dealer, so let's leave him out of this."

Todd stopped walking, and he turned to me and said, "All I ask, buddy, is if God forbid something happens to any one of them that you take care of all the legal bills. I know you will, but I just wanted to say it up front so I wouldn't have to bring it up later. But, trust me, nothing is gonna happen. I promise you."

I put my arm on Todd's shoulder and said, "All that goes without saying. If something happens, not only will I pay the legal bills but, as long as everyone keeps their mouth shut, they'll wind up with a seven-figure cash bonus when it's all over. Anyway, I trust you completely, Todd. I'm gonna give you the three million dollars to take back into the city, and I have no doubt it will end up in Switzerland within the week. There're only a handful of people in the world I would put that much trust in."

---

*Name has been changed.

Todd nodded solemnly.

Then I added, "On a separate note, Danny has another million to give you, but he won't have it until the middle of next week. I'll be up in New England with Nadine on the yacht, so call Danny and make plans to hook up with him, all right?"

Todd grimaced. "I'll do whatever you say, but I hate dealing with Danny. He's a fucking loose cannon; he does too many Quaaludes during the day. If he shows up with a million dollars in cash and he's all Luded out, I swear to God I'm gonna smack him in the face. This is serious shit, and I don't wanna be dealing with a slurring idiot."

I smiled. "Point well taken; I'll talk to him. Anyway, I gotta get back to the house. Nadine's aunt is in from England, and she's coming out here with Nadine's mother for dinner. I gotta get ready."

Todd nodded. "No problem. Just don't forget to tell Danny not to be fucked up when he meets me on Wednesday, okay?"

I smiled and nodded. "I won't forget, Todd. I promise."

Feeling satisfied, I turned toward the ocean and looked out to the edge of the horizon. The sky was a deep cobalt blue with just a sliver of magenta where the sky melted into the water. I took a deep breath . . .

And just like that I forgot.

CHAPTER 19

A LEAST LIKELY MULE

Dinner out! Westhampton! Or Jew-Hampton, as it was referred to by all those WASP bastards living down the road in Southampton. It was no secret that the WASPs sneered straight down their long, thin noses at the Westhamptonites, as if we were the sorts of Jews who'd just had our passports stamped at Ellis Island and were still dressed in long black coats and top hats.

Anyway, in spite of all that, I still considered Westhampton a fine place to keep a beach house. It was for the young and the wild, and, most importantly, it was full of Strattonites–the male Strattonites blowing obscene amounts of money on the female Strattonites, and the female Strattonites blowing the male Strattonites in return, in the Stratton version of a quid pro quo.

On this particular evening I was sitting at a table for four at Starr Boggs restaurant, athwart the dunes of Westhampton Beach, with two Quaaludes bathing the pleasure center of my brain. For a guy like me it was a rather minor dose, and I was in complete control. I had a terrific view of the Atlantic Ocean, which was a mere stone's throw away. In fact, it was so close that I could hear the waves breaking upon the shore. At 8:30 p.m. there was still enough light in the sky to turn the horizon into a swirling palette of purple and pink and midnight blue. An impossibly large full moon hung just over the Atlantic.

It was the sort of glorious view that served as an indisputable testament to the wonder of Mother Nature, which stood in sharp contrast to the restaurant itself, which was a total fucking dump! White metallic picnic tables were strewn about a gray wooden deck that was in desperate need of a fresh coat of paint and a serious desplintering. In fact, if you walked barefoot on the deck you were sure to end up in the emergency room at Southampton Hospital, which was the only institution in Southampton that accepted Jews, albeit reluctantly. Adding insult to injury, a hundred or so red, orange, and purple lanterns hung from thin gray wires that crisscrossed the roofless restaurant. It looked like someone had forgotten to take down last season's Christmas lights–someone with a severe alcohol problem. And then there were tiki torches, which were strategically positioned here and there. They gave off a feeble orange glow, making the place seem that much sadder.

But none of this–with the exception of the tiki torches–was the fault of Starr, the restaurant's tall, potbellied owner. He was a first-class chef, Starr, and his prices were more than reasonable. I had taken Mad Max here once, to provide him with a visual explanation of how my average Starr Boggs dinner bill ran $10,000. It was a concept he was having trouble grasping, since he wasn't aware of the special reserve of red wine that Starr stocked for me, the average price being $3,000 per bottle.

Tonight the Duchess and I, along with Nadine's mother, Suzanne, and the lovely Aunt Patricia, had already killed two bottles of Chateau Margaux, 1985, and were deep into our third–despite the fact that we hadn't ordered appetizers yet. But given the fact that Suzanne and Aunt Patricia were both half Irish, their proclivity for all things alcoholic was to be expected.

So far, the dinner conversation had been entirely innocuous, as I carefully steered things away from the subject of international money laundering. And while I had told Nadine what was going on with her aunt Patricia, I'd couched things in a way that made it all seem perfectly legit–glossing over the finer points, like the thousand and one laws we were breaking, and focusing on how Aunt Patricia would be getting her own credit card, allowing her to live out the twilight of her life in the lap of luxury. Anyway, after a few minutes of inside-cheek-chewing and some halfhearted threats, Nadine had finally bought into it.

At this particular moment Suzanne was explaining how the AIDS virus was a U.S. government conspiracy, not much different than Roswell or the Kennedy assassination. I was trying to pay close attention, but I was distracted by the ridiculous straw hats she and Aunt Patricia had decided to wear. They were larger than Mexican sombreros, and they had pink flowers around the brim. It was plainly obvious that the two of them weren't residents of Jew-Hampton. In fact, they looked like they were from a different planet.

And as my mother-in-law continued bashing the government, the delectable Duchess began nudging me under the table with the tip of her high heel, the unspoken message being: "Here she goes again!" I casually turned to her and gave her the hint of a wink. I couldn't get over how quickly she'd bounced back after Chandler's birth. Just six weeks ago she looked like she'd swallowed a basketball! Now she was back at her fighting weight–a hundred twelve pounds of solid steel–ready to smack me at the slightest provocation.

I grabbed Nadine's hand and placed it on the table, as if to show I was speaking for both of us, and said, "When it comes to your theories about the press and how everything's a pack of lies, I couldn't agree with you more, Suzanne. The problem is that most people aren't as insightful as you." I shook my head gravely.

Patricia picked up her wineglass, took a prodigious gulp, then said, "How convenient it is to feel that way about the press, especially since you're the one those bloody bastards keep bashing! Wouldn't you say, my love?"

I smiled at Patricia and said, "Well, that calls for a toast!" I raised my wineglass and waited for everyone to follow suit. After a few seconds I said, "To the lovely Aunt Patricia, who was blessed with the truly remarkable talent of being able to call a horse's ass a horse's ass!" With that we all clinked glasses and drank five hundred dollars' worth of wine in less than a second.

Nadine reached over to me and rubbed my cheek and said, "Oh, honey, we all know that everything they say about you is lies. So don't you worry, sweetness!"

"Yes," added Suzanne, "of course it's all lies. They make it seem as if you alone are doing something wrong. It's almost laughable when you think about. This all goes back to the Rothschilds, in the 1700s, and to J. P. Morgan and his brood, back in the 1900s. The stock market is just another puppet of the government. You can see . . ."

Suzanne was off again. I mean, there was no denying she was a little bit kooky–but who wasn't? And she was smart as a whip. She was a voracious reader, and she'd single-handedly raised Nadine and her younger brother, AJ, doing one hell of a job (at least with Nadine). And the fact that her ex-husband hadn't given her one ounce of support, financial or otherwise, made her accomplishment that much grander. She was a beautiful woman, Suzanne, with shoulder-length strawberry-blond hair and brilliant blue eyes. All in all, a good egg.

Just then Starr walked over to the table. He wore a white chef's jacket and a towering white chef's hat. He looked like a six-foot-four-inch Pillsbury Doughboy.

"Good evening," said Starr in warm tones. "Happy Labor Day to all of you!"

My wife, the aspiring people-pleaser, immediately popped up out of her chair like an eager cheerleader and gave Starr a pleasant peck on the cheek. Then she began the process of introducing her family. After a few wonderful minutes of meaningless small talk, Starr began explaining the evening's specials, starting with his world-famous pan-fried soft-shell crabs. But in less than a millisecond, I stopped listening and started thinking about Todd and Carolyn and my $3 million. How on earth were they going to get it all there without getting caught? And what about the rest of my cash? Perhaps I should have used Saurel's courier service? But that had seemed risky, hadn't it? I mean–to meet a complete stranger at a sordid rendezvous point and hand over that much money?

I looked over at Nadine's mother, who, by chance, was looking at me too. She offered me the warmest of smiles, an altogether loving smile, which I returned without hesitation. I had been very good to Suzanne. In fact, since the day I'd fallen in love with Nadine, Suzanne had never wanted for anything. Nadine and I bought her a car, rented her a beautiful home on the water, and gave her $8,000 a month in spending money. In my book, Suzanne was aces. She had never been anything but supportive of our marriage, and . . .

. . . then all at once the most devilish thought occurred to me. *Hmmm* . . . it was really too bad that Suzanne and Patricia couldn't carry some money over to Switzerland. I mean, really–who would ever suspect them? Look at them, in those stupid hats! What would be the chances that a Customs agent would ever stop them?

Zero! It had to be! Two old ladies smuggling money? It would be the perfect crime. But I instantly regretted thinking any such thought. Christ! If Suzanne got in trouble–well, Nadine would crucify me! She might even leave me and take Chandler. That was an impossibility! I couldn't live without them! Not in–

Nadine screamed, "Earth to Jordan! Hello, Jordan!"

I turned to her and gave her a vacant smile.

"You want the swordfish, right, baby?"

I nodded eagerly and kept smiling.

Then she added with great confidence, "And he also wants a Caesar salad with no croutons." She leaned over and gave me a wet kiss on the cheek, then sat back down in her seat.

Starr thanked us, complimented Nadine, and then went about his business. Aunt Patricia raised her wineglass and said, "I'd like to make another toast, please."

We all raised our glasses.

In a serious tone, she said, "This toast is to you, Jordan. Without you, none of us would be here tonight. And thanks to you, I'm moving into a larger flat, closer to my grandchildren"–I looked out the corner of my eye at the Duchess to gauge her response. She was chewing on the inside of her mouth! Oh, shit!–"and it's big enough so they can each have their own bedroom. You're a truly generous man, my love, and that's something to be very proud of. To you, my love!"

We all clinked glasses, then Nadine leaned over to me and gave me a warm, wonderful kiss on the lips, which sent the better part of five pints of blood rushing to my loins.

Wow! How wonderful my marriage was! And it was growing stronger every day! Nadine, myself, Chandler–we were a real family. Who could ask for anything more?

Two hours later I was knocking on my own front door, like Fred Flintstone after he'd been locked out by Dino, his pet dinosaur. "Come on, Nadine! Unlock the door and let me in! I'm sorry!"

From the other side of the door, the voice of my wife, dripping with disdain: "You're sorry? Why–you–little fuck! If I open this door I'm gonna smash your face in!"

I took a deep breath . . . and slowly exhaled. God, I hated when she called me little! Why did she have to call me that? I wasn't that little, for Chrissake! "Nae, I was only kidding around! *Please!* I'm not gonna let your mother carry money over to Switzerland! Now open the door and let me in!"

Nothing. No response, just footsteps. *God damn her!* What was she so mad about? It wasn't me who'd suggested that her mother bring a couple of million dollars over to Switzerland! She'd offered! Perhaps I had led her into it, but, still, she had made the official offer!

More forcefully this time: "Nadine! Open up the fucking door and let me in! You're overreacting!"

I heard more footsteps from inside the house, then the mail slot at waist level opened. Nadine's voice came through the slot. "If you want to talk to me, then you can talk to me through here."

What choice did I have? I bent down and–

SPLASH!

"Owwww, shit!" I screamed, wiping my eyeballs with the bottom of my white Ralph Lauren T-shirt. "That water's piping hot, Nadine! What the fuck is wrong with you? You could've burned me!"

The disdainful Duchess: "Could've burned you? I'm gonna do more than that before I'm through! How the fuck could you talk my mother into doing that? You don't think I know you manipulated her? Of course she's gonna offer after everything you've done for her! You just made it so fucking simple for her, you manipulative little bastard! You and your stupid fucking sales tactics or Jedi mind tricks or whatever the fuck you call them! You're a despicable human being!"

In spite of everything she'd said, it was the word *little* that wounded me most. "You better watch who you call little, or I'll smash you one and–"

"Just go ahead and try! If you lift a hand to me, I'll cut your balls off while you're sleeping and feed them to you!"

Christ! How could such a beautiful face spew out such terrible venom–and at her own husband! The Duchess had looked like an angel tonight, not to mention that she'd been showering me with kisses all night long! But then, after Patricia had finished making her toast, I caught a glimpse of her and Suzanne from a certain angle in those ridiculous straw hats, and they reminded me of the Pigeon Sisters from the movie *The Odd Couple.* I figured, what Customs agent in his right mind would stop the Pigeon Sisters?

And the fact that both of them carried British passports made the whole idea that much more plausible. So I launched a trial balloon, to see if either of them would be receptive to smuggling money for me.

My wife's voice, through the slot: "Come down here and look me in the eye and tell me that you won't let her do it."

"Come down there? Yeah, right!" I said mockingly. "You want me to look you in the eye? Why? So you can throw more boiling water in my face? What do you think, I'm fucking stupid or something?"

The toneless voice of the Duchess: "I'm not gonna throw more water at you. I swear on Chandler's eyes."

I stood my ground.

"You know, the problem is that my mother and Aunt Patricia think this whole thing is a giant fucking game. They both hate the government and they figure it's all for a good cause. And now that my mother has this thing in her mind, she's not gonna stop talking about it until you let her do it. I know her like a book. She thinks it's exciting–to walk through Customs with all that money and not get caught."

"I won't let her do it, Nae. I should have never brought it up in the first place. I just had too much wine. I'll talk to her tomorrow."

"You didn't have too much wine; that's the sad part. Even when you're straight you're a little devil. I don't know why I love you so much. It's me who's the crazy one, not you! I really oughta have my head examined–really! I mean, dinner was twenty thousand dollars tonight! Who spends twenty thousand dollars on dinner unless it's for a wedding or something? Nobody I know! But why would you care about that? You've got three million in the closet! And that's not fucking normal either.

"Contrary to what you might think, Jordan, I don't need all this. I just want to live a nice, quiet life, away from Stratton and away from all this madness. I think we should move before something bad happens." She paused. "But you'll never do it. You're addicted to all the power–and to all those idiots who call you the King and the Wolf! Christ, the Wolf! What a fucking joke that is!" I could hear the disgust oozing through the keyhole. "My husband, the Wolf of Wall Street! It's almost too ridiculous for words. But you can't see that. All you care about is yourself. You're a selfish little bastard. You really are."

"Stop calling me little, for Chrissake! What the fuck is wrong with you?"

"Aw, you're so sensitive," she said mockingly. "Well, get this, Mr. Sensitive: Tonight you're sleeping in the guest bedroom! And tomorrow night too! Maybe if you're lucky I might have sex with you next year! But that's a long shot!" A moment later I heard the door unlock . . . then the sound of her high heels clicking their way up the stairs.

Well, I guess I deserved it. But, still, what were the chances of her mother getting caught? Close to zero, one would think! It was just those stupid straw hats that she and Patricia were wearing that had made the thought bubble up to my brain. And the fact that I supported Suzanne financially counted for something, didn't it? After all, that was why she'd offered in the first place! Her mother was a sharp, decent lady, and deep down she knew that there was some unspoken IOU that I could cash in on if I really needed to. I mean, when all the bullshit was stripped away, nobody just *gave* out of the goodness of their own heart, did they? There was always some sort of ulterior motive, even if it was nothing more than the personal feeling of satisfaction you received from helping another human being, which in its own way was self-serving too!

On a brighter note, at least I'd had sex with the Duchess that afternoon. So a day or two without sex wouldn't be that difficult to handle.

CHAPTER 20

A CHINK IN THE ARMOR

The doleful Duchess had been half right and half wrong.

Yes, she'd been right about her mother insisting on playing a small role in "this fabulous adventure of mine," as she and Patricia had come to refer to my international money-laundering scheme. In fact, there had been no talking her out of it. But in both our defenses (Suzanne's and mine), it was a rather sexy notion, wasn't it? To stuff an obscene amount of money–$900,000, to be exact–into an oversize pocketbook and then throw it over your shoulder and walk straight through Customs without getting caught? Yes, yes, it was very sexy, indeed!

But, no, no, the Duchess had been wrong to worry herself sick over it. The simple fact was that Suzanne had breached the gauntlet on both sides of the Atlantic without a raised eyebrow–delivering the cash to Jean Jacques Saurel with a wink and a smile. Now she was safely back in England, where she would be spending the rest of September with Aunt Patricia, as the two of them basked in the glory of getting away with breaking a dozen or so laws.

So the Duchess had forgiven me and we were lovers once more–currently taking an end-of-summer vacation in the harbor town of Newport, Rhode Island. Joining us were my oldest friend, Alan Lipsky, and his soon to be ex-wife, Doreen.

At this particular moment it was just Alan and I, and we were walking along a wooden dock on our way to the yacht *Nadine*. We were shoulder to shoulder, but Alan's shoulder was a good six inches above mine. He was big and broad, Alan, with a barrel of a chest and a big thick neck. His face was handsome, in a Mafia hit man sort of way, with big, thick features and big, bushy eyebrows. Even now, dressed in a pair of light-blue Bermuda shorts, a tan V-neck T-shirt, and tan boating moccasins, he looked menacing.

Up ahead, I could see the *Nadine* towering above all the other yachts, its unusual tan color making it stand out that much more. As I drank up the glorious view, I couldn't help but wonder why on earth I had bought the fucking thing. My crooked accountant, Dennis Gaito, had begged me not to–reciting the age-old axiom: "The two happiest days for a boat owner are the day he buys his boat and the day he sells his boat!" Dennis was as sharp as a whip, so I hesitated–until the Duchess told me that buying a yacht was the stupidest thing she'd ever heard, which left me no choice but to immediately write a check.

So now I owned the yacht *Nadine,* which was 167 feet of floating heartache. The problem was that the boat was old, originally built for famed designer Coco Chanel back in the early 1960s. In consequence, the thing was noisy as hell and constantly breaking down. Like most yachts of that era, there was enough teakwood adorning the three massive decks to keep the crew of twelve on their hands and knees, with varnish brushes, from morning until night. Every moment I was on the boat it reeked of varnish, which made me nauseous.

Ironically, when the yacht was built it was only 120 feet long. But then the previous owner, Bernie Little, decided to extend it to make room for a helicopter. And Bernie–well, Bernie was the cunning sort of bastard who knew a sucker when he saw one. He quickly convinced me to buy the yacht after I'd chartered it a few times, using my love for Captain Marc to seal the deal (he gave me Captain Marc with the boat). Shortly thereafter, Captain Marc convinced me to build a jet-powered seaplane from scratch–his theory being that the two of us were avid scuba divers and we could fly the seaplane to uncharted waters and find fish that had never been hunted before. He'd said, "The fish will be so stupid we'll be able to pet them before we spear them!" It was a rather sexy prospect, I'd thought, so I gave him the green light to build it. The budget was $500,000, which quickly turned into a million.

But when we tried craning the seaplane onto the upper deck, we realized that the deck wasn't big enough. What with the Bell Jet helicopter, the six Kawasaki Jet Skis, the two Honda motorcycles, the fiberglass diving board and water slide–all of which were already on the top deck–there would no room for the helicopter to take off and land without colliding with the seaplane. I was in so deep with all this crap that I had no choice but to put the boat back in the shipyard and have it extended once more, for a cost of $700,000.

So the front had been pulled forward; the back had been pushed back; the yacht now looked like a 167-foot rubber band on the verge of snapping.

I said to Alan, "I'll tell you, I really love this boat. I'm glad I bought it."

Alan nodded in agreement. "She's a beauty!"

Captain Marc was waiting for me on the dock, looking as square as one of those Rock 'Em Sock 'Em Robots that Alan and I used to play with as kids. He was dressed in a white collared T-shirt and white boating shorts, both of which bore the *Nadine* logo–two gold-colored eagle's feathers bent around a royal-blue capital *N*.

Captain Marc said, "You got a bunch of phone calls, boss. One from Danny, who sounded higher than a kite, and then three more calls from a girl named Carolyn, with a heavy French accent. She said you need to call her right away, as soon as you get back to the boat."

Immediately my heart began thumping inside my chest. *Christ! Danny was supposed to meet Todd this morning and give him the million dollars! Shit!* All at once a thousand thoughts went flashing through my brain. Had something gone wrong? Had they somehow gotten caught? Were they both in jail? No, that was impossible, unless they were being followed. But why would someone be following them? Or maybe Danny had showed up stoned and Todd had knocked him out and Carolyn was calling to apologize. No, that was ridiculous! Todd would call himself, wouldn't he? *Fuck!* I had forgotten to tell Danny not to show up stoned!

I took a deep breath and tried to calm myself down. Maybe it was all just a coincidence. I smiled at Captain Marc and said, "Did Danny say anything?"

Captain Marc shrugged. "It was kinda hard to understand him, but he said to tell you that everything was cool."

Alan said, "Is everything okay? You need me to do anything?"

"No, no," I replied, breathing a sigh of relief. Alan, of course, having grown up in Bayside, knew Todd as well as I did. Still, I hadn't told Alan what was going on. It wasn't that I didn't trust him; there simply had been no reason to tell him. The only thing he was aware of was that I was going to need his brokerage firm, Monroe Parker, to buy a few million shares of Dollar Time from an unaffiliated overseas seller, which, perhaps, he assumed was me. But he had never asked (it would have been a serious breach of protocol). I calmly said, "I'm sure it's nothing. I just gotta make a couple of phone calls. I'll be downstairs in my bedroom." With that I took a small hop off the edge of the wooden dock and landed on the yacht, which was tied alongside it, lengthwise. Then I went downstairs to the master suite and picked up the satellite phone and dialed Danny's cell phone.

The phone rang three times. "Haaawoaaa?" muttered Danny, sounding like Elmer Fudd.

I looked at my watch: It was eleven-thirty. Unbelievable! He was stoned at eleven-thirty in the morning on a Wednesday, a workday! "Danny, what the fuck is wrong with you? Why are you so stoned at the office?"

"No, no, no! I zake off zaday"–*take off today*–"because I met Tazz"–*Todd*–"but doze you worry! It all go perfect! Iz done! Clean, no marks!"

Well, at least my worst fears were unfounded. "Who's minding the store, Danny?"

"I leave Blockhead and Wigwam there. Iz fine! Mad Max there too."

"Was Todd pissed at you, Danny?"

"Uh-huh," he muttered. "He crazy bastard, zat lumberjack! He pull out gun and point it at me and tell me I lucky I your friend. He shouldn't carry gun. Iz against the law!"

He pulled out a gun? In plain sight? That made no sense! Todd might be crazy, but he wasn't reckless! "I don't understand, Danny. He pulled out a gun in the street?"

"No, no! I give him briefcase in back of limo. We meet in Bay Terrace Zopping Zenter"–*Shopping Center*–"in za parking lot. It all go fine. I stay for only a second, then I drive away."

Christ almighty! What a scene that must've been! Todd in a black stretch Lincoln limousine, Danny in a black Rolls-Royce convertible, side by side in the Bay Terrace Shopping Center, where the next-nicest car was bound to be a Pontiac!

Once more I asked, "Are you sure everything went okay?"

"Yes, I sure!" he said indignantly, to which I slammed the phone down right in his ear, not so much because I was pissed at him but because I was the ultimate hypocrite–finding it annoying to speak to a stoned fool when I was sober.

I was about to pick up the phone and dial Carolyn when the phone started ringing. I took a moment to regard the phone, and at that very moment I felt like Mad Max, my pulse quickening with each terrible ring. But rather than answering it, I simply cocked my head to the side and stared at it with contempt.

On the fourth ring someone picked it up. I waited . . . and prayed. A moment later I heard a menacing little *beep* and then the voice of Tanji, Captain Marc's sexy girlfriend, saying, "It's Carolyn Garret for you, Mr. Belfort, on line two."

I paused for a brief moment to gather my thoughts and then picked up the handset. "Hey, Carolyn, what's going on? Is everything all right?"

"Oh, shit–thanks God I finally find you! Jordan, Todd is in jail and–"

I cut her off immediately. "Carolyn, don't say another word. I'm going to a pay phone and I'll call you right back. Are you home?"

"Yes, I home. I wait right here for your call."

"All right; don't move. Everything will be fine, Carolyn. I promise you."

I hung up the phone and sat down on the edge of the bed, in a state of disbelief. My mind was racing in a thousand different directions. I felt an odd feeling that I had never felt before. Todd was in jail. *In fucking jail!* How could it have happened? Would he talk? . . . No, of course not! If anyone lived by the code of omerta it was Todd Garret! Besides, how many years did he really have to live? He had a fucking lumberjack's heart beating inside him, for Chrissake! He was always saying how he was living on borrowed time, wasn't he? Perhaps a trial could be delayed until he was already dead. Immediately I regretted thinking any such thought, although I had to admit there was truth to it.

I took a deep breath–and tried to collect myself. Then I rose from the bed and made a quick beeline for the pay phone.

As I was walking down the dock it occurred to me that I had only five Quaaludes in my possession, which, given the current circumstances, was an entirely unacceptable number. I wasn't supposed to head back to Long Island for three more days, and my back had really been killing me . . . sort of. Besides, I'd been an angel for over a month now, and that was long enough.

The moment I reached the phone I picked it up and dialed Janet. As I punched in my calling-card number, I wondered if it would somehow make the call more traceable or, for that matter, more buggable. After a few seconds, though, I dismissed the thought as ridiculous. Using a calling card didn't make it any easier for the FBI to tap my phone conversation; it was the same as using quarters. Still, it was the thought of a careful, prudent man, so I commended myself for thinking it.

"Janet," said the prudent man, "I want you to go into the bottom right-hand drawer of my desk and count out forty Ludes; then give them to Wigwam and have him fly them up here on a chopper right now. There's a private airport a few miles from the harbor. He can land there. I don't have time to pick him up, so have a limo waiting for–"

Janet cut me off. "I'll have him there in two hours; don't worry about it. Is everything okay? You sound upset."

"Everything's fine. I just miscalculated before I left and now I'm out. Anyway, my back's been hurting, so I need to take the edge off." I hung up the phone without saying good-bye, then picked it right back up and dialed Carolyn at home. The moment she answered I was on her.

"Carolyn, is–"

"OhmyGod, I must tell you what is–"

"Carolyn, don't–"

"Going on with Tahad! He is–"

"Carolyn, don't–"

"In jail, and he said that–"

She refused to stop talking, so I screamed: *"Carrrrrrrolyn!"*

That got her.

"Listen to me, Carolyn, and don't talk. I'm sorry for yelling at you, but I don't want you to talk from your house. Do you understand?"

"Oui," she replied. Even now I noticed that during the heat of the moment she obviously found it soothing to speak in her own language.

"Okay," I said calmly. "Go to the nearest pay phone and call this number: area code 401-555-1665. That's where I am right now. Got it?"

"Yes," she replied calmly, switching back to English. "I write it down. I call you back in few minutes. I must get change."

"No, just use my calling-card number," I said, just as calmly.

Five minutes later the phone rang. I picked it up and asked Carolyn to read me the number off the pay phone she was at. Then I hung up, switched to the pay phone next to me, and dialed Carolyn's pay phone.

She immediately plunged into the details. ". . . so Tahad waiting in parking lot for Danny, and he finally show up in big-shot Rolls-Royce and he very stoned, swerving around shopping center, almost hitting other cars. So security guards call police because they think Danny driving drunk. He give money to Todd and he leave right away because Todd threaten to kill him for being stoned. But he leave Todd with briefcase. Then Todd saw two police cars with flashing lights and realize what is happening, so he run into video store and hide gun in video box, but police handcuff him anyway. Then police play back security video and see where he hide gun, and they find it and arrest him. Then they go to limousine and search and find money and take it."

Holy shit! I thought. The money was the least of my problems. The main problem was that Danny was a fucking dead man! He would have to leave town and never come back. Or make some sort of financial compensation to Todd, to buy him off.

Just then it occurred to me that Todd must've told all this to Carolyn over the telephone. And if he was still in jail, then he must've used the phone from–*Shit!* Todd was smarter than that! Why would he risk using a phone that was almost certainly tapped–to call his own house, nonetheless?

"When did you last speak to Todd?" I asked, praying there was some explanation.

"I not speak to him. His lawyer call me and tell me this. Todd call him and tell him to get bail money, and then Todd say I must leave to Switzerland tonight, before this become problem. So I book ticket for Tahad's parents and Dina and me. Rich will sign for Todd and I will give him bail money."

Christ almighty! This was an awful lot to take in. At least Todd had had enough common sense not to talk on the phone. And insofar as his conversation with his lawyer went, that would be privileged. Yet the most ironic part was that in the middle of the whole thing–while he was sitting in jail–Todd was still trying to get my money overseas. I didn't know whether to be appreciative of his unwavering commitment to my cause or angry over how reckless he was. I ran the whole thing through my mind, trying to put it all into perspective. The truth was that the police probably thought they'd stumbled onto a drug deal. Todd was the seller, which was why he had a briefcase full of cash, and whoever had been driving the Rolls-Royce was the buyer. I wondered if they had gotten Danny's license plate? If they had, wouldn't they have already picked him up? But on what grounds would they arrest him? In truth, they had nothing on Danny. All they had was a briefcase full of cash, nothing more. The main issue was the gun, but that could be dealt with. A good lawyer could most certainly get Todd off with probation and maybe a hefty fine. I would pay the fine–or Danny would pay the fine–and that would be that.

I said to the Bombshell, "Okay, you should go. Todd gave you all the specifics, right? You know who to go see?"

"Yes. I will see Jean Jacques Saurel. I have phone number and I know street very well. It is in shopping area."

"All right, Carolyn; be careful. Tell the same to Todd's parents and to Dina. And, also, call Todd's lawyer and tell him to let Todd know that you spoke to me and that he has nothing to worry about. Tell him that everything will be taken care of. And stress the word *everything,* Carolyn. You understand what I'm saying?"

"Yes, yes, I do. Don't worry, Jordan. Tahad love you. He would never say one word, no matter what. I promise you this with all my heart. He will sooner kill himself before he hurt you."

Those very words made me smile inwardly, even though I knew Todd was incapable of loving any soul on earth, especially himself. Yet Todd's very persona, the persona of the Jewish Mafioso, made it highly unlikely that he would roll over on me unless he was facing many years in jail.

Having worked things out in my mind, I wished the Bombshell a bon voyage and hung up the phone. As I headed back to the yacht, the only remaining question was whether or not I should call Danny and give him the bad news. Or perhaps it would be wiser to wait until he wasn't so stoned. Although, now that after the initial wave of panic had subsided, it wasn't such bad news, after all. It certainly wasn't good news, but it was more of an unexpected complication than anything else.

Still, there was no denying that those Quaaludes were going to be Danny's downfall. He had a serious problem with them, and perhaps it was time that he sought help.

BOOK III

CHAPTER 21

FORM OVER SUBSTANCE

January 1994

In the weeks following the parking-lot debacle, it became clear that the shopping center's surveillance cameras hadn't gotten a clear picture of Danny's license plate. But, according to Todd, the police were offering him a deal if he would tell them who'd been driving the Rolls-Royce. Todd, of course, had told them to eat shit and die, although I was somewhat suspicious that he was exaggerating a bit–laying a foundation for economic extortion. Either way, I had assured him that he would be taken care of, and in return he had agreed to spare Danny's life.

With that, the rest of 1993 passed without incident–which is to say that *Lifestyles of the Rich and Dysfunctional* continued unabated–and came to a bountiful close with the public offering of Steve Madden Shoes. The stock had leveled off at just over $8, and between my ratholes, bridge units, and proprietary trading commissions I had made over $20 million.

Over Christmas and New Year's, we took a two-week vacation in the Caribbean aboard the yacht *Nadine*. The Duchess and I partied like rock stars, and I had managed to fall asleep in just about every five-star restaurant between St. Bart's and St. Martin. I also managed to spear myself while scuba diving on Quaaludes, but it was only a flesh wound, and other than that I had made it through the trip mostly unscathed.

But vacation was over, and it was back to business now. It was a

Tuesday, the first week in January, and I was sitting in the office of Ira Lee Sorkin, Stratton Oakmont's gray-haired, mop-topped chief outside legal counsel. Like all prominent white-collar attorneys, Ike had once worked for the bad guys–or the good guys, depending on whom you asked, which is to say that Ike had once been a regulator. In his case, he had been Section Chief of the SEC's New York Regional Office.

At this particular moment he was leaning back in his fabulous black-leather throne, with his palms up in the air, saying, "You should be jumping for joy right now, Jordan! Two years ago the SEC sued you for twenty-two million bucks and was trying to shut down the firm; now they're willing to settle for three million bucks and let the firm off with a slap on the wrist. It's a complete victory. Nothing less."

I smiled dutifully at my blowhard of a lawyer, although deep down I felt conflicted. It was an awful lot to take in my first day back from Christmas vacation. I mean, why should I be so quick to settle, when the SEC hadn't found even one smoking gun against me? They had filed their suit more than two years ago, alleging stock manipulation and high-pressure sales tactics. But they had little evidence to support those claims, especially the stock manipulation, which was the more serious of the two.

The SEC had subpoenaed fourteen Strattonites, twelve of whom had placed their right hands on a stack of bibles and lied right through their teeth. Only two Strattonites had panicked and actually told the truth–admitting to using high-pressure sales tactics and such. And as a way of saying, "Thank you for your honesty!" the SEC had tossed them out of the securities industry. (After all, they had admitted wrongdoing under oath.) And what terrible fate had befallen the twelve who'd lied? Ah, such poetic justice! Every last one of them had walked away completely unscathed and was still working at Stratton Oakmont to this very day–smiling and dialing and ripping their clients' eyeballs out.

Still, in spite of my wonderful string of successes at fending off the bozos, Ira Lee Sorkin, a former bozo himself, was still recommending that I settle my case and put all this behind me. But I found myself struggling with his logic, inasmuch as "putting all this behind me" didn't just mean paying a $3 million fine and agreeing not to violate any more securities laws in the future; it also meant that I would have to accept a lifetime bar from the securities industry and leave Stratton Oakmont forever–with some additional language, I was certain, that if I were to somehow die and then figure out a way to resurrect myself, I would still be barred.

I was about to offer up my two cents when Sorkin the Great could remain silent no longer. "The long and short of it, Jordan, is that you and I made an excellent team, and we beat the SEC at their own game." He nodded at the wisdom of his own words. "We wore the bastards out. The three million you can make back in a month, and it's even tax-deductible. So it's time to move on with your life. It's time to walk off into the sunset and enjoy your wife and daughter." And with that, Sorkin the Great smiled an enormous boiling smile and nodded some more.

I smiled noncommittally. "Do Danny or Kenny's lawyers know about this?"

He flashed me a conspirator's smile. "This is strictly on the Q.T., Jordan; none of the other lawyers knows anything. Legally, of course, I represent Stratton, so my loyalty is to the firm. But right now you *are* the firm, so my loyalty is to you. Anyway, I figured that given the circumstances of the offer, you might want a few days to think it over. But that's all we have, my friend, a few days. Maybe a week at most."

When we were first sued, we had each retained separate legal counsel to avoid potential conflicts. At the time I had considered it a serious waste of money; now I was glad we had. I shrugged my shoulders and said, "I'm sure their offer isn't going away anytime soon, Ike. Like you said, we wore them out. In fact, I don't think there's anyone left at the SEC who even knows anything about my case." I was tempted to explain to him why I was so certain of that (my bug in the conference room), but I decided not to.

Ike the Spike threw his hands in the air and rolled his eyes up in his head. "Why do you wanna look a gift horse in the mouth, huh? The SEC's New York office has had huge turnover in the last six months, and morale is low. But that's only by coincidence, and it won't last forever. I'm talking to you like a friend now, Jordan, not your lawyer. You gotta settle this case once and for all, before a new set of investigators steps in and takes another crack at it. Eventually one of them might find something; then all bets are off."

I nodded slowly and said, "It was smart of you to keep this between us. If news leaks out before I have a chance to address the troops, they might panic. But I'll tell you that the thought of taking a lifetime bar doesn't exactly thrill me, Ike. I mean–*to never set foot in the boardroom again!* I don't even know what to say about that. That boardroom is my lifeblood. It's my sanity, and it's also my insanity. It's like the good, the bad, and the ugly all rolled up into one.

"Anyway, the real problem isn't gonna be with me; it's gonna be with Kenny. How am I gonna convince him to take a lifetime bar when Danny's staying behind? Kenny listens to me, but I'm not sure he'll listen if I tell him to walk away while Danny's allowed to stay. Kenny's making ten million dollars a year; he may not be the sharpest tool in the shed, but he's still smart enough to know that he's never gonna make this kinda money again."

Ike shrugged and said, "So let Kenny stay behind and have Danny take the bar. The SEC couldn't care less which of them stays and which of them goes. As long as *you're* gone, they're happy. All they want is to make a nice fat press release saying the Wolf of Wall Street is out of their hair, and then they'll be at peace. Would it be easier to convince Danny to leave?"

"That's not an option, Ike. Tell me how this would play out if we agreed to settle."

Ike paused, as if to gather his thoughts. After a few seconds he said, "Assuming you can convince Kenny, then both of you would sell your stock to Danny and then sign court orders permanently barring you from the brokerage business. The money for your fines can come directly out of the firm, so you won't have to take a dime out of your pocket. They'll want an independent auditor to come down to the firm and do a review and then make some recommendations. But that'll be no big deal; I can handle that with your compliance department. And that's it, my friend. It's very straightforward."

Ike added, "But I think you're putting too much stock in Danny. He's definitely sharper than Kenny, but he's stoned half the time. I know you enjoy your partying too, but you're always in good shape during business hours. Besides, for better or worse, there's only one Jordan Belfort in the world. And the regulators know that too–especially Marty Kupperberg, who's running the New York office right now. That's why he wants you out. He might despise everything you stand for, but he still respects what you've accomplished. In fact, I'll tell you a funny story: A couple of months ago, I was down at an SEC conference in Florida, and Richard Walker–who's the number-two man down in Washington right now–was saying that they need a whole new set of securities laws to deal with someone like Jordan Belfort. It got quite a chuckle from the audience, and he really hadn't said it in that derogatory a fashion, if you know what I mean."

I rolled my eyes. "Oh, yeah, Ike, I'm real proud of that; real proud, indeed! In fact, why don't you go call my mother and tell her what Richard Walker said? I'm sure she'll be very thrilled at the awesome respect her son inspires among the nation's top securities cop. Believe it or not, Ike, there was a time not that long ago when I was a nice Jewish boy from a nice Jewish family. Seriously. I was the kid who used to shovel driveways after snowstorms to make extra money. It's hard to imagine that less than five years ago I was able to walk into a restaurant without people looking at me funny."

I began shaking my head in amazement. "I mean–Jesus!–how the fuck did I let this whole thing spiral so far out of control? This wasn't what I intended when I started Stratton! I swear to God, Ike!" With that, I rose from my chair and stared out the plate-glass window at the Empire State Building. It wasn't all that long ago when I'd first gone to Wall Street as a stockbroker trainee, was it? I had taken the express bus–*the express bus!*–and had only had seven dollars left in my pocket. Seven fucking dollars! I could still remember the feeling of looking at all those other people and wondering if they felt as bitter as I did about having to take a bus to Manhattan to eke out a living. I remembered feeling bad for the older people–that they had to sit on those hard plastic seats and smell the diesel fumes. I remembered swearing I would never let myself end up that way, that somehow I would become rich and live life on my own terms.

I remembered getting off the bus and staring up at all those skyscrapers and feeling intimidated at the very power of the city, even though I had grown up just a few miles outside Manhattan.

I turned and faced Ike, and with nostalgia in my voice I said, "You know, Ike, I never wanted it to end up this way. I tell you the truth: I had good intentions when I started Stratton. I know that doesn't mean a lot right now, but, still . . . that really was the case five years ago." I shook my head once more and said, "I guess the road to hell *is* paved with good intentions, just like they say. I'll tell you a funny story, though: Do you remember my first wife, Denise?"

Ike nodded. "She was a kind, beautiful lady, as is Nadine."

"Yes. She was kind and beautiful, and she still is. In the beginning, when I started Stratton, she had this classic line. She said, 'Jordan, why can't you get a normal job making a million dollars a year?' I thought it was pretty funny at the time, but now I know what she was talking about. You know, Stratton's like a cult, Ike; that's where the real power is. All those kids look to me for every little thing. That was what was driving Denise crazy. In a way, they deified me and tried turning me into something I wasn't. I know that now, but back then it wasn't so clear. I found the power intoxicating. Impossible to refuse.

"Anyway, I always swore to myself that if it ever came down to it, I would fall on my sword and sacrifice myself for the sake of the troops." I shrugged my shoulders and smiled weakly. "Of course I always knew that was somewhat of a romantic notion, but that was how I'd always envisioned it.

"So I feel like if I throw in the towel right now and take the money and run, then I'm fucking over everyone; I'm leaving the brokers high and dry. I mean, the easiest thing for me would be to do what you said: take a lifetime bar and go off into the sunset with my wife and daughter. God knows I have enough money for ten lifetimes. But then I'd be fucking over all those kids. And I swore to every last one of them that I'd fight this thing to the bitter end. So how do I just pick up now and hightail it out of town—just because the SEC is giving me an exit ramp? I'm the captain of the ship, Ike, and the captain is supposed to be the last one off the boat, no?"

Ike shook his head. "Absolutely not," he replied emphatically. "You can't compare your SEC case to an adventure at sea. The simple fact is that by taking the bar you ensure the survival of Stratton. No matter how effective we are at foiling the SEC's investigation, we can't delay this thing forever. There's a trial date in less than six months, and you're not gonna find a jury of your peers very sympathetic to your cause. And there're thousands of jobs at stake, as well as countless families who depend on Stratton for their financial existence. By taking the bar you secure everybody's future, including your own."

I took a moment to consider Ike's wisdom, which was only partially true. In point of fact, the SEC's offer wasn't really that much of a surprise to me. After all, Al Abrams had predicted it. It had been at one of our countless breakfast meetings at the Seville Diner. Al said, "If you play your cards right, you'll wear the SEC down until there's no one left in the office who knows anything about your case. The turnover there is mind-boggling, especially when they get caught up in an investigation that's not going well.

"But never forget," he added, "that just because they settle, it doesn't mean it's over. There's nothing to stop them from coming right back at you with a new case the day after you settle the old one. So you need to get it in writing that there're no new cases pending. And even then there's still the NASD to contend with . . . and then the individual states . . . and then, God forbid, the U.S. Attorney's Office and the FBI . . . although chances are they would've already gotten involved if they were planning to."

With the wisdom of Al Abrams still in my mind, I asked Ike, "How do we know the SEC isn't planning on coming right back at us with another lawsuit?"

"I'll have it worked into the agreement," Ike replied. "The settlement will cover all acts up to the present. But remember–if Danny goes off the reservation again, there's nothing to stop them from bringing a new case going forward."

I nodded slowly, still unconvinced. "And what about the NASD . . . or the states . . . or, God forbid, the FBI?"

Sorkin the Great leaned back in his throne and crossed his arms once more, and he said, "There's no guarantee on that. I'm not gonna mislead you. It would be nice if we could get something like that in writing, but it doesn't work that way. If you want my opinion, though, I'll tell you that I think the chances are very slim that any other regulator will pick the case up. Remember, the last thing any regulator wants is to get involved with a losing case. It's a career killer. You saw what happened to all the lawyers the SEC assigned to the Stratton case: Every last one of them left the office in shame, and I can assure you that none of them got generous offers in the private sector. Most SEC lawyers are just there to gather experience and develop a track record. After they've made a name for themselves, they move on to the private sector, where they can make some real money.

"Now, exempt from that is the U.S. Attorney's Office. They'd have a lot more luck with the Stratton investigation than the SEC had. Funny things start to happen when criminal subpoenas are floating around. All those stockbrokers who were subpoenaed down to the SEC and supported you so admirably . . . well, they probably would've jumped ship if those same subpoenas had come from a grand jury.

"But that being said, I don't think the U.S. Attorney has any interest in your case. Stratton's out on Long Island, which is the Eastern District. And the Eastern District isn't particularly active with securities cases, unlike the Southern District, in Manhattan, which is very active. So that's my best guess, my friend. I think if you settle this thing right now and walk away, you can live your life happily ever after."

I took a deep breath and then let it out slowly. "So be it," I said. "It's time for peace with honor. And what happens if I go near the boardroom? Does the FBI show up at my door and arrest me for violating a court order?"

"No, no," answered Ike, waving the back of his hand in the air. "I think you're making more of this than it really is. In fact, theoretically, you could keep an office on the same floor, in the same building, as Stratton. For that matter, you could stand out in the hallway with Danny all day long and offer him your opinion on every little move he makes. I'm not encouraging you to do that or anything, but it wouldn't be illegal. You just can't force Danny to listen to you, and you can't spend half your day inside the boardroom. But if you wanted to drop in and visit once in a while, there would be nothing wrong with that."

All at once I found myself taken aback. Could it really be as easy as that? If the SEC were to bar me, could I really stay that much involved with the firm? If I could, and I could somehow make that known to all the Strattonites, then they wouldn't feel like I'd abandoned them! Sensing daylight, I asked, "And how much could I sell my stock to Danny for?"

"Anything you want," replied Ike the Spike, seeming to have no idea what my devilish mind was conjuring up. "That's between you and Danny; the SEC couldn't care less."

Hmmmm! Very interesting, I thought, with the righteous number of $200 million bubbling up into my brain. "Well, I guess I could come to a meeting of the minds with Danny. He's always been pretty reasonable when it comes to money. Although I don't think I'll keep an office on the same floor as Stratton. Perhaps I should take one a few buildings over. Whaddaya think, Ike?"

"I think that sounds like a good idea," replied Ike the Spike.

I smiled at my wonderful lawyer and went for broke: "I have only one more question, although I think I already know the answer. If I'm barred from the securities business, then theoretically I'm just like any other investor. I mean, I'm not barred from investing for my own account and I'm not barred from owning stakes in companies going public, right?"

Ike smiled broadly. "Of course not! You can buy stocks, you can sell stocks, you can own stakes in companies going public, you can do anything you want. You just can't run a brokerage firm."

"I could even buy Stratton new issues now, couldn't I? I mean, if I'm no longer a registered stockbroker, then that restriction no longer applies to me, right?" I said a silent prayer to the Almighty.

"Believe it or not," replied Ike the Spike, "the answer is yes. You would be able to buy as many shares of Stratton new issues as Danny would offer you. That's the long and short of it."

Hmmm . . . perhaps this could work out pretty well! In essence, I could become my own rathole, and not only at Stratton but at Biltmore and Monroe Parker too! "All right, Ike, I think I can convince Kenny to take a lifetime bar. He's been trying to convince me to help his friend Victor get into the brokerage business, and if I agree to, it'll probably seal the deal. But I need you to keep this quiet for a few days. If word of this gets out, all bets are off."

Sorkin the Great shrugged his beefy shoulders once more and then threw his palms up in the air and winked. No words were necessary.

Having grown up in Queens, I'd had the distinct pleasure of traveling on the Long Island Expressway, the LIE, a good twenty thousand times, and for some inexplicable reason this godforsaken highway seemed to be under perpetual construction. In fact, the section my limousine was traveling on right now–where the eastern portion of Queens meets the western portion of Long Island–had been under construction since I was five years old, and it didn't seem to be getting any closer to completion. A company had secured some sort of permanent construction contract, and they were either the most incompetent road pavers in the history of the universe or the savviest businessmen to ever walk the planet.

Whatever the case, the fact that I was less than three nautical miles from Stratton Oakmont hadn't the slightest bearing on when I might actually arrive there. So I settled back deep in my seat and did the usual: focused on George's wonderful bald spot and let it soothe me. *I wonder what George would do if he ever lost his job?* In fact, it wasn't only George who would be affected if I botched this thing but the rest of the menagerie too. If I were forced to cut back my expenses as a result of Danny not being able to keep Stratton in business, it would affect many people.

What would become of the Strattonites? For Chrissake, every last one of them would have to dramatically cut back their lifestyles or face immediate financial ruin. They would have to start living like the rest of the world–as if money meant something and you couldn't just go out and buy whatever the hell you wanted whenever the hell you pleased. What an unbearable thought!

From my perspective, the smart thing to do would be to walk away from this thing–clean. Yes, the prudent man wouldn't sell the firm to Danny for an exorbitant price . . . or take an office across the street . . . or run things from behind the scenes. It would be another case of the Wolf of Wall Street acting like Winnie the Pooh and sticking his head in the honeypot once too often. Look what had happened with Denise and Nadine: I had cheated on Denise dozens of times until . . . Fuck it. Why torture myself with that thought?

Anyway, there was no doubt that if I walked away, I wouldn't be risking what I already had. I wouldn't feel compelled to offer my advice, my guidance, nor would I even go near the boardroom to show any moral support for the troops. I wouldn't have any clandestine meetings with Danny or, for that matter, the owners of Biltmore and Monroe Parker. I would simply fade off into the sunset with Nadine and Chandler, just the way Ike had advised me to.

But how could I walk around Long Island knowing that I'd deserted the ship and left everybody hanging out to dry? Not to mention the fact that my plan with Kenny centered around my agreeing to finance Victor Wang, to assist him in opening Duke

Securities. And if Victor found out I was no longer behind Stratton, he would turn on Danny faster than lightning.

In truth, the only way to do this was to let everyone know that I still had an ax to grind at Stratton and that any attack on Danny was an attack on me. Then everyone would stay loyal, except, of course, Victor, who I would deal with on my terms, at the time of my own choosing–long before he was strong enough to wage war. The Depraved Chinaman could be controlled, so long as Biltmore and Monroe Parker stayed loyal and so long as Danny kept his head glued on straight and didn't try spreading his wings too fast.

Danny spreading his wings too fast: Yes, it was an important variable not to be discounted. After all, there was no doubt that eventually he'd want to run things according to his own instincts. It would be an insult to him if I tried holding on to the reins of power any longer than necessary. Perhaps there should be some sort of transition period that we verbally agreed to–a period of six to nine months, where he would follow my directives without question. Then, after that, I would slowly let him assume full control.

And the same would apply to Biltmore and Monroe Parker. They, too, would take orders from me, but only for a short period of time; then they would be on their own. In fact, their loyalty was so great that they would probably still make me just as much money, even if I didn't lift a finger. There was no doubt that would be the case with Alan; his loyalty was unquestioned, based on lifelong friendship. And Brian, his partner, owned only forty-nine percent of Monroe Parker–having agreed to that as a precondition to me coming up with the original financing. So it was Alan who called the shots there. And in the case of Biltmore, it was Elliot who owned the extra percentage point. And while he wasn't quite as loyal as Alan, he was still loyal enough.

Anyway, my holdings were so vast that Stratton represented only one aspect of my financial dealings. There was Steve Madden Shoes; there was Randall Franks and Saurel; and there were a dozen other companies that I currently owned stakes in that were preparing to go public. Of course, Dollar Time was still a complete disaster, but the worst of it was over.

Having worked things out in my mind, I said to George, "Why don't you get off the highway and take local streets. I need to get back to the office."

The mute nodded two times, obviously hating my guts.

I ignored his insolence and said, "Also, stick around after you drop me off. I'm gonna have lunch at Tenjin today. All right?"

Again the mute nodded, not uttering a single word.

Go figure! The fucking guy won't say a goddamn word to me, and here I am worrying what his life would be like without Stratton. Perhaps I was completely off the mark. Perhaps I owed nothing to the thousands of people who depended on Stratton Oakmont for their very livelihoods. Perhaps they would all turn on me in a New York second–and tell me to go fuck myself–if they no longer thought that I could help them. Perhaps . . . perhaps . . . perhaps . . .

How ironic it was that with all this internal debating I had missed one very important point: If I no longer had to worry about getting stoned inside the boardroom, there would be nothing to stop me from doing Quaaludes all day long. Without realizing it, I was setting the stage for some very dark times ahead. After all, the only thing holding me back now would be my own good judgment, which had a funny way of deserting me . . . especially when it came to blondes and drugs.

CHAPTER 22

LUNCHTIME IN THE ALTERNATIVE UNIVERSE

Every time the restaurant door opened, a handful of Strattonites came marching in to Tenjin, causing three Japanese sushi chefs and half a dozen pint-size waitresses to drop whatever they were doing and scream out, *"Gongbongwa! Gongbongwa! Gongbongwa!"* which was Japanese for good afternoon. Then they offered the Strattonites deep formal bows and changed their tone to a dramatic high-pitched squeal: "*Yo-say-no-sah-no-seh! Yo-say-no-sah-no-seh! Yo-say-no-sah-no-seh!"* which meant God only knew what.

The chefs ran over to greet the new arrivals, grabbing them by the wrists and inspecting their gleaming gold wristwatches. In heavily accented English, they would interrogate them: "How much watch cost? Where you buy? What car you drive to restaurant? Ferrari? Mercedes? Porsche? What kind golf club you use? Where you play at? How long for tee time? What your handicap?"

Meanwhile, the waitresses, who dressed in salmon-pink kimonos with lime-green rucksacks on their backs, rubbed the backs of their hands against the fine Italian wool of all those custom-made Gilberto suit jackets, nodding their heads approvingly, and making cooing sounds: "Ohhhhhhh . . . ahhhhhhhh . . . nice-a-fabric . . . so-a-soft!"

But then, as if by silent cue, they all stopped at precisely the same moment and returned to whatever it was they'd been doing. In the case of the sushi chefs, it meant rolling and folding and slicing and dicing. In the case of the waitresses, it meant serving oversize vats of Premium sake and Kirin beer to the young and the thirsty, and enormous wooden sailboats filled with overpriced sushi and sashimi to the rich and the hungry.

And just when you thought it was safe, the door swung open once more, and the madness repeated itself, as the wildly animated staff of Tenjin came swooping down on the next group of Strattonites and bathed them in Japanese pomp and circumstance, as well as heaping doses of what I was certain was unadulterated Japanese bullshit.

Welcome to lunch hour–Stratton style!

At this very moment, the alternative universe was exerting its full force on this tiny corner of planet earth. Dozens of sports cars and stretch limousines blocked traffic outside the restaurant, while inside the restaurant young Strattonites carried on their time-honored tradition of acting like packs of untamed wolves. Of the restaurant's forty tables, only two were occupied by non-Strattonites, or civilians, as we called them. Perhaps they had inadvertently stumbled upon Tenjin while searching for a quiet place to enjoy a nice relaxing meal. Whatever the case, there was no doubt they had been entirely unaware of the bizarre fate about to befall them. After all, as lunch progressed, the drugs would start kicking in.

Yes, the clock had just struck one and some of the Strattonites were already getting off. It wasn't hard to tell which of them were Luded out; they were the ones standing on the tabletops, slurring and drooling and reciting war stories. Fortunately, the sales assistants were required to stay in the boardroom–manning the phones and catching up on paperwork–so everyone still had their clothes on and nobody was rutting away in the bathrooms or under the tables.

I was sitting in a private alcove at the rear of the restaurant, watching this very madness unfold while pretending to listen to the ramblings of Kenny Greene who was spewing out his own version of unadulterated bullshit. Meanwhile, Victor Wang, the Depraved Chinaman, was nodding his panda-size head at everything his friend was saying, although I was certain he was only pretending to agree with him.

The Blockhead was saying, ". . . is the exact reason why you stand to make so much money here, JB. I mean, Victor is the sharpest guy I know." He reached over and patted the Depraved Chinaman on his enormous back. "Next to you, of course, but that goes without saying."

I smiled a bogus smile and said, "Well, gee, Kenny, thanks for the vote of confidence!"

Victor chuckled at his friend's idiocy, then flashed me one of his hideous smiles, causing his eyes to become so narrow they all but disappeared.

Kenny, however, had never really mastered the concept of irony. In consequence, he had taken my offering of thanks at face value and was now beaming with great pride. "Anyway, the way I figure it, it's only gonna take four hundred thousand or so in start-up capital to really get this thing off the ground. If you want, you can give it to me in cash and I'll filter it to Victor through my mother"–his mother?–"and you don't have to even worry about it leaving a bad paper trail"–a bad paper trail?–"because my mother and Victor own some real estate together, so they can justify it like that. Then we'll need a few key stockbrokers to help get the pump going and, most importantly, a big allocation of the next new issue. The way I figure it is . . ."

I quickly tuned out. Kenny was bursting at the seams with excitement, and every word that escaped his lips was utter nonsense.

Neither Victor nor Kenny was aware of the SEC's settlement offer. I wouldn't let them in on that for a few more days, not until both of them had gotten themselves so wet in the pants over the fabulous future of Duke Securities that Stratton Oakmont would seem all but expendable. Only then would I tell them.

Just then I caught a glimpse of Victor out of the corner of my eye, and I took a moment to regard him. Just looking at the Depraved Chinaman on an empty stomach made me want to eat him! Why this massive Chinaman looked so succulent had always baffled me, although it probably had most to do with his skin, which was smoother than a newborn baby's. And beneath that velvety soft skin were a dozen layers of lavish Chinese fat, which would be perfect for cooking; and beneath *that* were a dozen more layers of indestructible Chinese muscle, which would be perfect for eating; and on the very surface of it all, he sported the most delicious Chinese tint, which was the exact color of fresh tupelo honey.

The end result was that every time I laid eyes on Victor Wang, I envisioned him as a suckling pig, and I felt like shoving an apple in his mouth and sticking a skewer up his ass and throwing him on a rotisserie and basting him in sweet and sour sauce and then inviting some friends over to eat him–luau style!

". . . and Victor will always stay loyal," continued the Blockhead, "and you stand to make more money off Duke Securities than off Biltmore and Monroe Parker combined."

I shrugged my shoulders, then said, "Perhaps, Kenny, but that's not my primary concern here. Don't get me wrong–I'm planning on making a lot of money. I mean, after all, why shouldn't all of us make a lot? But what's most important to me here, what I'm really trying to accomplish, is to secure your and Victor's futures. If I can do that and make a few extra million a year at the same time, then I'll consider the whole thing a huge success." I paused for a few moments to let my bullshit sink in and tried getting a quick read on how they were taking my sudden change of heart.

So far so good, I thought. "Anyway, we have our SEC trial coming up in less than six months, and who knows how it'll end up? As good as things look, there may come a point when it might make sense to settle the case. And if that day comes, I want to make sure everybody has their exit visas stamped and ready. Believe it or not, I've actually wanted to get Duke up and running for a while now, but the issue of my Judicate stock has been hanging over my head. I still can't sell it for two more weeks, so everything we do has to be kept secret for now. I can't overestimate the importance of that. Understood?"

Victor nodded his panda head in understanding, and said, "I won't breathe a word to anybody. And as far as my Judicate stock goes, I don't even care about it. We all stand to make so much money on Duke that if I never get to sell a share I don't even give a shit."

At this point, Kenny chimed in: "You see, JB–I told you! Victor's head is in the right spot; he's completely with the program." Once more, he reached over and patted the Chinaman's enormous back.

Victor then said, "I also want you to know that I swear complete loyalty to you. Just tell me what stocks you want me to buy and I'll buy the shit out of them. You'll never see a share back until you ask for it."

I smiled and said, "That's why I'm agreeing to this, Victor, because I trust you and I know you'll do the right thing. And, of course, because I think you're a sharp guy and you'll make a big success of it." And words are cheap, I thought. In fact, all this goodwill on Victor's part was complete crap, and I was willing to bet my very life on it. The Chinaman was incapable of being loyal to anybody or anything, especially himself, who he would inadvertently fuck over to feed his own warped ego.

According to plan, Danny showed up fifteen minutes after we sat down, which I had calculated as the appropriate amount of time for Kenny to relish his moment of glory without Danny being there to rain on his parade. After all, he deeply resented Danny for having taken over his slot as my number one. Skipping over Kenny was something I'd felt bad about, but it was something I'd had to do. Still, it was a shame he had to take the fall with Victor, especially since I was certain that Kenny believed every word he said to me–about Victor staying loyal, and all the rest of that jargon. But Kenny's weakness was that he still looked at Victor through the eyes of a teenager. He still worshipped him as a successful coke dealer, while he was merely a successful pot dealer, which was one step down on the drug-dealing food chain.

Anyway, I had already had my sit-down with Danny when I got back to Stratton after my meeting with Ike–explaining my plan to him in intimate detail, holding back very little. When I was finished, his response had been the expected one.

"In my mind," he'd said, "you'll always own Stratton, and sixty cents of every dollar will always be yours. And that's whether you take an office down the street or you decide to sail your yacht around the world."

Now, an hour later, he had arrived at Tenjin, and he immediately poured himself a large cup of sake. Then he refilled all three of our cups and held up his own, as if to make a toast. Danny said, "To friendship and loyalty, and to getting scrummed by Blue Chips tonight."

"Here, here!" I exclaimed, and the four of us clinked our white porcelain cups together. Then we downed the warm fiery brew.

I said to Kenny and Victor, "Listen, I haven't really spoken to Danny about what's going on with Duke"–a lie–"so let me give him the quick rundown and bring him up to speed, okay?"

Victor and Kenny nodded, and I quickly plunged into the details. When I got to the subject of where Duke should be located, I turned to Victor and said, "I'll give you a couple of options: The first is to go to New Jersey, just over the George Washington Bridge, and open the firm there. Your best bet would be Fort Lee, or maybe Hackensack. Either way, you'll have no trouble recruiting there. You'll be able to pull kids from all over North Jersey and then some reverse commuters, kids living in Manhattan who are sick of working there. The second option would be to go into Manhattan itself; but that's a double-edged sword. On one side, there're a million kids there, so you won't have any trouble recruiting, but on the other side you're gonna find it hard to build loyalty there.

"One of the keys to Stratton is that we're the only game in town. I mean, just look at this restaurant, for example." I motioned with my head to all the tables. "All you see here are Strattonites. So what you have, Victor, is a self-contained society"–I resisted the urge to use the word *cult,* which was more appropriate–"where they don't get to hear the alternative point of view. If you open an office in Manhattan, your guys are gonna be having lunch with stockbrokers from a thousand different firms. It might not seem too important right now, but, trust me, in the future it will be important, especially if you start getting bad press or if your stocks start crashing. Then you'll be very happy that you're in a place where nobody's whispering negative things in your brokers' ears. Anyway, that being said, I'll still let it be your call."

Victor nodded his panda head slowly, deliberately, as if he were weighing the pros and cons. I found this to be almost laughable, insofar as the chances of Victor agreeing to go to New Jersey were slim and nil, and as the saying went, slim had already left town. Victor's giant ego would never allow him to pick New Jersey. After all, the state didn't resonate with wealth and success and, most importantly, a place for players. No, Victor would want to open his firm right in the heart of Wall Street, whether it made sense or not. And that was fine with me. It would make it that much easier to destroy him when the time came.

I had given the same speech to the owners of Biltmore and Monroe Parker, all of whom had originally wanted to open their firms in Manhattan. That was why Monroe Parker was tucked away in upstate New York and why Florida-based Biltmore had chosen to keep its office off Boca Raton's Maggot Mile, which was a name the press had given to the section of South Florida where all the brokerage firms were located.

In the end, it all came down to brainwashing, which had two distinct aspects to it. The first aspect was to keep saying the same thing over and over to a captive audience. The second aspect was to make sure you were the only one saying anything. There could be no competing viewpoints. Of course, it made things much easier if what you were saying was exactly what your subjects wanted to hear, which at Stratton Oakmont had been the case. Twice a day, every day, I had stood before the boardroom and told them that if they listened to me and did exactly as I said, they would have more money than they had ever dreamed possible and there would be gorgeous young girls throwing themselves at their very feet. And that was exactly what had happened.

After a good ten seconds of silence, Victor replied, "I see your point, but I think I can do really well in Manhattan. There're so many kids there that I can't imagine not filling the place up in two seconds flat."

The Blockhead then added, "And I bet Victor could give some kick-ass motivational meetings. So everyone's gonna love working for him. Anyway, I can help Victor with that. I've kept little notes on all your meetings, so I can go through them with Victor and we can . . ."

Oh, Christ! I quickly tuned out and began staring at the giant panda, trying to imagine what could possibly be going on inside that warped brain of his. He was actually a pretty smart guy, and he did have his uses. In fact, three years ago he had performed quite a service for me. . . .

It was just after I'd left Denise. Nadine hadn't officially moved in yet, so with no woman around, I decided to hire a full-time butler. But I wanted a gay butler, just like the one I'd seen on the show *Dynasty*–or was it *Dallas*? Anyway, the point was that I wanted a gay butler to call my own, and being as rich as I was, I figured I deserved it.

So Janet went on a quest to find me a gay butler, which, of course, she quickly did. His name was Patrick the Butler, and he was so gay that he had flames shooting out of his asshole. Patrick seemed like a pretty okay guy to me, in spite of being a bit tipsy once in a while, but I wasn't home that much, so I really had no idea what he was like.

When the Duchess moved in, she quickly assumed control over the household, and she started noticing a few things–like that Patrick the Butler was a rip-roaring alcoholic who went through sexual partners at a ferocious clip, or so he'd confided in the Duchess after his fudge-packing tongue had been lubricated by Valium and alcohol and God only knew what else.

It wasn't long after that that the shit hit the fan. Patrick the Butler made the sad mistake of assuming that the Duchess would be joining me at my parents' house for Passover dinner, so he decided to host a gay orgy for twenty-one of his friends, who formed a human daisy chain around my living room and then played naked Twister in my bedroom. Yes, it was quite a sight the Duchess (who was twenty-three at the time) had the pleasure of walking in to: all those homosexuals pressed together–butt to nut–rutting away like barnyard animals in our tiny Manhattan love nest, on the fifty-third floor of Olympic Towers.

It was from out the window of that very floor, in fact, that Victor ended up hanging Patrick the Butler, after it came to light that Patrick and his posse had stolen $50,000 in cash from my sock drawer. In Victor's defense, though, he hung Patrick out the window only after he'd asked him repeated times to return the stolen goods. Of course, his requests were punctuated by right crosses and left hooks, which had the effect of breaking Patrick's nose, rupturing the capillaries in both his eyes, and cracking three or four of his ribs. You would've thought Patrick would come clean and return the stolen money, wouldn't you?

Well, he didn't. In fact, Danny and I were there to witness Victor's act of savagery. It was Danny, more than anyone, who'd been talking tough–up until Victor threw the first punch and Patrick's face exploded into raw hamburger meat, at which time Danny ran to the bathroom and began vomiting.

After a while it seemed that Victor was getting a bit carried away and was on the verge of dropping Patrick out the window. So I kindly asked Victor to pull him back in, a request that seemed to deeply sadden Victor but that he followed nonetheless. When Danny emerged from the bathroom, looking worried and green, I explained to him that I had called the cops and they were coming to arrest Patrick the Butler. Danny was absolutely stunned that I would have the audacity to call the police after being the architect of Patrick's assault. But, again, I explained that when the police arrived I would tell them exactly what had happened, which was what I did. And to ensure that the two young policemen fully got my meaning, I gave each of them a thousand dollars in cash, at which point they nodded, removed their nightsticks from their NYPD utility belts, and began beating the shit out of Patrick the Butler all over again.

Just then my favorite waiter, Massa, came over to take our order. I smiled and said, "So tell me, Massa, what's good–"

But Massa cut me right off and asked, "Why you take limo today? Where Ferrari? Don Johnson, right? You like Don Johnson?" to which the two waitresses exclaimed, "Ohhhh, he Don Johnson . . . he Don Johnson!"

I smiled at my Japanese admirers, who were referring to my white Ferrari Testarossa, which was the exact car that Don Johnson had driven when he played Sonny Crockett in *Miami Vice*. It was just one more example of me playing out my adolescent fantasies. *Miami Vice* had been one of my favorite shows growing up, so I had bought a white Testarossa the moment I made my first million. I was slightly embarrassed by their Don Johnson reference, so I waved the back of my hand in the air and shook my head, then I said, "So what's on the menu to–"

But Massa cut me off once more. "You James Bond too! Have Aston Martin, like Bond. He have toys in car . . . oil . . . nails!" to which the waitresses exclaimed, "Ohhh, he James Bond! He kiss-kiss bang-bang! Kiss-kiss bang-bang!"

We all broke up over that one. Massa was referring to one of the most retarded blunders I'd ever made. It happened almost a year ago, after I'd rung the register to the tune of $20 million on a new issue. I was sitting in my office with Danny, and the Ludes were just kicking in, at which point I got a bug up my ass to start spending money. I called my exotic-car dealer and bought Danny a black Rolls-Royce Corniche convertible, for $200,000, and then I bought myself a racing-green Aston Martin Virage, for $250,000. But that hadn't done the trick, and I still felt like I needed to spend more money. So my exotic-car dealer offered to turn my Aston Martin into a true James Bond car–complete with an oil slick, a radar jammer, a license plate that slid back to reveal a blinding strobe light that would stop pursuers, as well as a naildrop box that, with a flip of a switch, would litter the road with spikes or nails or tiny land mines, if I could find an arms dealer to sell them to me. The cost: $100,000. Anyway, I went for the full monty, which had the effect of drawing so much power from the car's battery that the car hadn't worked right ever since. In fact, every time I took the car out for a drive, it would conk out on me. Now it just sat in my garage, looking nice.

I said to Massa, "Thanks for the compliment, but we're in the middle of discussing business, my friend." Massa bowed dutifully, recited the specials, and took our lunch order. Then he bowed again and left.

I said to Victor, "Anyway, let's get back to the issue of financing. I'm not comfortable with Kenny's mother being the one to write you the check. I don't care if the two of you are doing business together, unrelated or not. It's a red flag, so don't do it. I'll give you the four hundred thousand in cash, but I don't want any money flowing to you from Gladys. What about your own parents? Could you give the money to them and have them write you a check?"

"My parents aren't like that," replied Victor, in a rare moment of humility. "They're simple people and they wouldn't understand. But I can work something out with some overseas accounts that I have access to in the Orient."

Danny and I exchanged covert looks. The fucking Chinaman was already talking about overseas accounts before he'd even opened the doors to his own brokerage firm? What a depraved maniac he was! There was a certain logical progression to committing crimes, and the sort of crimes Victor was referring to came at the end of things, after you'd made your money, not before. I said to Victor, "That raises a different set of flags, but they're just as red. Let me think about it for a day or two, and I'll come up with some way to get you the money. Maybe I'll have one of my ratholes lend it to you. Not themselves but through a third party. I'll figure it out, so don't worry about it."

Victor nodded. "Whatever you say, but if you need any access to my overseas accounts just let me know, okay?"

I smiled a dead smile at him, then laid the trap: "All right, I'll let you know if I do, but I don't really dabble with that sort of stuff. Anyway, the final thing I want to talk about is how you should manage Duke's trading account. There are two different ways to do it: You can trade from either the long side or the short side. And both ways have their pluses and minuses. I'm not gonna go into complete detail right now, but I'll give you the long and short of it." I paused and smiled at my own pun, which had been entirely unintended. "Anyway, if you trade from the long side, you'll make a lot more money than if you trade from the short side. When I say trading long, I mean you'll be holding large blocks of stock in Duke's trading account; you can then move the price up and make money on what you're holding. Conversely, if you're short and the stock goes up, then you're gonna lose money. And during the first year all your stocks should be going up, so you need to stay heavily long if you want to make a lot of money. I mean, if you really wanna ring the register. Now, I won't deny that it takes a little bit of balls to do that–I mean, it can be a little nerve-racking sometimes–because your brokers won't always be able to buy all the stock you're holding. So your cash has a tendency to get tied up in inventory.

"But as long as you have enough guts and, for that matter, enough confidence to see it through, then when the slow period is over you'll make a bloody fortune on the way up. You follow what I'm saying, Victor? It's not a strategy for the weak; it's a strategy for the strong, and for those with foresight." With that I raised my eyebrows high on my forehead and threw my palms up in the air, as if to say, "Are we on the same page here?" Then I waited to see if the Blockhead would pick up on the fact that I'd just given Victor the worst trading advice in the history of Wall Street. The truth was that trading long was a recipe for disaster. By holding stock in the firm's trading account, you were risking everything. Cash was king on Wall Street, and if your trading account was tied up in stock you were vulnerable to attack. In a way, it was no different than any other business. Even a plumber who overstocked his inventory would find himself running low on cash. And when his bills came due–meaning rent, telephone, payroll–he couldn't offer to pay his creditors with plumbing supplies. No, cash was king in any business, and especially in this business, where your very inventory could become worthless overnight.

The proper way to trade was from the short side, which kept you flush in cash. While it was true that you would lose money as the prices of the stocks went up, it was the equivalent of paying an insurance premium. The way I had managed the Stratton trading account, I allowed the firm to take consistent losses in the day-to-day trading, which ensured that the firm would maintain a cash-rich position and be poised to ring the register on new-issue day. In essence I lost a million dollars a month by trading short but ensured that I could make ten million a month being in the IPO business. To me, it was so obvious that I couldn't imagine anybody trading any other way.

The question was would the Blockhead and the Chinaman pick up on it–or would Victor's ego feed right into the very insanity of trading long? Even Danny, who was sharp as a tack, had never fully grasped this concept, or perhaps he had but was such a born risk-taker that he was willing to put the health of the firm on the line to make a few extra million a year. It was impossible to say.

Right on cue, Danny chimed in and said to me, "I'll tell you the truth: In the beginning I was always nervous when you held major long positions, but over time . . . I mean . . . to see all the extra money being made"–he started shaking his head, as if to reinforce his very bullshit–"well . . . it's incredible. But it definitely takes balls."

Kenny: "Yeah, we've made a fortune trading that way. That's definitely the way to do it, Vic."

How ironic, I thought. After all these years Kenny still hadn't the foggiest notion of how I'd managed to keep Stratton at the pinnacle of financial health, in spite of all its problems. I had never traded long–not even once! Except, of course, on new-issue day, when I would let the firm go heavily long for a few carefully chosen minutes, as the price of the units was flying up. But I always knew there was a massive wave of buy tickets coming in at any moment.

Victor said, "I have no problem living with risk in my life. It's what separates the men from the boys. As long as I know the stock is going up, I'd put my last dime into it. Nothing ventured, nothing gained, right?" With that, the panda smiled, and once more his eyes disappeared.

I nodded at the Chinaman. "That's about the size of it, Vic. Besides, if you ever find yourself in a bad position, I'll always be there to support you until you get back on your feet. Just look at me as your insurance policy."

We raised our glasses for another toast.

An hour later I was walking through the boardroom with mixed emotions. So far everything was going according to plan, but what of my own future? What was to become of the Wolf of Wall Street? In the end, this whole experience–this wild ride of mine–would become a distant memory, something I would tell Chandler about. I would tell her how, once upon a time, her daddy had been a true player on Wall Street, how he'd owned one of the largest brokerage firms in history, and how all these young kids–kids who called themselves Strattonites–ran around Long Island, spending obscene amounts of money on all sorts of meaningless things.

Yes, Channy, the Strattonites looked up to your daddy, and they called him King. And for that brief time, right around when you were born, your daddy was, indeed, like a king, and he and Mommy lived just like a king and queen, treated like royalty wherever they went. And now your daddy is . . . who the hell is he? Well, perhaps Daddy could show you some of his press clippings, perhaps that would explain things . . . or . . . well, perhaps not. Anyway, everything they say about your daddy is lies, Channy. All lies! The press always lies; you know that, Chandler, right? Just go ask your nana, Suzanne; she'll tell you! Oh, wait, I forgot, you haven't seen your nana in a while; she's in jail with Aunt Patricia, for money laundering. Oops!

What a dark premonition that was! *Jesus!* I took a deep breath and pushed it aside. I was thirty-one years old and already on the road to becoming a has-been. A cautionary tale! Was it even possible to be a has-been at such a young age? Perhaps I was no different than one of those child actors who grows up to be ugly and gawky. What was that redhead's name from *The Partridge Family*? Danny Bona-douche-bag or something? But wasn't it better to be a has-been than a never-was? It was hard to say, because there was another side to that coin, namely, that once you got used to something it was hard to live without it. I had been able to live without the benefit of the mighty roar for the first twenty-six years of my life, hadn't I? But now . . . well, how could I possibly live without it after it had become so much a part of me?

I took a deep breath and steeled myself. I needed to focus on the kids–the Strattonites! They were the ticket! I had a plan and I would stick to it: the slow phaseout; keeping myself behind the scenes; keeping the troops calm; keeping peace among the brokerage firms; and keeping the Depraved Chinaman at bay.

As I approached Janet's desk, I noticed she had the grim expression on her face that spelled trouble. Her eyes were open a bit wider than usual and her lips were slightly parted. She was sitting on the edge of her seat, and the moment we locked eyes she rose from her chair and headed directly for me. I wondered whether she had somehow caught wind of what was going on with the SEC. The only people who knew were Danny, Ike, and myself, but Wall Street was a funny place like that, and news had a way of traveling remarkably fast. In fact, there was an old Wall Street saying that went: "Good news travels fast, but bad news travels instantly."

She compressed her lips. "I got a call from Visual Image, and they said they need to speak to you right away. They said it was absolutely urgent they talk to you this afternoon."

"Who the fuck is Visual Image? I've never even heard of them!"

"Yes you have; they're the ones who did your wedding video, remember? You flew them down to Anguilla; there were two of them, a man and a woman. She had blond hair and he had brown. She was dressed–"

I cut Janet off. "Yeah, yeah, I remember now. I don't need a full-blown description." I shook my head in amazement at Janet's memory for detail. If I hadn't cut her off she would have told me what color panty hose the girl wore. "Who was it that called: the guy or the girl?"

"The guy. And he sounded nervous. He said that if he didn't speak to you in the next few hours, it would be a problem."

A problem? What the fuck? That made no sense! What could my wedding videographer possibly need to speak to me about that was so urgent? Could it be something that happened at my wedding? I took a moment to search my memory . . . Well, it would be highly unlikely, in spite of the fact that I had received a warning from the tiny Caribbean island of Anguilla. I had flown down three hundred of my closest friends (friends?) for an all-expenses-paid vacation at one of the finest hotels in the world: the Malliouhana. It cost me over a million dollars, and at the end of the week the island's president informed me that the only reason everyone wasn't under arrest for drug possession was because I'd given the island so much business that they felt turning a blind eye was the least they could do. But he further assured me that everyone who'd attended would be on a watch list and that if they ever decided to come back to Anguilla they had best leave their drugs behind. That was three years ago though, so this couldn't have anything to do with that–or could it?

I said to Janet, "Get the guy on the phone. I'll take it in my office." I turned and started to walk away, then over my shoulder I said, "By the way, what's his name?"

"Steve. Steve Burstein."

A few seconds later the phone on my desk beeped. I exchanged quick hellos with Steve Burstein, the president of Visual Image, a small mom-and-pop operation somewhere on the South Shore of Long Island.

Steve said in a concerned tone: "Um . . . well . . . I don't know quite how to say this to you . . . I mean . . . you were really good to my wife and me. You . . . you treated us like guests at your own wedding. You and Nadine couldn't have been any nicer to us. And it was really the nicest wedding I've ever been to and–"

I interrupted him. "Listen, Steve, I appreciate the fact that you enjoyed my wedding, but I'm kind of busy right now. Why don't you just tell me what's going on."

"Well," he replied, "there were two FBI agents in here today and they asked me for a copy of your wedding video."

And just like that, I knew my life would never be the same again.

CHAPTER 23

WALKING A FINE LINE

Nine days after I'd received that poisonous phone call from Visual Image, I was sitting in world-famous Rao's restaurant in East Harlem, engaged in a heated debate with legendary private investigator Richard Bo Dietl, known simply to his friends as Bo.

Although we were at a table for eight, there would be only one other person joining us this evening, namely, Special Agent Jim Barsini* of the FBI, who was a casual friend of Bo's and, hopefully, would soon be a casual friend of mine too. Bo had arranged this meeting, and Barsini was due to arrive in fifteen minutes.

At this particular moment, Bo was doing the talking and I was doing the listening, or, more accurately, Bo was lecturing and I was listening and grimacing. The topic was an inspired notion I'd had to try to bug the FBI, which, according to Bo, was one of the most outlandish things he'd ever heard.

Bo was saying, ". . . and that's simply not the way you go about things, Bo." Bo had this odd habit of calling his friends Bo, which I found confusing sometimes, particularly when I was Luded out. Thankfully, I was able to follow him just fine tonight, because I was sober as a judge, which seemed like the appropriate state to be in when meeting an FBI agent for the first time, especially one

---

*Name has been changed.

who I was hoping to befriend–and then subsequently gather intelligence from.

Nevertheless, I did have four Ludes in my pocket, which at this very moment were burning a hole in my gray slacks, and in the inside pocket of my navy-blue sport jacket I had an eight ball of coke, which was calling my name in a most seductive tone. But, no, I was determined to stay strong–at least until after Agent Barsini went back to wherever it was FBI agents went back to after they ate dinner, which was probably home. Originally I had planned to eat light, so as not to interfere with my upcoming high, but right now the smell of roasted garlic and home-cooked tomato sauce was bathing my olfactory nerve in a most delicious way.

"Listen, Bo," continued Bo, "getting information out of the FBI isn't difficult in a case like this. In fact, I already got some for you. But listen to me–before I tell you anything–there are certain protocols you gotta follow here or else you're gonna get your ass caught in a sling. The first is that you *don't* go around planting bugs in their fucking offices." He started shaking his head in amazement. It was something he'd been doing a lot of since we sat down fifteen minutes ago. "The second is that you don't try bribing their secretaries–or anyone else, for that matter." With that, he shook his head some more. "And you don't follow their agents around, trying to find shit out about their personal lives." This time he shook his head quickly and began rolling his eyes up in his head, the way a person does after they've just heard something that defies logic in such a dramatic way that they have to shake off the effect.

I stared out the restaurant's window to avoid Bo's blazing gaze, at which point I found myself staring right smack into the gloomy groin of East Harlem and wondering why on earth the best Italian restaurant in New York City had to pick this fucking cesspool of a neighborhood for its location. But then I reminded myself that Rao's had been in business for over a hundred years, since the late 1800s, and Harlem was a different sort of neighborhood back then.

And the fact that Bo and I were sitting alone at a table for eight was a much bigger deal than it seemed–given the fact that a dinner reservation at Rao's needed to be booked five years in advance. In truth, though, getting a reservation at this quaint little anachronism was all but impossible. All twelve of the restaurant's tables were *owned,* "condo-style," by a select handful of New Yorkers, who more than being rich were very well connected.

Physically, Rao's was no great shakes. On this particular evening, the restaurant was decorated for Christmas, which had nothing to do with the fact that it was January 14. In August, it would *still* be decorated for Christmas. That was the way of things at Rao's, where everything was reminiscent of a much simpler time, where food was served family-style, and Italian music played from a fifties-style jukebox in the corner. As the night progressed, Frankie Pellegrino, the restaurant's owner, would sing for his guests, as men of respect congregated at the bar and smoked cigars and greeted one another Mafia-style, while the women stared at them adoringly, the way they did back in the good-old days, whenever those were. And the men would rise from their chairs and bow to the women each time they went to the bathroom, the way they did back in the good-old days, whenever those were.

On any given night, half the restaurant was filled with world-class athletes, A-list movie stars, and captains of industry, while the other half was filled with real-life mobsters.

Anyway, it was Bo, not I, who was the table's well-connected *owner*, and true to this tiny restaurant's star-studded list of patrons, Bo Dietl was a man whose star was seriously on the rise. Only forty years old, Bo was a legend in the making. Back in his day, in the mid 1980s, he was one of the most highly decorated cops in NYPD history–making over seven hundred arrests, in some of New York's toughest neighborhoods, including Harlem. He had made a big name for himself cracking cases that no one else could crack, finally jumping into the national spotlight after solving one of the most heinous crimes ever committed in Harlem: the rape of a white nun by two cash-strapped crack fiends.

At first glance, though, Bo didn't look that tough, what with his boyishly handsome face, perfectly coiffed beard, and slightly thinning light brown hair, which he wore combed straight back over his roundish skull. He wasn't a huge guy–maybe five-ten, two hundred pounds–but he was broad in the chest and thick in the neck, the latter of which was the size of a gorilla's. Bo was one of the sharpest dressers in town, favoring $2,000 silk suits and heavily starched white dress shirts with French cuffs and wiseguy collars. He wore a gold watch heavy enough to do wrist curls with and a diamond pinky ring the size of an ice cube.

It was no secret that much of Bo's success when it came to cracking cases had to do with his rearing. He was born and raised in a part of Ozone Park, Queens, where he was surrounded by mobsters on one side and cops on the other. In consequence, he developed the unique ability to walk a fine line between the two–using the respect he'd garnered with local Mafia chieftains to crack cases that couldn't be cracked through traditional means. Over time, he developed a reputation as a man who kept his contacts confidential and who used the information passed along to him only toward stamping out street crime, which seemed to get under his skin more than anything else. He was loved and respected by his friends, and he was loathed and feared by his enemies.

Never one to put up with bureaucratic bullshit, Bo retired from the NYPD at thirty-five and quickly parlayed his storied reputation (and even more storied connections) into one of the fastest-growing and most well-respected private security firms in America. It was for this very reason that two years ago I had first sought out Bo and retained his services–to build and maintain a first-class security operation within Stratton Oakmont.

More than once I had called upon Bo to scare away the occasional mid-level thug who made the mistake of trying to muscle in on Stratton's operations. Just what Bo would say to these people I wasn't quite sure. All I knew was that I would make one phone call to Bo, who would then "sit the person down," at which point I would never hear from them again. (Although one time I did receive a rather nice bouquet of flowers.)

At the upper levels of the Mob there was a silent understanding, independent of Bo, that rather than trying to muscle in on Stratton's operations, it was more profitable for the bosses to send their young bucks to work for us, so they could be properly trained. Then, after a year or so, these Mafioso plants would leave quietly–almost gentlemanly, in fact–so as not to disturb Stratton's operations. Then they would open Mafia-backed brokerage firms at the behest of their masters.

Over the last two years, Bo had become involved with all aspects of Stratton's security–even investigating the companies we were taking public, making sure that we weren't getting scammed by fraudulent operators. And unlike most of his competitors, Bo Dietl and Associates wasn't coming up with the sort of generic information any computer geek could pull off LexisNexis. No, Bo's people were getting their fingernails dirty, uncovering things one would think impossible to uncover. And while there was no denying that his services didn't come cheap, what you got was value for your money.

In point of fact: Bo Dietl was the best in the business.

I was still staring out the window when Bo said to me, "What's on your mind, Bo? You're staring out that fucking window like you're gonna find some answers in the street."

I paused for a brief moment, considering whether or not I should tell him that the only reason I'd considered bugging the FBI was because of the tremendous success I'd had at bugging the SEC, which was something *he'd* inadvertently paved the way for by introducing me to the former CIA guys who sold me the bugs behind his back. One of the bugs looked like an electrical plug, and it had been sticking in a wall outlet in the conference room for over a year, drawing power from the very outlet itself, so it never ran out of batteries. It was a wonderful little contraption!

Nevertheless, I decided now was not the time to share that little secret with Bo. I said, "It's just that I'm dead serious about fighting this whole thing. I have no intention of rolling over and playing dead because some FBI agent is running around asking questions about me. I have too much at stake here, and there are too many people involved just to walk away from this. So now that your mind's at ease, tell me what you found out, okay?"

Bo nodded, but before he answered me, he picked up a large glass of single-malt scotch and threw back what had to be three or four shots, as if it were no stronger than H_2O. Then he puckered up his lips. "*Whewwwww-boy!* That's the ticket!" Finally he plowed on: "For starters, the investigation is still in its early stages, and it's all being driven by this guy Coleman, Special Agent Gregory Coleman. No one else in the office has any interest in it; they all think it's a loser. And as far as the U.S. Attorney's Office goes, they're not interested either. The AUSA on the case is a guy named Sean O'Shea, and from what I hear, he's a pretty decent guy, not a scumbag prosecutor.

"There's a lawyer named Greg O'Connell who's a good friend of mine, and he used to work with Sean O'Shea. He reached out to Sean for me, and according to Greg, Sean couldn't give a rat's ass about your case. You were right when you said they don't do a lot of securities cases out there. They do more Mob-related stuff, because they cover Brooklyn. So in that respect you're lucky. But the word on this guy Coleman is he's very dogged. He talks about you like you're some kinda star. He holds you in very high regard, and not in the way you want. It sounds like he's a bit obsessed with the whole thing."

I shook my head gravely. "Well *that's* great to fucking hear! An obsessed FBI agent! Where did he come from all of a sudden? Why now? It must have something to do with the SEC settlement offer. Those bastards are double-dealing me."

"Calm down, Bo. It's not as bad as it seems. This has nothing to do with the SEC. It's just that Coleman is intrigued with you. Probably more to do with all the press you're getting than anything else, this whole Wolf of Wall Street thing." He started shaking his head. "All those stories about the drugs and the hookers and the big spending. It's pretty intoxicating stuff for a young FBI agent making forty grand a year. And this guy Coleman is young, in his early thirties, I think; not much older than you. So just think of the harsh reality of this guy looking at your tax return and seeing that you make more in an hour than he makes in a year. And then he sees your wife prancing across the TV screen."

Bo shrugged. "Anyway, the point I'm trying to make is that you should try keeping a low profile for a while. Maybe take an extended vacation or something, which makes perfect sense considering your SEC settlement. When is that gonna be announced?"

"I'm not a hundred percent sure," I replied. "Probably in a week or two."

Bo nodded. "Well, the good news is that Coleman's got a reputation for being a pretty straight shooter. He's not like the agent you're gonna meet tonight, who's a real fucking wild man. I mean, if you had Jim Barsini on your tail–well, it would be very bad news. He's already shot two or three people, one of them with a high-powered rifle after the perp had his hands up in the air. It was one of those things where he said, 'FBI–*bang!*–Freeze! Put your hands in the air!' You get the picture, Bo?"

Jesus Christ! I thought. My only salvation in this thing was a whacked-out FBI agent with an itchy trigger finger?

Bo plowed on: "So it ain't all bad, Bo. This guy Coleman isn't the sort of guy who's gonna fabricate evidence against you and go around threatening your Strattonites with life sentences, and he's not the sort of guy who's gonna terrorize your wife. But–"

I cut Bo off with great concern in my voice. "What do you mean, terrorize my wife? How can he drag Nadine into this? She hasn't done anything, except spend a lot of money." The mere thought of Nadine getting caught up in this sent my spirits plunging to unprecedented levels.

Bo's voice took on the tone of a psychiatrist talking a patient off the ledge of a ten-story building. "Now, calm down, Bo. Coleman's not a harassing sort of guy. All I was trying to say is that it's not unheard of for an agent to put pressure on a husband by going after his wife. But that doesn't apply in your situation, because Nadine's not involved in any of your business dealings, right?"

"Of course not!" I replied with great certainty, and then I quickly rifled through my business dealings to see if what I'd just said was true. I came to the sad conclusion that it wasn't. "The truth is I've done a couple a trades in her name, but nothing so bad. I'd say her liability is pretty much zero. But I'd never let it come to that, Bo. I'd sooner plead guilty and let them put me away for twenty years than let them indict my wife."

Bo nodded slowly and replied, "As would any real man. But my point is that they know that too, and they might view that as a point of weakness. Again, we're getting way ahead of ourselves here. The investigation is in its very early stages, more a fishing expedition than anything else right now. If you're lucky, Coleman will stumble onto something else . . . an unrelated case . . . and he'll lose interest in you. Just be careful, Bo, and you'll be fine."

I nodded. "You can count on it."

"Good. Well, Barsini should be here in a second, so let's go over a few ground rules. First, don't bring up your case. It's not that kinda meeting. It's just a bunch of friends shooting the shit. No talk of investigations or anything like that. You start by developing a casual friendship with him. Remember, we're not trying to get this guy to give you info he's not supposed to give you." He shook his head for emphasis. "The truth is that if Coleman *really* has a bug up his ass for you, there's nothing Barsini can do. It's only if Coleman doesn't have anything on you and he's just being a prick–then Barsini could say, 'Hey, I know the guy and he's not so bad, so why don't you cut him a break?' Remember, Bo, the last thing you want to be accused of is trying to corrupt an FBI agent. They'll throw you in jail for a long time for that."

Then Bo raised his eyebrows, and added, "But, on the flip side, there's some information that we *can* get from Barsini. See, the truth is that there are some things that Coleman might *want* you to know, and he can use Barsini as a conduit for that. Who knows? You might actually strike up a friendship with Barsini. He's a pretty good guy, actually. He's a crazy bastard but, then again, which of us isn't, right?"

I nodded in agreement. "Well, I'm not the judgmental type, Bo. I hate judgmental people. I think they're the worst sort, don't you?"

Bo smirked. "Right. I figured you'd feel that way. Trust me when I tell you that Barsini is not your typical FBI type. Maybe you could invite him on your yacht or something, especially if this whole Coleman thing turns out to be no big deal. Having a friend in the FBI is never a bad thing."

I smiled at Bo and resisted the urge to jump across the table and plant a wet kiss on his lips. Bo was a true warrior, an asset so valuable that it couldn't be calculated. How much was I paying him, between Stratton and personal? Over half a million a year, maybe more. And he was worth every penny. I asked, "What's this guy know about me? Does he know I'm under investigation?"

Bo shook his head. "Absolutely not. I told him very little about you. Just that you were a good client of mine as well as a good friend. And both of those statements are true–which is why I'm doing this, Bo, out of friendship."

In lockstep, I replied, "And don't think I don't appreciate it, Bo. I won't forget–"

Bo cut me off. "Here he is now." He gestured toward the window, to a fortyish man entering the restaurant. He was about six-two, two-twenty, and was sporting an extreme crew cut. He had gruff, handsome features, piercing brown eyes, and an incredibly square jaw. In fact, he looked like he belonged on a recruiting poster for a right-wing paramilitary group.

"Big Bo!" exclaimed the world's least likely FBI agent. "*Myyyyyy* man! What the fuck are you up to, and where the fuck did you find this restaurant? I mean–Jesus Christ, Bo–I could get some target practice in this neck of the woods!" He cocked his head to the side and raised his eyebrows, as if to imply the very logic of his observation. Then he added, "But, hey, that's not my concern. I only shoot bank robbers, right?" That last insane comment was directed at me, accompanied by a warm smile, to which Special Agent Barsini then added, "And you must be Jordan. Well it's nice to meet you, bud! Bo told me you got a kick-ass boat–or ship, actually–and he said you like to scuba dive. Let me shake your hand." He extended his hand to me. I quickly reached for it and was surprised to find that his hand was nearly twice the size of my own. After nearly pulling my arm out of my shoulder socket, he finally released me from his clutches and we all sat down.

I was about to continue the subject of scuba diving, but I never got the chance. Special Agent Madman was immediately off on a rant. "I'll tell you," he said with piss and vinegar, "this neighborhood's a real fucking cesspool." He shook his head in disgust and leaned back in his chair and crossed his legs, which had the effect of exposing the enormous revolver on his waist.

"Well, Bo," said Bo to Barsini, "you got no argument from me in that department. Know how many people I locked up when I worked this neighborhood? You wouldn't believe it if I told you. Half of them were the same fucking people over again! I remember this one guy, he was the size of a fucking gorilla. He snuck up behind me with a garbage-can lid and smashed me over the top of the head, nearly turning my lights out. Then he went after my partner, and he knocked him out cold."

I raised my eyebrows and said, "So what happened to the guy? Did you catch him?"

"Yeah, of course I did," replied Bo, almost insulted. "He didn't knock me out cold; he only fazed me. I came to while he was still whaling on my partner, and I took the lid from him and pounded him over the head for a few minutes. But he had one of those extra-thick skulls, like a fucking coconut." Bo shrugged, then finished his story with: "He lived."

"Well that's a damn fucking shame," replied the federal agent. "You're too soft, Bo. I woulda ripped out the guy's trachea and fed it to him. You know, there's a way to do that without even getting a drop a blood on your hands. It's all in the snap of the wrist. It makes a sort of popping sound, like"–the federal agent pressed the tip of his tongue to the roof of his mouth and compressed his cheeks and then released–*"POP!"*

Just then the restaurant's owner, Frank Pellegrino–also known as Frankie No, because he was always saying no to people who asked him for a table—came over to introduce himself to Agent Barsini. Frank was dressed so smartly, and matched so perfectly, and was so freshly pressed, that I would've sworn he'd just emerged from a dry cleaner. He wore a dark-blue three-piece suit with thick chalk-gray pinstripes. From out of his left breast pocket a white hanky debouched perfectly, flawlessly, brilliantly, in the sort of way only a man like Frankie could pull off. He looked rich and sixtyish, trim and handsome, and he had a unique gift of being able to make every last person at Rao's feel like they were a guest in his own home.

"You must be Jim Barsini," Frank Pellegrino said warmly. He extended his hand. "Bo told me all about you. Welcome to Rao's, Jim."

With that, Barsini popped out of his chair and began pulling Frank's arm out of its socket. I watched in fascination as Frank's perfectly coiffed grayish hair stayed stock-still while the rest of him shook like a rag doll.

"Jesus, Bo," said Frank to the real Bo, "this guy's got a handshake like a grizzly bear! He reminds me of . . ." and with that, Frank Pellegrino began expounding on one of his many tales of men with no necks.

I immediately tuned out, smiling every so often, while I quickly settled on the primary task at hand, which was: What could I possibly say, do, or, for that matter, give to Special Agent Barsini to entice him to tell Special Agent Coleman to leave me the fuck alone? The easiest thing to do, of course, would be to simply bribe Barsini. He didn't seem like a guy of such high moral standing, did he? Although perhaps this whole soldier-of-fortune thing would make him incorruptible, as if taking money for greed's sake would somehow dishonor him. How much did they pay an FBI agent? I wondered. Fifty grand a year? How much scuba diving could a man do on that? Not a lot. Besides, there was scuba diving and then there was scuba diving. I'd be willing to pay a pretty penny to have a guardian angel within the FBI, wouldn't I?

For that matter, what would I be willing to pay Agent Coleman to lose my number forever? A million? Certainly! Two million? Of course! Two million was chump change in the face of a federal indictment and the possibility of financial ruin!

Eh, who was I kidding? These thoughts were all pie in the sky. In fact, a place like Rao's served as a clear reminder that the government could never be trusted for the long term. It was only three or four decades ago when mobsters did whatever they wanted: They paid off the police force; they paid off politicians; they paid off judges; for Chrissake, they even paid off schoolteachers! But then came the Kennedys, who were mobsters themselves, and they viewed the Mob as competition. So they reneged on all the deals–all those wonderful quid pro quos–and . . . well, the rest was history.

". . . so that was the way he settled it back then," said Frankie No, finally completing his yarn. "Although he didn't actually kidnap the chef; he just held him hostage for a while."

With that, everyone, including me, started laughing hysterically, in spite of the fact that I'd missed ninety percent of what he'd said. But at Rao's, missing a story was merely incidental. After all, you kept hearing the same handful of stories over and over again.

CHAPTER 24

PASSING THE TORCH

George Campbell, my tongueless chauffeur, had just brought the limousine to a smooth, gentle stop at the side entrance to Stratton Oakmont, when he literally knocked me out of my seat by breaking his self-imposed vow of silence and asking, "Wha's gonna happen now, Mr. Belfort?"

Well, well, well! I thought. It's about time the old devil broke down and said a few words to me! And while his question might have seemed a bit vague, he had actually hit the nail right on the head. After all, in a little more than seven hours, at four p.m., I would be standing before the boardroom, giving a farewell speech to an army of extremely worried Strattonites, all of whom, like George, had to be questioning what the future had in store for them, financially and otherwise.

I had no doubt that in the days to come there would be many questions burning in the minds of my Strattonites. Questions like:

What would happen now that Danny was running the show? Would they still have desks in six months? And if they did, would they be treated fairly? Or would he favor his old friends and a few of the key brokers he dropped Ludes with? And what fate awaited the brokers who'd been friendlier with Kenny than with Danny? Would they be punished for that friendship? Or, if not punished, treated like second-class citizens? Was it possible for Broker Disneyland to endure? Or would Stratton slowly devolve into a run-of-the-mill brokerage firm, no better or worse than anyplace else?

I chose not to share any of those thoughts with George, and all I said was, "You have nothing to worry about, George. Whatever happens, you'll always be taken care of. Janet and I will get an office close by, and there's a thousand things Nadine and I need you for." I smiled broadly and made my tone very upbeat. "Just think, one day you'll be chauffeuring Nadine and me to Chandler's wedding. Can you imagine?"

George nodded and smiled broadly, revealing his world-class choppers, and he humbly replied, "I like my job very much, Mr. Belfort. You're the best boss I ever have. Mrs. Belfort too. Everybody love you two. It's sad you gotta leave here. It won't be the same no more. Danny ain't like you. He don't treat people good. People gonna leave."

I was too baffled over the first half of George's statement to even focus on the second half. Had he actually said he liked his job? And that he *loved* me? Well, admittedly, the whole love thing was a figure of speech, but there was no denying that George had just said he loved his job and respected me as a boss. It seemed ironic after everything I'd put him through: the hookers . . . the drugs . . . the midnight rides through Central Park with strippers . . . the gym bags full of cash that I'd had him pick up from Elliot Lavigne.

Yet, on the other hand, I had never disrespected him, had I? Even in my darkest and most decadent hours, I'd always made an effort to be respectful to George. While it was true that I'd had some very bizarre thoughts about him, I had never shared them with another living soul, except, of course, the Duchess, who was my wife, which made her exempt. And even then, it was all in good fun. I was not a prejudiced man. In fact, what Jew in their right mind could be? We were the most persecuted people on earth.

All at once I found myself feeling bad that I had ever questioned George's loyalty. He was a good man. A decent man. Who was I to read a thousand and one things into everything he said or, for that matter, didn't say?

With a warm smile, I said, "Truth is, George, no one can predict the future, certainly not myself. Who's to say what becomes of Stratton Oakmont? I guess only time will tell.

"Anyway, I remember when you first came to work for me, you used to try to open the limo door for me. You'd run around the side and try to beat me to it." I chuckled at the memory. "It used to drive you crazy. Anyway, the reason I never let you open the door for me was because I respected you too much to just sit in the back of the limo and pretend like I had a broken arm or something. I always thought of it as an insult to you."

Then I added, "But since today's my last day, why don't you open up the door for me, just once, and make believe you're a real fucking limo driver! Pretend like you're working for a fat-ass WASP. You can escort me into the boardroom. In fact, you might actually get a kick out of Danny's morning meeting. He should be giving it right now."

". . . and the study sampled more than ten thousand men," said Danny over the loudspeaker, "following their sexual habits for more than five years. I think you're gonna be absolutely shocked when I tell you some of the findings." With that, he pursed his lips, nodded his head, and began pacing back and forth, as if to say, "Prepare to hear the truly depraved nature of the male animal."

Jesus Christ! I thought. I'm not even gone yet and he's already running amok! I turned to George and took a moment to gauge his reaction, but he didn't seem that shocked. He had his head tipped to the side and a look on his face that so much as said, "I can't wait to find out how this whole thing relates to stocks!"

"You see," continued Danny, wearing a gray pinstripe suit and phony WASP glasses, "what the study found is that ten percent of the entire male population are stone-cold faggots." And here he paused to let the full implication of his words sink in.

Here comes another lawsuit! I looked around the room . . . and I saw a lot of confused looks, as if everyone was trying to make heads or tails of what he was saying. There were a few isolated snickers but no outright laughter.

Apparently, Danny wasn't pleased with the crowd's response—or lack thereof—so he plowed on with relish: "I say again," continued the man the SEC considered the lesser of two evils, "the study found that ten percent of the male population takes it up the ass! Yes, ten percent are fudge-packers! It's a huge number! Huge! All those men taking it up the Hershey Highway! Sucking cock! And–"

Danny was forced to give up his rant as the boardroom quickly degenerated into a state of pandemonium. The Strattonites began hooting and howling and clapping and cheering. Half the room was now standing; many were exchanging high-fives. But toward the front, in the section where the sales assistants were concentrated, no one was standing. All I could see were a bunch of long blond manes tilted at extreme angles, as the young females leaned over in their chairs and whispered in one another's ears, shaking their heads in amazement.

Just then George said in a confused tone, "I don' understand. What's this gotta do with the stock market? Why's he talkin' 'bout gay people?"

I shrugged my shoulders and said, "It's complicated, George, although there really is no reason other than that he's trying to create a common enemy, kind of like Hitler did in the thirties." And it's only by sheer coincidence, I thought, that he's not bashing black people right now. That very thought inspired me to add, "Anyway, you don't have to listen to this shit. Why don't you come back at the end of the day, around four-thirty, okay?"

George nodded and walked away, more nervous than ever, no doubt.

As I stood there, watching the morning riot, I couldn't help but wonder why Danny always distilled his meetings down to sex. Obviously, he was looking for a few cheap laughs, but there were other ways to get them, ways that didn't interfere with getting the hidden message across. The hidden message being that, in spite of everything, Stratton Oakmont was a legitimate brokerage firm trying to make its clients money–and the only reason it *wasn't* making its clients money was because of an evil conspiracy of short-sellers, who plagued the markets, like locusts, spreading vicious rumors about Stratton Oakmont and any other honest brokerage firm that stood in their way. And, of course, also embedded in that message was the fact that one day, in the not-so-distant future, the fundamental value of all these companies would come shining through, and the stocks would come roaring back, rising up like a phoenix amid the ashes, at which time all Stratton's clients would make a fortune.

I had explained this to Danny on numerous occasions, how

deep down all human beings (save a handful of sociopaths) were possessed with a subconscious desire to do the right thing. That was why a subliminal message was supposed to be embedded within each meeting–that when they smiled and dialed and ripped people's eyeballs out, they were fulfilling not only their own hedonistic desires of wealth and peer recognition but also their subconscious desire to do the right thing. Then and only then could you motivate them to achieve goals they had never dreamed themselves capable of.

Just then, Danny extended his arms out to the side, and slowly the room began to quiet down. He said, "Okay, now here's the truly interesting part, or, should I say, the disturbing part. See, if ten percent of all men are closet homosexuals, and there are one thousand men sitting in this room, that means that camping out within our midst are one hundred homos, looking to butt-fuck us every time we turn our backs!"

All at once heads began turning suspiciously. Even the little blond sales assistants were looking around–casting suspicious gazes from their heavily made-up orbital sockets. There was a low-level murmur in the room, which I couldn't quite make out. But the message was clear: "Find 'em and lynch 'em!"

I watched with great anticipation as a thousand necks craned this way and that . . . accusatory glances were thrown around the room by the hundreds . . . young, toned arms extended in all directions, each one with a pointed finger on the end of it. Then came some random screaming of names:

"Teskowitz* is a homo!"

"O'Reilly's* a fucking queer! Stand up, O'Reilly!"

"What about Irv and Scott*?" two Strattonites screamed in unison.

"Yeah, Scott and Irv! Scott blew Irv!"

But after a minute of finger-pointing and some not-so-baseless accusations against Scott and Irv, no one had come clean. So Danny lifted his arms once more and asked for quiet. "Listen," he said accusingly, "I know who some of you are, and there are two ways we can do this: the easy way or the hard way. Now, look: Everybody knows Scott blew Irv, and you didn't see Scott losing his job over it, did you?"

---

*Name has been changed.

From somewhere in the boardroom came the defensive voice of Scott: "I didn't blow Irv! It's just–"

Danny cut him off with a booming voice over the loudspeakers: "Enough, Scott, enough! The more you deny it, the more guilty you seem. So drop it! I just feel sorry for your wife and kids to have to be shamed by you like that." Danny shook his head in disgust and then turned away from Scott. "Anyway," continued Stratton's new CEO, "that heinous act had more to do with power than sex. And Irv has now proved to us that he's a true man of power–getting one of the junior brokers to blow him. So the whole act is exempt, and Scott is forgiven.

"Now that I've shown you how tolerant I am of that sort of behavior, isn't there one true man among you who has the balls–and, for that matter, the common fucking decency–to stand up and show themselves?"

Out of nowhere, a young Strattonite with a weak chin and an even weaker sense of judgment stood up and said in a loud, forthright voice, "I'm gay, and I'm proud of it!" And the boardroom went wild. In a matter of seconds, objects were flying in his direction like lethal projectiles. Then came hisses and catcalls, and then screams:

"You fucking homo! Get the fuck out of here!"

"Tar and feather the cocksucker!"

"Watch your drinks! He's gonna try to date-rape you!"

Well, I thought, this morning's meeting was officially over, called early on account of insanity. And what, if anything, had this meeting accomplished? I wasn't quite sure, other than it painted a truly grim picture of what was in store for Stratton Oakmont–starting tomorrow.

Why should I be surprised?

An hour later I was sitting behind my desk and using those five words to console myself, as I listened to Mad Max go ballistic on Danny and me over my buyout agreement. In short, the agreement called for Stratton to pay me $1 million a month for fifteen years, with most of it being paid under the terms of a noncompete agreement, meaning I was agreeing not to compete with Stratton in the brokerage business.

Nevertheless, in spite of the agreement raising a few eyebrows, it wasn't actually illegal (on the face of it), and I had been successfully able to bully the firm's lawyers into approving it although the collective wisdom was that while the agreement was legal, it didn't quite pass the smell test.

At this particular moment there was a fourth person sitting in my office, namely Wigwam, who so far hadn't really said much. But that was no surprise. After all, Wigwam had spent the better part of his youth eating dinner at my house, so he was acutely aware of Mad Max's capabilities.

Mad Max was saying, ". . . and you two morons are gonna get your tits caught in a wringer over this one. A hundred-eighty-million-dollar buyout? It's like pissing right in the SEC's face. I mean–Jesus fucking Christ! When are you two gonna learn?"

I shrugged. "Calm down, Dad. It's not as bad as it seems. It's a bitter pill I'm being forced to swallow, and the hundred eighty million serves as lubrication."

With a bit too much glee, Danny added, "Max, you and I are going to be working together for a long time, so why don't we just chalk this one up to experience, eh? After all, it's your own son who's getting the money! What could be so bad?"

Mad Max spun on his heel and stared Danny down. He took a world-class pull from his cigarette and puckered his lips into a tiny O. With a mighty exhale, he focused the smoke stream into a tight laser beam a half inch in diameter, and he projected it at Danny's smiling face with the force of a Civil War cannon. Then, with Danny still enveloped in his smoke cloud, he said, "Let me tell you something, Porush. Just because my son is leaving tomorrow, that doesn't mean I'm gonna show you any newfound respect. Respect has to be earned, and if this morning's meeting is any indication, maybe I should just go to the fucking unemployment office right now. Do you know how many laws you broke with that cockamamy routine of yours? I'm just waiting for a phone call from that fat bastard, Dominic Barbara. That's who that young fruitcake is gonna call with this shit."

Then he turned to me and said, "And why did you fashion this buyout agreement as a noncompete? How can you compete if you're already barred?" He took another pull from his cigarette. "It's you and that bastard Gaito who cooked up this crooked scheme. It's a fucking travesty, and I refuse to be a part of it." With that, Mad Max headed for the door.

"Two things, Dad, before you go," I said, holding up my hand.

With a hiss: "What?"

"First, the firm's lawyers all approved the agreement. And the only reason it's a hundred eighty million is because the noncompete has to be written off over fifteen years so we don't lose the full tax benefit. Stratton's paying me a million dollars a month, so fifteen years at a million a month is one hundred eighty million dollars."

"Spare me the quick math," he snapped. "I'm unimpressed. And as far as the tax code goes, I'm well aware of it, as well as your and Gaito's blatant disregard for it. So don't try snowing me, Mister Man. Anything else?"

Casually, I added, "We need to move tonight's dinner to six o'clock. Nadine wants to bring Chandler along so you and Mom can see her." I crossed my fingers and waited for the name *Chandler* to work its happy magic on Mad Max, whose face immediately began to soften at the mention of his only grandchild.

With a great smile and a slight British accent, Sir Max said, "Ohhh, what a wonderful surprise! Your mother will be thrilled to see Chandler. Well, righty-o, then! I'll call Mom and tell her the good news." Sir Max exited the office with a smile on his face and a bounce in his step.

I looked at Danny and Wigwam and shrugged. "There are certain key words that calm him down, and *Chandler*'s the most surefire of all. Anyway, you gotta learn them if you don't want him to have a heart attack right in the office."

"Your father's a good man," said Danny, "and nothing's gonna change for him around here. I look at him like my own father, and he can say and do whatever he wants until he's ready to retire."

I smiled, appreciative of Danny's loyalty.

"But more important than your father," he continued, "I'm already having problems with Duke Securities. In spite of Victor being in business for only three days, he's already spreading rumors that Stratton's on the way out and that Duke is the next great thing. He hasn't tried stealing any brokers yet, but that's coming next, I'm sure."

I looked at Wigwam. "What do you have to say about all this?"

"I don't think Victor's much of a threat," replied Wigwam. "Duke is small; they have nothing to offer anyone. They don't have any deals of their own or any capital to speak of, and they don't have a track record. I think Victor just has a big mouth he can't control."

I smiled at Wigwam, who had just confirmed what I already knew–that he was not a wartime consigliere and would be of little help to Danny in matters like these. In warm tones, I said, "You're mistaken, buddy. You got the whole thing backward. See, if Victor's smart, he'll realize he has everything to offer his new recruits. His greatest power is actually in his size–or lack of size, I should say. The truth is that at Stratton it's difficult for the cream to rise to the top; there're so many people in the way. So unless you know someone in management, you could be the sharpest guy in the world and you're still gonna be blocked from advancing, or at least advancing quickly.

"But at Duke, that doesn't exist. Any sharp guy can walk in there and write his own ticket. That's the reality. It's one of the advantages a small company has over a big company, and not just in this industry, in any industry. On the other hand, we have stability on our side and we have a track record. People don't worry about getting their paychecks on payday, and they know there's always another new issue around the corner. Victor's gonna try to undermine those things, which is why he's spreading the sorts of rumors he is right now." I shrugged my shoulders. "Anyway, I'll address that in this afternoon's meeting, and it's something *you,* Danny, need to start reinforcing during your own meetings, if you can get past all the homo-bashing shit. A lot of this is gonna be a war of propaganda–although three months from now it'll be a moot point and Victor'll be licking his wounds." I smiled confidently. "So, what else?"

"Some of the smaller firms are taking potshots at us," said Wigwam, in his usual glum tone. "Trying to steal a few deals, a broker here and there. I'm sure it'll pass."

"It'll pass only if you *make it* pass," I snapped. "Let word leak out that we're gonna sue any Stratton spin-off that tries stealing brokers. Our new policy is gonna be a heart for an eye." I looked at Danny and said, "Anybody else receive a grand-jury subpoena?"

Danny shook his head no. "Not that I'm aware of, at least not in the boardroom. So far it's just me, you, and Kenny. I don't think anyone in the boardroom knows there's an investigation."

"Well," I said, losing confidence daily, "there's still a good shot the whole thing is a fishing expedition. I should know something soon. I'm just waiting on Bo."

After a few moments of silence, Wigwam said, "By the way, Madden signed the escrow agreement and gave me back the stock certificate, so you can stop worrying about that."

Danny said, "I *told* you Steve's head is in the right place."

I resisted the urge to tell Danny that, as of late, Steve had been bashing him at unprecedented levels, saying Danny was incapable of running Stratton and I should focus more of my attention on helping him, Steve, build Steve Madden Shoes, which was showing greater potential than ever. Sales were growing at fifty percent a month–a month!–and they were still accelerating. But from an operational perspective, Steve was in way over his head, with manufacturing and distribution lagging far behind sales. In consequence, the company was getting a bad reputation with the department stores for delivering its shoes late. At Steve's urging, I'd been seriously considering moving my office to Woodside, Queens, where Steve Madden Shoes kept its corporate headquarters. Once there, I would share an office with Steve, and he would focus on the creative side and I would focus on the business side.

But all I said was, "I'm not saying Steve's head is in the wrong place. But now that we have the stock, it'll make it that much easier for him to do the right thing. Money makes people do strange things, Danny. Just have patience; you'll find out soon enough."

At one p.m. I called Janet in for a pep talk. Over the last few days she had been looking very upset. Today she seemed on the verge of tears.

"Listen," I said in a tone a father would use with a daughter, "there's a lot to be thankful for, sweetie. I'm not saying you don't have grounds to be upset, but you have to look at this as a new beginning, not an end. We're still young. Maybe we'll take it easy for a few months, but after that it'll be full steam ahead." I smiled warmly. "Anyway, for now we'll work out of the house, which is perfect, because I consider you a part of my family."

Janet began snuffling back tears. "I know. It's . . . it's just that I was here since the beginning, and I watched you build this from nothing. It was like watching a miracle happen. It was the first time I ever felt"–loved? I thought–"I don't know. When you walked me down . . . like a father would . . . I . . ." and with that, Janet broke down, crying hysterically.

Oh, Jesus! I thought. What had I done wrong? My goal had

been to console her, and now she was crying. I needed to call the Duchess! She was an expert at this sort of thing. Perhaps she could rush down here and take Janet home, although that would take too long.

Having no choice, I walked over to Janet and hugged her gently. With great tenderness, I said, "There's nothing wrong with crying, but don't forget that there's a lot to look forward to. Ultimately, Stratton's gonna fold, Janet; it's only a question of when; but since we're leaving *now,* we'll always be remembered as a success." I smiled and made my tone more upbeat. "Anyway, Nadine and I are having dinner tonight with my parents, and we're bringing Channy along. I want you to come too, okay?"

Janet smiled–smiled at the thought of seeing Chandler–and I couldn't help but wonder what that said about the state of our own lives, when only the purity and innocence of an infant could bring us peace.

I was fifteen minutes into my farewell speech when it dawned on me that I was giving the eulogy at my own funeral. But on the brighter side, I also had the unique opportunity of witnessing the reactions of all those attending my burial.

And just look at them sitting there, hanging on my every word! So many rapt expressions . . . so many eager eyes . . . so many well-formed torsos leaning forward in their seats. Look at those wildly adoring stares from the sales assistants with their lusty blond manes and their delectably plunging necklines and, of course, their incredibly loamy loins. Perhaps I should be planting subliminal suggestions deep inside their minds–that every last one of them should burn with the insatiable desire to blow me and then swallow every last drop of my very manhood, for the rest of their natural lives.

Christ, what a fucking pervert I was! Even now, in the middle of my own farewell speech, my mind was double-tracking wildly. My lips were moving up and down, as I went about the process of thanking the Strattonites for five years of undying loyalty and admiration, yet I still found myself questioning whether or not I should've banged more of the sales assistants. What did that say about me? Did it make me weak? Or was it only natural to want to bang them all? After all, what was the point of having the *power* if you didn't use it to get laid? In truth, I hadn't exploited that aspect of the power as much as I could have, or at least not to the extent Danny had! Would I come to regret that one day? Or maybe I'd done the right thing? The mature thing! The responsible thing!

All these bizarre thoughts were roaring through my head with the ferocity of an F-5 tornado, while self-serving words of wisdom gushed out of my mouth in torrents, without the slightest bit of conscious effort. And then I realized that my mind wasn't actually double-tracking (which it always did), but it was triple-tracking, which was truly fucking bizarre.

On track three there was an internal monologue, questioning the decadent nature of track two, which was focusing on the pros and cons of getting blown by the sales assistants. Meanwhile, track one was humming along uninterrupted, as my words to the Strattonites came tumbling from my lips like tiny pearls of self-serving wisdom, and the words were coming from . . . where? Perhaps from the part of the brain that works independently of conscious direction . . . or maybe the words were pouring out from sheer force of habit. After all, I'd given how many meetings over the last five years? . . . Two a day for five years . . . So with three hundred working days in a year, it translated into 1,500 working days, times two meetings per day, which equaled 3,000 meetings in total, minus whatever meetings Danny had given, which were probably ten percent of the total, subtracted from the gross number of 3,000 meetings, and the number 2,700 came into my mind just like that, but the tiny pearls of self-serving wisdom had continued tumbling from my lips as I did the math . . .

. . . and when I snapped back into the moment, I found myself explaining how the investment-banking firm of Stratton Oakmont was sure to survive–*sure to survive!*–because it was bigger than any one person and bigger than any one thing. And then I felt the urge to steal a line from FDR–who in spite of having been a Democrat, still seemed like a reasonably okay guy, although I'd recently been informed that his wife was a dyke–and I began explaining to the Strattonites how there was nothing to fear but fear itself.

It was at this point that I felt compelled to reemphasize how Danny was more than capable of running the firm, especially with someone as sharp as Wigwam at his side. But, alas, I still found myself looking at a thousand rolled eyeballs and an equal number of gravely shaking heads.

So now I felt it necessary to cross over the line of good judgment. "Listen, everyone: The fact that I'm being barred from the securities industry doesn't stop me from giving Danny advice. I mean–really! Not only is it legal for me to give Danny advice, but I can also give advice to Andy Greene, Steve Sanders, the owners of Biltmore and Monroe Parker, and, for that matter, to anyone else in this boardroom who's interested in hearing it. And just so you know, Danny and I have a tradition of eating breakfast and lunch together, and it's a tradition we have no intention of breaking just because of some ridiculous settlement I was forced to make with the SEC–a settlement that I made only because I knew that it would ensure Stratton's survival for the next hundred years!"

And with that came thunderous applause. I looked around the room. Ahhhh, such adoration! Such love for the Wolf of Wall Street! Until I locked eyes with Mad Max, who seemed to be blowing steam out of his fucking ears. What was he so fucking concerned about, anyway? Everybody else was eating this shit up! How come he couldn't simply join in the cheer? I resisted the urge to draw the obvious conclusion that my father was reacting differently because he was the only person in the boardroom who actually gave a shit about me and he was somewhat concerned at watching his son jump off a regulatory cliff.

For the sake of Mad Max, I added, "Now, of course, this will only be advice, and by the very definition of the word it means that my suggestions don't have to be followed!" to which Danny screamed from the side of the boardroom: "Yes, that's true, but why on earth would anyone in their right mind not follow JB's advice?"

Once again, thunderous applause! It spread through the boardroom like the Ebola virus, and soon the entire room was on its feet, giving the wounded Wolf his third standing ovation of the afternoon. I held up my hand for quiet, and I caught a pleasant glimpse of Carrie Chodosh, one of Stratton's few female brokers, who also happened to be one of my favorites.

Carrie was in her mid-thirties, which at Stratton made her a virtual antique. Nevertheless, she was still a looker. She'd been one of Stratton's first brokers–coming to me when she was flat broke, on the balls of her perfect ass. At the time, she was three months behind on her rent, and her Mercedes was being chased by a repo truck. You see, Carrie was another in a long line of beautiful women who had made the sad mistake of marrying the wrong man. After a ten-year marriage, her ex-husband refused to pay her a dime in child support.

It was a perfect segue, I thought, into Duke Securities and then into broaching the possibility of an FBI investigation. Yes, better to allude to the FBI now, to almost *predict* an investigation, as if the Wolf had seen it coming all along and had already prepared himself to fend off the attack.

Once more I held up my hand for quiet. "Listen, everyone–I'm not gonna lie to you here. Settling with the SEC was one of the toughest decisions I've ever made. But I knew that Stratton would endure no matter what. See, what makes Stratton so special, what makes it so unstoppable, is that it's not just a place where people come to work. And it's not just a business looking to turn a profit. Stratton is an idea! And by the very nature of being an idea it can't be contained, nor can it be quashed by a two-year investigation at the hands of a bunch of bozo regulators, who froze to death in our conference room and thought nothing of spending millions of taxpayer dollars to embark on one of the biggest witch hunts since the Salem witch trials!

"The very idea of Stratton is that it doesn't matter what family you were born into, or what schools you went to, or whether or not you were voted most likely to succeed in your high-school yearbook. The idea of Stratton is that when you come here and step into the boardroom for the first time, you start your life anew. The very moment you walk through the door and pledge your loyalty to the firm, you become part of the family, and you become a Strattonite."

I took a deep breath and pointed in Carrie's direction. "Now, everybody here knows Carrie Chodosh, right?"

The boardroom responded with hooting and howling and catcalling.

I raised my hand and smiled. "Okay, that was very nice. In case any of you weren't aware of it, Carrie was one of Stratton's first brokers, one of the original eight. And when we think of Carrie, we think of her the way she is today–a beautiful woman who drives a brand-new Mercedes; who lives in the finest condo complex on

Long Island; who wears three-thousand-dollar Chanel suits and six-thousand-dollar Dolce and Gabbana dresses; who spends her winters vacationing in the Bahamas and her summers in the Hamptons; you know her as someone who has a bank account with God only knows how much in it"–probably nothing, if I had to guess, since that was the Stratton way–"and, of course, everyone knows Carrie as one of the highest-paid female executives on Long Island, on pace to make over $1.5 million this year!"

Then I told them the state of Carrie's life when she came to Stratton and right on cue, the lovely Carrie responded in a loud, forthright voice: "I'll always love you, Jordan!" at which point the boardroom went wild once more, and I received my fourth standing ovation.

I bowed my head in thanks, then after a good thirty seconds I asked for quiet. As the last of the Strattonites retook their seats, I said, "Understand that Carrie's back was to the wall; she had a small child to worry about and a mountain of bills crashing down on her. She couldn't allow herself to fail! Her son, Scott, who happens to be an incredible kid, will soon be attending one of the finest colleges in the country. And thanks to his mother, he won't have to graduate owing a couple a hundred grand in student loans and then be forced to–" *Oh, shit!* Carrie was crying! I'd done it again! The second time in one day I'd brought a woman to tears! Where was the Duchess?

Carrie was crying so loudly that three sales assistants had surrounded her. I needed to hit my final points quickly and then end this farewell speech before someone else started crying. "Okay," I said. "We all love Carrie, and we don't want to see her cry."

Carrie held up her hand and said, through gooselike snorts, "I'm–I'm fine. I'm sorry."

"Okay," I replied, wondering what the appropriate response was to a crying female Strattonite during a farewell speech. Did such a protocol even exist? "The point I was trying to make was that if you think the opportunity for quick advancement doesn't exist anymore–that because Stratton is so big and so well-managed that your path to the top is somehow blocked–well, in the history of Stratton there's never been a riper time for someone to rise through the ranks and go straight to the top. And that, my friends, is a fact!

"The simple fact is, now that I'm leaving, there's a huge void Danny needs to fill. And where's he gonna fill it from? From the outside? From somewhere on Wall Street? No, of course not! Stratton promotes from within. It always has! So whether you just walked in the door, or if you've been here for a few months and just passed your Series Seven, or if you've been here for a year and just made your first million, then today is your lucky day. As Stratton continues to grow, there'll be other regulatory hurdles. And just like the SEC . . . we'll overcome those too. Who knows? Maybe the next time it'll be the NASD . . . or the states . . . or maybe even the U.S. Attorney's Office. Who can say for sure? After all, virtually every big Wall Street firm goes through that once. But all you need to know is that at the end of the day Stratton will endure and that from out of adversity comes opportunity. Maybe next time it'll be Danny who's standing up here, and he'll be passing the torch to one of you."

I paused to let my words sink in, and then began my close. "So good luck, everyone, and continued success. I ask you for only one favor: that you follow Danny the way you followed me. Pledge your loyalty to him the way you did to me. As of this very moment, Danny is in charge. Good luck, Danny, and Godspeed! I know you'll take things to a new level." And with that, I lifted the mike in the air in salute to Danny and received the standing ovation of a lifetime.

After the mob finally settled down, I was presented with a going-away card. It was three feet by six feet, and on one side, in big red block letters, it read, *To the World's Greatest Boss!* On either side were handwritten notes–brief accolades from each of my Strattonites–thanking me for changing their lives so dramatically.

Later, after I went inside my office and closed the door for the last time, I couldn't help but wonder if they would still be thanking me five years from now.

CHAPTER 25

REAL REALS

H*ow many reruns of* Gilligan's Island *can one man watch before he decides to stick a gun in his mouth and pull the trigger?*

It was a frigid Wednesday morning, and in spite of it being eleven a.m., I was still lying in bed, watching television. Forced retirement, I thought–it ain't no fucking picnic.

I'd been watching a considerable amount of TV over the last four weeks–too much, according to the doleful Duchess–and, as of late, I had become obsessed with *Gilligan's Island.*

There was a reason for that: While watching *Gilligan's Island* reruns, I made the shocking discovery that I was not the only Wolf of Wall Street. Much to my chagrin, there was someone sharing this not-so-honorable distinction with me, and he happened to be a bumbling old WASP who'd been unlucky enough to get himself shipwrecked on Gilligan's Island. His name was Thurston Howell III, and, alas, he truly *was* an idiot WASP. In typical WASP fashion he'd married a female of his species, an atrocious pineapple blond named Lovey, who was almost as great an idiot as he but not quite. Lovey felt it necessary to wear wool pantsuits, sequined ball gowns, and a full face of makeup, despite the fact that Gilligan's Island was somewhere in the South Pacific, at least five hundred miles from the nearest shipping lane where she would ever be seen by anyone. But WASPs are notorious overdressers.

I found myself wondering if it was only by sheer coincidence that the original Wolf of Wall Street was a bumbling moron or if my nickname was *meant* to be a slight–comparing Jordan Belfort to an old WASP bastard with an IQ of sixty-five and a penchant for bed-wetting. Perhaps, I thought glumly, perhaps.

It was all very sad, and very depressing too. On a brighter note, I had been spending a great deal of time with Chandler, who had just started talking. It was crystal clear now that my early suspicions had been confirmed, and my daughter was a certifiable genius. I found myself resisting the urge to regard my daughter from a physical perspective–knowing full well that I could and would cherish every last molecule of her no matter how she looked. But the fact remained that she was absolutely gorgeous and looking more and more like her mother with each passing day. Likewise, I found myself falling more deeply in love with her as I watched her personality unfold. She was a daddy's girl, and seldom a day went by when I didn't spend at least three or four hours with her, teaching her new words.

There were powerful feelings blossoming inside me, feelings I was entirely unfamiliar with. For better or worse, I came to the realization that I had never loved another human being unconditionally–including my wives and my parents. It was only now, since Chandler, that I finally understood the true meaning of the word *love*. For the first time, I understood why my parents had felt my pain–literally suffering alongside me–especially during my teenage years, when I'd seemed determined to waste my gifts. I finally understood where my mother's tears had come from, and I now knew that, I, too, would shed those very tears if my daughter were to end up doing what I had done. I felt guilty over all the pain I had caused my parents, knowing that it must have cut to their very cores. It was about unconditional love, wasn't it? It was the purest love of all, and up until now I had only been on the receiving end of it.

None of this diminished my feelings for the Duchess. Instead, it made me wonder if I could ever get to such a place with her, to that very level of comfort and trust where I could let my guard down and love her unconditionally. Perhaps if we had another child together, I thought. Or perhaps if we grew old together–truly old–and we both passed that point where the physical body dictates so much. Maybe then I would finally trust her.

As the days passed, I found myself looking to Chandler for a sense of peace, for a sense of stability, and for a sense of purpose in my life. The thought of going to jail and being separated from her was something that rested at the base of my skull like a deadweight, which would not be lifted until Agent Coleman had finished his investigation and found nothing. Only then would I rest easy. I was still waiting to hear back from Bo as to what intelligence he'd gathered from Special Agent Barsini, but he was having trouble nailing Barsini down.

And then there was the Duchess. Things had been going remarkably well with her. In fact, now that I had extra time on my hands, I was finding it much easier to hide my mushrooming drug habit from her. I had this wonderful program worked out where I would wake up at five in the morning, two hours before her, and drop my morning Ludes in peace. Then I would go through all four phases of my high–tingle, slur, drool, loss of consciousness–before she'd even wake up. Upon awakening, I would watch a few episodes of *Gilligan's Island* or *I Dream of Jeannie,* then spend an hour or so playing with Chandler. At noon, I would meet Danny for lunch at Tenjin, where we could be seen by all the Strattonites.

After the market closed, Danny and I would meet again, at which point we would drop Ludes together. This would be my second high of the day. I'd usually arrive home around sevenish–after I was well past the drool phase–and have dinner with the Duchess and Chandler. And while I was certain the Duchess knew what I was up to, she seemed to be turning a blind eye to things–thankful, perhaps, that I was at least making an effort not to drool in her presence, which, above all things, enraged her.

Just then, I heard the phone *beep.* "Are you awake yet?" asked Janet's obnoxious voice over the intercom.

"It's eleven o'clock, Janet. Of course I'm awake!"

"Well, you haven't surfaced yet, so how am I supposed to know?"

Unbelievable! She *still* showed me no respect, even now that she worked out of my house. It was as if she and the Duchess were constantly ganging up on me, poking fun at me. Oh, they pretended it was all in jest, all out of love, but it was all very raw.

And what grounds did those two women have for making fun of me? Seriously! In spite of the fact that I was barred from the securities industry, I'd still managed to earn $4 million in the month of February; and, this month, although it was only March 3, I'd already made another million. So it wasn't like I was some worthless sea slug, just lying in bed all day, doing nothing.

And what the fuck did the two of them do all day, huh? Janet spent most of her day doting on Chandler and bullshitting with Gwynne. Nadine spent her days riding those stupid horses of hers, then walking around the house dressed in an English riding ensemble of light-green stretch riding pants, a matching cotton turtleneck, and gleaming black leather riding boots that rose up to her kneecaps, as she sneezed and wheezed and coughed and itched from her intractable horse allergies. The only person in the house who truly understood me was Chandler, and maybe Gwynne, the latter of whom would serve me breakfast in bed and offer me Quaaludes for my back pain.

I said to Janet, "Well, I'm awake, so cool your fucking jets. I'm watching the Financial News Network."

Janet, the skeptic: "Oh, really? Me too. What's the guy saying?"

"Fuck off, Janet. What do you want?"

"Alan Chemtob is on the phone; he says it's important."

Alan Chemtob, aka Alan Chemical-tob, my trusted Quaalude dealer, was a real pain in the ass. It wasn't enough just to pay this societal leech fifty dollars a Quaalude and let him be on his way. Oh, no! This particular drug dealer wanted to be liked or loved or whatever the fuck he wanted. I mean, this fat bastard gave new meaning to the phrase *your friendly neighborhood drug dealer.* Still, he did happen to have the best Ludes in town: a relative statement in the world of Quaalude addiction, with the best Ludes coming from those countries where legitimate drug companies were still allowed to manufacture them.

Yes, it was a sad story. As was the case with most recreational drugs, Quaaludes had once been legal in the United States but were subsequently outlawed after it came to the DEA's attention that, for every legitimate prescription being written, there were a hundred bogus ones. Now there were only two countries in the world manufacturing Quaaludes: Spain and Germany. And, in both those countries, controls were so strict it was nearly impossible to get any meaningful supply . . .

. . . which was why my heart started beating like a rabbit's when I picked up the phone and Alan Chemical-tob said, "You won't believe this, Jordan, but I found a retired pharmacist who has twenty real Lemmons that've been locked inside his safe for almost fifteen years. I've been trying to pry them out of him for five years, but he'd never let them go. Now he's gotta pay his kid's college tuition, and he's willing to sell them for five hundred dollars a pill, so I thought you might be inter–"

"Of course I'm interested!" I resisted the urge to call him a fucking moron for even questioning my interest. After all, there were Quaaludes and there were *Quaaludes*. Each company's brand was of a slightly different formulation and, likewise, a slightly different potency. And no one had ever gotten it *more right* than the geniuses over at Lemmon Pharmaceuticals, which had marketed its Quaaludes under the brand name Lemmon 714. Lemmons, as they were called, were legendary, not only for their strength but for their ability to turn Catholic-school virgins into blow-job queens. In consequence, they had earned the nickname *leg openers*. "I'll take 'em all!" I snapped. "In fact, tell the guy if he'll sell me forty I'll give him a thousand bucks a pill, and if he'll sell me a hundred I'll make it fifteen hundred. That's a hundred fifty thousand dollars, Alan." Good God, I thought, the Wolf was a rich man! Real Lemmons! Palladins were considered real Ludes, because they were manufactured by a legitimate drug company in Spain, so if Palladins were Reals, then Lemmons were . . . *Real Reals!*

Chemical-tob replied, "He only has twenty."

"Shit! Are you sure? You're not glomming any for yourself, are you?"

"Of course not," replied Chemical-tob. "I consider you a friend, and I would never do that to a friend, right?"

What a fucking loser, I thought. But my response was slightly different: "I couldn't agree with you more, my friend. When can you be here?"

"The guy won't be home 'til four. I can be in Old Brookville around five." Then he added, "But make sure you don't eat."

"Oh, please, Chemical-tob! I resent the fact that you'd even suggest that." With that, I bid him safe passage. Then I hung up the phone and rolled around on my $12,000 white silk comforter like a kid who'd just won a shopping spree at FAO Schwarz.

I went to the bathroom and opened up the medicine cabinet and took out a box labeled *Fleet Enema*. I ripped it open, then pulled my boxers down to my kneecaps and rammed the bottle's pointed nozzle up my asshole with such ferocity that I felt it scrape the top of my sigmoid colon. Three minutes later, the entire contents of my lower digestive tract came pouring out. Deep down I was pretty sure that this wouldn't increase the intensity of my high, but, nonetheless, it still seemed like a prudent measure. Then I stuck my finger down my throat and vomited up the last of this morning's breakfast.

Yes, I thought, I had done what any sensible man would do under such extraordinary circumstances, perhaps with the exception of giving myself the enema before I'd made myself vomit. But I had washed my hands thoroughly with scalding hot water, so I redeemed myself for that tiny faux pax.

Then I called Danny and urged him to do the same, which, of course, he did.

At five p.m., Danny and I were playing pool in my basement, waiting impatiently for Alan Chemical-tob. The game was eight ball, and Danny had been kicking my ass for almost thirty minutes. As the balls clicked and clacked, Danny bashed the Chinaman: "I'm a hundred percent sure the stock is coming from the Chinaman. No one else has that much."

The stock Danny was referring to was Stratton's most recent new issue, M. H. Meyerson. The problem was that as part of my quid pro quo with Kenny, I had agreed to give Victor large blocks of it. Of course, the stock had been given with the explicit instructions that he wasn't to sell it back–and, of course, Victor had completely disregarded those instructions and was now selling back every share. The truly frustrating part was that by the very nature of the NASDAQ stock market, it was impossible to prove this transgression. It was all supposition.

Nevertheless, by process of elimination it wasn't too difficult to put two and two together: The Chinaman was fucking us. "Why do you seem so surprised?" I asked cynically. "The Chinaman's a depraved maniac. He'd sell the stock back even if he didn't have to, just to spite us. Anyway, now you see why I told you to stay short an extra hundred thousand shares. He's sold all he can sell, and you're still in perfect shape."

Danny nodded glumly.

I smiled and said, "Don't worry, buddy. How much of that other stock have you sold him so far?"

"About a million shares."

"Good. When you get to a million-five, I'm gonna turn the Chinaman's lights out, and–"

I was interrupted by the doorbell. Danny and I turned to each other and froze in place, our mouths agape. A few moments later, Alan Chemical-tob came thumping down the basement stairs and started in with the personal crap, asking, "How's Chandler doing?"

Oh, Jesus! I thought. Why couldn't he just be like any other drug dealer and hang out on street corners and sell drugs to schoolchildren? Why did he feel the need to be liked? "Oh, she's doing great," I replied warmly, *and can you hand over the fucking Lemmons*? "How are Marsha and the kids?"

"Oh, Marsha's Marsha," he replied, grinding his jaw like the true coke fiend that he was, "but the kids are doing fine." He did some more jaw-grinding. "You know, I'd really love to open up an account for the kids, if that's okay. Maybe a college fund or something?"

"Yeah, sure." *Just hand over the Ludes, you fat fuck!* "Call Danny's assistant and she'll take care of it, right, Dan?"

"Absolutely," replied Danny through clenched teeth. On his face was a look that said, "Hand over the fucking Lemmons or suffer the consequences!"

Fifteen minutes later, Alan finally handed over the Ludes. I took one out and examined it. It was perfectly round, just larger than a dime, and it had the thickness of a Honey Nut Cheerio. It was snow-white . . . very clean-looking . . . and had a magnificent sheen, which served as visible reminder that in spite of it resembling a Bayer aspirin, it was the furthest thing from it. On one side of the pill, the brand name, Lemmon 714, was etched in thick grooves. [illegible]n the other side was a thin line that ran the full diameter of the [illegible]nd the pill's circumference were the trademark beveled [illegible]

[illegible] "They're the real deal, Jordan. Whatever you [illegible]an one. They're not like the Palladins;

[illegible]ouldn't . . . and, ten minutes later, Danny and

I were well on the road to paradise. Each of us had swallowed one Real Real, and we were now in my basement gym, surrounded by floor-to-ceiling mirrors. The gym was packed with state-of-the-art Cybex equipment and enough dumbbells and barbells and benches and squat racks to impress Arnold Schwarzenegger. Danny was walking on a motorized treadmill at a brisk pace; I was on the StairMaster, climbing, as if Agent Coleman were chasing me.

I said to Danny, "Nothing kicks in a Quaalude better than exercise, right?"

"Absa-fuckin-lutely!" exclaimed Danny. "It's all in the metabolism; the faster, the better." He reached over and picked up a white porcelain sake cup. "And this is genius, by the way. Drinking hot sake after consuming a real Lemmon is inspirational. Like pouring gasoline on a raging fire."

I grabbed my own sake cup and reached over to clink cups with Danny. Danny tried too, but the two pieces of equipment were six feet apart, and we found ourselves just out of reach.

"Nice try," said Danny, giggling.

"At least I get an A for effort!" I giggled back.

The two giggling idiots toasted each other in the air and downed the sake.

Just then the door swung open, and there she was: the Duchess of Bay Ridge, in her lime-green riding ensemble. She took one aggressive step forward and struck a pose, with her head cocked to one side and her arms folded beneath her breasts and her legs crossed at the ankles and her back slightly arched. Then she narrowed her eyes suspiciously, and she said, "What are you two retards doing?"

Christ! An unexpected complication! "I thought you were going out with Hope tonight?" I asked accusingly.

"Ahhh . . . ahhh . . . chooo!" sneezed my aspiring horseback rider, giving up her pose. "My allergies were so bad I had . . . had . . . *ahhhh chooo*!" sneezed the Duchess once more. "I had to cancel on Hope."

"Bless you, young Duchess!" said Danny, using my wife's -
name.

The Duchess's reply: "Call me Duchess again, Danny, ar
pour that fucking sake over your head." Then, to me: "Co
side, I want to talk to you about something." With that, s

on her heel and headed to the other side of the basement, to a wraparound couch. It was just across from the indoor racquetball court, which had recently been converted into a clothing showroom in support of her latest aspiration: maternity designer.

Danny and I followed dutifully. I whispered in his ear: "You feel anything yet?"

"Nothing," he whispered back.

The Duchess said, "I was speaking to Heather Gold today, and she thinks it's the perfect time to get Chandler started horseback riding. So I want to buy her a pony." She nodded a single time, to emphasize her point. "Anyway, they have one there that's so cute, and it's not too expensive either."

"How much?" I asked, taking a seat beside the Duchess and wondering how Chandler was going to ride a pony when she hadn't even started walking yet.

"Only seventy thousand dollars!" answered a smiling Duchess. "Not bad, right?"

Well, I thought, if you'll agree to have sex with me while I'm getting off on my Real Real, then I'll gladly purchase this overpriced pony for you, but all I said was, "Sounds like a real fucking bargain. I didn't even know they made ponies that expensive." I rolled my eyes.

The Duchess assured me that they did, and then to reinforce her point she nuzzled up next to me so I could smell her perfume. "Please?" she said in an irresistible tone. "I'll be your best friend."

At that very moment, Janet came walking down the stairs with a great smile on her face. "Hey, everybody! What's going on down here?"

I looked up at Janet and said, "Come downstairs and join the fucking party!" Obviously, she missed the sarcasm, and a moment later the Duchess had recruited Janet into her camp, and the two of them were now talking about how fine Chandler would look on horseback, in a cute little English riding ensemble, which the Duchess could have custom-made for God only knew how much.

Sensing an opportunity, I whispered to the Duchess that if she would come into the bathroom with me and allow me to bend her over the sink, I would be more than happy to make a special trip to Gold Coast Stables tomorrow and purchase the pony, just as soon as the eleven o'clock showing of *Gilligan's Island* was finished, to which she whispered, "Now?" to which I nodded yes and said, "Please," three times fast, at which point the Duchess smiled and agreed. The two of us excused ourselves for a moment.

With little fanfare, I bent her over the sink and plunged inside her without even the slightest bit of lubrication, to which she said, "OW!" and then she sneezed and coughed again. I said, "Bless you, my love!" then I pumped in and out, twelve times fast, and came inside her like a rocket. Soup to nuts, the whole thing had taken about nine seconds.

The Duchess turned her pretty little head around and said, "That's it? You're done?"

"Uh-huh," I replied, rubbing my fingertips together and still feeling no tingles. "Why don't you go upstairs and use your vibrator?"

Still bent over the sink, the Duchess said, "Why are you so anxious to get rid of me? I know you and Danny are up to something. What is it?"

"Nothing; it's just business talk, sweetie. That's it."

"Fuck you!" replied an angry Duchess. "You're lying, and I know it!" And with one swift move, she pushed off the sink with her elbows and I went flying backward and smashed into the bathroom door with a tremendous force. Then she pulled up her riding pants, sneezed, looked in the mirror for a second, fixed her hair, pushed me off to the side, and walked out.

Ten minutes later Danny and I were alone in the basement, still stone-cold sober. I shook my head gravely and said, "They're so old they must've lost their potency. I think we should take another."

We did, and thirty minutes later: nothing. Not even one fucking tingle!

"Can you imagine this shit?" said Danny. "Five hundred bucks a pill, and they're duds! It's criminal! Let me check the expiration date on the bottle."

I tossed the bottle to him.

He looked at the label. "December '81!" he exclaimed. "They're expired!" He unscrewed the top and took out two more Lemmons. "They must've lost their potency. Let's each take one more."

Thirty minutes later we were devastated. We'd each taken three vintage Lemmons and hadn't gotten so much as a tingle.

"Well, that's about all she wrote!" I sputtered. "They're officially duds."

"Yeah," agreed Danny. "Such is life, my friend."

Just then, over the intercom, came the voice of Gwynne: "Mr. Belfort, it's"–*iz*–"Bo Dietl on the phone."

I picked up the receiver. "Hey, Bo, what's going on?"

His reply startled me. "I need to speak to you right now," he snapped, "but not on this phone. Go to a pay phone and call me at this number. You got something to write with?"

"What's going on?" I asked. "Did you speak to Bar–"

Bo cut me off: "Not on this phone, Bo. But the short answer is yes, and I have some info for you. Now go grab a pen."

A minute later I was inside my little white Mercedes, freezing my ass off. In my haste I had forgotten to put a coat on. It was absolutely frigid outside–couldn't have been more than five degrees–and at seven p.m. at this time of winter, it was already dark out. I started the car and headed for the front gates. I made a left turn onto Pin Oak Court, surprised to see a long row of cars parked on either side of the street. Apparently someone on my block was having a party. Wonderful! I thought. I just spent $10,000 on the worst Ludes in history, and someone is having a fucking celebration!

My destination was the pay phone at Brookville Country Club. It was only a few hundred yards up the road, and thirty seconds later I was pulling into the driveway. I parked in front of the clubhouse and walked up a half dozen red-brick steps, passing through a set of white Corinthian columns.

Inside the clubhouse were a row of pay phones against a wall. I picked one up, dialed the number Bo had given me, then punched in my credit-card number. After a few rings came the terrible news. "Listen, Bo," said Bo, from another pay phone, "I just got a call from Barsini, and he told me you're the target of a full-blown money-laundering investigation. Apparently this guy Coleman thinks you got twenty million bucks over in Switzerland. He has an inside source over there that's feeding him information. Barsini wouldn't get specific, but he made it sound like you got caught up in someone else's deal, like you didn't start off as the main target but now Coleman's made you the main target. Your home phone's probably tapped, and so is your beach house. Talk to me, Bo, what's going on?"

I took a deep breath, trying to keep myself calm and trying to figure out what to say to Bo . . . *but what was there to say?* That I had millions of dollars in the bogus account of Patricia Mellor and that my own mother-in-law had smuggled the money there for me? Or that Todd Garret had gotten popped because Danny was dumb enough to drive his car on Ludes? What was the upside of telling him that? None that I could think of. So all I said was, "I don't have any money in Switzerland. It must be some sort of mistake."

"What?" asked Bo. "I couldn't understand what you said. Say it again?"

Frustrated, I repeated: "I says, I zon't has azy muzzy ozzer in Swizzaziz!"

Sounding incredulous, Bo said, "What are you, stoned? I can't understand a word you're fucking saying!" Then, suddenly, in an urgent tone, he said, "Listen to me, Jordan–don't get behind the wheel of your car! Tell me where you are and I'll send Rocco for you! Where are you, buddy? Talk to me!"

All at once a warm feeling came rising up my brain stem, as a pleasant tingling sensation went ricocheting through every molecule of my body. The phone receiver was still at my ear and I wanted to tell Bo to have Rocco come pick me up at the Brookville Country Club, but I couldn't get my lips to move. It was as if my brain was sending out signals but they were being intercepted–or scrambled. I felt paralyzed. And I felt wonderful. I stared at the shiny metal face of the pay phone and cocked my head to the side, trying to find my own reflection . . . *How pretty the phone looked!* . . . So shiny it was! . . . And then all at once the phone seemed to be growing more distant . . . What was happening? . . . Where was the phone going? . . . *Oh, shit!* . . . I was falling backward now, tipping over like a tree that had just been chopped down. . . . *TIMBER!* . . . and then . . . *BOOM!* I was lying flat on my back, in a state of semiconsciousness, staring up at the clubhouse ceiling. It was one of those white Styrofoam dropped ceilings, the sort you find in an office. Pretty chintzy for a country club! I thought. These fucking WASPs were cutting corners on their own ceiling!

I took a deep breath and checked for broken bones. Everything seemed to be in working order. The Real Reals had protected me from harm. It had taken almost ninety minutes for these little fuckers to kick in, but once they had . . . *WOW!* I had gone straight past the tingle phase and right into the drool phase. Actually, I had discovered a new phase, somewhere between the drool phase and a state of unconsciousness. It was the . . . what was it? I needed a name for this phase. It was the cerebral palsy phase! Yes! My brain would no longer send clear signals to my musculoskeletal system. What a wonderful new phase! My brain was sharp as a tack, but I had no control of my body. Too good! Too good!

With a great deal of effort, I craned my neck and saw the receiver still swinging back and forth on its shiny metallic cord. I thought I could hear Bo's voice screaming, "Tell me where you are and I'll send Rocco!" although it was probably my imagination playing tricks on me. *Fuck it!* I thought. What was the point of trying to get back on the phone, anyway? I had officially lost the power of speech.

After five minutes on the floor, it hit me that Danny must be in the same condition. Oh, Jesus! The Duchess must be flipping out right now–wondering where I'd gone! I needed to get home. It was only a couple hundred yards to the estate, literally a straight shot. I could make the drive, couldn't I? Or perhaps I should walk home. But, no, it was too cold for that. I would probably die of frostbite.

I rolled onto all fours and tried standing up, but it was no use. Every time I lifted my hands off the carpet I tipped over to the side. I would have to *crawl* back to the car. But what was so bad about that? Chandler crawled, and she seemed to be fine with it.

When I reached the front door I propped myself onto my knees and grabbed the doorknob. I pulled open the door and crawled outside. There was my car . . . ten stairs down. Try as I might, my brain refused to let me crawl down the stairs, scared at the very possibility of what might happen. So I lay down flat on my stomach and tucked my hands beneath my chest and turned myself into a human barrel and began rolling down the stairs . . . slow at first . . . in complete control . . . and then . . . oh, shit! . . . There I go! . . . Faster . . . faster . . . *b-boom* . . . *b-boom* . . . *b-boom* . . . and I hit the asphalt parking lot with a mighty *thud*.

But, again, the Real Reals protected me from harm, and thirty seconds later I was sitting behind the steering wheel with the ignition on and the car in drive and my chin resting on the steering wheel. Hunched over the way I was, with my eyes barely peering over the dashboard, I looked like one of those blue-haired old ladies who drive in the left lane of the highway, doing twenty.

I pulled out of the parking lot, doing one mile an hour and saying a silent prayer to God. Apparently, He was a kind and loving

God, just like the textbooks say, because a minute later I was parked in front of my house, home in one piece. *Victory!* I thanked the Lord for being the Lord, and after a great deal of effort, I crawled my way into the kitchen, at which point I found myself staring up at the beautiful face of the Duchess. . . . *Uh-oh! I was in for it now!* . . . How angry was she? It was impossible to say.

And then all at once I realized that she wasn't angry. In fact, she was crying hysterically. Next thing I knew, she had crouched down, and she was giving me warm kisses all over my face and on the top of my head, as she tried speaking through her tears. "Oh, thank God you're home safe, sweetie! I thought I lost you! I . . . I"–she couldn't seem to get the words out–"I love you so much. I thought you crashed the car. Bo called here and said he was speaking to you on the phone and you passed out. And then I went downstairs and Danny was crawling around on his hands and knees, banging into the walls. Here, let me help you up, sweetie." She picked me up, led me over to the kitchen table, and placed me on a chair. A second later my head hit the table.

"You have to stop doing this," she begged. "You're gonna kill yourself, baby. I . . . I can't lose you. Please, look at your daughter; she loves you. You're gonna die if you keep this up."

I looked over at Chandler, and my daughter and I locked eyes, and she smiled. "Dada!" she said. "Hi, Dada!"

I smiled at my daughter and was about to slur back, *I love you,* when suddenly I felt two powerful sets of arms pulling me out of my seat and dragging me up the stairs.

Rocco Night said, "Mr. Belfort, you gotta get into bed and go to sleep right now. Everything's gonna be all right."

Rocco Day added, "Don't worry, Mr. B. We'll take care of everything."

What in the hell were they talking about? I wanted to ask them but I couldn't get the words out. A minute later I was alone in bed, still fully dressed but with the covers pulled over my head and the room lights out. I took a deep breath, trying to make sense of it all. It was ironic that the Duchess had been so nice to me, yet she had called the bodyguards to come take me upstairs, as if I were a naughty child. Well, fuck it! I thought. The royal bedchamber was very comfortable, and I would enjoy the rest of the cerebral palsy phase just like this, floating amid the Chinese silk.

Just then, the bedroom lights came on. A moment later someone pulled down my glorious white silk comforter and I found myself squinting into an extremely bright flashlight.

"Mr. Belfort," said an unfamiliar voice, "are you awake, sir?"

Sir? . . . Who the fuck is calling me sir? . . . After a few seconds, my eyes adjusted to the light and I found out. It was a policeman–two of them, actually–from the Old Brookville Police Department. They were dressed in full regalia–guns, handcuffs, shiny badges, the whole nine yards. One of them was big and fat with a droopy mustache; the other was short and wiry, with the ruddy skin of a teenager.

All at once I felt a terrible dark cloud descending on me. Something was very wrong here. Agent Coleman had sure worked fast! I was already getting arrested, and the investigation had barely begun! What happened to the wheels of justice grinding slowly? And why would Agent Coleman use the Old Brookville police to arrest me? They were like toy cops, for Chrissake, and their police station was like Mayberry RFD. Was this the way people got arrested for money laundering?

"Mr. Belfort," said the policeman, "were you driving your car?"

Uh-oh! Stoned as I was, my brain began sending emergency signals to my voice box–instructing it to clam up. "I zon't zo what zor zalkin azout," I said.

Apparently that response didn't go over too well, and next thing I knew I was being escorted down my spiral staircase with my hands cuffed behind my back. When I reached the front door, the fat policeman said, "You had seven different car accidents, Mr. Belfort: six of them were right here on Pin Oak Court, and the other was a head-on collision on Chicken Valley Road. That driver is on her way to the hospital right now with a broken arm. You're under arrest, Mr. Belfort, for driving under the influence, reckless endangerment, and leaving the scene of an accident." With that, he read me my rights. When he got to the part about not being able to afford an attorney, he and his partner began snickering.

But what were they talking about? I wasn't in any accident, much less seven accidents. God had answered my prayer and protected me from harm! They had the wrong person! A case of mistaken identity, I thought . . .

. . . until I saw my little Mercedes, at which point my jaw

dropped. The car was totaled out, from front to back. The passenger side, which I was now looking at, was completely smashed in, and the rear wheel was bent inward at an extreme angle. The front of the car looked like an accordion, and the rear fender was hanging on the ground. All at once I felt dizzy . . . my knees buckled . . . and next thing I knew . . . *bam!* . . . I was on the ground again, looking up at the night sky.

The two policemen bent over me. The fat one said in a concerned tone, "Mr. Belfort, what are you on, sir? Tell us what you're on so we can help you."

Well, I thought, if you'd be kind enough to go upstairs into my medicine cabinet, you'll find a plastic Baggie with two grams of cocaine in it. Please bring it to me and allow me to do a few blasts so I can even out, or else you'll be carrying me into the police station like an infant! But my better judgment prevailed, and all I said was: "You zot za zong zy!" *You got the wrong guy.*

The two policemen looked at each other and shrugged. They lifted me up by my armpits and walked me to the police car.

Just then the Duchess came running out, screaming in her Brooklyn accent, "Where the fuck do you think you're taking my husband? He's been home with me all night! If you guys don't let him go you'll both be working in Toys 'R' Us next week!"

I turned and looked at the Duchess. She was flanked by a Rocco on either side. The two policemen stopped dead in their tracks. The fat policeman said, "Mrs. Belfort, we know who your husband is, and we have several witnesses that he was driving his car. I suggest you call one of his lawyers. I'm sure he has many of them." With that, the policemen resumed walking me to their police car.

"Don't worry," screamed the Duchess, as I was being placed in the police car's rear seat. "Bo said he'll take care of it, sweetie! I love you!"

And as the police car pulled off the estate, all I could think of was how much I loved the Duchess and, for that matter, how much she loved me. I thought about how she'd cried when she thought she'd lost me, and how she stood up for me as the policemen were taking me away in handcuffs. Perhaps now, once and for all, she had finally proved herself to me. Perhaps now, once and for all, I could rest easy–knowing that she would be there for me in good times and bad. Yes, I thought, the Duchess truly loved me.

It was a short ride to the Old Brookville Police Station, which looked more like a quaint private home than anything else. It was white, with green shutters. It looked rather soothing, in fact. It would be a fine place, I thought, to sleep off a bad Quaalude high.

Inside were two jail cells, and pretty soon I found myself sitting in one of them. Actually, I wasn't sitting; I was lying on the floor with my cheek against the concrete. I vaguely remembered being processed–fingerprinted, photographed, and, in my case, videotaped–to bear witness to the extreme state of my intoxication.

"Mr. Belfort," said the police officer with his belly hanging over his gun belt like a roll of salami, "we need you to give us a urine sample."

I sat up–all at once realizing that I was no longer stoned. The true beauty of the Real Reals had come shining through once more, and I was now completely sober. I took a deep breath and said, "I don't know what you guys think you're doing, but unless I get a phone call right now you're gonna be in some deep shit."

That seemed to stun the bastard, and he said, "*Well,* I see whatever you were on finally wore off. I'll be happy to let you out of your cell, without handcuffs, if you promise not to run."

I nodded. He opened the cell door and gestured to a telephone on a small wooden desk. I dialed my lawyer's home number–resisting the urge to draw any conclusions as to why I knew my lawyer's home phone number by heart.

Five minutes later I was peeing in a cup, wondering why Joe Fahmegghetti, my lawyer, had told me not to worry about testing positive for drugs.

I was back inside my jail, sitting on the floor, when the policeman said, "Well, Mr. Belfort, in case you're wondering, you tested positive for cocaine, methaqualone, benzodiazepines, amphetamines, MDMA, opiates, and marijuana. In fact, the only thing you're not showing is hallucinogens. What's wrong, you don't like those?"

I offered him a dead smile and said, "Let me tell you something, Mr. Police Officer. As far as this whole driving thing is concerned, you got the wrong fucking guy, and as far as the drug test is concerned, I don't give a shit what it says. I have a bad back, and everything I take is prescribed by a doctor. So fuck off!"

He stared at me in disbelief. Then he looked at his watch and shrugged. "Well, either way it's too late for night court, so we're gonna have to take you to Central Booking in Nassau County. I don't think you've ever been there, have you?"

I resisted the urge to tell the fat bastard to go fuck himself again, and I turned away and shut my eyes. Nassau County lockup was a real hellhole, but what could I do? I looked up at the wall clock: It was just before eleven. Christ! I would be spending the night in jail. What a fucking bummer!

Once more I closed my eyes and tried to drift off to sleep. Then I heard my name being called. I stood up and looked through the bars–and I saw a rather bizarre sight. There was an old bald man in pin-striped pajamas staring at me.

"Are you Jordan Belfort?" he asked, annoyed.

"Yeah, why?"

"I'm Judge Stevens. I'm a friend of a friend. Consider this your arraignment. I assume you're willing to waive your right to counsel, right?" He winked.

"Yeah," I replied eagerly.

"Okay, I'll take that as a plea of not guilty to whatever it is you're being charged with. I'm releasing you on your own recognizance. Call Joe to find out when your court date is." With that, he smiled, wheeled about, and left the police station.

A few minutes later I found Joe Fahmegghetti waiting for me out front. Even at this time of night, he was dressed like a starched dandy, in an immaculate navy suit and striped tie. His salt-and-pepper hair was perfectly coiffed. I smiled at him and then held up one finger, as if to say, "Hold on a sec!" Then I peeked back into the police station and said to the fat policeman, "Excuse me!"

He looked up. "Yes?"

I shot him the middle finger and said, "You can take Central Booking and shove it up your ass!"

On the car ride home I said to my lawyer, "I'm in deep shit with that urine test, Joe. I tested positive for everything."

My lawyer shrugged. "Whaddaya worried about? You think I'd steer you wrong? They didn't actually catch you in the car, now, did they? So how can they prove those drugs were in your system while you were driving? Who's to say you didn't walk in the door and take a few Ludes and snort a little coke? And it's not illegal to have drugs in your system; it's only illegal to possess them. In fact, I'm willing to bet I'll get the whole arrest thrown out on the grounds that Nadine never gave the police permission to come on the property in the first place. You'll just have to pay for the damage to the other car–they're only charging you with one accident, because there were no witnesses to the others–and then you'll have to pay some hush money to the woman whose arm you broke. The whole thing won't run you more than a hundred thousand." He shrugged, as if to say, "Chump change!"

I nodded my head. "Where'd you find that crazy old judge? What a lifesaver he was!"

"You don't wanna know," replied my lawyer, rolling his eyes. "Let's just say he's a friend of a friend."

The remainder of the ride was spent in silence. As we pulled onto the estate, Joe said, "Your wife is in bed, pretty shaken up. So go easy on her. She's been crying for hours, but I think she's pretty much calmed down now. Anyway, Bo was here with her most of the night, and he was a big help. He left about fifteen minutes ago."

I nodded again, without speaking.

Joe added, "Just remember, Jordan: A broken arm is one thing, but no one can fix a dead body. You understand what I'm saying?"

"Yeah, Joe, but it's a moot point. I'm done with all that shit. Done for good." And we shook hands, and that was that.

Upstairs in the master bedroom, I found the Duchess lying in bed. I leaned over and kissed her on the cheek, then quickly undressed and climbed into bed with her. We stared up at the white silk canopy, our naked bodies touching at the shoulders and the hips. I grabbed her hand and held it in mine.

In a soft voice, I said, "I don't remember anything, Nae. I blacked out. I think that I–"

She cut me off. "Shhh, don't talk, baby. Just lie here and relax." She gripped my hand tighter, and we lay there silently for what seemed like a very long time.

I squeezed her hand. "I'm done, Nae. I swear. And this time I'm dead serious about it. I mean, if this isn't a sign from God, then I don't know what is." I leaned over and kissed her softly on the cheek. "But I gotta do something about my back pain. I can't live this way anymore. It's unbearable. And it's feeding into things." I took a deep breath and tried to calm myself. "I want to go to Florida and see Dr. Green. He has a back clinic down there, and they have a really high cure rate. But whatever happens, I promise you I'm done with drugs once and for all. I know Quaaludes aren't the answer; I know it'll end in disaster."

The Duchess rolled onto her side to face me, and she put her arm across my chest and hugged me gently. Then she told me that she loved me. I kissed her on the top of her blond head and took a deep breath to relish her scent. Then I told her that I loved her back and that I was sorry. I promised her that nothing like this would ever happen again.

I would be right about that.

Worse would.

CHAPTER 26

DEAD MEN TELL NO TALES

Two mornings later, I woke up to a phone call from licensed Florida real estate broker Kathy Green, wife of world-renowned neurosurgeon Dr. Barth Green. I had enlisted Kathy to find the Duchess and me a place to live while I was going through the four-week outpatient program at Jackson Memorial Hospital.

"You and Nadine will just adore Indian Creek Island," said a kindhearted Kathy. "It's one of the quietest places to live in all Miami. It's *so* serene and *so* uneventful. They even have their own police force–so given how security-conscious you and Nadine are, it's another plus."

Quiet and uneventful? Well, I *was* looking to get away from it all, wasn't I? So how much harm could I create in four short weeks, especially in a place as boring and peaceful as Indian Creek Island? A place where I'd be insulated from the pressures of a cold, cruel world, namely: Quaaludes, cocaine, crack, pot, Xanax, Valium, Ambien, speed, morphine, and, of course, Special Agent Gregory Coleman.

I said, "Well, Kathy, it sounds like just what the doctor ordered, especially the part about the place being peaceful. What's the house like?"

"The house is absolutely breathtaking. It's a white Mediterranean mansion with a red tile roof, and there's a boat slip big enough for an eighty-foot yacht . . ." Kathy's voice trailed off for a moment. ". . . which, I guess, wouldn't quite fit the *Nadine,* but perhaps you can buy a boat while you're down here, right? I'm sure Barth could help you with that." The sheer logic of her wacky suggestion oozed over the phone line with each of her words. "Anyway, the backyard is fabulous; it has an Olympic-size swimming pool, a cabana, a wet bar, a gas barbecue, and a six-person Jacuzzi overlooking the bay. It's absolutely perfect for entertaining. And the best part is that the owner's willing to sell the house, completely furnished, for only $5.5 million. It's quite a bargain."

Wait a second! Who said anything about wanting to buy a house? I was only going to be in Florida for four weeks! And why would I consider getting another boat when I despised the one I already had? I said, "To tell you the truth, Kathy, I'm not looking to buy a house right now, at least not in Florida. You think the owner would consider renting it for a month?"

"No," said a glum Kathy Green, whose hopes and dreams of a six percent real estate commission on a $5.5-million sale had just evaporated right before her big blue eyes. "It's only listed for sale."

"Hmmm," I replied, not quite convinced of that fact. "Why don't you offer the guy a hundred grand for the month and see what he says?"

On April Fool's Day, I was moving in and the owner was moving out–skipping and humming, no doubt, all the way to a five-star hotel in South Beach for the month. That aside, April Fool's Day was the perfect move-in date, given my discovery that Indian Creek Island was a sanctuary for a little-known endangered species called the Old Blue-haired WASP, which, as Kathy had previously indicated, was about as lively a species as the sea slug.

On the brighter side, in between my car accident and the back clinic I'd managed to jet into Switzerland and meet with Saurel and the Master Forger. My goal was to find out how the FBI had become aware of my Swiss accounts. To my surprise, though, everything seemed to be in order. The U.S. government had made no inquiries–and both Saurel and the Master Forger assured me they would be the first to know if it had.

Indian Creek Island was only a fifteen-minute car ride to the back clinic. And there was no shortage of cars; the Duchess had seen to that–shipping down a brand-new Mercedes for me and a Range Rover for herself. Gwynne had come to Miami too, to look after my needs, and she also needed a car. So I bought her a new Lexus, from a local Miami car dealer.

Of course, Rocco had to come too. He was like a part of the family, wasn't he? And Rocco *also* needed a car, so Richard Bronson, one of the owners of Biltmore, saved me the headache of buying yet another one and loaned me his red convertible Ferrari for the month. So now everyone was covered.

With lots of cars to choose from, my decision to rent a sixty-foot motor yacht to get myself back and forth to the clinic became ridiculous. It was $20,000 per week for four smelly diesel engines, a well-appointed cabin I would never set foot in, and a flybridge without a canopy, which resulted in a third-degree sunburn on my shoulders and neck. The boat came complete with an old white-haired captain, who shuttled me back and forth to the clinic at an average cruising speed of five knots.

At this particular moment we were on the Intracoastal Waterway, cruising north on our way back to Indian Creek Island from the clinic. It was a Saturday, a little before noon, and we'd been chugging along for almost an hour now. I was sitting atop the flybridge with Dollar Time's Chief Operating Officer, Gary Deluca, who bore a striking resemblance to President Grover Cleveland. Gary was bald, broad, grim-faced, square-jawed, and extremely hairy, especially on his torso. Right now we both had our shirts off and were basking in the sun. I had been sober for almost a month, which was a miracle unto itself.

Early this morning Deluca had accompanied me on my morning boat ride down to the clinic. It was a way for him to get some uninterrupted face time, and our conversation had quickly turned into a mutual bitching session over Dollar Time, whose future, we agreed, was hopeless.

But none of Dollar Time's woes were of Deluca's making. He had come after the fact–part of a workout team–and over the last six months he'd proven himself to be a first-class operations guy. I had already convinced him to move up to New York and become Chief Operating Officer of Steve Madden Shoes, which was in desperate need of someone with his operational expertise.

We had discussed all that earlier this morning, on the trip south. Now, on the trip north, we were discussing something I found infinitely more troubling, namely, his thoughts on Gary Kaminsky,

Dollar Time's CFO–the same CFO who'd introduced me to Jean Jacques Saurel and the Master Forger almost a year ago.

"Anyway," Deluca was saying, from behind a pair of wraparound sunglasses, "there's something strange about him that I can't put my finger on. It's like he's got a different agenda that has nothing to do with Dollar Time. Like the place is a front for him. I mean, a guy his age should be flipping out over the company going down the tubes, yet he couldn't seem to care less. He spends half his day trying to explain to me how we could divert our profits to Switzerland–which makes me wanna rip his fucking toupee off, considering we don't have any profits to divert." Gary shrugged. "Anyway, sooner or later I'll figure out what that bastard's up to."

I nodded slowly, realizing that my initial instincts about Kaminsky had been right on target. The Wolf had been very shrewd not to allow that toupeed bastard to worm his way into my overseas dealings. Still, I wasn't a hundred percent sure that Kaminsky hadn't smelled a rat, so I figured I'd launch a trial balloon in Deluca's direction. "I definitely agree with you. He's totally obsessed with the whole Swiss-banking thing. In fact, he actually pitched it to me." I paused, as if to search my memory. "Maybe a year ago, I think. Anyway, I went over there with him to check it out, but it seemed like more trouble than it was worth, so I took a pass. He ever mention anything to you?"

"No, but I know he's still got a bunch of clients over there. He's pretty tight-lipped about it, although he's on the phone to Switzerland all day long. I always make it a point to check the phone bill, and I'm telling you, he must make half a dozen overseas calls a day." Deluca shook his head gravely. "Whatever he's doing, it better be on the up and up–because if it's not, and his phone is tapped, he's gonna find himself in some deep shit."

I turned the corners of my mouth down and shrugged, as if to say, "Well, that's his problem, not mine!" But the truth was that if he were in constant contact with Saurel and the Master Forger, I would find it troubling. I said casually, "Just for curiosity's sake, why don't you pull the phone records and see if he keeps calling the same numbers over and over again. If he is, make some blind phone calls and see who he's speaking to. I'd be curious to find out, okay?"

"No problem. As soon we get back to the house I'll jump in the car and take a quick ride over to the office."

"Don't be ridiculous; the phone records will still be there on Monday." I smiled to reinforce my lack of concern. "Anyway, Elliot Lavigne should be at my house by now, and I really want you to meet him. He'll be a huge help to you in restructuring Steve Madden's operations."

"Isn't he kind of wacky?" asked Deluca.

"Kind of? The guy's a complete fucking loon, Gary! But he happens to be one of the sharpest guys in the apparel industry–maybe *the* sharpest guy. You just gotta catch him at the right time.

I'd first laid eyes on Elliot Lavigne four years ago, while I was vacationing in the Bahamas with Kenny Greene. I was lying by the pool at the Crystal Palace Hotel and Casino when Kenny came running up to me. I remember him screaming something like: "Hurry up! You gotta go into the casino right now and check this guy out! He's up over a million dollars, and he's not much older than you."

In spite of being skeptical over Kenny's version of things, I popped out of my lounge chair and headed for the casino. On the way, I asked, "What's the guy do for a living?"

"I asked one of the casino people," replied the Blockhead, whose use of the English language didn't include words like *dealer, pit boss,* or *croupier,* "and they said he's the president of some big Garment Center company."

Two minutes later I was staring at this young Garmento, in a state of utter disbelief. In retrospect, it's hard to say what bowled me over more: the sight of dashing young Elliot–who was not only betting $10,000 a hand but had the whole blackjack table to himself and was playing all seven hands at once, which is to say he was risking $70,000 on every deal–or the sight of his wife, Ellen, who appeared to be no more than thirty-five yet had already acquired a look that I had never seen before, namely, the look of the supremely rich and the supremely starved.

I was blown away. So I stared at these two anomalies for a good fifteen minutes. They seemed like an awkward couple. He was on the short side, very good-looking, with bushy, shoulder-length brown hair and a sense of style that was so fabulous he could walk around in a diaper and bow tie and you would swear it was the latest thing.

She, on the other hand, was short and had a thin face, thin nose, collapsed cheeks, bleached-blond hair, tan leathery skin, eyes that were too close together, and a body that was emaciated to near perfection. I figured she must have one of the world's great personalities–a loving, supportive wife of the highest order. After all, why else would this handsome young guy who gambled with the poise and panache of 007 be attracted to her?

I was slightly off the mark.

The next day Elliot and I happened to meet by the pool. We moved right past the normal pleasantries and plunged into what each of us did for a living, how much we were making, and how we'd arrived at this point in our lives.

Elliot, as it turned out, was the President of Perry Ellis, one of the Garment District's premier menswear companies. He didn't actually own the company; it was a division of Salant, a public company that traded on the New York Stock Exchange. So, in essence, Elliot was a salaried employee. When he told me his salary I nearly fell off my lounge chair: It was only $1 million a year, plus a small bonus of a few hundred grand, based on profitability. It was a paltry sum, in my book–especially with his penchant for high-stakes gambling. In point of fact, he seemed to be gambling two years' salary each time he sat down at the blackjack table! I wasn't sure whether to be impressed or contemptuous. I chose impressed.

Before departing, we exchanged phone numbers and promised that we would hook up back in the States. The subject of drugs never came up.

We met for lunch a week later, at a trendy Garment District hangout. Five minutes after we sat down, Elliot reached into his inside suit pocket and pulled out a small plastic Baggie filled with cocaine. He dipped a Perry Ellis collar stay inside; in one fluid motion he brought it to his nose and took a blast. Then he repeated the process once more, and then once more, and then once more again. Yet he had done it so fluidly–and with such nonchalance–that not a single soul in the restaurant noticed.

Then he offered me the Baggie. I declined, saying, "Are you crazy? It's the middle of the day!" to which he replied, "Just shut up and do it," to which I replied, "Sure, why not!"

A minute later I was feeling wonderful, and four minutes after that I was feeling miserable, grinding my teeth uncontrollably and in desperate need of a Valium. Elliot took pity on me. He reached into his pants pocket and pulled out two brown-speckled Quaaludes, and said, "Here, take these; they're bootlegs, so they have Valium in them."

"Do Ludes now?" I asked incredulously. "In the middle of the day?"

"Yeah," he snapped, "why not? You're the boss. Who's gonna say anything?" and he pulled out a couple more Ludes and swallowed the pills with a smile. Then he stood up and started doing jumping jacks in the middle of the restaurant to hasten the process of getting off. I took my own Ludes, since he seemed to know exactly what he was doing.

A few minutes later, a heavyset man walked into the restaurant, drawing a lot of attention. He looked sixtyish, and he reeked of wealth. Elliot said to me, "That guy's worth half a billion. But look how ugly his tie is." With that, Elliot picked up a steak knife and walked over to the big shot, hugged him, and then sliced his tie off, in the middle of the crowded restaurant. Then he removed his own tie, which was gorgeous, and turned up the big shot's collar, placed his tie around his neck, and made a perfect Windsor knot in less than five seconds flat, at which point the big shot hugged him and thanked him.

An hour later we were both getting laid by prostitutes, with Elliot introducing me to my first Blue Chip. And in spite of the fact that I had a terrible case of coke dick, the Blue Chip worked her oral magic on me, and I came like gangbusters–paying her $5,000 for her troubles, at which point she told me that I was very handsome and, despite the fact that she was a hooker, she was still marriage material, if I was interested.

Soon after, Elliot walked in the room and said, "Come on! Get dressed–we're going to Atlantic City! The casino is sending us a helicopter and they're gonna buy each of us a gold watch," to which I said, "I only have five grand on me," to which he replied, "I spoke to the casino, and they're gonna set you up with a half-million-dollar credit line."

I wondered why they were willing to advance me so much money, considering I had never gambled more than $10,000 in my entire life. But an hour later I found myself playing blackjack at Trump Castle to the tune of $10,000 a hand, as if it were no big deal. At the end of the night I walked away a quarter million richer. I was hooked.

Elliot and I began traveling around the world together; sometimes with wives, sometimes without. I made him my primary rathole, and he kicked me back millions in cash–using money he'd won at casinos. He was a first-rate gambler, and he was adding no less than two million a year to his bottom line.

Then came my divorce from Denise–and then my bachelor party in honor of my upcoming union to Nadine. This would mark a turning point in the life of Elliot Lavigne. The party was in Las Vegas at the Mirage Hotel, which had just opened and was considered the place to be. A hundred Strattonites flew in, accompanied by fifty hookers and enough drugs to sedate Nevada. We rounded up another thirty hookers from the streets of Vegas and had a few more flown in from California. We brought a half dozen NYPD cops along for the ride, the very cops I had been paying off with Stratton new issues. And once there, the NYPD cops quickly hooked up with local Vegas cops, so we hired a few of them too.

The bachelor party took place on a Saturday evening. Elliot and I were downstairs, sharing a blackjack table; there was a crowd of strangers surrounding us, as well as a handful of bodyguards. He was playing five of the seven available hands; I was playing the other two. We were each betting $10,000 per hand, we were both hot, and we were both higher than kites. I was five Ludes deep and had snorted no less than an eight ball of coke; he was five Ludes deep too and had snorted enough coke to ski-jump off. I was up $700,000; he was up over $2 million. Through clenched teeth and a grinding jaw, I said, "Less call is quis and zo upzairs and chess out da fezividees."

Of course, Elliot understood Lude-speak as well as I did, so he nodded and we headed upstairs. I was so stoned at this point that I knew I was done gambling for the evening; I made a pit stop at the cage and cashed out to the tune of $1 million. I tossed the cash into a blue Mirage knapsack and threw it over my shoulder. Elliot, though, wasn't done gambling yet, so he left his chips at the table, under armed guard.

Upstairs, we walked down a long hallway, at the end of which was a prodigious set of double doors. On either side of the doors was a uniformed police officer, standing watch. They opened the doors, and there was the bachelor party. Elliot and I walked into the room and froze: It was the reincarnation of Sodom and Gomorrah. The rear wall was floor-to-ceiling plate glass and looked out over the Strip. The room was filled with people dancing and carrying on. The ceiling seemed to be pressing down; the floor seemed to be rising up; the smell of sex and sweat mixed with the pungent smell of premium-grade sinsemilla. Music was blasting so loud that it seemed to resonate with my very gizzard. A half dozen NYPD cops were supervising the action, making sure everyone behaved themselves.

At the back of the room, a beastly pink-sheet hooker with orange hair and the face of a bulldog was sitting on a bar stool, stark naked and covered in tattoos. Her legs were spread wide open, and a line of twenty naked Strattonites were waiting to bang her.

In that very instant I became disgusted with everything my life stood for. It was a new Stratton low. The only solution was to go downstairs to my suite and take five milligrams of Xanax, twenty milligrams of Ambien, and thirty milligrams of morphine. Then I fired up a joint and fell into a deep dreamless sleep.

I woke up to Elliot Lavigne shaking my shoulders. It was early the next morning and he was calmly explaining to me how we needed to immediately leave Las Vegas, because it was too decadent. Happy to leave, I quickly packed my bags. But when I opened the safe it was empty.

Elliot yelled from the living room: "I had to borrow some money from you last night. I took a bit of a loss."

It turned out that he lost $2 million. A week later, he, Danny, and I went to Atlantic City so he could recoup some of his losses, and he lost a million more. Over the next few years he kept losing . . . and losing . . . until finally he lost it all. How much he actually lost was still a matter of speculation, although by most accounts it was somewhere between $20 million and $40 million. Either way Elliot had busted himself out. Completely broke. He was behind on his taxes, behind in his kickbacks to me, and he was physically a wreck. He weighed no more than a hundred thirty pounds, and his skin had turned the same brownish color as his bootleg Quaaludes, which made me that much gladder I took only pharmaceutical Quaaludes. (Always looking for a silver lining.)

So it was that I now sat in my backyard in Indian Creek Island, staring out at Biscayne Bay and the skyline of Miami. Also at the table were Elliot Lavigne, Gary Deluca, and Elliot's close friend, Arthur Wiener, who was fiftyish, balding, wealthy, and coke-addicted.

By the pool were the delectable Duchess, the emaciated Ellen, and Sonny Wiener, Arthur's wife. By one p.m. it was ninety degrees and there wasn't a cloud in the sky. At this particular moment, Elliot was trying to respond to a question I'd just posed to him, over what Steve Madden's goal should be with its business with Macy's, which seemed receptive to rolling out in-store Steve Madden shops.

"Za key za grozzing Mazzen wickly iz zoo zemand all zorz wiz Mazeez," said a smiling Elliot Lavigne, who was five Ludes deep and sipping on an ice-cold Heineken.

I said to Gary, "I think what he's trying to say is that we need to approach Macy's from a position of strength and tell them that we can't roll out in-store shops one by one. We need to do it region by region, with a goal of being in all stores across the country."

Arthur nodded. "Well said, Jordan; that was a fine translation." He dipped a tiny spoon into a coke vial he was holding and took a blast up his left nostril.

Elliot looked at Deluca and nodded and raised his eyebrows, as if to say, "You see, I'm not that difficult to understand."

Just then the Jewish skeleton walked over and said to her husband, "Elliot, give me a Lude; I'm out." Elliot shook his head no and shot her the middle finger.

"You're a real fucking bastard!" snapped the angry skeleton. "Just wait and see what happens next time you're out. I'll tell you to go fuck yourself too!"

I looked at Elliot, whose head was now bobbing and weaving. It was a clear sign that he was about to leave the slur phase and enter the drool phase. I said, "Hey, El: You want me to make you something to eat, so you can come down a bit?"

Elliot smiled broadly and replied, "Make me a zuld-claz cheezburzer!"

"No problem!" I said, and I rose from my chair and headed to the kitchen to make him a world-class cheeseburger. The Duchess intercepted me in the living room, wearing a sky-blue Brazilian bikini the size of kite string.

Through clenched teeth, she snapped, "I can't take Ellen for one more second! She's sick in the fucking head, and I don't want her in my house anymore. She's slurring and snorting coke, and the whole thing is fucking disgusting! You're sober almost a month now and I don't want you surrounded by this. It's not good for you."

I'd half-missed what the Duchess said. I mean–I'd heard every word, but I'd been too busy looking at her breasts, which she'd just had augmented to a small C-cup. They looked glorious. I said, "Calm down, sweetie; Ellen's not so bad. Besides, Elliot's one of my closest friends, so the matter's not up for discussion," and as the last few words escaped my lips, I knew I'd made a mistake. A split second later the Duchess took a swing at me. It was a full right cross with an open hand.

But having been sober for a month, I had catlike reflexes, and I easily dodged the blow. I said, "Cool your jets, Nadine. It's not so easy to smack me around when I'm sober, huh?" I flashed her a devilish smile, to which she grinned broadly, and then she threw her arms around me and said, "I'm so proud of you. It's like you're a different person now. Even your back's starting to feel better, right?"

"A little bit," I replied. "It's manageable now, but it's still not perfect. Anyway, I think I'm really over the hump with the Quaaludes. And I love you more than ever."

"I love you too," she said, pouting. "I'm only mad because Elliot and Ellen are evil. He's the worst influence on you, and if he stays here too long . . . well, you know what I'm talking about." She gave me a wet kiss on the lips and then pushed the curve of her stomach against mine.

Suddenly, with three pints of blood rushing to my loins, I found the Duchess's point of view making much more sense. I said, "I'll tell you what: If you agree to be my sex slave for the rest of the weekend, I'll put Elliot and Ellen up in a hotel–deal?"

The Duchess smiled broadly and rubbed me in just the right place. "You got it, sweetie. Your wish is my command; just get them outta here and I'm all yours."

Fifteen minutes later Elliot was slobbering over his cheeseburger, while I was on the phone with Janet, asking her to book Elliot and Ellen a hotel room at a plush hotel about thirty minutes away.

Out of nowhere, with his mouth still filled with cheeseburger, Elliot popped out of his chair and dove into the pool. A few seconds later he came up for air and waved me in for an underwater race. It was something we always did–betting which of us could swim the most laps underwater. Elliot was a strong swimmer, having grown up by the ocean, so he had a slight edge on me. But given his current condition, I thought I could take him. Besides, I'd been a lifeguard back in my teens, so I was a pretty strong swimmer too.

We each swam four laps: a tie. The Duchess came over and said, "Don't you think it's time you two schmucks grew up? I don't like when you play that game. It's stupid. And one of you is gonna get hurt." Then she added, "And where's Elliot?"

I looked at the bottom of the pool. I squinted. What the fuck was he doing? He was lying on his side? *Oh, shit!* All at once the sheer gravity of things hit me like a sledgehammer, and without thinking I dove down to the bottom of the pool to get him. He wasn't moving. I grabbed him by the hair–and with a mighty jerk of my right arm and the most powerful scissors kick I could muster, I yanked him off the bottom and headed for the surface. His body was almost weightless from the water's buoyancy. Just as we broke through the surface, I jerked my arm over to the right and Elliot went flying out of the water and landed on the edge of the pool, on the concrete. And he was dead. *Dead!*

"OhmyGod!" screamed Nadine, and tears began streaming down her face. "Elliot's dead! Save him!"

"Go call an ambulance!" I screamed. "Hurry up!"

I placed two fingertips over his carotid artery. No pulse. I grabbed his wrist and checked there. Nothing. *My friend is dead,* I thought.

Just then I heard a screeching sound; it was Ellen Lavigne. "Oh, God, no! Please don't take my husband! Please! Save him, Jordan! Save him! You can't let him die! I can't lose my husband! I have two children! Oh, no! Not now! Please!" She began sobbing uncontrollably.

I became aware of a crowd of people around me–Gary Deluca, Arthur and Sonny, Gwynne and Rocco, even the baby nurse, who had grabbed Chandler from the kiddie pool and rushed over to see what the commotion was. I saw Nadine running toward me, on her way back from calling the ambulance, and the words kept ringing in my ears–*Save him! Save him!* I wanted to give Elliot CPR, just like I'd been taught all those years back.

I really wanted to, but why should I? I thought. Wouldn't it be better if Elliot just died? He had the goods on me, and one of these days Agent Coleman would get around to subpoenaing his bank records, wouldn't he? At that very moment, as Elliot lay dead before me, I couldn't help but marvel at how convenient his death would be. *Dead men tell no tales* . . . Those five words began overtaking my mind, begging me not to resuscitate him, to let the secrets of our nefarious dealings die along with him.

And this man had been the scourge of my life–reintroducing me to Quaaludes after years of not taking them, getting me hooked on cocaine, and then going bad on me in the rathole game, which was tantamount to stealing my money. And all of it to fuel his gambling habit . . . and his drug addiction . . . and his IRS problems. Agent Coleman was no fool, and he would exploit those weaknesses, especially the IRS problems, where he would threaten Elliot with jail time. Then Elliot would cooperate against me and spill his guts. I should just let him die, for Chrissake, because . . . *dead men tell no tales* . . .

But in the background everyone was screaming: "Don't stop! Don't stop! Don't stop!" Suddenly it hit me: *I was already trying to resuscitate him!* As my conscious mind was debating things–something infinitely more powerful had already clicked inside me and was overriding my thoughts.

And at that very moment I found my mouth pressed against Elliot's mouth, and my lungs expelling air into his lungs, and then I lifted my head and began pumping Elliot's chest in rhythmic bursts. I stopped and took a moment to regard him.

Nothing! Shit! He was still dead! How could it be? I was doing everything right! Why wouldn't he come back?

All at once I remembered reading an article about the Heimlich maneuver and how it had been used to save a child who'd drowned, so I flipped Elliot onto his stomach and wrapped my arms around him. I squeezed as hard as I possibly could. *Snap! Crack! Crunch!* . . . In that very instant I realized I'd broken most of his ribs. So I flipped him back over to see if he'd started breathing, and he hadn't.

It was over. He was dead. I looked up at Nadine, and with tears in my eyes, I said, "I don't know what to do! He won't come back!"

And then I heard Ellen scream at the top of her lungs once more: "OhmyGod! My children! Oh, God! Please, don't stop, Jordan! Don't stop! You have to save my husband!"

Elliot was completely blue, the last flickers of light leaving his eyes. So I said a silent prayer and inhaled as deeply as I possibly could. With every last bit of force my lungs could muster, I shot a jet of air into him, and I felt his stomach blow up like a balloon. Then all at once the cheeseburger came up, and he vomited into my mouth. I started to gag.

I watched him take a shallow breath, then I stuck my face in the pool and washed the vomit out of my mouth. I looked back at Elliot and noticed his face looked less blue. Then he stopped breathing again. I looked at Gary and said, "Take over for me," to which Gary extended his palms toward me and shook his head, as if to say, "No fucking way!" and he took two steps backward to reinforce his point. So I turned to Elliot's best friend, Arthur, and asked him to do the same, and he reacted just as Gary had. So I had no choice but to do the most disgusting thing imaginable. I splashed water on Elliot's face as the Duchess sprang into action and cleaned the vomit off the sides of Elliot's mouth. Then I stuck my hand inside and scooped out partially digested cheeseburger meat, pushing his tongue down to clear an air passage. I put my mouth back on his mouth and began breathing for him again, while the others stood frozen in horror.

Finally I heard the sound of sirens, and a few moments later there were paramedics hovering over us. In less than three seconds they had a tube down Elliot's throat and had started pumping oxygen into his lungs. They gently placed him on a stretcher and then carried him off to the side of the mansion, under a shady tree, and stuck an IV in his arm.

I jumped into the pool and washed the vomit out of my mouth, still gagging uncontrollably. The Duchess came running over, holding a toothbrush and toothpaste, and I began brushing my teeth right in the pool. Then I jumped out and headed over to where Elliot was lying on the stretcher. By now there were half a dozen policemen there with the paramedics. They were desperately trying to get his heart beating at a normal rate, without success. One of the paramedics stuck his hand out to me and said, "You're a hero, sir. You saved your friend's life."

And just like that it hit me: I was a hero! Me! The Wolf of Wall Street! *A hero!* What a delicious ring those three words had! I desperately needed to hear them again, so I said, "I'm sorry, I missed what you said. Can you please repeat it?"

The paramedic smiled at me and said, "You're a hero, in the truest sense of the word. Not many men would have done what you did. You had no training, yet you did exactly the right thing. Well done, sir. You're a real hero."

Oh, Jesus! I thought. This was absolutely wonderful. But I needed to hear it from the Duchess, with her loamy loins and brand-new breasts, which would now be mine for the taking, at least for the next few days, because I, her husband, was a hero, and no female can refuse the sexual advances of a hero.

I found the Duchess sitting by herself on the edge of a lounge chair, still in a state of shock. I tried to find just the right words that would inspire her to call me a hero. I decided it would be best to use reverse psychology on her–to compliment her on how calm *she'd* remained and then praise her for calling the ambulance. This way she would feel compelled to return the compliment.

I sat down beside her and put my arm around her. "Thank God you called the ambulance, Nae. I mean, everyone else froze in place, except for you. You're a strong lady." I waited patiently.

She edged closer to me and smiled sadly. "I don't know," she said. "I guess it was just instinct more than anything else. You know, you see this sort of stuff in movies, but you never think it's gonna happen to you. You know what I mean?"

Un-fucking-believable! She didn't call me a hero! I would just have to get more specific. "I know what you mean. You never think something like this could happen, but once it does, well, instinct just takes over. I guess that's why I reacted the way I did." *Hello, Duchess! Get my drift, for Chrissake?*

Apparently she did, because she threw her arms around me and said, "OhmyGod! You were incredible! I've never seen anything like it. I mean . . . words just can't describe how brilliant you were! Everyone else was frozen in place and you . . ."

Christ! I thought. She kept gushing over me, but she refused to say the magic word!

". . . and you're . . . I mean . . . you're a *hero,* honey!" *There she goes!* "I don't think I've ever been prouder of you. My husband, the hero!" She gave me the wettest kiss imaginable.

In that very instant I understood why every young child wants to be a fireman. Just then I saw them carrying Elliot away on a stretcher. "Come on," I said. "Let's head over to the hospital and make sure they don't drop the ball after I worked so hard to save Elliot's life."

Twenty minutes later we were in the emergency room at Mount Sinai Hospital, and the early prognosis was unspeakable: Elliot had suffered some brain damage. Whether or not he would be a vegetable was still unclear.

On the way to the hospital, the Duchess had called Barth. Now I followed him into the critical-care room, which bore the unmistakable odor of death. There were four doctors and two nurses, and Elliot was lying flat on his back on an examining table.

Mt. Sinai wasn't Barth's hospital, yet apparently his reputation preceded him. Every doctor in the room knew exactly who he was. A tall one in a white lab coat said, "He's in a coma, Dr. Green. He won't breathe unassisted. His brain function is depressed, and he has seven broken ribs. We've given him epinephrine, but he hasn't responded." The doctor looked Barth straight in the eye and shook his head slowly, as if to say, "He's not going to make it."

Then Barth Green did the oddest thing. With complete and utter confidence, he walked right up to Elliot, grabbed him by the shoulders, put his mouth to Elliot's ear, and in a stern voice yelled, "Elliot! Wake up right this second!" He started shaking him vigorously. "This is Dr. Barth Green, Elliot, and I'm telling you to stop screwing around and open up your eyes right now! Your wife is outside and she wants to see you!"

And just like that, in spite of the last few words about Ellen wanting to see him–which would make most men choose death–Elliot followed Barth's instructions and opened his eyes. A moment later his brain function returned to normal. I looked around the room, and every last doctor and nurse was agape.

As was I. It was a miracle, performed by a miracle worker. I started shaking my head in admiration, and out of the corner of my eye I happened to see a large syringe filled with a clear liquid. I squinted to see what the label said. *Morphine.* Very interesting, I thought, that they would give morphine to a dying man.

All at once I was overtaken by this terrible urge to snatch the needle of morphine and inject myself in the ass. Just why, I wasn't sure. I had been sober for almost a month now, but that didn't seem to matter anymore. I looked around the room and everyone was hovering over Elliot, still in awe over this remarkable turn of events. I edged over to the metal tray, casually snatched the needle, and stuck it in my shorts pocket.

A moment later I felt my pocket growing warm . . . and then warmer . . . *Oh, sweet Jesus!* The morphine was burning a hole in my pocket! I needed to inject myself right this instant! I said to Barth, "That's the most incredible thing I've ever seen, Barth. I'm gonna go outside and tell everyone the good news."

When I informed the group in the waiting room that Elliot had made a miraculous recovery, Ellen began crying tears of joy and she threw her arms around me. I pushed her away and told her that I was in desperate need of a bathroom. As I started walking away, the Duchess grabbed me by the arm and said, "Are you okay, honey? You don't seem right."

I smiled at my wife and said, "Yeah, I'm fine. I just have to go to the bathroom."

The moment I turned the corner I took off like a world-class sprinter. I swung the bathroom door open, went inside one of the stalls, locked it, and then took out the syringe and pulled down my shorts and arched my back, so my ass was perched in the air. I was just about to plunge in the needle when disaster struck.

The needle was missing the plunger.

It was one of those newfangled safety needles, which couldn't be injected without first being put into a plunging mechanism. All I had was a worthless cartridge of morphine with a needle on the end of it. I was devastated. I took a moment to regard this needle. *A lightbulb!*

I pulled up my shorts and ran to the gift shop and purchased a lollipop, then ran back to the bathroom. I plunged the needle into my ass. Then I took the stick of the lollipop and pushed down on the center of the syringe until every last drop of morphine was injected. All at once I felt a keg of gunpowder exploding inside me, rocking me to my very core.

Oh, Christ! I thought. I must've hit a vein, because the high was overtaking me at an incredible rate. And just like that, I was down on my knees and my mouth was bone-dry, and my innards felt like they'd just been submerged in a hot bubble bath, and my eyes felt like hot coals, and my ears were ringing like the Liberty Bell, and my anal sphincter felt tighter than a drum, and I loved it.

And here I sat, the hero, on the bathroom floor, with my shorts pulled down below my knees and the needle still sticking in my ass. But then it occurred to me that the Duchess might be worried about me.

A minute later I was in the hallway, on my way back to the Duchess, when I heard an old Jewish woman say, "Excuse me, sir!"

I turned to her. She smiled nervously and pointed her index finger at my shorts. Then she said, "Your tushie! Look at your tushie!"

I had been walking down the hallway with a needle sticking out of my ass, like a wounded bull that had just been darted by a matador. I smiled at the kind woman and thanked her, then removed the needle from my ass, threw it in a garbage can, and headed back to the waiting room.

When the Duchess saw me she smiled. But then the room began to grow dark and . . . *Oh, shit!*

I woke up in the waiting room, sitting on a plastic chair. Standing over me was a middle-aged doctor in green surgical scrubs. In his right hand he was holding smelling salts. The Duchess was standing next to him, and she was no longer smiling. The doctor said, "Your breathing is depressed, Mr. Belfort. Have you taken any narcotics?"

"No," I said, forcing a weak smile for the Duchess. "I guess being a hero is very stressful, right, honey?" Then I passed out again.

I woke up in the back of a Lincoln limousine as it pulled into Indian Creek Island, where nothing exciting ever happens. My first thought was that I needed to snort some cocaine to even out. That had been my problem all along. To inject morphine without a balancing agent was a fool's errand. I made a mental note to never try that again and then thanked God that Elliot had brought coke with him. I would snatch it from his room and deduct it from the $2 million he owed me.

Five minutes later, the guesthouse looked like a dozen CIA agents had spent three hours searching for stolen microfilm. There were clothes strewn about everywhere, and every piece of furniture had been tipped over on its side. And still no cocaine! *Fuck!* Where was it? I kept searching–searching for over an hour, in fact, until finally it hit me: *It was that rat fuck, Arthur Wiener!* He'd stolen his best friend's cocaine!

Feeling empty and alone, I went upstairs to my sprawling master bedroom and cursed Arthur Wiener until I fell into a dreamless sleep.

CHAPTER 27

ONLY THE GOOD DIE YOUNG

June 1994

It seemed only appropriate that the offices of Steve Madden Shoes would be shaped like a shoe box. Actually, there were two shoe boxes: the one in the rear, which was thirty by sixty feet and housed a tiny factory, consisting of a handful of antiquated shoe-making machines manned by a dozen or so Spanish-speaking employees; and the shoe box in front, which was of similar size and housed the company's office staff, most of whom were girls in their late teens or early twenties, and all of whom sported the sort of multicolored hair and visible body piercings that so much as said, "Yes, I've also had my clit pierced, as well as both my nipples!"

And while these young female space cadets pranced around the office, teetering atop six-inch platform shoes—all bearing the Steve Madden label—there was hip-hop music blasting and incense burning and a dozen telephones ringing and countless new shoe styles in the designing and a smattering of traditionally garbed religious leaders performing ritual cleansings, and somehow it all seemed to work. The only thing missing was an authentic witch doctor performing voodoo, although I was certain that would come next.

Anyway, at the front of the aforementioned front shoe box was an even smaller shoe box—this one perhaps ten by twenty feet—which was where Steve, aka, the Cobbler, kept his office. And for the last four weeks, since mid-May, it was where I'd kept my office too. The Cobbler and I sat on opposite sides of a black Formica desk, which, like everything else in this place, was covered in shoes.

At this particular moment I was wondering why every teenage girl in America was going crazy over these shoes that, to me, were hideous-looking. Whatever the case, there was no denying that we were a product-driven company. There were shoes everywhere, especially in Steve's office, where they were scattered about the floor, hanging from the ceiling, and piled upon cheap folding tables and white Formica shelves, which made them seem that much uglier.

And there were more shoes on the windowsill behind Steve, piled so high I could barely see out that gloomy window into the gloomy parking lot, which, admittedly, was well suited to this gloomy part of Queens, namely, the gloomy groin of Woodside. We were about two miles east of Manhattan, where a man of my "somewhat" refined tastes was much better suited.

Nevertheless, money was money, and for some inexplicable reason this tiny company was on the verge of making boatloads of it. So this was where Janet and I would hang our hats for the foreseeable future. She was just down the hall, in a private office. And, yes, she, too, was surrounded by shoes.

It was Monday morning, and the Cobbler and I were sitting in our shoe-infested office, sipping coffee. Accompanying us was Gary Deluca, who, as of today, was the company's new Operations Manager, replacing no one in particular, because up until now the company had been running on autopilot. Also in the room was John Basile, the company's longtime Production Manager, who doubled as the company's Head of Sales.

It was rather ironic, I thought, but dressed the way we were you would have never guessed that we were in the process of building the world's largest women's shoe company. We were a ragtag lot–I was dressed like a golf pro; Steve was dressed like a bum; Gary was dressed like a conservative businessman; and John Basile, a mid-thirties chubster, with a bulbous nose, bald skull, and thick, fleshy features, was dressed like a pizza delivery boy, wearing faded blue jeans and a baggy T-shirt. I absolutely adored John. He was a true talent, and despite being Catholic, he was blessed with a true Protestant work ethic–whatever *that* meant–and he was a true seer of the big picture.

But, alas, he was also a world-class spitter, which meant that whenever he was excited–or simply trying to make a point–you'd best be wearing a raincoat or be at least thirty degrees in either direction of his mouth. And, typically, his saliva was accompanied by exaggerated hand gestures, most of which had to do with the Cobbler being a fucking pussy for not wanting to place large-enough orders with the factories.

Right now he was in the midst of making that very point. "I mean, how the fuck are we gonna grow this company, Steve, if you won't let me place orders for the fucking shoes? Come on, Jordan, you know what I'm talking about! How the fuck can I build"–*Shit!* The Spitter's Bs were his most deadly consonant, and he just got me in the forehead!–"relationships with the department stores when I don't have product to deliver?" The Spitter paused and looked at me quizzically, wondering why I had just put my head in my hands and seemed to be smelling my own palms.

I rose from my chair and walked behind Steve, in search of spit protection, and said, "The truth is I see *both* your points. It's no different than the brokerage business: Steve wants to play things conservative and not hold a lot of shoes in inventory, and you want to step up to the plate and swing for the fences so you have product to sell. I got it. And the answer is–you're both right and both wrong, depending on if the shoes sell through or not. If they do, you're a genius, and we'll make a ton of money, but if you're wrong–and they don't sell through–we're fucked, and we're sitting on a worthless pile of shit that we can't sell to anyone."

"That's not true," argued the Spitter. "We can always dump the shoes to Marshall's or TJ Maxx or one of the other closeout chains."

Steve swiveled his chair around and said to me, "John's not giving you the whole picture. Yeah, we can sell all the shoes we want to people like Marshall's and TJ Maxx; but then we destroy our business with the department stores and specialty shops." Now Steve looked the Spitter directly in the eye and said, "We need to protect the brand, John. You just don't get it."

The Spitter said, "Of course I get it. But we also have to *grow* the brand, and we can't grow the brand if our customers go to the department stores and can't find our shoes." Now the Spitter narrowed his eyes in contempt and stared the Cobbler down. "And if I leave this up to you," spat the Spitter, "we'll be a mom-and-pop operation forever. Fucking pikers, nothing more." He turned directly toward me, so I braced myself. "I'll tell ya, Jordan"–his spitball missed me by ten degrees–"thank God you're here, because this guy is such a fucking pussy, and I'm sick of pussyfooting around. We got the hottest shoes in the country, and I can't fill the fucking orders because this guy won't let me manufacture product. I'll tell you, it's a Greek fucking tragedy, nothing less."

Steve said, "John, do you know how many companies have gone out of business by operating the way you want? We need to err on the side of caution 'til we have more company-owned stores; then we can take our markdowns *in-house,* without bastardizing the brand. There's no way you can convince me otherwise."

The Spitter reluctantly took his seat. I had to admit I was more than impressed with Steve's performance, not just today but over the last four weeks. Yes, Steve was a Wolf in Sheep's Clothing too. Despite his outward appearance, he was a born leader–blessed with all the natural gifts, especially the ability to inspire loyalty among his employees. In fact, like at Stratton, everyone at Steve Madden prided themselves on being part of a cult. The Cobbler's biggest problem, though, was his refusal to delegate authority–hence, his nickname, the Cobbler. There was a part of Steve that was still a little old-fashioned shoemaker, which, in truth, was both his greatest strength and his greatest weakness. The company was doing only $5 million right now, so he could still get away with it. But that was about to change. It had been only a year ago that the company was doing a million. We were shooting for $20 million next year.

This was where I'd been focusing my attention over the last four weeks. Hiring Gary Deluca was only the first step. My goal was for the company to stand on its own two feet, without either of us. So Steve and I needed to build a first-class design team and operational staff. But too much too fast would be a recipe for disaster. Besides, first we needed to gain control of the operations, which were a complete disaster.

I turned to Gary and said, "I know it's your first day, but I'm interested to hear what you think. Give me your opinion, and be honest, whether you agree with Steve or not."

With that, the Spitter and the Cobbler both turned to our company's new Director of Operations. He said, "Well, I see both your points"–*ahhh, well done, very diplomatic*–"but my take on this is more from an operational perspective than anything else. In fact, much of this, I would say, is a question of gross margin–after markdowns, of course–and how it relates to the number of times a year we plan on turning our inventory." Gary nodded his head, impressed with his own sagacity. "There are complex issues here relating to shipping modalities, inasmuch as how and where we plan to take delivery of our goods–how many hubs and spokes, so to speak. Of course, I'll need to do an in-depth analysis of our true cost of goods sold, including duty and freight, which shouldn't be overlooked. I intend to do that right away and then put together a detailed spreadsheet, which we can review at the next board meeting, which should be sometime in . . ."

Oh, Jesus H. Christ! He was drizzling on us! I had no tolerance for operational people and all the meaningless bullshit they seemed to hold so dear. *Details! Details!* I looked at Steve. He was even less tolerant than me in these matters, and he was now visibly sagging. His chin was just above his collarbone and his mouth was agape.

". . . which more than anything else," continued the Drizzler, "is a function of the efficiency of our pick, pack, and ship operation. The key there is–"

Just then the Spitter rose from his seat and cut the Drizzler off. "What the fuck are you talking about?" spat the Spitter. "I just wanna sell some fucking shoes! I couldn't give two fucks about how you get them to the stores! And I don't need any fucking spreadsheet to tell me that if I'm making shoes for twelve bucks and selling them for thirty bucks then I'm making fucking money! Jesus!" Now the Spitter headed directly toward me with two giant steps. Out of the corner of my eye I could see Steve smirking.

The Spitter said, "Jordan, you gotta make a decision here. You're the only one Steve will listen to." He paused and wiped a gob of drool off his round chin. "I want to grow this company for you, but my hands are being tied behind my–"

"All right!" I said, cutting off the Spitter. I turned to the Drizzler and said, "Go ask Janet to get Elliot Lavigne on the phone. He's in the Hamptons." I turned to Steve and said, "I want Elliot's take on this before we make a decision. I know there's an answer to this, and if anyone has it it's Elliot." And, besides, I thought, while we're waiting for Janet to put him through, I'll have a chance to tell my heroic story again.

Alas, I never got the chance. The Drizzler was back in less than twenty seconds, and a moment later the phone beeped. "Hey, buddy, how ya doing?" said Elliot Lavigne through the speakerphone.

"I'm good," replied his hero. "But, more important, how are *you* doing, and how are your ribs feeling?"

"I'm recovering," replied Elliot, who'd been sober for almost six weeks now, which was a world record for him. "Hopefully, I'll be back to work in a few weeks. What's going on?"

I quickly plunged into the details, careful not to tell him whose opinion stood where–so as not to prejudice his decision. Ironically, it made no difference. By the time I was done, he already knew. "The truth is," said the sober Elliot, "this whole idea of not being able to sell your brand to discounters is more hype than reality. Every major brand blows out their dead inventory through the discount chains. It's a must. Walk into any TJ Maxx or any Marshall's and you'll see all the big labels–Ralph Lauren, Calvin Klein, Donna Karan, and Perry Ellis too. You can't exist without the discounters, unless you have your own outlet stores, which is still premature for you guys. But you have to be careful when you deal with them. You sell them in blips, because if the department stores know you're there on a consistent basis, you're gonna have problems."

"Anyway," continued the recuperating Garmento, "John's right for the most part; you can't grow unless you have product to sell. See, the department stores will never take you seriously unless they know you can deliver the goods. And as hot as you guys are right now–and I know you're hot–the buyers won't step up to the plate unless they're convinced you can deliver the shoes, and right now your reputation is that you can't. You gotta get your act together on that quick. I know it's one of the reasons why you hired Gary, and it's definitely a step in the right direction."

I looked at Gary to see if he was beaming, but he wasn't. His face was still set in stone, impassive. They were a weird bunch, these operations guys; they were steady Eddies, hitting singles all day long but never swinging for the fences. The thought of being one was enough to make me want to fall on my own sword.

Elliot plowed on: "Anyway, assuming you get your operations in order, John is still only half right. Steve has to consider the bigger picture here, which is to protect the brand. Don't kid yourselves, guys–at the end of the day, the brand is everything. If you fuck that up you're done. I can give you a dozen examples of brands that were red-hot once and then fucked up their name by selling to the discounters. Now you find their labels in a flea market." Elliot paused, letting his words sink in.

I looked at Steve and he was slumped over in his chair–the mere thought of the name *Steve Madden*–his own name!–being synonymous with the words *flea* and *market* had literally knocked the wind out of him. I looked at the Spitter; he was leaning forward in his seat, as if he were preparing to jump through the phone line to strangle Elliot. Then I looked at Gary, who was still impassive.

Elliot went on: "Your ultimate goal should be to license the Steve Madden name. Then you can sit back and collect royalties. The first thing should be belts and handbags, then move to sportswear and denim and sunglasses, and then everything else . . . your last stop being fragrance, where you can really hit it out of the park. And you'll never get there if John has his way in everything. No offense, John, but it's just the nature of the beast. You're thinking in terms of today, when you're red-hot. Eventually you'll cool down, though, and when you least expect it something won't sell through, and you'll wind up knee-deep in some retarded-looking shoe that no one outside a trailer park will wear. Then you'll be forced to go to the dark side and put the shoes where they don't belong."

At this point Steve interrupted. "That's exactly my point, Elliot. If I let John have his way, we'll end up with a warehouse full of shoes and no money in the bank. I'm not gonna be the next Sam and Libby."

Elliot laughed. "It's simple. Without knowing everything about your business, I'm willing to bet that the bulk of your volume comes from a handful of shoes–three or four of them, probably–and they're not the ridiculous-looking ones with the nine-inch heels and the metal spikes and zippers. Those shoes are what you guys create your mystique with–that you're young and hip and all that shit. But the reality is you probably sell hardly any of those *facockta* shoes, except maybe to some of the freaks down in Greenwich Village and in your own office. What you're really making your money on are your basic shoes–the staples, like the Mary Lou and the Marilyn, right?"

I looked at Steve and the Spitter, both of whom had their heads cocked to the side and their lips pursed and their eyes wide open. After a few seconds of silence, Elliot said, "I'll take that lack of response as a yes?"

Steve said, "You're right, Elliot. We don't sell too many of the crazy shoes, but those are the ones we're known for."

"That's exactly the way it should be," said Elliot, who six weeks ago couldn't tie two words together without drooling. "It's no different than those wild couture outfits you see on the runways in Milan. No one really buys that crap, but that's what creates the image. So the answer is to only step up to the plate with the conservative items–and only in the hottest colors. I'm talking about the shoes you know you're going to blow out, the ones you sell season after season. But under no circumstance do you risk serious money on a funky shoe, even if you guys are personally in love with it–and even if it's getting good reads in your test markets. Always err on the side of caution with anything that's not a proven winner. If something really takes off and you're short inventory, it'll make it that much hotter. Since you guys manufacture in Mexico, you can still beat the competition on the reorder.

"And on the rare occasions when you swing for the fences and you're wrong–then you dump your shoes to the discounters and take your loss right away. Your first loss is your best loss in this business. The last thing you want is a warehouse full of dead inventory. You also need to start partnering with the department stores. Let them know you'll stand behind your shoes, that if they *don't* sell you'll give them markdown money. Then they can put your shoes on sale and still maintain their margins. Do that, and you'll find the department stores closing out your garbage for you.

"On a separate note, you should be rolling out Steve Madden stores as fast as possible. You guys are manufacturers, so you get the wholesale markup *and* the retail markup. And it's also the best way to move your dead inventory–putting things on sale in your own stores. Then you don't risk fucking up the brand. And that's the answer," said Elliot Lavigne. "You guys are heading for the stars. Just follow that program and you can't lose."

I looked around the room, and everyone nodded.

And why wouldn't they? Who could argue with such logic? It was sad, I thought, that a guy as sharp as Elliot would throw his life away to drugs. Seriously. There was nothing sadder than wasted talent, was there? Oh, Elliot was sober now, but I had no doubt that as soon as his ribs were healed and he was back in the swing of things, his addiction would come roaring back. That was the problem with someone like Elliot, who refused to accept the fact that drugs had gotten the best of them.

Anyway, I had enough on my own plate to keep five people occupied. I was still in the process of crushing Victor Wang; I still had to deal with Danny, who was running amok at Stratton; I still had issues with Gary Kaminsky, who, as it turned out, spent half his day on the phone with Saurel, in Switzerland; and I still had Special Agent Gregory Coleman running around with subpoenas. So to focus on Elliot's sobriety was a waste of my time.

I had pressing issues to discuss with Steve over lunch, and then I had to catch a helicopter out to the Hamptons to see the Duchess and Chandler. Under those circumstances, I would have to say that the appropriate dosage of methaqualone should be small, perhaps 250 milligrams, or one Lude, taken now, thirty minutes before lunch, which would give me just the right buzz to enjoy my pasta while allowing me to escape detection at the hands of the Cobbler, who'd been sober for almost five years. A killjoy.

Then I would snort a few lines of coke just before I got behind the helicopter's controls. After all, I always flew best when I was on my down from Ludes but still crawling out of my own skin in a state of coke-induced paranoia.

Lunch on a single Lude! An innocuous buzz while dining in the armpit of Corona, Queens. Like most formerly Italian neighborhoods, there was still one Mafioso stronghold that remained, and in each stronghold there was always one Italian restaurant where the community congregated. And, without fail, it had the best Italian food for miles around. In Harlem, it was Rao's. In Corona, it was Park Side Restaurant.

Unlike Rao's, Park Side was a large, high-volume operation. It was decorated beautifully with a couple of tons of burled walnut, smoked mirrors, carved glass, flowering plants, and perfectly trimmed ferns. The bar was a Mob scene (literally!), and the food was to die for (literally!).

Park Side was owned by Tony Federici. In my book he was the best host in the five boroughs of New York City. Typically, you could find Tony walking around his restaurant in a chef's apron, holding a jug of homemade Chianti in one hand and a tray of roasted peppers in the other.

The Cobbler and I were sitting at a table in the fabulous garden section. At this particular moment we were talking about him replacing Elliot as my primary rathole.

"Fundamentally, I have no problem with it," I was saying to the greedy Cobbler, who had become obsessed with the rathole game, "but I have two concerns. The first is how the fuck are you gonna kick me back all the cash without leaving a paper trail? It's a lot of fucking money, Cobbler. And my second concern is that you're already Monroe Parker's rathole, and I don't want to be stepping on their toes." I shook my head for effect. "A rathole is a very personal thing, so I'd first have to clear it with Alan and Brian."

The Cobbler nodded. "I understand what you're saying, and as far as kicking back the cash goes, it won't be a problem. I can do it through our Steve Madden stock. Whenever I sell stock I'm holding for you, I'll just overpay you on it. On paper I owe you over four million dollars, so I have a legitimate reason to be writing you checks. And at the end of the day, the numbers will be so big, nobody's gonna be able to keep track of it anyway, right?"

Not such a bad idea, I thought, especially if we drew up some sort of consulting agreement where Steve would pay me money each year for helping him run Steve Madden Shoes. But the fact that Steve was ratholing 1.5 million shares of Steve Madden stock for me raised a more troubling issue—namely, that Steve owned hardly any stock in his own company. It was something that needed to be rectified now, lest it create problems down the road when Steve realized that I was making tens of millions and he was making only millions. So I smiled and said, "We'll work something out with the rathole. I think using the Madden stock is a pretty good idea, at least to start, but it leads to a more important subject, which is your lack of ownership in the company. We need to get you more stock before things really start to crank. You have only three hundred thousand shares, right?"

Steve nodded. "And a few thousand stock options; that's about it."

"Okay, well, as your general scheming partner, I strongly advise you to grant yourself a million stock options at a fifty percent discount to the current market. It's the righteous thing to do, especially since you and I are gonna be splitting them fifty–fifty, which is the most righteous part of all. We'll keep them in your name so NASDAQ won't flip a lid, and when it comes time to sell, you'll just kick me back along with everything else."

The Master Cobbler smiled and extended his hand toward me. "I can't thank you enough, JB. I never said anything, but it's definitely been bothering me a bit. I knew that when the time came, though, we would work it out." Then he rose from his chair, as did I, and we exchanged a Mafia-style hug, which in this restaurant didn't elicit a shrug from a single patron.

As we both retook our seats, Steve said, "But why don't we make it a million-five, instead? Seven-fifty for each of us."

"No," I said, with a pleasant tingle in my ten fingertips, "I don't like working with odd numbers. It's bad luck. Let's just round it off to two million. Besides, it'll be easier to keep track of–a million options for each of us."

"Done!" agreed the Cobbler. "And since you're the company's largest shareholder, we should bypass the hassle of a board meeting. It's all strictly legitimate, right?"

"Well," I replied, scratching my chin thoughtfully, "as your general scheming partner, I strongly advise you to refrain from using this word *legitimate,* except under the most dire circumstances. But since you already let the genie out of the bottle, I'll go out on a limb here and give this transaction a hearty two thumbs-up. Besides, this is something we *must* do, so it's not our fault. We'll chalk it up to a sense of fair play."

"I agree," said the happy Cobbler. "It's beyond our control. There are strange forces at work here that are far more powerful than a humble Cobbler or a not-so-humble Wolf of Wall Street."

"I like the way you think, Cobbler. Call the lawyers when you get back to the office and tell them to backdate the minutes from the last board meeting. If they give you a hard time, tell them to call me."

"No problem," said the Cobbler, who had just increased his stake by four hundred percent. Then he lowered his voice and changed his tone to one of a conspirator. "Listen–if you want, you don't even have to tell Danny about this." He smiled devilishly. "If he asks me, I'll tell him they're all mine."

Christ! What a fucking backstabber this guy was! Could he possibly think this made me respect him more? But I kept that thought to myself. "I'll tell you the truth," I said, "I'm not happy with the way Danny's running things right now. He's like the Spitter when it comes to holding inventory. When I left Stratton, the firm was short a couple million dollars of stock. Now it's basically flat. It's a real fucking shame." I shook my head gravely. "Anyway, Stratton's making more money *now* than ever, which is what happens when you trade long. But now Danny's vulnerable." I shrugged my shoulders. "Whatever. I'm done worrying about it. Regardless, I still can't cut him out."

Steve shrugged. "Don't take what I said the wrong way"–*Oh, really? How else am I supposed to take it, you fucking backstabber!*–"but it's just that you and I are gonna spend the next five years building this company. You know, Brian and Alan aren't thrilled with Danny either. And neither are Loewenstern and Bronson. At least that's what I hear through the grapevine. You're gonna have to let those guys go their separate ways eventually. They'll always be loyal to you, but they want to do their own deals, away from Danny."

Just then I saw Tony Federici heading our way, wearing his white chef's ensemble and carrying a jug of Chianti. So I rose to greet him. "Hey, Tony, how are you?"

I motioned to Steve and said, "Tony, I'd like you to meet a very close friend of mine: This is Steve Madden. We're partners in a shoe company over in Woodside."

Steve immediately rose from his chair, and with a hearty smile he said, "Hey, Tough Tony! Tony Corona! I've heard of you! I mean, I grew up out on Long Island, but even there everyone's heard of Tough Tony! It's a pleasure to meet you!" With that, Steve extended his hand to his newfound friend, Tough Tony Corona, who despised that nickname immensely.

I watched the Master Cobbler's bony, pale hand hover suspensefully in the air, waiting to be grasped by a return hand, which was nowhere in sight. Then I looked at Tony's face. He seemed to be smiling, although this particular smile was one a sadistic warden would offer a death-row inmate as he asked, "What would you like for your last meal?"

Finally, Tony did extend his hand, albeit limply. "Yeah, nice to meet ya," said a toneless Tony. His dark brown eyes were like two death rays.

"It's nice to meet you too, Tough Tony," said the increasingly dead Cobbler. "I've heard only the best things about this restaurant, and I plan on coming here a lot. If I call for a reservation, I'll just tell them I'm a friend of Tough Tony Corona! Okay?"

"Okay, then!" I said with a nervous smile. "I think we'd better get back to business, Steve." Then I turned to Tony and said, "Thanks for coming over to say hello. It was good seeing you, as always." I rolled my eyes and shook my head, as if to say, "Don't mind my friend; he has Tourette's syndrome."

Tony twitched his nose two times and then went on his way.

I sat down and shook my head gravely. "What the fuck is wrong with you, Cobbler? No one calls him Tough Tony! Nobody! I mean, you're a fucking dead man."

"What are you talking about?" replied the clueless Cobbler. "The guy loved me, no?" Then he cocked his head to the side nervously and added, "Or am I totally off base here?"

Just then, Alfredo, the mountainous maître d', walked over. "You have a phone call," said Mount Alfredo. "You can take it up front by the bar. It's quiet over there. There's no one around." He smiled.

I excused myself from the table and headed for the bar. "Hello?"

"Hi, it's me," said Janet. "You sound weird; what's wrong?"

"Nothing, Janet. What do you want?" My tone was a bit curter than usual. Perhaps the Lude was wearing off.

"Excuse me for fucking living!" said the sensitive one.

With a sigh: "What do you want, Janet? I'm having a bad time of it here."

"I have Victor Wang on the phone, and he said it's urgent. I told him that you were out for lunch, but he said he would hold on until you got back. I think he's an asshole, if you want to know my opinion."

Who–cares–about–your–fucking–opinion–Janet! "Yeah, well, put him through," I said, smiling at my own reflection in a smoked-glass mirror behind the bar. I didn't even look stoned. Or maybe I *wasn't* stoned. I reached into my pocket and pulled out a Spanish Quaalude, examined it for a brief second, and then threw it down–dry.

I waited for the sound of the Depraved Chinaman's panic-stricken voice. I had been shorting him into oblivion for almost a week now, and Duke Securities was up to its ears in stock. Yes, it was raining stock on Victor, and he was looking for my help, which I had every intention of giving him . . . sort of.

Just then came the voice of the Depraved Chinaman. He greeted me warmly and then began explaining how he owned more stock in this one particular company than there was physical stock. In fact, there were only 1.5 million shares in the entire float, and he was currently in possession of 1.6 million shares.

". . . and the stock is still pouring in," said the Talking Panda, "and I just don't understand how that's possible. I know Danny fucked me over, but even *he's* gotta be out of stock now!" The Chinaman sounded thoroughly confused–unaware that I had a special account at Bear Stearns that allowed me to sell as much stock as my little heart desired, whether I owned it or not and whether I could borrow it or not. It was a special kind of account called a prime-brokerage account, which meant I could execute my trades through any brokerage firm in the world. There was no way the Chinaman could figure out who was selling.

"Calm down," I said. "If you're having capital problems, Vic, I'm here for you–a hundred percent. If you need to sell me three or four hundred thousand shares, just say the word." That was about how much I was short right now, but I was short at higher prices, so if Victor was dumb enough to sell me the stock I would lock in a huge profit–and then turn around and reshort the stock again. Before I was done, the stock would be trading in pennies, and the Chinaman would be working on Mott Street, rolling wontons.

"Yeah," replied the Talking Panda, "that would really help. I'm running tight on capital, and the stock is already below five dollars. I can't afford it to drop anymore."

"No problem, Vic. Just call Kenny Kock at Meyerson; he'll buy fifty thousand share blocks from you every few hours."

Victor thanked me, and then I hung up the phone and immediately dialed Kenny Kock, whose wife, Phyllis, had been the minister at my wedding. I said to Kenny, "The Depraved Chinaman is gonna be calling you every few hours to sell you fifty thousand share blocks of *you know what*"–I had already shared my plan with Kenny and he was well aware that I was waging a secret war against the Chinaman–"so go out and sell another fifty thousand shares now, before we actually buy any from him. And then keep selling fifty thousand share blocks every ninety minutes or so. Make the sales through blind accounts, so Victor won't know where it's coming from."

"No problem," replied Kenny Kock, who was head trader at M. H. Meyerson. I had just raised $10 million for his company in an IPO, so I had unlimited trading authority with him. "Anything else?"

"No, that's it," I replied. "Just keep the sales small, in blocks of five or ten thousand. I want him to think it's coming from random short-sellers." *Ahh, a lightbulb.* "In fact, feel free to short as much as you want for your own account, because the stock's going to fucking zero!"

I hung up the phone, then went downstairs to the bathroom to do a few hits of coke. There was no doubt that I deserved it after my Academy Award–winning performance with Victor. I didn't feel a twinge of guilt over the rise and fall of Duke Securities. Over the last few months, he had fully lived up to his reputation as the Depraved Chinaman. He had been stealing Stratton brokers under the guise of them not wanting to work on Long Island anymore; he'd been selling back all the stock he owned of Stratton new issues and of course denying it; and he was openly bashing Danny, referring to him as a "bumbling buffoon" who was incapable of running Stratton.

So this was payback.

I was in and out of the bathroom in less than a minute, ingesting a quarter gram of coke in four enormous blasts. On my way back up the stairs, my heart was beating faster than a rabbit's and my blood pressure was higher than a stroke victim's, and I loved it. My mind was in overdrive and I had everything under control.

At the top of the stairs I found myself staring into the blimp-size chest of Mount Alfredo. "You have another phone call."

"Really?" I said, trying to hold my jaw in one place.

"I think it's your wife."

Jesus! The Duchess! How does she do that? She always seems to know when I'm up to no good! Although, since I was always up to no good, the law of averages dictated that she would always be calling at the wrong time.

With my head hung low, I walked over to the bar and picked up the phone. I would just have to bluff it out. "Hello?" I said open-endedly.

"Hi, honey. Are you okay?"

Am I okay? Such a pointed question! Very sneaky, this Duchess of mine. "Yeah, I'm fine, sweetie. I'm having lunch with Steve. What's up?"

The Duchess let out a deep sigh, then said, "I have bad news: Aunt Patricia just died."

CHAPTER 28

IMMORTALIZING THE DEAD

Five days after Aunt Patricia's death I was back in Switzerland, sitting in the wood-paneled living room of the Master Forger's house. It was a cozy place, about twenty minutes outside Geneva, somewhere in the Swiss countryside. We had just finished Sunday dinner, and the Master Forger's wife, who I'd come to think of as Mrs. Master Forger, had just loaded a beveled-glass coffee table with all sorts of fattening desserts–a fabulous array of Swiss chocolates, French pastries, rich puddings, and stinky cheeses.

I had arrived two hours ago, wanting to get right down to business, but the Master Forger and his wife had insisted on stuffing me with enough Swiss delicacies to choke a brood of Swiss mountain dogs. At this particular moment, the Forgers were sitting across from me, leaning back in a pair of leather reclining chairs. They had on matching gray sweat suits, which, to my eyes, made them look like matching Good Year blimps, but they were terrific hosts and had kind hearts to match.

Since Patricia's stroke and subsequent passing, Randall and I had had only one brief phone conversation–from a pay phone at the Gold Coast Equestrian Center, as opposed to the Brookville Country Club, which seemed to be cursed. He had told me not to worry, that he would take care of it. But he had refused to get specific over the phone, which, given the nature of our dealings, was understandable.

Such was the reason I had flown to Switzerland last night—to sit down with him face-to-face and get to the bottom of things.

This time, however, I was smart.

Rather than taking a commercial flight and running the risk of getting arrested for stewardess-groping, I had flown over on a private jet, a plush Gulfstream III. Danny had flown over too, and he was waiting for me at the hotel, which is to say there was a ninety percent shot that he was getting scrummed by four Swiss hookers.

So here I was, with a smile on my face and frustration in my heart, as I watched Randall and his wife devour the dessert table.

Finally I ran out of patience, and said with great kindness, "You know, you guys are truly wonderful hosts. I can't begin to thank you enough. But, unfortunately, I have to catch a flight back to the States, so if it's okay, Randall, can we get down to business now?" I raised my eyebrows and smiled bashfully.

The Master Forger smiled broadly. "Of course, my friend." He turned to his wife. "Why don't you start preparing dinner, my darling?"

Dinner? I thought. Sweet Jesus!

She nodded eagerly and excused herself, at which point Randall reached over to the coffee table and grabbed two more chocolate-covered strawberries, numbers twenty-one and twenty-two, if memory served me correctly.

I took a deep breath and said, "In light of Patricia's death, Randall, my biggest concern is how to get the money out of the UBP accounts. And, then, after that, what name do I use going forward? You know, one of the things that made me feel comfortable was being able to use Patricia's name. I really trusted her. And I loved her too. Who would've thought she'd pass away so fast?" I shook my head and let out a deep sigh.

The Master Forger shrugged and said, "Patricia's death is sad, of course, but there is no need to worry. The money has been moved to two other banks, neither of which has ever laid eyes on Patricia Mellor. All necessary documents have been created, and each of them bears Patricia's original signature, or what would certainly pass for it. The documents have been backdated to the appropriate dates, of course, before her death. Your money is safe, my friend. Nothing has changed."

"But whose name is it in?"

"Patricia Mellor's, of course. There is no finer nominee than a dead person, my friend. No one at either of the new banks has seen Patricia Mellor, and the money is in the accounts of your bearer corporations, to which you hold the certificates." The Master Forger shrugged, as if to say, "None of this is a big deal in the world of master forgery." Then he said, "The only reason I moved the money out of Union Banc is because Saurel has fallen out of favor there. Better safe than sorry, I figured."

Master Forger! Master Forger! He had turned out to be everything I'd hoped for. Yes, the Master Forger was worth his considerable weight in gold, or close to it. Still, he had managed to turn death into . . . *life!* And that was just how Aunt Patricia would have wanted it. Her name would live on forever in the seedy underbelly of the Swiss banking system. In essence, the Master Forger had immortalized her. Dying the way she had . . . so fast . . . she had never gotten the chance to say good-bye. Oh, but I'd be willing to bet that one of her final thoughts was a tiny worry that her unexpected passing would cause her favorite nephew-in-law a problem.

The Master Forger leaned forward and picked up two more chocolate-covered strawberries, numbers twenty-three and twenty-four, and started chomping. I said, "You know, Randall, I was very fond of Saurel when I first met him, but I'm having second thoughts now. He speaks to Kaminsky all the time, and it makes me uncomfortable. I'd just as soon not do any more business with Union Banc, if that's okay with you."

"I will always abide by your decisions," replied the Master Forger, "and in this case I think your decision is a wise one. But, either way, you need not worry about Jean Jacques Saurel. In spite of him being French, he still lives in Switzerland, and the United States government has no power over him. He will not betray you."

"I don't doubt that," I replied, "but it's not a matter of trust. I just don't like people knowing my business, especially a guy like Kaminsky." I smiled, trying to make light of the whole thing. "Anyway, I've been trying to reach Saurel for over a week now, but his office says he's away on business."

The Master Forger nodded. "Yes, he is in the United States, I believe. Seeing clients."

"Really? I had no idea." For some odd reason, I found that troubling, although I couldn't have explained why.

Matter-of-factly, Randall said, "Yes, he has many clients there. I know a few, but not most of them."

I nodded, dismissing my premonition as nothing more than worthless paranoia. Fifteen minutes later I was standing outside his front door, holding a doggie bag of Swiss delicacies. The Master Forger and I exchanged a warm hug. *"Au revoir!"* I said, which was French for *until I return.*

In retrospect, *good-bye* would have been much more appropriate.

I finally walked through the door of our Westhampton Beach house on Friday morning, a little after ten. All I wanted was to go upstairs and hold Chandler in my arms and then make love to the Duchess and go to sleep. But I never got the chance. I was home for less than thirty seconds when the phone rang.

It was Gary Deluca. "I'm really sorry to bother you," said the Drizzler, "but I've been trying to reach you for over a day. I thought you'd want to know that Gary Kaminsky got indicted yesterday morning. He's sitting in a Miami jail, being held without bail."

"Really?" I replied casually. I was in that state of extreme weariness where you can't fully fathom the consequences of what you're hearing, or at least not immediately. "What did he get indicted for?"

"Money laundering," Deluca said tonelessly. "Does the name Jean Jacques Saurel ring a bell?"

That one got me–woke me right the fuck up! "Maybe . . . I think I met him when I was in Switzerland that time. Why?"

"Because he got indicted too," said the Bearer of Bad News. "He's sitting in jail with Kaminsky; he's also being held without bail."

CHAPTER 29

DESPERATE MEASURES

As I sat in my kitchen, plowing through the indictment, I found the whole thing mind-boggling. How many Swiss bankers were there? There had to be at least ten thousand of them in Geneva alone, and I had to choose the one who'd been dumb enough to get himself arrested on U.S. soil. What were the chances of that? Even more ironic was that he'd gotten himself indicted on a completely unrelated charge, something having to do with laundering drug money through offshore boat racing.

Meanwhile, it didn't take the Duchess long to realize that something was terribly wrong, simply because I hadn't pounced on her the moment I'd walked through the door. But without even trying, I knew I couldn't get it up. I had resisted letting the word *impotent* enter my thoughts, because it had so many negative connotations to a true man of power, which I still considered myself to be, in spite of falling victim to the reckless behavior of my Swiss banker. So I preferred to think of myself as being a limp dick or a spaghetti dick, which was far more palatable than the heinous *I* word.

Either way, my penis had sought refuge inside my lower abdomen–shrinking to the size of a number-two pencil eraser–so I told the Duchess that I was sick and jet-lagged.

Later that evening I went into my bedroom closet and picked out my jail outfit. I chose a pair of faded Levi's, a simple gray

T-shirt with long sleeves (just in case it got cold inside the jail cell), and some old beat-up Reebok sneakers, which would reduce the chances of any seven-foot black men named Bubba or Jamal taking them from me. I had seen this happen in the movies, and they always took your sneakers before they raped you.

On Monday morning I decided not to go to the office–figuring it was more dignified to get arrested in the comfort of my own home rather than in the gloomy groin of Woodside, Queens. No, I would not allow them to arrest me at Steve Madden Shoes, where the Cobbler would view it as a perfect opportunity to fuck me out of stock options. The Maddenites would have to read about it on the front page of *The New York Times*, like the rest of the Free World. I would not give them the pleasure of seeing me taken away in handcuffs; that pleasure I would reserve for the Duchess.

Then something very odd happened–namely, nothing. There were no subpoenas issued, no unannounced visits from Agent Coleman, and no FBI raids at Stratton Oakmont. By Wednesday afternoon I found myself wondering what the fuck was going on. I'd been hiding out in Westhampton since Friday, pretending to be sick with a horrible case of diarrhea, which was basically true. Still, it now appeared that I was hiding for no good reason–perhaps I wasn't on the verge of being arrested!

By Thursday, the silence was overpowering and I decided to risk a phone call to Gregory O'Connell, the lawyer whom Bo had recommended. He seemed like the perfect person to gather intelligence from, since he had been the one who reached out to the Eastern District and spoke to Sean O'Shea six months ago.

Obviously, I wouldn't come clean with Greg O'Connell. After all, he was a lawyer, and no lawyer could be fully trusted, especially a criminal one, who couldn't legally represent you if he became aware that you were actually guilty. It was an outlandish concept, of course, and everyone knew that defense lawyers made their livings defending the guilty. But part of the game was an unspoken understanding between a crook and his lawyer, wherein the crook would swear innocence to his lawyer and the lawyer would put forward the crook's bullshit story to the court.

So when I spoke to Greg O'Connell I lied through my teeth, explaining how I'd gotten caught up in someone else's problem. I told him that my wife's family in Britain shared the same banker as some corrupt offshore boat-racers, which was, of course, a complete coincidence. As I went about running this first version of my bullshit story to my future lawyer–telling him all about the lovely Aunt Patricia, still alive and kicking, because I felt it made my case stronger–I started seeing thin rays of hope.

My story was entirely believable, I thought, until Gregory O'Connell said in a somewhat skeptical tone: "Where did a sixty-five-year-old retired schoolteacher come up with the three million in cash to get the account started?"

Hmmm . . . a slight hole in my story; probably not a good sign, I thought. Nothing to do but play dumb. "How am I supposed to know?" I asked matter-of-factly. Yes, my tone had been just right. The Wolf could be a cool character when he had to be, even now, under the most dire circumstances. "Listen, Greg, Patricia–may she rest in peace–was always going on about how her ex-husband was the first test pilot for the Harrier jump jet. I bet the KGB would have paid a bloody fortune for some hard intel on that project; so maybe he was taking cash from the KGB? As I recall, it was pretty cutting-edge stuff back then. Very hush-hush." *Christ!* What the fuck was I rambling about?

"Well, I'll make a few calls and get a quick heads-up," said my kind attorney. "I'm just confused about one thing, Jordan. Can you clarify whether your aunt Patricia is alive or dead? You just said she should rest in peace, but a couple of minutes ago you told me she lived in London. It would be helpful if I knew which of the two was accurate."

I had clearly dropped the ball on that one. I would have to be more careful in the future about Patricia's life status. No choice now but to bluff it out: "Well, that depends on which one bodes better for my situation. What makes my case stronger: life or death?"

"*Wellllllllllll,* it would be nice if she could come forward and say the money was hers, or, if not that, at least sign an affidavit attesting to that fact. So I would have to say that it would be better if she were alive."

"Then she's very much alive!" I shot back confidently, thinking of the Master Forger and his ability to create all sorts of fine documents. "But she likes her privacy, so you're gonna have to settle for an affidavit. I think she's in seclusion for a while, anyway."

Nothing but silence now. After a good ten seconds my lawyer finally said, "Okay, then! I think I've got a pretty clear picture here. I'll be back to you in a few hours."

An hour later I did receive a call back from Greg O'Connell, who said, "There's nothing new going on with your case. In fact, Sean O'Shea is leaving the office in a couple a weeks–joining the ranks of us humble defense attorneys–so he was unusually forthcoming with me. He said your whole case is still being driven by this Coleman character. No one in the U.S. Attorney's Office is interested in it. And as far as this Swiss banker goes, there's nothing going on with him in relation to your case, at least not now." He then spent a few more minutes assuring me that I was pretty much in the clear.

Upon hanging up, I dropped those first two hedge words, *pretty* and *much,* and held on to the last three, *in the clear*, like a dog with a bone. I still needed to speak to the Master Forger, though, to gauge the full extent of the damage. If he were sitting in a U.S. jail, like Saurel–or if he were in a Swiss jail, pending extradition to the United States–then I was still in deep shit. But if he wasn't–if he was in the clear too, still able to practice the little-known art of master forgery–then perhaps everything might work out for me.

I called the Master Forger from a pay phone at Starr Boggs restaurant. With bated breath, I listened to the troubling story of how the Swiss police had raided his office and seized boxes full of records. Yes, he was wanted for questioning in the United States, but, no, he was not officially under indictment, at least not to his knowledge. He assured me that under no circumstances would the Swiss government turn him over to the United States, although he could no longer safely travel outside Switzerland, lest he be picked up by Interpol on an international arrest warrant.

Finally, the subject turned to the Patricia Mellor accounts, and the Master Forger said, "Some of the records were seized, but not because they were specifically targeted; they were just scooped up with all the others. But have no fear, my friend, there is nothing in my records indicating that the money doesn't belong to Patricia Mellor. However, since she is no longer alive I would suggest that you stop doing business in those accounts until this whole thing blows over."

"That goes without saying," I replied, hanging on to the two words *blow* and *over*, "but my main concern isn't so much having access to the money. What I'm really worried about is Saurel cooperating with the U.S. government and saying that the accounts are mine. That would cause me a big problem, Randall. Perhaps if there were some documents that showed the money was clearly Patricia's, it would make a big difference."

The Master Forger replied, "But those documents already exist, my friend. Perhaps if you could give me a list of what documents might help you and what dates Patricia signed them on, I would be able to dig them out of my files for you."

Master Forger! Master Forger! He was still with me. "I understand, Randall, and I'll let you know if I need anything. But for right now, I guess it just makes the most sense to sit back and wait and hope for the best."

The Master Forger said, "As usual, we are in agreement. But until this investigation runs its course, you should steer clear of Switzerland. Remember, though, that I am always with you, my friend, and I will do everything in my power to protect you and your family."

As I hung up the phone, I knew my fortunes would rise and fall with Saurel. Yet I also knew that I had to get on with my life. I had to take a deep breath and suck it up. I had to get back to work, and I had to start making love to the Duchess again. I had to stop jumping out of my skin every time the phone rang or there was an unexpected knock at the front door.

And that was what I did. I reimmersed myself in the very insanity of things. I plunged into the building of Steve Madden Shoes and kept advising my brokerage firms from behind the scenes. I did my best to be a loyal husband to the Duchess and a good father to Chandler, in spite of my drug addiction. And as the months passed, my drug habit continued to escalate.

As always, I was quick to rationalize it, though–to remind myself that I was young and rich, with a gorgeous wife and a perfect baby daughter. Everyone wanted a life like mine, didn't they? What better life was there than *Lifestyles of the Rich and Dysfunctional*?

Either way, by mid-October, there were no repercussions from Saurel's arrest, and I breathed a final sigh of relief. Obviously, he had chosen not to cooperate and the Wolf of Wall Street had dodged another bullet. Chandler had taken her first steps and was now doing the Frankenstein walk–sticking her arms out in front of her, keeping her knees locked, and walking around stiffly. And, of course, the baby genius was talking up a storm. By her first birthday, in fact, she had been speaking full sentences–an astonishing achievement for an infant–and I had no doubt that she was well on the road to a Nobel Prize or at least a Fields Medal for advanced mathematics.

Meanwhile, Steve Madden Shoes and Stratton Oakmont were on divergent paths–with Steve Madden growing by leaps and bounds and Stratton Oakmont falling victim to ill-conceived trading strategies and a new wave of regulatory pressure, both of which Danny had brought upon himself. The latter was a result of Danny's refusal to abide by one of the terms of the SEC settlement–namely, for Stratton to hire an independent auditor of the SEC's choosing, who would review the firm's business practices and then make recommendations. One of these recommendations was for the firm to install a taping system to capture the Strattonites' phone conversations with their clients. Danny refused to comply, and the SEC ran into federal court and secured an injunction ordering the firm to install the taping system.

Danny finally capitulated–lest he be thrown in jail for contempt of court–but now Stratton had an injunction against it, which meant all fifty states had the right to suspend Stratton's license, which, of course, they slowly began doing. It was hard to imagine that after everything Stratton had survived, its demise would be tied to the refusal to install a taping system, which, in the end, hadn't made the slightest bit of difference. Within days Strattonites had figured out how to circumvent the system–saying only compliant things over Stratton's phone lines and then picking up their cell phones when they felt like going to the dark side. But the handwriting was now on the wall: Stratton's days were numbered.

The owners of Biltmore and Monroe Parker expressed their mutual desire to go their separate ways, to no longer do business with Stratton. Of course, it was done with the utmost respect, and they each offered to pay me a $1 million tribute on each new issue they took public. It amounted to somewhere around $12 million a year, so I gladly accepted. I was also receiving a million dollars a month from Stratton, pursuant to my noncompete agreement, as well as another four or five million every few months as I cashed out of large blocks of inside stock (144 stock) in the companies Stratton was taking public.

Still, I considered it a mere drop in the bucket compared to what I could make with Steve Madden Shoes, which seemed to be on a rocket ship to the stars. It reminded me of the early days of Stratton . . . those *heady* days . . . those *glory* days . . . in the late eighties and early nineties, when the first wave of Strattonites had taken to the phones and the insanity that had come to define my life had yet to take hold. So Stratton was my past, and Steve Madden was my future.

At this particular moment I was sitting across from Steve, who was leaning back in his seat defensively as the Spitter shot spit streams at him. Every so often, Steve would give me a look that so much as said, "The Spitter is relentless when it comes to ordering boots, especially since the boot season is almost over!"

The Drizzler was also in the room, and he was drizzling on us at every opportunity. Right now, though, the Spitter had center stage. "What's the big fucking deal about ordering these boots?" spat the Spitter. Because this morning's debate involved a word beginning with the letter *B,* he was doing an inordinate amount of spitting. In fact, each time the Spitter uttered the word *boot,* I could see the Cobbler cringe visibly. And now he turned his wrath on me. "Listen, JB, this boot"–*oh, Jesus!*–"is so fucking hot there's no way we can lose. You gotta trust me on this. I'm telling you, not a single pair will get marked down."

I shook my head in disagreement. "No more boots, John. We're done with fucking boots. And it's got nothing to do with whether or not they'll get marked down. It's about running our business with a certain discipline. We're going in eighteen different directions at the same time, and we need to stick to our business plan. We've got three new stores opening; we're rolling out dozens of in-store shops; we're about to pull the trigger on the unbranded business. There's only so much cash to go around. We gotta stay lean and mean right now; no huge risks this late in the season, especially with some leopard-skin fucking boot."

The Drizzler took this opening to do some more drizzling. "I agree with you, and that's exactly why it makes so much sense to move our shipping department down to Flor–"

The Spitter cut the Drizzler right off, using a word with a

double-*P,* the Spitter's second-deadliest consonant. "That's fucking *preposterous*!" spat the Spitter. "That whole fucking concept! I have no time for this shit. I gotta get some fucking shoes made or else we'll be out of fucking business!" With that, the Spitter walked out of the office and slammed the door behind him.

Just then the phone beeped. "Todd Garret's on line one."

I rolled my eyes at Steve, then I said, "Tell him I'm in a meeting, Janet. I'll call him back."

Janet, the insolent one: "*Obviously* I told him you're in a meeting, but he said it's urgent. He needs to speak to you right now."

I shook my head in disgust and let out a great sigh. What could be so important with Todd Garret–unless, of course, he had managed to get his hands on some Real Reals! I picked up the phone and said in a friendly yet somewhat annoyed tone, "Hey, Todd, what's going on, buddy?"

"Well," replied Todd, "I hate to be the bearer of bad news, but some guy named Agent Coleman just left my house and told me that Carolyn is about to get thrown in jail."

With a sinking heart: "For *what*? What did Carolyn do?"

I felt the world crash down on me when Todd said, "Did you know that your Swiss banker is in jail and he's cooperating against you?"

I clenched my ass cheeks for all they were worth and said, "I'll be there in an hour."

Like its owner, Todd's two-bedroom apartment was mean-looking. From top to bottom, the whole place was black, not an ounce of color anywhere. We were sitting in the living room, which was completely devoid of plant life. All I could see was black leather and chrome.

Todd was sitting across from me, as Carolyn paced back and forth on a black shag carpet, teetering atop some very high heels. Todd said to me, "It goes without saying that Carolyn and I will never cooperate against you, so don't even worry about that." He looked up at the pacing Swiss Bombshell and said, "Right, Carolyn?"

Carolyn nodded nervously and kept on pacing. Apparently Todd found that annoying. "Will you stop pacing!" he snarled.

"You're driving me fucking crazy. I'm gonna smack you if you don't sit down!"

"Oh, *fahak* you, Tahad!" croaked the Bombshell. "This no laughing business. I have two kids, in case you forget. It is all because of that stupid pistol you carry."

Even now, on the day of my doom, these two maniacs were determined to kill each other. "Will you two please stop?" I said, forcing a smile. "I don't understand what Todd's gun charge has to do with Saurel getting indicted."

"Don't listen to her," muttered Todd. "She's a fucking idiot. What she's trying to say is that Coleman found out what happened in the shopping center, and now he's telling the Queens District Attorney not to plea-bargain my case. A few months ago they were offering me probation, and now they're telling me I gotta do three years unless I cooperate with the FBI. Personally, I couldn't give a shit about that, and if I gotta go to jail I gotta go to jail. The problem is my idiot wife, who decided to strike up a friendship with your Swiss banker instead of just dropping off the money and not saying a word like she was supposed to. But, *nooooo,* she couldn't resist having lunch with the fuck and then exchanging phone numbers with him. For all I know she probably fucked him."

"You know," said a rather guilty-looking Bombshell, in her white patent leather go-to-hell pumps, "you got nerves upon nerves, dog-man! Who be you to throw stones in my direction? You don't think I know what you do with that steel-cage dancer from Rio?" With that, the Swiss Bombshell looked me directly in the eye and said, "Do you believes this jealous man? Will you please tell *Tahad* that *Jean Jacques* not like that? He is old banker, not ladies' man. Right, Jordan?" And she stared at me with blazing blue eyes and a clenched jaw.

An old banker? Jean Jacques? Jesus Christ–what a tragic turn of events! Had the Swiss Bombshell fucked my Swiss banker? Unreal! If she had just dropped off the money like she was supposed to, then Saurel wouldn't have even known who she was! But, no, she couldn't keep her mouth shut, and, as a result, Coleman was now connecting all the dots–figuring out that Todd's arrest in the Bay Terrace Shopping Center had nothing to do with a drug deal but with the smuggled millions of dollars to Switzerland.

"Well," I said innocently, "I wouldn't exactly characterize Saurel as an old man, but he's not the sort of guy who'd have an affair with another man's wife. I mean, he's married himself, and he never really struck me as being that way."

Apparently they both took that as a victory. Carolyn blurted out, "You see, dog-man, he is not like that. He is–"

But Todd cut her right off: "So why the fuck did you say he's an old man, then, you lying sack of shit? Why lie if you have nothing to hide, huh? Why, I . . ."

As Todd and Carolyn went about ripping each other's lungs out, I tuned out and wondered if there was any way out of this mess. It was time for desperate measures; it was time to call my trusted accountant Dennis Gaito, aka the Chef. I would offer him my humblest apology for having done all this behind his back. No, I had never actually told the Chef that I had accounts in Switzerland. There was no choice now but to come clean and seek his counsel.

". . . and what will we do for money now?" asked the Swiss Bombshell. "This Agent Coleman watch you like bird now"–*Did she mean hawk?*–"so you can no more sell your drugs. We will starve now for sure!" With that, the soon-to-be starving Swiss Bombshell–along with her $40,000 Patek Philippe watch, her $25,000 diamond-and-ruby necklace, and her $5,000 clothing ensemble–sat down in a black leather chair. Then she put her head in her hands and began to shake her head back and forth.

How very ironic that, at the end of the day, it was the Swiss Bombshell, with her bastardized English and gigantic boobs, who'd finally cut through all the bullshit and distilled things down to their very essence–it all came down to buying their silence. And that was fine with me; in fact, I had a sneaky suspicion it was fine with them too. After all, the two of them now had a pair of first-class tickets on the gravy train, and they would be good for many years to come. And if somewhere along the line the heat in the kitchen grew too hot, they could always apply for exit visas downtown, at the New York Field Office of the FBI, where Agent Coleman would be waiting for them with open arms and a smile.

That evening, in my basement in Old Brookville, Long Island, I was sitting on the wraparound couch with the Chef, playing a little-known game called Can You Top This Bullshit Story. The rules of the game were simple: The contestant spewing out the bullshit would try to make his story as airtight as possible, while the person listening to the bullshit would try to poke holes in it. In order to achieve victory, one of the contestants had to come up with a bullshit story that was so airtight that the other contestant couldn't poke a hole in it. And since the Chef and I were Jedi Masters of unadulterated bullshit, it was pretty obvious that if one of us could stump the other, then we could also stump Agent Coleman.

The Chef was boldly handsome, sort of like a trimmed-down version of Mr. Clean. He was in his early fifties and had been cooking the books since I was in grade school. I looked at him as an elder statesman of sorts, the lucid voice of reason. He was a man's man, the Chef, with an infectious smile and a million watts of social charisma. He was a guy who lived for world-class golf courses, Cuban cigars, fine wines, and enlightened conversation, especially when it had to do with fucking over the IRS and the Securities and Exchange Commission, which seemed to be his life's foremost mission.

I had already come clean with him this evening, baring my very soul and apologizing profusely for having done all this behind his back. I started bullshitting him even then, before the game had officially started, explaining that I hadn't brought him into my Swiss affair because it might've put him at risk. Thankfully, he'd made no effort to poke any holes in my feeble bullshit story. Instead, he'd responded with a warm smile and a shrug.

As I told him my tale of woe, I found my spirits sinking lower and lower. But the Chef remained impassive. When I was done, he shrugged nonchalantly and said, "Eh, I've heard worse."

"Oh, really?" I replied. "How the fuck could *that* be possible?"

The Chef waved his hand dismissively and added, "I've been in much tighter spots than this."

I'd been greatly relieved by those words, although I was pretty sure he was just trying to ease my worried mind. Anyway, we had started playing the game and now, after a half hour, we'd been through three evolutions of unadulterated bullshit. So far, there was no clear winner. But with each round our stories grew tighter and cleverer and, of course, more difficult to poke holes in. We were still hung up on two basic issues: First, how had Patricia come up with the initial $3 million to fund the account? And, second, if the money was really Patricia's, then why hadn't her heirs been contacted? Patricia was survived by two daughters, both of whom were in their mid-thirties. In the absence of a contraindicating will, they were the rightful heirs.

The Chef said, "I think the real problem is the outgoing currency violation. Let's assume this guy Saurel has spilled his guts, which means the feds are gonna take the position that the money made it over to Switzerland on a bunch of different dates. So what we need is a document that counteracts that–that says you gave all the money to Patricia while she was still in the United States. We need an affidavit from someone who physically witnessed you handing the money to Patricia in the U.S. Then, if the government wants to say different, we hold our piece of paper and say, 'Here ya go, buddy! We got our own eyewitness too!' "

As an afterthought, he added, "But I still don't like this business with the will. It smells bad. It's a shame Patricia's not alive. It would be nice if we could parade her downtown and have her say a few choice words to the feds, and, you know–*bada-beep bada-bop bada-boop*–that would be that."

I shrugged. "Well, I can't raise Patricia from the dead, but I bet I could get Nadine's mother to sign an affidavit saying that she witnessed me handing the money to Patricia in the United States. Suzanne hates the government, and I've been really good to her over the last four years. She really has nothing to lose, right?"

The Chef nodded. "Well that would be a very good thing, if she would agree to do it."

"She'll do it," I said confidently, trying to guess what temperature water the Duchess would be pouring over my head tonight. "I'll talk to Suzanne tomorrow. I just need to run it by the Duchess first. But, assuming I get it taken care of, there's still the issue of the will. It does sound kinda hokey that she wouldn't leave any money to her kids . . ." All at once a fabulous idea came bubbling into my brain. "What if we were to actually contact her kids and get them involved? What if we had them fly over to Switzerland and claim the money? It would be like hitting lotto to them! I could have Randall draw up a new will, saying the money I'd loaned Patricia was to come back to me but all the profits were to go to her children. I mean, if the kids went and declared the money in Britain, then how could the U.S. government make a case that the money was mine?"

"Ahhhhh," said a smiling Chef, "now you're thinking! In fact, you just won the game. If we can pull this whole thing together, I think you're in the clear. And I've got a sister firm in London that can do the actual returns, so we'll have control of things the whole way through. You'll get your original investment back, the kids'll get a five-million-dollar windfall, and we can move on with our lives!"

I smiled and said, "This guy Coleman is gonna flip his fucking lid when he finds out Patricia's kids went over and claimed the money. I bet you he's already tasting blood on his lips."

"Indeed," said the Chef.

Fifteen minutes later I found the soon-to-be-doleful Duchess upstairs in the master bedroom. She was sitting at her desk, thumbing through a catalog, and by the looks of her she wasn't just in the market for clothes. She looked absolutely gorgeous. Her hair was brushed out to perfection, and she was dressed in a tiny white silk chemise of such fine material that it covered her body like a morning mist. She had on a pair of white open-toe pumps with a spiked heel and sexy ankle strap. And that was all she wore. She had dimmed the lights, and there were a dozen candles burning, giving off a mellow orange glow.

When she saw me, she ran over to shower me with kisses. "You look so beautiful," I said, after a good thirty seconds of kissing and Duchess-sniffing. "I mean, you always look beautiful, but you look especially beautiful tonight. You're beyond words."

"Well, *thank you*!" said the luscious Duchess in a playful tone. "I'm glad you still think so, because I just took my temperature and I'm ovulating. I hope you're ready, because you're in big trouble tonight, mister!"

Hmmm . . . there were two sides to this coin. On the one side, how mad could an ovulating woman get at her husband? I mean, the Duchess really wanted another child, so she might shake off the bad news in the name of procreation. But on the flipside, she might get so angry she would throw on her bathrobe and go to fisticuffs. And with all those wet kisses she'd just showered on me, a tsunami of blood had gone rushing to my loins.

I dropped down to my knees and began sniffing the tops of her thighs, like a Pomeranian in heat. I said, "I need to talk to you about something."

She giggled. "Let's go over to the bed and talk there."

I took a moment to run that through my mind, and the bed seemed pretty safe. In truth, the Duchess wasn't any stronger than me; she was just an expert at using leverage, and the bed would minimize that.

On the bed, I maneuvered myself on top of her and I clasped my hands behind her neck and kissed her deeply, breathing in every last molecule of her. In that very instant I loved her so much that it seemed almost impossible.

She ran her fingers through my hair, pushing it back with gentle strokes. She said, "What's wrong, baby? Why was Dennis here tonight?"

The high road or the low road, I wondered, looking at her legs. And then it hit me: Why tell her anything? Yes! I would buy her mother off! What an inspired notion! The Wolf strikes again! Suzanne needed a new car, so I would take her tomorrow to buy one and then spring the idea of the phony affidavit on her during idle conversation. "Hey, Suzanne, you look really great in this new convertible, and, by the way, can you just sign your name here, right at the bottom, where it says signature? . . . Oh, what does *I swear under penalty of perjury* mean? Well, it's just legal jargon, so don't even waste your time reading it. Just sign it, and if you happened to get indicted we can discuss it then." Then I would swear Suzanne to secrecy and pray that she'd keep her mouth shut to the Duchess.

I smiled at the delectable Duchess and said, "It was nothing important. Dennis is taking over as auditor for Steve Madden, so we were going through some numbers. Anyway, what I wanted to tell you is that I want this baby as much as you do. You're the greatest mother in the whole world, Nae, and you're the greatest wife too. I'm lucky to have you."

"Aw, that's so sweet," said the Duchess, in a syrupy voice. "I love you too. Make love to me right now, honey."

And I did.

BOOK IV

CHAPTER 30

NEW ADDITIONS

August 15, 1995
(Nine Months Later)

"You little bastard!" screamed the delivering Duchess, sprawled out on a birthing table in Long Island Jewish Hospital. "You did this to me, and now you're stoned during the birth of our son! I'm gonna rip your lungs out when I get off this table!"

It was ten a.m., or was it eleven? Who knew anymore?

Either way, I had just passed out cold, my face on the delivery table, as the Duchess was in the middle of a contraction. I was still standing, though hunched over at a ninety-degree angle, with my head between her puffy legs, which were now propped up on stirrups.

Just then I felt someone shaking me. "Are you all right?" said the voice of Dr. Bruno, sounding a million miles away.

Christ! I wanted to respond, but I was just so damn tired. The Ludes had really gotten the best of me this morning, although I had my reasons for getting stoned. After all, giving birth is a very stressful business–for the wife *and* the husband–and I guess there are some things that women just handle better than men.

It had been three trimesters since that very candlelit evening, and *Lifestyles of the Rich and Dysfunctional* had continued unabated. Suzanne had kept my confidence, and Aunt Patricia's children had gone to Switzerland and claimed their inheritance. Agent Coleman, I assumed, had shit a pickle over the whole thing, and the last I'd heard of him was when he'd made an unannounced morning visit to Carrie Chodosh's house, threatening her with jail time and the loss of her son if she refused to cooperate. But those were desperate words, I knew, from a desperate man. Carrie, of course, had stayed loyal–telling Agent Coleman to go fuck himself, in so many words.

And as the first trimester had become the second, Stratton continued to spiral downward, no longer able to pay me a million dollars a month. But I'd been expecting that, so I'd taken it in stride. Besides, I still had Biltmore and Monroe Parker, and they were each paying me one million per deal. And further cushioning the blow was Steve Madden Shoes. Steve and I could hardly keep up with all the department-store orders, and the program Elliot had laid out was working like a charm. We had five stores now and plans to open five more over the next twelve months. We were also starting to license our name, initially with belts and handbags and moving on to sportswear. And most importantly, Steve was learning to delegate authority and we were well on the way to building a first-class management team. About six months ago, Gary Deluca, aka the Drizzler, had finally convinced us to move our warehouse to South Florida, and it had turned out to be a fine idea. And John Basile, aka the Spitter, was so busy trying to keep up with our department-store orders that his spit storms were becoming less and less frequent.

Meanwhile, the Cobbler was making money hand over fist–although not from Steve Madden Shoes. Instead, it was coming from the rathole game, with Steve Madden Shoes representing his future. But that was fine with me. After all, Steve and I had become the closest of friends and were spending most of our free time together. On the other hand, Elliot had succumbed once more to his drug addiction–sliding deeper and deeper into debt and depression.

At the beginning of the Duchess's third trimester I had my back operated on, but the procedure was unsuccessful–leaving me in worse shape than before. Perhaps I deserved it, though, because I had gone against the advice of Dr. Green, electing to have a local doctor (of dubious reputation) perform a minimally invasive procedure called a percutaneous disk extraction. The pain going down my left leg was excruciating and ceaseless. My only solace, of course, was Quaaludes, which I was always quick to point out to the Duchess, who was becoming increasingly annoyed at my constant slurring and frequent blackouts.

Nevertheless, she had fallen so deeply into the role of the codependent wife that she, too, no longer knew which way was up. And with all the money and the help and the mansions and the yacht and the sucking up at every department store and restaurant or wherever else we went, it was easy to pretend things were okay.

Just then, a terrible burning sensation under my nose–*smelling salts!*

My head immediately popped up, and there was the delivering Duchess, her gigantic pussy staring at me with contempt.

"Are you okay?" asked Dr. Bruno.

I took a deep breath and said, "Yeah, I'm zine, Dr. Bruno. I just got a little bit queasy *zrom* the blood. I need a splash some water on my face." I excused myself and ran to the bathroom, did two blasts of coke, and ran back to the delivery room, feeling like a new man. "Okay," I said, no longer slurring. "Let's go, Nae! Don't give up now!"

"I'll deal with you later," she snapped.

And then she began to push, and then she screamed, and then she pushed some more, and then she grit her teeth, and then suddenly, as if by magic, her vagina opened up to the size of a Volkswagen and–*pop!*–out came my son's head, with a thin coating of dark black hair. Next came a gush of water and then a moment later a tiny shoulder. Dr. Bruno grasped my son's torso and twisted him gently, and just like that he was out.

Then I heard, "*Waaaaahhhhhhhh* . . ."

"Ten fingers and ten toes!" said a happy Dr. Bruno, placing the baby on the Duchess's fat stomach. "You have a name yet?"

"Yes," said the fat, beaming Duchess. "Carter. Carter James Belfort."

"That's a very fine name," said Dr. Bruno.

In spite of my little mishap, Dr. Bruno was kind enough to allow me to cut the cord, and I did a good job. Having now earned his trust, he said, "Okay, it's time for Daddy to hold his son while I finish up with Mommy." With that, Dr. Bruno handed me my son.

I felt myself welling up with tears. I had a son. *A boy!* A baby Wolf of Wall Street! Chandler had been such a beautiful baby, and now I would get my first look at the beautiful face of my son. I looked down and–what the hell? He looked awful! He was tiny and scrunched up, and his eyes were glued shut. He looked like an underfed chicken.

The Duchess must've seen the look on my face, and she said, "Don't worry, honey. Most babies aren't born looking like Chandler. He's just a little premature. He'll be as handsome as his daddy."

"Well, hopefully he'll look just like his mommy," I replied, meaning every word. "But I don't care what he looks like. I already love him so much I wouldn't care if he had a nose the size of a banana." As I looked at my son's perfect, scrunched-up face, I realized there had to be a God, because this couldn't possibly be an accident. It was a miracle to create this perfect little creature from an act of love.

I stared at him for what seemed like a very long time, until Dr. Bruno said, "Oh, Jesus, she's hemorrhaging. Get the operating room ready now! And get an anesthesiologist in here!" The nurse took off like a bat out of hell.

Dr. Bruno regained his composure and calmly said, "Okay, Nadine, we have a slight complication. You have placenta accreta. What that means, honey, is that your placenta has grown too deeply into the uterine wall. Unless we can get it out manually, you could lose a great deal of blood. Now, Nadine, I'm gonna do everything possible to get it out clean"–he paused, as if trying to find the right words–"but if I can't, I'll have no choice but to perform a hysterectomy."

And before I even had a chance to tell my wife I loved her, two orderlies came running in and grabbed her bed and wheeled her out. Dr. Bruno followed. When he reached the door, he turned to me and said, "I'll do everything possible to save her uterus." Then he walked out, leaving Carter and me alone.

I looked down at my son, and I started to cry. What would happen if I lost the Duchess? How could I possibly raise two children without her? She was everything to me. The very insanity of my life depended on her making everything okay. I took a deep breath and tried to calm myself. I had to be strong for my son, for Carter James Belfort. Without even realizing it I found myself rocking him in my arms, saying a silent prayer to the Almighty, asking him to spare the Duchess and to bring her back to me whole.

Ten minutes later Dr. Bruno came back into the room. With a

great smile on his face, he said, "We got the placenta out, and you'll never believe how."

"How?" I said, grinning from ear to ear.

"We called in one of our interns, a tiny Indian girl, who has the most slender hands imaginable. She was able to reach up inside your wife's womb and manually pull out the placenta. It was a miracle, Jordan. A placenta accreta is very rare, and it's very dangerous. But it's fine now. You have a perfectly healthy wife and a perfectly healthy son."

And such were the famous last words of Dr. Bruno, the King of Jinxes.

CHAPTER 31

THE JOY OF PARENTHOOD

The next morning, Chandler and I were alone in the master bedroom, engaged in a heated debate. I was doing most of the talking, while she was sitting on the floor, playing with multicolored wooden blocks. I was trying to convince her that the new addition to the family would be a good thing for her, that things would be even better than before.

I smiled at the baby genius and said, "Listen, thumbkin, he's so cute and little, you're gonna fall in love with him the second you see him. And just think how much fun he'll be when he gets older; you'll be able to boss him around all the time! It's gonna be great!"

Channy looked up from her construction project and stared me down with those big blue eyes she'd inherited from her mother, and she said, "No, just leave him in the hospital." Then she turned back to her blocks.

I sat down next to the baby genius and gave her a gentle kiss on the cheek. She smelled clean and fresh, just the way a little girl should. She was a little more than two years old now, and her hair was a glorious shade of chestnut brown and fine as corn silk. It went down past her shoulder blades, and there were tiny curls on the bottom. I found the mere sight of her touching beyond belief. "Listen, thumbkin, we can't leave him at the hospital; he's part of the family now. Carter's your baby brother, and the two of you are gonna be best friends!"

With a shrug: "No, I don't think so."

"Well, I have to go to the hospital now and pick him and Mommy up, so either way he's coming home, thumbkin. Just remember that Mommy and I still love you just as much. There's enough love to go around for everybody."

"I know," she replied nonchalantly, still focusing on her construction project. "You can bring him. It's okay."

Very impressive, I thought. With a simple okay she had now accepted the new addition to the family.

Rather than going directly to the hospital, I had to make one quick stop along the way. It was an impromptu business meeting at a restaurant called Millie's Place, in the tony suburb of Great Neck, about a five-minute car ride from Long Island Jewish. My plan was to blow out of the meeting quickly and then pick up Carter and the Duchess and head out to Westhampton. I was running a few minutes late, and as the limo pulled up I could see Danny's boiling white teeth through the restaurant's plate-glass window. He was sitting at a circular table, accompanied by the Chef, Wigwam, and a lawyer named Hartley Bernstein, whom I was rather fond of. Hartley's nickname was the Weasel, because he was the spitting image of a rodent. In fact, he could have been a Hollywood stunt double for the comic book character BB Eyes from *Dick Tracy*.

Although Millie's Place wasn't open for breakfast, the restaurant's owner, Millie, had agreed to open the restaurant early to accommodate us. That was appropriate, considering that Millie's Place was where the Strattonites would come after each new issue to drink and eat and fuck and suck and drop and snort and do whatever else Strattonites did–and it was all done courtesy of the firm, which would receive a bill, between $25,000 and $100,000, depending on how much damage was done.

As I approached the table I noticed a fifth person sitting there: Jordan Shamah, Stratton's recently appointed Vice President. He was a childhood friend of Danny's and his nickname was the Undertaker, because his rise to power had little to do with his performance and more to do with his undermining every last soul who'd stood in his way. The Undertaker was short and pudgy, and his primary undertaking method was good old-fashioned back-stabbing, although he was also adept at character assassination and rumormongering.

I exchanged a quick round of Mafia-style hugs with my erstwhile partners-in-crime and then settled down in an armchair and poured myself a cup of coffee. The goal of the meeting was a sad one: to convince Danny to close down Stratton Oakmont, using the Cockroach Theory, which meant that before he actually closed Stratton he would first open a series of smaller brokerage firms—each of them owned by a front man—and then he would divide the Strattonites into small groups and shift them to the new firms. Once the process was complete, he would close Stratton and move himself to one of the new firms, where he could run it from behind the scenes, under the guise of being a consultant.

It was the generally accepted way for brokerage firms under regulatory heat to stay one step ahead—essentially, closing down and reopening under a different name, thereby starting the process of making money and fighting the regulators all over again. It was like stepping on a cockroach and squashing it, only to find ten new ones scurrying in all directions.

Anyway, given Stratton's current problems, it was the appropriate course of action, but Danny didn't subscribe to the Cockroach Theory. Instead, he had developed his own theory, which he referred to as Twenty Years of Blue Skies. According to *this* theory, all Stratton had to do was get past its current wave of regulatory hurdles, and it could stay in business for twenty more years. It was preposterous! Stratton had a year left at most. By now all fifty states were circling above Stratton like vultures over a wounded carcass, and the NASD, the National Association of Securities Dealers, had joined the party too.

But Danny was in complete denial. In fact, he had become a Wall Street version of Elvis in his final days—when his handlers would cram his enormous bulk into a white leather jumpsuit and push him onstage to sing a few songs. Then they would drag him back off before he passed out from heat exhaustion and Seconals. According to Wigwam, Danny was now climbing on top of desks during sales meetings and smashing computer monitors onto the floor and cursing the regulators. Obviously, the Strattonites ate this sort of shit up, so Danny was now kicking it up a notch–pulling down his pants and pissing on stacks of NASD subpoenas, to thunderous applause.

Wigwam and I locked eyes, so I motioned with my chin, as if to say, "Offer up your two cents." Wigwam nodded confidently and said, "Listen, Danny, the truth is I don't know how much longer I can even get deals through. The SEC's been playing four-corners defense, and it's taking six months to get anything approved. If we start working on a new firm now, I could be in business by the end of the year–doing deals for *all* of us."

Danny's reply wasn't exactly what Wigwam had hoped for. "Let me tell you something, Wigwam. Your motives are so obvious it's fucking nauseating. There's lots of time left before we need to consider cockroaching it, so why don't you take your fucking rug off and stay awhile."

"You know what, Danny? *Go fuck yourself!*" snapped Wigwam, running his fingers through his hair, trying to make it look more natural. "You're so drugged out all the time you don't even know which way is up anymore. I'm not wasting my life away while you drool in the office like a fucking imbecile."

The Undertaker saw an opportunity to put a hatchet in Wigwam's back. "That's not true," argued the Undertaker. "Danny doesn't drool in the office. Maybe he slurs once in a while, but even then he's always in control." Now the Undertaker paused, searching for a spot to inject his first dose of embalming fluid. "And you shouldn't be one to talk, by the way. You spend your whole day chasing around that smelly slut Donna, with her putrid armpits."

I was fond of the Undertaker; he was a real company guy–way too dumb to actually think for himself, expending most of his mental energy conjuring up devilish rumors about those he was looking to bury. But in this particular instance his motives were obvious: He had a hundred customer complaints against him, and if Stratton went under he would never be able to get registered again.

I said, "All right, enough of this shit–please!" I shook my head in disbelief; Stratton was totally out of control. "I gotta get to the hospital. I'm only here because I want the best for everyone. I personally couldn't care less whether or not Stratton pays me another dime. But I do have other interests–selfish interests, I admit–and they have to do with all the arbitrations being filed. A lot of them are naming me, in spite of the fact that I'm not with the firm anymore." I looked directly at Danny. "You're in the same position as me, Dan, and my sense is that even if there are Twenty Years of Blue Skies ahead, the arbitrations aren't gonna stop."

The Weasel chimed in: "We can take care of the arbitrations through an asset sale. We would structure it so that Stratton *sold* the brokers to the new firms, and, in return, they would agree to pay for any arbitration that came up for a period of three years. After that, the statute of limitations will kick in and you guys will be in the clear."

I looked at the Chef, and he nodded in agreement. It was interesting, I thought. I had never paid close attention to the wisdom of the Weasel. Unlike the Chef, who was a man's man–overflowing with charisma–the Weasel lacked those traits entirely. I had never thought him to be stupid; it was just that every time I looked at him, I imagined him nibbling a block of Swiss cheese. Nevertheless, his latest idea was brilliant. The customer lawsuits were troubling me, totaling more than $70 million now. Stratton was paying them, but if Stratton went belly-up, it could turn into a real fucking nightmare.

Just then Danny said, "JB, let me talk to you by the bar for a second."

I nodded, and we headed to the bar, where Danny immediately filled two glasses to the rim with Dewar's. He lifted one of the glasses, and said, "Here's to Twenty Years of Blue Skies, my friend!" He kept holding his glass up, waiting for me to join the toast.

I looked at my watch: It was ten-thirty. "Come on, Danny! I can't drink right now. I gotta go to the hospital and pick up Nadine and Carter."

Danny shook his head gravely. "It's bad luck to refuse a toast this early in the morning. You really willing to risk it?"

"Yes," I snarled, "I'm willing to risk it."

Danny shrugged. "Suit yourself," and he downed what had to be five shots of scotch. "Ho baby!" he muttered. Then he shook his head a few times and reached into his pocket and pulled out four Ludes. "Will you at least take a couple Ludes with me–before you ask me to shut the firm down?"

"Now you're talking!" I said, smiling.

Danny smiled broadly and handed me two Ludes. I walked over

to the sink, turned on the water, and stuck my mouth in the water stream. Then I casually stuck my hand in my pocket and dropped the two Ludes in there for safekeeping. "Okay," I said, rubbing my fingertips together, "I'm a ticking time bomb now, so let's make it fast."

I smiled sadly at Danny and found myself wondering how many of my current problems could be attributed to him? Not that I had deluded myself to the point where I was laying all the blame on his doorstep, but there was no denying that Stratton would have never spun this far out of control without Danny. Yes, it was true that I had been the so-called brains of the outfit, but Danny had been the muscle, the enforcer, so to speak–doing things on a daily basis that I could have never done, or at least couldn't have done and still looked at myself in the mirror each morning. He was a true warrior, Danny, and I didn't know whether to respect him or loathe him for it anymore. But above all I felt sad.

"Listen, Danny, I can't tell you what to do with Stratton. It's your firm now, and I respect you too much to tell you what you have to do. But if you want my opinion, I'd say close it down right now and walk away with all the marbles. You do it just the way Hartley said: You have the new firms assume all the arbitrations and then you get paid as a consultant. It's the right move, and it's the smart move. It's the move *I* would make if I were still running the show."

Danny nodded. "I'll do it, then. I just wanna give it a few more weeks to see what happens with the states, okay?"

I smiled sadly again, knowing full well that he had no intentions of closing down the firm. All I said was, "Sure, Dan, that sounds reasonable."

Five minutes later I had finished my good-byes and was climbing into the back of the limousine, when I saw the Chef coming out of the restaurant. He walked over to the limo and said, "In spite of what Danny's saying, you know he's never gonna close down the firm. They're gonna have to take him out of that place in handcuffs."

I nodded slowly and said, "Tell me something I don't know, Dennis." Then I hugged the Chef, climbed into the back of the limousine, and headed for the hospital.

It was only by coincidence that Long Island Jewish Hospital was in the town of Lake Success, less than a mile from Stratton Oakmont. Perhaps that was why no one seemed surprised as I made my way around the maternity ward passing out gold watches. I had done the same thing when Chandler was born and had made quite a splash then. For some inexplicable reason I got an irrational joy out of wasting $50,000 on people I would never see again.

It was a little before eleven when I finally completed my happy ritual. As I walked into the room where the Duchess was staying, I couldn't find her. She was lost amid the flowers. *Christ!* There were thousands of them! The room was exploding with color–fantastic shades of red and yellow and pink and purple and orange and green.

I finally spotted the Duchess sitting in an armchair. She was holding Carter, trying to give him his bottle. Once more, the Duchess looked gorgeous. Somehow she had managed to lose the weight in the thirty-six hours since she'd given birth, and she was now my luscious Duchess again. *Good for me!* She had on a pair of faded Levi's, a simple white blouse, and a pair of off-white ballet slippers. Carter was swaddled in a sky-blue blanket, and all I could see was his tiny face poking out from beneath it.

I smiled at my wife and said, "You look gorgeous, sweetie. I can't believe your face is back to normal already. You were still bloated yesterday."

"He won't take his bottle," said the maternal Duchess, ignoring my compliment. "Channy always took her bottle. Carter won't."

Just then a nurse walked into the room. She took Carter from the Duchess and started to give him his exit exam. I was still packing the bags when I heard the nurse say, "My, my, my, what wonderful eyelashes he has! I don't think I've ever seen such beautiful ones on a baby. Wait until he unfolds a bit. He's gonna be awfully handsome, I bet."

The proud Duchess replied, "I know. There's something very special about him."

And then I heard the nurse say, "That's strange!"

I spun on my heel and looked at the nurse. She was sitting in a chair, holding Carter–pressing a stethoscope against the left side of his chest.

"What's wrong?" I asked.

"I'm not sure," replied the nurse, "but his heart doesn't sound right." She seemed very nervous now, compressing her lips as she listened.

I looked over at the Duchess, and she looked like she'd just taken a bullet in her gut. She was standing, holding on to the side of the bedpost. I walked over and put my arm around her. No words were exchanged.

Finally the nurse said in a very annoyed tone: "I can't believe no one's picked this up. Your son has a hole in his heart! I'm certain of it. I can hear the backflow right now. It's either a hole or some sort of defect with one of the valves. I'm sorry, but you can't take him home yet. We need to get a pediatric cardiologist up here right now."

I took a deep breath and nodded slowly, vacantly. Then I looked at the Duchess, who was in tears–crying silently. In that very instant we both knew our lives would never be the same again.

Fifteen minutes later we were in the lower bowels of the hospital, standing in a small room filled with advanced medical equipment–banks of computers, monitors of various shapes and sizes, IV stands, and a tiny examining table, on which Carter was now lying naked. The lights had been dimmed and a tall, thin doctor was now in charge.

"There, you see it?" said the doctor. He was pointing his left index finger at a black computer screen, which had four amoebalike swaths in the center of it, two of them red, two of them blue. Each swath was the size of a silver dollar. They were interconnected and seemed to be draining into one another in a slow, rhythmic fashion. In his right hand he was holding a small device, shaped like a microphone, and he was pressing it against Carter's chest and moving it in slow, concentric circles. The red and blue pools were echoes of Carter's blood as it flowed through the four chambers of his heart.

"And there," he added. "The second hole–it's a bit smaller, but it's definitely there, between the atria."

Then he turned off the echocardiogram apparatus and said, "I'm surprised your son hasn't gone into congestive heart failure. The hole between his ventricles is large. There's a strong likelihood he'll need open-heart surgery in the next few days. How's he doing with his bottle? Is he taking it?"

"Not really," said the Duchess sadly. "Not like our daughter did."

"Has he been sweating when he feeds?"

The Duchess shook her head. "Not that I've noticed. He's just not that interested in feeding."

The doctor nodded. "The problem is that oxygenated blood is mixing with deoxygenated blood. When he tries to feed it puts a great strain on him. Sweating during feeding is one of the first signs of congestive heart failure in an infant. However, there's still a chance he might be okay. The holes are large, but they seem to be balancing each other out. They're creating a pressure gradient, minimizing backflow. If it weren't for that, he'd be exhibiting symptoms already. Only time can tell, though. If he doesn't go into heart failure in the next ten days, he'll probably be okay."

"What are the chances of him going into heart failure?" I asked.

The doctor shrugged. "About fifty-fifty."

The Duchess: "And if he does go into heart failure? Then what?"

"We'll start by giving him diuretics to keep fluid from building up in his lungs. There are other medications too, but let's not put the cart before the horse. But if none of the medications work, we'll need to perform open-heart surgery to patch the hole." The doctor smiled sympathetically. "I'm sorry to give you such bad news; we'll just have to wait and see. You can take your son home, but watch him carefully. At the first sign of sweating or labored breathing–or even a refusal to take his bottle–call me immediately. Either way, I'll need to see you again in a week"–*I don't think so, pal! My next stop is Columbia-Presbyterian, with a doctor who graduated from Harvard!*–"to take another echocardiogram. Hopefully, the hole will have started to close by then."

The Duchess and I immediately perked up. Sensing a ray of hope, I asked, "Do you mean it's possible that the hole could close on its own?"

"Oh, yes. I must have forgotten to mention that"–*Nice detail to leave out, slime bucket!*–"but if he doesn't have any symptoms in the first ten days, then that's most likely what'll happen. You see, as your son grows, his heart will also grow, and it'll slowly envelop the hole. By his fifth birthday it should be completely closed. And even if it doesn't close completely, it'll be so small that it won't give him a problem. So, again, it comes down to the first ten days. I can't stress it enough–watch him carefully! In fact, I wouldn't take my eyes off him for more than a few minutes."

"You don't have to worry about that," said a confident Duchess. "There's gonna be at least three people watching him at all times, and one of them is gonna be a registered nurse."

Rather than going to Westhampton, which was a good seventy miles to the east, we headed straight to Old Brookville, which was only fifteen minutes from the hospital. Once there, our families quickly joined us. Even the Duchess's father, Tony Caridi, the world's most lovable loser, showed up–still looking like Warren Beatty, and still looking to borrow money, I figured, once all the commotion died down.

Mad Max led the vigil, quickly turning into Sir Max–assuring the Duchess and me that everything would work out fine; then he went about making phone calls to various doctors and hospitals without losing his temper once. In fact, there would be no sign of Mad Max until the crisis resolved itself, at which point Mad Max would magically reappear–making up for lost time with vicious verbal tirades and belligerent smoking strategies. My mother was her usual self–a saintly woman who prayed Jewish prayers for Carter and offered moral support to the Duchess and me. Suzanne, the closet anarchist, chalked Carter's holes up to a government conspiracy, which included the doctors, who, for some inexplicable reason, were in on it.

We explained to Chandler that her brother was sick, and she told us that she loved him and that she was glad we decided to bring him home from the hospital. Then she went back to playing with her blocks. Gwynne and Janet stood vigil, too, but only after they'd recovered from six hours of hysterical crying. Even Sally, my lovable chocolate brown Lab, got into the act–setting up camp at the base of Carter's crib, leaving only for bathroom breaks and an occasional meal. However, the Duchess's dog, Rocky, evil little bastard that he was, couldn't have cared less about Carter. He pretended nothing was wrong and continued to annoy every person in the house–barking incessantly, peeing on the carpet, pooping on the floor, and stealing Sally's food from her dog bowl, while she was busy sitting vigil and praying with us like a good dog.

But the biggest disappointment was the baby nurse, Ruby, who came highly recommended from one of those WASPy employment agencies that specialize in providing wealthy families with Jamaican baby nurses. The problem started when Rocco Night picked her up from the train station, and he thought he smelled alcohol on her breath. After she'd finished unpacking her bags, he took it upon himself to search her room. Fifteen minutes later she was in the backseat of his car, being led away, never to be heard from again, at least by us. The only fringe benefit was the five bottles of Jack Daniel's that Rocco had confiscated from her, which were now in my downstairs liquor cabinet.

The replacement nurse showed up a few hours later. It was another Jamaican woman, named Erica. She turned out to be a real gem–instantly clicking with Gwynne and the rest of the crowd. So Erica joined the menagerie and stood vigil too.

By day four Carter still hadn't shown any signs of heart failure. Meanwhile, my father and I had made dozens of inquiries as to who the world's foremost pediatric cardiologist was. All our inquiries pointed to Dr. Edward Golenko. He was the Chief of Cardiology at Mount Sinai Hospital in Manhattan.

Alas, there was a three-month wait for an appointment, which quickly turned into a surprise cancellation the following day, after Dr. Golenko was made aware of the $50,000 donation I was planning to make to Mount Sinai's Pediatric Cardiology Unit. So on day five Carter was on another examining table, except this time he was surrounded by an elite team of doctors and nurses, who, after spending ten minutes marveling over his eyelashes, finally got down to business.

The Duchess and I stood silently off to the side, as the team used some sort of advanced imaging apparatus–looking much deeper into Carter's heart and with much greater clarity than with a standard echocardiogram. Dr. Golenko was tall, thin, slightly balding, and had a very kind face. I looked around the room . . . and counted nine intelligent-looking adults, all in white lab coats, all peering down at my son as if he was the most precious thing on earth, which he was. Then I looked at the Duchess, who, as usual, was chewing on the inside of her mouth. She had her head cocked in an attitude of intense concentration, and I wondered if she was thinking what I was thinking, which was: I had never been happier that I was rich than right now. After all, if anyone could help our son it would be these people.

After a few minutes of doctor-to-doctor medi-talk, Dr. Golenko smiled at us and said, "I have very good news for you: Your son's going to be just fine. The holes have already started closing, and the pressure gradient has eliminated any backflow between–"

Dr. Golenko never finished, because the Duchess charged him like a bull. Everyone in the room laughed as she threw her arms around the sixty-five-year-old doctor's neck, wrapped her legs around his waist, and started smooching him.

Dr. Golenko looked at me with a shocked expression, his face slightly redder than a beet, and he said, "I wish all my patients' moms were like this!" And everyone laughed some more. What a wonderfully happy moment it was! Carter James Belfort was going to make it! God had placed a second hole in his heart to balance out the first, and by the time he was five, both holes would be closed, Dr. Golenko assured us.

On the limo ride home, the Duchess and I were all smiles. Carter was sitting between us in the backseat, and George and Rocco were sitting up front. The Duchess said, "The only problem is that I'm so paranoid now, I don't know if I can treat him the way I treated Chandler. She was so big and healthy, I never thought twice about anything."

I leaned over and kissed her on the cheek. "Don't worry, sweetie. In a couple a days everything will be back to normal. You'll see."

"I don't know," said the Duchess. "I'm scared to even think what might happen next."

"Nothing's gonna happen next. We're over the hump now." And for the remainder of the ride I kept my fingers, toes, hands, legs, and arms crossed.

CHAPTER 32

MORE JOY

September 1995
(Five Weeks Later)

It was appropriate, I thought, for the Cobbler to be sitting on his side of the desk and wearing the proud expression of a man who had the world by the balls. For the calendar year 1996, we were shooting for $50 million in revenue, and each division was hitting stride simultaneously. Our department-store business was off the charts; our private-label business was booming; our licensing of the Steve Madden name was way ahead of schedule; and our retail stores, of which there were now nine, were making money hand over fist. On Saturdays and Sundays, in fact, there were lines out the doors, and Steve was becoming a celebrity of sorts, the shoe designer of first choice to an entire generation of teenage girls.

What *wasn't* appropriate was what he said to me next: "I think it's time to move out the Drizzler. If we get rid of him now, we can still take his stock options from him." He shrugged nonchalantly. "Anyway, if he works for us much longer, his options are gonna vest, and then we're fucked."

I shook my head in amazement. The true irony was that the amount of stock options the Drizzler owned was so minuscule that it didn't matter to anyone, except, of course, the Drizzler, who would be rocked if his stock options were to simply vanish into thin air–a victim of the fine print in his employment contract.

I said, "You can't do that to Gary; the guy has worked his ass off for us for over a year now. I'm the first to admit he's a royal pain in the ass sometimes, but, still, you just don't do that to one of your employees, especially one like Gary, who's been a hundred ten percent loyal. It's fucking wrong, Steve. And just imagine the signal it sends to everyone else. It's the sort of shit that destroys a company's morale. Everyone out there takes pride in their stock options; they make them feel like owners; they feel secure about their futures."

I took a weary breath, then added, "If we're gonna replace him, that's fine, but we give him what he's due, and a little bit extra, if anything. That's the only way to do it, Steve. Anything else is bad business."

The Cobbler shrugged. "I don't get it. You're the first one to make fun of the Drizzler, so why the fuck would you care if I take his stock options?"

I shook my head in frustration. "First of all, I only make fun of him so the day passes with a few laughs. I make fun of everyone, Steve, including myself and including you. But I actually love the Drizzler; he's a good man, and he's loyal as hell." I let out a great sigh. "Listen, I'm not denying that Gary might've outlived his usefulness, and maybe it *is* time to replace him with someone with industry experience, someone with a pedigree who can talk to Wall Street–but we can't take away his stock options. He came to work for us when we were still shipping shoes out of the back of the factory. And as slow as he moves, he's still done a lot of good things for the company. It's bad karma to fuck him."

The Cobbler sighed. "I think your loyalty is misplaced. He'd fuck us in two seconds if he had the chance. I've–"

Cutting off the Cobbler, I said, "No, Steve, he wouldn't fuck us. Gary has integrity. He's not like us. He lives by his word, and he never breaks it. If you want to fire him, that's one thing. But you should let him keep his stock options." I realized that by using the word *should,* I was giving Steve more power than he deserved. The problem was that, on paper, he was still the majority owner of the company; it was only through our secret agreement that I maintained control.

"Let me talk to him," said the Cobbler, with a devilish look in his eye. "If I can convince him to go peacefully, then why should you care?" He shrugged. "I mean, if I can get his stock options back, we can divide 'em up fifty–fifty, right?"

I dropped my chin in defeat. It was 11:30 a.m., and I felt so fucking tired. Too many drugs, I thought. And life at home . . . well, it hadn't been a bowl of cherries lately. The Duchess was still a wreck over Carter, and I had basically thrown in the towel on my back pain, which haunted me twenty-four hours a day now. I'd set October 15 as a tentative date to have my spine fused. That was only three weeks from now, and the very thought of it terrified me. I would be undergoing general anesthesia–going under the knife for seven hours. Who knew if I'd ever wake up? And even if I did, who was to say I wouldn't wake up paralyzed? It was always a risk when you underwent spine surgery, although with Dr. Green I was definitely in the best hands. Either way, I was going to be out of commission for at least six months, but then my pain would be gone once and for all, and I would have my life back. Yes, the summer of 1996 would be a good one!

Of course, I had used this as a rationalization to step up my drug habit, promising both Madden and the Duchess that once my back was fixed I would push the drugs aside and become the "real Jordan" again. In fact, the only reason I wasn't stoned right now was because I was just about to leave the office and pick up the Duchess in Old Brookville. We were heading into Manhattan for a romantic night together at the Plaza Hotel. It had been her mother's idea–that it would be good for us to get away from all the worry that seemed to have gotten the better of us since Carter's heart debacle. It would be an excellent chance to rebond.

"Listen, Steve," I said, forcing a smile, "I already have enough stock options and so do you. And we can always print more for ourselves, if we get the urge." I let out a great yawn. "Anyway, do whatever the fuck you want. I'm too tired to argue about it right now."

"You look like shit," said Steve. "I mean that in a loving way. I'm worried about you, and so is your wife. You gotta stop with the Ludes and coke or you're gonna kill yourself. You're hearing it from someone who knows. I was almost as bad as you"–he paused as if searching for the right words–"but I wasn't as rich as you, so I couldn't sink as deep." He paused again. "Or perhaps I sank just as deep, but it happened a whole lot quicker. But with you it could drag on for a long time, because of all your money. Anyway, I'm begging you–you gotta stop or else it's not gonna end well. It never does."

"Point taken," I said sincerely. "You have my promise that as soon as I get my back fixed I'm done for good."

Steve nodded approvingly, but the look in his eyes so much as said, "I'll believe it when I see it."

The brand-new, pearl-white, twelve-cylinder, 450-horsepower Ferrari Testarossa screamed like an F-15 on afterburners as I punched down the clutch and slapped the stick into fourth gear. *Just like that* another mile of northwestern Queens zipped by at a hundred twenty miles an hour, as I weaved in and out of traffic on the Cross Island Parkway with a joint of premium-grade sinsemilla dangling from my mouth. Our destination was the Plaza Hotel. With one finger on the wheel, I turned to a terrified Duchess and said, "Don't you just love this car?"

"It's a piece of shit," she muttered, "and I'm gonna fucking kill you if you don't put out that joint and slow down! In fact, if you don't, I'm not gonna have sex with you tonight."

In less than five seconds the Ferrari was doing sixty and I was putting the joint out. After all, I hadn't had sex with the Duchess since two weeks before Carter was born, so it had been over two months. Admittedly, after seeing her on the delivery table with her pussy looking big enough to hide Jimmy Hoffa, I hadn't been too much in the mood. And the fact that I'd been consuming an average of twelve Ludes a day, along with enough coke to send a band marching from Queens to China, hadn't done wonders for my sex drive.

And then there was the Duchess. She had stayed true to her word: Despite Carter remaining perfectly healthy, she was still on edge. Perhaps two nights at the Plaza Hotel would do us some good. I took one eye off the road and replied, "I'll gladly keep the speedometer below sixty, if you agree to fuck my brains out for the entire night; deal?"

The Duchess smiled. "It's a deal, but first you gotta take me to Barneys and then to Bergdorfs. After that, I'm all yours."

Yes, I thought, tonight was going to be a very good night. All I had to do was make it through those two overpriced torture chambers and then I'd be home free. And, of course, I'd keep it under sixty.

Barneys had been nice enough to rope off the top floor for us, and I was sitting in a leather armchair, sipping Dom Perignon, while the Duchess tried on outfit after outfit–spinning and twirling deliciously, pretending she was back in her modeling days. After her sixth spin, I caught a pleasant glimpse of her loamy loins, and thirty seconds later I was following her into the dressing room. Once inside, I attacked. In less than ten seconds I had her back against the wall and her dress hiked up above her waist and I was deep inside her. I was pounding her against the wall as we moaned and groaned, making passionate love to each other.

Two hours later, just after seven, we were walking through the revolving door of the Plaza Hotel. It was my favorite hotel in New York, despite the fact that it was owned by Donald Trump. Actually, I had a lot of respect for the Donald; after all, any man (even a billionaire) who can walk around town with that fucking hairdo and still get laid by the most gorgeous women in the world gives new meaning to the concept of being a man of power. Anyway, trailing us were two bellmen, holding a dozen or so shopping bags with $150,000 of women's clothing inside. On the Duchess's left wrist was a brand-new $40,000 Cartier watch studded with diamonds. So far, we'd had sex in three different department-store dressing rooms, and the night was still young.

But, alas, once inside the Plaza, things began to quickly go downhill. Standing behind the front desk was a rather pleasant-looking blonde in her early thirties. She smiled and said, "Back so soon, Mr. Belfort! Welcome! It's good to see you again!" Cheery, cheery, cheery!

The Duchess was a few feet to the right, staring at her new watch and, thankfully, still a bit wobbly from the Lude I'd convinced her to take. I looked at the check-in blonde with panic in my eyes and started shaking my head rapidly, as if to say, "Good God, my wife is with me! Pipe the fuck down!"

With a great smile, the blonde said, "We have you staying in your usual suite, on the–"

Cutting her off: "Okay then! That's perfect. I'll just sign right here! Thank you!" I grabbed my room key and yanked the Duchess toward the elevator. "Come on, honey; let's go. I need you!"

"You're ready to do it again?" she asked, giggling.

Thank God for the Ludes! I thought. A sober Duchess would never miss a trick. In fact, she'd already be swinging. "Are you kidding me?" I replied. "I'm always ready with you!"

Just then the resident midget came scampering by, in a lime-green Plaza outfit with gold buttons running up the front and a matching green cap. "Welcome back!" croaked the midget.

I smiled and nodded and kept pulling the Duchess toward the elevator. The two bellmen were still trailing us, carrying all our shopping bags, which I had insisted we bring to the room so she could try everything on for me again.

Inside the room, I tipped each bellman one hundred dollars and swore them to secrecy. The moment they left, the Duchess and I jumped on the king-size bed and started rolling around and giggling.

And then the phone rang.

The two of us looked at the phone with sinking hearts. No one knew we were here except Janet and Nadine's mother, who was watching Carter. *Christ!* It could only be bad news. I knew it in my very heart. I knew it in my very soul. After the third ring I said, "Maybe it's the front desk."

I reached over and picked up the phone. "Hello?"

"Jordan, it's Suzanne. You and Nadine need to come home right now. Carter has a hundred-and-five fever; he's not moving."

I looked at the Duchess. She was staring at me, waiting for the news. I didn't know what to say. Over the last six weeks she'd been as close to the edge as I'd ever seen her. This would be the crushing blow–the death of our newborn son. "We need to leave right now, sweetie. Carter's burning up with fever; your mom said he's not moving."

There were no tears from my wife. She just closed her eyes tightly and compressed her lips and started nodding. It was over now. We both knew it. For whatever reason, God didn't want this innocent child in the world. Just why, I couldn't figure out. But right now there was no time for tears. We needed to go home and say good-bye to our son.

Tears would come later. Rivers of them.

The Ferrari hit 125 miles per hour as we crossed over the Queens–Long Island border. This time, though, the Duchess's take on things was slightly different. "Go faster! Please! We have to get him to the hospital before it's too late!"

I nodded and punched down the accelerator, and the Testarossa took off like a rocket. Within three seconds the needle was pegged at 140 and still climbing–we were passing cars doing seventy-five as if they were standing still. Just why we'd told Suzanne not to take Carter to the hospital I wasn't quite sure, although it had something to do with wanting to see our son at home one last time.

In no time we were pulling into the driveway; the Duchess was running to the front door before the Ferrari had even come to a stop. I looked at my watch: It was 7:45 p.m. It was usually a forty-five-minute ride from the Plaza Hotel to Pin Oak Court: I had made it in seventeen minutes.

On our way back from the city, the Duchess spoke to Carter's pediatrician on her cell phone, and the prognosis was horrific. At Carter's age, an extreme fever accompanied by lack of movement pointed to spinal meningitis. There were two types: bacterial and viral. Both could be deadly, but the difference was that if he made it through the initial stages of viral meningitis, he would make a complete recovery. With bacterial meningitis, however, he would most likely live out the rest of his life plagued with blindness, deafness, and mental retardation. The thought was too much to bear.

I had always wondered how a parent learns to love a child who suffers from such things. Occasionally, I would see a small child who was mentally retarded playing in the park. It was a heart-wrenching affair–to watch the parents doing their best to create even the slightest bit of normalcy or happiness for their child. And I had always been awed by the tremendous love they showed their child in spite of it all–in spite of the embarrassment they might feel; in spite of the guilt they might feel; and in spite of the obvious burden it placed upon their own lives.

Could I really do that? Could I really rise to the occasion? Of course, it was easy to say I would. But words are cheap. To love a child whom you never really got to know, whom you never really had the chance to bond with . . . I could only pray that God would give me the strength to be that sort of man–a *good* man–and, indeed, a true man of power. I had no doubt my wife could do it. She seemed to have an unnaturally close connection to Carter, as he did to her. It was the way things had been between myself and Chandler, from the time she was old enough to be self-aware. Even now, in fact, when Chandler was inconsolable, it was always Daddy to the rescue.

And Carter, at less than two months old, was already responding to Nadine in that very miraculous way. It was as if her very presence calmed him, and soothed him, and made him feel that everything was just as it should be. One day I would be that close with my son; yes, if God would give me the chance, I most certainly would be.

By the time I made it through the front door, the Duchess already had Carter in her arms, swaddled in a blue blanket. Rocco Night had pulled the Range Rover to the front, ready to rush us to the hospital. As we headed out to the car I put the back of my hand to Carter's tiny forehead and was completely taken aback. He was literally *burning up* with fever. He was still breathing, albeit barely. There was no movement; he was stiff as a board.

On the way to the hospital the Duchess and I sat in the back of the Range Rover, and Suzanne sat in the front passenger seat. Rocco was an ex-NYPD detective, so red lights and speed limits were lost on him. And given the circumstances it was appropriate. I dialed Dr. Green, in Florida, but he wasn't home. Then I called my parents and told them to meet us at North Shore Hospital, in Manhasset, which was five minutes closer than Long Island Jewish. The rest of the ride was spent in silence; there were still no tears.

We ran into the emergency room, the Duchess leading the charge, with Carter cradled in her arms. Carter's pediatrician had already called the hospital, so they were waiting for us. We ran past a waiting room full of expressionless people, and in less than a minute Carter was on an examining table, being wiped down with a liquid that smelled like rubbing alcohol.

A young-looking doctor with bushy eyebrows said to us, "It looks like spinal meningitis. We need your authorization to give him a spinal tap. It's a very low-risk procedure, but there is always the chance of an infection or–"

"Just give him the fucking spinal tap!" snapped the Duchess.

The doctor nodded, seeming not the least bit insulted over my wife's use of language. She was entitled.

And then we waited. Whether it was ten minutes or two hours, it was impossible to say. Somewhere along the way his fever broke, dropping to 102. Then he started crying uncontrollably. It was a high-pitched, ungodly shriek, impossible to describe. I wondered if it was the sound an infant makes as he's being robbed of his very faculties, as if instinctively he was crying out in anguish, aware of the terrible fate that had befallen him.

The Duchess and I were sitting in light-blue plastic chairs in the waiting room, leaning against each other, hanging on by a thread. We were accompanied by my parents and Suzanne. Sir Max was pacing back and forth, smoking cigarettes in spite of the no-smoking sign posted on the wall; I pitied the fool who would ask him to put it out. My mother was sitting beside me, in tears. I had never seen her look so terrible. Suzanne was sitting beside her daughter, no longer talking about conspiracies. It was one thing for a baby to have a hole in his heart; it could be patched. But it was quite another for a child to grow up deaf, dumb, and blind.

Just then the doctor emerged through a pair of automatic double doors. He was wearing green hospital scrubs and a neutral expression. The Duchess and I popped up out of our chairs and ran over to him. He said, "I'm sorry, Mr. and Mrs. Belfort; the spinal tap came back positive. Your son has meningitis. It–"

I cut off the doctor: "Is it viral or bacterial?" I grabbed my wife's hand and squeezed it, praying for viral.

The doctor took a deep breath and let it out slowly. "It's bacterial," he said sadly. "I'm very sorry. We were all praying it would be viral, but the test is conclusive. We checked the results three times and there's no mistake." The doctor took another deep breath and then plowed on: "We've been able to get his fever down to a little over a hundred, so it looks like he's gonna make it. But with bacterial meningitis there's significant damage to the central nervous system. It's too soon to say exactly how much and where, but it usually involves a loss of sight and hearing and"–he paused, as if he were searching for the right words–"some loss of mental function. I'm very sorry. Once he's out of the acute stages we'll need to call in some specialists to assess how much damage was actually done. Right now, though, all we can do is pump him with high doses of broad-spectrum antibiotics to kill the bacteria. At this point, we're not even sure what bacteria it is; it seems to be a rare organism, not typically found in meningitis. Our head of infectious disease has already been contacted, and he's on his way to the hospital right now."

In a state of absolute disbelief, I asked, "How did he contract it?"

"There's no telling," replied the young doctor. "But he's being moved to the isolation ward, on the fifth floor. He'll be quarantined until we get to the bottom of this. Other than you and your wife, no one can see him."

I looked at the Duchess. Her mouth was hanging open. She seemed to be frozen solid, staring off into the distance. And then she fainted.

Up in the fifth-floor isolation unit, it was sheer bedlam. Carter was flailing his arms wildly, kicking and screeching, and the Duchess was pacing back and forth, crying hysterically. Tears were running down her face and her skin was an ashen gray.

One of the doctors said to her, "We're trying to get an IV in your son, but he won't remain still. At this age it can be very difficult to find a vein, so I think we're just going to stick the needle through his skull. It's the only way." His tone was rather nonchalant, entirely unsympathetic.

The Duchess was right on him. "You motherfucker! Do you know who my husband is, you bastard? You go back there right now and get an IV in his arm or I'll fucking kill you myself before my husband has the chance to pay someone to do it!"

The doctor froze in horror, mouth agape. He was no match for the sheer ferocity of the Duchess of Bay Ridge. "Well, what the fuck are you waiting for? Go!"

The doctor nodded and ran back over to Carter's hospital crib, lifting up his tiny arm to search for another vein.

Just then my cell phone rang. "Hello," I said tonelessly.

"Jordan! It's Barth Green. I just got all your messages. I'm so sorry for you and Nadine. Are they sure it's bacterial meningitis?"

"Yes," I replied, "they're sure. They're trying to get an IV in him, to pump him with antibiotics, but he's going crazy right now. He's kicking and screaming and flailing his arms–"

"Whoa, whoa, whoa," said Barth Green, cutting me off. "Did you just say he's flailing his arms?"

"Yes, he's going absolutely crazy, even as we speak. He's been inconsolable ever since his fever broke. It sounds like he's possessed by an evil–"

"Well, you can relax, Jordan, because your son doesn't have

meningitis, viral *or* bacterial. If he did, his fever would still be a hundred and six, and he'd be as stiff as a board. He probably has a bad cold. Infants have a tendency to spike abnormally high fevers. He'll be fine in the morning."

I was bowled over. How could Barth Green be so irresponsible as to create false hope like that? He hadn't even seen Carter, and the spinal tap was conclusive; they'd checked the results three times. I took a deep breath and said, "Listen, Barth, I appreciate you trying to make me feel better, but the spinal tap showed that he has some sort of rare org–"

Cutting me off again: "I really don't give a shit what the test showed. In fact, I'm willing to bet it was a contaminant in the sample. That's the problem with these emergency rooms: They're good for broken bones and an occasional gunshot wound, but that's about it. And this, well, this is absolutely *egregious* for them to have worried you like this."

I could hear him sigh over the phone. "Listen, Jordan, you know what I deal with each day with spinal paralysis, so I've been forced to become an expert on giving bad news to people. But this is complete horseshit! Your son has a cold."

I was taken aback. I had never heard Barth Green utter so much as a single curse. Could he possibly be right? Was it plausible that from his living room in Florida he could make a more accurate diagnosis than a team of doctors who were standing at my son's bedside using the world's most advanced medical equipment?

Just then Barth said in a sharp tone: "Put Nadine on the phone!"

I walked over and handed the phone to the Duchess. "Here, it's Barth. He wants to speak to you. He's says Carter's fine and all the doctors are crazy."

She took the phone, and I walked over to the crib and stared down at Carter. They'd finally been able to get an IV going in his right arm, and he had calmed down somewhat–only whimpering now and shifting uncomfortably in his crib. He really was handsome, I thought, and those eyelashes . . . Even now they stood out regally.

A minute later the Duchess walked over to the crib and leaned over and put the back of her hand to Carter's forehead. Sounding very confused, she said, "He seems cool now. But how could all the doctors be wrong? And how could the spinal tap be wrong?"

I put my arm around the Duchess and held her close to me. "Why don't we take turns sleeping here? This way one of us will always be with Channy."

"No," she replied, "I'm not leaving this hospital without my son. I don't care if I have to stay here a month. I'm not leaving him, not ever."

And for three straight days my wife slept by Carter's bedside, never leaving the room once. On that third afternoon, as we sat in the backseat of the limousine on our way back to Old Brookville, with Carter James Belfort between us and the words *It was a contaminant in the sample* ringing pleasantly in both our ears, I found myself in awe of Dr. Barth Green.

First I'd seen him shake Elliot Lavigne out of a coma; now, eighteen months later, he'd done this. It made me feel much more comfortable that he'd be the one standing over me next week with a scalpel in his hand–cutting into my very spine. Then I would have my life back.

And then I could finally get off drugs.

CHAPTER 33

REPRIEVES

(Three Weeks Later)

Just when I actually woke from my back surgery I'm still not sure. It was on October 15, 1995, sometime in the early afternoon. I remember opening my eyes and muttering something like "Uhhhh, fuck! I feel like shit!" Then all of a sudden I started vomiting profusely, and each time I vomited I felt this terrible shooting pain ricocheting through every neural fiber of my body. I was in the recovery room in the Hospital for Special Surgery in Manhattan, and I was hooked up to a drip that released titrated doses of pure morphine into my bloodstream each time I pushed a button. I remember feeling deeply saddened that I had to go through a seven-hour operation to get this sort of cheap high without breaking the law.

The Duchess was hovering over me, and she said, "You did great, honey! Barth said everything's gonna be fine!" I nodded and drifted off into a sublime state of morphine-induced narcosis.

Then I was home. It was perhaps a week later, although the days seemed to be melting into one another. Alan Chemical-tob was helpful–dropping off five hundred Quaaludes my first day home from the hospital. They were all gone by Thanksgiving. It was a feat of great manhood, and I was rather proud of it–to average eighteen Ludes a day, when a single Lude could knock out a two-hundred-pound Navy SEAL for up to eight hours.

The Cobbler came to visit and told me that he'd worked things out with the Drizzler, who had agreed to leave quietly with only a small fraction of his stock options. Then the Drizzler came over and told me that one day he would find the Cobbler in a dark alley and strangle him with his own ponytail. Danny visited, too, and told me that he was just about to cut a deal with the states, so there were definitely Twenty Years of Blue Skies ahead. Then Wigwam came over and told me that Danny had lost touch with reality–that there was no deal with the states–and that, he, Wigwam, was out hunting for a new brokerage firm, where he could set up shop just as soon as Stratton imploded.

As Stratton continued its downward spiral, Biltmore and Monroe Parker continued to thrive. By Christmas, they had completely cut ties with Stratton, although they continued to pay me a royalty of $1 million on each new issue. Meanwhile, the Chef stopped by every few weeks–giving me regular updates on the Patricia Mellor debacle, which was still in the process of winding down. There were some faint rumblings that the FBI was looking into the matter, but no subpoenas had been issued. The Chef assured me that everything would end up okay. He had been in touch with the Master Forger, who had been questioned by both the Swiss and United States governments, and he'd stuck to our cover story like glue. In consequence, Agent Coleman had hit a dead end.

And then there was the family: Carter had finally shaken off his rocky start and was thriving beautifully. He was absolutely gorgeous, with a terrific head of blond peach fuzz, perfectly even features, big blue eyes, and the longest eyelashes this side of anywhere. Chandler, the baby genius, was two and a half now, and she had fallen deeply in love with her brother. She liked to pretend she was the mommy–feeding him his bottle and supervising Gwynne and Erica as they changed his diaper. Chandler had been my best company, as I shuttled myself between the royal bedchamber and the basement's wraparound couch, doing nothing but watching television and consuming massive quantities of Quaaludes. In consequence, Chandler had become a Jedi Master at understanding slurred speech, which would stand her in good stead, I figured, if she happened to end up working with stroke victims. Either way, she spent the greater part of her day asking me when I would be well enough to start carrying her around again. I told her it would be soon, although I strongly doubted that I would ever make a full recovery.

The Duchess had been wonderful too–in the beginning. But as Thanksgiving turned into Christmas and Christmas turned into New Year's, she began to lose patience. I was wearing a full body cast and it was driving me up the wall, so I figured as her husband it was my obligation to drive her up the wall too. But the body cast was the least of my problems–the real nightmare was the pain, which was worse than before. In fact, not only was I still plagued with the original pain, there was a new pain now, which ran deeper, into the very marrow of my spine. Any sudden movement sent waves of fire washing through my very spinal canal. Dr. Green had told me that the pain would subside, but it seemed to be growing worse.

By early January I had sunk to new levels of hopelessness–and the Duchess put her foot down. She told me that I had to slow down with the drugs and at least try to resume some semblance of being a functioning human being. I responded with a complaint about how the New York winter was wreaking havoc on my thirty-three-year-old body. My bones, after all, had become very creaky in my old age. She recommended we spend the winter in Florida, but I told her Florida was for old people, and in spite of feeling old, I was still young at heart.

So the Duchess took matters into her own hands, and next thing I knew I was living in Beverly Hills, atop a great mountain that overlooked the city of Los Angeles. Of course, the menagerie had to come, too, to continue *Lifestyles of the Rich and Dysfunctional*–and for the bargain price of $25,000 a month I rented the mansion of Peter Morton, of Hard Rock Café fame, and settled in for the winter. The aspiring everything quickly reached into her bag of former aspirations, pulling out the one marked *aspiring interior decorator,* and by the time we moved in there was $1 million worth of brand-new furniture in the house, all arranged just so. The only problem was that the house was so enormous, perhaps 30,000 square feet, that I was considering buying one of those motorized scooters to get from one side of the house to the other.

On a separate note, I quickly realized that Los Angeles was merely a pseudonym for Hollywood, so I took a few million dollars and started making movies. It took about three weeks to realize that everyone in Hollywood (including me) was slightly batty, and one of their favorite things to do was: lunch. My partners in the movie business were a small family of South African Jews, who had been former investment-banking clients of Stratton. They were an interesting lot, with bodies like penguins and noses like needles.

In the third week of May my body cast came off. Fabulous! I thought. My pain was still excruciating, but it was time to start physical therapy. Maybe *that* would help. But during my second week of therapy I felt something pop, and a week later I was back in New York, walking with a cane. I spent a week in different hospitals, taking tests, and every last one of them came back negative. According to Barth I was suffering from a dysfunction of my body's pain-management system; there was nothing mechanically wrong with my back, nothing that could be operated on.

Fair enough, I thought. No choice but to crawl up to the royal bedchamber and die. A Lude overdose would be the best way to go, I figured, or at least the most appropriate since they had always been my drug of choice. But there were other options too. My daily drug regimen included 90 milligrams of morphine, for pain; 40 milligrams of oxycodone, for good measure; a dozen Soma, to relax my muscles; 8 milligrams of Xanax, for anxiety; 20 milligrams of Klonopin, because it sounded strong; 30 milligrams of Ambien, for insomnia; twenty Quaaludes, because I liked Quaaludes; a gram or two of coke, for balancing purposes; 20 milligrams of Prozac, to ward off depression; 10 milligrams of Paxil, to ward off panic attacks; 8 milligrams of Zofran, for nausea; 200 milligrams of Fiorinal, for migraines; 80 milligrams of Valium, to relax my nerves; two heaping tablespoons of Senokot, to reduce constipation; 20 milligrams of Salagen, for dry mouth; and a pint of Macallan single-malt scotch, to wash it all down.

A month later, on the morning of June 20, I was lying in the royal bedchamber, in a semivegetative state, when Janet's voice came over the intercom. "Barth Green is on line one," said the voice.

"Take a message," I muttered. "I'm in a meeting."

"Very funny," said the obnoxious voice. "He said he needs to speak to you now. Either you pick up the phone or I'm coming in there and picking it up for you. And put down the coke vial."

I was taken aback. How had she known that? I looked around the room for a pinhole camera, but I didn't see one. Were the

Duchess and Janet surveilling me? Of all the intrusions! I let out a weary sigh and put down my coke vial and picked up the phone. "Hewoah," I muttered, sounding like Elmer Fudd after a tough night out on the town.

A sympathetic tone: "Hi, Jordan, it's Barth Green. How ya holding up?"

"Never better," I croaked. "How about you?"

"Oh, I'm fine," said the good doctor. "Listen, we haven't spoken in a few weeks, but I've been speaking to Nadine every day and she's very worried about you. She says you haven't left the room in a week."

"No, no," I said. "I'm fine, Barth. I'm just catching my second wind."

After a few moments of uncomfortable silence, Barth said, "How *are* you, Jordan? How are you *really*?"

I let out another great sigh. "The truth is, Barth, that I give up. I'm fucking done. I can't take the pain anymore; this is no way to live. I know it's not your fault, so don't think I hold it against you or anything. I know you tried your best. I guess it's just the hand I was dealt, or maybe it's payback. Either way, it doesn't matter."

Barth came right back with: "Maybe you're willing to give up, but I'm not. I won't give up until you're healed. And you *will* be healed. Now, I want you to get your ass out of bed right now, and go into your children's rooms and take a good hard look at them. Maybe you're not willing to fight for yourself anymore, but how about fighting for them? In case you haven't noticed, your children are growing up without a father. When's the last time you played with them?"

I tried fighting back the tears, but it was impossible. "I can't take it anymore," I said, snuffling. "The pain is overwhelming. It cuts into my bones. It's impossible to live this way. I miss Chandler so much, and I hardly even know Carter. But I'm in constant pain. The only time it doesn't hurt is the first two minutes I wake up. Then the pain comes roaring back, and it consumes me. I've tried everything, and there's nothing I can do to stop it."

"There's a reason I called this morning," said Barth. "There's a new medication I want you to try. It's not a narcotic, and it has no side effects to speak of. Some people are having amazing results with it–people like you, with nerve damage." He paused, and I could hear him take a deep breath. "Listen to me, Jordan: There's nothing structurally wrong with your back. Your fusion is fine. The problem is you have a damaged nerve, and it's misfiring–or firing for no reason at all, to be more accurate. You see, in a healthy person, pain serves as a warning signal, to let the body know there's something wrong. But sometimes the system gets short-circuited, usually after a severe trauma. And then even after the injury is healed, the nerves keep firing. I suspect that's what's happening with you."

"What kind of medication is this one?" I asked skeptically.

"It's an epilepsy drug, to treat seizures, but it works for chronic pain too. I'll be honest with you, Jordan: It's still somewhat of a long-shot. It's not approved by the FDA for pain management, and all the evidence is anecdotal. You'll be one of the first people in New York taking it for pain. I already called it in to your pharmacy. You should have it in an hour."

"What's it called?"

"Lamictal," he replied. "And like I said, it has no side effects, so you won't even know you're on it. I want you to take two pills before you go to sleep tonight, and then we'll see what we see."

The following morning I woke up a little after 8:30 a.m., and, as usual, I was alone in bed. The Duchess was already at the stables, probably sneezing like a wild banshee. By noon, she would be back home, still sneezing. Then she would go downstairs to her maternity showroom and design some more clothes. One day, I figured, she might even try to sell them.

So here I was, staring up at the fabulously expensive white silk canopy, waiting for my pain to start. It'd been six years now of intractable agony at the very paws of that mangy mutt Rocky. But it wasn't shooting down my left leg, and there was no burning sensation in the lower half of my body. I swung my feet off the side of the bed and stood up straight, stretching my arms to the sky. I still felt nothing. I did a few side bends–*still* nothing. It wasn't that I felt less pain; I felt no pain whatsoever. It was as if someone had flipped off a switch and literally shut my pain off. It was gone.

So I just stood there in my boxer shorts for what seemed like a very long time. Then I closed my eyes and bit down on my lower lip and started to cry. I went over to the side of the bed, rested my forehead on the edge of the mattress, and continued to cry. I had given up six years of my life to this pain, the last three of which had been so severe that it'd literally sucked the life out of me. I had become a drug addict. I had become depressed. And I had done things while I was high that were unconscionable. Without the drugs I would have never let Stratton get so out of control.

How much had my drug addiction fueled my life on the dark side? As a sober man, would I have ever slept with all those prostitutes? Would I have ever smuggled all that money to Switzerland? Would I have ever allowed Stratton's sales practices to spiral so far out of control? Admittedly, it was easy to blame everything on drugs, but, of course, I was still responsible for my own actions. My only consolation was that I was living a more honest life now–building Steve Madden Shoes.

Just then the door swung open, and it was Chandler. She said, "Good morning, Daddy! I came to kiss away your boo-boo again." She leaned over and kissed my lower back, once on each side, and then she planted one kiss directly on my spine, just over my scar.

I turned around, tears still in my eyes, and took a moment to regard my daughter. She wasn't a baby anymore. While I'd been lost in my pain she'd given up her diaper. Her face was more chiseled now, and in spite of being less than three, she no longer spoke like a baby. I smiled at her and said, "Guess what, thumbkin? You kissed away Daddy's boo-boo! It's all gone now."

That got her attention. "It *is*?" she said, in a wondrous tone.

"Yeah, baby, it is." I grabbed her under her arms and stood up straight, lifting her over my head. "You see, baby? Daddy's pain is all gone now. Isn't that great?"

Very excited: "Will you play with me outside today?"

"You bet I will!" And I swung her over my head in a great circle. "From now on I'll play with you every day! But first I gotta go find Mommy and tell her the good news."

In a knowing tone: "She's riding Leapyear, Daddy."

"Well, that's where I'm going, then, but first let's go see Carter and give him a big kiss, okay?" She nodded eagerly and off we went.

When the Duchess saw me, she fell off her horse. Literally.

The horse had gone one way and she had gone the other, and now she was lying on the ground, sneezing and wheezing. I told her of my miraculous recovery, and we kissed—sharing a wonderful, carefree moment together. Then I said something that would turn out to be very ironic, which was: "I think we should take a vacation on the yacht; it'll be so relaxing."

CHAPTER 34

TRAVELING BADLY

A*hhh, the yacht* Nadine*!* In spite of despising the fucking boat and wishing it would sink, there was still something very sexy about tooling around the blue waters of the Mediterranean aboard a 170-foot motor yacht. In fact, all eight of us–the Duchess and I, and six of our closest friends–were in for quite a treat aboard this floating palace of mine.

Of course, one could never embark on such an inspired voyage without being properly armed, so the night before we departed I recruited one of my closest friends, Rob Lorusso, to go on a last-minute drug collection with me. Rob was the perfect man for the job; not only was he coming along on the trip but he and I also had a history with this sort of stuff–once chasing around a Federal Express truck for three hours during a raging blizzard, in a desperate search for a lost Quaalude delivery.

I had known Rob for almost fifteen years and absolutely adored him. He was my age and owned a small mom-and-pop mortgage company that did mortgages for the Strattonites. Like me, he loved his drugs, and he also had a world-class sense of humor. He wasn't particularly handsome–about five-nine, slightly overweight, with a fat Italian nose and a very weak chin–but, nevertheless, women loved him. He was that rare breed of man who could sit at a table with a bevy of beauties he'd never met before and fart and burp and belch and snort, and they would all say: "Oh, Rob, you're so funny! We love you so much, Rob! Please fart on us some more!"

His fatal flaw, though, was that he was the cheapest man alive. In fact, he was so cheap that it had cost him his first marriage to a girl named Lisa, who was a dark-haired beauty with a lot of teeth. After two years of marriage, she finally got fed up with him highlighting her portion of the phone bill, and she decided to have an affair with a local playboy-type. Rob caught her in the very act, and they were divorced shortly thereafter.

From there Rob started dating heavily, but each girl had some sort of deficiency–one had more arm hair than a gorilla; another liked to be wrapped in Saran Wrap during sex, while pretending she was a corpse; another refused to have any sex but anal sex; and still another (my personal favorite) liked to put Budweiser in her Cheerios. His latest girlfriend, Shelly, would be coming along on the yacht. She was rather cute, although she looked a bit like a hush puppy. Whatever the case, she had this odd habit of walking around with a Bible and quoting obscure passages. I gave her and Rob a month.

Meanwhile, as Rob and I spent our final hours gathering essentials, the Duchess crawled around our driveway, gathering pebbles. It was her first time leaving the children, and for some inexplicable reason it put her in the mood to do arts and crafts. So she made our kids a wish-box–a very expensive women's shoe box (in this case, the former home to a pair of $1,000 Manolo Blahniks) filled with tiny pebbles and then covered with a layer of tinfoil. On top of the tinfoil, the artful Duchess had glued two maps–one of the Italian Riviera and one of the French Riviera–as well as a dozen or so glossy pictures she'd cut out from travel magazines.

Just before we left for the airport, we went into Chandler and Carter's playroom to say good-bye. Carter was almost a year old now and he worshipped his older sister, although not nearly as much as he worshipped his mother, who could bring him to tears if she took a shower and didn't dry her hair before leaving the bathroom. Yes, Baby Carter liked his mother's hair blond, and when it was damp it was much too dark for him. Even the slightest glimpse of a damp-headed Duchess would cause him to point his finger at her hair and scream at the top of his tiny lungs: *"Noooooooooooooooo! Noooooooooooooooo!"*

I often wondered how Carter was going to react when he found out his mother's hair was only dyed blond, but I figured he'd work that out in therapy when he was older. Either way, at this particular moment he was in fine spirits, altogether beaming, in fact. He was staring at Chandler, who was holding court for one hundred Barbie dolls, which she'd arranged in a perfect circle around her.

The artful Duchess and I sat down on the carpet and presented our two perfect children with their perfect wish-box. "Anytime you miss Mommy and Daddy," explained the Duchess, "all you have to do is shake this wish-box and we'll know you're thinking of us." Then, to my own surprise, the artful Duchess pulled out a second wish-box, which was identical to the first, and she added, "And Mommy and Daddy will have our own wish-box too! So every time we miss you we're gonna shake our own wish-box, and then you'll know that we're thinking of you too, okay?"

Chandler narrowed her eyes and took a moment to consider. "But how can I know for sure?" she asked skeptically, not buying into the wish-box program as easily as the Duchess might've hoped.

I smiled warmly at my daughter. "It's easy, thumbkin. We'll be thinking of you night and day, so anytime you think we're thinking of you we are thinking of you! Think of it like that!"

There was silence now. I looked at the Duchess, who was staring at me with her head cocked to one side and a look on her face that said, "What the fuck did you just say?" Then I looked at Chandler, and she had her head cocked at the same angle as her mother. *The girls were double-teaming me!* But Carter seemed entirely unconcerned with the wish-box. He had a wry smile on his face, and he was making a cooing sound. He seemed to be taking my side in all this.

We kissed the kids good-bye, told them we loved them more than life itself, and headed for the airport. In ten days we'd see their smiling faces again.

The problems started the moment we landed in Rome.

The eight of us–the Duchess and I, Rob and Shelly, Bonnie and Ross Portnoy (childhood friends of mine), and Ophelia and Dave Ceradini (childhood friends of the Duchess)–were standing at the baggage claim at Leonardo da Vinci Airport, when an incredulous Duchess said, "I can't believe it! My bags have gone missing. I have no clothes now!" The last few words came out as a pout.

I smiled and said, "Relax, sweetie. We'll be like that couple who lost their bags in the American Express commercial, except we'll spend ten times as much as they did, and we'll be ten times higher while we're spending it!"

Just then, Ophelia and Dave walked over to comfort the doleful Duchess. Ophelia was a dark-eyed Spanish beauty, an ugly duckling that had become a gorgeous swan. The good news was that since she'd grown up ugly as sin, she'd had no choice but to develop a great personality.

Dave was entirely average-looking, a chain-smoker who drank eight thousand cups of coffee a day. He was on the quiet side, although he could be counted on to laugh at my and Rob's off-color jokes. Dave and Ophelia liked things to be boring; they weren't action junkies like Rob and me.

Now Bonnie and Ross walked over to join the fun. Bonnie's face was a mask of Valium and BuSpar, both of which she'd taken to prepare herself for the flight. Growing up, Bonnie was that nubile blonde who every kid in the neighborhood (including me) wanted to bang. But Bonnie wasn't interested in me. Bonnie liked her boys bad (and old too). When she was sixteen, she was sleeping with a thirty-two-year-old pot smuggler, who had already served a jail term. Ten years later, when she was twenty-six, she married Ross, after he'd just gotten out of jail for dealing cocaine. In truth, Ross wasn't really a coke dealer–just a hapless fool who'd been trying to help a friend. Still, he now qualified to bang the luscious Bonnie, who, alas, wasn't quite as luscious as she used to be.

Anyway, Ross was a pretty good yacht guest. He was a casual drug user, an average scuba diver, a decent fisherman, and was quick to run errands if the need arose. He was short and dark, with curly black hair and a thick black mustache. Ross had a sharp tongue, although only toward Bonnie, whom he was constantly reminding of her status as a moron. Yet, above all things, Ross prided himself on being a man's man, or at least an *outdoorsman*, who could brave the elements.

The Duchess still looked glum, so I said, "Come on, Nae! We'll drop Ludes and go shopping! It'll be like the old days. Drop and shop! Drop and shop!" I kept repeating those last three words as if they were the chorus of a song.

"I wanna speak to you in private," said a serious Duchess, pulling me away from our guests.

"What?" I said innocently, although not feeling all too innocent. Rob and I had gotten slightly out of control on the plane, and the Duchess's patience was wearing thin.

"I'm not happy with all the drugs you're doing. Your back is better now, so I don't get it." She shook her head, as if she was disappointed in me. "I always cut you slack because of your back, but now . . . well, I don't know. It doesn't seem right, honey."

She was being rather nice about it–very calm, in fact, and altogether reasonable. So I figured I owed her a nice fat lie. "Once this trip is over, Nae, I promise I'm gonna stop. I swear to God; this is it." I held my hand up like a Boy Scout taking an oath.

There were a few seconds of uncomfortable silence. "All right," she said skeptically, "but I'm holding you to it."

"Good, because I want you to. Now let's go shopping!"

I reached into my pocket and pulled out three Ludes. I cracked one in half and gave it to the Duchess. "Here," I said, "half for you, and two and a half for me."

The Duchess took her meager dose and headed for the water fountain. I followed dutifully. On the way, though, I reached back into my pocket and pulled out two more Ludes. After all, what's worth doing . . . is worth doing right.

Three hours later we were sitting in the back of a limousine, heading down a steep hill that led to Porto di Civitavecchia. The Duchess had a brand-new wardrobe, and I was so post-Luded I could barely keep my eyes open. There were two things I desperately needed: movement and a nap. I was in that rare phase of a Quaalude high called the movement phase, where you can't stand to be in the same spot for more than a second. It's the drug-induced equivalent of having ants in your pants.

Dave Ceradini noticed first. "Why are there whitecaps in the harbor?" He pointed his finger out the window, and all eight of us looked.

Indeed, the grayish water looked awfully rough. There were tiny whirlpools swirling this way and that.

Ophelia said to me, "Dave and I don't like rough water. We both get seasick."

"Me too," said Bonnie. "Can we wait until the water calms down?"

Ross answered for me: "You're such an imbecile, Bonnie. The boat's a hundred seventy feet long; it can handle a bit of chop. Besides, seasickness is a state of mind."

I needed to calm everyone's fears. "We have seasickness patches on board," I said confidently, "so if you get seasick, you should put one on as soon as we get on the boat."

When we reached the bottom of the hill, I noticed that we'd all been wrong. There were no whitecaps; there were waves . . . *Christ!* I'd never seen anything like it! Inside the harbor were four-foot waves, and they seemed to be crossing over one another, in no particular direction. It was as if the wind were blowing from all four corners of the earth simultaneously.

The limo made a right turn, and there it was: the yacht *Nadine,* rising up majestically, above all the other yachts. God–how I hated the thing! Why the fuck had I bought it? I turned to my guests and said, "Is she gorgeous or what?"

Everyone nodded. Then Ophelia said, "Why are there waves in the harbor?"

The Duchess said, "Don't worry, O. If it's too rough we'll wait it out."

Not a fucking prayer! I thought. *Movement . . . movement . . . I needed movement.*

The limo stopped at the end of the dock, and Captain Marc was waiting to greet us. Next to him was John, the first mate. They both wore their *Nadine* outfits–white collared polo shirts, blue boating shorts, and gray canvas boating moccasins. Every article of clothing bore the *Nadine* logo, designed by Dave Ceradini for the bargain price of $8,000.

The Duchess gave Captain Marc a great hug. "Why is the harbor so rough?" she asked.

"There's a storm that popped out of nowhere," said the captain. "The seas are eight to ten feet. We should"–*should*–"wait 'til it dies down a bit before we head to Sardinia."

"Fuck that!" I sputtered. "I gotta move right this fucking second, Marc."

The Duchess was quick to rain on my parade: "We're not going anywhere unless Captain Marc says it's safe."

I smiled at the safety-conscious Duchess and said, "Why don't you go on board and cut the tags off your new clothes? We're at sea now, honey, and I'm a god at sea!"

The Duchess rolled her eyes. "You're a fucking idiot, and you don't know the first thing about the sea." She turned to the group. "Come on, girls, the *sea god* has spoken." With that, all the women laughed at me. Then, in single file, they headed to the gangway and climbed aboard the yacht–following their cherished leader, the Duchess of Bay Ridge.

"I can't sit in this harbor, Marc. I'm heavily post-Luded. How far is Sardinia?"

"About a hundred miles, but if we leave now it's gonna take forever to get there. We'd have to go slow. You've got eight-foot waves, and the storms are unpredictable in this part of the Med. We'd have to batten down the hatches, tie everything down in the main salon." He shrugged his square shoulders. "Even then we might sustain some damage to the interior–some broken plates, some vases, maybe a few glasses. We'll make it, but I strongly advise against it."

I looked at Rob, who compressed his lips and gave me a single nod, as if to say, "Let's do it!" Then I said, "Let's go for it, Marc!" I pumped my fist in the air. "It'll be a fabulous adventure, one for the record books!"

Captain Marc smiled and started shaking his rectangular head. And we climbed aboard and prepared to shove off.

Fifteen minutes later, I was lying on a very comfortable mattress atop the yacht's flybridge, while a dark-haired stewardess named Michelle served me a Bloody Mary. Like the rest of the crew, she wore the *Nadine* uniform.

"Here you go, Mr. Belfort!" said Michelle, smiling. "Can I get you anything else?"

"Yes, Michelle. I have a rare condition that requires me to drink one of these every fifteen minutes. And those are doctor's orders, Michelle, so please set your egg timer or else I might wind up in the hospital."

She giggled. "Whatever you say, Mr. Belfort." She started to walk away.

"Michelle!" I screamed, in a voice loud enough to cut through the wind and the rumble of the twin caterpillar engines.

Michelle turned to me, and I said, "If I fall asleep, don't wake me up. Just keep bringing up the Bloody Marys every fifteen minutes and line them up next to me. I'll drink them when I wake up, okay?"

She gave me the thumbs-up sign and then descended a very steep flight of stairs that led to the deck below, where the helicopter was stowed.

I looked at my watch. It was one p.m., Rome time. At this very moment, inside my stomach sac, four Ludes were dissolving. In fifteen minutes I would be tingling away; fifteen minutes after that I'd be fast asleep. How relaxing, I thought, as I downed the Bloody Mary. Then I took a few deep breaths and shut my eyes. How very relaxing!

I woke up to the feeling of raindrops, but the sky was blue. That confused me. I looked to my right, and there were eight Bloody Marys lined up, all filled to the rim. I shut my eyes and took a deep breath. There was a ferocious wind howling. Then I felt more raindrops. *What the fuck?* I opened my eyes. Was the Duchess pouring water on me again? She was nowhere in sight, though. I was alone on the flybridge.

All of a sudden I felt the yacht dipping down in a most unsettling way until it reached a forty-five-degree angle, and then out of nowhere I heard a wild crashing sound. A moment later a thick wall of gray water came rising up over the side of the yacht, curled over the top of the flybridge, poured down–soaking me from head to toe.

What on God's earth? The flybridge was a good thirty feet above the water and–*oh, shit, oh, shit*–the yacht was dipping down again. Now I was being thrown on my side, and the Bloody Marys went flying on top of me.

I sat up straight and looked over the side and–*holy fucking shit!* The waves had to be twenty feet high, and they were thicker than buildings. Then I lost my balance. I was flying off the mattress now onto the teak deck, and the Bloody Mary glasses followed me, shattering into a thousand pieces.

I crawled over to the side, grabbed hold of a chrome railing, and pulled myself up. I looked behind the boat and–*Holy shit! The* Chandler*!* We were towing the *Chandler,* a forty-two foot dive-boat, by two thick dock ropes, and it was disappearing and reappearing in the peaks and troughs of these enormous waves.

I got back on all fours and started crawling over to the stairs. The yacht felt like it was breaking apart. By the time I'd crawled down the stairway to the main deck, I'd been soaked and banged around mercilessly. I stumbled into the main salon. The entire group was sitting on the leopard-print carpet, huddled in a tight circle. They were holding hands and wearing life vests. When the Duchess saw me, she broke from the group and crawled toward me. But then all at once the boat began tipping wildly to port.

"Watch out!" I screamed, watching the Duchess roll across the carpet and smash into a wall. A moment later an antique Chinese vase went flying across the main salon and smashed into a window above her head, shattering into a thousand pieces.

Then the boat righted itself. I dropped to my hands and knees and quickly crawled over to her. "Are you all right, baby?"

She gritted her teeth at me. "*You* . . . you fucking sea god! I'm gonna kill you if we make it off this fucking boat! We're all about to die! What's going on? Why are the waves so big?" She stared at me with her enormous blue eyes.

"I don't know," I said defensively. "I was sleeping."

The Duchess was incredulous. "You were sleeping? How the fuck could you sleep through this? We're about to sink! Ophelia and Dave are deathly ill. So are Ross and Bonnie . . . and Shelly too!"

Just then Rob came crawling over with a great smile on his face. "Is this a fucking rip or what? I always wanted to die at sea."

The doleful Duchess: "Shut the fuck up, Rob! This is as much your fault as my husband's. You two are complete idiots."

"Where are the Ludes?" sputtered Rob. "I refuse to die sober."

I nodded in agreement. "I have some in my pocket . . . Here," and I reached into my shorts pocket, pulled out a handful of Ludes, and handed him four.

"Give me one of those!" snapped the Duchess. "I need to relax."

I smiled at the Duchess. She was a good egg, my wife! "Here you go, sweetie." I handed her a Lude.

I looked up and Ross, the brave outdoorsman, was crawling over. He looked terrified. "Oh, Jesus," he muttered, "I've gotta get off this boat. I have a daughter. I . . . I . . . I can't stop vomiting! Please, get me off this boat."

Rob said to me, "Let's go up to the bridge and see what's going on."

I looked at the Duchess. "You wait here, honey. I'll be right back."

"Fuck that! I'm coming with you."

I nodded. "Okay, let's go."

"I'll stay down here," said the brave outdoorsman, and he started crawling back to the group with his tail between his legs. I looked at Rob, and we both started laughing. Then the three of us began crawling toward the bridge. On the way, we passed a well-stocked bar. Rob stalled in mid-crawl and said, "I think we should do some shots of tequila."

I looked at the Duchess. She nodded yes. I said to Rob, "Go get the bottle." Thirty seconds later Rob came crawling back, holding a bottle of tequila. He unscrewed the top and handed it to the Duchess, who took a giant swig. *What a woman!* I thought. Then Rob and I took swigs.

Rob screwed the top back on and threw the bottle against a wall. It smashed into a dozen pieces. He smiled. "I always wanted to do something like that."

The Duchess and I exchanged looks.

A short flight of stairs led from the main deck to the bridge. As we made our way up, two deckhands named Bill came barreling down, literally jumping over us. "What's going on?" I yelled.

"The diving platform just ripped off," screamed a Bill. "The main salon is gonna flood if we don't secure the rear doors." And they kept running.

The bridge was a beehive of activity. It was a small space, perhaps eight by twelve feet, and it had a very low ceiling. Captain Marc was holding on to the ship's antique wooden steering wheel with both hands. Every few seconds he would take his right hand off the wheel and work the two throttles, trying to keep the bow pointed in the direction of the oncoming waves. John, the first mate, was standing next to him. He was grasping a metal pole with his left hand to maintain his balance. With his right he held a pair of binoculars to his eyes. Three stewardesses were sitting on a wooden bench, their arms interlocked and tears in their eyes. Through wild bursts of static I heard the radio blaring: *Gale warning! This is a gale warning!*

"What the fuck is going on?" I asked Captain Marc.

He shook his head gravely. "We're fucked now! This storm is only getting worse. The waves are twenty feet and building."

"But the sky's still blue," I said innocently. "I don't get it."

An angry Duchess said, "Who gives a flying fuck about the color of the sky? Can't you turn us around, Marc?"

"No way," he said. "If we try to turn we're gonna get broadsided and tip over."

"Can you keep us afloat?" I asked. "Or should you call Mayday?"

"We'll make it," he replied, "but it's gonna get ugly. The blue skies are about to disappear. We're heading into the belly of a Force Eight gale."

Twenty minutes later I felt the Ludes taking hold. I whispered to Rob, "Give me some blow." I looked at the Duchess to see if she'd busted me.

Apparently she had. She shook her head and said, "You two are off your fucking rockers, I swear."

But it was two hours later–when the waves were thirty feet or better–that the shit really hit the fan. Captain Marc said, in the tone of the doomed: "Oh, shit, don't tell me . . ." Then an instant later he screamed, "Rogue wave! Hold on!"

Rogue wave? What the fuck was that? I found out a second later when I looked out the window–and everyone on the bridge screamed at once: "Holy shit! Rogue wave!"

It had to be sixty feet high, and it was closing fast.

"Hold on!" screamed Captain Marc. With my right hand, I grabbed the Duchess around her tiny waist and pulled her close to my body. She smelled good, the Duchess, even now.

All at once the boat began dipping at an impossibly steep angle, until it was pointing almost straight down. Captain Marc jammed the throttles to full power, and the boat jerked forward and we started rising up the face of the rogue wave. Suddenly the boat seemed to stop on a dime. Then the wave began curling over the top of the bridge, and it came slamming down with the force of a thousand tons of dynamite . . . *KABOOM!*

Everything went black.

It felt like the boat was underwater for forever, but slowly, painfully, we popped back up again–listing heavily to port now at a sixty-degree angle.

"Is everyone okay?" asked Captain Marc.

I looked at the Duchess. She nodded. "We're fine," I said. "How about you, Rob?"

"Never better," he muttered, "but I gotta pee like a fucking racehorse. I'm going downstairs to check on everyone."

As Rob made his way down the stairs, one of the Bills came barreling up, screaming, "The fore-hatch just blew open! We're going down by the bow!"

"Well, *that* kinda sucks," said the Duchess, shaking her head in resignation. "Talk about your shitty vacations."

Captain Marc grabbed the radio transmitter and pushed the button. "Mayday," he said urgently. "This is Captain Marc Elliot, aboard the yacht *Nadine.* This is a Mayday: We are fifty miles off the coast of Rome and going down by the head. We require immediate assistance. We have nineteen souls on board." Then he bent over and started reading off some orange-diode numbers from a computer monitor, giving the Italian Coast Guard our exact coordinates.

"Go get the wish-box!" ordered the Duchess. "It's downstairs, in our stateroom."

I looked at her as if she were a crazy person. "What are you–"

The Duchess cut me off. "Get the wish-box," she screamed, "right fucking now!"

I took a deep breath. "Okay, I will, I will. But I'm fucking starving to death." I looked at Captain Marc. "Can you have the chef whip me up a sandwich?"

Captain Marc started laughing. "You know, you really are one sick bastard!" He shook his square head. "I'll have the chef make us some sandwiches. It's gonna be a long night."

"You're the best," I said, heading for the stairs. "Can I also get some fresh fruit?" Then I ran down the stairs.

I found my guests in the main salon, in a state of panic, tied together with a dock rope. But I wasn't the least bit worried. Soon enough, I knew, the Italian Coast Guard would be here to rescue us; in a few hours from now we'd be safe and sound, and this floating albatross would be off my neck. I asked my guests, "You guys having a fun vacation?"

No one laughed. "Are they coming to rescue us?" asked Ophelia.

I nodded. "Captain Marc just called in a Mayday. Everything's gonna be fine, guys. I gotta go downstairs. I'll be right back." I headed for the stairs–but I was immediately knocked over by another massive wave and went crashing into a wall. I rolled back onto all fours and began crawling to the stairs.

Just then one of the Bills passed me, screaming, "We lost the *Chandler*! It snapped off!" and he kept running.

When I reached the bottom of the stairs I pulled myself up by a banister. I stumbled into my stateroom through ankle-deep water and there it was: the fucking wish-box, sitting on the bed. I grabbed it, made my way back up to the bridge, and handed it to the Duchess. She closed her eyes and started shaking the pebbles.

I said to Captain Marc, "Maybe I can fly the helicopter off the boat. I could take four people at a time."

"Forget it," he said. "With the seas like this it'd be a miracle if you made it up without crashing. And even if you did, it'd be impossible to land again."

Three hours later, the engines were still running but we were making no forward motion. There were four enormous container ships surrounding us. They had heard the Mayday and were trying to shield us from the oncoming waves. It was almost dark now, and we were still waiting to be rescued. The bow was pointing downward at a steep angle. Sheets of rain pounded against the window, the waves were thirty feet plus, and the winds were fifty knots or better. But we were no longer stumbling. We had our sea legs.

Captain Marc had been on the radio for what seemed like an eternity, talking to the Coast Guard. Finally, he said to me, "Okay, there's a helicopter hovering overhead; it's gonna lower down a basket, so get everyone up to the flybridge. We'll get the female guests off first, then the female crew members, then the male guests. The male crew will go last, and I'll go after them. And tell everyone, no bags allowed. You can take only what you can carry in your pockets."

I looked at the Duchess and smiled. "Well, there go all your new clothes!" She shrugged and said happily, "We could always buy more!" Then she grabbed me by the arm and we headed downstairs.

After I explained the program to everyone, I pulled Rob aside and said, "You got the Ludes?"

"No," he said grimly. "They're in your stateroom. It's completely flooded down there, maybe three feet of water–probably more by now."

I took a deep breath and let it out slowly. "I'll tell you, Rob: I got a quarter million in cash down there and I couldn't give a shit about it. But we gotta get those fucking Quaaludes. We have two hundred, and we can't leave 'em behind. It would be a travesty."

"Indeed," said Rob. "I'll get them." Twenty seconds later he was back. "I got shocked," he muttered. "There must be an electrical short down there; what should I do?"

I didn't answer. I just looked him straight in the eye and pumped my fist in the air a single time, as if to say, "You can do it, soldier!"

Rob nodded and said, "If I get electrocuted, I want you to give Shelly seven thousand dollars for a breast job. She's been driving me crazy about it since the day I met her!"

"Consider it done," I said righteously.

Three minutes later Rob was back with the Ludes. "*God,* that fucking hurt! I think I got third-degree burns on my feet!" Then he smiled and said, "But who's better than me, right?"

I smiled knowingly. "No one, Lorusso. You rule."

Five minutes later we were all up on the helicopter deck, and I was watching in horror as the basket swung back and forth a hundred feet in either direction. We were up there for a good thirty minutes–watching and waiting with sinking spirits–and then the sun dipped below the horizon.

Just then John came on deck, looking panic-stricken. "Everyone needs to come back downstairs," he ordered. "The helicopter ran out of fuel and had to go back. We're gonna have to abandon ship; we're about to sink."

I looked at him, astonished.

"Those are captain's orders," he added. "The life raft is inflated back by the stern, where the dive platform used to be. Let's go!" He motioned with his hand.

A rubber raft? I thought. In fifty-foot waves? *Get the fuck out of here!* It seemed like sheer lunacy. But it was captain's orders, so I followed dutifully, as did everyone else. We made our way to the stern, and the Bills were holding either end of a bright-orange rubber raft. The moment they placed it in the ocean it washed away.

"Okay, then!" I said with an ironic smile. "I think the rubber-raft idea is a definite loser." I turned to the Duchess and extended my hand toward her. "Come on; let's go talk to Captain Marc."

I explained to Captain Marc what had happened with the raft.

"God damn it!" he sputtered. "I told those kids not to put the raft in the water without tying it up first. . . . *Shit!*" He took a deep breath and regained his composure. "Okay," he said, "I want you two to listen to me: We're down to only one engine. If it goes, I won't be able to steer the boat anymore, and we're gonna get broadsided. I want you to stay up here. If the boat tips over, jump over the side and swim as far away as possible. There's gonna be a strong down current as the boat goes under, and it will try to suck you down with it. So just keep kicking for the surface. The water's warm enough to survive for as long as you have to. There's an Italian naval destroyer about fifty miles from here and it's on its way. They're gonna try another helicopter rescue with their Special Forces people. It's too rough for the Coast Guard."

I nodded and said to Captain Marc, "Let me go downstairs and tell everyone."

"No," he ordered, "you two are staying here. We could go down any minute and I want you together." He turned to John. "Go downstairs and explain everything to the guests."

Two hours later the boat was barely afloat when a crackling came over the radio. Another helicopter was overhead, this one from the Italian Special Forces.

"All right," said Captain Marc with an insane smile on his face, "here's the deal: They're gonna lower down one of their commandos on a winch, but first we gotta push the helicopter over the side to make room for him."

"You're shitting me!" I said, smiling.

"Oh, my God!" exclaimed the Duchess, putting her hand to her mouth.

"No," replied Captain Marc, "I shit you not. Let me go get the video camera; this one needs to be saved for posterity."

John stayed at the controls while Captain Marc and I headed up to the flight deck with both Bills and Rob. Once there, Captain Marc handed the video camera to one of the Bills and quickly undid the helicopter's restraints. Then he pulled me in front of the helicopter and put his arm around my shoulder. "Okay," he said, smiling, "I want you to say a few words to the studio audience."

I looked into the video camera and said, "Hey! We're pushing our helicopter into the Mediterranean. Isn't this fucking great?"

Captain Marc added, "Yeah! It's a first time in yachting history! Leave it to the owner of the yacht *Nadine*!"

"Yeah," I added, "and if we should all die, I want everyone to know that it was my idea to make this ill-conceived crossing. I forced Captain Marc into it, so he should still be given a proper burial!"

That ended our broadcast. Captain Marc said, "Okay–wait until we get hit by a wave and the yacht starts tipping to the right; then we'll all do a heave-ho at once." And just as the yacht tipped to the right, we all pushed upward and the helicopter went flying over the side of the deck. We ran to the side and watched it sink below the surface in less than ten seconds.

Two minutes later there were seventeen of us on the flight deck, waiting to be rescued. Captain Marc and John remained on the bridge, trying to keep the yacht afloat. A hundred feet above us, a double-bladed Chinook helicopter was in a stationary hover. It was painted military-green, and it was absolutely enormous. Even from a hundred feet, the thumping of the two main rotors was deafening.

Suddenly a commando jumped out of the helicopter and began descending on a thick metal cord. He was dressed in full Special Forces regalia, wearing a black rubber wet suit with a tight-fitting hood. He had a backpack over his shoulders and what looked like a speargun dangling from one of his legs. He was swinging back and forth in a wild arc, a hundred feet in either direction. When he was thirty feet above the boat, he grabbed his speargun, aimed it, and then harpooned the boat. Ten seconds later the commando was on the deck–smiling broadly and giving us the thumbs-up sign. Apparently he was having a ball.

All eighteen of us were lifted to safety. Yet there was a bit of chaos with all this women-and-children-first business, when a panic-stricken Ross (the formerly brave outdoorsman) knocked over Ophelia and the two Bills, made a mad dash for the commando, and took a running jump at him–wrapping his arms and legs around him and refusing to let go until he was off the boat. But that was okay with Rob and me, because we now had fresh material with which to rip Ross to shreds for the rest of his natural life.

Captain Marc, however, would go down with the ship. In fact, the last thing I saw before the helicopter pulled away was the yacht's stern, as it dipped below the water for the last time, and the crown of Captain Marc's square head, bobbing up and down amid the waves.

The nice thing about getting rescued by Italians is that the first thing they do is feed you and make you drink red wine; then they make you dance. Yes, we partied like rock stars aboard an Italian naval destroyer with the very Italian Navy. They were a fun-loving bunch, and Rob and I took that as a signal to get Luded out of our minds. Captain Marc was safe, thank God, and had been plucked out of the water by the Coast Guard.

The last thing I remember was the captain of the destroyer and the Duchess carrying me to the infirmary. Before they put the covers over me, the captain explained how the Italian government was making a big deal over the rescue–a public-relations coup, so to speak–so he was authorized to take us anywhere in the Med; the choice was ours. He recommended the Cala di Volpe Hotel in Sardinia, which he said was one of the nicest in the world. I nodded eagerly and gave him the thumbs-up sign, and said, "Zake me zoo Zarzinia!"

I woke up in Sardinia, as the destroyer pulled into Porto Cervo. All eighteen of us stood on the main deck, watching in awe as hundreds of Sardinians waved at us. A dozen news crews, each with a video camera, were anxious to film the idiot Americans who'd been foolish enough to sail out into the middle of a Force 8 gale.

On our way off the destroyer, the Duchess and I thanked our Italian rescuers and exchanged phone numbers with them. We told them that if they were ever in the States, they should look us up. I offered them money–for their bravery and heroism–and every last one of them refused. They were an incredible bunch–first-class heroes, in the truest sense of the word.

As we made our way through the throngs of Sardinians, it occurred to me that we'd lost all our clothes. For the Duchess, it was round two. But that was fine: I was about to receive a very large check from Lloyd's of London–which had insured the boat and helicopter. After we checked into the hotel, I took everyone shopping, guests and crew alike. All we could find was resort wear–exploding shades of pink and purple and yellow and red and gold and silver. We would be spending ten days in Sardinia looking like human peacocks.

Ten days later, the Ludes were gone and it was time to go home. It was then that I came up with the terrific idea to box up all our clothes and have them shipped back to the States, avoiding Customs. The Duchess agreed.

The next morning, a little before six, I went down to the lobby to pay the hotel bill. It was $700,000. It wasn't as bad as it seemed, though, because the bill included a $300,000 gold bangle studded with rubies and emeralds. I'd bought it for the Duchess somewhere around the fifth day, after I'd fallen asleep in a chocolate soufflé. It was the least I could do to make amends to my chief enabler.

At the airport, we waited two hours for my private jet. Then a tiny man who worked at the private-jet terminal walked up to me and said, in heavily accented English: "Mr. *Belforte*, your plane crash. Seagull fly in engine, and plane go down in France. It will not come to get you."

I was speechless. Did things like this happen to anyone else? I didn't think so. When I informed the Duchess, she didn't say a word. She just shook her head and walked away.

I tried to call Janet–to make new flight arrangements–but the phones were impossible to use. I decided that our best bet was to fly to England, where we could understand what the fuck people were saying. Once we got to London, I knew everything would be fine–until we were sitting in the back of a black London taxi and I noticed something odd: The streets were insanely crowded. In fact, the closer we got to Hyde Park, the more crowded it became.

I said to the pasty-faced British cabbie, "Why is it so crowded? I've been to London dozens of times and I've never seen it like this."

"Well, governor," said the cabbie, "we're having our Woodstock celebration this weekend. There are over half a million people in Hyde Park. Eric Clapton's performing, the Who, Alanis Morissette, and some others as well. It's going to be a jolly good show, governor. I hope you have hotel reservations, because there's scarcely a room anywhere in London."

Hmmm . . . there were three things that now astonished me: The first was that this fucking cabbie kept addressing me as "governor"; the second was that I happened to show up in London on the first weekend since World War II where there were no hotel rooms available in the entire city; and the third was that we all needed to go shopping for clothes again–which would be the Duchess's third time in less than two weeks.

Rob said to me, "I can't believe we gotta go buy clothes again. Are you still paying?"

I smiled and said, "Go fuck yourself, Rob."

In the lobby of the Dorchester Hotel, the concierge said, "I'm terribly sorry, Mr. Belfort, but we're booked solid for the entire weekend. In fact, I don't believe there's a room available anywhere in London. Feel free, though, to bring your party into the bar area. It's teatime, you know, and it would be my pleasure to offer you complimentary tea and finger sandwiches for all your guests."

I rolled my neck, trying to maintain my composure. "Could you call some other hotels and see if there're any rooms available?"

"Of course," he replied. "It would be my pleasure."

Three hours later we were still in the bar, drinking tea and munching on crumpets, when the concierge walked in with a great smile and said, "There's been a cancellation at the Four Seasons. It happens to be the Presidential Suite, which is particularly well-suited to your tastes. The cost is eight–"

I cut him off. "I'll take it!"

"Very well," he said. "We have a Rolls-Royce waiting for you outside. From what I hear, the hotel has a very nice spa; perhaps a *massage* might be in order after all you've been through."

I nodded in agreement, and two hours later I was lying faceup on a massage table, in the Presidential Suite of the Four Seasons Hotel. The balcony looked out over Hyde Park, where the concert was now under way.

My guests were gallivanting around the streets of London, shopping for clothes; Janet was busy at work, arranging flights on the Concorde; and the luscious Duchess was in the shower, competing with Eric Clapton.

I loved my luscious Duchess. Once again she'd proven herself to me, and this time under intense pressure. She was a warrior–standing toe to toe with me, facing down death, keeping a smile on that gorgeous face of hers all the while.

It was for that very reason, in fact, why I was finding it so difficult to maintain my erection right now, as a six-foot-tall Ethiopian masseuse jerked me off. Of course, I knew it was wrong to be getting a hand job from a masseuse while my wife was singing in the shower, twenty feet away. Yet . . . was there really any difference between getting a hand job and jerking myself off with my own hand?

Hmmm . . . I held on to that comforting thought for the remainder of my hand job, and the next day I found myself back in Old Brookville, ready to resume *Lifestyles of the Rich and Dysfunctional.*

CHAPTER 35

THE STORM BEFORE THE STORM

April 1997

As impossible as it might seem, nine months after the sinking of the yacht, my life had sunk to even deeper levels of insanity. I had found a clever way—an altogether *logical* way, in fact—to take my self-destructive behavior to a new extreme, namely, by changing my drug of choice from Quaaludes to cocaine. Yes, it was time for a change, I'd figured, with my chief motivating factor being that I was fed up with drooling in public places and falling asleep in inappropriate settings.

So, rather than starting off my day with four Quaaludes and a tall glass of iced coffee, I woke up to a gram of Bolivian marching powder—always careful to split the dose equally, a half gram up each nostril, so as not to deprive either side of my brain of the instantaneous rush. It was the *true* Breakfast of Champions. Then I'd round out my breakfast with three milligrams of Xanax, to quell the paranoia that was sure to follow. After that—and in spite of my back being completely pain-free now—I would take forty-five milligrams of morphine, simply because cocaine and narcotics were made for each other. Besides, since I still had a bunch of doctors prescribing me morphine, how bad could it be?

Either way, an hour before lunchtime I would take my first dose of Quaaludes—four, to be exact—followed by another gram of coke, to ward off the uncontrollable tiredness that was sure to follow. Of course, I still managed to consume my daily dose of twenty

Quaaludes, but at least now I was using them in a healthier way, a more productive way–to balance out the coke.

It was an inspired strategy, and it had worked perfectly, for a time. But like all things in life, there were a few bumps along the way. In this particular instance, the main bump was that I was sleeping only three hours a week, and by mid-April I was in the midst of a cocaine-induced paranoia that was so deep I'd actually taken a few potshots at the milkman with a twelve-gauge shotgun.

With a bit of luck, I figured, the milkman would spread the word that the Wolf of Wall Street was not a man to be trifled with, that he was armed and ready–fully prepared to ward off any intruder foolish enough to come on his property–even if his bodyguards were sleeping on the job.

Whatever the case, it had been in mid-December, four months ago, when Stratton was finally shut down. Ironically, it wasn't the states who'd lowered the boom on Stratton but the bumbling bozos at the NASD. They had revoked Stratton's membership–citing stock manipulation and sales-practice violations. In essence, Stratton had been shunned, and from a legal standpoint it was a deathblow. Membership in the NASD was a prerequisite for selling securities across state lines; without it, you might as well be out of business. So, reluctantly, Danny closed down Stratton, and the era of the Strattonite came to a close. It had been an eight-year run. Just how it would be remembered I wasn't quite sure, although I suspected the press wouldn't be kind to it.

Biltmore and Monroe Parker were still going strong and still paying me a million dollars per deal, although I considered it a distinct possibility that the owners, other than Alan Lipsky, were plotting against me. Just how and why, I wasn't quite certain, but such was the nature of plots–especially when the conspirators were your closest friends.

On a separate note, Steve Madden *was* plotting against me. Our relationship had completely soured. According to Steve, it had to do with me showing up at the office stoned, to which I'd said to him, "Go fuck yourself, you self-righteous bastard! If it weren't for me you'd still be selling shoes out of the trunk of your car!" True or not, the simple fact was that the stock was trading at thirteen dollars and it was on its way to twenty.

We had eighteen stores now, and our department-store business was booked out two seasons in advance. I could only imagine what he was thinking about me–the man who had taken eighty-five percent of his company and controlled the price of his stock for almost four years. Yet now that Stratton was out of business, I no longer had control over his stock. The price of Steve Madden Shoes was being dictated by the laws of supply and demand–rising and falling with the fortunes of the company itself, not the fortunes of any particular brokerage firm that was recommending it. The Cobbler *had* to be plotting against me. Yes, it was true: I had shown up at the office a bit stoned, and that was wrong, but, still, that was merely an excuse to force me out of the company and steal my stock options. And what was my recourse if he tried doing that?

Well, I had our secret agreement, but that covered only my original shares, 1.2 million of them; my stock options were in Steve's name, and I had nothing in writing. Would he try to steal them from me? Or would he try to steal everything–both my stock and my options? Perhaps that bald bastard had deluded himself, thinking I wouldn't have the balls to expose our secret agreement, that by its very nature it would cause both of us too many problems if I made it public.

He was in for a rude awakening. The chances of him getting away with stealing my stock and options were less than zero–even if it meant both of us going to jail.

As a sober, lucid man, I would've still had these thoughts, but in my current mental state they smoldered in my mind in a most venomous way. Whether Steve was planning to fuck me or not was wholly immaterial; he would never get the chance. He was no different than Victor Wang, the Depraved fucking Chinaman. Yes, Victor had tried to fuck me too, and I'd sent him back to Chinatown.

It was now the second week of April, and I hadn't been to Steve Madden Shoes in over a month. It was Friday afternoon, and I was home in my study, sitting behind my mahogany desk. The Duchess was already in the Hamptons, and the kids were spending the weekend with her mother. I was alone with my thoughts, ready for war.

I dialed Wigwam at his house and said, "I want you to call Madden and tell him that as escrow agent, you're giving him notice that you plan on liquidating a hundred thousand shares immediately. It comes out to about $1.3 million, give or take a few bucks. Tell him that pursuant to the agreement he has the right to sell his shares too, in ratio with me, which means he can sell seventeen thousand of them. Whether he decides to or not is his fucking decision."

Wigwam the Weak replied, "To get it done quickly I need his signature. What if he balks?"

I took a deep breath, trying to control my anger. "If he gives you a hard time, tell him that pursuant to the escrow agreement you're gonna foreclose on the note and sell the stock privately. You tell him that I've already agreed to buy it. And you tell that bald motherfucker that that'll give me a fifteen percent stake in the company, which means I'll have to file a 13D with the SEC, and then everyone on Wall Street's gonna know what a fucking cocksucker he is for trying to fuck me. You tell that motherfucker that I'm gonna make the whole thing public and that every fucking week I'm gonna keep buying more stock in the open market, which means I'm gonna keep filing updated 13Ds. You tell that cocksucker that I'm not gonna stop buying until I own fifty-one percent of his company, and then I'm gonna throw his bony ass right the fuck out of there." I took another deep breath. My heart was beating out of my chest. "And you tell that motherfucker if he thinks I'm bluffing, then he should climb inside a fucking bunker, because I'm about to unleash a nuclear bomb on his very fucking existence." I reached into my desk drawer and pulled out a Ziploc bag with a pound of cocaine in it.

"I'll do whatever you say," replied Wigwam the Weak. "I just want you to think about it for a second. You're the smartest guy I know, but you sound a bit irrational right now. As your lawyer I strongly advise you against making this agreement pub–"

I cut my lawyer right the fuck off. "Let me fucking tell you something, Andy: You have no fucking idea how little of a shit I give about the SE fucking C and the NAS fucking D." I opened the bag and grabbed a playing card off my desk, then dipped deep into the powder, scooping out enough cocaine to give a blue whale a heart attack. I dumped it onto the desktop. Then I bent over and stuck my face in it and started snorting. "And furthermore," I added, my face now covered in cocaine, "I couldn't give two shits about that Coleman motherfucker either. He's been chasing my ass around for four fucking years, and he still ain't got shit on me." I shook my head a few times, to try to get hold of the rush that was rapidly overtaking me. "And there ain't no fucking way I'm getting indicted over that agreement. It would be too anticlimactic for Coleman. He's a man of honor, and he wants to get me on something real. That would be like getting Al Capone on tax evasion. So fuck Coleman where he breathes!"

"Understood," said Wigwam, "but I need a favor from you."

"What?"

"I'm running short of money," said my lawyer, pausing for effect. "You know, Danny really fucked things up for me by not cockroaching it. I'm still waiting for my brokerage license to come through. Could you help me out in the interim?"

Unbelievable! I thought. My own fucking escrow agent was holding me up for money. *That toupeed motherfucker!* I should kill him too! "How much you need?"

"I don't know," he replied weakly, "maybe a couple hundred thousand?"

"Fine!" I snapped. "I'll give you a quarter million, now go call fucking Madden right fucking now and call me back and let me know what he said." I slammed the phone down without saying good-bye. Then I bent over and stuck my face back in the coke.

Ten minutes later the phone rang. "What did the motherfucker say?" I asked.

"You're not gonna like it," warned Wigwam. "He denies the existence of the escrow agreement. He says it's an illegal agreement and he knows you won't make it public."

I took a deep breath, trying to maintain control. "So he thinks I'm bluffing, huh?"

"Pretty much," said Wigwam, "but he said he wants to resolve things amicably. He's offering you two dollars a share."

I rolled my neck slowly in a great circle as I did the calculations. At two dollars a share he would be stealing more than $13 million from me, and that was just on the stock; he was also holding a million of my options, which had an exercise price of seven dollars. Today's market price–thirteen dollars–put them six dollars in the money. So that was another $4.5 million. All told, he was trying to steal $17.5 million from me. Ironically, I wasn't even that angry about it. After all, I had known it all along, from that very day in my office all those years ago, when I'd explained to Danny that his friend couldn't be trusted. It was for that very reason, in fact, why

I had made Steve sign the escrow agreement and hand over the stock certificate.

So why should I be angry? I'd been forced down a foolish path by the bozos at NASDAQ; I had been given no choice but to divest my stock to Steve, and I had taken all necessary precautions—preparing myself for this very eventuality. I ran the entire history of the relationship through my mind, and I couldn't find one mistake I'd made. And while there was no denying that showing up at the office stoned hadn't been good business on my part, it had absolutely nothing to do with what was going on here. He would have tried to fuck me either way; all the drugs had done was bring it to the surface quicker.

"All right," I said calmly. "I have to head out to the Hamptons now, so we'll take care of this first thing Monday morning. Don't even bother calling Steve back. Just get all the paperwork together for the stock purchase. It's time to go to war."

Southampton! WASP-Hampton! Yes, that was where my new beach house was. The time had come to grow up, and Westhampton was just a bit too *pedestrian* for the Duchess's discerning tastes. Besides, Westhampton was full of Jews, and I was sick and tired of Jews, despite being one. Donna Karan (a higher class of Jew) had a house just to the west; Henry Kravis (also a higher class of Jew) had a house just to the east. And for the bargain price of $5.5 million, I now owned a ten-thousand-square-foot gray and white postmodern contemporary mansion on the fabulous Meadow Lane, the most exclusive road on the entire planet. The front of the house looked out over Shinnecock Bay; the rear of the house looked out over the Atlantic Ocean; and the sunrises and sunsets exploded with a nearly indescribable palette of oranges and reds and yellows and blues. It was truly glorious, a vista worthy of the Wild Wolf.

As I passed through the wrought-iron gates at the front of the property, I couldn't help but feel proud. Here I was, behind the wheel of a brand-new royal-blue $300,000 Bentley turbo. And, of course, I had enough cocaine in the glove compartment to keep the entire town of Southampton dancing the Watusi from Memorial Day through Labor Day.

I had been to this house only once, a little over a month ago, when there was still no furniture. I'd brought a business associate named David Davidson here. Naming him that had been a cruel joke, although I found myself spending more time watching him blink his right eye than focusing on his name. Yes, he was a blinker, but only a one-sided blinker, which made it that much more disconcerting. Anyway, the Uniblinker owned a brokerage firm named DL Cromwell, which employed a bunch of ex-Strattonites; we were doing business together, making nothing but money. Yet the Uniblinker's most desirable trait–what I liked most about him–was that he was a coke addict, and on the very night I'd brought him to the house, we had first stopped at Grand Union and bought fifty cans of Reddi Wip. Then we sat on the bleached-wood floor and held the cans upright, pushed the nozzles to the side, and sucked out all the nitrous oxide. It was a helluva buzz, especially when we alternated each hit with two blasts of cocaine, one up either nostril.

It had been a banner evening, but nothing compared to what was in store for tonight. The Duchess had furnished the house–to the tune of $2 million of my not-so-hard-earned money. She was so very excited about it that she'd been spewing her aspiring-decorator bullshit ad nauseam, and all the while she never missed an opportunity to bust my balls for being a coke addict.

And fuck her for that! Who the hell was she to tell me what to do, especially when I'd become a coke addict for her benefit! After all, she had been threatening to leave me if I didn't stop falling asleep in restaurants. So that was why I'd switched to coke in the first place. And now she was saying things like: "You're sick. You've haven't slept in a month. You won't even make love to me anymore! And you only weigh a hundred thirty pounds. All you eat are Froot Loops. And your skin is green!" To have given the Duchess the Life and have her turn on me at the last second! Well, fuck her too! It was easy for her to love me when I was sick. All those nights when I was in chronic pain, she would come in and try to comfort me and tell me that she loved me no matter what. And now it turned out that it was all a clever plot. She could no longer be trusted. Fine. Good. Let her go her own way. I didn't need her. In fact, I didn't need anybody.

All these thoughts were roaring through my brain as I walked up the mahogany stairs and opened the front door to my latest mansion. "Hello," I said, in a very loud voice, stepping through the front door. The entire rear wall was glass, and I was looking at a panoramic view of the Atlantic Ocean. At seven p.m. at this time of spring, the sun was just setting behind me, on the bay side, and the water looked an interesting shade of Prince purple. Meanwhile, the house looked gorgeous. Yes, there was no denying that in spite of the Duchess being a world-class pain in the ass–a henpecking killjoy of biblical proportions–she had a flair for decorating. The entryway led to a vast living room. It was a wide-open space with soaring ceilings. There was so much furniture crammed into this place it was fucking mind-boggling. Overstuffed sofas and love seats and club chairs and wing chairs and ottomans were scattered this way and that, each one a separate seating area. All of this fabulous fucking furniture was white and taupe, very beachy, very shabby chic.

Just then came the royal greeting committee. It was Maria, the fat cook, and her husband, Ignacio, a mean-spirited little butler, who at four-foot-eight was a shade taller than his wife. They were from Portugal and prided themselves on providing service in the formal, traditional way. I despised them because Gwynne despised them, and Gwynne was one of the few people who truly understood me–she and my children. Who knew if these two could be trusted? I would have to keep a close eye on them . . . and, if necessary, neutralize them.

"Good evening, Mr. Belfort," said Maria and Ignacio in unison. Ignacio bowed formally and Maria curtsied. Then Ignacio added, "How are you this evening, sir?"

"Never better," I muttered. "Where's my loving wife?"

"She's in town, shopping," replied the cook.

"What a fucking surprise," I snarled, walking past them. I was carrying a Louis Vuitton travel bag, loaded with dangerous drugs.

"Dinner will be served at eight," said Ignacio. "Mrs. Belfort asked me to inform you that your guests will be here around seven-thirty, and if you could please be ready by then."

Oh, fuck her, I thought. "Okay," I sputtered. "I'll be in the TV room; please don't disturb me. I have important business to attend to." With that, I went into the TV room, flicked on the Rolling Stones, and broke out the drugs. The Duchess had instructed me to be ready by seven-thirty. What the fuck did that mean? That I should be dressed in a fucking tuxedo–or top hat and tails? What was I, a fucking monkey? I was wearing gray sweatpants and a white T-shirt, and that was just fucking fine! Who the fuck paid for all this shit? Me—that's who! And she had the nerve to be giving me orders!

Eight p.m., dinner is served! And who needs it? Give me Froot Loops and skim milk, not this chichi bullshit that Maria and the Duchess hold so dear. The dinner table was the size of a horseshoe pit. Still, the dinner guests weren't all that bad, with the exception of the Duchess. She was sitting across from me, on the other side of the pit. She was so far away I needed an intercom to converse with her, which was probably a good thing. Admittedly, she was gorgeous. But trophy wives like the Duchess were a dime a dozen, and the good ones wouldn't turn on me for no good reason.

Sitting to my right were Dave and Laurie Beall, who were up visiting from Florida. Laurie was a good blond egg. She knew her place in the general scheme of things, so she understood me. The only problem was that she was also under the influence of the Duchess, who'd crawled inside her very mind—planting subversive thoughts against me. So Laurie couldn't be fully trusted.

Her husband, Dave, was another story. He could be trusted—more or less. He was a big country bumpkin—six-two, two hundred fifty pounds of solid muscle. When he was in college he worked as a bouncer. One day someone had mouthed off to him, and Dave punched him in the side of the head and knocked his eye out. Rumor had it that the guy's eye was hanging by a couple of ligaments. Dave was an ex-Strattonite, who now worked at DL Cromwell. Tonight, I could count on him to repel intruders. In fact, he would do it with relish.

My other two guests were the Schneidermans, Scott and Andrea. Scott was a Bayside boy, although we hadn't been friends growing up. He was a confirmed homosexual who'd gotten married for inexplicable reasons, although, if I had to guess, it was to have children, of which he now had one, a daughter. He, too, was an ex-Strattonite, although he'd never possessed the killer instinct. He was out of the business now. He was here for only one reason: He was my coke dealer. He had a connection at the airport and was getting me pure cocaine from Colombia. His wife was innocuous–a chubby brunette with only a few words to say, none of which I found very interesting.

After four courses and two and a half hours of torturous conversation, it was finally eleven o'clock. I said to Dave and Scott, "Come on, guys, let's go into the TV room and watch a movie." I rose from my chair and headed for the TV room, with Dave and Scott in tow. I had no doubt the Duchess wanted to talk to me as little as I wanted to talk to her. And that was fine. Our marriage was basically over; it was only a matter of time now.

What happened next started with an inspired notion I had to divide up my cocaine stash into two separate snorting parties. The first party would commence now and consist of eight grams of powdered cocaine. It would take place here, in the TV room, and last for approximately two hours. Then we would adjourn to the game room upstairs, where we would play pool and darts and get whacked on Dewar's. Then, at two a.m., we would head back downstairs to the TV room and start the second snorting party, which would consist of a twenty-gram rock of ninety-eight percent pure cocaine. To snort it in one sitting would be a conquest worthy of the Wolf himself.

And follow this plan we did–right down to the very fucking letter, in fact–spending the next two hours snorting thick lines of cocaine through an 18-karat-gold straw, while we watched MTV with no sound and listened to "Sympathy for the Devil" on repeat mode. Then we went upstairs to the game room. When two a.m. rolled around, I said with a great smile, "The time has come to snort the rock, my friends! Follow me."

We walked back downstairs to the TV room and sat in our previous positions. I reached over for the rock and it was gone. Gone? How the fuck was that possible? I looked at Dave and Scott and said, "Okay, guys: Stop fucking around. Which one of you took the rock?"

They both looked at me, astonished. Dave said, "What are you, kidding me? I didn't take the rock! I swear on my kid's eyes!"

Scott added, in a defensive tone, "Don't look at me! I would never do something like that." He shook his head gravely. "Fucking around with another man's coke is a sin against God. Nothing less."

The three of us got down on our hands and knees and started crawling around on the carpet. Two minutes later we were looking at one another, dumbfounded–and empty-handed. I said skeptically, "Maybe it fell behind the seat cushions."

Dave and Scott nodded, and we proceeded to remove all the cushions. We found nothing.

"I can't believe this shit," I said. "It makes no fucking sense." Then a wild inspiration came bubbling up into my brain. Perhaps the rock fell *inside* one of the seat cushions! It seemed improbable, but stranger things had happened, hadn't they?

Indeed. "I'll be right back," I said, and I ran to the kitchen, full speed, and slid a stainless-steel butcher knife out of its wooden holder. Then I ran back to the TV room, armed and ready. The rock was mine!

"What are you doing?" asked Dave, in the tone of the incredulous.

"What the fuck do you think I'm doing?" I sputtered, dropping to my knees and plunging the knife into a seat cushion. I began throwing the foam and feathers on the carpet. The sofa had three seat cushions and an equal number of backrests. In less than a minute I'd shredded all of them. "Motherfucker!" I muttered. I switched my focus to the love seat, cutting the cushions open with a vengeance. Still nothing. Now I was getting pissed. "I can't believe this shit! Where'd the fucking rock go?" I looked at Dave. "Were we in the living room at all?"

He shook his head back and forth nervously. "I don't remember being in the living room," he said. "Why don't we just forget about the rock?"

"Are you fucking crazy or something? I'm gonna find that fucking rock if it's the last thing I do!" I turned to Scott and narrowed my eyes accusingly. "Don't bullshit me, Scott. We *were* in the living room, weren't we?"

Scott shook his head. "I don't think so. I'm really sorry, but I don't remember being in the living room."

"You know what?" I screamed. "You guys are both worthless pieces of shit! You know as well as I do that that fucking rock fell into a seat cushion. It's gotta be in there somewhere, and I'm gonna fucking prove it to you." I stood up, kicked the remains of the cushions out of my way, and walked through a littering of foam and feathers into the living room. In my right hand was the butcher knife. My eyes were wide open. My teeth were clenched in rage.

Look at all these fucking sofas! Fuck her if she thinks she can get away with buying all this furniture! I took a deep breath. I was on the edge. I needed to get a grip. But I had come up with a perfect plan–saving the rock until two in the morning. It could've been perfect and now all this furniture. Fuck it all! I dropped to my knees and went to work, making my way around the living room, stabbing wildly until every couch and chair was destroyed. Out of the corner of my eye, I saw Dave and Scott staring at me.

And then it hit me–it was inside the carpet! How fucking obvious! I looked down at the taupe carpet. How much did this fucking thing cost? A hundred thousand? Two hundred thousand? It was easy for her to spend my money. I started slicing up the carpet, like a man possessed.

A minute later, nothing. I sat on my haunches and looked around the living room. It was completely destroyed. Just then I saw a stand-up brass lamp. It looked human. With my heart palpitating out of my chest, I dropped the butcher knife. I picked the lamp up over my head and started swinging it the way the Norse god Thor swung his hammer. Then I released it in the direction of the fireplace, and it went flying into the stone . . . *CRASH!* I ran back over to the knife and picked it up.

Just then the Duchess came running out of the master bathroom, wearing a tiny white robe. Her hair was perfect and her legs looked glorious. It was her way of trying to manipulate me, to control me. It had worked in the past, but not this time. I had my guard up now. I was wise to her game.

"Oh, my God!" she screamed, putting her hand to her mouth. "Please, stop! Why are you doing this?"

"Why?" I screamed. "You want to know fucking why? Well, I'll tell you fucking why! I'm James fucking Bond looking for microfilm! That's fucking why!"

She looked at me with her mouth agape and her eyes wide open. "You need help," she said tonelessly. "You're a sick man."

Her very words enraged me. "Oh, fuck you, Nadine! Who the fuck are you to tell me I'm sick? What are you gonna do–try to take a swing at me? Well, come over and see what happens!"

All at once a terrible pain in my back! Someone was pushing me to the floor! Now my wrist was being crushed. "Oww, fuck!"

I screamed. I looked up and Dave Beall was on top of me. He squeezed my wrist until the butcher knife fell to the ground.

He looked up at Nadine. "Go back inside," he said calmly. "I'll take care of him. Everything's gonna be fine."

Nadine ran back into the master bedroom and slammed the door. A second later I heard the lock click.

Dave was still on top of me, and I turned my head around to face him and started laughing. "All right," I said, "you can let me up now. I was only kidding. I wasn't gonna hurt her. I was just trying to show her who's boss."

Clutching my right biceps with his enormous hand, Dave led me over to a seating area on the other side of the house–one of the few I hadn't destroyed. He placed me in an overstuffed club chair, looked up at Scott, and said, "Go get the vial of Xanax."

The last thing I remember was Dave handing me a glass of water and a few Xanax.

I woke up and it was nighttime, the following day. I was back in my office in Old Brookville, sitting behind my mahogany desk. Just how I got here I wasn't quite sure, but I did remember saying, "Thank you, Rocco!" to Rocco Day, for pulling me out of the car after I'd smashed it into the stone pillar at the edge of the estate on my way home from Southampton. Or had it been Rocco Night I'd thanked? Well . . . who really gave a shit? They were loyal to Bo, and Bo was loyal to me, and the Duchess didn't say much to either of them–so she hadn't crawled inside their minds yet. I would be on alert, though.

Where was the Doleful Duchess? I wondered. I hadn't seen her since the butcher-knife episode. She was home, but she was hiding somewhere in the mansion–hiding from me! Was she in the master bedroom? No matter. The important thing was my children; at least I was a good father. In the end, that's how I would be remembered: He was a good father, a family man at heart, and a wonderful provider!

I reached into my desk drawer and pulled out my Ziploc bag with nearly a pound of coke in it. I dumped it on my desktop and dropped my head into the pile and snorted with both nostrils simultaneously. Two seconds later I jerked my head up and muttered,

"Holy fucking Christ! Oh, my God!" and then I slumped back in my chair and started breathing heavily.

At that moment the TV volume seemed to increase dramatically, and I heard a gruff, accusing voice say: "Do you know what time it is right now? Where's your family? Is this your idea of fun—sitting in front of a television set at this hour of the morning—alone? Drunk, high, strung out? Look at your watch for a second, if you still have one."

What the fuck? I looked at my watch: a $22,000 gold Bulgari. Of course I still had one! I focused back on the TV. What a face! *Christ!* It was a man in his early fifties, enormous head, huge neck, menacingly handsome features, perfectly coiffed gray hair. In that very instant the name Fred Flintstone came bubbling up into my brain.

Fred Flintstone plowed on: "You want to get rid of me right now? How about getting rid of your disease right now! Alcoholism and addiction are killing you. Seafield has the answers. Call us today; we can help."

Unbelievable! I thought. How very fucking intrusive! I started muttering at the TV. "You motherfucking Fred Flintstone head—I'll kick your fucking caveman ass from here to Timbuktu!"

Flintstone kept talking. "Remember: There's no shame in being an alcoholic or an addict; the only shame is doing nothing about it. So call right now and take . . ."

I looked around the room . . . *there!* . . . a Remington sculpture on a green marble pedestal. It was two feet tall, made of solid brass—a cowboy riding a bucking bronco. I picked it up and ran toward the TV screen. With all the strength I could muster, I winged it at Fred Flintstone and . . . *CRASH!*

No more Fred Flintstone.

I addressed the shattered TV: "You motherfucker! I warned you! Coming into my fucking house and telling me I got a fucking problem. Look at you now, motherfucker!"

I walked back to my desk and sat down, then I dropped my bleeding nose into the pile of coke. But rather than snorting it, I simply rested my face in it, using it as a pillow.

I felt a slight twinge of guilt that my children were upstairs, but since I was such a wonderful provider all the doors were solid mahogany. There was no way anyone had heard a thing. Or that was what I'd thought until I heard heavy footsteps on the stairs. A second later came the voice of the Duchess: "Oh, my God! What are you doing?"

I lifted my head, fully aware that my face was completely covered in coke, and not giving a shit. I looked at the Duchess, and she was stark naked–trying to manipulate me with the possibility of sex.

I said, "Fred Flintstone was trying to come through the TV. But don't worry–I got him. You can go back to sleep now. It's safe."

She stared at me with her mouth open. She had arms crossed underneath her breasts, and I couldn't help but stare at her nipples. *What a shame the woman had turned on me.* She would be difficult to replace–not impossible, but difficult.

"Your nose is gushing blood," she said softly.

I shook my head in disgust. "Stop exaggerating, Nadine. It's barely even bleeding, and it's only because it's allergy season."

She started to cry. "I can't stay here anymore unless you go to rehab. I love you too much to watch you kill yourself. I've always loved you; don't ever forget that." And then she left the room, closing the door behind her but not slamming it.

"Fuck you!" I screamed at the door. "I don't got a fucking problem! I could stop anytime I want!" I took a deep breath and used my T-shirt to wipe the blood off my nose and chin. What did she think, that she could bluff me into rehab? Please! I felt another warm gush under my nose. I lifted the bottom of my T-shirt again and wiped away more blood. *Christ!* If I only had ether, I could make the cocaine into crack. Then I could just smoke the coke and avoid all these nasal problems. *But, wait!* There were other ways to make crack, weren't there? Yes, there were homespun recipes . . . something having to do with baking soda. There had to be a recipe for making crack on the Internet!

Five minutes later I had my answer. I stumbled to the kitchen, grabbed the ingredients, and dropped them on the granite countertop. I filled a copper pot with water and dumped in the cocaine and baking soda, then turned the burner on high and put a cover on it. I placed a ceramic cookie jar on top of the lid.

I sat down on a stool next to the stove and rested my head on the countertop. I started feeling dizzy, so I shut my eyes and tried to relax. I was drifting . . . drifting . . . *KABOOM!* I nearly jumped out of my own skin as my homespun recipe exploded all over the kitchen. There was crack everywhere–on the ceiling, floor, and walls.

A minute later the Duchess came running in. "Oh, my God! What happened? What was that explosion?" She was out of breath, almost panic-stricken.

"Nothing," I muttered. "I was baking a cake and fell asleep."

The last thing I remember her saying was: "I'm going to my mother's tomorrow morning."

And the last thing I remember thinking was: The sooner the better.

CHAPTER 36

JAILS, INSTITUTIONS, AND DEATH

The next morning—which is to say, a few hours later—I woke up in my office. I felt a warm, altogether pleasant sensation under my nose and on my cheeks. *Ahhh, so soothing it was. . . . The Duchess was still with me . . . cleaning me . . . mothering me . . .*

I opened my eyes and . . . alas, it was Gwynne. She was holding a very expensive white bath towel, which she'd dampened with lukewarm water, and she was wiping off the cocaine and blood that had caked on my face.

I smiled at Gwynne, one of the only people who hadn't betrayed me. Could she really be trusted, though? I closed my eyes and ran it through my mind. . . . Yes, she could. No two ways about it. She would see this through with me to the bitter end. In fact, long after the Duchess had abandoned me, Gwynne would still be there—taking care of me and helping me raise the children.

"Are you okay?" asked my favorite Southern belle.

"Yeah," I croaked. "What are you doing here on Sunday? Don't you have church?"

Gwynne smiled sadly. "Mrs. Belfort called me and asked me to come over today to keep an eye on the kids. Here, lift your arms up; I brought you a fresh T-shirt."

"Thanks, Gwynne. I'm kinda hungry. Can you bring me a bowl of Froot Loops, please?"

"They're *raight* there," she said, pointing to the green marble pedestal where the brass cowboy used to reside. "They're nice and soggy," she added, "just the way you like 'em!"

Talk about service! How come the Duchess couldn't be like that? "Where's Nadine?" I asked.

Gwynne pursed her full lips. "She's upstairs, packing an overnight bag. She's going to her mother's."

A terrible sinking feeling overtook me. It started in the pit of my stomach and spread to every cell of my body. It was as if my very heart and guts had been ripped out. I felt nauseous, ready to puke. "I'll be right fucking back," I sputtered, popping out of my chair and heading for the spiral staircase. I bounded up the stairs with a raging inferno burning inside me.

The master bedroom was just off the stairs. The door was locked. I started banging. "Let me in, Nadine!" No response. "It's my bedroom too! Let me in!"

Finally, thirty seconds later, the lock clicked open; but the door didn't follow suit. I opened the door and walked into the bedroom. On the bed was a suitcase filled with clothes, all neatly folded, but no Duchess. The suitcase was chocolate brown with the Louis Vuitton logo plastered all over it. Cost a fucking fortune . . . *of my money!*

Just then the Duchess came walking out of her Delaware-size shoe closet, carrying two shoe boxes, one under either arm. She didn't say a word, nor did she look at me. She just walked over to the bed and placed the shoe boxes next to the suitcase, then turned on her heel and headed back to the closet.

"Where the fuck do you think you're going?" I snapped.

She looked me in the eye with contempt. "I told you: I'm going to my mother's. I can't watch you kill yourself anymore. I'm done."

I felt a surge of steam rising up my brain stem. "I hope you don't think you're taking the kids with you. You're not taking my fucking kids–ever!"

"The kids can stay," she replied calmly. "I'm going alone."

That caught me off guard. Why would she be leaving the kids behind? . . . Unless it was some sort of plot. Of course. She was cagey, the Duchess. "You think I'm stupid or something? The second I fall asleep you're gonna come back here and steal the kids."

She looked at me with disdain and said, "I don't even know how to respond to that." She started walking back to the closet.

Apparently I wasn't hurting her enough, so I said, "I don't know where the fuck you think you're going with all these clothes. If you leave here, you leave with the shirt on your back, you fucking gold digger."

That one got her! She spun around and faced me. "Fuck you!" she screamed. "I've been the best wife to you. How *dare* you call me that after all these years! I've given you two gorgeous children. Waited on you hand and fucking foot for six fucking years! I've been a loyal wife to you–always! Never cheated on you once! And look what I got in return! How many women have you fucked since we're married? You . . . philandering piece of shit! Fuck you!"

I took a deep breath. "Say what you want, Nadine, but if you leave here, you leave with nothing." My tone was calm yet menacing.

"Oh, really? What the fuck you gonna do, light my clothes on fire?"

An excellent idea! And I yanked her suitcase off the bed, stomped over to the limestone fireplace, and threw all her clothes on top of a foot of kindling wood that was already there, waiting to be ignited with the push of a button. I stared down the Duchess; she was standing stock-still, frozen in horror.

Not satisfied with her reaction, I ran to her closet and ripped dozens of sweaters and shirts and dresses and skirts and pants off some very expensive-looking hangers. I ran back to the fireplace and threw them on top of the pile.

I looked at her again. Now she had tears in her eyes. Still not good enough. I wanted to hear her apologize, to beg me to stop, so I gritted my teeth in determination and bounded over to the desk where she kept her jewelry box. I grabbed the box, walked back over to the fireplace, and opened the lid and shook out all the jewelry on top of the pile. I reached over to the wall and placed my right index finger on a small stainless-steel button, and I stared her down. Now tears were streaming down her cheeks.

"Fuck you!" I screamed . . . and I pushed the button.

An instant later her clothes and jewelry were engulfed in flames. Without saying a word, she calmly walked out of the room, shutting the door behind her ever so gently. I turned back around and stared into the flames. Fuck her! I thought. It served her fucking right, making threats at me. Did she think I would let her walk all over me? I kept staring at the flames until I heard the sound of gravel kicking up in the driveway. I ran over to the window and saw the back of her black Range Rover peeling toward the front gate.

Good! I thought. Just as soon as the word got out that the Duchess and I were history, there would be women lining up at the door–*lining up!* Then we'd see who's boss!

Now that the Duchess was out of the picture, it was time to put on a happy face and show the children how wonderful life could be without Mommy. No more time-outs for Chandler; chocolate pudding for Carter whenever he felt like it. I took them out to the swing set in the backyard and we played together–while Gwynne, Rocco Day, Erica, Maria, Ignacio, and a few other members of the menagerie supervised the action.

We played together happily for what seemed like a very long time–an eternity, in fact, during which time we laughed and giggled and carried on and looked up to the blue dome of the sky and smelled the fresh spring flowers. Having kids was the best!

Alas, an eternity turned out to be only three and a half minutes, at which point I lost interest in my two perfect children and said to Gwynne, "You take over, Gwynne. I have some paperwork I need to go over."

A minute later I was back in my office, with a fresh pyramid of cocaine in front of me. And as a way of paying homage to Chandler's fascination with lining up all her dolls and holding court, I lined up all my drugs on the desktop and held court too. There were twenty-two of them, mostly in vials but some in plastic Baggies. How many men could take all these drugs and not over dose? None! Only the Wolf could! The Wolf, who'd built up his very resistance through years of careful mixing and balancing, going through the painstaking process of trial and error until he got it *just* right.

The next morning was war.

At eight a.m. Wigwam was sitting in my living room, pissing me off. In fact, he should've known better than to come to my house and try to expound on the U.S. securities laws–sketching only broad, meaningless strokes. Christ, I might've been deficient in many areas in life, but one of them wasn't U.S. securities laws. In fact, even after three months of basically no sleep–and even after the last seventy-two hours of complete insanity, during which time I'd consumed forty-two grams of cocaine, sixty Ludes, thirty Xanax, fifteen Valium, ten Klonopin, 270 milligrams of morphine, ninety milligrams of Ambien, and Paxil and Prozac and Percocet and Pamelor and GHB and God only knew how much alcohol–I still knew more about getting around U.S. securities laws than almost any man on the planet.

Wigwam said, "The main problem is that Steve never signed a stock power, so we can't just send the stock certificate over to the transfer agent and get it switched to your name."

In that very instant, as foggy as my mind was, I was still appalled at how much of an amateur my friend was. It was such a simple problem that I felt like spitting nails in his face. I took a deep breath and said, "Let me tell you something, you motherfucker. I love you like a fucking brother, but I'm gonna rip your fucking eyeballs out of your head next time you tell me what I can't do with this escrow agreement. You come over to my fucking house looking to borrow a quarter million dollars and you're worried about fucking stock powers? Jesus fucking Christ, Andy! We only need a stock power if we wanna sell the fucking stock, not if we want to buy the fucking stock! Don't you get it? This is a war of attrition, a war of *possession,* and once we gain possession of the stock we have the upper hand."

I softened my tone. "Listen to me: All you need to do is foreclose on the note pursuant to the escrow agreement and then you'll have a legal obligation to sell the stock to pay the note. Then you turn around and sell the stock to me at four dollars a share, and I write you a check, for $4.8 million, which covers the purchase price of the shares. Then you write a check right back to me for the same $4.8 million, to pay off the note, and that's that! Don't you get it? It's so simple!"

He nodded weakly.

"Listen," I said calmly, "possession is nine-tenths of the law. I write you a check right now and we officially have control of the stock. Then we file a 13D this afternoon, and we make a public announcement that I intend to keep buying more stock and start a proxy fight. It'll cause so much turmoil that it'll force Steve's hand. And each week I'll keep buying more stock and we'll keep filing updated 13Ds. It'll be in *The Wall Street Journal* every week–driving Steve crazy!"

Fifteen minutes later Wigwam was leaving my house, $250,000 richer and holding a check for $4.8 million. By this afternoon it would hit the Dow Jones newswire that I was attempting a takeover of Steve Madden Shoes. And while I really had no intention of doing so, I had no doubt that it would drive Steve crazy–and leave him little choice but to pay me fair market value for my shares. Insofar as my personal liability, I wasn't concerned. I had thought it through, and since Steve and I hadn't actually signed the secret agreement until a year after the underwriting, the issue of Stratton issuing a false prospectus was a moot point. The liability was more Steve's than my own, because as CEO, *he* was the one signing off on the SEC filings. I could plead ignorance–saying that I thought the filings were being done correctly. It wasn't plausible deniability at its best, but it was plausible deniability nonetheless.

Either way, Wigwam was now out of my hair.

I went back upstairs to the royal bathroom and started snorting again. There was a pile of coke on the vanity and a thousand lights ablaze–reflecting off the mirrors and the million-dollar gray marble floor. Meanwhile, I felt terrible inside. Empty. Hollow. I missed the Duchess so much, so terribly, yet there was no way to get her back now. After all, to give in to her would be to admit defeat–to admit that I had a problem and that I needed help.

So I stuck my nose in the pile and snorted with both nostrils at once. Then I swallowed a few more Xanax and a handful of Quaaludes. The key, though, wasn't the Ludes and Xanax. It was to keep my coke high in the very early stages–within that first wild rush where everything seems to make perfect sense and your problems seem a million miles away. It would require constant snorting–two thick lines every four or five minutes, I figured–but if I could keep myself at that very point for a week or so, then I could wait the Duchess out and watch her crawl back to me. It would require some serious drug-balancing, but the Wolf was up to the task . . .

. . . although if I fell asleep she would come for the kids and steal them. Perhaps I should just leave town with them, keep them out of her evil grasp, although Carter was a bit too small to travel with. He was still wearing a diaper and he was still very dependent on the Duchess. Of course, that would change soon, especially when he was ready for his first car and I offered him a Ferrari if he agreed to forget his mother.

So it made more sense just to leave town with Chandler and Gwynne. Chandler was wonderful company, after all, and we could travel around the world together as father and daughter. We would dress in the finest clothes and live a carefree life, while others looked on in admiration. Then, in a few years, I would come back for Carter.

Thirty minutes later I was back in the living room–conducting business with Dave Davidson, the Uniblinker. He was complaining about trading from the short side, that he was losing money as the stock went up. I couldn't have cared less, though; I just wanted to see the Duchess, to let her know about my plan to travel around the world with Chandler.

Just then I heard the front door open. A few seconds later I saw the Duchess walk past the living room and into the children's playroom. I was discussing trading strategies with the Uniblinker when she came walking back out, holding Chandler. My words were coming out automatically, as if on tape–and I heard the Duchess's soft footsteps heading to the basement, to the maternity showroom. She hadn't even acknowledged my presence, for Chrissake! She was taunting me, disrespecting me, *fucking enraging me!* I felt my heart beating out of my chest.

". . . so you make sure that you're around for the next deal," I continued, as my mind double-tracked wildly. "The key is, David, that you–excuse me for a second." I held up my index finger. "I gotta go downstairs and talk to my wife."

I stomped down the spiral staircase. The Duchess was sitting at her desk, opening mail. *Opening mail? The fucking nerve of her!* Chandler was lying on the floor next to her–holding a crayon, drawing in a coloring book. I said to my wife, in a tone laced with venom: "I'm going to Florida."

She looked up. "So? Why should I care?"

I took a deep breath. "I don't care if you care or not, but I'm taking Chandler with me."

She smirked. "I don't think so."

My blood pressure hit peak levels. "You don't think so? Well, go fuck yourself!" And I reached down, grabbed Chandler, and started running toward the stairs. Instantly, the Duchess popped out of her chair and started chasing me, screaming, "I'm gonna fucking kill you! Put her down! Put her down!"

Chandler started wailing and crying hysterically, and I screamed at the Duchess, "Go fuck yourself, Nadine!" I hit the stairs running. The Duchess took a flying leap and grabbed me around the thighs, desperately trying to keep me from going up the stairs.

"Stop!" she screamed. "Please, stop! It's your daughter! Put her down!" And she kept wriggling her way up my leg, trying to get a grip on my torso. I looked at the Duchess, and at that very instant I wanted her dead. In all the years we'd been married I had never raised a hand to her–until now. I placed the sole of my sneaker firmly on her stomach, and with one mighty thrust I kicked out–and just like that I watched my wife go flying down the stairs and land on her right side with tremendous force.

I paused, astonished, bewildered, as if I had just witnessed a wildly horrific act committed by two insane people, neither of whom I knew. A few seconds later Nadine rolled onto her haunches, holding her side with both hands–wincing in pain–as if she'd broken a rib. But then her face hardened again, and she got down on her hands and knees and tried crawling up the stairs this time, still trying to stop me from taking her daughter.

I turned from her and ran up the stairs, holding Chandler close to my chest and saying, "It's okay, baby! Daddy loves you and he's taking you on a little trip! It's gonna be okay." When I reached the top of the stairs I broke out into a full run, as Chandler continued to wail uncontrollably. I ignored her. Soon the two of us would be together, alone, and everything would be okay. And as I ran to the garage I knew that one day Chandler would understand all this; she would understand why her mother had to be neutralized. Perhaps when Chandler was much older–after her mother had been taught a lesson–they could reunite and have some sort of relationship. Perhaps.

There were four cars inside the garage. The white two-door convertible Mercedes was closest, so I opened the passenger door and put Chandler into the passenger seat and slammed the door. As I ran around the back of the car, I saw one of the maids, Marissa, looking on in horror. I jumped inside the car and started it.

Then the Duchess was throwing herself against the passenger

side of the car, banging on the window and screaming. I immediately hit the power-lock button. Then I saw the garage door starting to close. I looked to the right and saw Marissa's finger on the button. *Fuck it!* I thought–and I put the car into drive, stepped on the accelerator, and drove right through the garage door, smashing it to splinters. I kept driving full speed–smashing right into a six-foot-high limestone pillar at the edge of the driveway. I looked over to Chandler. She wasn't wearing a seat belt, but she was unharmed, thank God. She was screaming, crying hysterically.

All at once, some very disturbing thoughts began rising up my brain stem, starting with: What the fuck was I doing? Where the hell was I going? What was my daughter doing in the front seat of my car without a seat belt on? Nothing made sense. I opened the driver's side door and stepped outside and just stood there. A second later, one of the bodyguards came running over to the car, grabbed Chandler, and ran into the house with her. That seemed like a good idea. Then the Duchess came over to me and told me that everything would be all right and that I needed to calm down. She told me she still loved me. She put her arms around me and hugged me.

And there we stood. For how long I would never know, but pretty soon I heard the wailing of a siren, and then I saw flashing lights. And then I was in handcuffs, sitting in the back of a police car, craning my neck around and trying to catch a last glimpse of the Duchess before they took me to jail.

I would spend the rest of my day being shuttled around to different jail cells–starting with the cell in the Old Brookville Police Department. Two hours later they handcuffed me once more and drove me to another police department, where I was escorted into another jail cell, although this one was bigger and full of people. I spoke to no one and no one spoke to me. There was lots of yelling and screaming and carrying on, and the place was freezing cold. I made a mental note to dress warm if Agent Coleman ever came knocking on my door with an arrest warrant. Then I heard my name being called, and a few minutes later I was in the backseat of another police car–on my way to the town of Mineola, where the state courthouse was.

I found myself in court, in front of a female judge . . . *Oh, shit!*

My goose is cooked now! I turned to my dapper lawyer, Joe Fahmegghetti, and I said, "We're fucked now, Joe! This woman's gonna give me the death penalty!"

Joe smiled at me and put his arm on my shoulder. "Relax," he said. "I'll have you outta here in ten minutes. Just don't say a word until I tell you to."

After a few minutes of blah-blah-blahing, Joe bent over and whispered in my ear, "Say not guilty," so I smiled and said, "Not guilty."

Ten minutes later I was free–walking out of the courthouse with Joe Fahmegghetti by my side. My limo was waiting outside the courthouse at the curb. George was behind the wheel and Rocco Night was in the front passenger seat. They both climbed out, and I noticed that Rocco was carrying my trusty LV bag. George opened the limousine door without saying a word, while Rocco made his way around the back of the car. He handed me my bag and said, "All your stuff's in here, Mr. B, plus fifty thousand dollars in cash."

My lawyer quickly added, "There's a Learjet waiting for you at Republic Airport. George and Rocco will take you there."

All at once I was confused. It was the Duchess plotting against me! No two ways about it! "What the fuck are you talking about?" I sputtered. "Where are you taking me?"

"To Florida," said my dapper attorney. "David Davidson is waiting for you at Republic right now. He'll fly down with you to keep you company. Dave Beall will be waiting for you in Boca when you land." My attorney sighed. "Listen, my friend, you need to get away for a few days until we can resolve this with your wife. Or else you're gonna end up in jail again."

Rocco added, "I spoke to Bo, and he told me to stay up here and keep an eye on Mrs. B. You can't go home, Mr. B. She's got an order of protection against you; you'll get arrested if you come on the property."

I took a deep breath and tried to figure out whom I could trust... My attorney, yes... Rocco, yes... Dave Beall, yes... the dirty Duchess–*NO!* So what was the point of going home, anyway? She hated me and I hated her, and I would probably end up killing her if I saw her, and that would put a serious damper on my travel plans with Chandler and Carter. So, yes, perhaps a few days in the sun might do me some good.

I looked at Rocco and narrowed my eyes. "Is *everything* in there?" I asked accusingly. "All my medications?"

"I packed everything," said a weary-looking Rocco. "All the stuff from your drawers and inside your desk, plus the cash Mrs. Belfort gave us. It's all in there."

Fair enough, I thought. Fifty thousand dollars should last me a couple of days. And the drugs . . . well, there ought to be enough of them in there to get Cuba stoned for the rest of April.

CHAPTER 37

SICK AND SICKER

The sheer insanity of it! We were cruising along at 39,000 feet and there were so many cocaine molecules floating in the recirculated air that when I got up to go to the bathroom, I noticed that the two pilots were wearing gas masks. Good. They seemed like nice-enough guys, and I would hate to see them fail a drug test on my account.

I was on the run now. I was a fugitive! I needed to keep moving, to *maintain.* To rest was to die. To allow my head to come down, to allow myself to crash, to allow my thoughts to focus in on what had just happened, that was certain death!

Yet . . . why had it happened? Why had I kicked the Duchess down the stairs? She was my wife. I loved her more than anything. And why had I thrown my daughter into the passenger seat of my Mercedes and driven through a garage door without even buckling her seat belt? She was my most prized possession on earth. Would she remember that scene on the stairs for the rest of her life? Would she always visualize her mother crawling upward, trying to save her daughter from . . . from . . . what? . . . The coked-out maniac?

Somewhere over North Carolina I had admitted to myself that I was a coked-out maniac. For a brief moment, I had crossed over the line. But now I was back, sane, once more. Or was I?

I needed to keep snorting. And I needed to keep dropping,

dropping Ludes and Xanax and lots of Valium. I needed to keep the paranoia at bay. I needed to maintain my high at all costs; *to rest was to die . . . to rest was to die.*

Twenty minutes later the seat-belt sign came on, serving as a clear reminder that it was time to stop snorting, time to drop Ludes and Xanax–to ensure that we'd hit the ground in a state of perfect toxic poise.

As my attorney had promised, Dave Beall was waiting on the tarmac with a black Lincoln limousine behind him. Janet at work, I figured, already hooking me up with transportation.

Standing there with his arms crossed, Dave looked bigger than a mountain. "You ready to party?" I said buoyantly. "I need to find my next ex-wife."

"Let's go back to my house and relax," replied the Mountain. "Laurie flew to New York to be with Nadine. We got the whole house to ourselves. You need to get some sleep."

Sleep? No, no, no! I thought. "I'll get all the sleep I need when I'm dead, you big fuck. And whose side are you on, anyway? Mine or hers?" I took a swing at him, a full right cross that landed squarely on his right biceps.

He shrugged, apparently not feeling the sting of my blow. "I'm on your side," he said warmly. "I'm always on your side, but I don't think there's a war. You guys are gonna make up. Give her a few days to calm down; that's all the woman needs."

I gritted my teeth and shook my head menacingly, as if to say, "Never! Not in a million fucking years!"

Alas, the truth was somewhat different. I wanted my Duchess back; in fact, I wanted her back desperately. But I couldn't let Dave know that; he might slip, say something to Laurie, who would then say something to the Duchess. Then the Duchess would know that I was miserable without her, and that would give her the upper hand.

"I hope she drops fucking dead," I muttered. "I mean, after what she did to me, Dave? I wouldn't take her back if she were the last cunt in the world. Now, let's go to Solid Gold and get some strippers to give us blow jobs!"

"You're the boss," said Dave. "My orders are just to make sure that you don't kill yourself."

"Oh, really?" I snapped. "Who the fuck gave you those orders?"

"Everybody," said my big friend, shaking his head gravely.

"Well, then, *fuck* everybody!" I sputtered, heading to the limousine. "Fuck every last one of them!"

Solid Gold–what a place! A smorgasbord of young strippers, at least two dozen of them. As we made our way toward the center stage, I got a better look at some of these young beauties, and I came to the sad conclusion that most of them had been beaten over the head with an ugly stick.

I turned to the Mountain and the Uniblinker and said, "There're too many dogs in this place, but if we look hard enough I bet we can find a diamond in the rough." I craned my head this way and that. "Let's walk around a bit."

Toward the back of the club was a VIP section. An enormous black bouncer stood before a short flight of steps cordoned off by a red velvet rope. I headed straight for him. "How ya doing!" I said, in warm tones.

The bouncer looked down at me as if I were an annoying insect that needed to be squashed. He needed a little attitude adjustment, I reasoned, so I reached down into my right sock, pulled out a stack of $10,000 in hundreds, and peeled off half and handed it to him.

With his attitude now properly adjusted, I said, "Would you bring me the five hottest girls in this place, and then clear out the VIP section for my friends and me?"

He smiled.

Five minutes later we had the entire VIP section to ourselves. There were four reasonably hot strippers standing in front of us in their birthday suits and high heels. They were all decent-looking, but none of them was marriage material. I needed a true beauty, one I could parade around Long Island to show the Duchess once and for all who was boss.

Just then the bouncer opened the velvet rope and a naked teenager made her way up the steps, in a pair of white patent-leather go-to-hell pumps. She sat down next to me on the arm of the club chair, crossed her bare legs with complete insouciance, and then leaned over and gave me a peck on the cheek. She smelled of a mixture of Angel perfume and a tiny drop of her own musky aroma from dancing. She was gorgeous. She couldn't have been a day over eighteen. She had a great mane of light-brown hair, emerald-green eyes, a tiny button nose, and a smooth jawline. Her body was incredible–about five-five, a pair of silicone C-cups, a gentle curve to her tummy, and legs that rivaled the Duchess's. She had olive skin, and there wasn't a single blemish on it.

We exchanged smiles, and her teeth were even and white. In a voice loud enough to cut through the stripper music, I said, "What's your name?"

She leaned toward me until her lips were almost pressing against my right ear, and she said, "Blaze."

I recoiled and looked at her with my head cocked to one side. "What kinda fucking name is Blaze? Did your mother know you were gonna be a stripper when you were born?"

She stuck her tongue out at me, so I stuck my tongue back at her. "My real name is Jennifer," she said. "Blaze is my stage name."

"Well," I said, "it's very nice to make your acquaintance, Blaze."

"Awwww," she said, rubbing her cheek against mine. "You're such a little cutie!"

Little? Why . . . you . . . *little hooker in stripper's clothing! I oughta smash you one!* I took a deep breath and said, "What do you mean?"

That seemed to confuse her. "I mean you're . . . a cutie, and you have beautiful eyes, and you're young!" She offered me her stripper's smile.

She had a very sweet voice, Blaze. Would Gwynne approve of her, though? In truth, it was still too early to say if this one would make a suitable mother for the children.

"Do you like Quaaludes?" I asked.

She shrugged her bare shoulders. "I never tried one. What do they make you feel like?"

Hmmm . . . a novice, I thought. No patience to break her in. "How about coke? Have you tried that?"

She raised her eyebrows. "Yeah, I love coke! Do you have any?"

I nodded eagerly. "Yeah, mountains of it!"

"Well, then, follow me," she said, grabbing my hand. "And don't call me Blaze anymore, okay? My name is Jennie."

I smiled at my future wife. "Okay, Jennie. Do you like kids, by the way?" I crossed my fingers.

She smiled from ear to ear. "Yeah, I love kids. I wanna have a whole bunch one day. Why?"

"No particular reason," I said to my future wife. "I was just wondering."

Ahhh, Jennie! My very antidote to the backstabbing Duchess! Who even needed to go back to Old Brookville now? I could just move Chandler and Carter down to Florida. Gwynne and Janet would come too. The Duchess would have visitation rights, once a year, under court supervision. That would be fair.

Jennie and I passed away the next four hours in the manager's office, snorting cocaine, as she gave me private lap dances and world-class blow jobs, in spite of the fact that I hadn't been able to actually get it up yet. I was now convinced, however, that she would make a suitable mother for my children, so I said to the top of Jennie's head, "Hold on, Jennie. Stop sucking for a second."

She craned up her neck and offered me her stripper's smile. "What's wrong, sweetie?"

I shook my head. "Nothing's wrong. In fact, everything's right. I want to introduce you to my mother. Hold on a second." I pulled out my cell phone and dialed my parents' house in Bayside, which had had the same phone number for thirty-five years.

A moment later came my mother's concerned voice, to which I replied, "No, no, don't listen to her. Everything is fine. . . . A restraining order? So fucking what? I have two houses; she can keep one and I can keep the other. . . . The children? They'll live with me, of course. I mean, who could do a better job raising them than me? Anyway, that's not why I called, Mom; I called to let you know that I'm asking Nadine for a divorce. . . . Why? Because she's a backstabbing bitch, that's why! Besides, I already met someone else, and she's really nice." I looked over at Jennie, who was fairly beaming, and I winked at her. Then I said into the phone, "Listen, Mom, I want you to speak to my future wife. She's really sweet and beautiful and . . . Where am I right now? I'm in a strip club down in Miami. . . . Why? . . . No, she's not a stripper, or at least not anymore. She's putting all that behind her now. I'm gonna spoil her rotten." I winked at Jennie again. "Her name is Jennie, but you can call her Blaze if you want. She won't take offense at that; she's a very easygoing girl. Hold on—here she is."

I passed the cell phone to Jennie. "My mom's name is Leah, and she's very nice. Everyone loves her."

Jennie shrugged and grabbed the phone. "Hello, Leah? This is Jennie. How are you? . . . Oh, I'm fine, thanks for asking. . . . Yes, he's okay. . . . Uh-huh, yes, okay, hold on a second." Jennie put her hand over the mouthpiece and said, "She said she wants to speak to you again."

Unbelievable! I thought. That was very rude of my mother to blow off my future wife like that! I grabbed the phone and hung up on her. Then I smiled from ear to ear, lay back down on the couch, and pointed to my loins.

Jennie nodded eagerly, leaned over me, and started sucking . . . and grabbing . . . and yanking . . . and pulling . . . and then sucking some more. . . . Still, for the life of me I couldn't seem to get the blood flowing. But my young Jennie was a trooper, a determined little teenager she was, not about to quit without giving it a full college try. Fifteen minutes later she finally found that special little spot, and next thing I knew I was hard as a rock–fucking her mercilessly on a cheap white cloth couch and telling her that I loved her. She told me that she loved me too, at which point we both giggled. It was a happy moment for us as we marveled at how two lost souls could fall so deeply in love so quickly–even under these circumstances.

It was amazing. Yes, in that very instant–just before I came–Jennie was everything to me. Then an instant later I wished she would vaporize into thin air. A terrible sinking feeling washed over me like a hundred-foot tidal wave. My heart sank into the pit of my stomach. I visibly sagged. I was thinking of the Duchess: I missed her.

I needed to speak to her desperately. I needed for her to tell me that she still loved me and that she was still mine. I smiled sadly at Jennie and told her that I needed to speak to Dave for a second and that I'd be right back. I went out into the club, found Dave, and told him that if I didn't leave this place right this second I might kill myself, which would put him in deep shit, since it was his responsibility to keep me alive until things settled down a bit. So we left, without saying good-bye to Jennie.

Dave and I were sitting in the back of the limo, on our way to his house in Broken Sound, a gated community in Boca Raton. The Uniblinker had fallen in love with a stripper and stayed behind–and I was now considering slitting my wrists. I felt myself crashing; the cocaine was wearing off and I was falling from an emotional cliff. I needed to speak to the Duchess. Only she could help me.

It was two in the morning. I grabbed Dave's cell phone and dialed my home number. A woman's voice answered, but it wasn't the Duchess's.

"Who's this?" I snapped.

"It's Donna."

Oh, shit! Donna Schlesinger had been a friend of Nadine's since childhood. She would back Nadine to the hilt. I took a deep breath and said, "Let me speak to my wife, Donna."

"She doesn't want to talk to you right now."

That enraged me. "Just put her on the fucking phone, Donna."

"I told you," snapped Donna, "she doesn't want to talk to you."

"Donna," I said calmly, "I'm not fucking around here. I'm warning you right now that if you don't put her on the phone I'm gonna fly back to New York and stick a fucking knife through your heart. And then, when I'm done with you, I'm going after your husband, just on general principles." Then I screamed, "Put her on the phone right fucking now!"

"Hold on," said a very nervous Donna.

I rolled my neck, trying to calm myself down. Then I looked at Dave and said, "You know I didn't really mean that. I was just trying to make a point."

He nodded and said, "I hate Donna as much as you do, but I think you ought to let Nadine be for a couple of days. Just back off a bit. I spoke to Laurie, and she said Nadine is pretty shaken up."

"What else did Laurie say?"

"She said that Nadine won't take you back unless you go to drug rehab."

Just then over the cell phone: "Hi, Jordan, it's Ophelia. Are you okay?"

I took a deep breath. Ophelia was a good girl, but she couldn't be trusted. She was the Duchess's oldest friend, and she would want the best for us . . . but, still . . . the Duchess had crawled inside her mind . . . manipulated her . . . turned her against me. Ophelia could be an enemy. Still, she wasn't evil, so I found her voice somewhat calming. "I'm okay, Ophelia. Will you please put Nadine on the phone?"

I heard her sigh. "She won't come to the phone, Jordan. She won't speak to you unless you go to rehab."

"I don't need rehab," I said sincerely. "I just need to slow down a bit. Tell her I will."

"I'll tell her," said Ophelia, "but I don't think it'll help. Listen, I'm sorry, but I gotta go." And just like that she hung up the phone on me.

My spirits plunged even lower. I took a deep breath and dropped my head in defeat. "Unbelievable," I muttered under my breath.

Dave put his arm on my shoulder. "Are you all right, buddy?"

"Yeah," I lied, "I'm fine. I don't wanna talk right now. I just need to think."

Dave nodded, and we spent the remainder of the ride in silence.

Fifteen minutes later I was sitting in Dave's living room, feeling hopeless and desperate. The insanity seemed even worse now; my spirits had plunged to impossible depths. Dave was sitting next to me on the couch, saying nothing. He was just watching and waiting. In front of me was a pile of cocaine. My pills were on the kitchen counter. I had tried calling the house a dozen times, but Rocco had started to answer the phone. Apparently he'd turned against me too. I would fire him as soon as this was resolved.

I said to Dave, "Call Laurie on her cell phone. It's the only way I can get through."

Dave nodded wearily and started punching in Laurie's number on the cordless phone. Thirty seconds later I had her on the phone, and she was crying. "Listen," she said, snuffling back tears, "you know how much Dave and I love you, Jordan, but, please, I'm begging you, you gotta go to rehab. You gotta get help. You're about to die. Don't you see it? You're a brilliant man and you're destroying yourself. If you won't do it for yourself, then do it for Channy and Carter. Please!"

I took a deep breath and rose from the couch and started walking toward the kitchen. Dave followed a few steps behind. "Does Nadine still love me?" I asked.

"Yes," said Laurie, "she still loves you, but she won't be with you anymore unless you go to rehab."

I took another deep breath. "If she loves me she'll come to the phone."

"No," said Laurie, "if she loves you she *won't* come to the phone. You two are in this thing together; you're both sick with this disease. She might be even sicker than you for allowing it to go on so long. You need to go to rehab, Jordan, and she needs to get help too."

I couldn't believe it. Even Laurie had turned on me! I never would've thought it–not in a million years. Well, *fuck her!* And fuck the Duchess! And fuck every last soul on earth! Who gave a fucking shit anymore! I had already peaked, hadn't I? I was thirty-four and had already lived ten lifetimes. What was the point now? Was there anywhere to go but down? What was better, to die a slow, painful death or to go down in a blaze of glory?

Just then I caught a glimpse of the vial of morphine. There were at least a hundred pills inside, fifteen milligrams each. They were small pills, half the size of a pea, and they were a terrific shade of purple. I'd taken ten today, which was enough to put most men in an irreversible coma; for me, it was nothing.

With great sadness in my voice, I said to Laurie, "Tell Nadine I'm sorry, and to kiss the kids good-bye." The last thing I heard before I hung up the phone was Laurie screaming: "Jordan, no! Don't hang–"

In one swift movement I grabbed the vial of morphine, unscrewed the top, and poured out the entire contents into the palm of my hand. There were so many pills that half of them tumbled on the floor. Still, there were at least fifty, rising up in the shape of a pyramid. It looked beautiful; a purple pyramid. I threw them back and started chewing them. Then all hell broke loose.

I saw Dave running toward me, so I darted to the other side of the kitchen and grabbed a bottle of Jack Daniel's, but before I could put my lips to the bottle he was on me–knocking the bottle out of my hand and grabbing me in a bear hug. The phone started to ring. He ignored it and took me down to the floor, then stuck his tremendous fingers in my mouth and tried scooping the pills out. I bit his fingers, but he was so strong he overpowered me. He screamed, "Spit them out! Spit them out!"

"Fuck you!" I yelled. "Let me up or I'll fucking kill you, you big fuck!"

And the phone kept ringing, and Dave kept screaming, "Spit out the pills! Spit them out!" and I kept chewing and trying to swallow more pills until, finally, he grabbed my cheeks with his right hand and squeezed with tremendous force.

"Oww, fuck!" I spit out the pills. They tasted poisonous . . . incredibly bitter . . . and I had already swallowed so many of them it didn't really matter. It was only a matter of time now.

Holding me down with one hand, he picked up the cordless, dialed 911, and frantically gave the police his address. Then he threw down the phone and tried scooping more pills out of my mouth. I bit him again.

"Get your fucking paws out of my mouth, you big fucking oaf! I'll never forgive you. You're with *them*."

"Calm down," he said, picking me up like a bundle of firewood and carrying me over to the couch.

And there I laid, cursing him out for a solid two minutes, until I started to lose interest. I was getting very tired . . . very warm . . . very dreamy. It felt rather pleasant, actually. Then the phone rang. Dave picked it up, and it was Laurie. I tried listening to the conversation, but I quickly drifted off. Dave pressed the phone to my ear and said, "Here, buddy, it's your wife. She wants to speak to you. She wants to tell you that she still loves you."

"Nae?" I said, in a sleepy voice.

The loving Duchess: "Hey, sweetie, hang in there for me. I still love you. Everything's gonna be okay. The kids love you, and I love you too. It's all gonna be okay. Don't fall asleep on me."

I started to cry. "I'm sorry, Nae. I didn't mean to do that to you today. I didn't know what I was doing. I can't live with myself. . . . I'm . . . sorry." I sobbed uncontrollably.

"It's okay," said my wife. "I still love you. Just hang in there. It's all gonna be okay."

"I've always loved you, Nae, since the first day I laid eyes on you."

Then I overdosed.

I woke up to the most horrendous feeling imaginable. I remember screaming, "No! Get that thing out of my mouth, you fucker!" but not being sure exactly why.

I found out a second later. I was tied to an examining table in an emergency room, surrounded by a team of five doctors and nurses. The table was positioned upright, perpendicular to the floor. Not only were my arms and legs tied but there were also two thick vinyl belts affixing me to the table, one across my torso and the other across my thighs. A doctor in front of me, dressed in green hospital scrubs, was holding a long, thick black tube in his hand, the sort you would expect to find on a car radiator.

"Jordan," he said firmly, "you need to cooperate and stop trying to bite my hand. We have to pump your stomach."

"I'm fine," I muttered. "I didn't even swallow anything. I spit them out. I was only kidding."

"I understand," he said patiently, "but I can't afford to take that chance. We've given you Narcan to offset the narcotics, so you're out of danger now. But listen to me, my friend: Your blood pressure is off the charts and your heartbeat is erratic. What other drugs have you taken besides morphine?"

I took a moment to regard the doctor. He looked Iranian or Persian or something along those lines. Could he be trusted? I was a Jew, after all, which made me his sworn enemy. Or did the Hippocratic oath transcend all that? I looked around the room, and over in the corner I saw a very disturbing sight–two policemen, in uniform, with guns. They were leaning against a wall, observing. Time to clam up, I thought.

"Nothing," I croaked. "Only morphine, and maybe a bit of Xanax. I have a bad back. I got everything from the doctor."

The doctor smiled sadly. "I'm here to help you, Jordan, not to bust you."

I closed my eyes and prepared for the torture. Yes, I knew what was coming. This Persiranian bastard was gonna try to stick that tube down my esophagus, all the way into my stomach sac, where he would vacuum out the contents. Then he would dump a couple of pounds of black charcoal into my stomach to push the drugs through my digestive tract unabsorbed. It was one of the rare moments in my life when I regretted being well read. And the last thought I had before the five doctors and nurses attacked me and forced the tube down my throat was: *God, I hate being right all the time!*

An hour later my stomach sac was completely empty, except for the dump truck worth of charcoal they'd forced down my throat. I was still tied to the table when they finally removed the black tube. As the last inch of tubing slid up my esophagus, I found myself wondering how female porn stars were able to deep-throat all those enormous penises without gagging. I knew it was a strange thought to have, but, still, it was what had occurred to me.

"How you feeling?" asked the kind doctor.

"I have to go to the bathroom really bad," I said. "In fact, if you don't untie me I'm gonna take a dump right in my pants."

The doctor nodded, and he and the nurses began undoing my restraints. "The bathroom's in there," he said. "I'll come in there in a little while and check on you."

I wasn't quite sure what he'd meant by that, until the first salvo of gunpowder came exploding out of my rectum with the force of a water cannon. I resisted the urge to look inside the bowl to see what was coming out of me, but after ten minutes of exploding salvos I gave in to the urge and peeked inside the bowl. It looked like the eruption of Mount Vesuvius–pounds of dark-black volcanic ash exploding from my asshole. If I weighed a hundred thirty pounds this morning, I weighed only a buck twenty now. My very innards were inside some cheap porcelain toilet bowl in Boca Raton, Florida.

An hour later I finally emerged from the bathroom. I was over the hump now, feeling much more normal. Perhaps they'd sucked some of the insanity out of me, I thought. Either way, it was time to resume *Lifestyles of the Rich and Dysfunctional*; it was time to patch things up with the Duchess, curtail my drug intake, and live a more subdued lifestyle. I was thirty-four, after all, and the father of two.

"Thanks," I said to the kind doctor. "I'm really sorry for biting you. I was just a bit nervous before. You can understand, right?"

He nodded. "No problem," he said. "I'm just glad we could help."

"Could you guys call me a cab, please? I gotta get home and get some sleep."

It was then that I noticed that the two policemen were still in the room and they were heading directly for me. I had the distinct impression they weren't about to offer me transportation home.

The doctor took two steps back, just as one of the policemen pulled out a pair of handcuffs. Oh, Christ! I thought. Handcuffed again? It would be the Wolf's fourth time in chains in less than twenty-four hours! And what had I really done? I decided not to pursue that line of thinking. After all, where I was going I would have nothing but time to think about things.

As he slapped the cuffs on me, the policeman said, "Pursuant to the Baker Act, you're being placed in a locked-down psychiatric unit for seventy-two hours, at which point you'll be brought before a judge to see if you're still a danger to yourself or others. Sorry, sir."

Hmmm . . . he seemed like a nice-enough fellow, this Florida policeman, and he was only doing his job, after all. Besides, he was taking me to a psychiatric unit, not a jail, and that had to be a good thing, didn't it?

"I'm a butterfly! I'm a butterfly!" screamed an obese, dark-haired woman in a blue muumuu as she flapped her arms and flew lazy circles around the fourth-floor locked-down psychiatric unit of the Delray Medical Center.

I was sitting on a very uncomfortable couch in the middle of the common area as she floated by. I smiled and nodded at her. There were forty or so patients, mostly dressed in bathrobes and slippers and engaged in various forms of socially unacceptable behavior. At the front of the unit was the nurses' station, where all the crazies would line up every few hours for their Thorazine or Haldol or some other antipsychotic, to soothe their frazzled nerves.

"I gotta have it. Six point O two times ten to the twenty-third," muttered a tall, thin teenager with a ferocious case of acne.

Very interesting, I thought. I had been watching this poor kid for over two hours, as he walked around in a remarkably perfect circle, spitting out Avogadro's number, a mathematical constant used to measure molecular density. At first I was a bit confused as to why he was so obsessed with this number, until one of the orderlies explained that the young fellow was an intractable acidhead with a very high IQ, and he became fixated on Avogadro's number whenever a dose of acid hit him the wrong way. It was his third stay in the Delray Medical Center in the last twelve months.

I found it ironic that I would be put in a place like this–considering how sane I was–but that was the problem with laws like the Baker Act: They were designed to meet the needs of the masses. Either way, things had been going reasonably well so far. I had convinced a doctor to prescribe me Lamictal, and he, of his own volition, had put me on some sort of short-acting opiate to help with the withdrawals.

What troubled me, though, was that I'd been trying to call at least a dozen people on the unit's pay phone–friends, family, lawyers, business associates. I'd even tried reaching Alan Chemical-tob, to make sure he'd have a fresh batch of Quaaludes for me when I finally got released from this insane asylum, but I hadn't been able to get in touch with anyone. Not a soul: not the Duchess, my parents, Lipsky, Dave, Laurie, Gwynne, Janet, Wigwam, Joe Fahmegghetti, Greg O'Connell, the Chef, even Bo, who I could always get in touch with. It was as if I were being frozen out, abandoned by everyone.

In fact, as my first day in this glorious institution came to a close, I found myself hating the Duchess more than ever. She had completely forgotten about me, turned everyone against me, using that single despicable act I'd committed on the stairs to garner sympathy from my friends and business associates. I was certain that she no longer loved me and had uttered those words to me while I was overdosing only out of sympathy–thinking that perhaps I might actually kick the bucket and she might as well send me off to hell with one last bogus "I love you."

By midnight, the cocaine and Quaaludes were pretty much out of my system, but I still couldn't sleep. It was then, in the wee hours of the morning, on April 17, 1997, that a nurse with a very kind heart gave me a shot of Dalmane in my right ass cheek. And, finally, fifteen minutes later, I fell asleep without cocaine in my system for the first time in three months.

I woke up eighteen hours later to the sound of my name. I opened my eyes and there was a large black orderly standing over me.

"Mr. Belfort, you have a visitor."

The Duchess! I thought. She had come to take me out of this place. "Really," I said, "who is it?"

He shrugged. "I don't know his name."

My spirits sank. He led me to a room with padded walls. Inside was a gray metal desk and three chairs. It reminded me of the room the Swiss Customs officials questioned me in after I'd groped the stewardess, except for the padded walls. Sitting on one side of the desk was a fortyish man with horn-rimmed glasses. The moment we locked eyes he rose from his chair and greeted me.

"You must be Jordan," he said, extending his right hand. "I'm Dennis Maynard*."

Out of instinct I shook his hand, although there was something about him I instantly disliked. He was dressed like me, in jeans and sneakers and a white polo shirt. He was reasonably good-looking, in a washed-out sort of way, about five-nine, average build, with short brown hair parted to the side.

He motioned to a seat across from him. I nodded and sat down. A moment later, another orderly came in the room–this one a large, drunken Irishman, by the looks of him. Both orderlies stood behind me, a couple of feet back, waiting to pounce if I tried pulling a Hannibal Lecter on this guy–biting his nose off, while my pulse remained at seventy-two.

Dennis Maynard said, "I've been retained by your wife."

I shook my head in amazement. "What are you, a fucking divorce lawyer or something? Christ, that cunt works quick! I figured she'd at least have the decency to wait the three days 'til the Baker Act expired before she filed for divorce."

He smiled. "I'm not a divorce lawyer, Jordan. I'm a drug interventionist, and I've been hired by your wife, who still loves you, so you shouldn't be so quick to call her a cunt."

I narrowed my eyes at this bastard, trying to make heads or tails of what was going on. I no longer felt paranoid, but I still felt on edge. "So you say you've been hired by my wife, who still loves me? Well, if she loves me so much, why won't she visit me?"

"She's very scared right now. And very confused. I've spent the last twenty-four hours with her, and she's in a very fragile state. She's not ready to see you."

I felt my head fill with steam. This motherfucker was making a play for the Duchess. I popped out of my chair and jumped over the desk, screaming, "You cocksucker!" He recoiled, as the two orderlies lunged after me. "I'll have you stabbed to death, you piece of shit, going after my wife while I'm locked up in here. You're

*Name has been changed.

fucking dead! And your family's dead too! You don't know what I'm capable of."

I took a deep breath as the orderlies pushed me back down into my seat.

"Calm down," said the Duchess's future husband. "I'm not after your wife. She's still in love with you and I'm in love with another woman. What I was trying to say is that I've spent the last twenty-four hours with your wife talking about you, and her, and everything that's happened between you two."

I felt entirely irrational. I was used to being in control, and I found this lack of control wildly disconcerting. "Did she tell you that I kicked her down the stairs with my daughter in my arms? Did she tell you that I cut open two million dollars' worth of shabby-chic furniture? Did she tell you about my little baking disaster? I can only imagine what she said." I shook my head in disgust, not just over my own actions but over the Duchess airing our dirty laundry to a complete stranger.

He nodded and let out a chuckle, trying to defuse my anger. "Yeah, she told me about all those things. Some of them were pretty amusing, actually, especially the part about the furniture. I'd never heard that one before. But most of the things were pretty disturbing, like what happened on the stairs and in the garage. Understand, though, that none of this is your fault–or I should say none of these things makes you a bad person. What you are is a *sick* person, Jordan; you're sick with a disease, a disease that's no different than cancer or diabetes."

He paused for a second, then shrugged. "But she also told me how wonderful you used to be, before the drugs took hold. She told me how brilliant you were and about all your accomplishments and how you swept her off her feet when you first met. She told me that she never loved anyone the way she loved you. She told me how generous you are to everyone, and how everyone takes advantage of your generosity. And she also told me about your back, and how that exacerbated . . ."

As my interventionist kept talking, I found myself hanging on the word *loved*. He had said she *loved* me–past tense. Did that mean she no longer loved me? Probably so, I thought, because if she still loved me she would have come to visit me. This whole business of her being scared didn't make sense. I was in a locked-down psychiatric unit–how could I harm her? I was in terrible emotional pain. If she would just visit me–*even for a second, for Chrissake!*–and hug me and tell me that she still loved me, that would ease my pain. I would do it for her, wouldn't I? It seemed unusually cruel of her not to visit me after I'd almost committed suicide. It didn't strike me as the act of a loving wife–estranged or not–no matter what the circumstances.

Obviously, Dennis Maynard was here to try to convince me to go to rehab. And perhaps I would go, if the Duchess would come here and ask me herself. But not like this, not while she was blackmailing me and threatening to leave me unless I did what she wanted. Yet wasn't rehab what I wanted, or at least what I needed? Did I really want to live out my life as a drug addict? But how could I possibly live without drugs? My entire life was centered on drugs. The very thought of living the next fifty years without Ludes and coke seemed impossible. Yet there was a time, long before all this happened, when I'd lived a sober life. Was it possible to get back to that point, to turn back the clock, so to speak? Or had my brain chemistry been immutably altered–and I was now an addict, doomed to that very life until the day I died?

". . . and about your father's temper," continued the interventionist, "and how your mother tried to protect you from him but wasn't always successful. She told me everything."

I fought the urge to be ironic but quickly failed. "So did little Martha Stewart tell you how perfect *she* is? I mean, since I'm such damaged goods and everything, did she even get a moment to tell you anything about herself? Because she is perfect, after all. She'll tell you–not in so many words, of course–but she will tell you. After all, she's the Duchess of Bay Ridge."

The last few words gave him a chuckle. "Listen," he said, "your wife is far from perfect. In fact, she's sicker than you are. Think about it for a second: Who's the sicker one–the spouse who's addicted to drugs or the spouse who sits by and watches the person they love destroy themselves? I would say the latter. The truth is that your wife suffers from her own disease, namely, codependence. By spending all her time looking after you, she ignores her own problems. She's got as bad a case of codependence as I've ever seen."

"Blah, blah, blah," I said. "You don't think I know all this shit?

I've done my fair share of reading, in case no one's told you. In spite of the fifty thousand Ludes I've consumed, I still remember everything I've read since nursery school."

He nodded. "I haven't just met with your wife, Jordan; I've also met with all your friends and family, everyone who's important to you. And one thing they're all unanimous on is that you're one of the smartest men on the planet. So, that being said, I'm not gonna try to bullshit you. Here's the deal: There's a drug rehab in Georgia called Talbot Marsh. It specializes in treating doctors. The place is filled with some very smart people, so you'll fit in well there. I have the power to sign you out of this hellhole right now. You could be at Talbot Marsh in two hours. There's a limousine waiting for you downstairs, and your jet is at the airport, all fueled up. Talbot Marsh is a very nice place, and very upscale. I think you'll like it."

"What makes you so fucking qualified? Are you a doctor?"

"No," he said, "I'm just a drug addict like you. No different, except that I'm in recovery and you're not."

"How long you sober for?"

"Ten years."

"Ten fucking years?" I sputtered. "Holy Christ! How the fuck is that even possible? I can't go a day–an hour–without thinking about drugs! I'm not like you, pal. My mind works differently. Anyway, I don't need to go to rehab. Maybe I'll just try AA or something."

"You're past that point. In fact, it's a miracle you're still alive. You should've stopped breathing a long time ago, my friend." He shrugged. "But one day your luck's gonna run out. Next time your friend Dave might not be around to call 911, and you'll end up in a coffin instead of a psychiatric unit."

In a dead-serious tone, he said, "In AA we say there are three places an alcoholic or an addict ends up–jails, institutions, or dead. Now, in the last two days you've been in a jail and an institution. When will you be satisfied, when you're in a funeral home? When your wife has to sit your two children down and explain how they're never gonna see their father again?"

I shrugged, knowing he was right but incapable of surrendering. For some inexplicable reason I felt the necessity to resist him, to resist the Duchess–to resist everyone, in fact. If I were to get sober, it would be on my own terms, not on anyone else's, and certainly not with a gun to my head. "If Nadine comes down here herself, I'll consider it. Otherwise you can go fuck yourself."

"She won't come here," he said. "Unless you go to rehab she won't speak to you."

"Fair enough," I said. "Then you can both go fuck yourselves. I'll be out of here in two days; then I'll deal with my addiction on my own terms. And if it means losing my wife, so be it." I rose out of my chair and motioned to the orderlies.

As I was walking out of the room, Dennis said, "You may be able to find another beautiful wife, but you'll never find one who loves you as much as she does. Who do you think organized all this? Your wife's spent the last twenty-four hours in a state of panic, trying to save your life. You'd be a fool to let her go."

I took a deep breath and said, "A long time ago there was another woman who loved me as much as Nadine did; her name was Denise, and I fucked her over royally. Maybe I'm just getting what I deserve. Who knows anymore? But, either way, I'm not being bullied into rehab, so you're wasting your time. Don't come see me again."

Then I left the room.

The rest of the day was no less torturous. Starting with my parents, one by one my friends and family came into the psychiatric unit and tried to convince me to go to rehab. Everyone except the Duchess. How could the woman be so coldhearted, after I'd tried . . . what?

I resisted using the word *suicide*, even in my own thoughts—perhaps because it was too painful, or perhaps out of sheer embarrassment that the love or, for that matter, the obsession with a woman, even my own wife, could drive me to commit such an act. It was not the act of a true man of power, nor was it the act of a man who had any self-respect.

In truth, I had never actually intended to kill myself. Deep down, I knew that I'd be rushed to the hospital and my stomach would be pumped. Dave had been standing over me, ready to intervene. The Duchess wasn't aware of that, though; from her perspective, I had been so distraught over the possibility of losing her, and so caught up in the despair and desperation of a cocaine-induced paranoia, that I had tried to take my own life. How could she not be moved by that?

True: I had acted like a monster toward her, not just on the stairs but over the very months leading up to that heinous act. Or perhaps years. Since the early years of our marriage, I had exploited our unspoken quid pro quo–that by providing her with the Life, I was entitled to certain liberties. And while there might be a germ of truth to that notion, there was no doubt that I had stepped way over the line.

Yet, in spite of everything, I felt that I still deserved compassion.

Did the Duchess lack compassion? Was there a certain coldness to her, a corner of her heart that was unreachable? In truth, I had always suspected as much. Like myself–like everyone–the Duchess was damaged goods; she was a good wife, but a wife who'd brought her own baggage into the marriage. As a child, her father had all but abandoned her. She had told me the stories of all the times she got dressed up on Saturdays and Sundays–gorgeous even then she was, with flowing blond hair and the face of an angel–and waited for her father to take her to a fancy dinner or on the roller coaster at Coney Island or to Riis Park, the local beach in Brooklyn, where he could proclaim to one and all: "This is my daughter! Look how beautiful she is! I'm so proud she's mine." Yet she would wait on the front stoop for him, only to be disappointed when he never showed or even called to humor her with a lame excuse.

Suzanne, of course, had covered for him–telling Nadine that her father loved her but that he was possessed by his own demons that drove him to the life of a wanderer, to a rootless existence. Was I now feeling the brunt of that? Was her very coldness a result of the barriers she'd erected as a child that precluded her from becoming a compassionate woman? Or was I simply grasping at straws? Perhaps this was payback–for all the philandering, the Blue Chips and the NASDAQS, the three-a.m. helicopter landings, and sleep-talking about Venice the Hooker, and the masseuse and the groping of the stewardess . . .

Or was the payback more subtle? Was it a result of all the laws I'd broken? Of all the stocks I'd manipulated? Of all the money I'd smuggled to Switzerland? For fucking over Kenny Greene, the Blockhead, who had been a loyal partner to me? It was hard to say anymore. The last decade of my life was unspeakably complicated. I had lived the sort of life that people read about only in novels.

Yet, this had been my life. *Mine.* For better or worse, I, Jordan Belfort, the Wolf of Wall Street, had been a true wild man. I had always looked at myself as being bulletproof–dodging death and incarceration, living my life like a rock star, consuming more drugs than any thousand men have the right to and still living to tell about it.

All these thoughts were roaring through my head, as I closed out my second day in the locked-down psychiatric unit of the Delray Medical Center. And as the drugs continued to make their way out of my cerebrum, my mind grew sharper and sharper. I was on the rebound–ready to face the world with all my faculties; ready to make mincemeat out of that bald bastard Steve Madden; ready to resume my fight with my nemesis, Special Agent Gregory Coleman; and ready to win the Duchess back, no matter what it took.

The next morning, just after pill call, I was summoned back into the rubber room, where I found two doctors waiting for me. One was fat and the other was average-looking, although he had bulging blue eyeballs and an Adam's apple the size of a grapefruit. A glandular case, I figured.

They introduced themselves as Dr. Brad* and Dr. Mike* and immediately waved the orderlies out of the room. Interesting, I thought, but not nearly as interesting as the first two minutes of the conversation, when I came to the conclusion that these two were better suited as a stand-up comedy act than as drug interventionists. Or was that their method? Yes, these two guys seemed quite all right. In fact, I kind of liked them. The Duchess had flown them in from California, on a private jet, after Dennis Maynard informed her that the two of us hadn't hit it off too well.

So these were the reinforcements.

"Listen," said fat Dr. Brad, "I can sign you out of this shitty place right now and in two hours you can be at Talbot Marsh, sipping on a virgin piña colada and staring at a young nurse–who's now one of the patients because she got caught shooting Demerol

*Name has been changed.

through her nurse's skirt." He shrugged his shoulders. "Or you could stay here for another day and become better acquainted with butterfly-lady and math-boy. But I gotta tell ya, I think you'd be crazy to stay in this place one second longer than you have to. I mean, it smells like . . ."

"Shit," said the Glandular Case. "Why don't you let us sign you out of here? I mean, I have no doubt that you're crazy and everything, and you could probably use to be locked away for a couple of years, but not here–not in this shithole! You need to be in a classier loony bin."

"He's right," added fat-Brad. "All kidding aside, there's a limo downstairs waiting for us, and your jet's at Boca Aviation. So let us sign you out of this madhouse, and let's get on the jet and have some fun."

"I agree," added the Glandular Case. "The jet's beautiful. How much did it cost your wife to fly us here from California?"

"I'm not sure," I said, "but I'm willing to bet she paid top-dollar. If there's one thing the Duchess hates, it's a bargain."

They both laughed, especially fat-Brad, who seemed to find humor in everything. "The Duchess! I love that! She's a good-looking lady, your wife, and she really loves you."

"Why do you call her the Duchess?" asked the Glandular Case.

"Well, it's a long story," I said, "but I can't actually take credit for the name, as much as I'd like to. It came from this guy Brian, who owns one of the brokerage firms I do a lot of business with. Anyway, we were on a private jet, flying home from St. Bart's a bunch of Christmases ago, and we were all really hung over. Brian was sitting across from Nadine in the cabin, and he laid a humongous fart and said, 'Oh, shit, Nae, I think I just left a few skid marks with that one!' Nadine started getting pissed at him, telling him how uncouth and disgusting he was, so Brian said, 'Oh, excuse me; I guess the Duchess of Bay Ridge never laid a fart in her silk panties and left a few skid marks there!' "

"That's funny," said fat-Brad. "The Duchess of Bay Ridge. I like that."

"No, that's not the funny part. It's what happened next that was really funny. Brian thought his joke was so hysterical that he was doubled over laughing so he didn't see the Duchess rolling up the Christmas edition of *Town and Country* magazine. Just as he was lifting his head up, she popped out of her seat, took the most enormous swat at his head you could possibly imagine, and knocked him unconscious right on the plane. I'm talking out–fucking–cold! Then she sat back down and started reading her magazine again. Brian came to a couple of minutes later, after his wife threw a glass of water in his face. Anyway, ever since then the name stuck."

"That's incredible!" said the Glandular Case. "Your wife looks like an angel. I wouldn't think her the type to do something like that." Fat-Brad nodded in agreement.

I rolled my eyes. "Oh, you have no idea what she's capable of. She might not look tough, but she's strong as an ox. You know how many times she's beaten me up? She's especially good with water." I smiled and let out a chuckle. "I mean, don't get me wrong: I deserved most of the beatings. As much as I love the girl I haven't exactly been a model husband. But I still think she should've visited me. If she did, I'd already be in rehab, but now I don't wanna do it because I don't like being held hostage like this."

"I think she wanted to come," said fat-Brad, "but Dennis Maynard advised her against it."

"It figures," I sputtered. "He's a real piece a shit, that guy. As soon as all this is resolved I'm gonna have someone pay him a little visit."

The comedy team refused to engage with me. "Can I make a suggestion to you?" asked the Glandular Case.

I nodded. "Sure, why not? I like you guys. It's the other prick I hated."

He smiled and looked around conspiratorially. Then he lowered his voice and said, "Why don't you let us sign you out of here and take you to Atlanta and then just bolt out of the rehab after you check in? There're no walls or bars or barbed wire or anything like that. You'll be staying in a luxury condo with a bunch of wacky doctors."

"Yeah," said fat-Brad, "once we drop you in Atlanta, the Baker Act is nullified and you'll be free to go. Just tell your pilot not to leave the airport. If you don't like the rehab, just walk away."

I started laughing. "You two guys are unbelievable! You're trying to appeal to my larcenous heart, aren't you?"

"I'll do whatever it takes to get you to rehab," fat-Brad said.

"You're a nice guy and you deserve to live, not die at the end of a crack pipe, which is what's gonna happen if you don't get sober. Trust me–I speak from experience."

"You're a recovering addict too?" I asked.

"We both are," said the Glandular Case. "I'm sober eleven years. Brad is sober thirteen years."

"How is that even possible? The truth is I'd like to stop but I just can't. I wouldn't make it more than a few days, never mind thirteen years."

"You can do it," said fat-Brad. "Not for thirteen years, but I bet you make it through today."

"Yeah," I said, "I can make it through today, but that's about it."

"And that's enough," said the Glandular Case. "Today is all that matters. Who knows what tomorrow brings? Just take it one day at a time and you'll be fine. That's how I do it. I didn't wake up this morning and say, 'Gee, Mike, it's important to control your urge to drink for the rest of your life!' I said, 'Gee, Mike, just make it for the next twenty-four hours and the rest of your life will take care of itself.' "

Fat-Brad nodded. "He's right, Jordan. And I know what you're probably thinking right now–that it's just a stupid mind-dodge, like pulling the wool over your own eyes." He shrugged. "And it probably is, but I personally couldn't give a shit. It works, and that's all I care about. It gave me my life back, and it'll give you your life back too."

I took a deep breath and let it out slowly. I liked these guys; I really did. And I truly wanted to get sober. So much that I could *taste* it. But my compulsion was too strong. All my friends did drugs; all my pastimes included drugs. And my wife . . . well, the Duchess hadn't come to see me. With every terrible thing I'd done to her, I knew in my heart that I would never forget how she hadn't come to see me after I'd tried to commit suicide.

And, of course, there was the Duchess's side of things. Perhaps she would choose not to forgive me. I couldn't blame her for that. She had been a good wife to me, and I had paid her back by becoming a drug addict. I had had my reasons, I figured, but that didn't change things. If she wanted a divorce, then she was justified. I would always take care of her, I would always love her, and I would always make sure she had a good life. After all, she'd given me two gorgeous children, and she was the one who'd organized all this.

I looked fat-Brad straight in the eye and started nodding slowly. "Let's get the fuck outta this hellhole."

"Indeed," he said. "Indeed."

CHAPTER 38

MARTIANS OF THE THIRD REICH

The place seemed normal enough, at first glance.

The Talbot Marsh Recovery Campus sits on a half dozen immaculately landscaped acres in Atlanta, Georgia. It was only a ten-minute limo ride from the private airport, and I'd spent all six hundred seconds plotting my escape. In fact, before I'd deplaned, I gave the pilots strict instructions not to take off under any circumstances. It was me, after all, not the Duchess, I'd explained, who was paying the bill. Besides, there was a little something extra for them if they stayed awhile. They assured me they would.

So as the limo pulled into the driveway, I scoped out the terrain through the eyes of a prisoner. Meanwhile, fat-Brad and Mike the Glandular Case were sitting across from me, and true to their word there wasn't a cement wall, a metal bar, a gun tower, or a strand of barbed wire anywhere in sight.

The property gleamed brilliantly in the Georgia sunshine, all these purple and yellow flowers and manicured rosebushes and towering oaks and elms. It was a far cry from the urine-infested corridors of the Delray Medical Center. Yet something seemed a bit off. Perhaps the place was too nice? Was there really that much money in drug rehabs?

There was a circular drop-off area in front of the building. As the limo inched toward it, fat-Brad reached into his pocket and pulled out three twenties. "Here," he said. "I know you don't have any money on you, so consider this a gift. It's cab fare back to the airport. I don't want you to have to hitchhike. You never know what kind of drug-addicted maniac you'll run into."

"What are you talking about?" I asked innocently.

"I saw you whispering in the pilot's ear," said fat-Brad. "I've been doing this a long time, and if there's one thing I've learned it's that if someone's not ready to get sober, there's nothing I can do to force him. I won't insult you with the analogy of leading a horse to water and all that crap. But, either way, I figure I owe you the sixty bucks for making me laugh so hard on the way here." He shook his head. "You really are one twisted bastard."

He paused, as if searching for the right words. "Anyway, I'd have to say that this has been the world's most bizarre intervention. Yesterday I was in California, sitting in some boring convention, when I got this frantic call from the soon-to-be-late Dennis Maynard, who tells me about this gorgeous model who has a zillionaire husband on the verge of killing himself. Believe it or not, I actually balked at first, because of the distance, but then the Duchess of Bay Ridge got on the phone and she wouldn't take no for an answer. Next thing I know we're on a private jet. And then we met you, which was the biggest trip of all." He shrugged. "All I can say is that I wish you and your wife the best of luck. I hope you guys stay together. It would be a great ending to the story."

The Glandular Case nodded in agreement. "You're a good man, Jordan. Don't ever forget that. Even if you bolt out the front door in ten minutes and go straight to a crack den, it still doesn't change who you are. This is a fucked-up disease; it's cunning and baffling. I walked out of three rehabs myself before I finally got it right. My family ended up finding me under a bridge; I was living as a beggar. And the real sick part is that after they finally got me into rehab, I escaped again and went back to the bridge. That's the way this disease is."

I let out a great sigh. "I'm not gonna bullshit you. Even when we were flying here today–and I was busy telling you all those hysterical stories and we were all laughing uncontrollably–I was *still* thinking about drugs. It was burning in the back of my mind like a fucking blast furnace. I'm already thinking about calling my Quaalude dealer as soon as I get out of here. Maybe I can live without the cocaine, but not the Ludes. They're too much a part of my life now."

"I know exactly how you feel," said fat-Brad, nodding. "In fact, I still feel the same way about coke. Not a day goes by when I don't get the urge to do it. But I've managed to stay sober for more than thirteen years. And you know how I do it?"

I smiled. "Yeah, you fat bastard–one day at a time, right?"

"Ah," said fat-Brad, "now you're learning! There's hope for you yet."

"Yeah," I muttered, "let the healing begin."

We climbed out of the car and walked down a short concrete path that led to the front entrance. Inside, the place was nothing like I'd imagined. It was gorgeous. It looked like a men's smoking club, with very plush carpet, rich and reddish, and lots of mahogany and burled walnut and comfortable-looking sofas and love seats and club chairs. There was a large bookcase filled with antique-looking books. Just across from it was an oxblood leather club chair with a very high back. It looked unusually comfortable, so I headed straight for it and plopped myself down.

Ahhhhhh . . . how long had it been since I'd sat in a comfortable chair without cocaine and Quaaludes bubbling around inside my brain? I no longer had back pain or leg pain or hip pain or any other pain. There was nothing bothering me, no petty annoyances. I took a deep breath and let it out. . . . It was a nice, sober breath, part of a nice, sober moment. How long had it been for me? Almost nine years since I'd been sober. Nine fucking years of complete insanity! Holy shit–what a way to live.

And I was fucking starving! I desperately needed to eat something. Anything but Froot Loops.

Fat-Brad walked over to me and said, "Ya doing okay?"

"I'm starving," I said. "I'd pay a hundred grand for a Big Mac right now."

"I'll see what I can do," he said. "Mike and I need to fill out a few forms. Then we'll bring you in and get you something to eat." He smiled and walked off.

I took another deep breath, except this one I held in for a good ten seconds. I was staring into the very heart of the bookcase when I finally let it out . . . and just like that, in that very instant, the compulsion left me. I was done. No more drugs. I knew it. Enough was enough. I no longer felt the urge. It was gone. Why, I would never know. All I knew was that I would never touch them again.

Something had clicked inside my brain. Some sort of switch had been flipped and I just fucking knew it.

I rose from my chair and walked over to the other side of the waiting room, where fat-Brad and Mike the Glandular Case were filling out paperwork. I reached into my pocket and pulled out the sixty bucks. "Here," I said to fat-Brad, "you can have your sixty back. I'm staying."

He smiled and nodded his head knowingly. "Good for you, my friend."

Right before they left, I said to them, "Don't forget to call the Duchess of Bay Ridge and tell her to get in touch with the pilots. Or else they'll be waiting there for weeks."

"Well, here's to the Duchess of Bay Ridge!" fat-Brad said, making a mock toast.

"To the Duchess of Bay Ridge!" we all said simultaneously.

Then we exchanged hugs—and promises to keep in touch. But I knew we never would. They had done their job, and it was time for them to move on to the next case. And it was time for me to get sober.

It was the next morning when a new type of insanity started: sober insanity. I woke up around nine a.m., feeling positively buoyant. No withdrawal symptoms, no hangover, and no compulsion to do drugs. I wasn't in the actual rehab yet; that would come tomorrow. I was still in the detox unit. As I made my way to the cafeteria for breakfast, the only thing weighing on my mind was that I still hadn't been able to get in touch with the Duchess, who seemed to have flown the coop. I had called the house in Old Brookville and spoken to Gwynne, who'd told me that Nadine had dropped out of sight. She had only called in once, to speak to the kids, and she hadn't even mentioned my name. So I assumed my marriage was over.

After breakfast I was walking back to my room when a beefy-looking guy sporting a ferocious mullet and the look of the intensely paranoid waved me over. We met by the pay phones. "Hi," I said, extending my head. "I'm Jordan. How's it going?"

He shook my hand cautiously. "Shhh!" he said, darting his eyes around. "Follow me."

I nodded and followed him back into the cafeteria, where we sat down at a square lunch table, out of earshot of other human beings. At this time of morning the cafeteria had only a handful of people in it, and most of them were staff, dressed in white lab coats. I had pegged my new friend as a complete loon. He was dressed like me, in jeans and a T-shirt.

"I'm Anthony," he said, extending his hand for another shake. "Are you the guy who flew in on the private jet yesterday?"

Oh, Christ! I wanted to remain anonymous for once, not stick out like a sore thumb. "Yeah, that was me," I said, "but I'd appreciate it if you'd keep that quiet. I just want to blend in, okay?"

"Your secret's safe with me," he muttered, "but good luck trying to keep anything secret in this place."

That sounded a bit odd, a bit Orwellian, in fact. "Oh, really?" I said. "Why's that?"

He looked around again. "Because this place is like fucking Auschwitz," he whispered. Then he winked at me.

At this point, I realized the guy wasn't completely crazy, perhaps just a bit off. "Why is it like Auschwitz?" I asked, smiling.

He shrugged his beefy shoulders. "Because it's fucking torture here, like a Nazi death camp. You see the staff over there?" He motioned with his head. "They're the SS. Once the train drops you off in this place, you never leave. And there's slave labor too."

"What the fuck are you talking about? I thought it was only a four-week program."

He compressed his lips into a tight line and shook his head. "Maybe it is for you, but not for the rest of us. I assume you're not a doctor, right?"

"No, I'm a banker–although I'm pretty much retired now."

"Really?" he asked. "How are you retired? You look like a kid."

I smiled. "I'm not a kid. But why'd you ask me if I'm a doctor?"

"Because almost everyone here is either a doctor or a nurse. I'm a chiropractor, myself. There are only a handful of people like you. Everyone else is here because they lost their license to practice medicine. So the staff has us by the balls. Unless they say you're cured, you don't get your license back. It's a fucking nightmare. Some people have been here for over a year, and they're *still* trying to get their license back!" He shook his head gravely. "It's complete fucking insanity. Everyone's ratting each other out, trying to earn brownie points with the staff. Really fucking sick. You have no idea. The patients walk around like robots, spewing out AA crap, pretending they're rehabilitated."

I nodded, fully getting the picture. A wacky arrangement like this, where the staff had that much power, was a recipe for abuse. Thank God I'd be above it. "What are the female patients like? Any hot ones?"

"Just one," he answered. "A total knockout. A twelve on a scale from one to ten."

That perked me up! "Oh, yeah, what's she look like?"

"She's a little blonde, about five-five, unbelievable body, perfect face, curly hair. She's really beautiful. A real piece of ass."

I nodded, making a mental note to keep away from her. She sounded like trouble. "And what's the story with this guy Doug Talbot? The staff talks about him like he's a fucking god. What's he like?"

"What's he like?" muttered my paranoid friend. "He's like Adolf fucking Hitler. Or actually more like Dr. Josef Mengele. He's a big fucking blowhard, and he's got every last one of us by the balls–with the exception of you and maybe two other people. But you still gotta be careful, because they'll try to use your family against you. They'll get inside your wife's head and tell her that unless you stay for six months you're gonna relapse and light your kids on fire."

Later that night, at about seven p.m., I called Old Brookville in search of the missing Duchess, but she was still MIA. I did get a chance to speak to Gwynne, though; I explained to her that I'd met with my therapist today and I'd been subdiagnosed (whatever that meant) as a compulsive spending addict, as well as a sex addict, both of which were basically true and both of which, I thought, were none of their fucking business. Either way, the therapist had informed me that I was being placed on money restriction and masturbation restriction–allowed to possess only enough money to use in the vending machines and allowed to masturbate only once every few days. I had assumed that the latter restriction was enforced on the honor system.

I asked Gwynne if she could see her way clear to stick a couple a thousand dollars inside some rolled-up socks and then ship them UPS. Hopefully, they would get past the gestapo, I told her, but, either way, it was the least she could do, especially after nine years of being one of my chief enablers. I chose not to share my masturbation restriction with Gwynne, although I had a sneaky suspicion it was going to be an even bigger problem than the money restriction. After all, I had been sober only four days now, and I was already getting spontaneous erections every time the wind blew.

On a much sadder note, before I hung up with Gwynne, Channy came to the phone and said, "Are you in Atlant-ica because you pushed Mommy down the stairs?"

I replied, "That's one reason, thumbkin. Daddy was very sick and he didn't know what he was doing."

"If you're still sick, can I kiss away your boo-boo again?"

"Hopefully," I said sadly. "Maybe you can kiss away both our boo-boos, Mommy's and Daddy's." I felt my eyes welling up with tears.

"I'll try," she said, with the utmost seriousness.

I bit my lip, fighting back outright crying. "I know you will, baby. I know you will." Then I told her that I loved her and hung up the phone. Before I went to bed that night I got down on my knees and said a prayer–that Channy could kiss away our boo-boos. Then everything would be okay again.

I woke up the next morning ready to meet the reincarnation of Adolf Hitler, or was it Dr. Josef Mengele? Either way, the entire rehab–patients and staff alike–was getting together this morning in the auditorium for a regularly scheduled group meeting. It was a vast space with no partitions. A hundred twenty bridge chairs had been arranged in a large circle, and at the front of the room was a small platform with a lectern on it, where the speaker of the day would share his tale of drug-addicted woe.

I now sat as just another patient in a large circle of drug-addicted doctors and nurses (or Martians, from the Planet Talbot Mars, as I'd come to think of them). At this particular moment, all eyes were on today's guest speaker–a sorry-looking woman in her early forties who had a rear end the size of Alaska and a ferocious case of acne, the sort you usually find on mental patients who'd spent the better part of their lives on psychotropic drugs.

"Hi," she said in a timid voice. "My name is Susan, and I'm . . . uhhh . . . an alcoholic and a drug addict."

All the Martians in the room, including myself, responded dutifully, by saying, "Hi, Susan!" to which she blushed and then bowed her head in defeat–or was it victory? Either way, I had no doubt she was a world-class drizzler.

Now there was silence. Apparently, Susan wasn't much of a public speaker, or perhaps her brain had been short-circuited from all the drugs she'd consumed. As Susan gathered her thoughts, I took a moment to check out Doug Talbot. He was sitting at the front of the room with five staff members on either side of him. He had short snow-white hair, and he looked to be in his late fifties or early sixties. His skin was white and pasty, and he had the sort of square-jawed, grim expression that you would normally associate with a malevolent warden, the sort who looks a death-row inmate in the eye before he flips the switch on the electric chair and says, "I'm only doing this for your own good!"

Finally, Susan plowed on. "I've . . . been . . . uhhh . . . sober . . . for almost eighteen months now, and I couldn't have done it without the help and inspiration of . . . uhhh . . . Doug Talbot." And she turned to Doug Talbot and bowed her head, at which point the whole room rose to their feet and started clapping–the whole room except for me. I was too shocked at the collective sight of more than a hundred ass-kissing Martians trying to get their licenses back.

Doug Talbot waved his hand at the Martians and then shook his head dismissively, as if to say, "Oh, please, you're embarrassing me! I only do this job out of a love of humanity!" But I had no doubt that his happy hit squad of staff members were making careful notes as to who wasn't clapping loudly enough.

As Susan continued to drizzle, I began craning my head around–looking for the curly-haired blonde with the gorgeous face and the killer body, and I found her sitting just across from me, on the opposite side of the circle. She was gorgeous, all right. She had soft, angelic features–not the chiseled model features of the Duchess, but they were beautiful nonetheless.

Suddenly the Martians jumped to their feet again, and Susan took an embarrassed bow. Then she lumbered over to Doug Talbot, bent over, and gave him a hug. But it wasn't a warm hug; she kept her body far from his. It was the way Dr. Mengele's few surviving patients must've hugged him, at atrocity reunions and such–a sort of extreme version of the Stockholm syndrome, where hostages come to revere their captors.

Now one of the staff began doing a bit of her own drizzling. When the Martians stood this time, I stood too. Everyone grabbed the hands of the people on either side of them, so I grabbed too.

In unison, we bowed our heads and chanted the AA mantra: *"God, grant me the serenity to accept the things I cannot change, the courage to change the things I can, and the wisdom to know the difference."*

Now everyone began clapping, so I clapped too–except this time I was clapping with sincerity. After all, in spite of being a cynical bastard, there was no denying that AA was an amazing thing, a lifesaver to millions of people.

There was a long rectangular table at the back of the room with a few pots of coffee on it and some cookies and cakes. As I headed over, I heard an unfamiliar voice yelling: "Jordan! Jordan Belfort!"

I turned around and–*Holy Christ!*–it was Doug Talbot. He was walking toward me, wearing an enormous smile on his pasty face. He was tall, about six-one, although he didn't look to be in particularly good shape. He wore an expensive-looking blue sport jacket and gray tweed slacks. He was waving me toward him.

At that very instant, I could feel a hundred five sets of eyes pretending not to look at me–no, it was actually a hundred fifteen sets of eyes, because the staff was pretending too.

He extended his hand. "So we finally meet," he said, nodding his head knowingly. "It's a pleasure. Welcome to Talbot Marsh. I feel like you and I are kindred spirits. Brad told me all about you. I can't wait to hear the stories. I got a few of my own–nothing as good as yours, I'm sure."

I smiled and shook my new friend's hand. "I've heard a lot about you too," I replied, fighting back the urge to use an ironic tone.

He put his arm on my shoulder. "Come on," he said warmly, "let's go to my office for a while. I'll drop you off later this afternoon. You're being moved up the hill to one of the condos. I'll drive you there."

And just like that, I knew this rehab was in serious trouble. I had the owner–the unreachable, the one and only Doug Talbot–as my new best buddy, and every patient and staff member knew it as well. The Wolf was ready to bare his fangs–even in rehab.

Doug Talbot turned out to be a decent-enough guy, and we spent a good hour exchanging war stories. In fact, as I was soon to find out, virtually all recovering drug addicts share a morbid desire to play a game of "Can You Top the Insanity of My Addiction." Obviously, it didn't take long for Doug to realize that he was seriously outmatched, and by the time I'd gotten to the part where I'd cut open my furniture with a butcher knife he'd heard enough.

So he changed the subject and began explaining how he was in the midst of taking his company public. Then he handed me some documents, to illustrate what a terrific deal he was getting. I studied them dutifully, although I found it difficult to focus. Apparently something had clicked off in my brain insofar as Wall Street was concerned too, and I failed to get that usual rush as I looked through his papers.

Then we climbed into his black Mercedes and he drove me to my condo, which was just down the road from the rehab. It wasn't actually part of Talbot Marsh, but Doug had a deal worked out with the management company that ran the complex, and about a third of the fifty semiattached units were occupied by Talbot's patients. Another profit center, I figured.

As I was getting out of his Mercedes, Doug said, "If there's anything I can do for you, or if any of the staff or the patients aren't treating you right, just let me know and I'll take care of it."

I thanked him, figuring there was a ninety-nine percent chance I would be speaking to him about that very issue before the four weeks were out. Then I headed into the lion's den.

There were six separate apartments in each town house, and my particular unit was on the second floor. I walked up a short flight of stairs and found the front door to my unit wide open. My two roommates were inside, sitting at a circular dining-room table made of some very cheap-looking bleached wood. They were writing furiously in spiral notebooks.

"Hi, I'm Jordan," I said. "Nice to meet you guys."

Before they even introduced themselves, one of them, a tall, blond man in his early forties, said, "What did Doug Talbot want?"

Then the other one, who was actually very good-looking, added, "Yeah, how do you know Doug Talbot?"

I smiled at them and said, "Yeah, well, it's nice to meet you guys too." Then I walked past them without saying another word, went into the bedroom, and closed the door. There were three beds inside, one of which was unmade. I threw my suitcase next to it and sat down on the mattress. On the other side of the room was a cheap TV on a cheap wooden stand. I flicked it on and turned on the news.

A minute later my roommates were on me. The blond one said, "Watching TV during the day is frowned upon."

"It's feeding your disease," said the good-looking one. "It's not considered right thinking."

Right thinking? *Holy Christ!* If they only knew how demented my mind was! "Well, I appreciate your concern over my disease," I snapped, "but I haven't watched TV in almost a week, so if you don't mind, why don't you just keep out of my fucking hair and worry about your own disease? If I want to engage in wrong thinking, then that's what I'm gonna do."

"What kind of doctor are you, anyway?" asked the blond one accusingly.

"I'm not a doctor, and what's the story with that phone over there?" I motioned to a tan Trimline phone sitting on a wooden desk. Above it was a small rectangular window in desperate need of a cleaning. "Are we allowed to use it or would that be considered wrong thinking too?"

"No, you can use it," said the good-looking one, "but it's for collect calls only."

I nodded. "What kind of doctor are you?"

"I used to be an ophthalmologist, but I lost my license."

"And how about you?" I asked the blond one, who was definitely a member of the Hitler youth. "Did you lose your license too?"

He nodded. "I'm a dentist, and I deserved to lose my license." His tone was entirely robotic. "I'm suffering from a terrible disease and I need to be cured. Thanks to the staff at Talbot Marsh I've made great strides in my recovery. Once they tell me I'm cured, I'll try to get my license back."

I shook my head as if I'd just heard something that defied logic, then I picked up the phone and started dialing Old Brookville.

The dentist said, "Talking for more than five minutes is frowned upon. It's not good for your recovery."

The eye doctor added, "The staff will sanction you for it."

"Oh, really?" I said. "How the fuck are they gonna find out?"

They both raised their eyebrows and shrugged innocently.

I smiled a dead smile at them. "Well, excuse me, because I got a couple a phone calls to make. I should be off in about an hour."

The blond one nodded, looking at his watch. Then the two of them headed back into the dining room and plunged back into their recoveries.

A moment later, Gwynne answered the phone. We exchanged warm greetings, then she whispered, "I sent you down a thousand dollars in *yer* socks. Did ya get it yet?"

"Not yet," I said. "Maybe it'll come tomorrow. More importantly, Gwynne, I don't want to put you on the spot anymore with Nadine. I know she's home and that she won't come to the phone, and that's okay. Don't even tell her I called. Just answer the phone each morning and put the kids on for me. I'll call around eight, okay?"

"Okay," said Gwynne. "I hope you and Mrs. Belfort patch things up. It's been very quiet 'round here. And very sad."

"I hope so too, Gwynne. I really hope so." We spoke for a few more minutes before I said good-bye.

Later that evening, just before nine, I received my first personal dose of Talbot Marsh insanity. There was a meeting in the living room for all the town house's residents, where we were supposed to share any resentments that had built up during the day. It was called a ten-step meeting, because it had something to do with the tenth step of Alcoholics Anonymous. But when I picked up the AA book and read the tenth step–which was to continue to take a personal inventory and when you were wrong, to promptly admit it–I couldn't imagine how this meeting applied to it.

Whatever the case, eight of us were now sitting in a circle. The first doctor, a dweeby-looking bald man in his early forties, said, "My name is Steve, and I'm an alcoholic, a drug addict, and a sex addict. I have forty-two days sober."

The other six doctors said, "Hi, Steve!" And they said it with such relish that if I didn't know better, I would've sworn they'd just met Steve for the first time.

Steve said, "I have only one resentment today, and it's toward Jordan."

That woke me up! "Toward me?" I exclaimed. "I haven't said two words to you, pal. How could you possibly resent me?"

My favorite dentist said, "You're not allowed to defend yourself, Jordan. That's not the purpose of this meeting."

"Well, excuse me," I muttered. "And just what is the purpose of this crazy meeting, because for the life of me I can't figure it out."

They all shook their heads in unison, as if I were dense or something. "The purpose of this meeting," explained the Nazi dentist, "is that harboring resentments can interfere with your recovery. So each night we get together and air any resentments that may've built up during the day."

I looked at the group, and every last one of them had turned the corners of his mouth down and was nodding sagely.

I shook my head in disgust. "Well, do I at least get to hear why good old Steve resents me?"

They all nodded, and Steve said, "I resent you over your relationship with Doug Talbot. All of us have been here for months–some of us for close to a year–and none of us has ever gotten to speak to him. Yet he drove you home in his Mercedes."

I started laughing in Steve's face. "And that's why you resent me? Because he drove me home in his fucking Mercedes?"

He nodded and dropped his head in defeat. A few seconds later the next person in the circle introduced himself, in the same retarded way, and then he said, "I resent you, too, Jordan, for flying here in a private jet. I don't even have money for food and you're flying around in private planes."

I looked around the room and everyone was nodding in agreement. I said, "Any other reasons you resent me?"

"Yes," he said, "I also resent you for your relationship with Doug Talbot." More nodding.

Then the next doctor introduced himself as an alcoholic, a drug addict, and a food addict, and he said, "I have only one resentment, and it is also toward Jordan."

"Well, gee willikers," I muttered, "that's a fucking surprise! Would you care to humor me as to why?"

He compressed his lips. "For the same reasons they do, and also because you don't have to follow the rules around here because of your relationship with Doug Talbot."

I looked around the room and everyone was nodding in agreement.

One by one, all seven of my fellow patients shared their resentments toward me. When it was my turn to speak, I said, "Hi, my name is Jordan, and I'm alcoholic, a Quaalude addict, and a cocaine addict. I'm also addicted to Xanax and Valium and morphine and Klonopin and GHB and marijuana and Percocet and mescaline and just about everything else, including high-priced hookers, medium-priced hookers, and an occasional streetwalker, but only when I feel like punishing myself. Sometimes I take an afternoon massage at one of those Korean joints, and I have a young Korean girl jerk me off with baby oil. I always offer her a couple hundred extra if she'll stick her tongue up my ass, but it's sort of hit or miss, because of the language barrier. Anyway, I never wear a condom, just on general principles. I've been sober for five whole days now, and I'm walking around with a constant erection. I miss my wife terribly, and if you *really* want to resent me I'll show you a picture of her." I shrugged. "Either way, I resent every last one of you for being total fucking pussies and trying to take your life's frustrations out on me. If you really want to focus on your own recoveries, stop looking outward and start looking inward, because you're all complete fucking embarrassments to humanity. And, by the way, you are right about one thing–I *am* friends with Doug Talbot, so I wish you all good luck when you try ratting me out to the staff tomorrow." With that, I broke from the circle and said, "Excuse me; I gotta make a few phone calls."

My favorite dentist said, "We still need to discuss your work detail. Each person in the unit has to clean an area. We have you down for the bathrooms this week."

"I don't think so," I sputtered. "Starting tomorrow there's gonna be maid service in this joint. You can talk to her about it." I walked into the bedroom, slammed the door, and dialed Alan Lipsky to tell him about the very insanity of the Talbot Martians. We laughed for a good fifteen minutes and then started talking about old times.

Before I hung up, I asked if he'd heard anything from the Duchess. He said he hadn't, and I hung up the phone sadder for that fact. It had been almost a week now, and things were looking grim with her. I flicked on the TV and tried shutting my eyes, but, as usual, sleep didn't come easily. Finally, sometime around midnight, I did fall asleep–with another day of sobriety under my belt and a raging hard-on inside my underwear.

The next morning, eight o'clock sharp, I called Old Brookville. The phone was picked up on the first ring.

"Hello?" said the Duchess softly.

"Nae? Is that you?"

Sympathetically: "Yes, it's me."

"How are you?"

"I'm okay. Hanging in there, I guess."

I took a deep breath and let it out slowly. "I . . . I called to say hi to the kids. Are they there?"

"What's wrong?" she said sadly. "You don't wanna talk to me?"

"No, of *course* I want to talk to you! There's nothing in the world I want more than to talk to you. I just didn't think you wanted to talk to me."

Kindly: "No, that's not true. I do want to talk to you. For better or worse, you're still my husband. I guess this is the *worse* part, right?"

I felt tears coming to my eyes, but I fought them down. "I don't know what to say, Nae. I . . . I'm so sorry for what happened. . . . I . . . I–"

"Don't," she said. "Don't apologize. I understand what happened, and I forgive you. That's the easy part, forgiveness. Forgetting's a different story." She paused. "But I do forgive you. And I want to go on. I want to try to make this marriage work. I still love you, in spite of everything."

"I love you too," I said, through tears. "More than you know, Nae. I . . . I don't know what to say. I don't know how it happened. I . . . I hadn't slept in months and"–I took a deep breath–"I didn't know what I was doing. It's all a blur."

"It's my fault as much as yours," she said kindly. "I watched you killing yourself and just stood there and did nothing. I thought I was helping you, but I was really doing the opposite. I didn't know."

"It's not your fault, Nae, it's mine. It's just that it happened so slowly, over so many years, that I didn't see it coming. Before I knew it I was out of control. I've always considered myself a strong person, but the drugs were stronger."

"The kids miss you. I miss you too. I've wanted to speak to you for days now, but Dennis Maynard told me I should wait until you were fully detoxed."

That rat fuck! I'll get that bastard! I took a deep breath, trying to calm myself down. The last thing I needed was to lose my temper with the Duchess on the phone. I needed to prove to her that I was still a rational man, that the drugs hadn't permanently altered me. "You know," I said calmly, "it's a good thing you got those second two doctors to come to the hospital"–I refused to use the words *psych unit*–"because I despised Dennis Maynard more than you can imagine. I almost didn't go to rehab because of him. There was something about him that just rubbed me the wrong way. I think he had a thing for you." I waited for her to call me crazy.

She chuckled. "It's funny you say that, because Laurie thought the same thing."

"Really?" I said, with contract murder in my heart. "I thought I was just being paranoid!"

"I don't know," said the luscious Duchess. "At first I was too much in shock to pick up on it, but then he asked me to go to the movies, which I thought was a bit out of line."

"Did you go?" The most appropriate method of death, I figured, would be blood loss through castration.

"No! Of course I didn't go! It was inappropriate for him to ask. Anyway, he left the next day and that was the last I heard of him."

"How come you wouldn't come see me in the hospital, Nae? I missed you so bad. I thought about you all the time."

There was a long silence, but I waited it out. I needed an answer. I was still struggling as to why this woman, my wife–who obviously loved me–wouldn't come visit me after a suicide attempt. It made no sense.

After a good ten seconds, she said, "At first I was scared because of what happened on the stairs. It's hard to explain, but you were like a different person that day, possessed or something. I don't know. And then Dennis Maynard told me I shouldn't come see you until you went to rehab. I didn't know whether he was right or wrong. It wasn't like I had a road map to follow, and he was supposedly the expert. Anyway, all that matters is that you went to rehab, right?"

I wanted to say no, but this wasn't the time to start an argument. I had the rest of my life to argue with her. "Yeah, well, I'm here, and that's the most important thing."

"How bad are the withdrawals?" she asked, changing the subject.

"I haven't really had any withdrawals, or at least any I could feel. Believe it or not, the second I got here I lost the urge to do drugs. It's hard to explain, but I was sitting in the waiting room and all of a sudden the compulsion just left me. Anyway, this place is kind of wacky, to say the least. What's gonna keep me sober is not Talbot Marsh; it's me."

Very nervous now: "But you're still gonna stay there for the twenty-eight days, right?"

I laughed gently. "Yeah, you can relax, sweetie; I'm staying. I need a break from all the madness. Anyway, the AA part is really good. I read the book and it's awesome. I'll go to meetings when I get home, just to make sure I don't relapse."

We spent the next half hour talking on the phone, and by the end of the conversation I had my Duchess back. I knew it. I could feel it in my bones. I told her about all my erections and she promised she would help in that department just as soon as I got home. I asked her if she would have some phone sex with me, but she declined. I would keep after her about that, though. Eventually, I figured, she would break down.

Then we exchanged *I love you*s and promises to write each other every day. Before I hung up I told her that I would call her three times a day.

The next few days passed uneventfully, and before I knew it I had made it a full week without doing drugs.

Each day we were given a few hours of personal time, to go to the gym and such, and I quickly insinuated myself into a small cadre of kiss-ass Martians. One of the doctors–an anesthesiologist who'd had a habit of anesthetizing himself while his patients were on the table under his care–had been at Talbot Marsh for over a year, and he'd had his car shipped down. It was a piece-of-shit gray Toyota hatchback, but it served its purpose.

It was about a ten-minute car ride to the gym, and I was sitting in the right backseat, wearing a pair of gray Adidas shorts and a tank top, when I popped an enormous woody. It was probably the vibrations from the four-cylinder engine, or maybe it was the bumps in the road, but something had sent a couple a pints of blood to my loins. It was a huge, rock-hard erection, the sort that presses against your underwear and needs to be adjusted and then readjusted, lest it drive you insane.

"Check this out," I said, pulling down the front of my gym shorts and showing the Martians my penis.

They all turned and stared. Yes, I thought, it looked good. Despite my height, God had been very kind to me in that department. "Not too shabby!" I said to my doctor friends, as I grabbed my penis and gave it a few yanks. Then I slapped it against my stomach, which created a rather pleasant *thud*.

Finally, after the fourth *thud*, everybody started laughing. It was a rare moment of levity at Talbot Marsh, a moment between guys, a moment between Martians, where the normal societal niceties could be stripped away, where homophobia could be entirely ignored, and men could be just that: men! I had a fine workout that afternoon, and the rest of the day passed uneventfully.

The following day, just after lunch, I was sitting in an astonishingly boring group therapy session. My counselor strolled in, asking to see me.

I couldn't have been happier–until two minutes later, when we were sitting in her small office and she cocked her head to the side at a very shrewd angle and said, using the tone of the Grand Inquisitor, "So, how are you, Jordan?"

I turned the corners of my mouth down and shrugged. "I'm okay, I guess."

She smiled warily and asked, "Have you been having any urges lately?"

"No, not at all," I said. "On a scale of one to ten, I would say my urge to do drugs is a zero. Maybe even less than that."

"Oh, that's very good, Jordan. Very, very good."

What the fuck? I knew I was missing something here. "Um, I'm a bit confused. Did someone tell you that I was thinking about using drugs?"

"No, no," she said, shaking her head. "It has nothing to do with that. I'm just wondering if you've had any other urges lately, anything other than drugs."

I searched my short-term memory for urges but came up blank, other than the obvious urge to bolt out of this place and go home to the Duchess and fuck her brains out for a month straight. "No, I haven't had any urges. I mean, I miss my wife and everything and I'd like to go home and be with her, but that's about it."

She pursed her lips and nodded her head slowly, then she said, "Have you been having urges to expose yourself in public?"

"What?" I snapped. "What are you talking about? What do you think, I'm a flasher or something?" I shook my head in contempt.

"Well," she said gravely, "I received three written complaints today, from three separate patients, and they all say you exposed yourself to them–that you pulled down your shorts and masturbated in their presence."

"That's a complete load of crap," I sputtered. "I wasn't jerking off, for Chrissake. I just yanked on it a few times and slapped it against my stomach so we could all hear the sound. That's all. What's the big deal about that? Where I come from, a little bit of nudity between men isn't anything to write home about." I shook my head. "I was just fucking around. I've had an erection since I got to this place. I guess my dick is finally waking up from all the drugs. But since it seems to bother everyone so much, I'll keep the snake in its cage for the next few weeks. No big deal."

She nodded. "Well, you have to understand that you traumatized some of the other patients. Their recoveries are very fragile at this point, and any sudden shock could send them back to using."

"Did you just say *traumatized*? Give me a fucking break! Don't you think that's a bit extreme? I mean . . . Jesus! These are grown men we're talking about! How could they have been traumatized by the sight of my dick, unless, of course, one of them wants to suck on it. You think that might be it?"

She shrugged. "I couldn't say."

"Well, I'll tell you that no one in that car was traumatized. It was a moment between guys, that's all. The only reason they ratted me out was because they want to prove to the staff that they're cured or rehabilitated or whatever. Anything it takes to get their fucking licenses back, right?"

She nodded. "Obviously."

"Oh, so you know that?"

"Yes, of course I know that. And the fact that they all reported you makes me seriously question the status of their own recoveries." She smiled the smile of no hard feelings. "Either way, it doesn't change the fact that your behavior was inappropriate."

"Whatever," I muttered. "It won't happen again."

"Fair enough," she said, handing me a sheet of paper with some typing on it. "I just need you to sign this behavioral contract. All it says is that you agree not to expose yourself in public again." She handed me a pen.

"You're shitting me!"

She shook her head no. I started laughing as I read the contract.

It was only a few lines, and it said just what she'd indicated. I shrugged and signed it, then rose from my chair and headed for the door. "Is that it?" I snapped. "Case closed?"

"Yes, case closed."

As I headed back to my therapy session, I had this strange feeling that it wasn't. These Talbot Martians were a strange lot.

The next day it was time for another roundtable discussion. Once more, all hundred five Martians and a dozen or so staff members sat in a great circle in the auditorium. Doug Talbot, I noticed, was conspicuously absent.

So I closed my eyes and prepared for the drizzle. After ten or fifteen minutes I was soaking wet and half asleep, when I heard: ". . . Jordan Belfort, who most of you know."

I looked up. My therapist had taken over the meeting at some point, and now she was talking about me. Why? I wondered.

"So rather than having a guest speaker today," continued my therapist, "I think it would be more productive if Jordan shared with the group what happened." She paused and looked in my direction. "Would you be kind enough to share, Jordan?"

I looked around the room at all the Martians staring at me, including Shirley Temple with her wonderful blond curls. I was still a bit confused as to what my therapist wanted me to say, although I had a sneaky suspicion that it had something to do with me being a sexual deviant.

I leaned forward in my seat, stared at my therapist, and shrugged. "I have no problem talking to the group," I said, "but what is it that you want me to say? I have lots of stories. Why don't you pick one?"

With that, all hundred five Martians turned their Martian heads toward my therapist. It looked like the two of us were engaged in a tennis match. "Well," she said therapeutically, "you're free to talk about whatever you want in this room. It's a very safe place. But why don't you start with what happened in the car the other day, on the way to the gym?"

The Martians turned their heads back to me. Through laughter, I said, "You're kidding me, right?"

Now the Martians looked back at my therapist . . . who pursed her lips and shook her head, as if to say, "Nope, I'm dead serious!"

How ironic, I thought. My therapist was giving me center stage.

How glorious! The Wolf–back in action! I loved it. The fact that the room was half females made it all the better. The SEC had taken away my ability to stand before the crowd and speak my piece, and now my therapist had been kind enough to restore that power to me. I would put on a show the Martians would never forget!

I nodded and smiled at my therapist. "Is it okay if I stand in the middle of the room and talk? I think better when I'm moving."

A hundred five Martian heads turned back to my therapist. "Please, feel free."

I walked to the center of the room and stared into the eyes of Shirley Temple. "Hi, everybody! My name is Jordan, and I'm an alcoholic and a drug addict and a sexual deviant."

"Hi, Jordan!" came the hearty response, accompanied by a few chuckles. Shirley Temple, however, had turned beet-red. I had been staring right into her enormous blue eyes when I'd referred to myself as a sexual deviant.

I said, "Anyway, I'm really not much for talking in front of crowds, but I'll try my best. Okay, where should I begin? Oh, my erections–yes, that's the most appropriate place, I guess. Here's the root of the problem. I spent the last ten years of my life with my dick in a state of seminarcosis as a result of all the drugs I was doing. I mean, don't get me wrong, I wasn't impotent or anything like that, although I will admit that there were about a thousand or so times I couldn't get it up because of all the coke and Ludes."

Scattered laughter now. *Ah, the Wolf of Wall Street! Let the games begin!* I raised my hand for quiet.

"No, seriously, this isn't a laughing matter. See, for the most part, when I couldn't get it up, I was with hookers, and that was about three times a week. So I was basically throwing my money out the window–paying upward of a thousand dollars a pop and not being able to even sleep with them. It was all very sad, and very expensive too.

"Anyway, they usually succeeded in the end–at least the good ones did–although it took a bit of coaxing with toys and such." I turned the corners of my mouth down and shrugged, as if to say, "Sex toys are nothing to be ashamed about!"

There was great laughter now, although without even looking I could tell it was the sound of female Martian laughter. My suspicions were confirmed when I looked around the room and saw all the female Martians staring at me with terrific smiles on their kind Martian faces. Their Martian shoulders bounced up and down with each and every giggle. Meanwhile, the male Martians were shooting daggers at me with their Martian eyes.

I waved my hand dismissively and soldiered on: "No matter, no matter. You see, the irony is that when I was with my wife I never really had that problem. I could always get it up with her–or at least usually–and if you saw her you'd understand why. But when I started snorting a quarter ounce of coke a day, well, I was having trouble with her too.

"Yet now that I haven't touched a drug in over a week, I think my penis is undergoing some sort of strange metamorphosis, or maybe a reawakening. I've been walking around with an erection twenty-three hours a day . . . or maybe even more." A huge burst of female Martian laughter. I looked around the room. Oh, yes, I had them! They were mine now! The Wolf, spinning his yarn for the ladies! Center stage!

"Anyway, I thought some of the men here would appreciate my plight. I mean, it seemed only logical that other people would be suffering from this terrible affliction too, right?"

I looked around the room and all of the female Martians were nodding in agreement, while the male Martians were shaking their heads back and forth, staring at me with contempt. I shrugged. "So, anyway, here's where the problem started. I was sitting in the car with three other male patients–dickless patients, I'm now thinking–and we were driving to the gym, and I think it was the vibrations from the engine or maybe it was the bumps in the road, but, whatever it was, out of nowhere I got this huge erection!"

I looked around the room, carefully avoiding the blazing gazes of the male Martians–relishing instead the adoring looks of all the female Martians. Shirley Temple was licking her lips in anticipation. I winked at her, and I said, "Anyway, it was just a harmless moment between guys, that's all. Now, I won't deny that I yanked on the snake a few times"–a burst of female Martian laughter–"and I won't deny that I slapped it against my stomach once or twice"–more laughter–"but it was all done in jest. It wasn't like I was yanking on it ferociously, trying to make myself come in the backseat of the car, although I wouldn't pass judgment on anyone who did. I mean, to each his own, right?" An unidentified female

Martian screamed, "Yeah, to each his own!" to which the rest of the female Martians started clapping.

I held up my hand for quiet, wondering how long the staff would let this go on. I suspected they would let it go on indefinitely. After all, for every second I spoke there was some insurance company receiving a bill for each of these hundred five Martians. "So, to sum it up, to tell you what's really bothering me about this whole affair, is that the three guys who turned me in, whose names will go unmentioned–although if you come up to me afterward I'll gladly tell you exactly who they are, so you can avoid them–they all laughed and joked about it while we were in the car. No one confronted me or even hinted that they thought what I was doing was in poor taste."

I shook my head in disgust. "You know, the truth is that I come from a very dysfunctional world–a world of my own construction–where things like nudity and prostitutes and debauchery and all sorts of depraved acts were all considered normal.

"In retrospect, I know it was wrong. And I know it was insane. But that's now . . . *today* . . . as I stand here a sober man. Yeah, today I know that midget-tossing is wrong and that getting scrummed by four hookers is wrong and that manipulating stocks is wrong and that cheating on my wife is wrong and falling asleep at the dinner table or on the side of the road or crashing into other people's cars because I fell asleep at the wheel, I know all these things are wrong.

"I'm the first one to admit that I'm the furthest thing from a perfect person. I'm actually insecure and humble, and I embarrass easily." I paused, changing my tone to dead seriousness. "But I refuse to show it. If I had to choose between embarrassment and death, I'd choose death. So, yeah, I'm a weak, imperfect person. But one thing you'll never find me doing is passing judgment on other people."

I shrugged and let out a very obvious sigh. "Yeah, maybe what I did in the car was wrong. Perhaps it was in bad taste and it was offensive. But I challenge any person in this room to make a case that I did it with malice in my heart or to try to fuck up someone else's recovery. I did it to make light of a terrible situation I'm in. I've been a drug addict for almost a decade now, and although I might appear to be somewhat normal, I know I'm not. I'll be leaving here in a couple of weeks, and I'm scared shitless to go back into the lion's den, to go back to the people, places, and things that fueled my habit. I have a wife, whom I love, and two children, whom I adore, and if I go back out there and relapse I'll destroy them forever, especially my children.

"Yet, here, in Talbot Marsh, where I'm supposed to be surrounded by people who *understand* what I'm going through, I've got three assholes trying to undermine my recovery and get me thrown out of this place. And that's really sad. I'm no different than any one of you, male or female. Yeah, maybe I got a few extra bucks, but I'm scared and worried and insecure about the future, and I spend the better part of my day praying that everything's gonna wind up okay. That one day I'll be able to sit my kids down and say, 'Yes, it's true I pushed Mommy down the stairs once while I was high on cocaine, but that was twenty years ago, and I've been sober ever since.' "

I shook my head again. "So next time any of you consider reporting me to the staff, I would urge you to think twice. You're only hurting yourself. I'm not getting thrown out of this place so fast, and the staff is a lot smarter than you people think. And that's all I have to say. Now, if you'll excuse me, I'm getting an erection, so I need to sit down to avoid embarrassment. Thank you." I waved my hand in the air, as if I were a political candidate on the campaign trail, and the room broke out into thunderous applause. Every last female Martian, every last staff member, and about half the male Martians rose to their feet, giving me a standing ovation.

As I took my seat, I locked eyes with my therapist. She smiled at me, nodded her head, and pumped her fist in the air a single time, as if to say, "Good for you, Jordan."

The next thirty minutes was open discussion, during which the female Martians defended my actions and said that I was adorable, while some of the males of the species continued their attack against me and said that I was a menace to Martian society.

That evening I sat my roommates down and said, "Listen, I'm sick and tired of all the crap that's going on around here. I don't want to hear about how I forget to put the toilet seat down and how I talk too much on the phone or how I breathe too loud. I'm done. So here's the deal. You guys are both desperate for cash, right?"

They nodded.

"Fine," I said. "Here's what we're gonna do. Tomorrow morning you're gonna call my friend Alan Lipsky, and he's gonna open accounts for you at his brokerage firm. By tomorrow afternoon you'll each have made five grand. You can have the money wired wherever you want. But I don't want to hear another fucking peep out of either of you until I leave this place. That's less than three weeks from now, so it shouldn't be too difficult."

Of course they both called the next morning, and of course it greatly improved our relationship. Nevertheless, my problems at Talbot Marsh were far from over. But it wasn't the luscious Shirley Temple who would complicate things. No, my problems came from my desire to see the Duchess. I'd heard through the Martian grapevine that, under rare circumstances, the staff granted furloughs. I called the Duchess and asked her if she would fly down for a long weekend, if I got approval.

"Just tell me where and when," she'd replied, "and I'll give you a weekend you'll never forget."

It was for that very reason that I now sat in my therapist's office, trying to get a furlough. It was my third week on planet Talbot Marsh and I hadn't gotten myself into any new trouble, although it was common knowledge among the Martians that I was attending only twenty-five percent of the group therapy sessions. But no one seemed to care anymore. They realized that Doug Talbot wasn't going to toss me and that in my own offbeat way I was being a positive influence.

I smiled at my therapist and said, "Listen, I don't see what the big deal is if I leave on a Friday and come back on a Sunday. I'm gonna be with my wife the whole time. You've spoken to her, so you know she's with the program. It'll be good for my recovery."

"I can't let it happen," said my therapist, shaking her head. "It would be disruptive to the other patients. Everybody's up in arms as it is about the alleged special treatment you get around here." She smiled warmly. "Listen, Jordan, the policy is that patients aren't eligible for furloughs until they've been at the rehab for at least ninety days–and had perfect behavior. No flashing or anything."

I smiled at my therapist. She was a good egg, this lady, and I had grown close to her over the last few weeks. It had been shrewd of her that day, putting me before the crowd and giving me a chance to defend myself. I would find out only much later that she'd spoken to the Duchess, who had informed her of my ability to sway the masses, for good or ill.

"I understand you have rules," I said, "but they weren't designed for someone in my situation. How could I be held to a rule that requires a ninety-day cooling-off period when my entire stay is only twenty-eight days?" I shrugged, not thinking too highly of my own logic until a wonderful inspiration came bubbling up into my sober brain. "I have an idea!" I chirped. "Why don't you let me stand in front of the group again and make another speech? I'll try to sell them on the fact that I deserve a furlough, even though it goes against institutional policy."

Her response was to put her hand to the bridge of her nose and start to rub. Then she laughed softly. "You know, I almost want to say yes, just to hear what line of shit you're gonna give the patients. In fact, I have no doubt you'd convince them." She let out a few more chuckles. "It was quite a speech you made two weeks ago, by far the best in Talbot Marsh history. You have an amazing gift, Jordan. I've never seen anything like it. Just out of curiosity, though, what would you say to the patients if I gave you the chance?"

I shrugged. "I'm not really sure. You know, it's not like I ever plan out what I'm gonna say. I used to give two meetings a day to a football field full of people. I did it for almost five years, and I can't remember a single time that I ever thought about what I was going to say before I actually said it. I usually had a topic or two that needed to be hit on, but that was about the extent of it. Everything else was spur of the moment.

"You know, there's something that just happens to me when I stand before a crowd. It's hard to describe, but it's like all of a sudden everything becomes very clear. My thoughts start rolling off my tongue without even thinking about them. One thought just leads to another and then I get on a roll.

"But to answer your question, I'd probably use reverse psychology on them, explain how letting me go on a furlough is good for their own recovery. That life, as a whole, isn't fair, and that they should get used to it now in a controlled environment. Then I'd follow it up by making them feel bad for me–telling them what I did to my wife on the stairs and how my family was on the verge of being destroyed because of my drug addiction, and how having this visit now would probably make the difference between my wife and me staying together or not."

My therapist smiled. "I think you should figure out a way to put your abilities to good use; figure out some way where you get your message across, except this time do it for the greater good, not to corrupt people."

"Ahhh," I said, smiling back, "so you've been listening to me all these weeks. I wasn't sure. Anyway, maybe I will one day, but for right now I just wanna get back to my family. I plan on getting out of the brokerage business altogether. I have a few investments to wind down and then I'm done forever. I'm done with the drugs, the hookers, the cheating on my wife, all the crap with the stocks, everything. I'm gonna live out the rest of my life quietly, out of the limelight."

She started to laugh. "Well, somehow, I don't think your life's gonna turn out that way. I don't think you're ever gonna live in obscurity. At least not for very long. I don't mean that in a bad way. What I'm trying to say is that you have a wonderful gift, and I think it's important for your recovery that you learn to use that gift in a positive way. Just focus on your recovery first–and stay sober–and the rest of your life will take care of itself."

I dropped my head and stared at the floor and nodded. I knew she was right, and I was scared to death about it. I desperately wanted to remain sober, but I knew the odds were heavily against me. Admittedly, after learning more about AA it no longer seemed like a patent impossibility, just a long shot. The difference between success and failure, it seemed, had a lot to do with getting grounded into AA as soon as you left rehab–finding a sponsor you identified with, someone to offer hope and encouragement when things weren't going your way.

"How about my furlough?" I asked, raising my eyebrows.

"I'll bring it up at tomorrow's staff meeting. At the end of the day, it's not up to me, it's up to Dr. Talbot." She shrugged. "As your primary therapist I can veto it, but I won't. I'll abstain."

I nodded in understanding. I would talk to Talbot before they had their meeting. "Thank you for everything," I said. "You've only got me for another week or so. I'll try to stay out of your hair."

"You're not in my hair," she replied. "In fact, you're my favorite, although I'd never admit it to anyone."

"And I won't tell anyone." I leaned over and hugged her gently.

It was five days later, a Friday, in fact, a little before six p.m., and I was waiting on the tarmac at the private terminal at Atlanta International Airport. I was leaning against the rear bumper of a black stretch Lincoln limousine, staring up into the northern sky through sober eyes. I had my arms folded beneath my chest and an enormous erection in my pants. I was waiting for the Duchess.

I was ten pounds heavier than when I'd arrived, and my skin glowed once more with youth and health. I was thirty-four and I had survived the unspeakable–a drug addiction of biblical proportions, a drug addiction of such insanity that I should have died long ago, of an overdose or a car accident or a helicopter crash or a scuba-diving accident or one of a thousand other ways.

Yet here I stood, still retaining all my faculties. It was a beautiful, clear evening with a tiny, warm breeze. At this time of the day, this close to summer, the sun was still high enough in the sky that I was able to catch sight of the Gulfstream long before its wheels touched the runway. It seemed almost impossible that inside that cabin was my beautiful wife, who I'd put through seven years of drug-addicted hell. I wondered what she was wearing and what she was thinking. Was she as nervous as I was? Was she really as beautiful as I remembered? Would she still smell as glorious? Did she still really love me? Could things ever be the same?

I found out the moment the cabin door opened and the luscious Duchess emerged with her fabulous mane of shimmering blond hair. She looked gorgeous. She took a single step forward, and then, in typical Duchess fashion, she struck a pose, with her head cocked to one side and her arms folded beneath her breasts and one long bare leg slewed out to the side, in a statement of defiance. Then she just stared at me. She had on a tiny pink sundress. It was sleeveless and a good six inches above her knee. Still holding her pose, she compressed those luscious lips of hers and started shaking her little blond head back and forth, as if to say, "I can't believe this is the man I love!" I took a step forward and threw my palms up in the air and shrugged.

And we just stood there, staring at each other for a good ten seconds, until all at once she gave up her pose and blew me a world-class double kiss. Then she spread her arms out, did a little pirouette to announce her arrival to the city of Atlanta, and came running down the stairs with a great smile on her face. I started running toward her, and we met in the middle of the asphalt tarmac. She threw her arms around my neck and took a tiny jump and wrapped her legs around my waist. Then she kissed me.

And we held that kiss for what seemed like an eternity as we breathed in each other's scent. I spun around in a 360, still kissing her, until we both started giggling. I pulled my lips away and buried my nose into her cleavage and sniffed at her, like a puppy dog. She giggled uncontrollably. She smelled so good it seemed almost impossible.

I pulled my head back a few inches and stared into those vivid blue eyes of hers. I said, in a dead-serious tone: "If I don't make love to you right this second, I'm gonna come right here on the tarmac."

The Duchess's response was to revert to her baby voice: "Aw, my poor little boy!" *Little? Unbelievable!* "You're so horny you're about to burst, aren't you?"

I nodded eagerly.

The Duchess went on: "And look how young and handsome you look now that you've gained a few pounds and your skin's not green anymore. Too bad I have to teach you a lesson this weekend." She shrugged. "There'll be no lovemaking until July Fourth."

Huh? "What are you talking about?"

In a very knowing tone: "You heard me, love-bug. You've been a very bad boy, so now you're gonna have to pay the price. First you have to prove yourself to me before I let you stick it in again. For now you only get to kiss me."

I giggled. "Get out of here, you nut!" I grabbed her hand and started pulling her toward the limousine. "I can't wait until July Fourth! I need you now–right this second! I wanna make love in the back of the limousine."

"Nope, nope, nope," she said, shaking her head back and forth in an exaggerated way. "It's only kisses this weekend. Let's see how you behave over the next two days, and then maybe on Sunday I'll think about going further."

The limo driver was a short, sixtyish, white cracker named Bob. He wore a formal driver's cap, and he was standing by the rear door, waiting for us. I said, "This is my wife, Bob. She's a duchess, so treat her accordingly. I bet you don't get that much royalty down here, now, do you?"

"Oh, no," said a very serious Bob. "Not much of it at all."

I compressed my lips and nodded gravely. "I thought as much. Anyway, don't be intimidated by her. She's actually very down to earth, right, honey?"

"Yeah, very down to earth. Now shut the fuck up and get in the goddamn limo," spat the Duchess.

Bob froze in horror, obviously taken aback at how someone with as royal a bloodline as the Duchess of Bay Ridge could use such language.

I said to Bob, "Don't mind her; she just doesn't want to seem too uppity. She's saves her stuffy side for when she's back in England, with the other royals." I winked. "Anyway, all kidding aside, Bob, being married to her makes me a duke, so what I'm thinking is that since you're gonna be our driver for the whole weekend, you might as well just address us as the Duke and the Duchess–just to clear up any confusion."

Bob bowed formally. "Of course, Duke."

"Very well," I replied, pushing the Duchess into the backseat by her fabulous royal bottom. I climbed in behind her. Bob slammed the door and then headed to the plane to collect the Duchess's royal baggage.

I immediately yanked up her dress and saw that she wasn't wearing any panties. I pounced. "I love you so much, Nae. So, so much!" I pushed her down on the rear seat, lengthwise, and pressed my erection against her. She moaned deliciously, wriggling her pelvis against mine, giving me the benefit of a little friction. I kissed her and kissed her until after a few minutes she extended her arms and pushed me off.

Through giggles: "Stop, you silly boy! Bob's coming back. You'll have to wait until we get back to the hotel." She looked down and saw my erection through my jeans. "Aw, my poor little baby"–*little? Why always little?*–"is ready to burst!" She pursed her lips. "Here, let me rub it for you." She reached down with the palm of her hand and started rubbing the outline of my erection.

I responded by hitting the divider button on the overhead console. As the partition slid shut, I muttered, "I can't wait for the hotel! I'm making love to you right here, Bob or no Bob!"

"Fine!" said a frisky Duchess. "But it's only a sympathy fuck, so it doesn't count. I'm still not making love to you until you prove to me that you've become a good boy. Understood?"

I nodded, giving her puppy-dog eyes, and we started ripping off each other's clothes. By the time Bob made it back to the limo, I was already deep inside the Duchess, and the two of us were moaning wildly. I put a forefinger to my lips and said, "Shhhhhh!"

She nodded, and I reached up and pressed the intercom button. "Bob, my good man, are you there?"

"Yes, Duke."

"Splendid. The Duchess and I have some very urgent business to discuss, so please don't disturb us until we get to the Hyatt."

I winked at the Duchess and motioned to the intercom button with my eyebrows. "Off or on?" I whispered.

The Duchess looked up, and started chewing on the inside of her mouth. Then she shrugged. "You might as well leave it on."

That's my girl! I raised my voice and said, "Enjoy the royal show, Bob!" And with that, the sober Duke of Bayside, Queens, began making love to his wife, the luscious Duchess of Bay Ridge, Brooklyn, as if there were no tomorrow.

CHAPTER 39

SIX WAYS TO KILL AN INTERVENTIONIST

My dog needs an operation . . . my car broke down . . . my boss is an asshole . . . my wife's a bigger asshole . . . traffic jams drive me crazy . . . life's not fair . . . and so forth and so on . . .

Yes, indeed, it was drizzling something awful in the rooms of Alcoholics Anonymous in Southampton, Long Island. I'd been home for a week now, and as part of my recovery I'd committed to doing a Ninety-in-Ninety, which is to say: I had set a goal to attend ninety AA meetings in ninety days. And with a very nervous Ducshess watching me like a hawk, I had no choice but to do it.

I quickly realized it was going to be a very long ninety days.

The moment I stepped into my first meeting, someone asked me if I'd like to be the guest speaker, to which I'd replied, "Speak in front of the group? Sure, why not!" What could be better than that? I figured.

The problems started quickly. I was offered a seat behind a rectangular table at the front of the room. The meeting's chairperson, a kind-looking man in his early fifties, sat down beside me and made a few brief announcements. Then he motioned for me to begin.

I nodded and said, in a loud, forthright voice, "Hi, my name is Jordan, and I'm an alcoholic and an addict."

The room of thirty or so ex-drunks responded in unison: "Hi, Jordan; welcome."

I smiled and nodded. With great confidence, I said, "I've been sober for thirty-seven days now and–"

I was immediately cut off. "Excuse me," said an ex-drunk with gray hair and spidery veins on his nose. "You need to be sober ninety days to speak at this meeting."

Why, the insolence of the old bastard! I was absolutely devastated. I felt like I'd gotten on the school bus without remembering to put my clothes on. I just sat there, in this terribly uncomfortable wooden chair, staring at the old drunk and waiting for someone to drag me off with a hook.

"No, no. Let's not be too tough," said the chairperson. "Since he's already up here, why don't we just let him speak? It'll be a breath of fresh air to hear a newcomer."

Impudent mumbles came bubbling up from the crowd, along with a series of insolent shrugs and contemptuous head-shakes. They looked angry. And vicious. The chairperson put his arm on my shoulder and looked me in the eyes, as if to say, "It's okay. You can go on."

I nodded my head nervously. "Okay," I said to the angry ex-drunks. "I've been sober for thirty-seven days now and–"

I was cut off again, except this time by thunderous applause. *Ahhh, how wonderful!* The Wolf was receiving his first ovation, and he hadn't even gotten going yet! Wait 'til they hear my story! I'll bring the house down!

Slowly, the applause died down, and with renewed confidence I plowed on: "Thanks, everybody. I really appreciate the vote of confidence. My drug of choice was Quaaludes, but I did a lot of cocaine too. In fact–"

I was cut off again. "Excuse me," said my nemesis with the spider veins, "this is an AA meeting, not an NA meeting. You can't talk about drugs here, only alcohol."

I looked around the room, and all heads were nodding in agreement. *Oh, shit!* That seemed like a dated policy. This was the nineties now. Why would someone choose to be an alcoholic yet shun drugs? It made no sense.

I was about to jump out of my chair and run for the hills, when I heard a powerful female voice yell, "How dare you, Bill! How dare you try to drive away this young boy who's fighting for his life! You're despicable! We're all addicts here. Now, why don't you just shut up and mind your own business and let the boy speak?"

The boy? Had I just been called a boy? I was almost thirty-five now, for Chrissake! I looked over at the voice, and it was coming from a very old lady wearing granny glasses. She winked at me. So I winked back.

The old drunk sputtered at Grandma, "Rules are rules, you old hag!"

I shook my head in disbelief. Why did the insanity follow me wherever I went? I hadn't done anything wrong here, had I? I just wanted to stay sober. Yet, once again, I was at the center of an uproar. "Whatever," I said to the chairperson. "I'll do whatever you want."

At the end of the day, they let me speak, although I left the meeting wanting to wring the old bastard's neck. From there, things continued to spiral downward when I went to an NA–Narcotics Anonymous–meeting. There were only four other people in the room; three of them were visibly stoned, and the fourth had even fewer days sober than me.

I wanted to say something to the Duchess, to tell her that this whole AA thing wasn't for me, but I knew she'd be devastated. Our relationship was growing stronger by the day. There was no more fighting or cursing or hitting or stabbing or slapping or water-throwing–nothing. We were just two normal individuals, living a normal life with Chandler and Carter and twenty-two in domestic help. We had decided to stay out in Southampton for the summer. Better to keep me isolated from the madness, we figured, at least until my sobriety took hold. The Duchess had issued warnings to all my old friends: They were no longer welcome in our house unless they were sober. Alan Chemical-tob received a personal warning from Bo, and I never heard from him again.

And my business? Well, without Quaaludes and cocaine, I no longer had the stomach for it, or at least not yet. As a sober man, problems like Steve Madden Shoes seemed easy to deal with. I'd had my lawyers file a lawsuit, while I was still in rehab, and the escrow agreement was now public. So far, I hadn't gotten myself arrested over it, and I suspected I never would. After all, on the face of it, the agreement wasn't illegal; it was more an issue of Steve having not disclosed it to the public–which made it his liability more than mine. Besides, Agent Coleman had faded off into the sunset long ago, hopefully never to be heard from again. Eventually, I would have to settle with the Cobbler. I had already resigned myself to that fact, and I no longer gave a shit. Even in my most depraved emotional state–just before I'd entered rehab–it wasn't the money that had been driving me crazy but the idea of the Cobbler trying to snatch my stock and keep it for himself. And that was no longer a possibility. As part of a settlement he would be forced to sell my stock to pay me off, and that would be that. I would let my lawyers deal with it.

I had been home for a little over a week when I came home one evening from an AA meeting and found the Duchess sitting in the TV room–the very room where I had lost my twenty-gram rock six weeks ago, which the Duchess had now admitted to having flushed down the toilet.

With a great smile on my face, I said, "Hey, sweetie! What's–"

The Duchess looked up, and I froze in horror. She was visibly shaken. Tears streamed down her face, and her nose was running. With a sinking heart, I said, "Jesus, baby! What's wrong? What happened?" I hugged her gently.

Her body was trembling in my arms when she pointed to the TV screen and said through tears, "It's Scott Schneiderman. He killed a police officer a few hours ago. He was trying to rob his father for coke money and he shot a policeman." She broke down hysterically.

I felt tears streaming down my cheeks as I said, "Jesus, Nae, he was here just a month ago. I . . . I don't . . ." I searched for something to say but quickly realized that no words could describe the magnitude of this tragedy.

So I said nothing.

A week later, on a Friday evening, the seven-thirty meeting at Our Lady of Poland Church had just begun. It was Memorial Day weekend, and I was expecting the usual sixty minutes of torture. Then, to my shock, the opening words from the meeting's chairperson came in the form of a directive–stating that there would be no drug-drizzling allowed, not under his watch. He was creating a Drizzle-Free Zone, he explained, because the purpose of AA was to create hope and faith, not to complain about the length of the checkout line at Grand Union. Then he held up an egg timer for public inspection, and he said, "There's nothing that you can't say in less than two and a half minutes that I have any interest in hearing. So keep it short and sweet." He nodded once.

I was sitting toward the back, next to a middle-aged woman who looked reasonably well kept, for an ex-drunk. She had reddish hair and a ruddy complexion. I leaned over to her and whispered, "Who is that guy?"

"That's George. He's sort of the unofficial leader here."

"Really?" I said. "Of this meeting?"

"No, no," she whispered, in a tone implying that I was seriously out of the loop, "not just here, all over the Hamptons." She looked around conspiratorially, as if she were about to pass on a piece of top-secret information. Then, sotto voce, she said, "He owns Seafield, the drug rehab. You've never seen him on TV?"

I shook my head no. "I don't watch much TV, although he does look somewhat familiar. He–*ohmygod!*" I was speechless. It was Fred Flintstone, the man with the enormous head who'd popped on my TV screen at three in the morning, inspiring me to throw my Remington sculpture at his face!

After the meeting ended, I waited until the crowd died down and then went up to George and said, "Hi, my name is Jordan. I just wanted you to know that I really enjoyed the meeting. It was terrific."

He extended his hand, which was the size of a catcher's mitt. I shook it dutifully, praying he wouldn't rip my arm out of its socket.

"Thanks," he said. "Are you a newcomer?"

I nodded. "Yeah, I'm forty-three days sober."

"Congratulations. That's no small accomplishment. You should be proud." He paused and cocked his head to the side, taking a good hard look at me. "You know, you look familiar. What'd you say your name was again?"

Here we go! Those bastards in the press–there was no escaping them! Fred Flintstone had seen my picture in the paper, and now he was going to judge me. It was time for a strategic subject change. "My name's Jordan, and I gotta tell you a funny story, George: I was in my house up the Island, in Old Brookville, and it was three in the morning . . ." and I proceeded to tell him how I threw my Remington sculpture at his face, to which he smiled and replied, "You and a thousand other people. Sony should pay me a dollar for every TV they sold to a drug addict who smashed their

TV after my commercial." He let out a chuckle, then added skeptically, "You live in Old Brookville? That's a helluva nice neighborhood. You live with your parents?"

"No," I said, smiling. "I'm married with children, but that commercial was too–"

He cut me off. "You out here for Memorial Day?"

Jesus! This wasn't going according to plan. He had me on the defensive. "No, I have a house out here."

Sounding surprised: "Oh, really, where?"

I took a deep breath and said, "Meadow Lane."

He pulled his head back a few inches and narrowed his eyes. "You live on Meadow Lane? Really?"

I nodded slowly.

Fred Flintstone smirked. Apparently, the picture was growing clearer. He smiled and said, "And what did you say your last name was?"

"I didn't. But it's Belfort. Ring a bell?"

"Yeah," he said, chuckling. "A couple a hundred million of them. You're that kid who started . . . uh . . . what's it called . . . Strathman something or other."

"Stratton Oakmont," I said tonelessly.

"Yeah! That's it. Stratton Oakmont! Holy Christ! You look like a fucking teenager! How could you have caused so much commotion?"

I shrugged. "The power of drugs, right?"

He nodded. "Yeah, well, you bastards took me for a hundred large in some crazy fucking stock. I can't even remember the name of it."

Oh, shit! This was bad. George might take a swing at me with those catcher's mitts of his! I would offer to pay him back right now. I would run home and get the money out of my safe. "I haven't been involved with Stratton for a long time, but I'd still be more than happy to–"

He cut me off again. "Listen, I'm really enjoying this conversation, but I gotta get home. I'm expecting a call."

"Oh, I'm sorry. I didn't mean to hold you up. I'll come back next week; maybe we can talk then."

"Why, you going someplace now?"

"No, why?"

He smiled. "I was going to invite you over for a cup of coffee. I live just down the block from you."

With raised eyebrows, I said, "You're not mad about the hundred grand?"

"Nah, what's a hundred grand between two drunks, right? Besides, I needed the tax deduction." He smiled and put his arm on my shoulder, and we headed for the door. He said, "I was expecting to find you in the rooms one of these days. I've heard some pretty wild stories about you. I'm just glad you made it here before it was too late."

I nodded in agreement. Then George added, "Anyway, I'm only inviting you over to my house under one condition."

"What's that?" I asked.

"I wanna know the truth about whether you sank your yacht for the insurance money." He narrowed his eyes suspiciously.

I smiled and said, "Come on, I'll tell you on the way!"

And just like that I walked out of the Friday night meeting of Alcoholics Anonymous with my new sponsor: George B.

George lived on South Main Street, one of the premier streets in the estate section of Southampton. It was one notch down from Meadow Lane, insofar as price was concerned, although the cheapest home on South Main would still set you back $3 million. We were sitting across from each other, on either side of a very expensive bleached-oak table, inside his French country kitchen.

I was in the middle of explaining to George how I planned to kill my interventionist Dennis Maynard, just as soon as my Ninety-in-Ninety had been completed. I had decided that George was the appropriate person to speak to about such an affair after he told me a quick story about a process server who came on his property to serve a bogus summons on him. When George refused to answer the door, the process server started nailing the summons to his hand-polished mahogany door. George went to the door and waited until the process server had the hammer in an upstroke, then he swung open the door, punched the process server's lights out, and slammed the door shut. It had all happened so fast that the process server couldn't describe George to the police, so no charges were filed.

". . . and it's fucking despicable," I was saying, "that this bastard calls himself a professional. Forget the fact that he told my wife not to come visit me while I was rotting away in the loony bin! I mean, that alone is grounds to have his legs broken. But to invite her to the movies to try to coax her into bed, well, that's grounds for *death*!" I shook my head in rage and let out a deep breath, happy to finally get things off my chest.

And George actually agreed with me! Yes, in his opinion my drug interventionist did deserve to die. So we spent the next few minutes debating the best ways to kill him–starting with my idea of cutting off his dick with a pair of hydraulic bolt cutters. But George didn't think that would be painful enough, because the interventionist would go into shock before his dick hit the carpet and bleed out in a matter of seconds. So we moved on to fire–burning him to death. George liked that because it was very painful, but it worried him because of the possibility of collateral damage, since we would be burning his house down as part of the plan. Next came carbon monoxide poisoning, which we both agreed was far too painless, so we debated the pros and cons of poisoning his food, which, in the end, seemed a bit too nineteenth century. A simple botched-burglary attempt came to mind, one that turned into murder (to avoid witnesses). But then we thought about paying a crack addict five dollars to run up to the interventionist and stab him right in the gut with a rusty knife. This way, George explained, he would bleed out nice and slow, especially if the stab wound was just over his liver, which would make it that much more painful.

Then I heard the door swing open and a female voice yell, "George, whose Mercedes is that?" It was a kind, sweet voice, which happened to have a ferocious Brooklyn accent attached to it, so the words came out like: *"Gawge, whoze Mihcedees is that?"*

A moment later, one of the cutest ladies on the planet walked in the kitchen. As big as he was, she was tiny–maybe five feet, a hundred pounds. She had strawberry-blond hair, honey-brown eyes, tiny features, and perfect Irish Spring skin, smattered with a fair number of freckles. She looked to be in her late forties or early fifties, but very well preserved.

George said, "Annette, say hello to Jordan. Jordan, say hello to Annette."

I went to shake her hand, but she moved right past it and gave me a warm hug and a kiss on the cheek. She smelled clean and fresh and of some very expensive perfume, which I couldn't quite place. Annette smiled and held me out in front of her by my shoulders, at arm's length, as if she were inspecting me. "Well, I'll give you one thing," she said matter-of-factly, "you're not the typical stray George brings home."

We all broke up over that one, and then Annette excused herself and went about her usual business, which was making George's life as comfortable as possible. In no time flat, there was a fresh pot of coffee on the table, as well as cakes and pastries and donuts and a bowl of freshly cut fruit. Then she offered to cook me a full-blown dinner, because she thought I looked too thin, to which I said, "You should've seen me forty-three days ago!"

And as we sipped our coffee, I kept going on about my interventionist. Annette was quick to jump on the bandwagon. "He sounds like a real bastard"–*bahstid*–"if you ask me," said the tiny Brooklyn firecracker. "I think you got every right in the world to wanna chop his *cojones* off. Don't you, Gwibbie?"

Gwibbie? That was an interesting nickname for George! I kinda liked it, although it didn't really suit him. Perhaps Sasquatch, I thought . . . or maybe Goliath or Zeus.

Gwibbie nodded and said, "I think the guy deserves to die a slow, painful death, so I want to think about it overnight. We can plan it out tomorrow."

I looked at Gwibbie and nodded in agreement. "Definitely!" I said. "This guy deserves a fiery death."

Annette said to George, "And what are you gonna tell him tomorrow, Gwib?"

Gwib said, "Tomorrow I'm gonna tell him that I want to think about it overnight and then we can plan it out the next day." He smiled wryly.

I smiled and shook my head. "You guys are too much! I knew you were fucking around with me."

Annette said, "*I* wasn't! I think he does deserve to have his *cojones* chopped off!" Now her voice took on a very knowing tone. "George does interventions all the time, and I've never heard of the wife being left out of it, right, Gwib?"

Gwib shrugged his enormous shoulders. "I don't like passing

judgment on other people's methods, but it sounds like there was a certain *warmth* missing from your intervention. I've done hundreds of them, and the one thing I always make sure of is that the person being intervened on understands how much he's loved and how everyone will be there for him if he does the right thing and gets sober. I would never keep a wife away from her husband. Ever." He shrugged his great shoulders once more. "But all's well that ends well, right? You're alive and sober, which is a wonderful miracle, although I question whether or not you're really sober."

"What do you mean? Of course I'm sober! I have forty-three days today, and in a few hours I'll have forty-four. I haven't touched anything. I swear."

"Ahhh," said George, "you have forty-three days without drinking and drugging, but that doesn't mean you're actually *sober.* There's a difference, right, Annette?"

Annette nodded. "Tell him about Kenton Rhodes,* George."

"The department-store guy?" I asked.

They both nodded, and George said, "Yeah, but actually it's his idiot son, the heir to the throne. He has a house in Southampton, not far from you."

With that, Annette plunged into the story. "Yeah, you see, I used to own a store just up the street from here, over on Windmill Lane; it was called the Stanley Blacker Boutique. Anyway, we sold all this terrific Western wear, Tony Lama boo–"

George, apparently, had no patience for drizzling even from his own wife, and he cut her right off. "Jesus Christ, Annette, what the hell does that have to do with the story? No one cares what you sold in your goddamn store or who my tenants were nineteen years ago." He looked at me and rolled his eyes.

George took a deep breath, puffing himself up to the size of an industrial refrigerator, and then slowly let it out. "So Annette owned this store up by Windmill Lane, and she used to park her little Mercedes out in front. One day she's inside the store waiting on a customer, and she sees through the window this other Mercedes pulling in behind her car and hitting her rear bumper. Then, a few seconds later, a man gets out with his girlfriend, and without even leaving a note he goes walking into town."

---

*Name has been changed.

At this point, Annette looked at me and raised her eyebrows, and she whispered, "It was Kenton Rhodes who hit me!"

George shot her a look and said, "Right, it was Kenton Rhodes. Anyway, Annette comes out of the store and sees that not only did he hit the back of her car but he also parked illegally, in a fire zone, so she calls the cops and they come and give him a ticket. Then, an hour later, he comes walking out of some restaurant, drunk as a skunk; he's goes back to his car and looks at the parking ticket and smiles, and then he rips it up and throws it in the street."

Annette couldn't resist the temptation to chime in again: "Yeah, and this *bahstid* had this smug look on his face, so I ran outside and said, 'Let me tell you something, buddy–not only did you hit my car and make a dent but you got the nerve to park in a fire zone and then just rip the ticket up and throw it on the floor and litter."

George nodded gravely. "And I happened to be walking by as all this is happening, and I see Annette pointing her finger at this smug bastard and screaming at him, and then I hear him call her a bitch, or something along those lines. So I walk up to Annette and say, 'Get in the damn store, Annette, right now!' and Annette runs inside the store, knowing what's coming next. Meanwhile, Kenton Rhodes is mouthing off to me something fierce, as he climbs inside his Mercedes. He slams the door shut and starts the car and hits the power-window button, and the thick tempered glass starts sliding up. Then he puts on this enormous pair of Porsche sunglasses–you know, the big ones that make you look like an insect–and he smiles at me and gives me the middle finger."

I started laughing and shaking my head. "So what did you do?"

George rolled his fire hydrant of a neck. "What did I do? I wound up with all my might and I hit the driver's side window so hard that it smashed into a thousand pieces. My hand landed directly on Kenton Rhodes's left temple and knocked him unconscious, and his head fell right in his girlfriend's lap, with those obnoxious Porsche sunglasses still on his face–except now they were all cockeyed."

Through laughter, I said, "You get arrested?"

He shook his head. "Not exactly. See, now his girlfriend was screaming at the top of her lungs: 'OhmyGod! OhmyGod! You killed him! You're a maniac!' And she jumps out of the car and runs over to the police station to get a cop. A few minutes later, Kenton Rhodes is just coming to, and his girlfriend is running back with a cop, who happens to be my good friend Pete Orlando. So she runs over to the driver's side and helps Kenton Rhodes out of the car and brushes all the glass off him, and then the two of them start barking away at Pete Orlando, demanding that he arrest me.

"Annette comes running out, screaming, 'He ripped up a ticket, Pete, and he threw it on the floor! He's a goddamn litterbug and he parked in a fire zone!' to which Pete walks around the back of the car and starts shaking his head gravely. Then he turns to Kenton Rhodes and says, 'You're parked in a fire zone; move your car right now or I'm having it towed.' So Kenton Rhodes starts muttering under his breath, cursing out Pete Orlando as he gets in his car and slams the door shut. Then he turns on the ignition and puts the car in gear and starts backing up a few feet, at which point Pete holds up his hand and yells, 'Stop! Get out of the car, sir!' So Kenton Rhodes stops the car and gets out and says, 'What now?' and Pete says, 'I smell alcohol on your breath; you're gonna have to take a sobriety test.' And now Kenton Rhodes starts muttering at Pete: 'You don't know who the fuck I am!' and all the rest of that crap–and he was still muttering curses a minute later when Pete Orlando arrested him for drunk driving and slapped the cuffs on him."

The three of us cackled for what had to be at least a minute; it was my first sober belly laugh in almost ten years. In fact, I couldn't remember the last time I'd laughed so hard. The story had a message, of course–that back then George was newly sober, which is to say he wasn't really sober at all. He might've stopped drinking, but he was still acting like a drunk.

Finally, George regained his composure and said, "Anyway, you're a smart guy, so I think you got the point."

I nodded. "Yeah, that wanting to kill my interventionist is not the act of a sober man."

"Exactly," he said. "It's okay to think about it, to talk about it, to even make jokes about it. But to actually act on it–that's the point where the question of sobriety raises itself." He took a deep breath and let it out slowly. "I've been sober for more than twenty years now, and I still go to meetings every day–not just so I won't drink alcohol but because, for me, sobriety means a lot more than not getting drunk. When I go to meetings and I see newcomers like you, it reminds me of how close I am to the edge and how easy it would be to slip off. It serves as a daily reminder not to pick up a drink. And when I see the old-timers there, people with thirty-plus years–even more sobriety than myself–it reminds me of how wonderful this program is and how many lives it's saved."

I nodded in understanding and said, "I wasn't really gonna kill my interventionist, anyway. I just needed to hear myself talk about it a bit, to vent." I shrugged and shook my head. "I guess when you look back at it now, you must be shocked that you actually did something like that to Kenton Rhodes. With twenty years sober, now you'd just turn the other cheek at an asshole like that, right?"

George gave me a look of pure incredulity. "You fucking kidding me? It wouldn't matter if I had a hundred years sober. I'd still knock that bastard out just the same!" And we broke down hysterically once more, and we kept laughing and laughing, all the way through that wonderful summer of 1997, my first summer of sobriety.

In fact, I kept right on laughing–as did the Duchess–as we grew closer to George and Annette, and our old friends, one by one, faded into the woodwork. In fact, by the time I was celebrating my first year of sobriety, I had lost touch with almost everyone. The Bealls were still around, as were some of Nadine's old friends, but people like Elliot Lavigne and Danny Porush and Rob Lorusso and Todd and Carolyn Garret could no longer be in my life.

Of course, people like Wigwam, and Bonnie and Ross, and some of my other childhood friends still showed up for an occasional dinner party and whatnot–but things would never be the same. The gravy train had officially stopped running, and the drugs, which had been the glue, were no longer there to hold us together. The Wolf of Wall Street had died that night in Boca Raton, Florida, overdosing in the kitchen of Dave and Laurie Beall. And what little of the Wolf still remained was extinguished when I met George B., who set me on a path of true sobriety.

Exempt from that, of course, was Alan Lipsky, my oldest and *dearest* friend, who'd been there long before any of this happened, long before I'd ever had that wild notion of bringing my own version of Wall Street out to Long Island–creating chaos and insanity among an entire generation of Long Islanders. It was sometime in the fall of 1997 when Alan came to me, saying that he couldn't take it anymore, that he was sick and tired of losing his clients' money and that he'd rather do nothing than keep Monroe Parker open. I couldn't have agreed more, and Monroe Parker closed shortly thereafter. A few months later Biltmore followed suit, and the era of the Strattonite finally came to a close.

It was around the same time when I finally settled my lawsuit with Steve Madden. I ended up settling for a little over $5 million, a far cry from what the stock was actually worth. Nevertheless, as part of the settlement Steve was forced to sell my stock to a mutual fund, so neither of us got the full benefit. I would always look at Steve Madden as the one that got away, although, all in all, I still made over $20 million on the deal–no paltry sum, even by my outrageous standards.

Meanwhile, the Duchess and I had settled into a quieter, more modest lifestyle, slowly reducing the menagerie to a more reasonable level, which is to say, twelve in help. The first to go were Maria and Ignacio. Next came the Roccos, whom I'd always liked but no longer considered necessary. After all, without cocaine and Quaaludes fueling my paranoia, it seemed somewhat ridiculous to have a private security force working in a crimeless neighborhood. Bo had taken the dismissal in stride, telling me that he was just happy I'd made it through this whole thing alive. And while he never actually said it, I was pretty sure he felt guilty about things, although I don't think he was aware of how desperate my drug addiction had become. After all, the Duchess and I had done a pretty good job of hiding it, hadn't we? Or perhaps everyone knew exactly what was going on but figured as long as the goose kept laying his golden eggs, who cared if he killed himself?

Of course, Gwynne and Janet stayed on, and the subject of them being my chief enablers (outside the Duchess) was never brought up. Sometimes it's easier to let sleeping dogs lie. Janet was an expert at burying the past, and Gwynne being a Southerner–well, to bury the past was the Southern way. Whatever the case, I loved both of them, and I knew they both loved me. The simple fact is that drug addiction is a fucked-up disease, and the lines of good judgment become very murky in the trenches, especially when you're living *Lifestyles of the Rich and Dysfunctional.*

And speaking of chief enablers, there was, of course, the luscious Duchess of Bay Ridge, Brooklyn. I guess she turned out all right in the end, didn't she? She was the only one who'd stood up to me, the only one who had cared enough to put her foot down and say, "Enough is enough!"

But as the first anniversary of my sobriety came and went, I began to notice changes in her. Sometimes I would catch a glimpse of that gorgeous face when she wasn't aware I was looking, and I would see a faraway look in her eye, a sort of shell-shocked look, peppered with a hint of sadness. I often wondered what she was thinking at those moments, how many unspoken grudges she still held against me, not just for that despicable moment on the stairs but for everything–for all the cheating and philandering and falling asleep in restaurants and wild emotional swings that went hand in hand with my addiction. I asked George about that–what he thought she might be thinking and if there was anything I could do about it.

With a hint of sadness in his voice, he told me that this whole affair hadn't played itself out yet, that it was inconceivable that Nadine and I could've gone through what we had and then just sweep things under the rug. In fact, in all the years he'd been sober he'd never heard of anything like this; the Duchess and I had broken new ground in terms of dysfunctional relationships. He likened Nadine to Mount Vesuvius–a dormant volcano that one day was sure to explode. Just when and with how much ferocity he wasn't quite sure, but he recommended that the two of us go into therapy, which we didn't. Instead, we buried the past and moved on.

Sometimes I would find the Duchess crying–sitting alone in her maternity showroom with tears streaming down her cheeks. When I'd ask her what was wrong, she would tell me that she couldn't understand why all this had to happen. Why had I turned away from her and lost myself in drugs? Why had I treated her so badly during those years? And why was I such a good husband now? In a way, it only made it worse, she'd said, and with each act of kindness I now showed her, she felt that much more resentful that it couldn't have been that way all those years. But then we would make love, and all would be well again, until the next time I found her crying.

Nonetheless, we still had our children, Chandler and Carter, and we found solace in them. Carter had just celebrated his third birthday. He was more gorgeous than ever now, with his platinum-blond hair and world-class eyelashes. He was a child of God, watched over since that terrible day in North Shore Hospital when they'd told us that he would grow up without his faculties. How ironic it was that since that day he hadn't had so much as a runny nose. The hole in his heart was almost closed now, and it had never given him a day's problems.

And what of Chandler? What of my little thumbkin, the former baby genius, who had kissed away her daddy's boo-boo? Well, as always, she was still a daddy's girl. Somewhere along the way she had earned the nickname "the CIA," because she spent a good part of her day listening to everyone's conversations and gathering intelligence. She had just turned five, and she was wise beyond her years. She was quite a little salesperson, using the subtle power of suggestion to exert her very will over me, which, admittedly, wasn't all that difficult.

Sometimes I would look at her while she was asleep–wondering what she would remember about all this, about all the chaos and insanity that had surrounded her first four years, those all-important formative years. The Duchess and I had always tried to shield her from things, but children are notoriously keen observers. Every so often, in fact, something would trigger Channy and she would bring up what had happened on the stairs that day–and then she would tell me how happy she was that I had gone to Atlant-ica so Mommy and Daddy could be happy again. I found myself crying inwardly at those moments, but she'd change the subject just as quickly, to something entirely innocuous, as if the memory hadn't touched her viscerally. One day I would have some explaining to do, and not just about what had happened on the stairs that day but about everything. But there was time for that–lots of time–and at this point it seemed prudent to allow her to enjoy the blissful ignorance of childhood, at least for a while longer.

At this particular moment, Channy and I were standing in the kitchen in Old Brookville, and she was pulling on my jeans and saying, "I want to go to Blockbuster to get the new *Rugrats* video! You promised!"

In truth, I hadn't promised anything, but that made me respect her even more. After all, my five-year-old daughter was assuming the sale on me–making her case from a position of strength, not weakness. It was 7:30 p.m. "Okay," I said, "let's go right now, before Mommy gets home. Come on, thumbkin!" I extended my arms toward her and she jumped into them, wrapped her tiny arms around my neck, and giggled deliciously.

"Let's go, Daddy! Hurry up!"

I smiled at my perfect daughter and took a deep, sober breath, relishing her very scent, which was glorious. Chandler was beautiful, inside and out, and I had no doubt that she would grow strong, one day making her mark on this world. She just had that look about her, a certain sparkle in her eye that I'd noticed the very moment she was born.

We decided to take my little Mercedes, which was her favorite, and we put the top down so we could enjoy the beautiful summer evening. It was a few days before Labor Day, and the weather was gorgeous. It was one of those clear, windless nights, and I could smell the first hints of fall. Unlike that fateful day sixteen months ago, I seat-belted my precious daughter into the front passenger seat and made it out of the driveway without smashing into anything.

As we passed through the stone pillars at the edge of the estate, I noticed a car parked outside my property. It was a gray four-door sedan, maybe an Oldsmobile. As I drove past it, a middle-aged white man with a narrow skull and short gray hair parted to the side stuck his head out the driver's side window and said, "Excuse me, is this Cryder Lane?"

I hit the brake. Cryder Lane? I thought. What was he talking about? There was no Cryder Lane in Old Brookville or, for that matter, anywhere in Locust Valley. I looked over at Channy and felt a twinge of panic. In that very instant I wished I still had the Roccos watching over me. There was something odd and disturbing about this encounter.

I shook my head and said, "No, this is Pin Oak Court. I don't know any Cryder Lane." At that moment I noticed there were three other people sitting in the car, and my heart immediately took off at a gallop . . . *Fuck–they were here to kidnap Channy!* . . . I reached over, placed my arm across Chandler's chest, and looked her in the eyes and said, "Hold on, sweetie!"

As I stepped on the accelerator, the rear door of the Oldsmobile swung open and a woman popped out. She smiled, then waved at me and said, "It's okay, Jordan. We're not here to hurt you. Please don't pull away." She smiled again.

I put my foot back on the brake. "What do you want?" I asked curtly.

"We're from the FBI," she said. She pulled a black leather billfold from her pocket and flipped it open. I looked . . . and, sure enough, those three ugly letters were staring me in the face: F-B-I. They were big block letters, in light blue, and there was some official-looking writing above and below them. A moment later the man with the narrow skull flashed his credentials too.

I smiled and said ironically, "I guess you guys aren't here to borrow a cup of sugar, right?"

They both shook their heads no. Just then the other two agents emerged from the passenger side of the Oldsmobile and flashed their credentials as well. The kind-looking woman offered me a sad smile and said, "I think you should turn around and bring your daughter back inside the house. We need to talk to you."

"No problem," I said. "And thanks, by the way. I appreciate what you're doing."

The woman nodded, accepting my gratitude for having the decency to not make a scene in front of my daughter. I asked, "Where's Agent Coleman? I'm dying to meet the guy after all these years."

The woman smiled again. "I'm sure the feeling is mutual. He'll be along shortly."

I nodded in resignation. It was time to break the bad news to Chandler: There would be no *Rugrats* this evening. In fact, I had a sneaky suspicion there would be some other changes around the house, none of which she would be too fond of–starting with the temporary absence of Daddy.

I looked at Channy and said, "We can't go to Blockbuster, sweetie. I have to talk to these people for a while."

She narrowed her eyes and gritted her teeth. Then she started screaming: "No! You promised me! You're breaking your word! I want to go to Blockbuster! You promised me!"

As I drove back to the house she kept screaming–and then she continued to scream as we made our way into the kitchen and I passed her to Gwynne. I said to Gwynne, "Call Nadine on her cell phone; tell her the FBI is here and I'm getting arrested."

Gwynne nodded without speaking and took Chandler upstairs. The moment Chandler was out of sight, the kind female FBI agent said, "You're under arrest for securities fraud, money laundering, and . . ."

Blah, blah, blah, I thought, as she slapped the cuffs on me and recited my crimes against man and God and everyone else. Her words blew right past me, though, like a gust of wind. They were entirely meaningless to me, or at least not worth listening to. After all, I knew what I'd done and I knew that I deserved whatever was coming to me. Besides, there would be ample time to go over the arrest warrant with my lawyer.

Within minutes, there were no less than twenty FBI agents in my house–dressed in full regalia with guns, bulletproof vests, extra ammo, and whatnot. It was somewhat ironic, I thought, that they would dress this way, as if they were serving some sort of high-risk warrant.

A few minutes later, Special Agent Gregory Coleman finally reared his head. And I was shocked. He looked like a kid, no older than me. He was about my height and he had short brown hair, very dark eyes, even features, and an entirely average build.

When he saw me, he smiled. Then he extended his right hand and we shook, although it was a trifle awkward, what with my hands being cuffed and everything. He said, in a tone of respect, "I gotta tell you, you were one wily adversary. I must've knocked on a hundred doors and not a single person would cooperate against you." He shook his head, still awestruck at the loyalty the Strattonites had for me. Then he added, "I thought you'd like to know that."

I shrugged and said, "Yeah, well, the gravy train has a way of doing that to people, you know?"

He turned the corners of his mouth down and nodded. "Definitely so."

Just then the Duchess came running in. She had tears in her eyes, yet she still looked gorgeous. Even at my very arrest, I couldn't help but take a peek at her legs, especially since I wasn't sure when I'd see them again.

As they led me away in handcuffs, the Duchess gave me a tiny peck on the cheek and told me not to worry. I nodded and told her that I loved her and that I always would. And then I was gone, just like that. Going where I hadn't the slightest idea, but I figured I would end up somewhere in Manhattan and then tomorrow I would be arraigned in front of a federal judge.

In retrospect, I remember feeling somewhat relieved–that the chaos and insanity would finally be behind me. I would do my time and then walk away a sober young man–a father of two and a husband to a kindhearted woman, who stood by me through thick and thin.

Everything would be okay.

EPILOGUE

THE BETRAYERS

Indeed, it would have been nice if the Duchess and I had lived happily ever after–if I could have done my time, and then walked out of prison into her kind, loving embrace. But, no, unlike a fairy tale, this part of the story doesn't have a happy ending.

The judge had set my bail at $10 million, and it was then, on the very courthouse steps, that the Duchess dropped the D-bomb on me.

With icy coldness, she said, "I don't love you anymore. This whole marriage has been a lie." Then she spun on her heel and called her divorce lawyer on her cell phone.

I tried reasoning with her, of course, but it was no use. Through tiny, bogus snuffles, she added, "Love is like a statue: you can chip away at it for only so long before there's nothing left."

Yes, that might be true, I thought, if it weren't for the fact that you waited until I got indicted to come to that conclusion, *you backstabbing, gold-digging bitch*!

Whatever. We separated a few weeks later, and I went into exile at our fabulous beach house in Southampton. It was a rather fine place to watch the walls of reality come crashing down on me–listening to the breaking waves of the Atlantic Ocean and watching the breathtaking sunsets over Shinnecock Bay, while my life came apart at the seams.

Meanwhile, on the *legal* front, things were going even worse. It was on my fourth day out of jail when the U.S. attorney called my lawyer and told him that unless I pleaded guilty and became a government witness he was going to indict the Duchess too. And while he didn't get specific on the charges, my best guess was that she was going to be indicted for conspiracy to spend obscene amounts of money. What else was she guilty of, after all?

Either way, the world was upside down. How could I, the one at the very top of the food chain, rat out those beneath me? Did giving up a multitude of smaller fish offset the fact that I was the biggest fish in town? Was it a matter of simple mathematics: that fifty guppies added up to a single whale?

Cooperating meant that I would have to wear a wire; that I would have to testify at trials and take the witness stand against my friends. I would have to spill my very guts, and disclose every last drop of financial wrongdoing from the last decade. It was a terrible thought. An absolutely horrendous thought. But what choice did I have? If I didn't cooperate they would indict the Duchess and take her away in handcuffs.

An indicted Duchess in handcuffs. I found that notion rather pleasing, at first. She would probably reconsider divorcing me if we were both under indictment, wouldn't she? (We would be like birds of a feather, flocking together.) And she would be a much less desirable catch to another man if she had to report to a probation officer each month. No two ways about it.

But, no, I could never let that happen. She was the mother of my children, and that was the beginning and the end of it.

My lawyer cushioned the blow by explaining that everyone cooperated in a case like mine–that if I went to trial and lost I would get thirty years. And while I could have gotten six or seven years with a straight guilty plea, that would've left the Duchess exposed, which was entirely unacceptable.

So I cooperated.

Danny was also indicted; and he also cooperated, as did the boys from Biltmore and Monroe Parker. Danny ended up serving twenty months, while the rest of the boys got probation. The Depraved Chinaman was indicted next. He cooperated, too, and was sentenced to eight years. Then came Steve Madden, the Cutthroat Cobbler, and Elliot Lavigne, the World-Class Degenerate, both of whom pleaded guilty. Elliot got three years; Steve, three and a half. And, finally, came Dennis Gaito, the Jersey Chef. He went to trial and was found guilty. Alas, the judge gave him ten years.

Andy Greene, aka Wigwam, was never tried; and Kenny Greene, aka the Blockhead, was indicted many years later, a stock-fraud case having nothing to do with Stratton. Like the rest of the clan, he also cooperated, and he served one year.

Along the way, the Duchess and I fell in love again; the only problem was that it was with other people. I went as far as getting engaged, but broke it off at the last second. She, however, got married, and remains married to this day. She lives in California, just a few miles from me. After a few rocky years, the Duchess and I finally buried the hatchet. We get along terrific now–partly because she happens to be a great lady, and partly because her new husband happens to be a great man. We share custody of the kids, and I see them almost every day.

Ironically, it would be more than five years from the time I was indicted until I actually went to jail–serving twenty-two months in a federal prison camp. What I would have never guessed, though–not in a million years, in fact–was that those last five years would be as insane as the ones before them.

ACKNOWLEDGMENTS

Countless thanks to my literary agent, Joel Gotler, who after reading three pages of a very rough manuscript told me to drop everything I was doing and become a full-time writer. He's been a coach, an advisor, a psychiatrist, and, above all, a true friend. Without him, this book would have never been written. (So, if your name is in it, blame him, not me!)

I'd also like to thank my publisher, Irwyn Applebaum, who believed in me from the very beginning. It was his vote of confidence that made the difference.

Immeasurable thanks to my editor, Danielle Perez, who did the work of three editors–turning a 1,200-page manuscript into a 500-page book. She's an amazing lady, with a style and grace all her own. Over the last nine months her favorite nine words to me were: "I'd hate to see what your liver looks like!"

Many thanks to Alexandra Milchan, my one-woman army. If every author were lucky enough to have an Alexandra Milchan, there would be a lot less starving authors in the world. She's tough, kind, brilliant, and as beautiful on the inside as she is on the outside. She's definitely her father's daughter.

And many thanks to my good friends Scott Lambert, Kris Mesner, Johnnie Marine, Michael Peragine, Kira Randazzo, Marc Glazier, Faye Greene, Beth Gotler, John Macaluso, and to all the waiters and waitresses at the restaurants and coffeehouses I wrote this book in–the girls at Chaya and Skybar and Coffee Bean, and Joe at Il Boccaccio.

And, lastly, I thank my ex-wife, the Duchess of Bay Ridge, Brooklyn. She's still the best, despite the fact that she orders me around as if I were still married to her.